The Rise of

Mystery Babylon

Vol. 1: The Way of Cain

Brett Lee Thomas

Parallel World Books

The Rise of Mystery Babylon
The Way of Cain (Vol. 1)

ISBN-13: 978-0-9995257-0-8
Parallel World Books

Cover photos courtesy of Adi Nes

Emails:
theriseofmysterybabylon@protonmail.com
brettleethomas@protonmail.com

www.theriseofmysterybabylon.com

Those who cannot remember the past
are condemned to repeat it.

- George Santayana

Table of Contents

Preface

The Ancient Parallel to Today's World: "The Days of Noah"

You have to know the ***past*** *to understand* ***the present****.*
- Carl Sagan[1]

There is much in this book that was common knowledge in the past - those ancient of days. Life was very different; the whole world was very different back then. The people in the past probably thought and did things that, today, might sound surprising to many of us. Yet, there are *some* ideologies and ways of life - practiced back then - which are surprisingly similar to those which are practiced today. Why? What is going on? Why the return of much of these elements of the past? Could there actually be a *parallel*, of what might have went on - then to now?

The Two Parallel Worlds

But as the ***days of Noe (i.e. Noah)*** *were, so shall also the coming of the Son of man be.*
- Mat. 24:37 (KJV)

Just what do these prophetic words mean; spoken by Jesus Christ himself?[2] Two thousand year ago, Jesus' disciples asked him to describe the "end times," and what would be the approaching signs. As the above explanation seems to provide, there was going to be a *parallel* between two eras of existence - how life was lived *in the days of Noah (Noe)* and *how life would be lived in some era of the future*.

This verse tells us so much: if the lifestyles of the two seem to match, then it gives us a pretty good clue to understanding whether or not we might be near the end of our age - the so-called "end times." Also, this gives us a rationale for understanding why God had destroyed the working order of the ancient world - at the time of Noah. Obviously, they were **sinning** immensely. There were severe cracks in their ideologies and ways of living.

So, if we *truly* want to discover what good and evil probably is, in our present age, then all we need to do is discover what might have gone on back then, and use it to help develop a model for the future. Obviously, if these lifestyles of old were wrong enough for God to pass a horrible *judgment* upon the entire world, then there must be some merit to this comparison.

The purpose of this book, first off, is to show the reader much of what could have gone on back then - in the times of early Genesis; and how there could actually be a *parallel* of two eras of existence. In our current times, we are bombarded - via so many angles - with people telling us what they feel *might* be right and what *might* be wrong. Beauty is in the eye of the beholder today. There are so many diverse opinions being thrown around, that a lot of us do not have a solid moral foundation anymore. From the ancient side of this parallel, however, we can absolutely learn about what was right and wrong back then. The utilization of this knowledge really helps us to understand how to solidify our own moral foundations in our daily walk.

What is Bringing it All Back

There is something truly evil out there - something beyond our world - lurking in the shadows of everyday life; something which has continually manipulated cultures, politics, and religion throughout history. This is the force the Bible coins *Mystery Babylon.*

> *And upon her forehead was a name written,* ***MYSTERY, BABYLON****...*
> - *Rev.* 17:5 (KJV)

The word *Babylon* has almost always been the headquarters of the greatest religious apostasy ever known; both literally and symbolically - the true enemy of the Bible. The city itself was lost over the years; but this "capital of corruption" has continued on, in many different forms, as a symbol of all that is against God. And, on top of it, there are *mysteries* associated with this once-ancient city. There were cultural, political, and religious *systems*, established in these earliest of times, which have continued on, throughout the empires, throughout world changes. All of what began around Babylon would eventually manifest itself into many different forms, to many different faces. *That* is why the Bible calls it ***Mystery*** *Babylon* - it resides under the surface of so much. These same systems are ever-working to help manipulate us: the way we think, the attitudes we take, the god(s) we believe in, etc.; with hopes to bring our world right back to the same existence as was at the earliest times of Babylon, itself.

Is the future just like the past? Does history *truly* repeat itself? And, what is working to bring so much of these same ancient ideologies and ways of life back to us… *again*?

> *The result of the* **serpent** *nature in mankind is the conglomerate world* **system** *- economic, political, and religious - prophetically called* **Mystery Babylon***… he is "that ancient serpent called the devil and Satan, which deceiveth the whole world"…* ("The World System", n. d., p. 2)[3]

Just who or what would be *the Serpent* in this whole scheme of things? What *system* is bringing our world right back to the same state as in Noah's day? Could this *Serpent* be thc same *Serpent* who deceived Eve back in the earliest part of Genesis; in the time of the Garden of Eden?

This first volume (*The Way of Cain*) will concentrate on earth's history before, and leading up to, Babylon - the time of this *Serpent;* as well as what socio/cultural influences this Serpent might have had on this world. The second volume (*The Tower of Babel*) will take us deeper into the era of Babylon, and *beyond* - diving more into the political and religious elements of Serpent influence. The Serpent's role in our past (and present) begins through the discovery of what went on in early Genesis; especially up to the time people lived in *the days of Noah*. That is how we uncover the secrets of *Mystery Babylon*.

Obscured History, and Meant to Stay That Way

> *When words* **lose their meaning**, *people will lose their liberty.*
> *- Confucius*

Words were manipulated back then, as well as today. Why don't we already know all about the *serpent* and *Mystery Babylon*? Why have so many of us, seemingly, been kept "in the dark" about what would be in the pages of this book? Could the information contained herein have been, for the most part, obscured for a *reason*?

To begin our quest, we'll dive into many of the little-known, or obscured, interpretations of early stories in the Bible. This information comes from a variety of ancient texts; texts which could help us understand the truth of these stories, and our world, unlike we have ever seen before. Since the Bible does not deliver the exact detail, it might be necessary to search other ancient texts, to help "fill in the gaps" on what might be the *entire* story. Once we know the whole story, the *mysteries* of ancient Babylon become more and more clear.

There are those who say that *Genesis* and *Revelation* are the books of the Bible that Satan hates the most; the reason being that Revelation exposes his plans for the future, and Genesis **exposes** his plans for the past. So, it is for these very reasons that full comprehension of these ancient stories are so **vital**. They are the framework for understanding the Serpent, *Mystery Babylon*, and how our world is being manipulated - for the *worse*. Since a lot of our history was changed, or even obscured, over the years, the probability of any previous exposure was in a relative state of inactivity… until now. The detailed discovery into these ancient stories of Genesis can provide the means for discovering what so many of us might have been missing, all of these years.

To make these stories "complete," the author will incorporate the most accurate, the most relevant, and the most respected ancient parallel works of Genesis first; down to the most questionable. We *can* come up with <u>one</u> conglomerated "story" of these early times, which also helps us to identify the most definitive *parallel* of these ancient times of Noah.

Putting it all together, however, wasn't easy. The information in these books had to have been brought together in a way similar to how one would assemble a jigsaw puzzle. It took a while; yet, the end-result is very telling. It is important that we study these earliest, and most original, texts for one all-important reason:

The farther you are away from the originals the farther you are away from the ***truth****.*
- Unknown

These books help to bring an essence of probably *truth* to our history - truth as close as ancient texts could provide. Ultimately, these expositions contained herein could allowance for another, more compelling view of Biblical history, as well as ways to help us strengthen our foundations of religious belief. It, ultimately, helps to "blow the lid off" of information which has been hidden from us… for too long.

The theme of this book is **twofold**: one, to understand how these serpent systems of Babylon work; and (as a *result* of this knowledge), two, to strengthen our own moral and religious foundations! Many of us do what we are told, as spoken of by politicians and religious authorities. Many of us concentrate on good, or positive, elements of Christianity, for example; and our world. Few of us fully comprehend how our **enemies** would work against us. We must also learn, and understand, *this* side of the political and religious coins. We need to know *all* of what we may be up against, in this world, to survive. As they say: it's best to "know thy enemy."

"Out of Touch" Ideals?

It all might begin to sound somewhat simple, at first. But, in actuality, there is a lot in the way of one's easy comprehension of *Mystery Babylon*, and what it's all about - that's probably by design. There's no scientific proof to almost everything in this book; that's for sure. One's comprehension relies on *belief*: a belief in these ancient sources, as well a belief in the Bible's original Hebrew and Greek.

Also, a lot of this book deals with elements of our world that many might find fantastic; even downright folklore (especially regarding the supernatural: transgressions of fallen angels, existence of demons, etc). It seems there's a lot of work against our understanding, already:

> *The late eighteenth and early nineteenth centuries saw a massive decline in the popularity of the Christian Church in many parts of Protestant Europe... churches everywhere were being neglected and left to fall into ruin under the impact of Newtonian science and the arrival of the Industrial Revolution. In an age of reason and learning, there were little place for the alleged transgressions of* ***angels***, ***fallen*** *or otherwise. Most of the general public were simply not interested...*
>
> (Collins, 1996, p. 20)[4]

The ancients, however, believed in a lot of these fantastic elements. They even attributed most of the supernatural as more than just folklore. So, just because many, today, may try to ridicule a lot of this information doesn't mean that it never existed, or isn't relevant *today*. The world truly is a complex network of intricate and interrelated processes. Who's to say that these supernatural elements of our ancient past actually disappeared, or went anywhere! As the Bible clearly states: "there is *nothing new* under the sun."

True; a number of people, today, might read this book and claim, "this is just one man's *opinion*." There is no proof. But, in the book's defense, these volumes are not filled with a bunch of wild speculation, or pet-theories. The author, for the most part, just lets the ancient texts, and accredited authors, speak *for themselves*.

When it all boils down to is this: even the "big bang theory," and the theory of evolution, are - at best - only *theories*. They are only the consensus of *opinion*. No one is alive today who could *definitively* tell us what happened back then because no one was alive back then! In this day and age, it's easy to assume that there will be a consensus against the contents of this book. This is the age of science; the age of reason. That doesn't mean that there isn't more beyond what we can see and touch. It also doesn't mean that these texts of old should be tossed aside, or discounted, because of their age... or their contents.

We'll see that there are many people, today, who seem to have *a stake* in telling us what they think that *should* be our history; as well as what they think our morality *should* be. There is politics in everything; even though we might not see it.

If this is true, then how do we find the real story? How do we know what ways to follow? It takes an open mind. An open mind to "other" sources of information on our planet could help us to truly understand why things are the way they are today; and could greatly assist the reader in the understanding of this book - as well as their world at hand. Sometimes, we need to wade through the vast array of "smoke and mirrors" presented before us, in order to find *true* answers in our world. We need to get *beyond* so many of the predetermined ***denials*** we face, to discover what we may have been missing all of these years!

So, to begin to reinterpret some of the widely-held thoughts about our past, and also to begin to expose what this ancient system of *Babylon* is all about, let's look at what might have really went on... "*in the beginning*."

Chapter 1

In the Beginning…
With A Gap In Between

Earth ***made*** *waste and empty by judgment.*
- *Gen.* 1:1-2 (The Scofield Bible, notes)

If we want to delve into some of the more obscure viewpoints of religious theology, we really need to take a good, hard look at a few alternate views of early Genesis. As we begin to discover these early accounts, we might begin to discover the ancient side of this *parallel*. So, to begin, we really do need to start at the beginning - *in the beginning*.

Creationists tell us the earth was up to 12,000 years old; evolutionists say billions. Which is right? Could there be another scenario, a scenario that might be something a little different… somewhere in between; a scenario that might even give us an entirely new way to look at our world?

Many of us who are religious were taught God created the world in six days; and then rested on the seventh. For centuries we have accepted this story, and other early stories in Genesis, as absolute truth. We trusted men who first translated the Bible into English, and that they made no mistakes in their translation. What if these people were not entirely correct in their interpretations? What if the original language of the Bible could, perhaps, say something *different* than what these early translators portrayed? What if there could be more to these early stories than we were always taught?

To start off, if we look at a few of these alternate, ancient texts, we already get a different interpretation on world creation:

> *In the beginning God created* ***numerous worlds****, destroying* ***one after the other*** *as they failed to satisfy Him. All were inhabited by man, a thousand generations of whom He cut off, leaving no record of them.* (Graves and Patai, 1964, p. 45)[1]

Strange; this may sound a little more like our modern view of *evolution* than it does the Bible. Evolutionists often may hold that the ecosystem of our earth was destroyed, and "brought back to life," again and again - even six or seven times. There were numerous worlds, before ours, which did not make it; case in point: the rise and fall of the dinosaurs. To clarify our stance in this book, however, the author wants to make something totally clear: this book is *not* trying to promote the theory of evolution, nor compromise Biblical scripture in any way. On the other extreme, we are not trying to make the Bible "fit in" with our modern, secular view of the world. What we want to do is to show that there could be *another* way to look at Biblical creation, as well these early stories of Genesis. If they show some similarities to the evolutionary view, then so be it.

There *could* be coincidences between the two, as we'll see; but that doesn't mean they are totally related. With all of this said and done, let's now see that there could be something very interesting on the horizon: a totally different, *but Biblically sound*, view of our early days!

As many may know, the Old Testament was originally written in Hebrew; and the New Testament in Greek. As the old saying goes, "if you really want to understand the Bible, you should read it in its original Hebrew." So, to gather the whole story of these early *days of Noah*, we attempted to do just that, whenever possible. Most of us know that English was not the original language of the Bible. No matter how well the Bible was translated, no matter how many variable translations we have out there, the English word cannot *totally* grasp the original meanings of the Hebrew. As with the English language, there could be more than *one* meaning to each Hebrew word in the Bible. Because of this fact, could there be different meanings - entirely different elements - to some of these stories? Could our ancient Biblical history, in fact, be different? What this may point to is a simple concept: perfect words, *imperfect translations*.

The learned scholars who translated King James Bible probably translated the words with the best of intentions. They probably believed most of what had always been *taught*; and used their preconceived notions to affect their interpretations. It's simple. The Creation of Genesis 1 is a perfect example of this. The attempt to keep up with tradition may have swayed them to insert *one* meaning of the original Hebrew over another; just to make it all sound "correct." Once we look at the original Hebrew words in more detail, here, and discover the *other* ways of which these words could be used, a *whole new realm* of possibilities might begin to open up! If there truly could be variations in these early stories, how significant could that be? How much could this change the way we look at our religious and political views on the world, today? Quite a bit (as we'll see). This will be a permeating theme, throughout this book.

Elements of these early stories could have been left out (or beautifully concealed) - either accidentally, or for very good reason: they might actually help us discover the Serpent's *true* nature; the origin of *Mystery Babylon*; among other things. The understanding of these obscured elements could also help determine just *who* or *what* is behind attempts to bring back these same thoughts and ideals (those of "the days of Noah") back into our mainstream.

Genesis and Revelation

To begin to grasp these concepts, we need to take a good look at the books of Genesis and Revelation; arguably two of the most important books in the Bible. This first volume will concentrate more on Genesis; the second on both Genesis and Revelation. The reason we need to understand so much about Genesis is because Genesis gives us this ancient parallel of the *Days of Noah* - the "background" to it all, if you may. Revelation gives us the modern equivalent. If we dare challenge what most of the modern Christian population have accepted as the *only* story of the Bible, if we dare desire to find what *really* could be influencing our world "behind the scenes," let's continue further.

The Gap Between the Worlds

One interesting but obscured theory must arise - first off - in regards to the beginnings of biblical creationism. This theory is fairly old. Obviously, most of us have never heard of it. This is one example of a school of thought where our modern populous has been kept "in the dark." This first theory, commonly known as **the *Gap Theory***, is an incredible way of looking at our creation. It could really turn assumptions within the first chapter of Genesis "on its ear."

This theory, along with the rest of the alternate views of the book, requires the reader to maintain a sense of openness, and possibility. We will discuss a number of other topics besides this Gap Theory. The relevance of *angels* to our world, for example, will be discussed in great detail. If we believe the Bible is the word of God, then, hopefully, we will believe in angels also; for the ancients who scribed the Bible into words surely believed in them! Ultimately, there is nothing in this book which intentionally contradicts the words of the Bible. We only offer other possible interpretations of it all. Science, as well, might not support a lot of the following information, but what elements of the supernatural/religious world *would it really support*?

The Gap Theory is the first to shed light on what we have been missing, all of this time. It's quite simple: the first verse of the Bible signifies the *beginning* of God's creation. Between the first and second verses there was a **gap** in time. The exact expanse of time between these two verses is unknown. Other people, animals, and whatever might have existed during this time also was unknown. The *original* creation could have taken place "in the beginning" (Gen. 1:1), and at least one "re-creation" could have occurred since then. This trend may have continued since this time - another "re-creation;" and another; and another… all the way up to the time of the "Six-Day Creation" of Genesis. There was a "gap" in between the first creation (of everything), and our present *world's* creation.

As the Bible states:

In the beginning God created the heaven and the earth.
- *Gen.* 1:1 (KJV)

The next verse, then, says:

And the earth was without form, and void...
- *Gen.* 1:2 (KJV)

According to C.I. Scofield, Thomas Chalmers, and other scholars, it was just before the time most of us have heard about - the "Six-Day Creation" - that something terrible had happened. The Scofield KJV Bible, for example, gives us an explanation for what may have happened:

Earth made waste and empty by judgment.

There are clues in the Bible that also might support this theory. As we'll see, the planet *itself* might even be extremely old; and there could have been at least *one* "destruction and re-creation" sequence before our present era - with the "Six-Day Creation" kicking it all of. Could there have been a major *catastrophe* occurring right before our "Six-Day Creation" of Genesis?

As we look at these first two verses of Genesis, we may need to look closer into the original Hebrew. If we accept the modern postulate of creationism, the "beginning" of our **current** world occurred somewhere in the area of **six thousand years ago** - because this was, more or less, the time Adam and Eve were said to have been placed in the Garden of Eden. With the Gap Theory, however, we cannot assume *this* time was also the time of the *formation* of planet earth. That could have been long before.[2]

As we look more into the first verse of the Bible, we have a curious anomaly:

In the beginning God created the ***heaven*** *and the earth.*
- *Gen.* 1:1 (KJV)

We notice the word *heaven* is *in the singular*. This verse clearly states there were *one* heaven, and one earth, created at this beginning. As we read further, at the end of our "Six-Day Creation," we are provided with another statement:

Thus the ***heavens*** *and the earth were finished, and all the host of them.*
- *Gen.* 2:1 (KJV)

> *These are the generations of the* ***heavens*** *and of the earth when they were created, in the day that the LORD God made the* ***earth and the heavens****...*
>
> \- *Gen.* 2:4 (KJV)

The above two verses, as already stated, describe the time just *after* the "Six-Day Creation" of Genesis 1. Curiously, the word *heaven*, now, is in the plural. Why do we now have it as *plural*? Could this mean that, at the end of this "Six-Day Creation," there were *additional* heavens already created? Was the "Six-Day Creation" the actual beginning of our entire creation as a planet, or just the *latest* in a chain of "destruction" and "re-creation" events? It seems the Bible has a lot more support towards the *latter* suggestion.

The word *beginning*, in Genesis 1:1, comes from the Hebrew word *reshiyth*. *Reshiyth* means "first in place, time, order or rank."[3] Could this have signified a *first* creation, or the *first* harmonized world - in a *cycle* of them? Could there have been a second, a third; even more?

The Differences Between the Words "Earth" and "World"

> *Before the mountains were brought forth, or ever thou hadst formed the* ***earth*** *and the* ***world****, even from everlasting to everlasting, thou art God.*
>
> \- *Psa.* 90:2 (KJV)

In the Bible, we have another anomaly here - seemingly. As we see in the verse above, the words *earth* and *world* look like they represent two distinct terms - two different things. Simply, we might be able to theorize that the *world* (such as in the above) represents a **present, organized order of things** (on our planet); the *earth* represents the physical **planet** itself. The *world*, then, would advance, beyond the simple definition of a physical planet - becoming an organized cosmos, or makeup or the planet. If we look at it this way, we could also postulate that there might have been more than *one* formulated and reformulated *world* - or organized cosmos - on the earth; perhaps several (with the "Six-Day Creation" of Genesis 1 being the latest).

One of the Greek words, in the New Testament, often translated as the English "world" is *kosmos*. The word *kosmos*, in Classical Greek, represents "a harmonious order, system or arrangement" - a type of *established order*.[4] If we connect this with the above, then our physical planet could have been created by God, a long time ago; and this organized, harmonious order to the earth we see today was fashioned at the exact same time as the "Six-Day Creation" - and only in the neighborhood of six thousand years ago. The first harmonized *order* of the planet could have changed a number of times - destroyed and refashioned over time.

> *Now Moses saith in the beginning of the Pentateuch, "In the beginning God made the heavens, and the* ***earth existed of old****"...* - *Bakhayla Mikael*[5]

Whatever went on during the times "of old" - before our previous *world* - we just don't know. Maybe we weren't supposed to know. We don't know why God wasn't satisfied with the organized *worlds* before us, or why they were all destroyed. One thing we can surmise - that our present world (the world of the "Six-Day Creation") was formed from the ashes of a former world's undistinguishable ruin; "reworked" by God, once again.[6]

More Than One World?

There seems to be Scriptural evidence that describes how at least one *world* was created by God:

> *Through faith we understand that the* ***worlds*** *were framed by the word of God, so that things which are seen were not made of things which do appear.*
> - *Heb.* 11:3 (KJV)

> *Hath in these last days spoken unto us by his Son, whom he hath appointed heir of all things, by whom also he made the* ***worlds****...* - *Heb.* 1:2 (KJV)

Even though the ancients may have known of the planets of our solar system, the above might not be referring to them, here! The Greek word for *worlds*, above, is *aion*. Interestingly, this word was not used, here, in the context of space, but of *time*. It does not only mean a "perpetuity of time," but also "a period of time" or an "age"... just like the Hebrew word for *beginning* in Genesis 1:1.[7] In other words, the original Greek might be referring to these *worlds* as in being in a succession of *order* - one simultaneous world after another (rather than *separate*, distinct planets).[8]

The root for the Greek word *aion* is *aei*, which can also mean "at any and every time: when according to the circumstances something is or ought to **be done again**."[9] So, it further supports our thought: each time one world was destroyed, the planet was made up anew, or refashioned again; much like plot of land which was "baptized" by a good rain spell.

Interestingly:

> *Remember this, and shew yourselves men: bring it again to mind, O ye transgressors. Remember the **former things** of old: for I am God, and there is none else... Declaring the **end from the beginning**, and from **ancient times** the things that **are not yet done**...*
> - *Isa.* 46:9-10 (KJV)

The more we ponder the possibilities of our planet having more than one *world*, the more sense verses like the above seem to make.

A World Formed Without Form, And Void?

> *And the earth was **without form**, and **void**...*
> - *Gen.* 1:2 (KJV)

As we now see, the Hebrew word *tohuw* was translated into the English as "without form." *Tohuw*, however, can also mean "laid waste," "that which is wasted;" as well as a "place of chaos," "vanity," or "confusion."[10] The Hebrew *bohuw* was translated into the English *void*, which can also mean a state of "waste," or "emptiness."[11] Put them all together, and we have *another* possible scenario of our beginnings; as implied by the above verse:

And the earth was ***laid to waste****, and* ***emptied****...*
- *Gen.* 1:2 (in retranslation)

This seems a lot different than what so many of us have assumed about the "Six-Day Creation." Common thought on creation is that the world, at the beginning of our "Six-Day Creation," was **created** in a vain, or an empty, wasted state - without form, void. Now, one question that logically might follow after this is: was the planet created to be this way, or *did it become* this way?

The following verse of the Bible seems to give us an answer:

For thus saith the LORD that created the heavens; God himself that formed the earth and made it; he hath established it, he created it ***not in vain****, he formed it* ***to be inhabited****: I am the LORD; and there is none else.*
- *Isa.* 45:18 (KJV)

Clearly, God *established* a working order to the earth (i.e. a *world*) at some time; and formed it ***not in vain***. It must have reached that state later on. God did not create the earth *without form* and *void*; but rather to **be inhabited** in an established, organized way! The Bible seems to make it clear that the world did *not* start out like evolutionist would want to make us believe - it was structured, clean, and organized cosmos. It *began* that way; and, for whatever reason, did not last.

The World "Was"

And the earth **was** *without form, and void...*
- *Gen.* 1:2 (KJV)

The English use of the word ***was,*** in this verse, also stands out as somewhat of a convincer for the Gap Theory. The English *was* originates in the Hebrew word *hayah.*[12]

Looking at *Strong's Concordance and Lexicon*, we clearly see that the word means "to be," "to come to pass," or to "come about." *Hayah*, also, can mean "to happen" or to "fall out." Again, with this in mind, we see the verse could take on a whole new meaning:

> *In the beginning God created the heaven and the earth. And the earth **had fallen out; to be laid to waste**, and **emptied**...* - *Gen.* 1:1-2 (in retranslation)

As we see, this could also represent a *point of change* - time for a *destruction* and *recreation* event to occur. Simply:

> *If the Hebrew verb were **eue**, "was" would be an accurate translation; but it is **eie**, the **causative** form of be which means become. This causative form (eie) appears more than twenty times in chapter one of Genesis alone, and everywhere denotes **a change**, and not mere existence.* (Johnson, 2004, p. 205)[13]

The translators of the 1611 King James Version probably thought the world was created in six days; as so many of faith do today! They probably inserted the English words *they* thought were right; to make everything fit in with what most around them have always perceived. As we look into these *other* possible meanings of the original Hebrew, however, we begin to discover how the words of the Bible could take on a whole new meaning.

The "Foundation of This World"

As we've already postulated, the established *world* before our own might have been destroyed, for whatever reason; which left God to do something entirely different the next time. At that moment, He began to set up the foundation for a *new* world. The word *foundation* can also be of some significance, in regards to this Gap Theory.

To begin, the English word *foundation*, in the New Testament, comes from the Greek *katabole*. Interestingly enough, the word *katabole* actually originates from the word *kataballo* - a compound word made up of *ballo* ("to cause, to throw") and *kata* (down").[14]

As we now see, in the original Greek - the root of the word for *foundation* - also may signify something that was "caused" to be, or "thrown," down. Could this *foundation*, then, represent the period when an established cosmos was "thrown down," "cast down," "descended," or "fell" - only to be *set back up* again in another way?[15] The *foundation* of a planetary *world*, here, seems to represent the turning point of a whole new era:

> *For we which have believed do enter into rest, as he said, As I have sworn in my wrath, if they shall enter into my rest: although the works* ***were finished*** *from the* ***foundation*** *of the world.* - *Heb.* 4:3 (KJV)

The above states the works of God were *already in place*, or were already *finished*, by the time of our world's foundation. What does this mean? Could it be that each *foundation* was the representation of a time when a former world was *thrown down*, and a whole new organized cosmos (or world) was about to take its place?

> *And forgettest the LORD thy maker, that hath stretched forth the heavens, and laid the* ***foundations*** *of the earth... I am the LORD they God... I may plant the heavens, and lay the* ***foundations*** *of the earth...* - *Isa.* 51:13-16 (KJV)

Note the *plural* use of the word *foundation*, here - as one era of work being completed, with another (among a number) arising out of the ashes. This could easily signify that the happened more than once.

Throughout these examples, we may begin to understand how the Gap Theory could gather momentum. Yet, there is one powerful verse of the Bible which seems to provide evidence towards its disproval:

> *Wherefore, as by* ***one man*** *sin entered into the* ***world****, and death by sin; and so death passed upon all men, for that all have sinned.* - *Rom.* 5:12 (KJV)

This verse, according to many, is thought to be "proof-positive" that there was no previous world before Adam. There was one man who brought sin into our world, according to this verse; so how could there be anything before Adam… right? It's totally understandable to conclude this, but we have to remember the context of how the word *world* was used, here. We know how it could mean something *different* than the physical planet. The original Greek word for *world* - *kosmos* - seems to put things right back into perspective, here. Adam brought sin into our *present* "organized order of things," and not the whole time frame of the planet. Simple! There might have been sin before our current world; and this verse doesn't deny that there could have been more than one organized cosmos, or *world* - it only affirms that Adam was the person who brought sin into *this* world![16]

So, if Adam was only the one who brought sin into *our* world, then could there have been a similar situation on our planet, before this destruction? Could there have been human beings on the earth before this flood, bringing it to a point where God felt He *had* to pass judgment? Did this particular *world* go through its own version of our up-and-coming "end times?"

> *The concept of pre-Adam civilizations was well accepted by early sages. Also in support of the notion of lost civilizations, we read in Psalms (105:8) the words: "He hath remembered his covenant for ever, the world which he commanded to a* ***thousand generations****"... The Talmud reveals that this verse indicates that God's Law, the Torah, was given to Moses and all the Hebrews at Mount Sinai* ***after the elapse of 1,000 human generations****. Since Moses was of the 26th generation following the first progenitor the human race, this indicates* ***some 974 generations before Adam****.* (Killian, p. 29-30)[17]

We recall, from the beginning of this chapter, one author summarized this all as the following:

> *In the beginning God created* ***numerous worlds****, destroying* ***one after the other*** *as they failed to satisfy Him. All were inhabited by man, a thousand generations of whom He cut off, leaving no record of them.* (Graves and Patai, 1964, p. 45)[18]

"Being Overflowed With Water"

The following verse also seems to state something so intriguing, in support of our Gap Theory:

Whereby the world that ***then was****, being overflowed with water, perished...*
- *II Pet.* 3:6 (KJV)

Interestingly, as we know, the original Greek word for *world* is *kosmos*.[19] What "world that then was" are we talking about here? Could these verses be referring to a flood, such as the flood of Noah… or a flood *before* our present *world*? Could this flood of water represent what happened before the world *that was our own*? Interestingly, our current world, according to the Bible, has been called *this* ***present*** *evil world* (Gal. 1:14). Maybe, before this present, organized world, there was another world - with its own story, and its own destruction via a flood. Obviously, we see in the beginning of our Six-Day Creation:

...and darkness was *upon the face of the* ***deep****. And the Spirit of God moved upon the* ***face of the waters****.* - *Gen.* 1:2 (KJV)

Seems that had to have been some kind of water catastrophe, here - a catastrophe which, perhaps, inundated a great deal of the planet's former *world*. This was why the Spirit of God would be hovering over the face of so much *water*, here - it may have been the remnants of the previous world's destruction.

If there could have been *a number* of these destroyed-and-recreated *worlds* to our planet, could the earth, indeed, be much *older* than young Creationists may have thought? Science theorizes the planet is up to a few billions of years old. Could this lead to the possibility of science and the Bible having at least *some* common ground, here, as far as the planet's age?

Pre-Adamic Flood Vs. Noachic Flood

What about all of that *water* on the earth, in early Genesis? Did that help destroy man's existence before the *world* of our own?

<u>*Psa.* 90:</u>
2 *Before the mountains were brought forth, or* ***ever though hadst formed the earth and the world****, even from everlasting to everlasting, thou art God.*
3 *Thou turnest man to destruction; and sayest, Return, ye children of men...*
4 *Thou carriest them away as with a* ***flood****...*

Could some of the biblical references to a flood **not** be just the flood of Noah, but a flood that destroyed the entire world before Adam?

We recall, from Genesis 1:2, that a blanket of water covered the earth, just before the time of Adam's formation:

And the spirit of God moved upon the face ***of the waters****.*
- *Gen.* 1:2 (KJV)

Since God had to "let the dry land appear" (Gen. 1:9), in our "Six-Day Creation," then it's easy to assume the surface of the earth was covered with water in vast quantities.

We also see, from the previously-mentioned II Peter 3:6:

Whereby the world ***that then was****, being overflowed with* ***water****, perished...*
- *II Pet.* 3:6 (KJV)

Obviously, a lot of people have speculated (and still do) that this was regarding *Noah's* flood. Yet, the Bible might be mentioning, what could be, *another* flood - a flood with a lot of the same destructive attributes.

How so? Let's look at some possible reasons:

<u>*2 Sam. 22:*</u>
2 *And he said, The LORD is my rock, and my fortress, and my deliverer;*
3 *...thou savest me from violence.*
5 *When the waves of death compassed me, the floods of ungodly men made me afraid;*
8 *Then the earth* ***shook and trembled****; the foundations of heaven* ***moved and shook****, because he was wroth.*
10 *He bowed the heavens also, and came down; and darkness was under his feet.*
12 *And he made* ***darkness*** *pavilions round about him,* ***dark waters****, and thick clouds of the skies.*
15 *And he sent out arrows, and scattered them; and discomfited them.*
16 *And the channels of the sea appeared,* ***the foundations of the world were discovered****, at the rebuking of the LORD.*

In the flood mentioned above, the earth "shook and trembled;" arrows came and scattered the inhabitants; water and darkness were the result. The Bible does not mention any of this during Noah's flood. In almost a mirror image of the above verses, we have:

<u>*Psa. 18:*</u>
1 *I will love thee, O LORD, my strength.*
4 *The sorrows of death compassed me, and the floods of ungodly men made me afraid.*
7 *Then the earth* ***shook and trembled****; the foundations also of the* ***hills moved*** *and were* ***shaken****, because he was wroth.*
9 *He bowed the heavens also, and came down: and darkness was under his feet.*
11 *He made* ***darkness*** *his secret place; his pavilion round about him were dark waters and thick clouds of the skies.*
12 *At the brightness that was before him his thick clouds passed,* ***hail stones*** *and* ***coals of fire****.*
13 *The LORD also thundered in the heavens, and the Highest gave his voice; hail stones and coals of fire.*
14 *Yea, he sent out his* ***arrows****, and scattered them; and he shot out* ***lightnings****, and discomfited them.*
15 *Then the channels of* ***waters*** *were seen, and* ***the foundations of the world were discovered*** *at thy rebuke, O LORD.*

Again, we have the *hailstones*, *lightning* and *coals of fire* launched upon the earth. We have great *earthquakes*, and mountains *shaking*. Although all of this could have occurred during the flood of Noah, nothing was mentioned in the Biblical account as the same. Interestingly, the word "**foundations**" was used in both of these. Could this be actually describing a turning point - a flood which occurred before the **foundation** of our own world? In both of these above verses, they end with the mention of a **new** foundation discovered - a new *world* after the destruction, seemingly! There was no new world after Noah's flood. As well, Noah's world wasn't *completely* destroyed; there was no *new* foundation to be had.

In the next set of verses, "foundations" was used again:

<u>*Psa.* 104:</u>
4 *Who maketh his angels, spirits; his ministers a flaming fire:*
5 *Who laid the **foundations** of the earth, that is should not be removed forever.*
6 *Thou coveredst it with the **deep** as with a garment: that **waters** stood above the mountains.*
7 *At thy rebuke they (the angels) fled; at the voice of thy **thunder** they hasted away.*
8 *They go up by the mountains; they go down by the valleys unto the place which thou hast founded for them.*
9 *Thou hast set a bound **that they may not pass over**; that they **turn not again** to cover the earth.*

Whoever may have lived during this time did not survive this disaster; whenever it occurred. The following verses, similar to the above, seem to go a little further:

*I beheld the earth, and, lo, it **was without form**, and **void**; and the heavens, and they had **no light**.* - *Jer.* 4:23

Wow, this is surprising. Even though this verse sounds like it should be in Genesis Chapter 1, it is in the Book of Jeremiah. It is similar to the situation of Genesis 1:2-3: "And the earth was without form, and void;" as well as God saying "let there be light." Could this verse of Jeremiah be describing this same time - the time before Adam? As we read further, we see, in the same chapter of Jeremiah:

<u>*Jer.* 4:</u>
24 *I beheld the **mountains**, and, lo, they trembled, and all the hills moved lightly.*
25 *I beheld, and, lo, there was **no man**, and all the birds of the heavens were fled.*
26 *I beheld, and, lo, the fruitful place was a wilderness, and all the cities thereof were broken down at the presence of the LORD, and by his fierce anger.*

27 *For thus hath the LORD said, The whole land shall be desolate; yet will I not make a full end.*
28 *For this shall the earth mourn, and the* ***heavens above be black****; because I have spoken it, I have purposed it, and will not repent, neither will I turn back from it.*

Jeremiah 4:25, again, makes it known that *there was no man* in the world, around this time. This could not be Noah's flood - we know there were survivors, there! Again, we also see that the mountains moved and trembled about - again, not mentioned in Noah's flood. The word "trembled," interestingly enough, comes from the Hebrew word *raash*, which means *to undulate*. Assumedly, there was a great shock, or earthquake, which *undulated* this former world before Adam. These shocks caused the mountains to rise and fall, and move from side to side; in smooth, wave-like motions.[20] The Hebrew word translated into English, above, as "moved lightly" is *qalal*, which means "to be light in the sense of weight." So, we see that the mountains must have moved around like waves in the ocean; the hills tossed about like featherweights. There seems to have been *major* cataclysmic change in *this* flood, a change which *shook* the earth to its core! In Noah's flood, however, there were no earthquakes or shaking of mountains; nothing like this.

The above verses also makes it known that "there was no light;" as well as says "the heavens above became black." This could easily be construed as more of a *permanent* result, rather than as a temporary, storm-darkened sky (as in what most-probably happened in Noah's flood).

There are another set of verses which say almost the same as the above:

Job 9:
4 *He... is mighty in strength...*
5 *Which* ***removeth the mountains****, and they know not: which* ***overturneth*** *them in his anger.*
6 *Which* ***shaketh*** *the earth* ***out of her place****, and the pillars thereof tremble.*
7 *Which commandeth the* ***sun****, and* ***it riseth not****; and* ***sealeth*** *up the stars.*

Interesting, though: we see, here, that the Lord shook the earth "out of her place." Again, major change happened at this time. What really happened here, in these examples… and *when*?

According to another ancient source, we have another anomaly: after the flood of Noah, God assures Noah that, "…therefore I will not **again** destroy together all living as **I have done**."[21] Interesting: maybe He *did* bring a flood upon the earth more than once. The ancient historian, *Philo*, also interprets this same promise to Noah in much of the same way, but with a little more:

> *…therefore I (God) will not now proceed to smite all living flesh* ***as I have done at other times****…*
>
> - *Works of Philo Judaeus* Questions and Answers on Genesis 2(54)[22]

Could these *other times* be the times before our "Six-Day Creation?" Why don't we already know more about these ancient times, then?

No Memory of Former Things?

From the former verses, we may be able to assume that, in the flood before Adam (the so-called "pre-Adamic" flood), the former world was entirely cut off, and all human life ended.[23] This was an abrupt halt to everything; there was no direct genetic link of any ancient human beings to our modern day.[24] We have an interesting example of information which might support this: a 12,000 year-old strand of human hair, reportedly, was discovered in Woodburn, Oregon, in 2001: "DNA analysis of hair follicles found at the site have so far failed to find a match with any known human racial type living on earth today," says William Orr, the professor who analyzed it. "The geneticists found the hair didn't match any Asian hair DNA. It didn't match African, European. It didn't match anything."[25] Interesting: this hair's DNA had *no* match with any modern-day human. Why? Could the reason be that those who existed before the Adamic flood were all wiped out? As we recall, in Jeremiah:

> *I beheld, and, lo, there was* ***no man****…*
>
> - *Jer.* 4:25 (KJV)

As we'll soon discover, this could be a reason why there weren't a lot of written accounts regarding the time before our own world's foundation. This could also be the reason why we, as human beings, do not have some sort of "collective memory" of anything before the Adamic flood. We don't have a lot except, possibly, these divinely inspired words of the Bible.[26]

The Bible also says that:

There is no remembrance of former things...
- *Eccl.* 1:11 (KJV)

Maybe this information is something God feels we really don't need to know too much about. Although we may not know a lot about the Pre-Adamic flood, that doesn't mean it never happened.

Willingly Ignorant?

As we begin of our journey through the earliest parts of Genesis, we seem to have some scriptural evidence of a world before our "Six-Day Creation." If this is the case, then why do so many people - Christian and not so - scoff at this possibility? Why have so many scoffed at the Gap Theory? Why do so many learned people of the past, and in this day and age, automatically seem to debunk these thoughts - as well as others this book will put in front of you? The answer is simply:

*...for the time will come when they will **not** endure sound doctrine; but after their own lusts shall they heap to themselves teachers, having itching ears; And they shall **turn away their ears** from the truth, and shall be turned unto **fables**.*
- *II Tim.* 4:3-4 (KJV)

*...This people honoreth me with their lips, but their heart is far from me. Howbeit in vain do they worship me, teaching for doctrines the commandments of men. For laying aside the commandment of God, ye hold **the tradition of men**... ye reject the commandment of God, that ye may keep your own **tradition**.*
- *Mark* 7:6-9 (KJV)

The following verses also seem to affirm that in the **last days** (our modern times, maybe?) there will be people who *scoff* at the very idea of most any thoughts - other than their own. Please notice the last verse in the following block, especially:

<u>*II Pet.* 3:</u>
3 *Knowing this first, that there shall come in the last days scoffers, walking after* ***their own lusts****,*
4 *And saying, Where is the promise of his coming? for since the fathers fell asleep, all things continue as they were from the beginning of the creation.*
5 *For this they* ***willingly*** *are* ***ignorant of****, that by the word of God the heavens were* ***of old****, and the earth standing out of the* ***water*** *and in the* ***water****...*

II Peter, here, states that people will become "willingly ignorant of" the word of God. The Greek word for *willingly*, here, simply means "to choose." People will either *choose* to believe what they always were taught (i.e. tradition) or *choose* to be ignorant of things that could actually be truth. How true, today.

They *willingly* hold to their traditions as valid. They do not want to accept change; nor open their ears to any other theories which might abound. Sound like today? Sounds like a good reason why so many of us have not heard of the Gap Theory? How often are scientists willing to accept anything *other* than their own pet theories (such as evolution)? Anything else is shouted down. Even beyond the scientific community, how often do people want to hear *anything* that's not "politically correct," or different than commonly held traditions of society and culture? Today, the Bible has even been *demoted* to a collection of false stories, or myths. And, the above verses clearly state that people will be *willingly* ignorant of so much that out there, *even* the possibility that "the heavens were of old" and the earth was once "in the water." Well; what might *this* mean, then? The next verses of this chapter seem to clear up any confusion:

<u>*II Pet.* 3:</u>
6 *Whereby* ***the world*** *that* ***then was****, being overflowed with water,* ***perished****:*
7 *But the heavens and the earth,* ***which are now****, by the same word are kept in store, reserved unto fire against the day of judgment and perdition of ungodly men.*

Wow! This explains so much. It seems to mention a world that was once in and out of the water. Then, this same world was overflowed with water; and perished. Finally, there is a heaven and earth (i.e. a world) which are here ***now***.

Why Don't More People Question Tradition?

There are a number of fossils which tell us there could be a lot more to our history than only 6,000 years. Science claims the world is much older than this - maybe it is. That doesn't necessarily mean Bible is false, however. A lot of the upcoming stories and theories on early stories of Genesis might sound as unbelievable as the Gap Theory - at first. But, that's why this book was written: to give us a chance to see the *other* side of things we were trying to be *steered away* from - the *other* side to culture, politics, and religion. This is all important; and deserves an audience, too. Maybe the Bible isn't as full of unscientific *myths* as many portray it to be. Maybe there was something to all of the above verses, and the Gap Theory, itself - knowledge that some "powers that be" feel is knowledge we shouldn't know, or doesn't support their agenda(s).

It's time to try to make sense of the "politically incorrect," and see these words for what they really may be saying!

> *Thou sendest forth thy spirit, they are created: and thou* ***renewest*** *the face* ***of the earth****.* - *Psa.* 104:30 (KJV)

Maybe there is a lot more truths to the Bible than we were previously taught, or had ever thought.

More Biblical Re-interpretations

Also, we should realize that our focus of life, today, doesn't really have to depend on knowing all of the information *before* this time of Adam and Eve. We no longer live in that world. Do we really need to comprehend *all* of what happened before our present world? What we really need to do is to concentrate on the world *that is now* - with this Gap Theory knowledge in the back of our minds.

Since the Bible is the *book of the generations of Adam* (Genesis 5:1), it is a book that is concerned more with the world that existed *since* his formation. Any hints of a world before our own were probably divinely inserted - to help us question secular tradition and manipulation.

As we begin to take our next steps in understanding *more* of these hidden tidbits of obscured knowledge, we'll take a deeper look at the stories of early Genesis. From these, we will probably be able to "fill in the gaps" of so much that the Bible has left out; and help us get as close to the *entire* story of our past as we can. Why do we want to do this? They say that understanding the past is a key to our future. The reason we try to decipher what happened, so long ago, and why, is because it just might be the first step in helping find the *truth* of who or what we are, where we come from, and just what direction we might be heading, as a whole.

As well, we do this research to help us expose just who might *willingly* be trying to conceal all of this information; and why. Genesis and Revelation are indeed the books of the Bible which seem to have been the *most* misinterpreted, and also *most* misunderstood. The reason why is simple: these books help expose those responsible for wanting to keep us "in the dark," as a civilization. The **Serpent's** system does not want exposure: much like an animal who runs and hides after being found hiding under a rock - a rock which has just been turned over.

So, as we continue onward, let's discover more alternate views of the "Six-Day Creation" - up to the Garden of Eden, and beyond.

Chapter 2

Angels From "The Well of Lost Souls"

When he (God) comes, Fire shall be ***darkness*** *in the midnight black.*
- *Sibylline Oracles* 1st Fr. (notes)[1]

...thy (God's) judgments are a great ***deep****...*
- *Psa.* 36:6 (KJV)

In the last chapter, we discovered how the world might actually be a lot *older* than many have previously thought. We've also postulated how the organized cosmos on earth could have been destroyed, and refashioned; all the way up to the "Six-Day Creation" of Genesis 1! In this chapter, we may discover that most every man, angel - whoever occupied our planet in the worlds past - *died*; or somehow *fell* from their present state of being. We'll, soon, get more into how all of it might have gone down.

Although our former *world* might have been destroyed, could there have been anyone who survived… into this one? Did *anything* of special significance pass on, from one world to another? To answer this, we must begin to sound a little esoteric. We need to go into the spiritual realm of understanding here: what *if* spiritual remnants of the former world were brought back, into our own world, by God (and not via reincarnation). What if the spiritual part of individuals - their *soul* - were cast down into some **dark**, temporary **state of abyss** (at the time of the previous world's destruction); and was brought **back up again**, into the world of our "Six-Day Creation?" And *why*?

This becomes an intriguing - and most difficult - topic to delve into, here; but, the Bible *does* seem to get into this topic quite a bit (believe it or not). As we'll soon discover, the words ***darkness*** and ***deep***, as in the above quotes, often show up in Biblical narratives; as well as other ancient texts. What do they stand for? *Why* are they used? And, most importantly, *what does it all mean* to our expose on the Serpent, and *Mystery Babylon*?

First, we'll discover that these two words could stand for an actual *place*, or *abode* - a spiritual place, actually. This place could also be thought of as a "Well of Lost Souls," if you will. This *Darkness*, and the *Deep*, could then be considered an actual *place* where spiritual *remnants* of our former world (i.e. the *souls* of everyone alive during that time) would be stored - up to the destruction of a previous world. It would be a place where these souls would just site; ready and waiting for whatever God had in store for them, next! Think *hell*, here. Think *purgatory*. Think *hades*. All of these have some similarities to the Darkness and the Deep, but are **not** quite the same.

Anyhow, these "remnants" would be comprised of, for the most part, *human* souls; possible *angelic* souls thrown in there, as well - *whatever* might have been destroyed at this time of God's judgment. Sounds a little difficult to understand; it might even sound a little like reincarnation - until we read, further.

First off, the Bible makes an interesting statement: that we were *already* accounted for *before the foundation* of this world:

> *According as he hath chosen us in him* ***before the foundation*** *of the world.*
> - *Eph.* 1:4 (KJV)

> *Then shall the King say unto them... Come, ye blessed of my Father, inherit the kingdom prepared for you* ***from the foundation*** *of the world...*
> - *Mat.* 25:34 (KJV)

How does this happen? How would we even be thought of, before the foundation of this world? Could the possibility be that each one of us was a part of God's plan *before* the foundation of this present world? And, if this is so, we now need to ask ourselves: why would *we* be so relevant if there wasn't even any part of us in existence yet? Could there have been a piece of us already there, before our world's creation? To a number of us, these ideas might begin sound like they're going down a totally *unbiblical* pathway; but they aren't. It takes a bit to explain - but it leads to some totally fascinating ways to look at, and interpret, these earliest parts of the "Six-Day Creation." So, a bit of an open mind is required here, because it will begin to sound a little complex - but it will *all pay off*, in the end!

So, to advance ourselves deeper into the understanding of early Genesis, we need to really comprehend what the *Darkness* or *Deep* may have *really* stood for; and the significance they may have once had on our very souls! To begin, here, we need to dive into even *more* esoteric topics; and, first, decipher what would be considered the spiritual "antithesis" of such a dismal place known as the *Darkness* or *Deep*. Let's look deep into what the Bible calls "*the Light*."

Divisions of "Light" and "Dark"

As we proceed, one thought which may come into the minds of many might be: if no *physical* human being was able to be pass on, from our former *world,* could something *spiritual* have passed - from one *world* to another? Could human *souls* have gone through? And; what about any *angelic* beings which might have existed during the previous world? What if *they* became a part of God's destruction, here, as well?

All individuals - at the time of God's judgment - were silenced at this time. What if some of them (human or angel) really didn't *deserve* such a harsh judgment, seemingly? What if some, at the time, were living pious lives; and fell as a victim of circumstance - just at the wrong place at the wrong time? It seemed God used a "carpet-bombing" approach to His judgment; destroying everything and everyone - regardless of their moral stance. If something like this happened - a destruction which essentially wiped the whole planet out of sentient beings - wouldn't it be up to God to devise a plan to be fair to the just? It's quite possible the previous world didn't have the same pathways to reaching heaven as we do today. God is a fair God.

All of this might sound like a stretch, or conjecture; but there *are* some interesting interpolations of traditional Christian beliefs which *really* could be looked upon in other, *different* ways. Let's see…

The "Light of Face"

We continue our look at early Genesis, with the second half of Genesis 1, verse 2:

<u>*Gen.* 1:</u>
2 *...and **darkness** was upon the face of the **deep**. And the spirit of God moved upon the face of the **waters**.*
3 *And God said, Let there be **light**: and there was light.*

As many people might accept, there are *two* "hemispheres" of existence to our planet: the natural and *the supernatural*; the corporeal and *the spiritual*. Most of us understand common, everyday meanings to words we are bringing up, here. Could this *darkness*, the *deep*, and *water* all have deeper, supernatural meanings, though? How about the word *light* (as compared to the word *darkness*)? Could the two, somehow, be looked upon as some kind of *spiritual* extremes, as well?

As we already know, the *world* could have a couple of different meanings, beyond the obvious. There could be more meanings to light and darkness, as well:

<u>*Gen.* 1:</u>
4 *And God saw the **light**, that it was good: and God divided the light from **the darkness**.*
5 *And God called the light Day, and the darkness he called Night. And the evening and the morning were the first day.*

This type of *light*, for example, could be referring to some supernatural, divine "light," of sorts. The English word for *light*, in the above, comes from the Hebrew *owr*, which could also symbolize *the light of someone's face*. Often, the features of one's *face* were defining perceptions of people in the ancient of days. A person's race, color, national identity, and other outward factors of their existence were often summed up by one looking at predominant *facial* features. So, *light*, in the Bible, could often be used in conjecture with the *brightness* (or *countenance*) of one's face (as in Job 29:24, Psa. 4:7, 44:4, and Psa. 104:15, for example). Even Proverbs 16:15 states that, "when the king's *face* shineth…" Could the word *light*, in these above verses, also be referring to the *bright countenance*, or *shine*, *of one's face*? What beings would have a bright, shining countenance such as this?

*O Lord, is there in the world another god besides You, who created **angels** and filled **them with light**...*
- *First Book of Adam and Eve (The Conflict of Adam and Eve with Satan)* 27:10[2]

Supernatural/spiritual beings - also known as **angels** - were traditionally thought to have possessed the ability to be "*of the light*," or to show *light*. The ancient Christian theologian, *Augustine*, once made this statement:

*Where Scripture speaks of the world's creation, it is not plainly said whether or when the **angels** were created... when all things, which are recorded to have been completed in six days, were created and arranged, how should the angels be omitted, as if they were not among the works of God, from which on the seventh day He rested?... There is no question, then, that if the angels are included in the works of God during these six days, they are that **light** which was called Day... For when God said, Let there be light, and there was light, if we are justified in understanding in this light the **creation of the angels**, then certainly they were created partakers of the eternal light which is the unchangeable Wisdom of God, by which all things were made... so that they, being illumined by the Light that created them, might themselves become light and be called Day... The true Light, which lights every man that comes into the world, John 1:9 - this Light lights also every pure angel, that he may be light not in himself, but in God...* - *Augustine* City of God 11:9[3]

The word *light* has also been defined as:

- *Spiritual awareness; illumination.*
- *A prominent or distinguished person; a **luminary**.*[4]

In the Bible, there are many examples of this *light* as a symbol of God, godliness, as well as some sort of *angelic* illumination.

*...LORD, lift thou up the **light** of thy **countenance** upon us.*
- *Psa.* 4:6 (KJV)

*...God is **light**, and in him is no darkness at all.*
- *I John* 1:5 (KJV)

The Elohim

Seemingly **alone**, the Bible says that God created and reformulated the heavens and the earth. Curiously enough, however, by the *end* of our "Six-Day Creation," God had a group of angels with Him (Gen. 2:1). Some schools of thought believe that, collectively, God and his angels might have been known as the *Elohim*, or *bene Elohim*.[5] If this could be the case, just *when* did He pick up these angels; and where from? Could the *light* of the First Day (i.e. Gen. 1:3) actually be a group of angels - ones He formed, or called up, at this time… beings with a *light* or *shine* in their *face*?[6]

Angelic Beings "Created" on Day One?

> *...These are the holy angels of God, who were **first** created...*
> - *Shepherd of Hermas* Visions 3:4[7]

> *...on the **First** Day... God created... the hosts which are invisible (that is to say, the **Angels**...), and all the ranks and companies of Spiritual beings...*
> - *Cave of Treasures* The Creation. First Day[8]

> *For on the **first** day He (God) created... all the spirits which serve before him - the **angels**...*
> - *Book of Jubilees* 2:2 (also 2:8)[9]

On the **first** day, did God lay out the groundwork for the *supernatural* cosmos, as well as the natural? It states, in the classic *Legends of the Jews*, that God taught the biblical Enoch (a great teacher of ancient days) about the creation of all things; such as earth, man, and the ***light***.[10] We also see that:

> *I commanded **in** the very **lowest parts**, that **visible** things should come down from **invisible**...*
> - *2 Enoch* 25:1[11]

> *...God revealed unto him (Enoch) great secrets, which even the angels do not know. He told him how, out of the **lowest darkness**, the visible and invisible were created...*
> (Ginzberg, 1909, p. 135)[12]

As we see, out of the lowest *darkness* God had brought the visible and invisible… the visible and invisible *what*? Could the *invisible* be angelic beings, here? And, if they were, who would be the *visible*, then - *human* beings?

> *...He (God) willed, and heaven, earth, water, air, fire,* ***and the angels*** *and* ***darkness****, came into being...*
> - *Book of the Bee* Ch. II[13]

What about the *Darkness*? Is it *really* considered some abode for lost souls of our previous *world*?

The Dark Extreme

So, if we look at Genesis, Chapter 1, again:

> *Gen.* 1:
> 2 *...and* ***darkness*** *was upon the face of the deep.*
> 3 *And God said, Let there be* ***light****: and there was light.*

The above verses of Genesis say that the *darkness was upon the face of the deep*, and *light* brought up soon after. So, could this *Light* have come from that "holding area" of human and angelic souls - the *Darkness*?[14] Could they be angels? Does this all sound fantastic? Let's read further:

> *...God... commanded the light to shine* ***out of darkness****...*
> - *II Cor.* 4:6 (KJV)

Could this stand for the "opposite" state of *darkness* and *dreariness* - angelic *light*?

> *...from whom if an angel turned away, he becomes impure, as are all those who are called unclean spirits, and* ***are no longer light in the Lord****, but* ***darkness*** *in themselves, being deprived of the participation of* ***Light*** *eternal...*
> - *Augustine* City of God 11:9[15]

> *...(He created) the **abysses** and the **darkness**, eventide (and night)...*
> - *Book of Jubilees* 2:2[16]

> *This earth is above the **water**, and, below the **Ocean**, is the **awful abyss of water**, and below the abyss is a rock, and below the rock is SIOL (Sheol – i.e. Hell, Hades, etc.), and below SIOL is the wind, and under the wind is the boundary of **darkness**.*
> - *Bakhayla Mikael*, p. 12[17]

So, to move further, we now need to take a look into this alternate, supernatural term - the *opposite* of what a bright, lively state of being; such as an angel would have. Being *dark*, or being in *darkness*, can also mean:

- absence of light; lacking enlightenment
- characterized by gloom; dismal
- having depth
- concealed or secret; mysterious; obscure
- exhibiting or stemming from evil characteristics or forces[18]

One biblical resource (figuratively) defines *darkness* as misery, destruction, death, ignorance, or wickedness.[19] And, along these same lines, the word *night* also could mean:

- a time or condition of gloom, obscurity, ignorance, or despair
- a time or condition marked by absence of moral or ethical values[20]

So, we know *darkness* and *night* can be considered close in a number of ways; as well, seemingly in sharp contrast to the concepts of *light* and *day*. Colossians 1:13 even stated that some **angels** possessed the powers of *darkness*! So, we have an idea what *light*, *angels*, and the *brightness of day* might signify (to many); could there be some angelic significance to the *darkness*?

> *Ye are all the children of **light**, and the children of the day: we are not of the **night**, nor of **darkness**.*
> - *I Cor.* 5:5 (KJV)

II Cor. 6:
14 *Be ye not unequally yoked together with unbelievers: for what fellowship hath righteousness with unrighteousness? and what communion hath* ***light*** *with* ***darkness****?*
15 *And what concord hath* ***Christ*** *with* ***Belial****? or what part hath* ***he that believeth*** *with an* ***infidel****?*

Maybe there are angels out there, which, either *came up* from the darkness, or were *of the darkness*, in some way. We've already postulated there could be a "well" of sorts - a "holding place" of souls from our previous world. If we could associate some angels with *light*, naturally, one might be able to associate *lost* or *negative* souls with this place of *darkness* - a place of souls who were, perhaps, in some sort of unenlightened state.

There is a good deal of ancient written evidence to support this; even in the Bible! Ancient Jewish lore, for example, mentions a place for souls of the unborn are kept, known as *the Guff*. Could this be the same thing? Could the *Darkness* represent some gloomy place of *unenlightened absence* - where souls of our previous world would temporarily be held - until it was time for God to do something with them?[21]

> *...in mythology the underworld was imagined as a* **chthonic** *place of* **darkness**, *contrasting with the celestial realm...*
> ("Black and White Dualism", n. d., p. 1)[22]

...the word *chthonian*, in the above, literally means, "belonging to the earth" or "in, under, or beneath the earth."[23]

The Darkness... Upon the Deep

So, if the *Darkness* could be some actual, *spiritual* plane of existence beneath our world, then could the *Deep* also have a deeper, supernatural significance, here - representing some sort of watery "area," perhaps, which surrounds this *Darkness*?[24] Let's see.

Thy righteous is like the great mountains; thy ***judgments*** *are* ***a great deep****...*
\- *Psa.* 36:6 (KJV)

If we acknowledge that there could be some validity to *supernatural* elements of these above words, then we might be able to assume that God designated a huge number of dead souls to enter this *Darkness* at one time. This dark, holding cell was located in the bottom of some spiritual abyss; way beneath the waters that covered most of the previous world. The abyss, itself, was known as the ***Deep***.

Interestingly, there *are* Biblical meanings which seem to support this hypothesis, with the *deep* being equated to:

\- the deepest part of the sea (e.g. Psa. 69:15)
\- a state of **chaos** (e.g. Gen. 1:2)[25]
\- **the grave** or abyss (e.g. Rom. 10:7, Luke 8:31)
\- the bottomless **pit**, or hell (e.g. Rev. 9:1-2, 11:7, and 20:13)

If we absorb how the *deep* was used in the Bible, we could conclude that it means a whole lot more than just some portion of a body of water:

> *It is not unreasonable, then, to see "the deep" in Genesis signifying something greater than simply deep water... it has other shades of meaning as well, including the abyss and the grave... The Deep does refer to the ocean. But it also symbolic of a* ***judgment*** *against wrongdoing and bolsters the overall feel that all things* ***are not right*** *in creation as the opening passage of Genesis unfolds.* (Quayle, 2005, p. 16-17)[26]

What it all boils down to is simple: we've already postulated that our previous world, and every one of this world's inhabitants (at the time), were destroyed in a massive, destructive flood. This was just before the "Six-Day Creation" of Genesis, Chapter 1. The *Darkness of the Deep* represents a gloomy, 'holding area:' a supernatural area which held the previous world's (human and angelic) souls. The following seems to point towards this, as well:

*Or, Who shall descend into the **deep**? (that is, to bring up Christ again from the **dead**).*
- *Rom.* 10:7 (KJV)

Luke 8:
30 *And Jesus asked him, saying, What is thy name? And he (the demon-possessed man) said, Legion: because many devils were entered into him.*
31 *And they besought him that he would not command them to go out into the **deep**.*

God, upset with our previous world, enacted His own judgment, here. Destruction blanketed the entire planet. There poured the *souls* of every human and angelic being alive at the time - the righteous with the unrighteous; the good with the evil; the dedicated with the indifferent. The souls of **everyone** were bunched together into this one place. It was literally the enactment of the famous phrase, "destroy them all. God knows His own."

No, this was not hell. This was not eternal damnation. It wasn't even a place of Purgatory. It was just the place where God decided to hold the future inhabitants the *new* world He was going to bring about.

At the time of Genesis 1:2, the time was ripe for God to "hover over the face of the waters," and then take action. The time was ripe to "sort them out." Thus began our "Six-Day Creation." If anyone believes in places such as Hell, Hades, or Heaven, then their postulation might not be too far off - just "tweaked" a little. We'll soon see what this *Darkness upon the Deep* has to do with the rest of Genesis, and *Mystery Babylon.*

But, Isn't This Reincarnation?

On the surface, this entire concept might begin to sound **a lot** like pagan reincarnation. There might be some similarities on the surface, but there are some *major* differences:[27]

*The first earth age was inhabited by us, by our souls in a different form... in this earth age we have flesh bodies because we were created and formed from the dust of the earth... Your spirit (your intellect) and your soul will either live forever or will be consumed in the lake of fire (hell)... Every soul goes through each earth age **only one time**, but it is the **same one soul**... So this second earth age... became necessary so as to allow every soul to come through it and make a **choice** between following God or* *following satan... God placed a veil between this earth age and the first so that we cannot know what side we were on in that revolt, nor do we possess any memory of it... this is not saying there is any reincarnations... Each soul can only pass through each earth age* ***one*** *time; just like we live in this earth age but we can also live in the next earth age,* ***referred to as Heaven****... what would be the use of this earth age, which itself is nothing more than a* ***proving*** *ground, a place and a time for us to decide whom we will love and follow?*

("When Was the Beginning?", n. d., p. 8-12)[28]

It's the *ages* of the world that had changed - *not* our souls! We are not progressing "upward" *on our own* - towards some "god-like" state of immortality, as the typical believer of reincarnation would have us believe. None of this happened without the hand of God, refashioning the world into what *He* wanted it to be, next! This is not the same as reincarnation, at all.

As we may recall:

Whereby the world that ***then was****, being overflowed with water, perished...*

- *II Pet.* 3:6 (KJV)

The world of the past was abruptly halted, leading to God's regeneration; next would be His decision on what to do with all of what He had just destroyed. So, with this knowledge in mind, we see that:

He shook the earth and then covered it with water, to give it a good cleansing. This was NOT Noah's flood, because everything on the earth perished! Everything. After God "washed" away those evil rudiments, He began to prepare this old earth for a new age... By allowing His children to be born ***as innocent babes****, through their mother's womb, they would have no remembrance of that great rebellion in the world* ***that then was****.* ("3 World Ages", n. d., p. 1)[29]

The victims of this blanket destruction would not have any remembrance of the world *that then was*. As a result, those *human* souls not brought back up as the *light* (i.e. former *angelic* souls) were allowed one more chance in the world... the world *which is* ***now*** (II Pet. 3:6-7). Any souls placed in the *Darkness of the Deep* - human or angelic - would now be brought up, by God, and placed *somewhere* (and, at *some time*) in His brave new world:

> *...on the First Day of the Week the Spirit of holiness, one of the Persons of the Trinity, hovered* ***over the waters****, and through the hovering thereof over the face of the waters, the waters were blessed so that they might become producers of* ***offspring****... As the mother-bird maketh warm her young by the embrace of her closely covering wings, and the young birds acquire form through the warmth of the heat which [they derive] from her, so through the operation of the Spirit of holiness, the Spirit... the leaven of the* ***breath of life*** *was united to the waters when He hovered over them.*
> - *Cave of Treasures* The Creation. First Day[30]

So, why might God have *hovered* over the waters, in such a way? Simply, some of the individuals terminated at the time of the previous world's judgment might have been *undecided*: they did not know yet, or decide (in their own hearts) whether or not to follow God. *Now*, in regards to these individuals, *this* was their second chance. In this brave new world, *they* will have another opportunity - to make a decision on just where their loyalty lies. *Now*, our present world would become a **proving ground** for a number of ancient, undecided souls... those of the past. There is more.

The Good, The Bad, and the Undecided

> *II Pet. 3:*
> 6 *Whereby the world that* ***then was****, being overflowed with* ***water****, perished:*
> 7 *But the heavens and the earth,* ***which are now****, by the same word are kept in store, reserved unto fire against the day of judgment and perdition of ungodly men.*

In regards to their relationship with God, some souls of our previous world may have leaned more towards following *good*; others leaned towards *evil*. Still others were not sure which direction they were heading. In the world before our own, there must have been some people absolutely faithful to God. There also may have been angels in vicinity of the earth's atmosphere. Some of these could, very well, have been those brought up as ***angels*** in our present world - as the *Light*.[31] Because of their obedience, God may have granted them *splendor* and *radiance* in this world of today. They did not have to go through this decision-making process as other souls previously sent to the Darkness. So, now (according to some), this council of angelic beings, along with God Himself, could have been considered *bene Elohim* - God and his angels.[32] The "good" souls were now brought back up.

Back in the *Darkness*, however, undecided souls were still not able to reach this worthy plateau; so they had to live again, as human beings, in this modern world. Thus began our new, modern version of spiritual warfare - the struggle of each undecided soul to make the most important choice of his or her life.[33] Although much of this all, at first, might be a little hard to swallow, there *are* scriptural passages (as well as information from other ancient texts) to back up most of what is postulated here!

Here is one interesting ancient, non-Biblical interpretation of our present world's formation. As we'll see, it's very *similar* to the beginning verses of Genesis - with elements of our above theory, as well:

> *Here is what the Ancient Egyptians said about the First Time, Zep Tepi, when the gods ruled in their country: they said it was a golden age during which the* ***waters of the abyss*** *receded, the primordial* ***darkness*** *was banished, and* ***humanity****, emerging into the light, was offered the gifts of civilization.* (Hancock, 1995, p. 381)[34]

A lot of ancient mythology, in fact, cited some sort of universal *chaos* as the beginning of our present world. Let's look at another mythological account which might bring much of this together.

Other Non-Biblical Accounts

The Greek philosopher *Orpheus* stated that, in the beginning, there was ***Time***.[35] Another Greek, *Hesoid*, said much the same thing. Why? Interestingly enough, Time could also have been known as *the Eternal*. Could *Time* and *the Eternal*, in fact, be a pagan definition of the biblical God? Could this be the *Eternal*, the *Alpha and Omega*, the *Beginning and the End* (Rev. 22:13) of scripture?

As one easily might suppose, pagan accounts were often in sharp, diametric contrast to the religious teachings of the ancient Hebrews, and the Bible. Pagans, then, often considered the God of the Bible as some insignificant, negative, deity; or some universal *invariant*. The universal invariant - *Time* - could be thought of as negative in the way that it eventually causes a person to be *old, useless*, or *worthless*. Labeling God as *Time*, indeed, in sharp contrast to the Creator God we know of, in the Bible.

The pagan Greeks also held that from *Time* proceeded *Chaos*: the bottomless abyss holding the Night.[36] From Chaos also came forth *Erebus*: the covered *pit*.[37] Well, what is this bottomless abyss - this *pit* - they were talking about: could it be the *Darkness of the Deep*?

The ancient Greeks also referred to a daughter of *Chaos* as the *Night* (or *Nyx*) - the ***darkness*** which inhabited our primordial living space![38] So, what does this mean? Could the *Chaos* of the Greeks, here, be the same thing as the *chaos* of Genesis 1:2? Again, we may have the very same *postulation* of creation; only from a different perspective. All of this, eventually, will help us in our venture of deciphering just what the *Serpent*, and *Mystery Babylon*, is. So, as we begin to discover other parallels of biblical insights, we'll need to move further ahead - beyond the *first day* of creation - to help us in our goal of understanding all of this obscured knowledge. Let's go.

The Second Day - The Firmament

Gen. 1:
6 *And God said, Let there be a **firmament** in the midst of the waters, and let it divide the waters from the waters.*
7 *And God made the firmament, and divided the waters which were under the firmament from the waters which were above the firmament: and it was so.*
8 *And God called the firmament Heaven. And the evening and the morning were the second day.*

Let's, first, take a look at the *second* day of our present world's "creation." In regards to understanding this book, we just need to know a little about the *firmament*, and what it is. It refers to a vast canopy of water, now placed in the higher regions of our atmosphere, by God.[39] This expanse of water was said to have covered the earth, from the time of the

"Six-Day Creation," all the way to the flood of Noah. It was said to be able to give protective qualities to all of the living creatures of the world - shielding them from the harmful effects of the sun, as well as solar radiation. This also allowed people to live a lot longer than they do today, as well as granting plants and animals the same. It even allowed some plants and animals to grow much *larger* that we see them, today.

This *firmament* seems to be hinted *further*, in other parts of the Bible:

> *Praise him, ye heavens of heavens, and ye* ***waters*** *that* ***be above the heavens****.*
> - *Psa.* 148:4 (KJV)

Beyond the above, what might another reason God may have had, with regards to His creation of this canopy? One reason might be: there was already a great deal of water on the earth at the beginning of our "Six-Day Creation" (see Gen. 1:2). Maybe some this water God positioned to go *up*, into the atmosphere, to clear the earth of a little. After all, He needed to find a place to put all of this water covering the earth at the time, to allow dry land to appear.

Interestingly enough, the talk of a firmament may even give us *further* hints to what might have happened before our previous world - as well as what brought it to such a *demolished* state. According to one modern theory, dying stars (such as the sun) were said to have the ability to give off a great deal of *water*. One expert is stated as thus: "some of the hydrogen of those dying stars produced great quantities of waters across the cosmos."[40] Could this excess water be the result of some near-flying celestial body, which was, once, destroyed near the earth? Did a "star," or some celestial object, explode right next to the earth, bringing a flood of water upon it? Could the possible death of the previous world's "sun" have caused the earth to flood with water?

From Genesis, Chapter 1, we may be able to assume that there was, once upon a time, a source of *light* to our previous world - a source which was, since, destroyed. The reason we could assume this is because there was a "great light" which had to be created by God on the **fourth** day - a light also known as our *sun*. Logic follows that: if the world before our "Six-Day Creation" had turned *dark* - as Genesis, Chapter 1 suggests it did - then it was probably because the source of the world's *light* was already destroyed. It necessitated the recreation of *another* light source.

If this "sun" of our previous world did, indeed, collapse, then there forms a postulation on what could have happened next: "...because there was no gravity via this former 'sun,' the planet's former clouds and atmosphere had no attractive force to keep them in suspension. They also descended, in moisture, to the earth surface, and helped bring water that flooded the earth."[41] So, now, the planet was flooded with water. And it came time for God to find a place to put all of it.

He easily could have placed some above the earth (as the firmament), and allotted most of the rest to retreat, down into the great caverns, or wells, of the earth. We're not sure exactly how He accomplished all of this; but science, today, *does* allow for the possibility of great quantities of water to be located deep beneath the earth's surface... amounts vast enough to fill oceans.

Beyond being a place to relocate some of this water, the firmament could have been put in place for, yet, another reason: God wanted to divide the waters in this way to signify a "new," reconfigured, cosmos - something entirely different than the world before.[42] As we'll soon discover, God seemed to have *refashioned* certain parts of our planet in this world (such as placing water up in the firmament), and had to *create* other parts, outright... maybe because some parts - such as the sun - were totally destroyed.

The "Sea"

Along these same lines, we now get insight into *another* often-misunderstood term of the Bible: the ***Sea***. One of the greatest biblical arguments *against* the previous-chapter's *Gap Theory* lies in the following verse:

> *For* ***in six days*** *the LORD* ***made*** *heaven and earth, the* ***sea****, and all that in them is, and rested the seventh day...* - *Ex.* 20:11 (KJV)

Wow, how damaging to our Gap Theory - sounds pretty open and shut, in our case... or *does it*? The verse states that it took *only six days* for God to create the heavens and the earth - contrary to anything else. Yet, to find *true* meanings of a verse, we sometimes need to look at the original Hebrew words, here. Another important thing to consider, here, is how a verse is used *in context* with its surrounding verses. They tell us what the verse actually might be saying…

First, for example, the Hebrew word for *made*, in the above verse, is the word *asah*: meaning "to do," "fashion," or "accomplish." Interestingly enough, it is **not** the same as the Hebrew word used for "created" in Genesis 1:1! This, right off the bat, supports our theory that these two acts represent two different periods of time – one for the creation of the planet, and the other, possibly, a *reorganization* of some former world. Could the above verse, then, only be referring to some *reorganization* of a previous world? Also, when we look at the *context* of which this one verse resides, we further begin to understand what it all might mean.

Let's take a look at some of the verses which are directly before it:

<u>*Ex.* 20:</u>
9 *Six days shalt thou labour, and do all thy* ***work****:*
10 *But the seventh day is the sabbath of the LORD thy God: in it thou shalt not do any work, thou, nor thy son, nor thy daughter, thy manservant, nor thy maidservant, nor thy cattle, nor thy stranger that is within thy gates:*
11 *For in six days the LORD* ***made*** *heaven and earth, the sea, and all that in them is, and rested the seventh day: wherefore the LORD blessed the sabbath day, and hallowed it.*

Again, these verses seem to represent the time frame when God was giving Moses the Ten Commandments. He wanted to instruct the Israelites to keep Sabbath; and not work. And, if we look at the *context* of these verses, we clearly see that they refer to *work*, and the concept *of work*: simply, one should work for *six* days, and rest on the seventh… just like God did with the "Six-Day Creation." The formation of our world designated a pattern for His people to follow, later on, here. This, again, could be describing the six-day formation of our worldly cosmos - not necessarily the beginning of the planet, itself.

We also notice, in the above, that God made *the* ***sea***. Now, what was the sea, here; in actuality? Was it a plain body of water; or could it be something *deeper*? We recall there was a watery *chaos* on the earth, around the time of our current world's formation; so He really didn't need to create any seas of *water*, here - the whole planet was filled with water, at the time of day 1. This *Sea* may have been the name of something *else*, beyond water. Let's see.

Looking at a verse in the book of Revelation, we also discover:

And I saw a new heaven and a new earth: for the first heaven and the first earth were passed away; and there was ***no more sea****.* - *Rev.* 21:1 (KJV)

Well, this verse in Revelation seems to parallel the above verse in Exodus, in a few ways. And, we also need to ask ourselves, in this situation: does this above verse of Revelation state that there will be *no more water* on the earth, in future times? As well, what would be so important about God only desiring to remove a large expanse of water from the earth, here?

It, more likely, seems to mean that God would want to eliminate a certain characteristic of our **present world** - a supernatural/spiritual characteristic of our world, known as *the* ***Sea***. Let's see what this *Sea* might actually be:[43]

<u>*Job* 38:</u>
1 *Then the LORD answered Job out of the whirlwind, and said...*
4 *Where wast thou when I laid the* ***foundations*** *of the earth? declare, if thou hast understanding...*
8 *Or* ***who shut up the sea*** *with doors, when it brake forth, as if it had issued out of the womb?*
9 *When I made the cloud the garment thereof, and thick darkness a swaddlingband for it...*

The above verses seem to state that: when God laid the foundations of the earth, He *then*, shut up the **sea**! At the foundation of our current world - at the time of the "Six-Day Creation" - God decided to close up a particular place. Could this *particular place* be related to the ***Darkness of the Deep***? Did God "shut up" the place where He emptied a lot of souls present, since at the end of our previous world? To get more of a definitive answer, let's move on - to the Third Day.

The Third Day

<u>*Gen.* 1</u>:
9 *And God said, Let the waters under the heaven be gathered together unto one place,
and let the dry land appear: and it was so.*
10 *And God called the dry land Earth; and the gathering together of the waters called
he **Seas**: and God saw that it was good.*

The gathering of waters, in the above verses, is known as *Seas*.[44] Note the *plural* use of this word, here. The *Sea* - in the previous verses of Exodus and Revelation - is set in the **singular**. Could *this* Sea be something else - the name of one *specific* place, possibly?

> *And forgettest the LORD thy maker, that hath stretched forth the **heavens**, and laid the foundations of the earth... I am the LORD they God, **that divided the sea**... I may plant the heavens, and lay the **foundations** of the earth...*
>
> \- *Isa.* 51:13-6 (KJV)

In our "Six-Day Creation," we've postulated that God *divided* the souls in the *Darkness of the Deep*; and slowly ushered them back into our current world. So, logic dictates that: at the end of our current era, there really shouldn't be any more souls **left** in this *Darkness* to bring up, right? And, if this was the case, there really wouldn't be much of a need to retain, at least this section, of a holding place such as this - i.e. there would be **no more sea**! We recall the above verse of Revelation, stating there *would be no more Sea.* If we've reached the end of our present existence - at this point of Revelation - then it might be a ripe time for God to bring on the "end times": the *last* of these undecided *souls* of the previous world would have already been born!

So, this *Sea*, most probably, is not just a body of water, but another way to describe the *Darkness of the Deep* - a *deep* <u>*sea*</u> of spiritual/supernatural *darkness*, deep below the earth… and more evidence in support of our theory.

Let's move further, and see what unconventional ideas the rest of these creation days have in store for us!

The Sun and Its Light - The Fourth Day

<u>*Gen.* 1:</u>
14 *And God said, Let there be lights in the firmament of the heaven to divide the day from the night; and let them be for signs, and for seasons, and for days, and years:*
15 *And let them be for lights in the firmament of the heaven to give* ***light upon the earth****: and it was so.*
16 *And God* ***made two great lights****; the greater light to rule the day, and the lesser light to rule the night: he made* ***the stars also****.*
17 *And God set them in the firmament of the heaven to give light upon the earth,*
18 *And to rule over the day and over the night, and to divide the light from the darkness: and God saw that it was good.*
19 *And the evening and the morning were the* ***fourth*** *day.*

Next, we see that: it was during *this* day (and *not the first*) that God created a sun - a *new* sun (as well as moon); and created them *outright*. Obviously, logic tells us that the world before this time must have been in darkness, *still*… at least, up to this point. This further provides us evidence for the validity of that *Light* (on the First Day) as being something more than just physical *light*, such as *the sun*… because the sun was not created until the fourth **day**![45]

The prophet *Job*, below, seems to be referring to what might happen when God decides to take judgment. Could Job have been referring to the time of God's destruction of our previous world, here? If possibly, then the verses also seem to confirm how the sun, at one time in our distant past, might not have been around to show light:

<u>*Job* 9:</u>
4 *He (God)… is mighty in strength…*
5 *Which removeth the mountains, and they know not: which overturneth them in his anger.*
6 *Which shaketh the earth out of her place, and the pillars thereof tremble.*
7 *Which commandeth the* ***sun****, and* ***it riseth not****; and sealeth up the stars.*

Could it have been destroyed, at the end of our previous world; necessitating it to be brought back, again, in Day *Four*?

More Angels Formed on This Day, As Well?

Also, what did Job mean, in the same set of verses, regarding *the* ***stars***?

<u>*Job* 9:</u>
7 *Which commandeth the sun, and it riseth not; and* ***sealeth up the stars****.*

It also states, in Genesis 1:16, "He made the stars" during the fourth day. Now, why would God need to *make* stars at this time? Were they destroyed, along with the previous world, and need to be reconfigured in such a way; or could this mean something *more*?[46]

Another interpretation of the word *stars*, here, could also signify that God had the desire to fashion more *angels* at the time of the fourth day - not the *Light* of the first. These were a different bunch of angels; but, angels, nonetheless.

The Bible sometimes uses the word *star* in the same context as the word *shining ones*, as well as angels:[47]

When the morning ***stars*** *sang together, and all the sons of God shouted for joy?*
- *Job* 38:7 (KJV)

Strong's Lexicon equated that the original Hebrew word for *stars*, in the above, as a figurative word for "brothers," for "numerous progeny," or for "personifications." Could these "stars" have represented *other* groups of angels, brought up by God, at this time?

<u>*Psa.* 104:</u>
4 *Who maketh his* ***angels****, spirits; his ministers a flaming fire:*
5 *Who laid the* ***foundations*** *of the earth...*

One interesting commentary (on the above verses) seems to give us further proof:

In mentioning the angels in the context of the creation of the heavens, waters, and earth, this psalm (104:4-6) seemed to be saying that God had created the angels ***at the same time*** *as these other things.* (Kugel, 1997, p. 59)[48]

So, if these might have represented *angels*, then they could have been some of the angels from our previous world, left over from the formation of the first-day's group - the *Light*. *Who* was exactly *who*, here - and why God did things exactly this way - might forever remain a mystery to us. But, what is important to understand is that different groups of angels may have been brought up by God; at different times, and for different reasons. And, we've also postulated where, at least, their souls came from: the *Darkness* of the *Deep*… the deepest part of some spiritual/supernatural *Sea* beneath us. So, why is this all important? We'll soon need to discover a lot more about *angels* in their own right: why were they put back on the planet; the capacity of these angels to do right (as well as to harm); and the impact they would have on the entire world, to come.

Another question that might, naturally, arise out of this all: are we just going to talk about angels, here? What about the *other* souls who were left in the deep, dark depths of the supernatural *Sea*, up to this time? Quite possibly, in day ***Five***, it became high time for God to bring another group of individuals up, onto the earth - as *human beings*.

Chapter 3

The Pre-Adamites

*And Adam gave names to every **animal**, **and** to the **birds of the heaven**, and to every **beast of the open field**. But for Adam, no partner was found like himself.*

- *Genizah Manuscripts* Gen. 2:20[1]

The above is a pseudo-biblical account of creation - at the time of the first man, *Adam*; and how he was supposed to name each animal. If we notice, in the above, he **also** gives names to the *birds of the heaven* and every *beast of the open field*. Now, wait a minute: why notate these two groups separately if they're all were considered *animals*? And, possibly, if these two groups weren't necessarily animals, here - just what were they? There are other ancient sources, including the Bible, who often list these "birds" and "beasts" in the same way. Why?

As we also see, in the above, Adam was looking for a partner - a helpmate or a wife - at the same time he was told to provide them their names. Now, *why* would Adam want to look for a wife *among these lowly animals*, here? What reason would Adam do this, if he had nothing to choose from? Reportedly, this was *before* the time that Eve was created. So, the question now arises: was Adam *really alone* at this time? Could Adam have been, subtly, looking for a *human* mate, within the social construct he was facing, here? Might there have been even *more* to the Garden of Eden than so many of us have once assumed?

In this chapter, we hope to show ancient written evidence - even *in the Bible* - that points towards there being *other* groups of people on the earth here; people existing slightly before, and during, this early time of Adam… known as the ***pre-Adamites***. Let's take a look at the *Fifth Day*, and discover there could, quite possibly, have been *other* groups of people formed at this time; and what their reasons to be might have been, within the Garden.

Day Five - Out of the Darkness

> *The LORD by wisdom hath* ***founded the earth****; by understanding hath he established the heavens. By his knowledge the depths* ***are broken up****...*
> - *Prov.* 3:19-20 (KJV)

> *Dead things* ***are formed*** *from* ***under the waters****, and the inhabitants thereof.*
> - *Job* 26:5 (KJV)

As we already recall (from Chapter 2, *Angels From "The Well of Lost Souls"*), there could have been a great many *souls* to be brought up from the previous world - from the supernatural/spiritual *Sea*. The next souls to come forth from this *Darkness* of the *Deep* would be *human beings* - the undecided having to make, what would be, the greatest decision of their lives. God assuredly knew about *each* individual, and their moral leanings, before the foundation of the world (Eph. 1:4, Mat. 25:34):

> *But ye are a* ***chosen*** *generation, a royal priesthood, an holy nation, a peculiar people; that ye should shew forth the praises of him who hath called you* ***out of darkness*** *into his marvellous light...*
> - *I Pet.* 2:9 (KJV)

Interesting choice of wording, here: God knew "who was who," even when their souls were still in the *Darkness*.

The ***Sea***, as we've already postulated, was another name for this watery *chaos*, which leads us to this next verses of Genesis:

> *And God said, Let the* ***waters*** *bring forth abundantly the moving creature* ***that hath life****...*
> - *Gen.* 1:20 (KJV)

As we see, Genesis 1:20 may have stated that God commanded waters out of the ***Sea*** - the supernatural *Darkness* of the *Deep* - to bring forth, abundantly, moving creatures which *hath life*. Well, what does this mean? Just *who* might be these moving creatures? Are they animals; or something more? And, what is the significance of the words "that hath life," here?

Our next postulation begins with these three words. When we look at the original Hebrew for these words, they are represented by the word ***nephesh***. The word *nephesh* not only means to be "living," have "breath," or "life," but also to have "a higher intelligence," or "soul."[2] Now, what kinds of beings possess this *higher intelligence*?

The Hebrew for the words "bring forth abundantly" (in the above verse) is *sharats*; which means "to multiply," to "bring forth," "swarm," and even "creep." The Hebrew for "moving creature" (in the above) is *sherets*; which signifies "creeping" or "swarming things." Put them together (using these alternate, Hebrew meanings) and we get a very different layout than the King James Version:

> *Let the waters bring forth the swarming (human?) creatures who* ***have a soul****...*
> - *Gen.* 1:20 (in retranslation)

Again, what beings truly have such a *nephesh*, or "higher intelligence," other than human beings, or angels? What animals would have this particular type of *soul*?

In the next verse, we have:

> *And God created great whales, and* ***every living creature that moveth****, which the waters brought forth abundantly, after their kind...*
> - *Gen.* 1:21 (KJV)

In this verse, the Hebrew *nephesh* is missing. Could the former verse, here (Gen. 1:20) refer to the time when God brought up beings who had *a soul*, and the latter (Gen. 1:21) be the time when He fashioned sea-dwelling animals? Note the word "And," in the beginning of the verse above: could this signify "the next step" of God's creation process, maybe - human beings being brought up *first*; and *then* the formation of the animals?

Groups of Human Souls

> *And Elohim said, Let the waters swarm abundantly with moving creatures that have life... **Everything swarmed at the same time**, both good waters of holiness and evil waters of **the other side**... they were intermingled...*
>
> - *Zohar* Safra Det'zniuta 38[3]

We already surmised that all the vanquished souls of the previous world were made to swarm together, in the *Darkness* - the good, the bad, the undecided… all of them. And, we've already postulated that *angels* may have already been brought up as the *Light* (on the First Day); with God bringing up other angels - possibly known as *the stars* - on the Forth. The rest of the souls down there - *human* souls - could have been brought up at *this* time, and put into respective groups (to be known as *the pre-Adamites*).

Let's look at some of these possibilities; and what the Bible may have notated them as:

- **The *Fowl of the Air***
- **The *Beast of the Field* and/or *Cattle***
- **The *Creeping Thing That Creepeth***
- **The *Adamites***

So, just *who* were these groups? Why name them as animals? Interestingly, these **same** groups would not only be mentioned at the beginning of our "Six-Day Creation," but a thousand years later - as going aboard and coming off of Noah's ark! They were even mentioned 1500 years after this! But, why - why would these names be associated with animals? Why does it all seem so strange?

Bird, Beast, and Creature… Now, Not Politically Expedient!

If we look at the names of these above groups, obviously, they don't sound like groups of people. Why would the Bible do anything like this? Isn't it insulting to even suggest? We have to remember, first, that the Bible wasn't written in today's language - things were very different back in ancient times. In the Biblical era, this type of labeling wasn't out of the ordinary; sometimes, it wasn't even meant to sound offensive. That's just how it was.

The ancient Israelites, for example, stated that some Gentiles (non-Jews) acted like animals.[4] Some were called "beasts" and "creatures;" others were even referred to as "dogs:"[5]

> *His watchmen [are] blind: they are all ignorant, they [are] all dumb* ***dogs****, they cannot bark; sleeping, lying down, loving to slumber. Yea, [they are] greedy dogs [which] can never have enough, and they [are] shepherds [that] cannot understand: they all look to their own way, every one for his gain, from his quarter.*
>
> \- *Isa.* 56:10-11 (KJV)

> *For without [are]* ***dogs****, and sorcerers, and whoremongers, and murderers, and idolaters, and whosoever loveth and maketh a lie.*
>
> \- *Rev.* 22:15 (KJV)

As stated, some of these references weren't necessarily meant to be insulting:

> *For the* ***creature*** *was made subject to vanity, not willingly, but by reason of* ***him*** *who hath subjected the same in hope...* - *Rom.* 8:20 (KJV)

> *And (Jesus) he said unto them, Go ye into all the world, and preach the gospel to every* ***creature****.* - *Mark* 16:15 (KJV)

> *Therefore if any man be in Christ, he is a new* ***creature****: old things are passed away; behold, all things are become new.* - *II Cor.* 5:17 (KJV)

Obviously, these verses weren't referring to animals, here - they were talking about people. Could this be the real meaning of the following?

> *And God said, Let the waters bring forth abundantly the moving* ***creature*** *that* ***hath life****...* - *Gen.* 1:20 (KJV)

It was not only the ancient Israelites who talked like this; practically all nations talked in this same way. Just because they were referred to as *animals*, that doesn't mean they were! That's just the way it was. That's just another way the ancients might have used to "classify" a particular group of individuals (in some cases, according to how they *related* to the elements around them)! For example: a human being was sometimes associated with a "beast" because of their occupation - they worked around animals. There wasn't a lot to assist people in these days - there were no cities, nor paper, nor schools. The animals were one of the few things around that people could use to associate their thoughts with, to turn into symbols of something, etc..

In the Bible, there were eight different Hebrew and Greek words translated into our word *beast*. Each word, as we know, can mean different things in different contexts. In ancient times, almost everybody understood that some of these words were used for these ways. Since thoughts and perceptions have changed over the years, the men who translated the Bible into English may have begun to perceive these *beasts* as ***only*** animals. As a result of their misconceptions, the *real* meanings could have been taken out of many verses! These misconceptions can truly hurt our interpretation of the Bible - especially when we need to discover the real truths of these early times.

Let's first look at one group: the *Fowl of the Air*.

The Fowl of the Air

> *And God said, Let the waters bring forth abundantly the moving creature that hath life, and* ***fowl*** *that may fly above the earth in the open firmament of heaven.*
>
> \- *Gen.* 1:20 (KJV)

There could have been a few reasons why this group was called *Fowl of the Air*... something *beyond* what one might think, regarding how it might look in our everyday, natural world. Another thought that might come to one's mind is: should this title *even be* a correct one? Well, in ancient times, the word *bird* and *fowl* were, often, used interchangeably.[6] The only major difference between the two (at least in today's world) is that these *fowl* are birds destined to be consumed by mankind (such as *ducks*, *chickens*, *quails*, etc.).

But, the *deeper* Biblical meaning behind this group of individuals, probably, may be one of the most difficult things for us to swallow, overall! Yet, we really need to bring this possible interpretation of the group to *light*, because these *Fowl* (or *birds*) come up, time and time again, in Biblical phrases! They may not have a direct importance to *Mystery Babylon*, as well; but, they *do*, in a number of ways, help us to get a grasp on what *Mystery Babylon* is all about. So, an *open mind* might need, here, in this case, to absorb all of this.

To lay it out, plain and simple: the *Fowl of the Air* could, actually, be another group of human, or ***human-like*** individuals… brought up from the *Darkness of the Deep*. They were not *totally* human, but not totally angelic, either… but, somewhere *in between*. This also means that - in ways - they, probably, had some higher, angelic-like qualities to them, as well! Since they were almost human, they could live their lives on earth as human beings - for the most part… but they had something more to them. Let's explain.

During the Fourth Day (of the "Six-Day Creation"), God, reportedly, formulated the Garden of Eden (according to certain ancient sources). This was His attempt to establish a new, organized society of people, in this world. And, beginning in the *Fifth* Day, groups of humanoid, or human-like, individuals were going to be brought up from the *Darkness*, for this task of repopulation - helping to work in, or around, the Garden. Some of these new groups would probably assist in the domestication of animals; some might work the fields; some may even help with the Garden's maintenance. Still other may possess *angelic-like* qualities, to help them in their daily duties (whatever they might be). This latter group, here, could have been the reason why these *Fowl of the Air* were brought up: there may have been some tasks to perform, in the Garden, by which only a group of individuals with angelic-like characteristics might be able to perform!

> *When were the **angels** created?... They were created on the fifth day, for it is written, "And let **fowl** fly above the earth" (Gen. 1:20)... (Thus angels too **fall** within the category of **beings that fly**, and were created on the same day as all flying creatures.)...*
> - *Genesis Rabbah* 1:3 (& notes)[7]

Does this sound fantastic? Well, as we'll soon see, it all may, indeed, not be too far from what the Bible consistently says about *birds*, and *fowl*, in a number of verses! It's interesting to note that (such as, in the above work) - beyond the linking of *fowl* with *angels*, here - we see that fowl and angels "fall within the category of **beings that fly**." Now, in order to cement the theory that these *birds* and *fowl* actually might be linked to *angelic beings*, we need to understand some of the words associated with *both*. Let's view some of the words Scripture might link, here to *bird* or *fowl*: such as to *fly*, to have *wings*, *heaven*, the *air*, etc..

First, we see that, in the Bible, a *bird*, essentially, equates to any sort of "flying animal." Well, we've already understood (above) how Biblical references to *beasts*, *creatures*, and *animals* could, in certain contexts, be referring to human beings! The Bible even seems to suggest that these *birds* and *fowl* could, in some circumstances, be referring to angelic beings, as well:

> *And he cried mightily with a strong voice, saying, Babylon the great is fallen, is fallen, and is become the habitation of devils, and the hold of every foul spirit, and a cage of every unclean and hateful* ***bird****...* - *Rev.* 18:2 (KJV)

The Biblical reference to the *bird*, in the above, isn't in regards to an innocent swallow. In another Biblical verse (containing the *same* original Hebrew word used for *bird*, in the above), we have:

> *And I saw an angel standing in the sun; and he cried with a loud voice, saying to all the* ***fowls*** *that fly in the midst of heaven, Come and gather yourselves together unto the supper of the great God...* - *Rev.* 19:17 (KJV)

We see, in the above, that angels are speaking to all of the "fowls that fly in the midst of heaven" - and telling them they should gather in the midst of God. Of course, angels would be talking to *other angels*, or *angelic-like beings*, here… in order to invite them to such a supper. They would have *no* reason to invite ordinary hawks and eagles to sup with God, obviously!

Now, whatever specific qualities these angelic *birds* or *fowl* might have had (over people); exactly what they might have looked like; and whatever specific roles they might have had in the Garden; we don't know, for sure. One could guess they had positions which required the use of supernatural knowledge, or super-human ability - all of which a normal human being couldn't provide.

We, now, see an example of these *Fowl of the Air* - and their presence - all the way back in the Garden of Eden. In one ancient source - *The Book of Adam* - we have a story, regarding Adam and Eve. Eve was really upset at Adam, and didn't know where he was. She made an interesting plea to the beings of her immediate area:

> *Is there none among the* ***birds****, who would go to him and tell him (Adam), "Come help Eve, your spouse." I beg of you, all you* ***races of heaven****, and when you go to the east, relate my present sufferings to my lord (Adam).* - *Book of Adam* 19:2[8]

Again: what animals of ancient times could *talk*? What birds were of a *race*, in the past? And, why would Eve even want to call out to *animals*, anyhow, and have them relay the words to Adam? Could these "birds," again, just be another group of beings: *angels*, or humans with *angelic-like* qualities?[9]

Later on, in the same story, Adam eventually finds Eve, and she says to him:

> *My lord, Adam, have you not heard the sound of my tears... have not the* ***birds of the heavens*** *and the beasts of the earth informed you, for I begged them all that they tell you about it...* - *Book of Adam* 20:2[10]

Again, which animals are able to engage in rational conversation, like this... except for *human beings* and/or *angels*?

One could assume that, in the Bible, a *bird* or *fowl* represents a "flying animal," or "flying creature." And, if we assume that *birds* or *fowl* could be lumped together with any beings which *can fly*, let's come to terms with some of the *other* possible meanings of *flying*, or to *fly*. The Bible also seems to hint to this ability as one "passing," as one's "swiftness;" or as one's ability to move through the air "by means of wings." Now, what significance could this all have, here? Could other definitions of *flying*, here, be related to one's *swiftness* - or, their *swiftness* of *passing* through the "veil"... of one world to another? In other words, could this be one's ability to come into, and go back out of, our natural, terrestrial world? Angels, reportedly, have the ability to "fly" - or disappear - from our natural world... to the supernatural/spiritual. One moment, they're there, right in the midst of our human presence; the next minute, they seem to have, swiftly (and totally), vanished from the plane of our existence. Call it one's ability to become *invisible*!

And, on top of this: what about one's ability to fly, or move through the air, by means of *wings*? What could this all mean? The Biblical take on *wings* could, in ways, be symbolic of one's strength, or endurance. Obviously, the *Fowl of the Air*, with their supernatural abilities, could have been considered one of great strength, and also power. A *wing*, as well, could refer to a "flank," a "side-piece," or an "extreme body or part of an army."[11] In other words: could each member of these *Fowl of the Air* be considered as part of *a larger group*, or a *flank*? Could these *Fowl* have been known to be a "tightly-knit" group - a group which usually sticks together, for the most part (in physical locality, ideology, etc.)? If so, both of these descriptions might be a couple of characteristics of these *Fowl*. This is all the same as one mentioning a lion tamer - which opens up a person's mind to picture what a person, such as this, might look like (i.e. holding a chair; snapping a whip, etc.).

There is more: let's also look at why these *Fowl* might have been known as the ***Fowl of the Air***. By looking at the original Hebrew for *air*, here (as Strong's H8064 - *shamayim*), one might discover how it actually comes from an unused Hebrew root - which means *to be lofty*. Assuredly, angels (or even angelic-like beings) are very *lofty* in nature! The word *air*, in the Bible, could also be equated to words, such as "intelligence" or "information." And, as we know, angels easily could have thought to be endowed with a great deal of intelligence, and knowledge. So often, words such as *air* could have more than one meaning, or significance.[12]

***Air** spirits... were everywhere, **moving invisibly on their wings** above the world.*
(Curran, 2010, p. 65)[13]

And, on top of all this, the word *air* could even (in the Bible) be equated to words such as *heaven*, or *sky*. The word *heaven* is especially important, in this conversation. The Bible, essentially, lets us know there are *3* heavens, overall: the first is the natural world's region or expanse (i.e. the firmament above our heads), in which one may be able to see the sky above, the sun, and the stars. The second is the spiritual or supernatural realm - around us, and over us (of which Sammael/Satan, sorry to say, is the ruling authority over, now). This heaven, not only, represents the realm where the angels of Satan could access, but, represents the realm by which any of the angels of God could enter, and swiftly move through (if desired). And, the third heaven stands for the residence of God, and all He desires to be with Him. This heaven is way, way beyond this planet, and our galaxy, itself. So, now, we see the word *heaven* could, easily, stand for so much - especially, anything in the supernatural, or spiritual, realm:[14]

> ...*the cities* are *great and walled up to heaven...*
> - *Deut.* 1:28 (KJV)

> ...*Father, I have sinned against heaven, and before thee,*
> - *Luke* 15:18 (KJV)

So, if we really think about it: if these *Fowl of the Air* do possess angelic-like qualities, then couldn't they have - more appropriately - been renamed the *Fowl **of the Heaven***? Arguably, *yes* - and the Bible does seem to give us verses where this is so. Interestingly enough, the Hebrew word for *air* - often used in the *Fowl of the Air* (i.e. Strong's H8064 - *shamayim*) - was translated into English as *air* only 21 times (in the Old Testament)... compared to it being translated a whopping 398 times *as heaven*![15] So, if we think of it in these terms, the word *heaven* seems to be a little more practical (if not easier) to rename these beings, more appropriately, as *Fowl **of the Heavens*** (which, also, makes them sound a lot more angelic, as well)!

So, in conclusion, here, these *birds* or *Fowl* (in the Bible) could, actually, be a lot more than just animals - they could be representative of beings who actually *are* from heaven; or, at least, possess some of the elements which came from *heaven*! These beings might be able to move - swiftly - back and forth... through the realm of which one might consider to be the *heavenly* realm! All of this seems to bring us a lot closer towards being able to associate these *Fowl* with their origins - *heaven*, or that which is *heavenly*! And, we see, now, there could be *a lot more* to these Biblical *birds* and *fowl* than we once thought - as their actually being a part of a *semi-spiritual* race of beings, on earth (rather than just a group of falcons, or cock-a-toos).

Next, we'll see that, not only would the *Fowl of the Air* be a part human part angelic group of beings, the Biblical *Beasts of the Earth* could, also, represent *another* group of human beings, here… beyond just being a group of large, terrestrial animals. As we've already seen (in *The Book of Adam* quote, above), *both* groups could have been intelligent, rational beings - and *both* could have worked in the Garden of Eden.

> *My lord, Adam, have you not heard the sound of my tears... have not the birds of the heavens and* ***the beasts of the earth*** *informed you, for I begged them all that they tell you about it...*
> - *Book of Adam* 20:2

Let's, now, take a look at the *rest* of these human groups; to, now, be formed on the *Sixth* Creation Day.

The Sixth Day

Angels might have already been fashioned. Now, we see that even humans with angel-like qualities might have been already fashioned. So, in the *Sixth* Day, the time became ripe for the formation of human beings - those of which we are familiar with, today. The Sixth Day seems to have been reserved for the rest of the souls from the *Darkness* - now placed on the earth, together, in groups.

> *And God said, Let the earth bring forth the living creature (soul) after his kind, cattle, and creeping thing, and* ***beast of the earth*** *after his kind: and it was so.*
> - *Gen.* 1:24 (KJV)

Seems we have three more groups here, coming into fruition.

The English word *beast* (in the above) originates in the Hebrew word *chay*. The Hebrew *chay* could either stand for "soul," "beast," or "living creature." With traditional beliefs of King James translators at hand, their intent on interpreting the *Beasts (or Chay) of the Earth* group as some group of animals seems to be forefront. They probably assumed these *Chay of the Earth (or Field)* were animals, as with the aforementioned *Fowl*. Again, we'll continue to use the original Hebrew words, here (such as *Chay*; not *beast*), when we describes these groups; because it seems a little more appropriate to use these titles, rather than trying to equate a group of people to *beasts*, for example.

These ways to label these groups apparently goes beyond the Bible. In other ancient texts, such as the *Book of Jasher*, we see that the groups the *Beasts of the Field* and the *Fowl of the Air* were mentioned apart from those of the animal kingdom; as if they were not in the same ballpark:

> *...I (God) will gather to thee all the* ***animals*** *of the earth, the* ***Beasts of the Field*** *and the* ***Fowls of the Air****... And thou (Noah) shalt go and seat thyself by the doors of the ark, and all the* ***beasts****, the* ***animals****, and the* ***fowls****, shall assemble... And the Lord brought this about on the next day, and* ***animals****,* ***Beasts*** *and* ***Fowls*** *came...*
>
> \- *Book of Jasher* 6:1-3

> *And the Lord sent all the* ***Beasts and animals*** *that stood round the ark.*
>
> \- *Book of Jasher* 6:25

Why name these groups individually, and separate them from the "animals," if they're all the same? Wouldn't it be easier just to combine them all, and say "animals," rather than mention specific groups, such as this?

How about in the Bible? Does the Bible give *more* evidence that these *beasts* could indeed be people, in some cases? As we'll now see, there were people in the Bible referred to as *beasts*:

> *...The Cretians are always liars, evil* ***beasts****...*
>
> \- *Titus* 1:12 (KJV)

In another example, some people from the city of Ephesus were thought of as *beasts*.

If after the manner of men I have fought with ***beasts*** *at Ephesus, what advantageth it me, if the dead rise not? let us eat and drink; for to morrow we die.*
- *I Cor.* 15:32 (KJV)

These were obviously talking about people. How about the following:

The ***beast (chay) of the field*** *shall honour me...*
- *Isa.* 43:20 (KJV)

We need to ask ourselves: what kind of animal *knows how to honor*?

In another example: we know how domesticated animals subsist only on grass, hay, or cereals; none of them are really flesh-eating. The *Beast of the Field*, in the Bible, often could have been considered flesh-eating creatures (Gen. 9:3-5). Some were even known to be *cannibals* (II Sam. 21:10). There is more:

... thus said the Lord God; ***Speak*** *unto every feathered* ***fowl****, and to every* ***beast of the field****, Assemble yourselves, and come; gather yourselves on every side to my sacrifice that I do sacrifice for you... that ye may eat* ***flesh****, and drink* ***blood****... And I will set my glory among the* ***heathen****, and all the heathen shall see my judgment that I have executed, and my hand that I have laid upon them.*
- *Ezek.* 39:17 (KJV)

Again, these Fowl and Beasts were *spoken* to, as well as thought of as flesh-eating *heathen*. Now, who speaks to animals anyway? Animals really don't know their own moral character; and, assuredly, don't really care much about morality. There really needs to be a second look at the words "fowl" and "beast" in the Bible - more than what's commonly portrayed.

If the *Chay of the Field* could actually be a group of people - possibly even a people *who had some sort of intimate connection with the fields of the Garden maybe* - then we might be able to see that there's a lot *more* to our "Six-Day Creation" than most anyone thought.

The Behemah

And God said, Let the earth bring forth the living creature (soul) after his kind, ***cattle****, and creeping thing, and beast of the earth after his kind: and it was so.*
- *Gen.* 1:24 (KJV)

Going back to Genesis 1:24, and we'll see another Hebrew word - ***behemah*** - which was also translated into English as *beast*, or *cattle*. Could this represent still another group of people?

Interestingly enough, one major dictionary defines a *behemah* as "**someone** or something that is abnormally large and powerful" or "**a person** of exceptional importance and reputation."[16] Other dictionaries, such as Merriam-Webster (www.merriam-webster.com), also seem to confirm this: one archaic definition of *beast* has it as "a contemptible **person**," or "something formidable difficult to control or deal with." And, on top of it, the word *cattle* could also be defined as, "**human beings** especially in masse (or, in a group)."

As well, another closely-related word to the English *cattle* is the word *chatel* (or *chattel*). This word could also be used to signify a "slave," or "bondman." So, now that we have some evidence, could some of the *beasts* of the Bible, and elsewhere, have been *human beings* - maybe even designated (or bonded) to work in the Garden of Eden? Could the *Chay of the Field*, possibly, have been *in the field* for some sort of purpose? Maybe this group cared for the *domesticated animals* of the Eden - the first shepherds, or animal caretakers - the keeper of cattle, whatever.[17] Maybe certain groups of people, in the Garden, had certain roles, or functions to fill.

In another example, the following verse of the Bible describes *the Sabbath* - the Jewish time of rest:

But the seventh day is the sabbath of the LORD thy God: in it thou shalt ***not do any work****, thou, nor thy son, nor thy daughter, thy manservant, nor thy maidservant, nor thy cattle (****behemah****), nor thy stranger that is within thy gates...*
- *Ex.* 20:10 (KJV)

As we see, the *Behemah* are listed right alongside the *people* who work. Why? Why would *animals* need to take a break, this same way? That is, unless they are *not* animals, of course.

And, as with the *Chay*, these *Behemah* are also thought to have the capacity to be moral and immoral - something that only *humans* have:

> *I said in mine heart, God shall judge the righteous and the wicked: for [there is] a time there for every purpose and for every work. I said in mine heart concerning the estate of the sons of men, that God might manifest them, and that they might see that they themselves are **beasts** (behemah).* - *Eccl.* 3:18 (KJV)

Some people *could* act as an uncivilized as a *beast*, or as an animal… that's a fact. This sort of name-calling still exists today; in many forms. There is more.

The Creeping Thing That Creepeth

> *And God said, Let the earth bring forth the living creature (soul) after his kind, cattle, and **creeping thing**, and beast of the earth after his kind: and it was so.*
> - *Gen.* 1:24 (KJV)

Our last group of the three - the *Creeping Thing that Creepeth* - could, in theory, refer to *everyone* not involved in any of the serving positions in the Garden. Let's explain why. If the Bible is truly the "book of the generations of the Adam" (Genesis 5:1) as it claims, the *Creeping Thing that Creepeth*, is seems, were not too significant to the famous man Adam. It not that they weren't important as individuals, it's just, it seems, that they were not really part of the working order of the Garden of Eden - if we go with the thought that, perhaps, these individual groups each had their own role, alongside of Adam. The *Owph (or Fowl) of the Air* seemed to surround Adam and Eve in the Garden of Eden, as we have already read, possibly there to assist them in some fashion; the *Chay (Beast) of the Field*, quite possibly, could have been to be there to work the fields, or assist in farming; and the *Behemah* (*Cattle)* there to help work with the animals. But, the *Creeping Thing that Creepeth* did not have much of an occupation, at least as far as we know.

As before, the Hebrew word ***Remes*** will be used to replace the English *Creeping Thing*; so as to dignify this group of people more, as well. Although there isn't a lot about the *Remes* (*Creeping Thing*) *that Creepeth*, the fact they were another part of the mistranslation eventually will help shed light on the possibility of pre-Adamites here in the Garden; as we will see.

Was it only *occupation* which differentiated the groups, one might ask? Could these groups be different, somehow, by their *outward* appearance? That seems the million-dollar question. Not only could individuals of each group be recognized by outward appearance, how about differentiating them by the ways that a majority of them acted; or the ways they communicated with each other? Were they each of a different *race*, possibly? We don't know for sure. Yet, as time goes on - and our research amplifies on these topics - mounting evidence will help us to speculate further.

The Adamites

What about *Adam*, and the group that was contained this "first man?" What about the group that Adam was a part of? As we read on:

<u>*Gen.* 1:</u>
25 *And God made the beast of the earth after his kind, and cattle after their kind, and every thing that creepeth upon the earth after his kind: and God saw that it was good.*
26 *And God said, Let us make* <u>**man**</u> *in our image, after our likeness…*

Here, one final group of human beings is mentioned: the group *Adam* (also known as the *Adamites*). This, obviously, was the group that *Adam*, himself, belonged to. This was also the group commonly associated with the word ***man*** or *mankind* - not saying that there were not living, breathing men in the other groups, of course. Yet, the word *man* actually comes from the Hebrew word *Adam*; which, as one could guess, was considered the leader of this group. That's probably why the whole group was named after him.

Tradition, of course, tells us that there was only *one* man - Adam - formed at this time; and that's all. We have scriptural evidence, however, that might tell us there were a lot *more* than one Adam, or Adamite, created around the time of the above verses:

> *So God created man in his own image, in the image of God created he him;* ***male*** *and* ***female*** *created he* ***them****.* - *Gen.* 1:27 (KJV)

It's obvious: God created an entire *group* of people on the Sixth Day - *male* and *female*; and not just one man. The next question that might logically follow, then, is: *why* were we always led to believe *one* and only one man named Adam was formed? And, if there were more, *what* would be so special about this one Adamic group?

To Have Dominion?

> *...and let* **them** *have dominion over the fish of the sea, and over the fowl of the air, and over the cattle, and over all the earth, and over every creeping thing that creepeth upon the earth.* - *Gen.* 1:26 (KJV)

The Adamites were to have dominion over the animals, over the fish of the sea, **and** over these other groups of people. Interesting… but where might one go with all of this?

It's pretty obvious the Adamites were given control over the animal kingdom; but there may be a little more to it. And, as far as understanding how the *fish* of the world would relate to this all, let's develop this postulation: first, one could assume the Adamites were to have dominion over the swimming animals of the sea - the *real* fish of the world. But, could there be something more to all of this? Were the Adamites to have dominion over a group of *living beings* here, mistranslated (again) as "fish?"

We know the *Sea* could be another name for that *Darkness of the Deep*; could the "fish," here, also refer to something more *supernatural* - spiritual *souls* coming from the *Sea*, maybe? Could Adam have dominion over any of the **angelic** "fish" (or souls) coming from that spiritual *Sea*? Common sense would dictate there wasn't a group of human beings known as *fish*; but we might be able to assume that Adam and the

Adamites were granted dominion over the *angelic* souls who surrounded them. Makes sense; especially when we assume there might have been angelic souls brought up, already; as well as the *Owph (Fowl) of the Air*.

If they had dominion, they, obviously, did not have it for very long. Most of us know Adam would lose his authority over all that was the Garden. We'll soon learn how these Adamites, as well as these early angels, had a play in the Garden of Eden; and what could have happened to this working order of things.

Not the Father of the Human Race?

Before we proceed, a lot of skepticism might begin to show its head about this, right about now - *especially* about any mention of these extra groups of pre-Adamites! Understandable… to a degree. Most of us might be able to swallow that Adam was the first human being - and father of humanity! Still other people think we, somehow, may have evolved; over a long period of time. Maybe there is a *third* option: let's also contemplate the validity of there being up to *five* groups of people on earth by this time.

For the quick *naysayer* - who might totally disagree with this possibility - we need to look at one of their most prominent schools of thought they often use… *against* the validity of the pre-Adamites. Their argument seems centered around one particular verse in the Book of Acts:

> *And hath made of one* ***blood*** *all nations of men for to dwell on all the face of the earth, and hath determined the times before appointed, and the bounds of their habitation…*
> - *Acts* 17:26 (KJV)

Adam was the first human being, according to Biblical tradition; and the rest of the human race descended from him; right? This verse, indeed, seems to support that idea. Since all of us are of ***one*** *blood*, then how can we come from the *Darkness*; and be made to branch out into various human groups? It doesn't make sense. If we're of one blood, we obviously come from one man.

Yet, if we look deeper into this verse, we discover the word *blood* was *not even in a good deal of early Bible versions*![18] It may have even been added later on; to make the verse seem more "readable." And, in versions where the word *blood* is inserted, we'll soon see the original Greek could mean something much more.[19]

Regardless, beyond whether this addition is just or not, the verse *still* implies that we are all of one blood… or *does* it? Of course, if we take the verse *out of context* it looks as though we are all of the same blood. But, we recall how dangerous it is to take verses out of context, in the Bible. And, when we insert the verse back *into* the original text, and look at other possible meanings for the Greek words used in vicinity of this English *blood*, we see the verse might take on a whole new meaning.

<u>*Acts* 17:</u>
24 *God that made the world and all things therein, seeing that he is Lord of heaven and earth, dwelleth not in temples made with hands;*
25 *Neither is worshipped with men's hands, as though he needed any thing, seeing he giveth to all life, and breath, and all things;*
26 ***And He (God) made of one (one's bloodshed) to be for all nations of men to dwell upon, on all the face of the earth, having determined the appointed times and boundaries of the habitation of men.***
(in retranslation)
27 *That they should seek the Lord, if haply they might feel after him, and find him, though he be not far from every one of us…*

These verses obviously refer to how people should not worship idols; only God. And, learning, now, that another possible meaning for the original Greek word for *blood*, here (in the minority of versions of which it was added), also means *bloodshed*. If we look at the verse in these contexts, now, the meaning of it all becomes totally clear: the *one* referred to **Jesus**, obviously; and how *his sacrifice of blood* would set the foundation for the workings of man on earth - in the past, and the future! Yet, the translators tried to use words - even *add additional words* - to "fit it all in" with their own assumptions. Again: a **perfect original - *imperfect* translation**.

Most Christians were taught that we *all* came from Adam; even though science, today, has established the various races do *not* all have the same genetic makeup.[20] Why have we been taught this? Maybe there's something *deeper* to it all.

In one interesting example, the so-called *Mongolian Spot* is almost entirely evident in some races, but not in others. Why? How could this be? Although, as human beings, we are all the same in numerous ways, we must understand that there are differences in people we can't ignore… simply.

What, then, is Behind All of this Disbelief Today?

> *Knowing this first, that there shall come in the last days* ***scoffers****, walking after their own lusts…*
> - *II Pet.* 3:3 (KJV)

In the last few hundred years or so, we, as a human race, have had another serious struggle to deal with (as far as reinterpreting the words of the Bible): "political correctness." Especially in today's world, Biblical translators might feel the need to translate words that may sound *inoffensive* to other people, even though it will compromise the integrity of the document. They might feel the need to **remove**, alter, or somehow *change*, whatever in the Bible they deem bigoted, insensitive, or in any way offensive (just like adding *blood* into the above verse, to force a meaning). They want the Bible pleasing to *everyone*, or may want to rectify the words of the Bible to fit the current views or standards of science and/or secular society. Whatever the reason for these changes, the attempts to change what the Bible might have originally said can be most devastating or damaging to the individual; especially when they are trying to decipher and understand true meaning.

As Peter stated in the above, the people of the last days *scoff* at the words of the Bible; and try to interpret in the ways that they want - which is ***exactly*** **what is going on today**. Today, it's not really what the Bible *says* that's important it's what people *think* it **should** say! Again, it might sound good if we, as the human race, are all the same; if we act the same; or if we come from the same origin - even though these thoughts may not be grounded in Biblical reality.

There are those who also want to "absorb" the Bible with modern-day rules of *science*. With these people, the concept of pre-Adamites does not set very well with them. **Evolutionists** also work hard to push the belief in Monogenism - a theory that states we all have a common origin.[21] Their reasons for believing this, however, are a little different than those in the Christian world. According to these people, our human race was not created by God; but came from two "ape-like" ancestors. From some semi-human "Adam" and "Eve," there was a gradual evolution of the species - into us, today. This gradual slope of improvement was essential for any type of **gene-mutation** or **survivalist adaptation** to take place… which allows, according to them, for a species to improve. The pre-Adamite theory hurts those trying to convert us to this modem of thought… because it says **practically the opposite**: a creator *God* actually fashioned different groups of people, since the beginning of our world. And, as time marches on, the human race would, more or less, maintain the *same* physical existence as when it was first created - replicating "*kind after kind.*"

It's so crucial that we don't take the Bible out of context, in these verses; or maintain a blind eye to what the Holy Scriptures might *really* be trying to portray. They trouble with these word changes - done for the sake of science / "political correctness" - are loud and clear: you change the words of the Bible and you could change the meaning; change the meaning and you could change ***history***; change history and you could change **reality**.

What about all of what we postulated so far: the Gap Theory, the Well of Lost Souls (i.e. the *Darkness*, the *Deep*, or the *Sea*), and now the pre-Adamites wouldn't these all definitely disrupt the "politically correct" apple cart of our modern world? Wouldn't these disrupt modern science; or a lot of what people may *want* to be for our history? Wouldn't science and political correctness give people *reasons* to cover up these alternate concepts?

To move further into this, let's discuss this unique creation of the Adamite group; *their* contribution to the Garden of Eden; as well as one member of this group. This member would become a major focus of the early Bible; the most prestigious man of his time; and, well into the future. He was the one most of us know, today, as the viceroy of the Garden of Eden: **Adam**.

Chapter 4

The Adam is Formed

Disposed he the wild ***races*** *of the* ***beasts****,*
And to us mortals made subordinate
All ***cattle****; the God-formed one (****Adam****) made chief*
Of all things; and subordinate to man
He put all variegated forms of life,
And things that are incomprehensible.
- *Sibylline Oracles* 2nd Fr. 13-18[1]

Some apparent mistranslations of the Bible and other works are now already beginning to be explained, it seems. As we've already seen, there indeed could be a *gap* between the actual creation of our planet and the "Six-Day Creation" of Genesis 1; there could be such a thing as the *Well of Lost Souls*; phrases such as *Beast of the Field* and *Fowl of the Air* might not only stand for a group of animals, here. What's the "next-step" in our reinterpretation of early Genesis? It's the formation of the most famous man, known as *Adam*!

Adam was absolutely human; no doubt about it. Yet, what's so significant about this *one* man? Why would the Bible be known as the *book of the generations of* ***Adam*** (Gen. 5:1)?

Man Vs. Human Being

...although Adam was the first man he was not the first human being...
(Bristowe, 1927, p. 17)[2]

The word *man* and *Adam* are often used synonymously in the Bible, and in our everyday lives. This doesn't point to, in any way, that other groups of pre-Adamites weren't composed of men, or anything; that's not what we're saying. What this points to is: early off, the word *man* could easily have been used to describe Adam, and his group -

the *Adamites*. Yet, because so many of us may have thought that Adam was the first and only man of his time, we naturally associated the word *man* stood for the males in every group. But, with the information we have at hand, another theory develops: Adam may have been the father of some, but not the father of every living *human being*.

The *Adamites* - the group associated with *Adam* - were, as we see, the last members of this regenerated world to be brought up. The end of God's reformulation of our world would eventually head towards one particular man: last, *but not least*, Adam.[3]

This One Particular Man

The year was approximately 4000 B.C.. Even though there were probably a number of angels around at this time, and, even though there were at least four groups of humans brought up from the *Darkness*, the *Adamites* - the group Adam belonged to - were now on the scene.

As we recall, in the latter-half of the sixth day, we have:

<u>*Gen.* 1:</u>
26 *And God said, Let us make* **man** *(Adam) in our image, after our likeness: and let them have dominion over the fish of the sea, and over the fowl of the air, and over the cattle, and over all the earth, and over every creeping thing that creepeth upon the earth.*
27 *So God created man in his own image, in the image of God created he him; male and female created he them.*

In actuality, the formulation of the Adamites seems to have been mentioned *two* times in Genesis; in *two* separate chapters. Why would it do this? Why? This has baffled Biblical scholars in the past… at least, until *now*. Quite probably, the above verses represented the time for this *entire group* of Adamites to be formed. Soon after, in the next chapter of Genesis, the single man - *Adam* - was formed.

> *In 1655, Isaac de la Peyreira, a converted Jew, published a curious treatise on the Pre-Adamites. Arguing upon Romans v. 12-14, he contended that there were two creations of man;* ***that recorded in the first chapter of Genesis*** *and that described in the second chapter* ***being distinct****.* (Baring-Gould, 1881, p. 28)[4]

We recall, in the first chapter:

> *And God said, Let us make* **man** *(the Adamites) in our image, after our likeness... male and female created he* **them***.* - *Gen.* 1:26-27 (KJV)

Now, in the second chapter, we have:

> *And the LORD God formed man (the man,* **Adam***) of the dust of the ground, and breathed into his nostrils the breath of life; and man (the man, Adam) became a living soul.* - *Gen.* 2:7 (KJV)

In Genesis 1:27, the Bible states that, "male and female created he **them**" - obviously a plural reference, here… more than one individual formulated. Genesis 5:2, again, seems to confirm that there was more *than one* person fashioned at this time:

> *Male and female created he* **them***; and blessed* **them***, and called* **their** *name* **Adam** *(the* **Adamites***?), in the day when they were created.* - *Gen.* 5:2 (KJV)

We see that God called *their* name *Adam*. If we think about it, if there was only one man formed at this early part of Genesis, why would He call *their* name Adam? And, why mention the same event twice - unless there were two *separate*, and *distinct*, formations?

The next thing for us to understand is how the word *man* was used in the Bible. In Genesis Chapter 2, the Hebrew words for *Adam* were configured slightly different than in Chapter 1. In Chapter 1, the word *Adam* is one single word.[5] In Chapter 2, the word *Adam* is accompanied by another word - the word *the*.[6] This *the*, in grammar, is recognized as the *article*, here. So, why these differences? If we put these two words together we get ***The Adam***. And, when this article is added in Scripture, the word *Adam* becomes emphatic (which means one's "self," "this very," "this same," or "this same man Adam").[7] In other words, *The Adam* stands for *one particular man* named *Adam*, apart from the others - him, and him *alone*.[8]

The word *Adam* without the article could easily stand for the rest of the Adamites - *the group* Adam.

What's So Special About this One Man?

> *And the LORD God said the angels who ministered before Him, Behold,* ***Adam is sole on the earth****, as* ***I am sole*** *in the heavens above; and it will be that they will arise from him who will know to discern between good and evil.*
>
> \- *Targum Pseudo-Jonathan* III[9]

God had something special planned for this one man. Adam was going to be formed in a different way; at a *different* time; and, yes, for a *different reason*.

> *...God created Adam with own hand...*
>
> \- *al-Tabari: The History of al-Tabari - Vol. I: General Introduction and From the Creation to the Flood* The Story of Adam 87[10]

Adam, we know, being a member of the *Adamites*, seemed a group already made in somewhat of a special way: in the image of God and his angels.

> <u>*Gen.* 1:</u>
> 26 *And God said, Let us make man (the Adamites) in* ***our*** *image, after* ***our*** *likeness...*
> 27 *So God created man in his* ***own*** *image, in the image of God created he him; male and female created he them.*

Male and female **Adamites** were formed in this same image - the group; not just Adam. Even beyond, as we'll see, the formation of this one "self-same" Adamite would go one step further, beyond the creation of these Adamites. The word *God*, in the above verses (and other verses of Scripture), might actually stand for the *Elohim* - *God and His* *angels*. So, we see that Adam was, not only, given this same image and likeness of God and His angels, he would be given something more - animation by the *breath of* God himself!

> *And the LORD* ***God*** *formed man (Adam) of the dust of the ground, and* ***breathed into his nostrils*** *the breath of life****; and man (Adam)*** *became a living soul.*
> - *Gen.* 2:7 (KJV)

Special formation by God. God made the solitary Adam "a living soul." Could this mean that he did not have a soul which came from the *Darkness*, like the others? As the above verse states, "*The Lord God* formed man…" The words "LORD God," in this verse, seem to state something different than other verses, where we show "God," as in the Elohim (i.e. *God and his angels*). The "LORD God," in this verse, very well represents God in the singular (a.k.a. *Lord of the Angels*, *Jehovah Elohiym*, etc.). In other words, God *himself* came down to form Adam. He was not accompanied by any angels, at this time. *He* breathed the breath of life into this man; and established him into a living soul. For some reason, it seemed to make a difference. This was the primary reason Adam, as one man, was formed in a fairly special way.

> *…he became… like potter's clay untouched by fire. When, after that… God blew the spirit into him…*
> - *al-Tabari: The History of al-Tabari - Vol. I: General Introduction and From the Creation to the Flood* The Story of Adam 91[11]

> *…Adam… the most free and perfect of His creatures… the only one that was animated by His breath…* - *Legends of the Mussulmans* Adam[12]

To gather us even more support for this postulation, there seems to be a difference in the words the Bible uses to describe the way God formed the Adamites, compared to how He formed Adam. The Adamites (of Genesis Chapter 1) were **created** (i.e. the Hebrew word *bara*); the solitary man Adam (in Genesis Chapter 2) was ***formed*** (i.e. the Hebrew *yatsar*). Again, the reason for the different wording was probably to show this one particular Adamite was *made* differently.

Already, the *living soul* of Adam made him distinct:

> *...the "living soul" breathed into Adam raised him above some previously created race.* (Bristowe, 1927, p. 16-17)[13]

> *Adam was created with a spiritual* ***soul****, and that from Adam the Jewish race was descended, whereas the Gentile nations issued from the loins of the pre-Adamites.* (Baring-Gould, 1881, p. 28)[14]

> *When God gave a* ***pure inspiration*** *to your body on the earth, you were* ***separated*** *from every strong creature the day your* ***soul*** *was formed. When you were* ***brightly*** *created in the likeness of* ***God's shape****, when every dear creature was told that it should come to do you reverence.* - *Saltair na Rann* 1789-1796[15]

Let's look at more of what the Bible has to say.

In Our Image and Likeness...

> *And God said, Let us make man (the Adamites) in our* ***image****, after our likeness...* - *Gen.* 1:26 (KJV)

So, what is this *image* of God? The word *image* comes from an ancient Hebrew word meaning "to shade."[16] This word was commonly used to describe a spirit of the supernatural; or something ghost like. The word *image*, as well, could be defined as "likeness" or "resemblance." The group *Adam* seemed to be in the same *image* as God – in, maybe, a similar spiritual or physical appearance (or outer form) as what God, or his angels, might represent.

> *The Hebrew word for "image" in all these passages is tzelem... meaning "shadow" or "reflection"... Human beings... are similar to their mastery of the spiritual and physical dimensions of the Maker.* (Quayle, 2005, p. 23-24)[17]

If the other groups were human beings as well, then how could just the Adamites be of this different image? Makes no sense. In the New Testament, however, the word *man* (in its original Greek) comes from the word *anthropos* - a word which could mean a "countenance," or "man-faced."[18] In other words, the Adamites quite possibly could have had a similar *countenance*, or outer "shine," as the Elohim did (God and His angels).[19] They may have glowed brightly, as one might picture how an angel would.

We know that people of these ancient times would, quite often, identify each other by the features of their face. Could these early Adamites have that brightness, or shine, to their face, as well as their bodies? These Adamites could have also been fairly large and tall, compared to the rest of the human beings - also like some of the angels of the day were thought to be. ***Adam*** was occasionally described as having both the "light of face" (or "shine") about him, as well as a large height.[20] We'll soon see that, in ancient times, the thought of someone having a large height - or being a *giant* - could be symbolic, or *real.* Some individuals of this early were called *giants* because they were, in fact, very powerful and influential - a *giant* of their day.[21] We're not saying that there were never any *real* giants in the ancient world, however - quite the contrary. We'll see that there were probably *real* giants on the earth in these ancient of times; but that will be in another chapter. What we have now, at this point of time, is that - however you might describe him - Adam was truly powerful and influential in his brave, new world; similar to the angels who subsisted around him!

"The Thinker"

> *And God said, Let us make man (the Adamites) in our image, after our* **likeness**...
> - *Gen.* 1:26 (KJV)

There is more: what about this "likeness" of God? The word *likeness* originated from Hebrew words which could mean, "to be like," a "similitude," "**imagination**" or "**thought**." Could being "in the likeness of God" refer to one's following righteous *ways* of God; righteous ways of *imagination* or *thought*? Could this be the tendency to, morally, approach God; and take on the same overall thought pattern as the One above?

> *...the first people are not, like Adam, said to have received the inestimable gift of intellect... (a) "reflective or intellectual life"...*
> (Bristowe, 1950, p. 91-92)[22]

> *...and there was in the body of Adam the inspiration of a speaking spirit, unto the illumination of the eyes and the hearing of the ears.*
> *- Targum Pseudo-Jonathan* II[23]

This could be the same as a person possessing a similar "heart" as another.

Adam was known, by some ancient sources, as the *Thinker* - the one who possessed a specific *style* of thought.[24]

> *...**Adam**... was in the **mind** (or, **thought**) of God aforetime...*
> *- Bakhayla Mikael* p. 8[25]

> *...the spirit came to Adam by way **of his head**.*
> *- al-Tabari: The History of al-Tabari - Vol. I: General Introduction and From the Creation to the Flood* The Story of Adam 91[26]

Maybe Adam was appointed to run the garden because of his rationality, sensibility, and consciousness - thoughts considered akin to the thoughts of God?

> *In Sanskrit literature the first man is called Manu or Menu... The fact that the word "Man" meant a **thinker** Professor Max Muller writes: "Man, a derivative root, means to think. From this we have the Sanskrit Manu, **originally** the thinker, then man." (Lectures. Vol I.p.425).* (Bristowe, 1927, p. 16-17)[27]

> *...he (God) created man in the **likeness** of his own form, and put into him eyes to see, and ears to hear, and **heart** to reflect, and **intellect** wherewith to **deliberate**.*
> *- 2 Enoch (The Book of the Secrets of Enoch)* 65:2[28]

From the following ancient text, Adam was given the opportunity to name all of the animals he had dominion over. We'll see how his utilizing this "likeness of God" could have had an effect on his decision-making:

> *(Adam speaking to God...) And Thy will was that I should name them all, one by one, with a suitable name. But* ***Thou gavest me understanding and knowledge, and a pure heart and a right mind from Thee****, that I should name them* ***after Thine own mind*** *regarding the naming of them.*
>
> \- *First Book of Adam and Eve (The Conflict of Adam and Eve with Satan)* 34:8[29]

Even though the *Adamites* may have had some of the same moral values and thoughts as the Elohim, it would be *Adam* and his direct descendents who would retain this direct breath (or soul) from God. Again, we are not saying the Adamites were *better* than any other group of human beings, here - only that there were differences; or may have been. And, it was Adam's bright, outwardly image, his great height, as well as his different ways of thought, which gave him the ability to judge (and handle) the major responsibility of his day - managing the Garden of Eden.

> *Remember, O Lord that... Thou hast fashioned Adam, our father, in the* ***likeness*** *of Thy glory; Thou didst breathe a breath of life into his nostrils and, with* ***understanding, knowledge*** *Thou didst give him... Thou didst make him to rule over the Garden of Eden which Thou didst plant...*
>
> \- *The Words of the Heavenly Lights (4Q504)* Fr. 8 recto[30]

This was to be his job in this world. Again, we are not trying to infer any type of *superiority* of one group (or person) over another, but *somebody* had to run the garden; and, in this case, Adam was the person God assigned to do it all.

...And Also From Different Material

> *And the LORD God... took dust from the place of the house of the sanctuary, and from the four winds of the world, and mixed from all the waters of the world...*
>
> \- *Targum Pseudo-Jonathan* II[31]

The Bible states our physical, moral bodies came from elements of this earth - that's fairly common-place. The Adamites, according to one ancient source, were thought to be "those who were of the ground."[32] The name *Adam*, also, could be a name signifying *his own place of origin.*[33] Following this train of logic, Adam, the man, may have been named so because God brought him up from one **specific kind** of dirt (unlike the other individuals). Why does this matter? Let's see.

In Genesis 1:24-26, the other groups of human beings (previously mentioned) were also said to be brought up from the ground; but, interestingly enough, it was the Adamites alone that were said to have come up from one, specific type of *red* ground. *Adam* was brought up from something even *more* significant than this same *red* ground: the *dust* of this red ground! Now, what's the significance of all this?

Again, we see that Adam was a single - and significant - formation, apart from the others. This *dust* that Adam was made from was even, in some respects, considered fine *dust* (or, even a form *of clay*):[34]

> *Now, for what reason did God make Adam out of these four materials unless it were [to show] that everything which is in the world should be in* ***subordination*** *to him through them? He took a grain from the earth in order that everything in nature which is formed of earth should be subject unto him; and a drop of water in order that everything which is in the seas and rivers should be his; and a puff of air so that all kinds [of creatures] which fly in the air might be given unto him; and the heat of fire so that all the beings that* ***are fiery in nature****, and* ***the celestial hosts****, might be* ***his helpers****.* - *Cave of Treasures* The Creation of Adam[35]

As we'll see, Adam - the man of dust - was given dominion over the other groups of people, as well as the angelic souls around him! How could a "man of the ground" be put on a higher level, or plateau, over the angels?

God's Favorite - Red and White Dust?

So, if we begin to follow the average man's rationale at this time, its easy to begin to gather some rather negative assumptions about God: He "plays favorites." It seems that God, obviously, favored Adam and the Adamites more than he did other groups of people. We also might begin to assume, following the train of logic, that He would create His groups of human beings in some sort of *order*: maybe, the workers of the garden first; and on to the top "manager." Sounds rational. He began, way in the depths of that spiritual *Sea*, to take souls out, and formulate them into groups of *Owph*, *Chay*, and *Behemah*, for example… those who were on par to serve Adam; or, somehow, work in the garden. Ultimately, He would work Himself up, to creating the final prize of His creation: *Adam*, himself![36] We also know that Adam was fashioned directly from God's image and likeness; which, in and of itself, might begin to sound somewhat racist, or supremacist, to some. Yet, if we really look at the Bible, we'll discover there are a **number** of discrepancies to this whole way of thinking - elements that really counteract all of these assumptions. Let's see how.

We begin by looking at Adam's physical characteristics.

The name *Adam*, as we've already postulated, has Hebrew roots in a word which means, "to be red," "to cause to show red," or be "ruddy."[37] And, since the name *Adam* comes from a word that stands for "red earth," we'll learn another unique characteristic of this man:

> *…**reddish clay** suggests the presence of iron oxide, which is the mineral that makes blood red and accounts for the red-faced countenance of blushing. The same root turns up in the Biblical Hebrew as "Admoni"… where the description is commonly interpreted as "red-haired" or "ruddy".*
>
> ("Wikipedia, the Free Encyclopedia, *Adam*", n. d., p. 5)[38]

The word *ruddy* simply stands for the ability of one to *show red* in their face - as with their ability *to blush*. The word *Adam*, also, could mean one *who is fair* (or *handsome*).

Put them all together, and we see Adam's name might relate to the fairness - or *whiteness* - of Adam's skin.[39] Also, as we know, the ability to *blush* is evident in most people of the Caucasian race. So, can we conclude that, Adam was named to because he had fair, white skin; as well as rosy (**red**) cheeks?[40]

The rest of the Adamites, obviously, were pretty much the same. The chosen descendants of Adam, a.k.a. the *Israelites*, obviously had this same complexion, over time. There's a verse in the Bible which described some Israeli people as: "…purer than snow, they were whiter than milk, they were more ruddy in body than rubies (Lam. 4:7)." Ezra had the ability to "*blush*" (Ezra 9:6). Solomon, son of the Jewish King David, was, also, said to have had a lover. This lover - the Queen of Sheba - described him as:

My beloved is ***white*** *and* ***ruddy****, the chiefest among ten thousand.*
- *Song of Sol.* 5:10 (KJV)

Noah, another descendent of Adam, was described in much the same way:

And his body was ***white*** *as snow and* ***red*** *as the blooming of a rose…*
- *1 Enoch* 106:2[41]

As most surmise, Jesus was white, as well. It seems Adam must have looked the same as these direct descendents, if he was their father. "Well… so what?" One might ask. Does that mean that God "saved the best for last," here? Just because Jesus and others were Jewish, and probably had the same skin color as Adam, did God assign the *white* Adamites as some sort of *superior* group? We'll soon see this, clearly, was **not** the case.

The Bible does state that human beings were made "a little lower than the angels (Psa. 8:5)." If this was the case, then one could naturally follow the summation that God should have created the higher, angelic beings *first*; with Adam *next*… because he was a little lower than the angels. After this, He should have created those who worked the Garden, etc.; and so on. It all seems logical. Yet, in actuality, the angels (as we've already surmised) were created *first* - **followed by** all the rest of the groups of people! ***Then*** Adam and the Adamites were created last. Why weren't they created in some sort of ascending/descending order?

Also, if Adam was *really* fashioned for greatness over other people, then why wouldn't God have made Adam out of the *best* of materials on earth? Those other groups of human beings, including the Adamites, were formed out of solid ground; **Adam** was formed out of plain *dust*. We'll now see that *dust*, to the ancients, was not the most worthy of materials to form something, or someone, out of.

Dust could have a *whitish* to *reddish* hue. In ways, this could further provide a clue of Adam's fair skin, and his ruddiness (or, his ability to blush red).[42] This dust, regardless if it was colorful, was often considered a material of very *low* quality.[43] The Hebrew meaning for *dust* (in Gen. 2) not only stands for "dry earth," but also "ashes," "debris;" or even "rubbish." Psalms 104:29 seems to express dust as *the* ***lowness*** *and fragility of* *human nature*.[44] Interesting. Sometimes, *dust* and ***dung*** were even used interchangeably![45] Now, it really doesn't sound too wonderful - and not a picture-perfect example of Adam's superiority, as well.

If Adam was truly a superior person - better than everyone else - wouldn't God have created him right after these angels, and use the *best* of ingredients? The logic behind this all is simple: humility. The birth of Jesus - the savior of the world - even took place in a *manger*, or a *cave*; and not some wonderful palace. Whatever it was, it simply was a lowly den, with animals all around! **Humility** is obviously one of the ways of God, not superiority!

> Gen. 2:
> 8 *And the LORD God planted a garden eastward in Eden; and there he put the man whom he had formed.*
> 15 *And the LORD God took the man, and put him into the garden of Eden to* ***dress it*** *and* ***to keep it****.*

We see in the above that God did not appoint Adam to sit on some throne; He did not appoint him to some wonderful position of authority; He apportioned Adam to *till the ground* - to be lead **farmer**. Adam's position on earth, although he was the leader of the pack, was only a manager - a man with the responsibility to oversee the dressing of a garden.[46] Of course it would be logical to think that Adam was considered *superior*, because of some elements of his origins; but now we know how God works - and He doesn't work that way.

With all of this said and done, knowing that God did not "play favorites" (as far as the five groups of the world), we also have to surmise that *someone* had to be the leader; there had to be some sort of hierarchy to this Garden; and to the world. There has to be organization in every cosmos! And, we've been taught that there's even a hierarchy of *angels* in the spiritual realm. So, why would the world below be any different?

To top it all off, if we consider all of the horrible things that resulted from the fall of Adam in the Garden, we really can't be too happy with Adam, overall. Adam - an Adamite - messed up everything for the rest of the human race. Even with his unique creation, *he* was the one who helped usher sin into this world… not the other groups. Not to say that other members of other groups may not have even ended up in the same situation; that's not the point. What we're getting at is: *superior*, not quite… at least, as far as how God would work things in this world. It seems clear that God wants *everyone* to understand the truth: that no matter *what* the circumstances of one's birth - no matter what one's position in life may be - *nobody* (except Jesus Christ, of course) should be put on a pedestal… above anything *other* than a flawed human being that they really are.

The Seventh Day - All Was Good (At Least Temporarily)

> <u>*Gen.* 1:</u>
> 28 *And God blessed* ***them****, and God said unto them, Be fruitful, and multiply, and replenish the earth, and subdue it.*
> 31 *And God saw every thing that he had made, and, behold, it* ***was very good****. And the evening and the morning were the sixth day.*
>
> <u>*Gen.* 2:</u>
> 1 *Thus the heavens and the earth were finished, and all the* ***host of them****.*

We've already postulated there were a *host* of angels already around, during the time of Adam's formation. The Hebrew word for *host* (*tsaba*), above, most probably included the angels, as well.[47] A number of ancient sources stated that the Adamites - especially *Adam* - were given control over *even these* angelic beings. As we'll see, man's authority over angels would become a problem to the whole layout of the ancient Garden; a problem which, eventually, would affect the entire planet.

At the end of the "Six-Day Creation," God was satisfied with His attempt to replenish earth. Our current world was ready to go, with Adam, the angels, human beings with angelic-like qualities, and the other human groups into the mixture. Our organized, functional *world* was now in order - there was a new harmony to the cosmos. As we recall:

Disposed he the wild races of the beasts,
And to us mortals made subordinate
*All cattle; the God-formed one (**Adam**) made chief*
*Of all things; and **subordinate** to man*
He put all variegated forms of life,
*And things that are **incomprehensible**.*
- *Sibylline Oracles* 2nd Fr. 13-8[48]

Everyone had a purpose. It all seemed to work, at this early time; that's why Adam had to have workers *under* him - the people of the different groups, as well as the angels, all probably had roles; somewhere. They all knew his or her place, at least for the time being.

One Man to Manage… or Mismanage

With so much going on, this became a primary reason why there had to be a special person in charge, to manage this entire working order.

Gen. 2:
5 *...and there was not a man to till the ground.*
7 *And the LORD God formed man (**Adam**) of the dust of the ground...*

With Adam now created, we'll now discover something more: there probably was one *more* reason why the garden needed a "manager": our world, even back then, wasn't exactly free and clear of potentially new problems. The world of the "Six-Day Creation," even though it was refashioned to be **very *good***, it wasn't perfect.

First off, we see:

As Dr. Kitto writes: "To dress and keep the Garden of Eden, Adam not only required the necessary implements, but also the knowledge of operations for insuring future produce, the use of water and the various trainings of the plants and trees."
(Bristowe, 1927, p. 29)[49]

There was work to be done, as with any garden: people actually had to work - to sweat and toil some - for their sustenance.[50] Even though their work wasn't really too hard, *a little* human effort was needed to ensure the survival of the plants:

> *...in spite of all this, man obtains his food in toil and trouble.*
> - *Chronicles of Jerahmeel* 6:14[51]

The people worked around Adam, in a small community.[52] Looking at how our world looks *now*, we know that this working arrangement under Adam did not last. Next, the question that most naturally might arise is: if our world was fashioned so wonderfully back then - if it was made so *very good* - then *how* could anything go wrong? What could have happened to Adam's authority, to destroy this special, organized cosmos?

As we'll see, there were those - all the way from *the beginning* of this world - who began to resent Adam's position in the Garden; and even desired him to fall. Adam's control of this garden would indeed be temporary. The days of Adamite dominion over the working cosmos would be on a sliding scale. The era of our world being "very good" (i.e. Gen. 1:31) would soon end; and was about to.

Chapter 5

Adam and the Angels: Dissension in the Garden

*And God saw every thing that he had made, and, behold, it **was** very good.*
- *Gen.* 1:31 (KJV)

As we stated in the chapter previous, things in the world were *good* - the harmonized order of the world was even considered *very good* - but not perfect. We'll soon discover that, because *some* inhabitants were about to utilize their own "free will," dissension would arise. There would be those who had a problem with the way things were - a problem with Adam's authority. There would soon be "trouble in Paradise."

The first major accomplishment after the "Six-Day Creation" of Genesis was, obviously, the Garden of Eden. The word *Eden* could relate to words such as "delight," "pleasure," as well as "paradise."[1] It may have even had a mountain close by - the "gateway" mount to God Himself.[2] Possibly created on the Third Day, the Garden was truly a beautiful place: where everything seemed to go good; there was no pain; and everyone seemed to be happy.

The word *Eden* could also be equated with a "plain," or plot of "uncultivated land." From this, we might be able to gather that the Garden was, indeed, located on some open, uncultivated plain. Another meaning of the word *Edin* (in ancient Akkadian myth) is a "steppe," or a "terrace."[3] If *Edin* could have been the same as the Biblical Eden, then the Garden could have been a raised (or stepped) agricultural plot of land - a stepped terrace. Some ancient sources even stated that the Garden was a **walled enclosure**.[4] Why might this be significant? Let's see.

According to one ancient source, Eve proclaimed:

*God set us to **guard** the Garden...*
- *Penitence of our Forefather Adam* [44]17.3[5]

An interesting question that, naturally, might follow is: if the world was created so *very good*, then why would the Garden need to be placed on a stepped plateau; or why would it need to contain surrounding walls? Who or what would the Garden need protection from, in this way?[6]

The Fall of Angels Before Our World

Around this time, there could have been at least **three** groups of angels around Adam - all who had "fallen from grace" because of the use of their own free will.[7] These highly-esteemed angels would rebel against God, and eventually get demoted from their once-lofty positions. The first couple of occurrences could have taken place right around the time that God created Adam. The third probably occurred around a thousand years later. There was trouble brewing, on account of these angels.

Beyond these dissensions, there might have even been a rebellion of angels *before* the reformation of our current world! The prophet Jeremiah speaks of something interesting:

> Jer. 4.
> 24 *I beheld the mountains, and, lo, they trembled, and all the hills moved lightly.*
> 25 *I beheld, and, lo, there was no man, and all the* ***Fowl*** *(or birds)* ***of the Air*** *(or, the heavens) were fled.*
> (in retranslation)

Could these tragic events be describing the destruction of our previous world? And, if this was so, could there have been a group similar to the *Fowl of the Air* before our current world - who had *fled*! Maybe some of these angelic, or angelic-like, groups *fled* the destruction - being swept up by God and allowed to escape; whatever.[8] As we've already understood, some of these spiritual *Birds* (or *Owph*) might have been brought back into our world, by God, at the beginning of our "Six-Day Creation."

As we begin to look at these three angelic dissensions, we'll discover that the *first* group of beings who fell could have been purely *heavenly* beings - their souls had not come up from *the Darkness*. The second and third incidents could have involved angelic beings who probably served in similar capacities to those human (and angelic-like) *Fowl of the Air*.

There were angels, all around our atmosphere, whose role it was to "help out;" or, otherwise, make sure the world was a better place… assisting whomever God dictated that they should. Instead, as we'll see, a number of these angels would help turn the world in **the *opposite* direction**. What happened, and why?

Leader of the First Group?

Looking further into Biblical clues, we, possibly, have the name of at least two angelic groups who may have existed for a long time - maybe even before the time of our world's foundation:

> Job 38:
> 1 *Then the LORD answered Job out of the whirlwind, and said...*
> 4 *Where wast thou when I laid the foundations of the earth? declare, if thou hast understanding...*
> 7 *When the* ***morning stars*** *sang together, and all the* ***sons of God*** *shouted for joy?*
>
> Job 1:
> 6 *Now there was a day when the* ***sons of God*** *came to present themselves before the Lord, and* ***Satan*** *came* ***also*** *among them.*

Here, we see there are the *Morning Stars* and *the Sons of God*. The *Sons of God* are in both of the above verses; so it's pretty easy to attempt to link them as one group. Let's concentrate a little more, here, on those *Morning Stars*. We already know there were, most probably, angels of *Light* who were formed on the First Day. Could the *Light* be the same these *Morning Stars*? They both seem to be known for their illuminous, star-like countenances.

What about the famous angel Satan (or Lucifer)? Could he have, at one time, been a member of this *Light*; or even a leader of them? Was he a Son of God; or, what was he exactly? The Bible *does* say that Satan once appeared as an angel of *Light* (II Cor. 11:14); and he was also known as *Son of the Morning* (in Isa. 14:12).

And when he (Satan) was in the heavens, in the realms of ***light****, he knew naught of darkness.*

- First Book of Adam and Eve (The Conflict of Adam and Eve with Satan) 13:4[9]

At least, we know that Satan may have related to some of these angels, in some way. Could they have all been part of the same illuminous group?[10]

Whomever Satan was in charge of, and whatever group *he* was from, he apparently was among the *first* to dissent from Adam's position in the Garden. Why? What could have happened to allow him to feel this way?

Former Ruler of the World?

(God speaking) Adam has life on earth, and I created a garden in Eden in the east… I made the heavens open to him, that he should see the angels singing the song of victory, and the gloomless ***light****; And he was continuously in paradise, and the devil understood that I* ***wanted to create another world****, because Adam was lord on earth, to rule and control it. The devil is the evil spirit of the lower places... and he understood his condemnation and the sin which* ***he had sinned before****...*

- 2 Enoch (The Book of the Secrets of Enoch) 31:1-5[11]

Who was this *devil*? Was it Satan; or was it someone else? Apparently, for whatever reason, this devil may have been brought down from heaven - in the world before our own - to run things on the earth… and it all didn't work out.[12] As we recall from our chapter on the *Gap Theory*, evil probably did not begin in the time of Adam; it was probably present *before* the foundation of our world. That's why God had to destroy it! So, another question which might naturally arise, here, is: who or what might have brought about this previous world's destruction?

According to certain ancient sources, including Mormon thought, God intended the angel *Sammael* (a.k.a. Satan) to rule this previous world. Sammael was once in a lofty position, sent down from his official position in heaven to rule the planet. He was, at one time, the overseer and musician of God's heavenly court. We don't know if he was satisfied with his new assignment on the earth, but something went horribly wrong with his dominion over the planet. As a punishment, this angel *lost* his position as the world's ruler; and he also was not able to ascend back into his former abode, in heaven. We have some ancient commentaries on this:

> *...he belonged to the* ***remnant*** *of the jinn (angels) who* ***were on earth****. They shed blood and caused corruption on it.*
>
> \- *al-Tabari: The History of al-Tabari - Vol. I: General Introduction and From the Creation to the Flood* The Story of Iblis 84 (also 81)[13]

> *...****they*** *cast the world into ruins, were themselves* ***driven*** *from the* ***world in ruin****...*
>
> \- *Genesis Rabbah* 26:7[14]

> ***Before*** *the Lord God [created] earth, he created the nine divisions of angels for the service of his divinity. Now the wicked Sadael and Beliar were the heads of the divisions of Satan; they were adorn gloriously, and were higher than all the angels and all the divisions of the angels... But the detestable Satan did not want to bless God and was arrogant in his heart... And the Lord God commanded the... great Gabriel, and the terrible Michael, and nine divisions of the angels, and they fall upon Sadael and all his attendants, smote them, and cast them down like hail from a cloud.*
>
> \- *Armenian Apocryphal Adam Literature* Transgression 1-4[15]

Apparently, Sammael (or Satan) rebelled in his position, and his punishment was laid out before him.[16] Jesus even spoke of the Adversary as the "Prince of this World" (John 16:30). Could this be because Satan may have once ruled the world?[17]

> *...before Adam, the jinn (i.e. angels) were on the earth. God sent Iblis to act among them as judge. He did so conscientiously for a thousand years, so that he eventually was called "arbiter." God called him thus and reveled to him His name. At that, he became filled with haughtiness. He became self-important and caused terror, hostility, and hatred among those to whom God had sent him as arbiter. This is assumed to have caused them to fight so bitterly on earth for two thousand years that their horses waded in the blood of (those killed). They continued. This is (meant by) God's word: "Were We wearied by the first creation? No! Rather they are in uncertainty about a new creation (at the end of the world)," and (by) the statement of the angels: "Will You place on (earth) one who will cause corruption on it and shed blood?" At that, God sent a fire that consumed them. They continued. When Iblis saw the punishment that had descended upon his people, he ascended to heaven. He stayed with the angels worshiping God in heaven as zealously as did no other creature.*
>
> \- *al-Tabari: The History of al-Tabari - Vol. I: General Introduction and From the Creation to the Flood* The Story of Adam 85-86[18]

Who was this *Iblis*? Was he Satan; or another angel? Apparently, whoever he was, he seemed to be around before the formation of our new world. So, to "let the cat out of the bag" somewhat early, here, we'll soon discover that there may have been *two* angelic beings - two leaders - known as the "devil," all throughout ancient texts… with Satan (or Sammael) being one of them. The other will become more apparent to us, as time goes on. But, for now, the important thing to understand is that there could have been more than *one* leader of angels which went rouge, back then.

Whatever happened before our time, whatever brought on our previous world's destruction, would have assuredly brought on some action by God against any of those involved in any misdoings. Apparently, we see, in the above, that Iblis (whomever he might be) felt really afraid of God's wrath; and tried to do whatever it took to save his own skin. Assuredly, if God was a forgiving God (which He is), then there must be *some* type of punishment to meet each heavenly/earthly crime. We will soon see what these two leaders, and a number of other angels, did; and what mitigated their punishments to follow.

To release some more information a little early, we'll now discover that a number of ancient sources say that certain angels, in punishment, would be *lowered* in their angelic "rank," or their overall position in the heavens: from a prince, or leader of many, to only a couple of steps in spiritual "rank" above Adam![19] This would upset some angels to the extreme; and make them even more spiteful.

So, in order to get to the nitty-gritty of what brought on all of this dissension, let's begin to put all of the pieces together.

The Angel's Replacement

> *Certain of the angels having fallen, God made* ***men****, that they might take* ***their vacated places****.* (Baring-Gould, 1881, p. 21)[20]
>
> *…Which to those rebel angels prohibited return… he stopped their service…* ***In their room*** *he created* ***mankind****… May He give them strength, never to neglect his world.* (Bristowe, 1950, p. 39)[21]

The above works follow the ancient presumption that, through the "Six-Day Creation," mankind was to be created to *fill the void* left by the dissension of a number of ungrateful, fallen angels![22] And, this event, apparently, took place before the formation of our current world. One man, in particular, would usher in a lot of problems:

> *And God the beneficent, because of* ***Satan's arrogance****, created earthen* ***Adam*** *to fill the place of the fallen angels.*
> - *Armenian Apocryphal Adam Literature* Transgression 1[23]

Mankind, especially *Adam* himself, would even be formed to replace the authority of the highest angels on the earth, at the time. Why? The devil, and any other angels "in charge," would have probably felt a little taken back, by it; and might have wanted to get back at least *some* sense of worthiness and dignity, in their eyes. Regardless of how these lead angels may have felt about Adam, even regardless of how any of them might have tried to get back into God's graces, they *still* may have went too far - in God's eyes - to go back to what it once was; and *some* kind of response (by God) to it all had to be on the horizon:

> *When Iblis saw the punishment that had descended... he ascended to heaven. He stayed with the angels worshiping God in heaven as zealously as did no other creature. He* ***continued to do so, until*** *God created* ***Adam****...*
> - *al-Tabari: The History of al-Tabari - Vol. I: General Introduction and From the Creation to the Flood* The Story of Adam 86[24]

Adam's Dominion Questioned

> *When the Holy One, blessed be He (i.e. God), desired to create man, He said to the angels, "Let us make man in our image..." He wanted to make him a leader over all the angels above, so that* ***he might govern*** *all the angels and* ***they would be under his rule****...*
> - *Zohar* Beresheet A20[25]

> *God... made* ***him*** *ruler over all the earth and of all the jinn (i.e. angels)...*
> - *al-Tabari: The History of al-Tabari - Vol. I: General Introduction and From the Creation to the Flood* The First House on Earth 130[26]

Soon before the formation of human beings, God went to his accompanying angels (i.e. the *Light*) and said, "Let us make man in our image" (Gen. 1:26). On top of this, God wanted angels, and any other groups of human beings around, to understand one more thing about His final formulation - Adam:

> *Just as all of you praise Me in the heights of heaven so he (**Adam**) professes My Unity on earth...* - *Pirke deR. Eliezer* XIII[27]

Adam, especially, was given the crown of glory and honor - dominion over all of the works of God's hands - including these surrounding angels.[28] Adam was to be *revered* as the new, supreme leader:[29]

> *...**Adam** walked about the Garden of Eden like one of the ministering angels.*
> - *Chronicles of Jerahmeel* 6:13[30]

He, according to one source, was even given knowledge *beyond* these angels! According to *The Traditions of the Jews*, even the upper angels of heaven were not permitted to know some of the privileged information Adam was privy to. He was able to take some of these 'upper secrets,' and write down in his own special book, as a reference.[31] A number of these angels quickly began to gripe about this whole set-up. As things would progress, God was to advance Adam's position even further:

> *And again, when he (God) bringeth in the firstbegotten into the world, he saith, And let all the **angels** of God worship him.* - *Heb.* 1:6 (KJV)

We already know (via Psa. 8:5) that man was made a *little* lower than the angels. Now, not only were these angels commanded to respect Adam, they were also to bow down to him, in and subjugation - not worship him as a god; but, ultimately, recognize him as the leading authority on earth. Adam, assuredly, felt honored; but also remained humble throughout it all.[32]

> *The animals all came to bow down to Adam and worship him, Adam directed them to all worship* ***God****, as ruler of the earth.* (Baring-Gould, 1881, p. 26)[33]

He probably held to a standard such as the following:

> *Do not rejoice that the* ***spirits submit to you****, but rejoice that your names are written in Heaven.* - *Luke* 20:20 (KJV)

He followed the attitude of God: *humility*; which solidified the authority of Adam in God's eyes. Some angels weren't angry, and didn't complain. There were those, however, who would not have any of it. Their subjection to a being they deemed *inferior* was more than a good number could handle.

> *Adam has so much inherent glory and power the angels* ***quaked*** *and* ***were dismayed****, and* ***prayed to God*** *to remove this overwhelming, vast presence which he had made...* (Baring-Gould, 1881, p. 26)[34]

There would, soon, be a vast migration of angels *away* from God's present, reorganized cosmos, here - they just couldn't accept *Adam* as the one ruling over them. This would result in angels *falling* in heavenly hierarchy; in rank… at least somewhat. The world, as Adam inherited it, was about to change.

A Major Problem - Free Will

> *(God) gave* ***angels*** *the perfection of a created nature... He gave them* ***freedom****.* (Baring-Gould, 1881, p. 15)[35]

Because of *free will*, the working order of our world was about to become extremely ***fragile*** - open to outside influences. This Garden of Eden - the wonderful place that it was - needed to be elevated and secured with walls for this very reason.

The Angel of Will

As the Bible tells us, Satan was once the high musician, and guardian, of God's heavenly throne. As we'll see, some of his musical talent could have even been brought down to the Garden of Eden. We've now discover that there were angels in the Garden who provided an atmosphere of harmony and solace, due to their singing abilities.[36] The devil, as well, may have found it advantageous to utilize some of this talent, as well:

> Ezek. 28:
> 12 ...*Thus saith the Lord GOD; Thou sealest up the sun, full of wisdom, and perfect in beauty.*
> 13 *Thou hast been in* ***Eden*** *the garden of God... the workmanship of thy* ***tabrets*** *and of* ***thy pipes*** *was prepared in thee in the day that thou wast created.*
> 14 *Thou art the anointed cherub that covereth; and I have set thee so: thou wast upon the holy mountain of God; thou hast walked up and down in the midst of the stones of fire.*
> 15 *Thou wast perfect in thy ways from the day that thou wast created, till* ***iniquity*** *was found in thee.*
> 16 *By the multitude of thy merchandise they have filled the midst of thee with violence, and thou hast sinned: therefore I will cast thee as profane* ***out of the mountain of God****: and I will destroy thee, O covering cherub, from the midst of the stones of fire.*

In the above, we see that it was around the time of the Garden of Eden that the devil / Satan was about to have *another* falling out. Through his rebellion, he was about to lose any position of authority he might have once maintained, and be demoted even *further*.

Envy of the Devil

> *And the ministering Angels came down and rejoic'd before him (the man)... But when Sammael descended, and saw the glory that Adam was plac'd in, and the ministering Angels serving him at his Wedding, he* ***envied*** *him.*
> (Eisenmenger, 1748, p. 195)[37]

> *Through the devil's* ***envy*** *death entered the world, and those who are on his side suffer it.*
> - *Wisd.* 2:24[38]

Whatever power the devil still might have had over this new world of ours, he was about to lose it. It was around this time that God told the angels of earth's atmospheric heaven to "bow yourselves down" - and this was also directed at the devil.[39] Interestingly enough, the first racist of our world not be a white Adam; it was not the Adamites; it was no one of whom we might assume it would be - it was actually the devil.

The devil, Satan, whatever you might call him, was probably once an angel of the heavenly realm, since he, at one time, was able to guard God's throne. Heavenly angels seem to have a body made, primarily, out of some sort of divine **fire**.[40]

> *And the Jinn (i.e. angel) race, We had created* ***before****, from the* ***fire*** *of a scorching wind.* - *The Qur'an* 015:027[41]

> *The ensigns of Sammael and all his princes, and all his lords, have the resemblance of a red fire…* (Eisenmenger, 1748, p. 192)[42]

Adam, as we know, was fashioned from the earth's *dust* - a substance that, at the time, was of very little significance. And, as if it wasn't enough to be demoted to a lower position in this world, the devil - an angel of fire - was now ordered to *prostrate* himself *low* (in his eyes), before some created man of dust. He was around longer; he was stronger… he was even said to have dominated the previous world, for one time. Why should a son of fire have to bow to this son of clay?[43] It was at this point that the devil spoke up:

> *And when the prince of the lower order of angels saw what great majesty had been given unto Adam, he was jealous of him from that day, and he did not wish to worship him. And he said unto his hosts, "Ye shall not worship him, and ye shall not praise him with the angels. It is meet that ye should worship me, because I am fire and spirit; and not that I should worship a thing of dust, which hath been fashioned of* ***fine dust****"…* - *Cave of Treasures* The Revolt of Satan, and the Battle in Heaven[44]

The devil thought the *opposite* should occur - that man should be bowing to *him* instead.[45] Because God created Adam in His *own* image, He wanted Adam to be the new light of the world, and bring forth human children "of the Light." Some of the actual angels of *Light* had other ideas.[46] Very envious and scornful, the pride and free will of this devil allowed his thoughts to spiral down; even further:[47]

> *...and God the Lord spake: "Here is Adam. I have made thee in our image and likeness." And Michael (the angel) went out and called all the angels saying: "Worship the image of God as the Lord God hath commanded." And... he (Satan talking) called me and... I said to him... "I will not worship an inferior and younger being (than I). I am his senior in the Creation, before he was made was I already made. It is his duty to worship me." When the angels, who were under me, heard this, they refused to worship him. And Michael said... "if thou wilt not worship him, the Lord God will be wrath with thee." And I said, "If He be wrath with me,* ***I will set my seat above the stars of heaven*** *and* ***will be like the Highest****."*
>
> \- *Vita Adae Et Evae* 13:2-15:3[48]

A lot of similarities exist between this account and the book of Isaiah:

<u>*Isa.* 14:</u>
12 *How art thou fallen from heaven, O Lucifer (a.k.a. Satan), son of the morning! how art thou cut down to the ground, which didst weaken the nations!*
13 *For thou hast said in thine heart, I will ascend into heaven, I will exalt my* ***throne*** *above the stars of God: I will sit also upon the mount of the congregation, in the sides of the north:*
14 *I will ascend above the heights of the clouds; I will be like the most High.*

God responded to the devil's rebellion:

> *And his name was called "Sâṯânâ" (i.e. Satan) because he turned aside [from the right way]... (he) would not render obedience to God, and of his own free will he asserted his independence and separated himself from God. But he was swept away out of heaven and fell, and the fall of himself and of all his company from heaven took place... And the apparel of their* ***glorious state*** *was stripped off them...*
>
> \- *Cave of Treasures* The Revolt of Satan, and the Battle in Heaven[49]

The devil, now, lost even more of his previous, angelic "estate:"

> *(God speaking) But the wicked Satan who continued not in **his first estate**, nor kept his faith... though I had created him... so that I hurled him down...*
> - *First Book of Adam and Eve (The Conflict of Adam and Eve with Satan)* 6:7[50]

Once having a great countenance of *light*, the devil, and more and more of his accomplices, were to *further* lose what they all once had.

> *O Adam, so long as the good angel was obedient to Me, a bright **light** rested on him and on his hosts. But when he transgressed My commandment, I deprived him of that bright nature, and he became dark... he transgressed, and I made him fall from heaven upon the earth; and it was this darkness that came upon him.*
> - *First Book of Adam and Eve (The Conflict of Adam and Eve with Satan)* 13:2-5[51]

In one interesting ancient text, Satan actually explains to Adam, in detail, his own position:

> *Satan also wept loudly and said to Adam. "All my arrogance and sorrow came to pass because of you; for, because of you I went forth from my dwelling; and because of you I was alienated from the throne of the cherubs... You did nothing to me, but I came to this measure because of you, on the day on which you were created"... Then Michael summoned all the angels... He called me and said, "You too, bow down to Adam." I said "Go away, Michael! I shall not bow down to him who is posterior to me... Thereupon, God became angry with me and commanded to expel us from our dwelling and to cast me and my angels, who were in agreement with me, to the earth; and **you** were at the same time in the Garden... I had gone forth from the dwelling of **light**"...* - *Penitence of our Forefather Adam* 12.1-16.2[52]

Another Punishment - Not to be Allowed in the Garden

> *God cast him (Satan?) out what had been before an angel of the earth, and keeper of terrestrial things, and **a guardian of Paradise**.*
> (Baring-Gould, 1881, p. 18)[53]

In consequence of his arrogance, Satan was no longer admitted into the Garden of Eden, as he once had![54] Apparently, the walls around the Garden also provided some sort of *spiritual* blockage for undesirables, as well as a physical. Satan was even made to feel *afraid* in Adam's presence, eventually.[55] Although he had all of these restrictions, he *still* maintained a lot of his power; and began, eventually, to want - desperately - a way to break this cycle of Adam's authority.

Let's look more at least one major angel involved in this insurrection - Satan, the angel also known as **Sammael** - and what he once had, what he was reduced to, and what he might have done to upstart Adam's authority. Why do we need to know all of this information about such a negative topic? As they say: "*know thy enemy*." We need to know what we're up against - just like Adam needed to.

Samma-el

Satan's proper name (of old) was *Sammael*.[56] Something happened in this powerful angel's mind to lead him in some opposing direction of God, and God's ways. It is important to know exactly who this Sammael is, so that we can understand what Adam was up against - and we, today, *still* might be up against.

Sammael was once thought to be among highest-ranking angels; among their various classes.[57] He had, and still has, many other obscure names, and/or avatars. Among his other avatars, Sammael was also known as the *End of all Flesh*, the *Dog*, as well the *Strange God*.[58] *Sammael* also means *The Blind One* or *Poison of God* - the poison (of information, knowledge, etc.) that ends a man's life.[59] He also, in ancient times, was known as the *angel of desolation*, *destruction*, or *death*.[60] We don't know, for sure, if this title came about from something he did in the past, or whether he was appointed to these duties somewhere, in some world.

His most infamous name, however, is *Satan*. Under this title, he eventually would be allowed to accuse human beings in front of God: as the official "prosecutor" of God's court, if you will.[61] This is also where we get one meaning of the word ***devil***, meaning "slanderer" or "malignant accuser."[62] Any *devil* is considered an all-around moral deviant, whether it's in reference to Satan himself, or not.

Finally, Satan was also known as the *Leviathan*:

In that day the LORD with his sore and great and strong sword shall punish leviathan the piercing serpent, even leviathan that ***crooked serpent****; and he shall slay the dragon that [is] in the* ***sea****.* - *Isa.* 27:1 (KJV)

He (Satan) is call'd Leviathan. In the Treatise entitled Emek hammeleck, we have the following passage ... "And Gabriel shall hereafter hunt the Leviathan, that is, Sammael; as it is said 'Canst thou draw out Leviathan with a hook?'"
(Eisenmenger, 1748, p. 189)[63]

Leviathan has long been paired with references to the *Sea*. Why? Does the leviathan live in the physical sea, or something - or could it be something more *spiritual*? The *Fish of the Sea*, as we've already postulated, could also stand for those human and angelic souls once in the *Darkness*, or *Deep*… that supernatural *Sea* beneath the earth. Could this be the *sea* that leviathan "swims in?"

The "fish being" idea also doubtless relates to the Shining Ones (angelic and/or other beings) arriving out of the waters of ***the great Deluge****, or Deluges recorded in the myths of many different* ***cultures****.* (Gardiner and Osborn, 2006, p. 145)[64]

(The pagan fish/sea god) Oannes is the emblem of priestly, esoteric wisdom; he comes out ***from the sea****, because the "great* ***deep****," the water, typifies... the secret doctrine.*
(M.P. Blavatsky, n.d.)[65]

The fish-man was one of the esoteric symbols of the initiate in that ancient culture [Babylon]. No doubt it was taught that the man or woman who had so developed themselves as to have free ***access*** *to* ***the Spiritual world*** *could be regarded as being* ***dual****. Such people would be regarded as being equally content to walk on the Earthly plane or* ***swim*** *in the* ***watery****.* (David Ovason, n.d.)[66]

According to *Gesenius's Lexicon*, the Hebrew origins of the English *fish*, in the Bible, could *indeed* mean something else. It originates in the root-word *dagah*, which is also associated with words such as "to multiply," to "increase," and to "cover:"[67] What could this signify?

...to cover (like... to cover over; hence to be dark)... this verb is applied to multitude and plenty covering over everything (compare... a ***great company****... a* ***great multitude****...).* ("Gesunius's Lexicon - *dagah*", n. d., p. 1)[68]

Again, it is really important that we look at the original Hebrew words, here, for Biblical verses: could the *fish* of some segments of the Bible actually refer to a great **company** of angelic (and/or human) souls - souls who once may have resided, or still do, in the *Darkness*, or *Deep*, or the *Sea*? We see that:

> *...where a god dies, that is, ceases to exist in human form, his life passes into the **waters** where he is buried; and this again is merely a theory to bring the **divine water** or the divine **fish** into harmony with anthropomorphic ideas.*
>
> (Mackenzie, 1915, p. 28)[69]

Its obvious Sammael was concerned about Adam. He didn't like the fact God allowed Adam to have dominion over all living beings - including the *fish (or angelic) around him.*[70] The *Zohar* has a very interesting comment, regarding the Genesis 1:26 verse:

> *... "and let them have dominion over the fish of the sea" ... meaning the ministers in the sea from the sphere of the **serpent**...* - *Zohar* Mishpatim 18[71]

Obviously, there was a reason Satan was also known as the *Leviathan*: he was once leader of a great **company**, or *sea*, of angelic souls! It would be no big deal if he ruled over salmon and trout. Since Adam was also considered as having authority over the *Fish of the Sea*, Sammael may have took this as an attack on his dominance and authority; and brought his grievances to other groups of angelic individuals, as well.

> *...the wicked Sammael (Satan) made a covenant with all the **upper gods** (i.e. angels?) against his Lord, because the Holy and Blessed God had said to Adam and Eve, "And have dominion over the **fish of the Sea**." How can I prompt them that they sin, and be driven out before me? Then came he with all his **hosts**...*
>
> (Eisenmenger, 1748, p. 193)[72]

Obviously, Satan wouldn't have cared so much about things - even enough to plot out something against Adam - if these *Fish of the Sea* were **only** lowly fish.

The Allies of Satan's Cause

We've already seen that:

> *It is written... "and let them have dominion over the fish of the sea" (Beresheet 1:26), meaning the* ***ministers*** *of the sea from the* ***sphere*** *of the serpent...*
>
> \- *Zohar* Mishpatim 18[73]

Satan began to recruit angels - the former angels under his "sphere," undoubtedly - towards his new cause. One source stated he probably had 130 die-hard angelic ministers of authority behind him.[74] Interestingly enough, these allies of his were known as, according to one ancient source, *Shells* or *Barks*. Why? The reason is example:

> *...the princes encompass his throne as a* ***shell*** *surrounds its fruit.*
>
> (Eisenmenger, 1748, p. 187)[75]

These minsters had soon become devoted to their leader in thought and deed.[76] The first fall of angels, as noted in the Bible, could possibly have involved angels of *fire* (or, some of those angels of *Light*?). They became totally devoted to Satan's cause; of which was their undoing - God was watching. Things don't get by Him. Their allegiance caused God to have to do what He had do, and *demote* entire groups.

The Second Wave of Envious Ones

Other groups would become dissident to Adam, soon after; and follow in Satan's footsteps. These angels would, possibly, be a little different, however. They would not be angels who come, strictly, from the upper heavens (like Satan). No. These would be a lower order of angelic beings; closer to human beings in a number of ways. We'll see that further grumbling took place between these lower-classes of angels and their human manager, as well.

The complaints of this angelic class would be made public through one of the first tasks the new manager, Adam, was to be engaged in - and there would also be a **competition** set up, to decide "who was who." Let's see.

The Competition for a Help-Mate

Adam, as we know, was assigned the job of dressing and keeping the Garden - the top manager of this whole process. One of the first responsibilities Adam was assigned to was to *name* practically every living being around him - animals *and* (as we'll see) human beings! Adam was, also, fairly lonely, throughout this time... possibly because a lot of other human beings around him had significant others; and he didn't. The manager had a job to do; and not a lot of time to spend looking for a mate. God noticed this, and, during this whole "naming" process, probably brought a number of *women* in front of him - hoping that Adam would find himself **a mate**.[77]

> *And Adam gave names to every animal,* ***and*** *to the birds of the heaven, and to every beast of the open field. But for Adam,* ***no partner*** *was found like himself.*
>
> - *Genizah Manuscripts* Gen. 2:20[78]

The Bible stated, somewhat, the same thing:

<u>*Gen. 2:*</u>

18 *And the LORD God said, It is not good that the man should be alone; I will make him an* ***help meet*** *for him.*

19 *And out of the ground the LORD God formed every Chay (Beast) of the Field, and every Owph (Fowl) of the Air; and brought them unto Adam to see what he would call them: and whatsoever Adam called* ***every living soul*** *(a.k.a. "creature"), that was the name thereof.*

20 *And Adam gave names to all Behemah, and to the Owph (Fowl) of the Air, and to every Chay (Beast) of the Field; but for Adam there was not found* ***an help meet*** *for him.*

(in retranslation)

You'll notice, in the above, that Adam seemed to give names to a couple of pre-Adamite groups, here, as well. Interestingly, this *does* help support the postulation the *Owph of the Air* and *Chay of the Field* were groups of human beings, and not just animals: why would groups of *animals* need to have been brought in front of Adam… for a possible helpmate?

In the above, we see Genesis 2:19 stated that, "out of the ground the LORD God formed…," also of which might not be entirely correct. Again, we look at the original *Hebrew* to find some answers. We know that God formed the *Chay of the Field* in Genesis 1:24 and *Owph of the Air* in Genesis 1:21 - at different times. In the above verse, we see that there's really no reason for God to form them "out of the ground" again, if they already were once! What could the Bible *really* be saying here?

The Hebrew word for *ground*, here, could also mean "a specific plot of land," or even "the whole inhabited earth." And, the word *formed* could also mean to "plan," to be "predetermined," or "pre-ordained."[79] When we look at this verse with these other Hebrew meanings, it all makes sense:

<u>*Gen. 2:*</u>
19 *And* ***on one specific plot of land*** *the LORD God* ***pre-ordained to have*** *every*
Chay (Beast) of the Field, and every Owph (Fowl) of the Air brought down unto
Adam to see what he would call them: and whatsoever Adam called every living
soul *(a.k.a. creature), that was the name thereof.*
20 *And Adam gave names to all Behemah (Cattle), and to the Owph (Fowl) of the Air,*
and to every Chay (Beast) of the Field; but for Adam there was not found ***an help***
meet *for him.*
(in retranslation)

A particular plot of land was chosen for the "meeting" event to occur; maybe in a field around the Garden.

We also see, in the above, that those with a *soul* came in front of Adam (the Hebrew *nephesh*, again); translated into English as *creature*, here. As we've already surmised, those who had a soul - or, the *nephesh* - probably meant those living creatures with ***human*** souls (but, of course, the early King James translators, here, forced themselves to not see this as anything else than animals). So, Adam allowed *human* workers to pass by him; naming them as they walked along. Subtly, he was *also* looking for **a wife**, out of all of these, at the same time. Obviously… Adam wasn't going to marry an animal!

> *What is that which is said in Genesis 2:23, Bone of my Bone, and Flesh of my Flesh. This Passage teaches us, that he (Adam) had coition with* ***beasts*** *(Chay, and others maybe?), both wild and tame, of every Kind; but his Mind could not be satisfied 'till he cohabited with* ***Eve****… 'Tis said by Some of the Sages, That the first Man had carnal Knowledge of all* ***Animals*** *(i.e. humans?), but could not be induc'd to chuse (choose) any one of them to be* ***his Wife****.* (Eisenmenger, 1748, p. 22)[80]

Maybe he wanted a human being closer to him, in a number of ways. Even though the people he had before him may have sufficed his desires to some degree, he was probably looking for that "perfect" woman - one who thought like him; had similar interests; looked a lot like him; whatever. It seems, in the Bible, Adam grew a little weary, because he did not have a suitable woman close to him (in a number of ways). Some of us may recall, after Eve came into being, Adam stated this new wife was "bones of my bones" and "flesh of my flesh." He was very happy she was close to him, in many regards.

But, before this, it seems that God arranged to have women from at least three different groups of pre-Adamites (the *Chay of the Field*, the *Owph of the Air*, and the *Behemah*) to have their shot with Adam - one by one. Adam may have tried to make a relationship work with these women, but, on a personal level, didn't seem to find the right connection. It's not that these women weren't worthy enough; it was more probable that Adam was some sort of perfectionist - wanting more of a clone of himself, to love. We're not sure the exact reason why Adam was so picky, here.

Incidentally, an astute eye would notice that we only have the members from three different pre-Adamite groups, here. What about the *Remes (Creeping Thing) that Creepeth*? Why didn't God bring them in front of Adam, at this time? Maybe it was because they really didn't work much the Garden. We postulated already that this *Remes* group might not have had much of a working role in the Garden; so, God, quite possibly, didn't feel they were in "the thick of things" enough to put them in there. Another possibility might arise - that Adam could have already once **had** a wife from one of these

Remes; and it didn't work out. We don't know for sure. Why didn't Adam choose from the other Adamites, as well? Same reason?

Lilith - Woman Left Out

> *...and the first Eve - that is,* ***Lilith*** *- found him (Adam)...*
> - *Chronicles of Jerahmeel* 23:1[81]

Speaking of relationships which don't work, there is a mountain of ancient evidence which suggests that Adam could have been married, or at least in a sexual relationship, at least one time *before* he would be united with Eve. It could have been slightly before the formation of Eve that Adam may have already concluded he had the perfect mate. The Bible might even allude to this, as well:

> *Why had not God created Eve at the same time that He created Adam? Moreover, when Eve finally was created, why did Adam say, "****This time*** *[in some translations, "This* ***at last****"] bone of bones and flesh of my flesh"... (Gen. 2:23). To ancient interpreters, both questions seemed to suggest that Eve was not Adam's first mate...*
> (Kugel, 1997, p. 113)[82]

According to a number of ancient sources, ***Lilith*** was his first help meet, or wife![83] Some sources stated he was created out of this same dust (or mud/clay) as Adam.[84] Possibly, since she was formed from this same *dust*, Adam may have been under the assumption that she would be a suitable wife. There were other sources, however, which said that Lilith was formed from a slightly *different* mixture, which might have helped allow for friction between the two.[85]

Though Adam wanted to make Lilith his wife, and have her respect him as her husband, she wasn't having any part of it, eventually. Apparently, it seemed that Adam was trying to be head of the household, and Lilith was *against* these "roles."[86] Regardless of being from the same dust, they just did not get along.

Lilith did not want to lie under Adam during sex, nor submit to him sexually. Since she was from the same dust that Adam was, she figured she didn't have to lie underneath him![87] She wanted to be on the same **level** as Adam, in whatever they did; even *higher*. Adam complained to God about it, and Lilith ran away. She would abandon her wifely duties, and continually leave the Garden. Eventually, she was reported to have consorted (had sex) with other human and angelic beings around her. God brought her back to Adam a few times, but she kept doing the same. Eventually, Lilith would soon be ousted; for good.

> *...(after Lilith) became proud and a vexation to her husband, God expelled her from paradise.* (Baring-Gould, 1881, p. 34)[88]

Eve, as many probably know, was created from Adam's *rib*. Again, a woman came on the scene; closer to Adam (as he wished). For whatever reason, she more compatible:

> *...when he (Adam) saw the woman fashioned from his rib, "This is now bone of my bone, and flesh of my flesh," which is as much as to say, Now God has given me a wife and companion, suitable for me, taken from my bone and flesh, but* ***the other wife*** *he gave me was not of my bone and flesh, and therefore not a suitable companion and wife for me.* (Baring-Gould, 1881, p. 34)[89]

Adam, most probably, believed that someone taken *strait out* of his own flesh may now work. Maybe; maybe not.

Another Reason for this "Naming of the Animals"

Beyond the naming of people, beyond the possible naming of any animals, as well - even beyond Adam looking for a help meet - there was **one more** reason for Adam's undertaking, at this time. According to ancient sources, there were angels who *challenged* Adam's knowledge and understanding of the world he lived in; which was a major indicator - at least in their minds - of his authority.

According to one source, "The according qualities with which Adam was blessed... aroused the **envy** of the angels."[90]

> *The angels then began to envy him (Adam), saying, "Indeed, God will now* ***love him*** *more than He does us; if we can entice him to sin he will be destroyed from the earth."*
> *- Chronicles of Jerahmeel* 22:1[91]

These angels thought they were superior in *every* way; and, from their very make-up, more knowledgeable. They did not want God to love this man as much as He did. Naturally, all of this would prompt them to continually desire to challenge Adam's intellect.[92]

The following verses of the Bible seem to give us more insight on the dissension of these angelic beings - strait from their own mouths:

> <u>*Psa.* 8:</u>
> 3 *When I consider thy heavens, the work of thy fingers, the moon and the stars, which thou hast ordained;*
> 4 *What is* ***man****, that thou art mindful of him? and the son of man, that thou visitest* ***him****?*
> 5 *For thou hast made him a little lower than the angels, and hast* ***crowned him with glory and honour****.*
> 6 *Thou madest him to have* ***dominion over the works of thy hands****; thou hast put all things under his feet...*

They continually complained to God about the man. And God eventually would grant them their time to prove themselves. Now, the naming each human being (and animal) would become a **test** between these angels and Adam - whoever could do it *better* would, naturally, be considered more knowledgeable; and be considered worthy enough to be in the top position of authority.

Dissidence of these Angels "Of Old"

As we recall, a good number of angels in this world were, most probably, *brought up*, from the previous world. Apparently, God may have even allowed these angels memories and knowledge of this previous world - the world the Bible might refer to as that world which was "*of old*." These angels, then, may have easily understood "how the world worked" before our "Six-Day Creation;" as well as any of the *negative* elements which may have comprised this world! This knowledge would, continually, prove to be a powerful commodity to these angelic beings. So, now, armed with this previous-world knowledge, the angels may have believed they would have a way to show Adam what an "upper hand" really was! The competition had begun.

Angel Verses Adam

God, now, set up the contest: whoever could name *all* of the human beings and animals placed in front of them would be deemed the more capable being; the loser to submit to the winner's authority. This should settle it, at least in the minds of everyone.[93] Back and forth, Adam and the angels attempted to name each animal. People and animals came in front of Adam, and he named every one (Gen. 2:20).[94] The angels tried, but could not name them all. God, according to one source, could have even prompted Adam to win.[95] Whatever way it turned out, Adam accomplished this feat, and become the victor over all. This also was **proof-positive** Adam was more capable, at least to these grumbling angels.

> *Then God said to the angels, "Were you not saying, What is man, that Thou shouldst remember him? Now his **wisdom** is greater than yours!"*
>
> - *Chronicles of Jerahmeel* 22:1[96]

When the angels failed in their endeavor, they were taken back.[97] Instead of reconciling with their defeat, everything seemed to get worse - they allowed free will and pride to get the better of them.

Angels to Burn

These angels, then, became so angry and envious that it became even harder for them to bow down. Ultimately, their inner rage turned into thoughts of revenge. According to some ancient sources, there were at least *two* distinct groups of angels who wanted action against Adam. Immediately God would put a stop to it. Another source stated that some of these angels tried to consume the Adamites (most notably Adam) with fire; but the protecting hand of God stopped them in their tracks. He allowed Adam to go about his business - unscathed.

As a consequence, God eliminated the "glow" of a group of the angelic *light* for their insolence; He even *burnt up* some of them.[98] God would not let any rebellious angels stop His plans for Adam, and his role on earth:

> *God created some (angelic) creatures and said: "Prostrate yourselves before Adam!" They replied: We shall not do that... He set a fire to consume them. He then created other creatures... They refused, and God sent a fire to consume them.*
> - *al-Tabari: The History of al-Tabari - Vol. I: General Introduction and From the Creation to the Flood* The Story of Iblis 84[99]

> *At the time the Holy One, blessed be He... said to them: Would ye advise me to create a man? And they asked Him: What will be his deeds? And He related before them such and such. They explained before Him: Lord of the Universe, what is the mortal, that Thou rememberest him, and the son of men, that Thou thinkest of him? [Ps. vii. 5]. He then put His little finger among them and they were all* ***burnt****. And the same was with the second coetus.* - *Babylonian Talmud* Sandhedrin, Chap. XI[100]

The punishment of some obviously became a reflection of their fiery, overly-passionate thoughts.[101] They were burnt, or made blackened, on the *outside* for their dark, negative thoughts of envy, hate, and revenge on the *inside*.

Era of the "Fallen Ones" - Now Known as Nephilim

As if these disfigurements weren't enough, many of these accursed angels were probably **demoted**, in rank or status; and given a new name: **the *Nephilim*** (or, the "Fallen Ones").

> *How, you may well ask, can they (the Nephilim) subsist in this world? Rabbi Chiya said that they are among those referred to as "****Birds which fly upon the earth****."*
> - *Zohar* Beresheet B69[102]

Again, we see a reference to *birds* or *fowl* as having some type of angelic connection (remember the *Owph (or Fowl) of the Air*, for example). These "fallen" angels, also known as the **Nephilim**, were so-named because, with their attempts to bring the organized world of Adam to a fallen state, they, *themselves*, fell![103]

> *...those angels wanted to denounce him. They asked the Holy One, blessed be He (God), "What is man, that you are mindful of him" (Tehilim 8:5), **for he is bound to sin** before you? Why, therefore, do you want us to be under him? The Holy One, blessed be He (God), replied, **If you were down below on earth like he**, you would sin more than he does.* - *Zohar* Beresheet A20[104]

Once with angelic qualities way above the average man, these angels had, now, even lost a lot of that. Their latest act of sacrilege caused them, in their fall, to be *physically* demoted - to have most of the *same attributes* as human beings![105]

Sammael (i.e. Satan) and the heavenly angels probably were not created using elements of our planet. They were fashioned in true, *spirit* form. Henceforth, these beings really could not transform themselves into human form at will. But, angels such as the Nephilim probably could.[106]

> *And these, as we have discussed, appear to men in the form of human beings. And how, you may ask, do they transform themselves from the shape of an angel to that of human beings? As we have learned, they can transform themselves into all kinds of shapes, and when they come down into this world, they clothe themselves with **the garments of earth's atmosphere** and **take on human form**.*
>
> - *Zohar* Beresheet B69[107]

Yet, their *demotion* - their *loss of 'estate'* - was a further blow to them, on so many levels!

> *...there are heretical accounts which suggest that when angels sin they "clothe themselves with the corruptibility **of the flesh**."* (Godwin, 1990, p. 86)[108]

This probably made them a lot less powerful than they were before - and even more resentful to Adam. They wanted Adam to go down *even* more now! So, let's take a look at a couple leaders of the Nephilim, and see what they did to further expedite their cause against Adam, and all of mankind.

Azza, Uzza, and Azazel

A few prominent angelic beings of the day were known as *Azza*, *Uzza*, and *Azazel*.[109] According to the *Third Book of Enoch*, these were angels who openly and continually made the most complaints about Adam. Two of them, Azazel and Azza, were notorious in ancient written works (Azazel was even synonymous with the so-called "scapegoat" of the Bible; in Lev. 16:8).

Azazel, though, had quite an interesting story about him: according to one source, even before the beginning of our "Six-Day Creation," Azazel was disagreeing with God! Apparently, God *already* chose the bloodline of what would be His people (i.e. Israel) in the beginning of our world, with Adam to be the patriarch. Azazel knew of this, and had a prediction about the future. He reminded God that Adam's future descendents could eventually fall, and believed that his descendents would not turn out to be the great nation God set them out to be. God, however, did not falter; He continued on with His creation, forming Adam anyway. According to another source, Azazel was even commanded by God to go and fetch the dust for Adam's formation - probably in response to all of his bickering!

This angel, and fifty-or-so of his fellow *Nephilim* (or *fallen* angels), were all forced to give up their lofty positions, because of these continual complaints. *Now*, they were told to take on a new role for their insolence: to be mid-level "managers" of the Garden of Eden![110] Worse yet, at least to them, they felt the "sting" of looking a lot like, as well as taking on an, overall, general role as human beings! To them, it was a massive step in the spiritual "gutter."

These angels, then, began to cry out: "If we do not take counsel against this man so that he sin before his Creator, then we will not prevail against him!"[111] So, this became their new rallying cry; their new goal - to make Adam fail at *any* price.

Azazel was the lead angel of these Nephilim, and possibly many more. He played a very sinister role in the organized construct under Adam - speaking to people with a forked tongue. He probably strolled around the Garden – under another, very-famous name! We've mentioned earlier that Sammael (or Satan) may not have been the ***only*** *leader of angelic dissidents at this time* - can we guess who the *other* largely-problematic leader of angels might be? Yes, he was *in* the Garden of Eden; and, yes, he was someone that most of us have heard of.

It's, now, time to learn who the other half of this whole "conspiracy of *devils*" was…

Chapter 6

The Spoiler of the Garden

*And with guile **I** cheated thy (Adam's) wife and caused thee to be expelled through her (doing) from thy joy and luxury, as **I** have been driven out of my glory.*
- *Vita Adae Et Evae* 16:4[1]

Enter One of the Most Infamous Ones of Them All!

Adam was placed in the garden; as priest, king, and prophet over the land. He, as one might also assume, was head of those other groups of people, and angels, around him. Assuredly, he was to be the example of God's "image" and "likeness" throughout the Garden, and beyond - to show others how to think and act.[2] Eve, now, was formed - created from Adam's rib; and would be there to accompany him as his second wife. Coming straight from the body of Adam, himself, they, seemingly, were the perfect couple.

Adam and Eve, of course, were allowed entry into this "paradise on earth." Others, as we've postulated, were *not*. According to one ancient source, some groups of people - such as the *Chay* and *Behemah* - were, not only, assigned to help manage the garden's cultivation, but also to help *guard* it.[3] Who or what, again, would they have to guard it *from* is an interesting concept for us to ponder. According to one ancient source, *The Book of the Cave of Treasures*, "in it (the Garden) dwelt the souls of the **righteous**. The souls of sinners dwelt in a deep place, outside Eden."[4] Apparently, as well, the walls were to keep out any and all of those who might not have been the most righteous. Only a limited few of these fallen angels (or Nephilim) were, probably, allowed in - those with "mid-level" management positions. And, we also know, because of Adam's dominion over it, Satan, Lilith, and angels who truly despised Adam were definitely out. Yet, there may have been *one* angel allowed access to the Garden; and possibly in the position to do something about that pesky little Adam.

There was one more angel, besides Satan, who wanted Adam to fail, as well. This someone, also, was in an elevated position at one time; but lost out… due to Adam. This was an angel who may have even decided to go into a "pact" with Satan, himself; in order to bring the man down. Now, this same angel, also, was in the right position to spoil Adam's authority; and overthrow the Garden's entire working order. He was the angel's "way in."

Although the aforementioned angels - Azazel and Azza - were considered well-known throughout ancient texts, the former could have been the one bent on this destruction. **Azazel**, a mid-level "manager" of the Garden of Eden, could actually have been one of the most infamous characters of Biblical history - the ***Serpent*** of the Garden of Eden!

The Garden's Serpent - A Fallen Angel?

> *Before that time it (the serpent) had legs like other animals and according to one rabbinic tradition was* ***like a man*** *in appearance, standing upright on two legs. Therefore, the man representations of the temptation which depict the serpent as a snake curled round the Tree of Knowledge are really based on a* ***misunderstanding*** *of the scriptural text.* (Goldstein, 1933, p. 4)[5]

Many have concluded the Serpent was nothing more than an animal - a snake. As we look deeper into these alternate sources, even *the Bible*, we see evidence that this Serpent might actually be something more. If we think about it, how could an *animal* deceive Eve so badly? How could a lowly snake turn the entire world of the Garden upside down - unless there was something *more* to him, in the first place? One portion of an ancient Babylonian hymn - the *Penitential Hymn* - has the following:

13. *Which to those* ***rebel angels*** *prohibited return*
14. *he (God) stopped their service, and sent them to the gods who were his enemies*
15. *In their room he created mankind.*
16. *The first (Adam) who received life, dwelt along with him.*
17. *May he give them strength, never to neglect his word,*
18. *Following the* ***serpent****'s voice...*[6]

According to what so many of us have been taught, a winding, slithery animal convinced Eve to disobey God, and she listened to him! It is quite possible, however, that the Serpent was actually an **angelic being**; one of many angelic beings who were sentenced to become less angelic, and more and more human, in God's brave new world. He was one of those angelic beings reduced in spiritual rank or stature, mainly because of his continual, nonstop complaining. Really… how could a small reptile be able to talk to Eve in the first place? And, if he did, Eve really didn't seem too *surprised* that an animal would begin to have a conversation with her… right?

According to one ancient source, the Serpent was considered a *beast*, just like the similar namesakes of the *Chay of the Field* and the *Behemah.*[7] Was he the same? Apparently, as we postulated, there were Chay and Behemah around the garden, to help out in the fields and the domestication of the animals. The Bible even states the Chay and Behemah could have had something in common with this Serpent.

> *Now the serpent was more* ***subtil*** *than any* ***Beast (i.e. Chay?) of the Field*** *which the LORD God had made…* - *Gen.* 3:1 (KJV)

Could this imply that the *Serpent* was, either associated with these people in some way; or, most probably, was a mid-level ***leader*** of them?[8] Also, in the Bible, the word *beast* could be another term for an angelic being (c.f. Rev. 6:1). Put them both together and we see that: maybe the Serpent was either a mid-level manager of many human individuals who worked around the Garden, or he was much more *subtil*, or *shrewd*, that almost any other terrestrial angel in the vicinity.

Either way, the Serpent was, quite possibly, just *below* the position of Adam's authority in Eden - demoted because of his vocal insolence.

An Angel - in Serpent Form?

> *So it appears there were three distinct orders of* ***angels*** *in the lower echelons. At the top were the seven Archangel chiefs, who were known as* ***the aristocratic two-eyed serpents****…* (Godwin, 1990, p. 71)[9]

We recall that Sammael (Satan) was also known as the *Leviathan* of the Sea. In the Talmud, however, the Leviathan is also known as the "strait or upright **Serpent**," or "crooked **serpent.**"[10]

Could this "Serpent" have been an angel, now in some sort of physical, corporeal, nearly-human form?[11] If he was some sort of fallen angel, did he resemble a serpent, in any way, walking around the earth? What could he have looked like? What exactly was he all about?

Characteristics of This Serpent

We'll now get into how an angel such as the Serpent could, so often, be associated with an actual serpent, or snake. Could these terrestrial angelic beings actually have *serpentine-like* features that we could have seen? From the preponderance of the ancient written evidence, the answer to that would, most probably, be *no*… and *yes*. What that means is: some ancient sources stated that the Serpent had human-like extremities; such as hands and feet.[12] One holy text of the ancient *Zoroastrian* faith, for example, cited the evil spirit - the father of the daevas (i.e. demons) - was *serpent-like*, and with legs.[13] Another text said that he ate *food*, just like a human would.[14] The same aforementioned *Zoroastrian* spirit was said to even have had a male *sexual organ*. Talk of serpents flourished all over ancient pagan mythology and religion.

There are, still, a number of other ancient reports of human-like beings with *serpentine* characteristics walking the earth - with characteristics especially evident *in their face*.[15] These humanoids were also said to have shined like a bright *star* - much like one would how picture an angel would, if they appeared for a man to see.[16] Still another source stated these serpents had brilliant, pale-white skin.[17] Still another source stated that the angels once under the Serpent's authority had "serpentine" features to their face… even though they had the overall form and shape of a man. If we assemble information to be had on these ancient serpentine beings, we could come to some kind of general conclusion about them: it seems that, the *more* these beings head towards living life as a terrestrial human being on the earth, the *more* human they will probably look! It's fairly simple.

We've already alluded to the concept of certain angels coming *solely* from heaven; therefore, because of their physical make-up, they really wouldn't have any physical way to manifest themselves into resembling human beings on earth. But, there *are* other angels, such as the Serpent and Nephilim, who were of a slightly *lower* "class;" and *could* manifest themselves into a human-like appearance (given it was their place to do so). To head back towards their *original* appearance - into more of a *spiritual* being - would, then, point them back in the direction of showing their *true*, serpentine "colors." If, for example, they manifested themselves into looking like a human being of our terrestrial world, for whatever reason, it would only be *temporarily*. And, when seen by people on this earth, they still might possess *somewhat* of a serpentine appearance, somewhere - because they haven't *totally* changed into an earthly, terrestrial being. But, if they've been *demoted* from their original angelic nature and/or spiritual "rank" by God (such as the Serpent and the Nephilim), they continually might look closer and closer to a human being, as long as they lost more and more of their former angelic state… until they would become almost indistinguishable from neighboring terrestrial human beings on the earth!

Here are a couple of ancient written texts, which provide us a couple of curious examples of these *temporary* serpent manifestations on the earth.

"The Cloak of Feathers"

The following quote comes from the ancient work, *The Second Book of Enoch*. A couple of large, brightly-shining angels - even identified as having *wings* - manifested themselves in front of a human being:

> *And there appeared to me two* ***men****, exceedingly big, so that I never saw such on earth; their faces were shining like the sun… with* ***clothing*** *and singing of various kinds in appearance purple, their* ***wings*** *were brighter than gold…*
>
> \- *2 Enoch (The Book of the Secrets of Enoch)* 1:6[18]

It appears these angels looked *somewhat* like men; but the observing people knew they were also something *more*. These angels, in the above, were also said to be wearing some type of purple *cloak*; and appeared to have *wings*. What could this mean?

Another ancient work - *The Testament of Amram* - stated almost the same thing. *Amram*, the father of Moses, apparently had a dream one night, or a vision, about one particular angel.[19] In his description, he described an angel who looked like a *serpent*; also wearing a colored cloak:

> *His looks were frightening [like those of a* ***vip]er****, and his* ***[ga]rm[en]ts*** *were multi-coloured and he was extremely dark... And afterwards I looked and behold... by his appearance and his* ***face*** *was like that of an* ***adder****...*
>
> \- *The Testament of Amram (4Q544)* f #1[20]

First, could these garments, as mentioned above, be the same as that *cloak* worn by the angels in *The Second Book of Enoch* (also, above)? There were reportedly *other* angelic beings, in other ancient works, said to have worn a *winged* cloak, when appearing to human beings.[21] These angels were said to have been "clothed like **birds**, with *wings* for garments."[22] Other accounts record angels as wearing a *feathered* cloak. Could this be one reason why so many angels, so often, were said to have had "*wings*?" To the human eyes, witnessing an angel wearing a *feathered* cloak might easily have appeared to be looking like the angel had some manner of wings!

Interestingly enough, we've already postulated how the *(Owph) Fowl of the Air* were human beings - with angelic qualities; yet, they were called *fowl*. Also, we've seen how some angels were referred to as *birds*. Could the above information give us even *more* credence towards accepting all of this as reality?

Next, we return to the above quote:

> *And afterwards I looked and behold... by his appearance and his* ***face*** *was like that of an* ***adder****...* - *The Testament of Amram (4Q544)* f #1[23]

And, what about the description of certain serpentine angels as having a face like an *adder* (or a *viper*)? Interestingly enough, there have even been a number of ancient figurines found possessing *these same* facial characteristics. They were found in the ancient lands of *Ubaid* (a part of ancient Mesopotamia), as well as the land of *Jarmo* (in ancient Iraqi Kurdistan).[24] Could these figurines actually be a description of these serpentine angels - those who manifested themselves into being able to be seen by people, long ago?

The Dragon

There is another famous symbol in ancient mythology - *the* ***dragon***. The dragon has long been a famous symbol in ancient mythologies, all around the world. This Serpent of the Garden, according to some ancient sources, was also known to be a *dragon*.[25] Well, just what is *a dragon*? The Bible makes mention of a "great dragon" (in Rev. 12:3, 12:9), as well a "fiery, flying serpent" (in Isa. 30:6).[26] We'll soon see how the Serpent was also considered to be "*fiery*" - a strongly emotion and passionate angelic being, bent on change in the Garden, and overall destruction.

The Bible has even more on these apparent correlations:

> *In that day the LORD with his sore and great and strong sword shall punish leviathan the piercing* ***serpent****, even leviathan that crooked* ***serpent****; and he shall slay the* ***dragon*** *that is in the sea.* - *Isa.* 27:1 (KJV)

> *And he laid hold on the* ***dragon****, that old* ***serpent****, which is the* ***Devil****...*
> \- *Rev.* 20:2 (KJV)

We see how they both seem to be equated. Revelation 12:9 also said this *old Serpent* was a ***he***... and not an animal. Could these serpentine angels - especially the *Serpent* himself - be the origins of so many of the *serpent*, "*bird-men*," or *dragon* stories one may come across, throughout ancient religious history and mythology?

What is important, now, to understand about these serpentine angels is how they may have looked more serpentine in their original, spiritual form; and how they could have become more and more *human* - when forced to live a terrestrial life, in our natural world. Also, it's good to know that *all* serpents of the spiritual realm were not necessarily *evil* - just the ones who turned away from God, and followed other pathways and/or individuals (such as the Serpent, and the Nephilim). As well, it's important that we look more into the *thoughts* and *attitudes* of these serpentine angels - what may or may not have been going on in their minds… looking at the Serpent, for example, following his "demotion;" and *what* motivated them to do what, we'll see, he did. If this Serpent was, *indeed*, an angel with serpentine features - now *demoted* to look more and more like a man (because of his negativity towards God) - *then* what? What would be *his* next step of recourse? And, what ways would he use to reposition himself - or at least try to - in order to regain some sort of dignity he felt he once had; or he felt he *deserved*?

Let's look more into *these* elements of the Serpent, to gather more insight into what may have *really* happened in the Garden.

Nachash - His Biblical Name

> *He is called… the old serpent… the erect serpent, or else only* ***Nachasch****, i.e. serpent.* (Eisenmenger, 1748, p. 187-9)[27]

If we substitute the original Hebrew word for *serpent*, in Genesis 3:1, we have:

> *Now* ***Nachash*** *was more subtil than any beast of the field which the LORD God had made…* - *Gen.* 3:1 (in retranslation)

As we see, the Serpent *does* seem to have more of a proper name in the Bible. The word *Nachash* seems to be a descriptive title, however - relating to how the individual may have *thought*, or *related* to others. The word *Nachash* has been associated with a "whisperer," "magician," "enchanter," or "hypnotist."[28] One reason for Nachash's association with this Serpent, and these specific words, might lie with his *approach* to how he manipulated Eve.

The above verse stated Nachash was more "subtle" than anyone around him. Could he have acted much like a Serpent would, in this respect: passing himself off as a man who has something to hide; whispering; acting *subtly*, etc.?

The name *Nachash* could also be associated with the Arabic words *Chanas* or *khanasa*: meaning, "he departed, drew off, lay hid, seduced, or slunk away."[29] Again, Nachash, by acting and speaking in these mysterious ways, could have *hid* his true **intentions** from Eve - until, of course, his opportunity to "strike." Snakes, in their own right, aren't particularly too clever, dangerous, or annoying animals… but they seem to be able seduce their prey - quite well!

As one might picture a snake trying to carry out a conversation, Nachash would converse with Eve in a soft-spoken, subtle-like *hiss*. We recall that one of the meanings of *Nachash* is "enchanter." Was the Serpent able to seduce others, at least in part, by his enchanting words? We recall Satan was in charge of *music* in heaven - did the Serpent also use some of these musical techniques of wordplay?[30]

Let's look more at this mysterious, cunning being; and how he truly had similarities to a fallen angel.

The Fiery Seraphim

In *The Companion Bible* we have an interesting interpretation of the word *Nachash*:

> *In Genesis 3 we have neither allegory, myth, legend, nor fable, but literal historical facts set forth, and emphasized by the use of certain Figures of speech... All the confusion of thought and conflicting exegesis have arisen from taking literally what is expressed by Figures, or from taking figuratively what is literal... Hence, in Chaldee it (Nachash) means brass or copper, because of its* ***shining****... In the same way Saraph, in Isaiah 6:2, 6, means a burning one, and, because the serpents mentioned in Num. 21 were burning, in the poison of their bite, they were called Saraphim, or Seraphs... Nachash is thus used as being interchangeable with* ***Saraph****. Now, if Saraph is used of a serpent because its bite was burning, and is also used of a celestial or spirit being (a burning one), why should not Nachash be used of a serpent because its appearance was shining, and be also used of a* ***celestial or spirit-being*** *(a shining one)... The Nachash, or serpent, who beguiled Eve (II Cor. 11:3) is spoken of as "an* ***angel*** *of light" in v. 14. Have we not, in this, a clear intimation that it was not a snake, but a* ***glorious shining being****, apparently an* ***angel****, to whom Eve paid such great deference, acknowledging him as one who seemed to possess superior knowledge, and who was evidently a being of a superior knowledge, and who was evidently a being of a superior (not an inferior) order?* - *The Companion Bible* Appx. 19[31]

The title *Nachash* could also stand for a "shining one."[32] From the above, we clearly gather that *Nachash* might have, was, been a shining being - a *Seraph*, or a *Seraphim*. We see, in the above, a *Seraphim* is a high-ranking angel, with human attributes.[33] Could the Serpent once have been one of these glorious *Seraph*; now demoted to work in the Garden of Eden?[34]

The word *Seraphim* can come from either *seraph* (meaning, "to burn") or the noun *seraph* (which means "fiery, flying **serpent**").[35] In the Bible, a *Seraph* was considered a "fiery, flying **serpent**" a number of times (e.g. Num. 21:8, Deut. 8:15, Isa. 14:29 & 30:6). Is there a connection, here?

A few more literary works describe the Seraphim:

> *The Seraphim are identical with the Chalkadri... and, probably, also with the "**serpents**" of I Enoch...*
> - *3 Enoch (The Hebrew Book of Enoch)* 26:8 (notes)[36]

> *...the Seraphim are more identified with the **serpent** or dragon than any other angelic order.* (Godwin, 1990, p. 25)[37]

Another literary work describes the *Seraphim* as very tall angels, with six wings: one pair for flying; one for covering their eyes in front of God; and one for covering their "feet" (or, their *genitalia*).[38]

> *Now the angels have **phalli**, hearken unto [Isaiah 6:2 and Ezekiel 1:12] the prophet, who saith, 'With two of their wings they covered their faces, with two others they covered their feet, with two others they covered their hands, and with two others they covered their **phalli**'...* - *Bakhayla Mikael* p. 17[39]

Interesting, these angels also have *phalli*. Could they work like human beings, possibly? We clearly will find even *more* interesting characteristics of this Serpent, to come.

One of Many Titles

Beyond the name *Nachash*, the Serpent, as we've already postulated, has other names. We've already postulated he could have been the angel *Azazel*. One ancient source, *The Apocalypse of Abraham* (in 23:7-12, 14:5-6, and 31:5), stated the tempter of the Garden was a "serpent," or a "dragon." And, the same was described as "having hands and feet like a man's, on his back… wings." It all seems to fit into our theory about how the Serpent was, actually, a Seraphim, a Seraphim known as *Nachash*. On top of this, the same *Apocalypse of Abraham* provides another name to the Serpent:

> *...this is Adam... this is Eve. And he who is between them is the impiety of their behavior unto perdition,* ***Azazel*** *himself.*
>
> \- *Apocalypse of Abraham* 23:11-12[40]

The angel *Azazel*, according to another ancient source, was described "as being like a **Serpent** in appearance, having hands and feet like a man, with… wings" - very similar to the above description of *Nachash*.[41] According another source, he was also considered the *old Serpent*, and ***Seducer*** *of Mankind*.[42]

There is more.

Strong… In Rebellion

The word *Azazel*, itself, stands for the "strong one of God," or "of whom God strengthened."[43] These affiliations might sound somewhat positive on the surface - and maybe there could have been a reason for this… at one time. But, after his fall, all of this could also take on a negative tone. Instead of Azazel being a mighty warrior of God's resolve, he *now* could have become "belligerent towards God," or one strong in *his* rebellion.[44]

According to some sources, the Serpent was also an angel known as *Gadriel*, *Gadreel*, or *Katriel*.[45] The word *Gadriel*, itself, means, "God is my helper;" but, again, it could also take on a negative tone: as "he intrigued or revolted."[46]

Gadriel and Azazel *do* seem to possess similarities with each other, as well as with Nachash. Gadriel had hands and feet; with six wings on each side of his back. Azazel had a lot of the same.[47] Gadriel was known for teaching men how to create tools, weapons of war; and how to kill other people in an effective manner.[48] Azazel would also be known for showing mankind how to forge metals and create articles of war, such as swords, knives, shields and breastplates. Most importantly, Gadriel and Azazel both were known for one more thing - being the angel who *led Eve astray*.[49]

From what we can surmise, then, Nachash, Azazel, and Gadriel were all probably one in the same - the *Serpent*. And, from all of the above, it seems more *probable* there could be something much more to this vengeful, man-hating Serpent being something *more*… beyond just a slithering, talking animal.

Thoughts of the Serpent

Now that we established that the Serpent could have been something more: an angel who had lost his former, spiritual estate - we must now ask ourselves: just what *thoughts* could have been behind such an important decision… to move away from God? Why would he do something so drastic, which caused him to lose out on so much he once had?[50] There a number of answers to this.

Let's begin to delve into the Serpent's thoughts and motivations.

> *Adam was upright and straightforward, it being said of him, "Behold, Adam is one of us" (Gen. 3:22), as* ***one of the ministering angels****... Adam reclined in the Garden of Eden, while ministering angels, hovering over him, roasted flesh and strained wine for him.*
> (Goldin, 1929, p. 20)[51]

To serve the *man*? Not the *other way around*? Certain emotions began to well up within the Serpent:

> *But when the* ***Serpent*** *came and saw the Honour that was done them he cast an* ***envious*** *eye upon them, and was full of* ***Passion*** *and Spite against them.*
> (Eisenmenger, 1748, p. 196)[52]

*Had **envy** not wormed its way into his (the serpent's) soul, he…would have lived happily with Adam and Eve… it was precisely his **wisdom** that led to his undoing.*
(Frankel, 1989, p. 28)[53]

Had the Serpent not been cursed, he would have been a great benefit to man…
(Jung, 1974, p. 69)[54]

We now see what would have been some of the reasons behind the Serpent's thoughts. One commentary stated the Serpent may have actually begun his dissension with statements such as the following:

***I** will… be king of the whole earth: I will walk with my body erect, and eat of all the **dainties** of the world.* (Eisenmenger, 1748, p. 198)[55]

We already know, according to the Bible, the Serpent was very *subtle*. And, the above word *dainty* comes from an archaic Middle English word for "high esteem," "dignity," or "worth."[56] It could also stand for "fastidiousness," "scornful," "despising," "arrogant," or as "having high and often capricious standards." In other words, the Serpent became proud and arrogant in his thoughts - simply, he wanted to go after royal luxuries of this world.[57] In this case, the word *subtle* probably relates to how the Serpent was capable of using his intelligence for these deceptive purposes: to be deceitful and crafty - ultimately, for his own advantage.[58]

*The word **subtle** does not mean clever as we think of it in English. The Hebrew word, **aruwm**, could be cunning in an evil sense, but most scholars, such as Ferrar Fenton, define the word as "more impudent:" as a person who does **not know his place** or **station** in life. You might also define it as "cock" or lacking in modesty. So, if you mix immodest, cocky, contemptuous, cunning and impudent into one Hebrew word, then you can imagine what "subtle" means in this verse.*
("Star Wars, Lesson Seven", n. d.)[59]

As we could guess, his arrogance and cockiness already had led to the downfall of his previous angelic estate:

*His name was **Azazil**. He was one of the most **zealous** and **knowledgeable** of the angels. That led him to **haughtiness**.*

- *al-Tabari: The History of al-Tabari - Vol. I: General Introduction and From the Creation to the Flood* The Story of Iblis 83[60]

Another interpretation of Genesis 3:1 substitutes the word "*subtle*" with:

*...the serpent... He Who Waits in Ambush was more **smooth-tonged / slier** than any other life in the field...* (Halevi, 1997, p. 166)[61]

*And the serpent was the **shrewdest** of all the beasts of the open field...*

- *Genizah Manuscripts* Gen. 3:1[62]

Adding further to the association with *subtle*, the word *shrewd* could stand for one being "mischievous," "abusive," or even "dangerous."[63] In other words, the Serpent's knowledge would, eventually, become a dangerous thing to individuals around him. To top it off, he might have even had some knowledge of the world *of old* - our previous world - and used it all as a means to his *own* ends. What does all of this mean?

A Knowledge of Their Past

Another of the more sinister meanings of *Nachash* is, "to acquire knowledge through **experience**."[64] How old was the Serpent, to gather this experience? It seems obvious he didn't just jump on the scene the same time Adam was formed. Since this Serpent may have had an understanding of the *world of old*, he would have known what happened to *bring it all down*; and *also* how to manipulate people who might have lived in these times. Could the Serpent have used his inner cockiness, imprudence, and immodesty to achieve his goals, along with this knowledge?

As already stated, Azazel could easily have been one of the angels who existed before our "Six-Day Creation." In a number of ancient works (even the Bible), Azazel and Sammael/Satan *both* were considered that ***old*** Serpent (or, the Serpent ***of old***). Could it be because they were both had, once, lived in this *world of old* - in the era of the *old world*, or the *times of old*... simply, the world before our own?[65]

If the Serpent was actually an angel - forced to live on the earth, now, as a terrestrial being due to his insolence - we have to ask: what might have *really* transpired here, between the Serpent and Eve, the woman? It wasn't just a snake talking to a human being. It was two intelligent beings talking to one another.

What all *could* have possibly transpired? The answer may shock us all.

And, was Nachash (or Azazel) the *only* fallen angelic being to confront Eve, in the Garden? What about Sammael/Satan? What part could *he* have had in this whole up-and-coming attempt to dethrone mankind?

The Serpent's Crusade - To Corrupt Adam

> *Iblis (the Serpent?) said to angels Don't be afraid of that one Adam for I sold, and he is hollow. When I am given authority over him, I shall **ruin him**.*
> *- al-Tabari: The History of al-Tabari - Vol. I: General Introduction and From the Creation to the Flood* The Story of Adam 91[66]

From the evidence, we see the Serpent, most probably, could have been an angel. We have so many names. As many of us have been taught, the Serpent of Genesis 3 was considered to be **Satan** himself. Was this true?

As we postulated, the Serpent was lowered in position and rank. Satan (and some of his fellow angels of fire) also rebelled against Adam formation, and authority; and were also lowered in position and rank. Because Sammael (or Satan) and his angels were made of purely angelic *fire*, they cannot really do anything - physically - on this earth. Azazel and other angelic serpents, on the other hand, could… if demoted. So, we know the two were both upset about Adam; and were fairly equal in thought - why not join forces?

As we also previously stated, there may have been walls around the Garden of Eden, to keep Sammael/Satan and other undesirables out. They could not influence Adam and Eve in any way, as long as they were spiritually protected by Eden's fortifications. The Serpent, however, may have been in a position to do something, because:

> ***Azazil** (a.k.a. Azazel - the Serpent)... was one of the dwellers and **cultivators** on earth.*
> *- al-Tabari: The History of al-Tabari - Vol. I: General Introduction and From the Creation to the Flood* The Story of Iblis 83[67]

And, *he* had access to the Garden.

> *The jinn were dwellers of the earth from **among the angels**.*
> *- al-Tabari: The History of al-Tabari - Vol. I: General Introduction and From the Creation to the Flood* The Story of Iblis 83[68]

> *They were called jinn because they were **the keepers of Paradise**... Iblis (the Serpent?) was a keeper (of Paradise).*
> *- al-Tabari: The History of al-Tabari - Vol. I: General Introduction and From the Creation to the Flood* The Story of Iblis 80[69]

The Serpent - the terrestrial angel of the bunch - had that one thing non-terrestrial angels (such as Sammael/Satan) did **not** have... a way to make a difference. This subtly became both the Serpent and Sammael's golden opportunity.

Two Sides of the Same Plot

> *And God said unto Adam, "See Satan's love for thee, who pretended to give thee the Godhead and greatness; and, behold, he burns thee with fire, and seeks to **destroy thee** from off the earth."*
> *- First Book of Adam and Eve (The Conflict of Adam and Eve with Satan)* 46:4[70]

All of these dissenting angels around Adam probably had the same thought in common: "If we do not take counsel against this man so that he sin before his Creator, we cannot prevail against him."[71] The reason for their intention to corrupt man was simple: to negate *their* current positions in the world. They thought that, by making Adam fall, *this* would help them again to recover the power they had once lost... because of Adam. They wanted to be elevated back to the positions they once had.

Some ancient sources state that *this* was also the time Sammael (Satan) approached the Serpent (Nachash, Azazel, or Gadriel), and a conversation arose:

> *...the devil (Satan) told the serpent, "I (hear) that you are wiser than all the animals (human beings?)... for Adam gives food to all the animals (human beings?), thus* ***also to you****. When then all the animals (i.e. human beings?) come* ***to bow down*** *before Adam from day to day and from morning to morning, every day, you* ***also*** *come to bow down.* ***You were created <u>before</u> him****... and you bow down before this little one! And why do you eat (food) inferior to Adam's and his spouse's and not the good fruit of paradise? But come and hearken to me so that we may have Adam expelled from the wall of paradise just as* ***we are outside****. Perhaps we can re-enter somehow to paradise"... "Be a sheath for me and I will speak to the woman through your mouth a word by which we will trick (them)."* - *Book of Adam* [44]16.3a-16.4[72]

Interestingly, we seem to have *more* ancient evidence there were other people on the earth, here, besides Adam. It seems clear that the "animals," in the above, were not actually animals at all. What kind of animal feels the obligation to *bow down* to anyone?

Upon Satan's proposal, we'll see how the Serpent agreed to help him out. Satan then (symbolically) *rode* atop of the Serpent, as one would don a horse. What this means is that, in a spiritual way, Satan was probably allowed to *possess* the Serpent; and speak through his body.[73] Satan now found a door to enter his world, via the mouth.[74] It was for this reason that a variety of sources assumed Azazel and Satan may have been **identical**, or that Satan was the *only* Serpent. But, actually, there could have been *two* individuals bent on Adam's destruction.[75]

The combination of these two (Satan and the Serpent) were probably conglomerated, in the Bible, as the one Serpent.[76] Yet, together, they both waited for the opportunity to undermine Adam and Eve - the Serpent, with Satan possessing him... all to deceive them, and gain control of their world, once again.

Another version of this same account, above, is as follows:

> *...the devil (Satan) went to Adam's lot, where the male creatures were... And the devil spake to the serpent saying, "Rise up, come to me and I will tell thee a word whereby thou mayst have profit." And he arose and came to him. And the devil saith to him: "I hear that thou art wiser than all the beasts, and I have come to counsel thee. Why dost thou eat of Adam's* ***tares*** *and not of paradise? Rise up and we will cause him to be cast out of paradise, even as we were cast out through him." The serpent saith to him, "I fear lest the Lord be wroth with me." The devil saith to him: "Fear not, only be my vessel and I will speak through thy mouth words to deceive him." And instantly he hung himself from the wall of paradise, and when the angels ascended to worship God, then Satan appeared in the form of an angel and sang*

hymns like the angels... And I (Eve speaking) bent over the wall and saw him, like ***an angel****. But he saith to me... "What are thou doing in paradise?" And I said to him. 'God set us to guard and to eat of it.' The devil answered* ***through*** *the mouth* ***of the serpent****... "Follow me."* - *Apocalypse of Moses / Apocalypsis Mosis* 16:1-18:6[77]

A Twisted Conversation With Eve

Interestingly enough, one source cites the time set for Eve's seduction as some sort of twisted *remembrance*:

...some say that... Satan was deposed from his degree... on the sixth day, when he envied Adam, who was created in the image of God... but in that sixth hour of the sixth day, when he was cast out, he ***approached to seduce****...*

- *Barhebraeus* Gen. 3:1-4[78]

The stage was now set. Eve was all alone, one afternoon. In some sort of sick act of remembrance, the Serpent arose, and went to confront her. He was going to use every trick up his proverbial sleeve to deceive this newly-formed woman. He obviously was endowed with gifts of knowledge of our previous world, with self-awareness and reason, as well as the understanding of free will and suggestion. The Serpent's abilities, here, allowed him to question Eve's own rationale, to make her think *twice* about what God said, and also to feel insecure about her rationales. This would, then, enable the Serpent to badger Eve with questions such as, "Yea, hath God said (in Gen. 3:1);" and make her *doubt* God's word.

Let's discover how the Serpent used his subtlety, his own worldly knowledge, and another method of manipulation - a method which, when set into place, was about to plague the **rest of our world** from that point on: a practice known as *fornication*.[79]

Chapter 7

Fornication With the "Other Side"

> *...(Sammael/Satan) did not change his intelligence as far as (his) understanding of righteous and sinful things. And he understood* ***his condemnation*** *and the sin which* ***he had sinned before****, therefore he conceived thought against Adam, in such form he* ***entered*** *and* ***seduced*** *Eva (i.e. Eve)...*
>
> *- 2 Enoch (The Book of the Secrets of Enoch)* 31:5[1]

Things in our world were about to become a lot more *complex*. The Serpent had knowledge of the world *before* our own. Sammael/Satan did *too*, assuredly. They both felt the need to bring down Adam, in any way possible. We, now, know there could have been a little more to their motives besides envy, jealousy, and anger:

> *He (the Serpent) saw Adam and Eve, in blissful ignorance of shame, happy in their love, and he became jealous and envious... (A) main purpose, however, of the Serpent is not the death of Adam, but* ***the possession*** *of his widow Eve. Because he saw their* ***joys of love****, he* ***lusted*** *after Eve.* (Jung, 1974, p. 68-69)[2]

Wow. It seems the more like human beings these angels are forced to become, the more passions, desires, and physical "needs" - like human beings - they also take on! There was no doubt about it: the terrestrial Serpent was *male* - and Satan knew it. According to ancient sources, this angel-turned-human began to have human *sexual passions*, as well.[3] Satan could have finalized the contract between him and the Serpent by allowing the Serpent to possibly partake in one unique opportunity: the richest, most luscious "food" in the garden - *Eve* ***herself***![4]

> *(The historian) Philo regards the serpent as a symbol of pleasure, including* ***sexual*** *lust.* (McClausland, 1872, p. 130)[5]

With more and more human passions, there was another "factor of life" the Serpent seemed to notice around him - *women*. Interestingly, the Bible begins to talk about the Serpent right *after* the verse, "And they **were both naked**, the man and his wife, and were not ashamed (Gen. 2:25)." Could the Serpent have noticed Adam and Eve, and how they were both naked, and began to desire her, as well? The couple (Adam and Eve) seemed to enjoy a wonderful paradise. Maybe another thought went along with the Serpent's deal with Satan is: "**I** will destroy Adam and *marry* Eve, and truly rule."[6]

If we think about it, if the Serpent was an animal - an ordinary reptile - he would *not* have had any desire for Eve, of course. Only a *man*, or a humanoid being, would have sexual desires for a woman.[7] All of these thoughts might sound completely contrary to Biblical teaching, here; but, as we'll see, Scripture may even start to give us hints towards this all being a reality! Layered within the verses of Genesis and Revelation, there could be a number of obscure pieces of information about these early stories of Genesis - some we never really thought of. Could this be an example of a story element which was obscured, or translated differently, to make it sound like something else? And, *why*? There really could, in actuality, be a lot more to this temptation of Eve than many of us may have assumed.

One ancient source seems to make a comparison: comparing *Eve's* actions to another woman:

> *(A heroic mother expressing principles to her children)... "**I** was a pure virgin and did not go outside my father's house; but I guarded the rib from which woman (Eve) was made. No **seducer** corrupted me... nor did the Destroyer, the deceitful **serpent**, defile the purity of **my virginity**."* - *4 Maccabees* 18:7-8[8]

In other words: this woman had not allowed herself to be sexually seduced - unlike *Eve*. If the Serpent *did* seduce Eve with sexual coition, then that throws a whole new light on this whole temptation of the Garden! As well, the implications of this *one* act could, very well, have continued on, to affect them for the rest of their lives, as well as other people from then on... as we shall see!

Soft Target

What about the seduction of Eve? Did something in this manner *really* happen? The Serpent might have considered Eve an easier target for his manipulation than Adam. Either way, they set out to do anything they could, to achieve their nefarious goals. The Serpent / Satan assumed that, according to one ancient source, the man would probably be a little more hardheaded - when confronted with their plan.[9] Also, since Satan knew the Serpent was *male*, he probably assumed sexual tension might spring up, between the two… which, as well, might work towards the Serpent's advantage.

Obviously, this Serpent, unlike *real* serpents, was endowed with *human-like* reason. Snakes don't really talk with a rational mind. He also, most probably, knew from past experiences of the world before that a woman may be more prone to *listen to all creatures* (including terrestrial angels), as well as have more compassion.[10] Because of all of these attributes, the Serpent probably concluded Eve as the best target - a "softer" target, if you will. He (they) needed to find some way in. They didn't care how they got into the Garden, to do their dirty work. The target was now in scope. The time was nigh for Eve's seduction.

When a conversation arose, Eve informed the Serpent of the one *law* that they had - the one and only law: to *not* eat the fruit of just one tree. This tree was known as the *Tree of the Knowledge of Good and Evil*. One of the Serpent's acts of trickery may have involved her thoughts about being a mother, and having children. Apparently, Eve understood the possibility; and longed to have children right away. So, the Serpent decided to try to convince her that the Tree of Knowledge could actually *allow* a greater chance for her fertility![11] With her interested, the Serpent was on-par towards being able to twist any questions about the tree which might arise.

Another twist of the Serpent would involve Eve's knowledge and authority in the Garden. Again, in the following quote, please try to picture the *beasts*, here, as *human beings* - either the *Chay (Beasts) of the Field* or the *Behemah (Cattle)*.

Eve speaking:

> *...while I was guarding my own portion (of paradise)... the devil came to Adam's portion. And there were **beasts** there... for the Lord had also divided the **beasts** between us. All (that were) male He had given to Adam, and all (that were) female, He had given to me. **And we each had fed our own ones**.*
>
> - *Book of Adam* [44]15:3-4[12]

Apparently, Adam and Eve were in charge, not only of guarding the Garden, but with helping to cultivate it, and redistribute food to the masses. According to one ancient source, the Serpent made it known to Eve: "I am distressed for you, for you are like the **animals**... but I, I do not desire your ignorance" (*The Book of Adam* [44]18.1). In other words, the Eve acted like an animal - probably saying she acted like one of the people who worked the field... and not a manager.[13] He tried to undermine Eve's authority; as well as haughtily tried to show her how much wisdom/experience *he* had in this brave new world. Ultimately, he set out to show Eve how *she* should have been the one to actually *look to him*, and take *his* superior words to heart.

The Serpent, then, accosted Eve with the famous: "Yea, hath God said?" In other words, he said, "What? What are you putting your faith in, here - regarding this tree? No. You are actually being hood-winked! God is, in reality, deceiving you; don't you see that? The fruit of the tree does not cause death; it actually brings forth *life*! It, in actuality, confers **wisdom**; not punishment. You're a fool. God is just keeping you in ignorance, on purpose."[14]

Although it wasn't really like this at all - and God clearly warned Eve that death would result from the eating of this fruit - the Serpent tried to convince her that the *opposite* was true... that God's "death," here, would actually confer her life![15] She could maintain a better way of life, in the end, as well as bare *new* life (via a child), through this tree... if only she had the sense to partake of it the way the Serpent said!

The Serpent, also, began to convince Eve that, since she and Adam were created *last*, God might create *other* beings to be superior over them, in power and in knowledge. She'd better act fast. If she didn't do something about it, *now*, then she would be left behind. She eventually concluded that: if only she ate the fruit of this tree, **she** could become more like a god; and able to create new worlds, as well... like God. A lot of this potential hidden knowledge and power left Eve curious; and in want. She thought this was her chance to gain some sort of divine "enlightenment."

Yet, some knowledge may have been hidden from Adam and Eve - by God - for a good reason: it could lead to one's death and destruction, if taken lightly. Satan uses these same tricks today - he tries to preach the *opposite* as reality; he plays on our desires to look "behind the curtain"… to know *more*. The Serpent began to capitalize on Eve's curiosity, compassionate thoughts, and human tendencies to want to advance. Assuredly, God already figured out there could be potential problems looming within the conversation between the Serpent and Eve:

> *Then I commanded thee concerning the tree, that thou eat not thereof. Yet I knew that Satan,* ***who deceived himself****, would also deceive thee.*
> - *First Book of Adam and Eve (The Conflict of Adam and Eve with Satan)* 13:16[16]

Eve wanted to try the fruit. And, in one final condition of her acceptance, the Serpent allowed Eve access to this "power" if, and *only* if, he had one guarantee in return - that she gave the same fruit to Adam, and make him eat.[17] Eve was still a little hesitant about jumping at this opportunity. So, to counter, the Serpent may have had one more trick up his sleeve.

Beguiled - Wholly Seduced?

As one ancient source stated, it was around this time that "the woman was **inflamed** by the Serpent."[18] What could be the meaning of this word "inflamed," here? Let's take a good look at what the Bible said happened:

> *…And the woman said, The serpent* ***beguiled*** *me, and I did eat.*
> - *Gen.* 3:13 (KJV)

Did the Bible *leave out* an important part to this story, or not? Could it have provided hints to *something else* which might have been going on, at this time? What does the word *beguiled* mean in this verse? Could it stand for something *more* than just casual, verbal seduction?

If we look in the Bible, we see that the way *beguiled* may have really been implied in this above instance:

> *...for I have espoused you to one husband, that I may present [you as] a chaste* ***virgin*** *to Christ. But I fear, lest by any means, as the serpent* ***beguiled*** *Eve through his subtilty, so your minds should be corrupted from the simplicity that is in Christ.*
> - *II Cor.* 11:1-3 (KJV)

Paul, the writer of this verse, wanted people to come to Christ as untainted as a virgin; not like the Serpent who, on the contrary, tainted Eve. Could this mean that Eve, no longer, was a **virgin** after her exchange with the Serpent? Could he have *beguiled* her - or *wholly* seduced her?

> *Possibly, the lure of a snake is unconsciously* ***sexual****.*
> (Pember, 1975, p. 127)[19]

Was *sexuality* another modem to help seduce her, emotionally?[20] It's totally understandable why so many people have never heard of this possibility, or would automatically dismiss it - thank you "political correctness." That doesn't mean this never happened. There, assuredly, have been a *number* of attempts to obscure this possibility, all the way back to ancient times. It was for a *reason*, as we shall see.

Even though this extra element to the story might sound a little outrageous, or impossible, at this time, there *are* a good number of ancient and modern scholarly works which do allude to *sex* as a possible element of Eve's seduction:[21]

> *(Eve speaking)... And he (the serpent) put upon the fruit which he gave me to eat the poison of his wickedness, that is, of his* ***desire****, for desire is the head (another version: has root and origin) of all sin.* - *Schatzhohle* III[22]

The Serpent was envious of Adam, on account of Eve. And having ***polluted*** *her, he inveigled her to eat of the forbidden fruit.* (Eisenmenger, 1748, p. 21)[23]

...the serpent had intercourse with Eve and injected filth into her...
- *Zohar* Pekudei 21[24]

The ***Talmud*** *tells us how the serpent in the Garden of Eden had sexual relations with Eve and injects its filth into her, which affected all her descendants.*
(Unterman, 1991, p. 150)[25]

Even ancient *pagan* texts, some with accounts similar to this story of Genesis, point towards a sexual encounter between a serpent and their "Eve-like" character:

In a story preserved in the prologue of Gilgamesh, Enkidu and the Underworld, the goddess Inanna (i.e. Eve?) gains knowledge of ***sex*** *by descending to earth and eating from various plants and fruits. She transplants the huluppu tree from the Euphrates to her own garden, but a wicked serpent made its nest amongst the roots of the tree. This tale* ***connects*** *the serpent to the garden, and with the presence of Inanna, the* ***theme of sexuality****.* ("Wikipedia, *Eve*", n. d., p. 4)[26]

At the time the Serpent seduced Eve with subtle words, he could have begun to work on her… on a whole *other* level! He began to caress her; touched her in certain areas; and, ultimately, began to provide her with more knowledge about her own body than she probably ever experienced before! Now engaged in an act of coition - within their newfound sexual frenzy - Eve probably gave in; and agreed to eat the fruit of the Tree of Knowledge. Within the agreement of the pact they made, Eve had to fulfill her promise: to give the fruit to *Adam*, as well. The Serpent got what he wanted, on so many levels. The rest of this story is much the same as in the Bible.

After their coitus, and after she ate the fruit, she *instantly* saw the Serpent's true colors. The Angel of Death (i.e. Sammael/Satan) also begun to make himself visible to Eve at this time; which really shocked her. It was also the time she realized she had made a *grave* error. This fallen angel had now helped bring death into Eve's world; he destroyed her authority over others; and, ultimately, he told her to go and do the same thing to Adam. Interestingly enough, the name *Azazel* (i.e. the Serpent) was also known to be the angel of death and destruction![27] Doesn't this further help confirm that he and Satan *both* were considered "the Serpent" of this incident?

The "Evil Inclination" Planted

What could have happened, at the time of their sexual union? According to many ancient sources, upon the completion of their copulation, the Serpent injected his so-called "**evil inclination**" into Eve. This "evil inclination" seems to represent a supernatural "poison," or "disease," of sorts. It was also known as the Serpent's *filth*: a "built in" desire for evilness, or destruction, in people. Eve and her descendants, then, would begin to feel these same ways; and carry on these negative thoughts; as well as those so-called "animal instincts." Although eating this fruit *did* allow Eve to gain the knowledge (or discernment) of good and evil, she also acquired *other* carnal, and otherwise "worldly," thoughts and desires. These *carnal* thoughts would, in one way or another, often negatively affect the human race, from then on.[28]

The Poison of Lust

> *(Eve speaking)... (and) he went and poured upon the fruit the poison of his wickedness, which is* ***lust****, the* ***root and beginning of every sin****, and he bent the branch on the earth and I took of the fruit and I ate.*
>
> \- *Apocalypse of Moses / Apocalypsis Mosis* 19:3[29]

Eve began to develop new desires - especially *lustful* desires. What exactly is *lust*, according to the Bible? One ancient source stated that *Azazel* (the Serpent) would, in the future, also be known as the angel who taught women how to enjoy *sexual* pleasures, and acts of sexual promiscuity.[30] He would also be known for teaching women how to use makeup, as well as how to wear all kinds of costly stones - all to make themselves look more sexually appealing. Interestingly, these all seem to involve *sex*.

> *And the whole earth has been corrupted through the works that were taught by Azazel: to him* ***ascribe all sin****.* - *1 Enoch* 10:8[31]

Eve's newfound knowledge allowed her the ammunition for fulfilling her promise to the Serpent - to seduce Adam. She needed to "finish the deal," which ultimately would help spread the Serpent's "evil inclination" throughout the rest of their early world.

Beastliness Incarnate

> *(The Serpent) goes in unto Eve and infests her with* ***lasciviousness****... in spite of all his superiority to his fellow beasts, he left some* ***beastliness*** *in Eve...*
> (Jung, 1974, p. 76)[32]

Lasciviousness is just one example of this Biblical **lust**.[33] These desires often seem to represent one's intent to take something of this world, and use it to put their selves *equal* to God; or *above* God, in a way. Sex could also be used in much of this same way: a personal route towards achieving a "god-like" state of worthiness or enlightenment. This one act between the Serpent and Eve seemed to have laid the groundwork for so much *more* corruption in our world to come; as we shall see.

Come One, Come All

Eve felt good, at least during their sexual exchange, because of these newfound feelings and sexual euphoria. After it was over, however, she quickly began to feel *guilt* for allowing herself to take this particular route. In fact, she soon began to feel *very* despondent - terrible. The desire for these "enlightened" thoughts, as well as the use of sexuality in this way, began to weigh on her. She also had the feeling she just altered the present order of things, and endangered everything, and everyone, around her.

Because of these negativities, she, then - with her newfound *lust* - felt the desire *not* to be alone, in shame. She knew she had to seduce Adam, as well - not only to honor the Serpent's request, but also to bring him down… of course, so she wouldn't have to suffer those feelings by herself![34] If she was going to falter, and live as a fallen human being, then she wanted to do it *with* Adam. If she was going to die, then he was going to die with her. Also, Adam was not going to have a chance with another woman… if she could help it.[35] She probably knew about Lilith, and the potential of Adam to be with *her* again, if she wasn't around - all of this would eventually prove too much for Eve to handle, emotionally, unless she *did* something.

One ancient source stated that Eve even gave the fruit of the Tree of Knowledge to animals around her; and possibly other *people*, as well. It was all done to allow Eve to feel better about her situation, at least a little bit. Hoping to bring most everything and everyone down with her didn't really help her, in the end; it only served to make her feel worse:

> *…I have sinned before your* ***elect angels****… I have sinned before the generations of the heavens. I have sinned before the* ***birds (Owph?) of the heavens****. I have sinned before the* ***beasts (Chay?) of the earth****. I have sinned against you, God, by my greed, against* ***all your creatures*** *(i.e. people?).* - *Book of Adam* [45]32.2[36]

Animals, as we know, don't really care about who might have sinned against them! They mainly care about eating; or being eaten. Interesting how she mentions two groups of living beings: the *Owph (Fowl) of the Air* and *Chay (Beasts) of the Field*. Could this also further support our postulation that these beings were actually two groups of *people* who lived and worked in the Garden around her?

Continuing on, we discover that, in regards to Eve's newfound sadness, the Serpent had something to say:

> *Then the beast (the Serpent / Satan) replied to her and told Eve, "It is not from our greed(iness) that your discontent and your weeping come, but your discontent and your weeping come from your own greed(iness), for at the beginning of creation, it was you who harkened to the beast, the serpent. How did you dare open your mouth and eat of the tree of which God had commanded you not to eat?"*
>
> - *Book of Adam* [38]11.1-[38]11.2[37]

Sad; but true. Eve harkened to a beast (i.e. an angel?), or a leader of them, over God; and now was starting to pay the price. When she first encountered Adam, he knew that something bad had happened. He quickly became aware of her attempts to make him eat, as well.

Throughout her narrative, Adam began to perceive something:

*He (Adam) had thought... a **beast** had entered paradise...*
- *Book of Adam* [44]21.2[38]

Did one of these *Chay (Beasts) of the Field*, or a *leader* of them, do something they weren't supposed to?[39] Adam eventually summed up what happened to his wife. He was aware that she may have done something unsavory with the Serpent... and he didn't want any part of it. Eve tearfully pleaded with Adam, and could have even tried to seduce him sexually; the same way the Serpent had with her. Adam - feeling for Eve - debated for almost three hours on what he should do.

In the end, Adam eventually made a decision: "Eve, I love you. I would rather die with you than outlive you... God could never console me with another woman equaling your loveliness!" He did give in, and ate the forbidden fruit. Another ancient account shows Eve coming to Adam *without* her heavenly splendor; and, when asked why, she refused to tell Adam *why* until he ate the forbidden fruit.[40] Even though he *knew* he was doing something wrong, in this case, Adam's rationale was simple: to show his *love* for Eve. It may sound noble by today's standards; but, of course, it was **disobedient** to God. He should have obeyed his Lord, and not do what might have sounded good to *him* at the time. He was just as wrong as Eve, in this all. He should have not given in to his *own* interpretation of what was right and wrong, here.

These two exchanges (between the Serpent and Eve and between Eve and Adam) may have given rise to another important thing going on, here: ***fornication***.

Fornication and Adultery

*But thou... pouredst out thy **fornications** on every one that passed by... How weak is*

> *thine heart, saith the Lord God, seeing thou doest all these things, the work of an imperious whorish woman... But as a wife that committeth* ***adultery****, which taketh stranger instead of her husband! They give gifts to all whores: but thou givest thy gifts to all thy lovers, and hirest them... Wherefore, O Harlot, hear the word of the LORD... (because) thy filthiness was poured out, and thy nakedness discovered through thy whoredoms with thy lovers...* - *Ezek.* 16:15-36 (KJV)

Both Adam and Eve, according to many ancient sources, seemed to be seduced by some type of sexual seduction. Both were given seductive words, as well. Both eventually gave in to the seduction... which cost them. Yet, regardless, Adam and Eve both *chose* their destiny; even if it was through their *own* sexual seduction. The woman chose her destiny, by allowing the Serpent to have his way with her, and following his path. The man, in this sense, did the same thing!

We seem to have an interesting quote, in regards to this whole understanding:

> *That tree was from the tree of knowledge of good and evil (Gen. 2:9, 17). Upon eating from the tree, Eve was aware of what she had done. She now had the* ***knowledge*** *of evil and she was aware that she had sinned against God. In that knowledge, and having fallen, she then offered the fruit from the tree to Adam. Adam was not deceived (I Tim 2:14). He knew when he saw Eve that she* ***had*** *sinned, because she had lost the spiritual glow that results from being in close spiritual harmony with God. Moses had this same glow when he came down from Sinai (Ex 34:29-30). Adam* ***elected*** *to eat the fruit, knowing what he was doing. His* ***love*** *for Eve (whom he knew had sinned) was greater than his love of God. This is a tactic used time and again by Satan. The downfall of God's people* ***is frequently through the temptations of godless women*** *(see Numbers 25:1-9)... The same basic scenario is being* ***repeated after the Garden of Eden****, only on a larger scale.* ***There is a wholesale abandonment of God and his righteous ways for women known to be in sin****. This is what God calls* ***fornication****, not referring only to a sexual sin, but the sin of mixing the righteous with the wicked, truth with evil. (One example of this is the word fornication as attributed to the* ***harlot church*** *in Rev 17:4 and 18:3). This sin was so prevalent, and so blatant, a rejection of God that it could not be allowed to continue indefinitely.* ("There Were Giants on the earth... The Nephilim", n. d., p. 2)[41]

This is another way to define the act of *fornication*. This definition of *fornication* goes beyond "sex outside of marriage." It doesn't just relate to *sex*; it relates to *intent*: Eve being able to *help* change Adam's mind, through manipulation and seduction. Fornication was committed, in this case, because the two went *beyo*nd some innate, or occasional, drive for *sex*, and used it *in other ways*. Eve mixed sex's original purpose with something evil - as a means to accomplish **her ends**… *disparaging* the other individual, in the process.

This type of fornication occurred throughout the Bible, even though many, today, probably won't recognize it as *fornication*. It happened between Sampson and Delilah, David and Bathsheba, and many more.[42] Again, it wasn't *sex* as the problem, but *the way it was used*. A lot of men (and women) were turned away from their original thought and deed because of seductions such as this… this is how fornication gives sex a bad name.

Satan / the Serpent also used sex, here, as a means for their own ends, as well.

> *For so long as he (Adam) was by himself, as accorded with such solitude, he went on growing like to the world and like God... But when woman too had been made...* ***love*** *enters in... and this desire likewise engendered* ***bodily pleasure****, that pleasure which is the beginning of wrongs and violation of law, the pleasure for the sake of which men bring on themselves the life of mortality and wretchedness in lieu of that of immortality and bliss.*
>
> - *Works of Philo Judaeus* On the Creation 151-152 (also 165-166)[43]

Doing what he thought was the "right thing," it clearly wasn't, in the end. Adam and Eve brought their negative situation upon themselves.

In the same vein of fornication, *adultery* is, not only, defined as one partner having sex outside of a committed marriage, but someone (usually a woman) who had sexual relations with someone *other* than her husband. What's the big deal, with this? What parallels can we see with this and what may have happened in the Garden?

> *Indeed, every act of sexual intercourse which has occurred between those* ***unlike*** *one another is* ***adultery****.*
>
> - *Gospel of Philip*[44]

Interestingly enough, some thoughts on adultery could have easily originated in the Garden of Eden, here: Eve reached out, and had sexual relations with someone other than Adam. Also, Eve might very well have had sex with a terrestrial, angelic being… one *unlike* her in many ways. We're not talking about the mixing of different groups of pre-Adamites, here; we're talking about a human woman mating with one of these terrestrial angelic beings. We'll soon see that this type of *adultery* - human, with someone "not-exactly" human - would be greatly *abhorred* by God in the future; and we'll also see *why*.

The Loss of Adam's Angelic-Like State

Now, the time for Adam's temptation had come and gone. He failed. Adam would have been God's representative to the entire world if he would have only resisted; but he didn't. Now, when he fell, everything and everyone around him also fell. The whole organized world - epitomized in the Garden - would never be the same. The Angel of Death showed his true colors to Eve, and now Eve showed Adam elements of the Evil Inclination… Satan / the Serpent were indeed victorious.

Adam fell, in many ways - never to return to this former state… and this included his once-great height, and brilliant countenance.[45]

> *And on thee, O Adam, while in My garden and obedient to Me, did that* ***bright light*** *rest also. But when I heard of thy transgression, I deprived thee of that bright light.*
> - *First Book of Adam and Eve (The Conflict of Adam and Eve with Satan)* 13:6-7[46]

Now Adam, Eve and everyone around them were to become familiar with the concepts of misery and death, and all they could bring.[47] The entire world, it seems, went down with them. The *Chay of the Field*, the *Behemah*, and the *Owph of the Air* probably began to think twice about their working positions, now. Their leaders both made huge errors. Why would they respect either Adam or Eve, and their positions of authority, anymore? The *Chay of the Field* may have no longer had the desire to work the fields; the *Behemah* may have no longer had the desire to domesticate the animals. Probably, the animals were beginning to act a little uncontrollable by now, anyhow; for the curse of the Fall also extended to all that surrounded Adam… even the animals. Possibly, the *Owph (Fowl) of the Air* may have lost most of the positive, angelic qualities they had. All were affected.

Anyone who may have had something remotely to do with the Garden may have felt the desire to *lose* his or her original role. Adam's power and authority over the people, and over the earth, was gone.[48]

Animals now began to live without order. Many became wild, aggressive; even hungry for blood. Some ancient sources stated that both animals and man now had their teeth "turned on edge" (i.e. sharpened), because of the Fall - the "law of the jungle" began. Negative elements to our planet were sprouting up all over, beyond the plant kingdom - thorns and thistles were beginning to sprout up, everywhere.

Death was all around Adam. The world was no longer *very good*. Battles for superiority and survival began to take place. Even human beings began to act *wild*; and, overall, turn more uncivilized:

> *And the* ***beasts*** *(angels?, humans?) of whom you ruled shall rise up against you. You shall be weakened because you have not kept my commandments.*
>
> \- *Book of Adam* [44]24.4[49]

Adam, because of all these changes, most probably felt the worst, out of everyone else around him. The following ancient verse, coming from a work loosely known as "The Cry of Adam," described how Adam felt totally despondent for his actions (please notice how he seems to mention the *Owph of the Air*, the *Chay of the Field*, and the *Behemah* here, as well):

> *O* ***birds (Fowl?) of the heavens****, come down to me and see my weeping!*
> *O* ***beasts (Chay?)****, see me who am tormented!*
> *O* ***wild animals (i.e. Behemah?)****, look at me, who am ashamed!*
> *Have pity on me, who was once your lord, sovereign, and king, but am now equal to you,* ***but more unworthy****!*
>
> \- *Armenian Apocryphal Adam Literature* Repentance 20[50]

Assuredly, Eve, and other women around her, began to rebel against the men in their lives. Not only had Adam lost his authority over human beings and animals, he probably lost authority over his own wife.

The fallen angels - the Nephilim - felt vindicated! They also felt like they could break away from *their* own traditional roles. According to Hebrews 2:5, our future world will *not* be under the dominion of angels around us. Logically, if this is the case, one could easily assume that they *currently* have dominion over our world. Before the Fall of Adam, the opposite was probably true - *man* had dominion over the angels of the world.

We have another interesting quote:

> *Woe for the loss of a great servant. For had not the* ***serpent*** *been cursed, every Israelite would have had two valuable serpents... to bring him costly gems, precious stones and pearls. Moreover, one would have fastened a thong under its tail, with which it would bring forth earth for his garden and waste land...*
>
> \- *Babylonian Talmud* Sanhedrin 59a[51]

As the above source stated, a person *might have had* two serpentine angels - angelic servants - to aid them in their daily life and work… if Adam didn't fall, that is. After Adam's fall, mankind had to resort to stubborn mules and beasts of burden, to help them with their more-difficult work. Adam allotted the world so much pain, hardship, and toil. The *dominion* of Adam and possibly those in his group (i.e. the Adamites) would never fully return.[52] This chaos-in-the-making was exactly what the Serpent / Satan wanted.

> *And the woman said, "It is the serpent who instructed me." And he (God) cursed the serpent, and called him "****devil.****"* - *Testimony of Truth*[53]

Hence, our current, worldly "set-up" began.

The Curses Pronounced - On Adam

> *Then the Lord became angry at them, and said to Adam, "Because you have done this, and you did not listen to my counsel, but hastily listened to* ***your wife's*** *counsel, thorns will spring forth to you in place of this immortal plant."*
>
> \- *Armenian Apocryphal Adam Literature* Transgression 41[54]

God, no doubt, was very angry. And, the time had come for all involved to pay the price for their disobedience. The punishments began to be dealt - they had to - to Adam, to Eve, *and* to the Serpent.

> Gen. 3:
> 17 *And unto Adam he said, Because thou hast hearkened unto the voice* ***of thy wife****,*
> *and hast eaten of the* ***tree****, of which I commanded thee, saying, Thou shalt not eat*
> *of it: cursed is the ground for thy sake; in sorrow shalt thou eat of it all the days of*
> *thy life;*
> 18 *Thorns also and thistles shall it bring forth to thee; and thou shalt eat the herb of*
> *the field;*
> 19 *In the sweat of thy face shalt thou eat bread, till thou return unto the ground; for*
> *out of it wast thou taken: for dust thou art, and unto dust shalt thou return.*

Adam was given at least *three* curses for his disobedience. Interestingly enough, they all seemed to have to do with *working the ground* - probably because that was, once, his ultimate responsibility. Adam ate of a forbidden tree in the garden, now the ground was forbidden from being truly bountiful, because of it. Another one of Adam's punishments was that he, now, had to work by "the sweat of his brow."[55] If we think about this, it might be logical to assume that, before this time, Adam really *did not have* to work by the sweat of his brow (obviously, because there would be no punishment if he already had). But, *why* didn't he? Again, it was probably because there were a number of **other** human beings around - to work the Garden! Adam lived in a Garden… and he really didn't seem to sweat *at all* by working it? This seems to give us even further scriptural proof that there were probably other groups of people - the *pre-Adamites* - in, and around, the Garden of Eden. These were probably the ones who helped Adam with all his work.

Yet, now, Adam was ordered to do the same thing as the rest of his helpers and servants![56] Adam was also ordered to eat food of the field (Gen. 3:18); not the wonderful fruits of paradise he was once used to.

> *For the next seven days, they could find nothing fit to eat, only food for cattle and wild beasts.*
> (Frankel, 1989, p. 32)[57]

Now, the thoughts of having to work - without *quickly* achieving one's satisfying sustenance - began to make Adam *shiver* with stress and nervousness:[58]

"(God said)... and thou shalt eat the herb of the field." When Adam heard that the Holy One blessed be He told him "And thou shalt eat the herb of the field," his limbs trembled. He said before Him: "Lord of the Universe! Shall I and my cattle eat in one crib?" The Holy One blessed be He replied: "Considering that they limbs ***trembled*** *(at the thought), thou shalt eat bread in the sweat of thy brow."*

(Jung, 1974, p. 75)[59]

Through his fear, Adam began to show how much he respected God, in regards to his punishments, here. He seemed deeply concerned about what he did; and his inner emotions began to manifest, all over. God noticed his uneasiness, and began to show mercy on him. Adam, after this, became calm; and ended up being more at *ease* to accept God's overall judgment, now.[60]

The Serpent, and his reactions, would become a different story, however.

Curses on the Serpent

...whoever sets his eyes on that which is not his is not granted what he seeks and what he possesses is taken from him. We thus find it with the primeval ***serpent*** *[in the Garden of Eden] which set its eyes on that which was not proper for it; what it sought was not granted to it and what it possessed was taken from it. The Holy One, blessed be He (i.e. God), said: I declared: Let it be* ***king*** *over every animal and beast; but now, Cursed art thou above all cattle and above every beast of the field.*

\- *Babylonian Talmud* Sotah 9a-9b[61]

The reason a lot of people could have believed this Serpent was an actual *animal* seems to revolve around the *curses* that God pronounced on him. We have:

And the LORD God said unto the serpent, Because thou hast done this, thou art cursed above all cattle (Behemah?), and above every beast (Chay?) of the Field; ***upon thy belly*** *shalt thou go, and* ***dust shalt thou eat*** *all the days of thy life...*

\- *Gen.* 3:14 (KJV)

We see that the Serpent was made to crawl *on its belly*, and also to *eat dust*. Most of the Bible could, for the most part, be taken *literally*. This above verse, however, does not necessarily point towards a literal meaning. The reason is simple: people then, as today, had their ways of saying things. Quite probably, these two were ancient Hebrew *idioms*, *methods of thought*, or *figures of speech* - known as *Hebraisms*. In ancient Israel, the terms "upon thy belly" and "dust shalt thou eat" were, in ancient times, often used as expressions of *degradation*. What sort of animal goes around, and eats *dust*, anyhow?

After his fornication with Eve, the *Serpent* - Satan's vessel - wasn't going to escape without any sort of punishment. He didn't have total victory, here. He was already "demoted," once before - by God - for his insolence. Even though he helped upstart the whole program at the Garden of Eden, God had something in store for him, once again.

The Serpent (i.e. Azazel) once walked about with an erect, cocky posture, as one could guess, with the desire to eat "*dainties*" of the world. Now, he was about to lose all of it. Well, what might those *dainties* be?

Once, the Serpent may have had authority over the *Behemah* (the animal domesticators?) and the *Chay of the Field* (the land workers?); as well as the rest of the Adamite and pre-Adamite groups. Now, he was cursed above them all (in Gen. 3:14)! He would be considered **lower** than other people around him; possibly in a number of ways - *This time*, it was probably *not* a manipulation of what he looked like, or of his physical form.

Let's look at all of this, a little deeper.

"Upon Thy Belly…"

"upon thy belly shalt thou go" - *a Hebraism (an idiom, figure of speech, etc.) for utter* ***defeat**... **humiliation**.*

- *The Companion Bible* Appx. 19[62]

First, we see that the above phrase is a *derogatory* term - aimed at the Serpent.[63] If we look at one example of this phrase, in the Bible, we see:

> *Wherefore hidest thou thy face, and forgettest our affliction and our oppression? For our soul is bowed down to the dust:* ***our belly*** *cleaveth* ***unto the earth****.*
>
> \- *Psa.* 44:23-24 (KJV)

The Serpent and other serpentine angels, now, would be lowered in their "estates" even further - with practically *no* angelic qualities, anymore. And this would go way beyond the physical…

They, as with any other sinful human being, would be destined to suffer a worldly "death," as well as damnation by God… by living the same type lives as any other human being was about to. Not only was his former position in the Garden about to end, the Serpent would suffer something he never really had to face, before: feelings of human *defeat*, *humiliation*, and *low self-esteem*. His *mind* was also sentenced to feel "low," and experience those feelings one might describe, today, as "**insecurity**." His punishment would now extend to his *thoughts*, his *feelings*, and all of his *perceptions of himself* - now, given *all* of the negativities a human individual might feel who's mindset is "down in the dumps"… but, with him, it's about to be *so much* worse.

> *"(God speaking) Thou has said, Thou wilt be king over the whole world: thou shalt therefore be cursed above all cattle. Thou hast said, Thou wilt walk with thy body* ***erect****; therefore upon thy belly shalt thou creep. Thou hast said, Thou wilst eat of all the dainties of the world; therefore* ***dust*** *shalt thou eat off the days of thy life."*
>
> (Eisenmenger, 1748, p. 198)[64]

"…Dust Shalt Thou Eat"

<u>"dust shalt thou eat"</u> - *a Hebraism (an idiom, figure of speech, etc.) for constant, continuous* ***disappointment****,* ***failure****, and* ***mortification****.*

\- *The Companion Bible* Appx. 19[65]

We recall, from Adam's formulation, that *dust* was not a very worthy substance to behold, or be created out of. We recall that *dust*, even, could be associated with dung, or worthlessness - a sign of one's own *humility*.[66] Adam was fashioned from it; but Satan / the Serpent would now be made to *feel* like it.

We see examples of this use of "*dust*" throughout the Bible:

> *...and his enemies shall **lick the dust**.*
> - *Psa.* 72:9 (KJV)

> *...they shall bow down to thee with their **face toward the earth**, and **lick up the dust**...* - *Isa.* 49:23 (KJV)

A serpent doesn't eat dust - it eats only small animals. It only eats meat. This gives us further validity to our thoughts about his angelic origin. The Bible must speak truth, here; and, again, it *does*. This seems to further validate that both of God's statements, here, were referring to some inner *degradation* of the mind; with the only physical changes were the loss of any former angelic qualities that they may have had left.

Even the Serpent's present, physical body would suffer degradation, swiftly; from then on:

> *But he turned to the serpent (in great wrath) and said: "Since thou hast done this... thou shalt feed on **dust** all the days of thy life... There shall **not be left thee ear** nor **wing**, nor **one limb** of all that with which thou dist ensnare them in thy malice and causedst them to be cast out of paradise; and I will put enmity between thee and his seed"...* - *Apocalypse of Moses / Apocalypsis Mosis* 26:1-4[67]

We also, possibly see, from the above, that even the *sexual organ* of the Serpent – what he used to further seduce Eve - would be another part of this degradation. His senses (such as his hearing), his swiftness, his overall power - even his *penis* - probably would not work very well in the future, or would quickly give him a good deal of "earthly" problems, throughout the rest of his mortal life.

He was now to suffer all the negatives this world had to offer (in which he helped to create)… but at much *more* of a *rapid* pace than others. He helped created this world; the time had come from him to lie in the bed he helped to make.

> *(Satan / the Serpent have)... slid from the upper height to the nether region... (as well, they) shalt chew **earthly** things.* - *Barhebraeus* Gen. 3:14[68]

> *...dark and noisome shall be the serpents dwelling.*
> (Baring-Gould, 1881, p. 43)[69]

Instead of him ruling with all of this "dainties" (i.e. wonderful things) he once had, he now would begin to lose it all… even fathering descendants who would continue to suffer the same; and, ultimately, start giving the world a whole lot of problems. The Serpent - as an ultimate punishment - was cursed to suffer the rest of his life by having fits of mental anguish; with feelings of misery, worthlessness, and self-torment.[70]

> *...what he (the serpent) desired was not given him, and what he possessed was taken from him.* (Halevi, 1997, p. 204)[71]

> *"(God speaking to the serpent)... they shall have healing and* ***thou*** *shalt have no healing."* (Jung, 1974, p. 71)[72]

> *Some of the angels by an act of free will obeyed the will of God, and in such obedience found perfect happiness; other angels by an act of free will rebelled against the will of God, and in such disobedience found* ***misery****.*
> (Baring-Gould, 1881, p. 16)[73]

Curses Upon Eve

> *Thereupon God imposed punishment on Adam for yielding to a woman's counsel... Eve He punished by* ***childbirth*** *and* ***its attendant pains****, because she had* ***deluded*** *(deceived) Adam, even as the serpent had* ***beguiled*** *her.*
> - *Falvius Josephus* Jewish Antiquities 1:45-50[74]

Eve would have a few punishments dished out to her, as well. Interestingly, we see most of hers were associated with ***sex*** - probably an ironic *response* to the act that she and the Serpent participated in.

> *Unto the woman He (God) said,* ***Multiplying****, I will* ***multiply thy affliction*** *by the* ***blood of thy virginity****...* - *Targum Pseudo-Jonathan* III[75]

Possibly, because she was no longer a virgin at this time, her *bloodshed* meant a lot to these punishments, as well. Again, God probably distributed punishments *measure for measure*, here; as He often does.

In the Bible, we have *these* curses placed upon Eve:

- *a greatly multiplied sorrow when she experiences pregnancy*
- *sorrow when she brings forth children* (*Gen.* 3:16)

Sorrow and pain would now be a necessary part of human conception. Eve may have brought these sorrows upon herself, and her fellow womankind after her (it seems), because of her act of coition with the Serpent. She, once, wanted to be *fruitful* by eating of the Tree of Knowledge, and be able to multiply - now she'll suffer in her ability to multiply because of it.

A woman's cries would, now, come from a deep, psychological repentance of the process of human generation. From that point on, once a woman undertakes the responsibility of childbearing - especially at the point of giving birth - they will suffer a general, sometimes almost unbearable, anguish:

> *...and on that occasion you shall come near to losing your life from your great anguish and pains.* (Halevi, 1997, p. 204)[76]

> *...your giving birth will be changed* ***into death****.*
> - *Armenian Apocryphal Adam Literature* Transgression[77]

When God punished Eve, He could have said something like the following:

> *Since thou hast hearkened to the serpent... thou shalt be in throes of travail and intolerable agonies; thou* <u>*shalt*</u> <u>*bear*</u> <u>*children*</u> *in much* ***trembling*** *and in one hour thou shalt come to the birth... But thou shalt confess and say: "Lord, Lord, save me, I will turn no more to the* ***sin of the flesh****." And on this account, from thine own words I will judge thee, by reason of the enmity which the enemy* ***has planted in thee****.*
> - *Apocalypse of Moses / Apocalypsis Mosis* 25:1-4[78]

This tells us so much. The word *trembling*, in the above text, could equate to one "with great sorrow."[79] And, it says that when a woman gives birth, she often might think or say something such as, "no more will I ever want to have sex again!" Ancient sources proclaim that these thoughts of a woman - at the moment of childbirth - might actually represent their own, subconscious, attempt to make *atonement* for Eve's sin!

On top of this, the "bite" of the Serpent's coitus also seemed to have ended Eve's run as a *maiden*; which brought her to the point where she may no longer have felt "innocent." Their act, also (according to one ancient source) had begun to activate Eve's *menstrual* cycle (as well as menstrual cycles of all women after her)... again, these things seemed to all be an *ironic* style of punishment - running in *exact correlation* to what she did in the Garden.[80]

> *Now, you, Eve, as you* ***caused the tree to bleed****, you* ***will bleed*** *every new moon.*
> *- al-Tabari: The History of al-Tabari - Vol. I: General Introduction and From the Creation to the Flood* God's Testing of Adam 107[81]

Apparently, menstrual pains seemed to be another side effect of her sin in the Garden. According to the Bible, a woman, now, will have:

> *...a desire to be with her husband again, or to her husband when she has travail, and he will rule over her.* - *Gen.* 3:16 (in retranslation)

From this point on, when Eve argues with her husband, at first she might be angry, cynical, or negative; then she will be a little afraid; and, ultimately, she'll want to return to him. Why? Could Eve's desire to again be with Adam, in part, be the result of her seduction by the Serpent? By her "going astray" with some other male, sexually, as with the Serpent, here, have brought *this* curse on to her - to assure that she eventually *goes back* to the same man she was with, before?

> *(May you, Eve)... give birth to many fruits... and you will* ***harden your heart*** *in view of the great* ***combat*** *which the* ***serpent constituted*** *in you. (But may you) return at once to the same point, may you* ***bear your offspring*** *in hurt and return in pity to your husband...* - *Book of Adam* [44]25.1-4[82]

All of these newfound desires of Eve, now, seem to be with her on an unconscious level… as well as on an unconscious level with a good deal of women, after her. As a result, Eve, and, therefore, women in general, would become a lot more *emotional* than they ever might have, before:

> *Eve shall be afflicted with variety of* ***strange affections****.*
> (Baring-Gould, 1881, p. 43)[83]

Apparently, the reason she seemed to have a greater amount of affliction was because she seemed to be *less* repentant than Adam, after being exposed as a sinner, by God; which led her further down the "totem pole" of authority (between she and her husband).

> *And toward your husband will be your* ***turning****, and he will have dominion over you, whether to admit or find fault.* - *Targum On Genesis* 3:16[84]

Interesting: the word *turning*, in the above, seems of special significance:

> *Now, "turning" was the ordinary Hebrew word for repentance. So it must have seemed that the whole point of this verse (if we understood as "turning") was that Eve had been* ***unrepentant*** *when she was reproached by God in the openings words of Gen. 3:16... Unlike her husband, she showed no remorse. As a result, she was then* ***further*** *sentenced...* (Kugel, 1998, p. 143)[85]

Adam shivered, and God took pity on him. Eve, at first, did not… at least until God showed her He wasn't kidding, and sentenced her *more*.

According to another source, the meaning of the word *Eve* could, actually, be equivalent to "*a serpent*."[86] We see, in the following ancient text, that God spoke this to Eve:

The serpent was thy serpent, and ***thou*** *wast Adam's serpent.*
- Genesis Rabbah 23:2[87]

In other words, Eve was to Adam as what the Serpent was *to her*: the temptress, the seducer.[88]

Adam - Not a Part of the Transgression

I Tim. 2:
14 ...*Adam was not deceived, but the woman being deceived was* ***in the transgression***.
15 ***Not*** *withstanding she shall* ***be saved in childbearing***.

Notice that "childbearing" was mentioned right *after* Eve was suggested to be "in the transgression." Again, the two seem to be related, possibly, here: one could have been in consequence *of the other*, it seems. What that probably means is this: the Serpent committed a *transgression* by fornicating with Eve in this way; Eve also committed a transgression by fornicating with Adam, the same way. Adam did not turn around, and fornicate with anyone else, here… the process stopped with him, in this case. Not saying that men could never commit fornication with women, here, it's just that - in the Garden - the Serpent and the woman were the only two guilty of this act. Eve eventually would be *saved* from her transgression, though, in the end. Because, via *her descendants* - from umbilical cord to umbilical cord - a **seed** of Adam would eventually be born… one who would become savior of the world, and have the authority to resolve these wrongs that were committed in the Garden. And this savior would be known by a name most of us know: *Jesus Christ*.[89] We'll, soon, look at these concepts much deeper.

The Curse of Seed on the Earth

Speaking of this, there *could* have been **one** more *important* outcome of this transgression, between Eve and the Serpent. There could be one more consequence that would plague the Adamites, and other people of the Garden, until the end of time. What if something actually *resulted* from this sexual union?

> *And Eve said to Adam: "Live thou, my Lord, to thee life is granted, since thou hast committed neither* ***the first*** *nor* ***the second error****. But I have erred and been led astray."*
> - *Vita Adae Et Evae* 18:1-2[90]

Well, what's this first ***and second*** error, here? Obviously, she committed the first error of eating forbidden fruit of the Tree of the Knowledge of Good and Evil. Could a second **error** of Eve involve her having *sex* with this Serpent?

Interestingly enough, shortly after the above verse, we have:

> *And she made there a booth, while she had in her* ***womb*** *offspring of three months old.*
> - *Vita Adae Et Evae* 18:3[91]

What if something *did* come out of their coition? How *this* really might complicate her entire world! What if there *was* a little more than regret which resulted from her sexual experience - what if she **was** pregnant?

You'll notice that she was seemed to be *with child* soon after being seduced by the Serpent, in the above. It seems she may have already known she was pregnant, here - on track to bring forth her first child. If there was to be one, what were the circumstances surrounding this birth? And, if the Serpent was possibly the father, what effect would his offspring have on the world to come?

Chapter 8

The Offspring

> *(God, speaking to the Serpent)... And I will put enmity between thee and the woman, and between* **thy seed** *and her seed...* - *Gen.* 3:15 (KJV)

The above was a prophecy, given by God, given directly to the Serpent, himself.

First off, what do we mean by "thy seed?" God was talking to the Serpent, here. What seed… are we talking about the seed of baby snakes, here? How could a little enmity (or hatred) between women and slithery, slimy snakes be of such an importance, in regards to what happened in the Garden? There are plenty of animals in the world that scare people. Why *enmity* is so *noteworthy*, here, to be included by God, in His statement? These words do seem to go quite beyond one's irrational paranoia about snakes, here. And, just *who's* "seeds" might we be referring to, in this case?

As we recall, God was making this statement - right after a possible copulation between Eve and the Serpent. Maybe their coition would, now, set the stage for two separate **bloodlines** to be born - the human descendants of Adam and Eve **and** the descendants of Eve and the Serpent! If this was the case, then the above verse, actually, will become the **focal point** of so much in this book! It's so important, as we shall see.

It's quite possible Eve and the Serpent could have been able to spawn **offspring**, because of their actions. If this did, indeed, happen, this particular offspring would go on, to be in conflict with Eve and many of her descendants from that point on (as we shall see). Could *this* be why it was important enough to be mentioned, here, by God? According to a number of ancient sources, *this* is actually what happened: two separate bloodlines would come about, through Eve, here - and something big was on the horizon; something big was about to unfold, here.

Through seduction, ancient sources tell us that the Serpent could have even tried to have offspring with Eve *more than once* - in the future; as well as try it with other women! It would be through these pregnancies that entire groups of people, collectively thought of (at least in Jewish thought) as the *mixed multitudes*, would come together.

The offspring which would spring right from the Serpent and Eve - the "patriarch" of all of these groups of mixed multitudes - would go on to launch one of the most important struggles of our time![1] Just *who* might this offspring be; and what affect would *he* have on the world around him? Let's look more at the prophecy, who "he" was, and what might this all might *really* mean.

The Head and Heel

> *...I will put enmity between thee and the woman, and between thy seed and her seed...*
> - *Gen.* 3:15 (KJV)

Next, after proclaiming the **prophecy** (above), God prophesied what would, eventually, be the result of it: a *savior* would eventually arise from these seed lines, and provide a solution to all of the problems which originated in the Garden:

> *...it (the savior) shall* ***bruise*** *thy head, and thou shalt bruise his heel.*
> - *Gen.* 3:15 (KJV)

In other words, this *savior* would be none other than *Jesus Christ*.[2] As we see, in the below, God said to the Serpent:

> *Let the precious cross* ***which my Son*** *will take upon the earth condemn you (the Serpent) because of the deceit by which you deceived Adam. But may you again be* ***crushed*** *and* ***broken*** *because of the evil of your heart. And I will set enmity between you and the offspring of the woman: she will lay in wait for your head and you will lay in wait for her heel until the day of judgment.*
> - *Book of Adam* [44]26.3-4[3]

So this simply means that: the descendants of Eve - sometime, somewhere - would bring forth an individual who would **crush**, or **break**, the "head" (i.e. *power*) of the Serpent - the *hold* the Serpent now had over the world (as result of the fall of Adam). In the process, however, this particular individual would have his *own* heel bruised. All of this, of course, referred to the sacrifice of Jesus Christ - and how he would have his "heel" bruised (by being crucified). But, he would rise again, from the dead, and defeat (or crush) the spiritual power the devil had on the world, up to then.[4]

Let's explain this in a little more detail. *Strong's Concordance* gives us a couple of Hebrew meanings for the English *bruise*, here: to "snap at," to "overwhelm," or to "cover." So, another interpretation of it all might be: the seeds of the Serpent would, throughout the ages, continually try to snap "at the **heels** of Christ, groveling in the battle, while Christ, the Lion of Judah, snaps at the **head** of the serpent," crushing his skull.[5] The descendants of the Serpent - those with blood of the Serpent - will, from this point of time on, try to inflict some type of suffering on the bloodline of Adam. This would continue, all the way up to the time of Christ's birth.

These Serpent descendants have (as we'll see) tried, throughout history, to either somehow compromise, or even *destroy*, the Adamic seed line… to stop baby Jesus from ever coming into existence! Again, all of this was to try to destroy the savior's purpose, here, on the earth. But, in the end, most of us know what happened - these "Serpent-seeds" were defeated, at least in that attempt… Jesus was born. The savior *did* crush the power the Serpent had over the entire world by his sacrifice.

> *…all Satan's plans and plots, policy and purposes, one day will be finally* ***crushed*** *and ended, never more to mar or hider the purposes of God.*
> - *The Companion Bible* Appx. 19[6]

A very powerful reason for Christ's existence, here! The main punishment of Adam and Eve was *death*. Yet, through *Christ's* death, burial and resurrection, Jesus' sacrifice will "snap" (or break) the head of this Serpent - his spiritual authority over the world. How he will do that is, through his *resurrection*, he would defeat the hold, or power, that *death* has on the world, here. He'll break the punishment of which Adam and Eve helped usher into our existence. One verse states it very well:

> *…as the children are partakers of flesh and blood, he (Jesus) also himself likewise took part of the same; that through* ***death*** *he might destroy him that had the power of death, that is, the* ***devil****…* - *Heb.* 2:14 (KJV)

With Jesus' unblemished sacrifice on the cross, the road was paved for human existence to make atonement with God, from then on. There is more.

The Poison "Head"

> *...it (the savior) shall bruise thy **head**...*
> - *Gen.* 3:15 (KJV)

If we think about it, the *head* of a snake is exactly where the poison sac is. As well, the *head* of any animal is also where their ***thought processes*** occur. Likewise, the *mouth* of the snake represents the point where *poison* flows out of.[7] Well, if we follow that train of parallel logic: how about *the rest* of our mouths? Could there be a connection to some kind of "poison" and rhetoric coming out of individuals? Looking at it another way: could this "head," represented above, actually be a symbol of ***theology***, ***philosophy***, or any of the ***schools of thought*** which might be portrayed by the Serpent, and his seeds? Could the "poison" which comes out of their mouths actually symbolize some sort of ***theological*** "poison," here?

> *(God speaking to the serpent)... and the poison of death shall be **in thy mouth**...*
> - *Targum Pseudo-Jonathan* III[8]

Interestingly enough, *we'll* soon see the major players - the ones largely responsible for railroading Jesus to his execution - might, very well, have been among those who promoted those ideologies steeped within elements of the Serpent's "head." Most of them, at the time, might have even been a part of the Serpent's bloodline, *as well* (as we shall see)!

Adam to Jesus

One thing *is* for certain: the seed line of the first, unique Adam, here, was needed to start the groundwork for these descendant seeds… those who would lead to the "last Adam" - *Jesus Christ*:

> <u>*I Cor.* 15:</u>
> 45 *And so it is written, The* ***first*** *man (**Adam**) was made a living soul; the* ***last Adam*** *was made a quickening spirit.*
> 47 *The first man is of the earth, earthy; the second man is the Lord from heaven.*

The Greek word for *man*, in the above, is *anthropos*. It not only means *man*, but a *special* kind of man. It represents a man distinguished, "from beings of a different order."[9] In other words, Adam was a little different because he was given life by *the direct* breath of God, himself (as the Bible noted) - which is a *special* designation. His role on earth, after the Fall, would be to pass on his special seed (i.e. his special *breath*, *soul*, etc.) to the last "Adam" - Jesus Christ. Any other seed just won't do, here, in regards to God's proclamation. Any other seed just wasn't the apportioned one… simple.

> *The First Adam lived to die; The Second Adam died to live. Go, and imitate the penitence of the First Adam; Go, and celebrate the Goodness of the Second Adam.*
> (Alvarez, 1713)[10]

If we look at the genealogy of Jesus, we *do* seem to see a special significance to his seed line. The lineage of Jesus, in the Book of Luke (and, also Matthew), makes note of Jesus' **seed line**; which (listed in reverse order) begins with Jesus himself. As we notice, it does go all the way back to *Adam*. And, let's take a look at what is noted at the end of this list (noting the generations of Jesus, here - practically going all the way back at the beginning, to *Adam*):[11]

> *…(we have Cainan being)… the son of Enos, which was the son of Seth, which was the son of Adam, which was* ***the son of God****.* - *Luke* 3:38 (KJV)

Adam's special circumstance - as a "son" of God, here - will help to establish the whole up-and-coming narrative of the Bible. Yes, **the Bible is the story of *one particular man*: Adam**, down his family bloodline, to the eventual savior.

> *This is the book **of the generations of Adam**. In the day that God created man, in the likeness of God made he him...* - *Gen.* 5:1 (KJV)

This is the underlying thread behind the entire Old Testament! Of course, this doesn't mean that every other bloodline in the world is not important, or doesn't matter - it's just that the savior of the world needed to be of *some* blood line. In this case, it belonged to the blood line of the man who helped cause this worldly ruckus; the one who actually begun his existence from the breath of God. A fitting choice.

Although the unique, outward qualities of Adam (i.e. his height, his brilliant, "angelic-like" countenance, etc.) would fade, the special significance of his seed line would not. This seed line would *have* to survive, and continue on, if this prophecy of God was to be fulfilled:

> *(In regards to Jesus Christ, himself)... He (God) hath appointed heir of all things, by whom also he made the worlds; Who being in the brightness of his glory, and the express **image** of his person...* - *Heb.* 1:2-3 (KJV)

So, as a result - in order to keep this seed "alive" - there, quite often, needed to be the *separation* of Adam's seed, throughout the ages… in order to *deter* any possible means to compromise to it; to assure birth of a savior for our world.

The Necessity for Untainted Seed

> *By a profound principle of genetic science, discovered only recently, the blood line, or type, is determined through the **male**, or father, and thus the blood of Christ was technically, and truly, not tainted by the **curse of Adam** as it is in the rest of humanity, since Jesus did not have **an earthly father**. The **same sinless blood** was poured out at Calvary for all whom are redeemed in Christ. No other death could have accomplished the substitutionary atonement and the propitiation of His*

righteousness unto us. (Unruh, n. d.)[12]

The **male** seed was important for this very reason. And, since Jesus was born of a virgin, he did not have the Serpent's curse within him. The rest of the world's human offspring, from this time, would; because the *evil inclination* was inherited by them. And, on top of this, Adam was different than the Serpent and Eve - in regards to the Fall:

> *...in such form he (the serpent) entered and seduced Eva, but* ***did not touch*** *Adam...*
> - *2 Enoch (The Book of the Secrets of Enoch)* 31:5[13]

> *...Adam* ***was not deceived****, but the woman being deceived was in the transgression.*
> - *I Tim.* 2:14 (KJV)

Those of this seed of Adam were not perfect or anything. But, since Adam did *not* participate in that horrible transgression of the garden - ***fornication*** - he wasn't as liable for as much pain and suffering as Eve and the Serpent were. And, as a result, Jewish law seemed to be more favorable to the male; treating them with higher regard. Not only was he to remain head of the family, the *man* was also to remain the example of God's code of morality on earth. Although this might not sound fair to some, today, that's simply the way it was back then - and the occurrences at the **Garden of Eden** were behind most all the reasons why.

The Force of Separation

Even though Adam may have been given a "lighter sentence," here, he still wasn't very happy with what happened, overall. Apparently angered by how things turned out between him and his wife, he made an interesting, but appropriate, revelation:

> *And Adam called his wife's name Eve; because she was the* ***mother*** *of all living...*
> - *Gen.* 3:20 (KJV)

Wow; this sounds a little like a compliment - Adam noted that Eve was the *matriarch* of all of mankind! That's a nice comment… or is it? Would one think that Adam was really *happy* with Eve, at this moment? He may have just discovered that she copulated with another individual - a being *just under him*, in rank and authority! The Serpent, obviously, was an individual that Adam knew quite well; and probably worked closely with. What a blow.

Adam also listened to *Eve*, and her pleas. She probably seduced him, sexually. And, now, the world he once knew had *forever* changed. Adam, at the time, probably wasn't really in the mood to compliment his wife, here; but, rather, comment on this whole "seed line" prophecy of which God laid out, before him!

The original Hebrew word for *mother*, in this verse, is *em*. It doesn't only mean "mother;" but, according to *Strong's Concordance*, it also stands for "a point of departure or division." So, if we recall the above prophecy (in Gen. 3:15), we, indeed, see that there was to be *a split* - a **division** of *enmity* between descendents of Eve and the descendants of the Serpent. And, Eve, because of her situation, became **the focal point** of this whole division! Adam probably *did* identify this as such; and made this comment to her!

> *And Adam called his wife's name Eve; because she was the* ***point of division*** *between all the living human beings…* - *Gen.* 3:20 (in retranslation)

The descendants of this Serpent - through Eve - would work to *separate*, or *divide*, themselves from Adam; as well as anyone who might think like him. They also would work to *divide* other people away from Adam, and bring them towards *their* ways of thinking. As we recall, the *head* of the Serpent was symbolic of where all this **mental propaganda** might have spewed out; like *poison*.[14] *Thoughts* and *ways of thinking* are what truly can be used to *divide* people - no doubt about that. One ancient source even stated the first offspring of Eve and this Serpent would be known as "the ***divider*** of the kingdom."[15] *Now* we know why!

Armed with this understanding, just *who was* this offspring of Eve - the one who, reportedly, would cause so much turmoil on our entire planet? Let's see.

Time to Leave the Garden

> *The LORD God sent him forth from the garden of Eden, to till the ground from whence he was taken.* - *Gen.* 3:23 (KJV)

Now, Adam (and the rest of the human race) was about to go to work, and work *hard* - no more life of leisure, for the most part. The time was nigh for Adam and Eve to physically *depart* from the Garden of Eden, itself.[16] And, the foundation of this Genesis 3:15 Prophecy (also known as the ***Protoevangelium***) was soon to be set into place - descendants of Eve would soon be born. And, when God makes a prophecy, it **has** to come true - that's just the way a perfect God works. So, the divisions of these two lines of offspring were about to form; and Adam may have already had an idea what was about to occur!

According to one ancient source "the union of Adam and Eve was consummated **after** the expulsion from Paradise."[17] Whether Adam and Eve copulated before or after they left the garden, it's still a good possibly a third party - the *Serpent* - was, now, in the middle of their entire relationship… in a *big* way; a *child* of the Serpent may have already been in Eve's womb!

One ancient work has an angel, now, approaching Eve; and beginning to confide in her about how to correctly manage what might be growing, inside her:

> *If you had not been brought help… you would have conceived such a thorn that you could not have rescued yourself from your sufferings. Rise up now and prepare yourself to* ***give birth to a child****.* - *Book of Adam* 21.2[18]

To Eve's surprise, she found out she was, indeed, with child. Let's look at some reasons why *Adam* may have had suspicions that this particular child wasn't his.

And Adam Knew Eve…

> *And Adam* ***knew*** *Eve his wife; and she conceived…*
> - *Gen.* 4:1 (KJV)

When one reads this verse, it seems obvious that Adam *knew* his wife (or had *sex* with his wife), and their first offspring was ***Cain*** - simple. To many, this is proof that Adam was the father of Cain - right? Possibly not.

We have some interesting thoughts about this verse: many have assumed that the word *knew*, in the above, practically just means "to have sex with." We also know the original language of the Bible was Hebrew; and there were people who translated these words according to what definition *they* thought was right; or what *they* were always *taught*. Yet, again: to find what the original words might really be saying, here, we need to dig a little deeper; going beyond the realms of assumption.

The Hebrew for *knew*, in the above, really comes from *two* Hebrew words: *yada* and *eth.*[19] The word *yada* means, "to know (a person carnally)," yes… but it can **also** mean to "recognize," "discern," or "acknowledge." The other word, *eth*, is untranslatable in English, but is rooted in a word that means, "sign," "distinguishing mark," or "omen." Put them *together*, and we could have:

> *And Adam eventually* ***acknowledged*** *the* ***distinguishing sign*** *that had come upon Eve…*
> - *Gen.* 4:1 (in retranslation)

On top of this, the Hebrew word for *conceived*, in the above, could also stand for one being "with child." So, to top it off, we could have another way to word this entire verse:

> *And Adam eventually* ***acknowledged*** *the* ***distinguishing sign*** *that had come upon Eve; that she was* ***with child****, and realized she was about to give birth…*
> - *Gen.* 4:1 (in retranslation)

Wow. The Bible can't really state it much clearer *than that*. Adam *understood* that his wife was pregnant; and what it all meant, here. We have other interpretations to further back this up:

> *Adam knew his wife, not in the sexual sense, but knew* ***something about her****.*
> (Kugel, 1997, p. 86)[20]

What is the meaning of "knew?" (He knew) that she had conceived.
- *Pirke deR. Eliezer* XXI[21]

Adam *knew* she was pregnant, by looking at her bulge; and then went on, to make a conclusion about it, in his mind. Sounds a lot different than what the King James' translators tried to portray, and most other translations - but, *now* we know why! They felt the need to follow tradition; they translated things according to how *they were taught*; they didn't want any interpretations out there *other* than what their establishment teachers "pushed" on them.

Yet, regardless, we still see there could easily be another, **relevant** interpretation of the word *knew*: "the time had come when Adam and Eve were expelled from the Garden, and Adam took his wife away from there, with the *knowledge* she was already pregnant. From there, they settled to the east of the Garden."[22]

The Serpent, indeed, drove a wedge between Adam and Eve, by this insemination… one they can't really ignore.

The Offspring of Amalek

And Adam ***knew*** *his wife, who had conceived by the angel* ***Sammael****, was pregnant…*
(Eisenmenger, 1748, p. 198)[23]

We already have a number of names for the Serpent: Nachash, Gadriel, Azazel, etc.. and, we know others name for Sammael: Satan, Lucifer, etc.. Let's look at *one* more title the Serpent may have had, back then; as well as about the child he was instrumental in bringing forth.

The word *El* has been defined as the English form of God.[24] As we recall, from an earlier section, some hypothesized the word *El-ohim* might stand for "God and his angels." So, a *strange El*, then, could represent an *El* (i.e. a "*false god*") who was of the *strange* kind (i.e. one who had "fallen").

So, as we'll see (below), the following ancient source describes how women of the time, even *Eve*, began to mate with these fallen angels, or strange "El's," around them;

and how their unions began to form an entire group of offspring, sometimes known as *strange* offspring. These would be those groups of "mixed multitudes," as we've already mentioned - and many of these individuals would act just like God said they would: be at *enmity* with Adam, his descendants of Adam, and anyone who might follow their ways of living. So, we *now* have another name for the Serpent:

> *These are all mixed among Yisrael (Israel), but none of them is cursed as* ***Amalek****, who is the evil* ***Serpent****, a Strange El: The one who uncovers all nakedness in the world. This means that it... causes incest in the world. It is the murderer. From it, all murders in the world originate, and its spouse is the potion of death of idol-worship. So the three transgressions of idol-worship, incest and bloodshed derive from... Amalek, who* ***is the serpent*** *and another El. They are all related to the aspect of Samael, who has many different aspects, but they are not the same. Samael, who is from the side of the Serpent, is the most cursed of them all.*
>
> - *Zohar* Beresheet A29

According to this ancient source, incest, murder, and idol-worship seemed to have originated from the *Serpent* of the Garden - a.k.a. ***Amalek***. The descendents of Amalek, as well, would go on to form a significant group of "mixed multitudes" - known as the ***Amalekites***.

Interestingly enough, ancient sources stated these Amalekites *would* survive, and thrive, throughout the ages - up to the time of Israel, and far *beyond*. Again, probably the most famous member of this group of mixed multitudes was also said to be a direct child of *Amalek* - his own son.

> *Having been made pregnant by the* ***seed of the devil****... she brought forth a* ***son****.*
>
> - *Tertullian* On Patience 5:15[25]

> *And I will put enmity between thee and the woman, and between the seed* ***of thy son****, and the seed of her sons...*
>
> - *Targum Pseudo-Jonathan* II[26]

We see, in the above, that Amalek was the origin of those who commit **murder**. Who, in the Bible, was the most *famous* figure who committed murder - the *first* murder? Who was the Serpent's son? Who was Amalek's son? Yes, this represents all the same person - none other than the first son of Eve… one the Bible makes known as **Cain**![27]

Cain

Could **the Serpent** actually be the father of Cain, and not Adam?[28]

> *(Cain)… who, on account of the foulness of the murder which he had committed, has* ***nothing in him*** *resembling his father (or Adam, his presumptive father), either in* ***body or soul****.*
>
> \- *Works of Philo Judaeus* Questions and Answers on Genesis 1(81)[29]

Maybe the reason Cain did not resemble Adam, here, was because Adam really **was not** his father!

> *Now afterward, she bore Cain - (the serpent's) son, begotten on Eve's "shadow," or physical body, by… (the serpent's) act of raping her… The posterity of Cain are therefore the offspring of devils.* - *The Reality of the Rulers*[30]

> *The descendants of Kayin (Cain), after he (Kayin) was driven from the face of the earth, are strange creatures…* - *Zohar* Vayishlach 28[31]

Again, in the above, we see the word *strange* is used. We know how this could stand for one who is a descendent of a *strange* god - a fallen angel. One way or another, we'll discover more of how the Serpent probably had everything to do with the birth of Cain; and not Adam![32]

There have been other theories on this whole thing: some ancient sources have even speculated there could have been an "infusion" of the Serpent's seed with Adam's seed, somehow:

> *Samael begot the spirit, the soul of Cain, Adam became his bodily father…*
>
> (Jung, 1974, p. 79)[33]

Know then, Cain was form'd from the impurity, and that drop which the serpent injected into Eve: but as it was impossible, without the mixture of Adam's seed, for the spirit to cloath itself with a human body, and be brought forth into this world; so the seed of Adam furnish'd means for the cloathing it with a body.
(Eisenmenger, 1748, p. 197)[34]

It's possible; a mixture, such as this. But, it's much more simplistic to accept the possibility that the terrestrial Serpent alone *could* father children, just like any other human being (because of his *demotion* by God); and that Cain was purely the Serpent's son - lock, stock, and barrel.

As we'll see, these angelic/human unions would produce offspring such as Cain, in vast numbers. This, even, was not the only account of a *serpent-like* angel (i.e. a Seraphim) having offspring like this, in the past. In the *Book of Enoch*, for example, a **serpent** angel named *Taba'et* fathered a human offspring.[35] We'll soon see this will become *a lot more* commonplace. Whatever way Cain may have been conceived, he probably had seed of *the Serpent*, somewhere - and that other descendants of these terrestrial angels would go on to be major components of other groups of individuals after the Fall - the so-call *strange* or *mixed multitudes*.

Let's look more at Cain, here.

Cain - A "Shining One"

What is the meaning of the word "knew?" He knew that she had conceived. And she saw his likeness that it was **not** *of the earthly beings...* (Jung, 1974, p. 78)[36]

...Cain was not of Adam's seed, **nor** *after his likeness, nor after his image... The Pal. Targum to Gen 5:3 adds: "... Eve had borne Cain, who was not like to him" (i.e. Adam).* *- Pirke deR. Eliezer* XXII[37]

Adam, as we've postulated already, had a shining, "angelic-like" appearance before his fall. After his sinned, however, he would lose most of it. Cain, interestingly enough, was also **born** with somewhat of a brilliant countenance; a lot brighter than Adam. In fact, he looked a lot more like the other *angels* around the Garden might have looked!

(Cain's) shape was not like that of other men.
(Eisenmenger, 1748, p. 197)[38]

*...And his **face** was not like that of other human beings, and all those who descend from him are called "Bene Elohim".* (Jung, 1974, p. 78)[39]

As we've stated, angels could also be thought of as, "stars," "luminaries," or "angels of light."[40] Baby Cain had a lot of the same:

*Cain's color was that of the **stars**.*
- *Book of Adam* 21.3a[41]

Angels, even these fallen, terrestrial angels on the earth, probably still possessed a degree of *countenance* within them; and even were able to pass it on to their descendants (at least for a while).

The Shocking Moment

And, Eve probably *knew* what the angels around her looked like; and, then, could have convinced herself a terrestrial angel may have planted seed in her - by reason of her exclamation in the Bible:[42]

<u>*Gen.* 4:</u>
1 *And Adam knew Eve his wife; and she conceived, and bare Cain, and said, I have gotten a man **from the LORD**.*
2 *And she again bare his brother Abel.*

Another translation has it like this:

<u>*Gen.* 4:</u>
1 *And Adam knew Eve his wife; and she conceived, and bare Cain, and said, I have gotten a man **from an angel of the LORD**.*
2 *And she again bare his brother Abel.*
- *The Jerusalem Translation*

Apparently, she thought she conceived Cain through the Lord, or some angel of the Lord. The fact that Cain had a similar seraphic or "shining" countenance gives us credence that **Cain's birth** might have been shocking to Adam and Eve - he didn't look like either of them. Eve may have even been frightened of her child; and wished to kill him.[43] It seems Cain wasn't the *only* one born at this time. Eve, apparently, was pregnant with more than one child (as we shall see)! Her other son, Abel, here, probably had a similar "angelic" illumination about him. Both looked as if they were conceived by an angel.

If the two did come from a fallen angel, Cain and Abel must have *both* been shockingly bright to Adam and Eve. At least, we can conclude that Eve did not think her son came from Adam - it's pretty obvious, from the above, ***who*** she thought her son was from:

> *And Adam knew his wife, who **had desired the Angel**; and she conceived, and bare Kain; and she said, I have acquired a man, **the angel of the Lord**.*
> - *Targum Pseudo-Jonathan* IV[44]

Who Cain was really from, and the ways he would follow the rest of his life, really sets the stage for the rest of this book! We'll see… it's all so important.

Gotten From the Lord?

We remember the verse:

> *And Adam knew Eve his wife; and she conceived, and bare Cain, and said, I have **gotten** a **man** from the LORD.* - *Gen.* 4:1 (KJV)

Eve stated, here, that she had *gotten* a man from the Lord. Now, from whom was he "gotten" for sure? Let's, again, look at this original verse, with a bit of additional information:

> *And Adam knew his wife, who had conceived by the angel Sammael, was pregnant, and bare Cain, whose resemblance was like the upper (Creatures) and not like the lower. And she said, I have* ***got the man, the angel of the Lord****.*
>
> (Eisenmenger, 1748, p. 198)[45]

Interestingly, a couple of meanings of this name *Cain* are "gotten," "acquired," and "possession."[46] What's the significance of the above words, as relation to Cain? Could this give us further evidence Cain was *acquired*, or *gotten*, by another source… instead of Eve's husband? Interestingly enough, we also notice, here, that Eve calls this newly-born son a *man* at this time; and not a child. A man, obviously, represents a human being who's already grown up. Why not call him a "baby?"[47]

> *…this divinely begotten child could appropriately be called a* ***man*** *(rather than a "****baby****") because* ***angels*** *are* ***frequently called "man"*** *in the Bible (see Gen. 18:2, 32:24, and elsewhere). Thus, some ancient interpreters concluded that Cain had in fact been half-human, half-angelic creature begotten by the devil.*
>
> (Kugel, 1997, p. 87)[48]

The "Promised Seed" - Already, in Her Lifetime?

> *…there has broken out another heresy also… that they magnify Cain* ***as if he*** *had been conceived of some* ***potent Virtue*** *which operated in him…*
>
> ("The Gospel of Judas: Cain - Cainites - Kenite - Rechabites", n. d., p. 15)[49]

We recall the prophecy of Genesis 3:15 - concerning the seeds of Eve and seeds of the Serpent: "it shall bruise thy head, and thou shalt bruise his heel…." As we'll see, at the birth of Cain, Eve could have thought something *else*: her own salvation, and salvation of the world, might already be at **hand**! Because Cain had such as brilliant countenance, maybe Eve thought her child was the "promised seed" of God! Maybe, the Genesis 3:15 Prophecy was already being fulfilled! Was Cain her inception of "the Christ?"

Maybe Eve was starting to live a little in denial. Maybe, by looking her son's angelic *shine*, Eve may also have started rationalizing to herself that his shine might be a sign *of something "good."* Maybe she thought Cain's birth, no matter the real circumstances, was a positive. Maybe one with angelic blood *could* do good things. Maybe her son *could* do wonders for the world, later on, because of these circumstances - blinding herself to the *real* truth of it all. Maybe she hoped Cain would, ultimately, be one "from the Lord," or from an angel of the Lord - who could do something wonderful and relevant.

> *It may be well here to note that whenever the word 'Lord' is printed in our English Bibles in capitals, its Hebrew Equivalent is Jehovah - a term which marks the idea of the* **covenant** *God. Apparently she connected the birth of her son with* ***the immediate fulfillment*** *of the promise concerning the Seed...*
> ("The World Before the Flood and The History of the Patriarchs", n. d., p. 5-6)[50]

The word *covenant* means "promise." Eve may not have been the most up-to-date on how pregnancy really worked. Maybe she thought that, somehow, God allowed Cain to be born this way to give *her* the promised seed **right away**; on who would counter-balance the Serpent's sin in her life. Maybe Cain could solve all of her problems, over time. Maybe her concern at his appearance was nothing more than some over-zealous theory.

Most of us know how conception works, now-a-days. In actuality, one, today, could assume that Cain's angelic appearance probably pointed him towards *the opposite* direction of one who could actually be the prophesied "savior!" An angry, envious terrestrial angel as a father - bent on the world's destruction - probably wouldn't help Cain's case… if he was the one who was the prophesied "Christ-child."

Yet, if Eve - in some subconscious desire to continually find ways to "undo" what she helped spawn in the Garden - continued to often perpetuate these thoughts about Cain, what affect might this have on Cain, throughout his years? What about his descendants? Might Cain, and his offspring, begin to think that *they* were something special, indeed? Might Cain begin to think that, maybe, he *could have been* something like a prophesied savior?

Although the Bible made it clear the savior would be born of a seed of *Adam*, maybe Cain's descendants would have been told - all the way back to Cain himself - that *they* were something special; that they were of the prophesied seed! A typical mother usually wants the *best* for her child - regardless who the real father is; and, most of the time, wants to put him in the *best* possible light as she could. Any and all of these thoughts, however, would greatly complicate matters in Cain, and a great deal of other individuals.

If we think about it, if Cain's descendants began take on the view that *they* were the only right ones (in this whole argument), then this could usher in a *sibling rivalry* unlike the world had ever seen - a rivalry which would continue to the end of time… with each side thinking of *themselves* as being part of the "divine light!" What about the ideological *thoughts* of either seed line? Wouldn't this easily begin to develop into some long, drawn-out battle of wills and ideology, between the two? Apparently, that's *exactly* what was going to happen, between these two seed lines; and it all began with *Cain*.

More About This "Possessor"

Cain, from his very beginning, had become *notorious* to many of those around him. We have written evidence, in the ancient *Book of Adam*, which shows Cain as the son of the Serpent; as well as shows that there were *more* people around at this time (beyond Adam and Eve). At the time of Cain's birth, Eve reportedly had a *midwife*: a woman used to assist her in a child's delivery.[51] This midwife, somehow, was able to sense *the real truth* about Cain from the get-go.

Soon after his birth, the young lad began to mature - incredibly fast.

> *He fell into the hands of the midwife and (at once) he began to pluck up the grass, for in his mother's hut grass was planted.* - *Book of Adam* 21.3a[52]

Even as a baby, he was said to have gotten up, grabbed a blade of grass, and then gave it to his mother! According to other ancient sources, he was able to get up, possibly even *walk*, not too long after his birth. All of this was miraculous - "angelic-like."

> *Some interpreters apparently understood that the baby Cain was born with abilities well beyond his years.* (Kugel, 1997, p. 85)[53]

Whatever the situation, here; the wondrous acts of baby Cain could have been a prelude to how *good* of a farmer Cain would eventually become (and, possibly, *more*, as we'll see).[54] Let's take that blade of grass he supposedly picked up, and gave to his mother: as we'll soon see, this "blade" could have also been some type of *reed*, *stick*, or *stalk*. Interestingly enough, a stick, according to some ancient texts, was the exact weapon Cain would use to commit murder![55] Could these acts, as a baby, show everyone around Cain what might, eventually, become elements of his own destiny, *later on*?

Interestingly enough, this is also where we get some of the *other* meanings for the name *Cain*: "acquired" and "possession." Soon after his birth, Cain wanted to *possess* whatever was around him. Right off the bat, he grabbed for a blade of grass. We'll soon see that Cain would be *grabbing* for a lot more, later in life - attempting to *seize almost everything and everyone* he could, around him![56]

Back to our story: once this midwife saw Cain's attempt to grab this stalk, she quickly sensed something about him, and his character. She, then, made an interesting interpretation at this very point, in regards to his future stay on this earth:

> *The midwife replied to him (Cain) and told him, "God is just that he did not at all leave you in my hands. For, you are Cain, the perverse one, killer of the good, for you are the one* ***who plucks up*** *the fruit bearing tree, and* ***not*** *him who plants it. You are the bearer of* ***bitterness*** *and not of sweetness." And the power (an angel) told Adam, "Remain by Eve until she had done with the infant what I have taught her."*
>
> \- *Book of Adam* 21:3b-21:3c[57]

Wow, an angel of the Lord had to come, and intervene between the two. What a story we have here. The midwife was so set on what she sensed that an angel had to tell Adam to remain by his wife; as well as watch over Cain. Now, why would God have to *already* take some kind of action to protect Cain? Maybe the midwife already understood *who* Cain was, *who* he was **really** from, and what he was going to be in the future. She knew already he was *of the Serpent*, and wanted to destroy him instantly!

As we'll see, there may have been reasons for her deadly thoughts.

And Adam Begat…

We have another Biblical "proof" of Cain's significance to the **Serpent's** seed line. When we look at Biblical references to the genealogy of Christ, we'll see: "so-and-so *begat* so-and-so." The word *begat* simply means, "so-and-so male had a son from his own seed." The Bible states things, in a way, to *assure* the reader there wouldn't be any doubt - there wouldn't be any *doubt* to one's own offspring! Interesting, though, the word *begat* was first mentioned in the Bible - **not** with Cain or Abel - but with Adam's son ***Seth*** (Gen. 5:3)! Nowhere in Scripture does it state that Adam *begat* either Cain or Abel!

Adam's son *Seth* was also the first son - according to the Bible - who looked *similar* to Adam, as a baby (Gen. 5:3)! These facts could easily lead us to believe that Cain and Abel were not *begat* by Adam - even according to the Bible! If they weren't *begat* by Adam, then ***who***? The ancient, written evidence for the **angelic** significance of Cain's birth seems to be coming more and more apparent, now.

Adam and Cain also seemed to have had differences, on a number of *other* levels:

> *…Adam **(is) not (cursed)**, but the earth is cursed because of him, lest the curse should **pass over** upon the just who are of his seed, as from Cain, **who was cursed, upon** his seed.* - *Barhebraeus* Gen. 3:17[58]

In other words, God wasn't exactly happy with this sexual situation between Eve and the Serpent; and was even more upset when Cain was born - because he would be trying to infiltrate other people around him! And, regarding any of the curses now upon the earth: Cain and his generations would probably find it somewhat *harder* to overcome a lot of the negativities now present in our world, compared to Adam, his generations, and the rest of the planet (as a result). God did not want human beings and these terrestrial angels to mate. That was not part of His "kind-after-kind" plan of human reproduction in this world. But, now, the devil also *begat* on this planet - throwing the first monkey-wrench into what was once God's magnificent, almost-perfect recreation.

Regardless, being of Cain's blood, or seed line, wasn't in any way meant to be a death sentence, here; one just might have to be a little more careful, and maybe even work a little harder, at life (because of God's anger). Even though God may have not wanted these offspring on the planet, He still is a loving God. Even these offspring could do right by God… if they wanted to. Now, we'll see one such person of this particular blood line, and how he was able to *do* just that.

Twin Sons, Plus a Whole Lot More

> *These folk recount another tale, according to which, they say, the* ***devil*** *came to Eve and united with her as a* ***man*** *with a woman and begot on her Cain* ***and Abel****... For, they say,* ***they*** *were physically begotten from the* ***devil's*** *sperm...*
>
> \- *The Archontics According to St. Epiphanius* 40.5.3-4[59]

As we'll see, the Serpent could have sired **Cain**… *as well as* **Abel**. Ancient sources tell us that, in early times, when human beings were born, they were often born as *twins*.[60] Could these two characters of the Bible also be twins - both sons of a fallen, angelic being?[61] We recall our Biblical interpretation:

> Gen. 4:
> 1 *And Adam* ***eventually acknowledged the distinguishing sign*** *that had come upon Eve; that she* ***was with child****, and* ***realized*** *she was about to give birth to Cain, and, after the birth, she said, I have gotten a man through an angel of the LORD.*
> (in retranslation)

The next verse follows with:

> Gen. 4:
> 2 *And she* ***again*** *bare his brother Abel.*

The word *again* could easily signify, "without **adding** any further qualification as in the case of Cain."[62] In other words, the two births did not need to be noted any differently because were not **different**. The word *again* could also mean to "add," "augment," or "continue on." Interestingly, one ancient Jewish Rabbi stated:

> *...as it is said, "And she conceived, and bare (**with**) Cain" (Genesis 4:1). At that hour she had an additional capacity for child-bearing (as it is said), "And she **continued** to bear his brother Abel" (ibid. 2).* - *Pirke deR. Eliezer* XXI[63]

In other words, Eve's labor, here, could have been "augmented," or "continued," at this time - continued by Abel's *birth*.[64] Could both have come out of the womb at the same time? Were they twins?

Let's look at the above verse again, inserting these other, possible Hebrew meanings:

> *And she **continued on** with the birthing process, and bore his brother Abel.*
> - *Gen.* 4:2 (in retranslation)

Abel, obviously, then, would have been *another* offspring of Eve and the Serpent.

> *No wonder that **Abel**... meant "serpent shining" and that Cain was thought to be of serpent descent... According to Hyde Clarke and C. Staniland Wake in Serpent and Siva Worship, Abel (Mbale) and Cain (Kane/can) are names given to elder and younger brothers. Abel resolves into **Ab** (Snake) and **El** (God/shining)...*
> (Gardiner, 2006, p. 18)[65]

And, according to the Bible, it was in *the process of time* that Cain and Abel were required to make an offering unto God (Gen. 4:3). In other words, Cain and Abel were required to give an offering, once *they both reached a certain age*. The Bible seems to infer they both did their sacrifice on the same day![66] So, if they would have come to age on **the same day**, logic dictates they probably were born on the same day! That's exactly what the Bible seems to say, here - and reason enough to conclude that they were born together, on the same day; *and* from the same seed.

One Father - Different Attitudes

Ialdabaoth... The first and chief ruler... Called... ***Samael***
(a.k.a. Sammael or the serpent)...
Abel. A ***just*** *son of Ialdabaoth and Eve.*
Cain. An ***unjust*** *son of Ialdabaoth and Eve.*
- *Secret Book According to John* Mythic Char. II- III[67]

As we see, the two probably could have been of the same father; but, now we see they didn't necessarily *act* the same. One ancient name for Cain was *Adiaphotos* - "full of light." As we know, Cain had this bright countenance from birth… makes sense. Abel, on the other hand, was also known as *Amilabes* - "well-minded."[68] Could it be that Abel, **even though** he was a seed of the Serpent, *still* could have managed to be a just and worthy person?

Cain was certainly not the prophesized seed; neither was Abel (because they both had blood of the Serpent). Yet, the two seemed to have been different - on so many levels:

According to Dr. Keith Bertrand of the Department of Theriogenology. University of Georgia, the blood of the mother never mingles with her child, the blood of twins ***do*** *intermingle. This it is possible that Abel might well have had some of the seed of Satan in him, and this may also be a reason why Almighty God saw so it that he did not produce any "questionable" Seed Line.*

("Star Wars - Lesson Eight", n. d., p. 4-5)[69]

Although he may have been a very righteous individual, this was the obvious reason Abel couldn't carry on the Holy seed line of Adam - he needed to be of this direct seed of Adam. Regardless, that doesn't mean that he couldn't be in God's favor, and accepted by God! Abel *chose* to do right - he utilized his free will and wanted to honor God in positive ways. Interestingly enough, this gives us absolute proof that, no matter who you are - even a **son of the Serpent himself** - you can ***choose*** to follow a proper path, if you want to! Anyone could be in God's favor - if they *choose* to!

Seeing Abel rising in the ranks of God's favor, Cain began to have a sullen, bad attitude. He went *out* from the presence of the Lord - both symbolically *and literally* - to do things his *own* way; to try to dwell in areas where he thought he could be more alone… and more away from God.

> *...even by the same father, different kinds of seeds can come forth out of the same womb. It will either be a spiritual seed of God or a religious seed of the devil. One will believe every word and promise of God, the other will despise God's word and make His promises of none effect. The twins of Isaac and Rebekah (Jacob and Esau, for example) showed a type of what could come forth...*
>
> (Gan, n. d., p. 17)[70]

Cain started out on a different course in life: Abel, a lover of righteousness; Cain, wholly intent upon possessing worldly things, and wholly intent on absorbing whatever he could around him.[71] As with that blade of grass he wanted to possess (while a baby), Cain continued to want to possess whatever he could; even what other people might have had.

The Spark of Evil

Most of us already know, from the Bible, that Cain was the first murderer. Let's look at how this murder could have occurred, and the facts which surrounded it. Let's discover what went on in Cain's mind - to allow such a dastardly deed to take place!

> *After Adam and his wife sinned, and the serpent had intercourse with Eve and injected filth into her, Eve bore Cain. He had the shape from above and from below... Therefore, he was the first to bring* ***death*** *into the world, caused by his side, as he came from the filth of the serpent. The* ***nature of the serpent is to lurk*** *so* ***as to kill****, and his issue, Cain,* ***learned his ways****.* - *Zohar* Pekudei 21[72]
>
> *Of the* ***mixed multitude*** *it is written: "Now the serpent was craftier than any beast of the field" (Beresheet 3:1). Here, "craftier" means to do* ***evil*** *more than all the other animals... the members of the mixed multitude are the children of* ***the primordial Serpent*** *(a.k.a. the serpent of "****old****") that seduced Chavah (Eve) by the tree of knowledge, so the mixed multitude is indeed the impurity that the Serpent injected into Chavah. From this impurity, which is considered the mixed multitude,* ***Kayin*** *(Cain) came forth and* ***slew*** *Hevel (Abel)...* - *Zohar* Beresheet A28[73]

Not only was Cain physically *different* than Adam, the Adamites, and the pre-Adamites; he would become different in *thoughts*, *attitudes*, and *ways of life*. Cain seemed to have inherited some of the same personality traits as his father, the Serpent. The Serpent was cocky, imprudent, and self-absorbed; Cain began to act in these same ways, as well. These inherited tendencies would allow for the *ease* of Cain's readiness to act on improper thoughts he might have had! Cain's rationales could have easily led him to act in unpredictable ways, and in acts of violence.

> *Know then, that Cain was formed from the impurity... that drop which the serpent injected into Eve.* (Eisenmenger, 1748, p. 197)[74]

The Child Destined for Sorrow - Abel

We, already, know a number of alternate meanings for the name *Cain*. Abel, on the other hand, has some too: his name could also stand for "breath," "mist," "nothingness," as well as "fading away" - all appropriate meanings for what, soon, would happen to him![75] A major reason, according to many ancient sources, Cain would become so angry and hateful against his brother would be over a woman. She was another element of our world that Cain wanted, desperately, to *possess*.

This woman was, in fact, said to be one of Cain's own sisters. One ancient source stated that: when Adam looked at Cain's face (as a newborn), he instantly began to conclude that Cain would be ill-tempered, later on in life.[76] He just felt it. One of Cain's sisters, however, was beautiful. She seemed to have a good-tempered face to Adam. This sister must really have been gorgeous; because she was even said to have looked like her mother, Eve.[77]

The opposite was for Abel. Adam seemed to see a good-tempered face. And, there were also sisters born which seemed to be ill-tempered, as well - just like Cain. Adam may not have been too keen about his sons marrying their own sisters; but it was permissible in the day. As a result, Adam began the process to unite each son with a "similar" sister - the two ill-tempered ones together; and two good-tempered ones together. Cain, however, wanted the **beautiful**, good-tempered sister for his own!

So, one major reason for Cain's continued aggression towards Abel, up to the murder, was probably because of this desire.[78] Cain, somewhere in his mind, began to take Adam's intention as some type of plot - to *disgrace* him, or make him feel inferior. He may have assumed Adam plotted against him *on purpose*. These insecure and utterly irrational interpretations, in his mind, were fueling his emotional *fire*.

Cain, as the Serpent, wanted things to go his *own* way.[79] Adam was the "father;" Cain the "son" - Cain should have **obeyed**. Regardless of how Cain felt, Adam tried to do what seemed right in his own mind; and still wanted to be fair to everybody. According to one ancient source, Adam even attempted to allow Cain a chance to *prove* himself worthy of the sister… through his up-and-coming sacrifice! If Cain's sacrifice proved to be a good one, then Adam may change his mind. But, it had to be *good* - what God wanted.

The time for their sacrifices was upon them. Adam could have set it all up as an opportunity for Cain to show him - and God - his true *character*. Let's see how it all panned out, and what Cain *actually* did.

Chapter 9

The Cockatrice

*"...out of the **serpent's** root shall come forth a **cockatrice**."*
- *Isa.* 14:29 (KJV)

a cockatrice (or basilisk) - *a legendary **serpent** or **dragon** with lethal breath and glance*[1]

Would this first son of the Serpent become, in a number of ways, the *successor* of his father?[2] Let's see.

The Sacrifice

The up-and-coming sacrifices of Cain and Abel would determine Adam's decision - whoever cared enough about their *own* sacrifice, and about the law that God had given them, would not only have the satisfaction of doing things right, but also get the beautiful and good-tempered woman as wife.[3] This was Cain's proving ground.

Yet:

...Abel was a keeper of sheep, but Cain was a tiller of the ground.
- *Gen.* 4:2 (KJV)

As we've stated, there were signs around Cain, even at his birth, which indicated he might be a good tiller of the ground in future times. We remember that, after being born, Cain picked up a piece of vegetation, and gave it to his mother (as if he had some natural *inkling* towards the earth). Abel, on the other hand, would end up leaning towards a sheep herding career. Thus began a world of difference between the two brothers; not only in lifestyles, but, now, **in their *sacrifices***, as well.

Hence Cain assisted in production of food for the primeval family, while Abel's duties were concerned with their religious services and clothing.

(Pember, 1975, p. 118)[4]

Now, it was the time for each to give a sacrifice - a **blood** sacrifice. *Blood*, even back then, seemed necessary for the *remission* of one's sin. It seemed important - at least to God![5] Cain, however, began to think his sacrifice could be done his *own* way - using whatever elements *he* wanted to add! His thoughts, now, were beginning to betray him.

At the time of the sacrifice, he thought it would be good to put some of his *vegetables* out. Why not? He grew them… that would be fair showing of his labor. It looked good to *him*. Abel, on the other hand, did what he was instructed - he slaughtered a lamb, and (as messy as it all might sound) poured the lamb's blood on the altar. Let's look at what the Bible says happened next:

Gen. 4:
3 *And in the process of time it came to pass, that Cain brought of the fruit of the ground an offering unto the LORD.*
4 *And Abel, he also brought of the firstlings of his flock and of the fat thereof. And the LORD had respect unto Abel and to his offering.*
5 *But unto Cain and to his offering he had not respect.*

Topping it off, Cain went to his sacrifice with a *haughty* attitude. He strutted on the scene, assumed *his* ways were right, and presented whatever he felt was just. With his Serpent-like pride, he may have even concluded that he was *entitled* to some sort of acceptance - *just* for doing it! He made the effort… and he should get something out of it (according to him)! Was he just acting like his father, here?

Abel, the younger, had respect for ***justice*** *and, believing that God was with him in all his actions, paid heed of* ***virtue****… Cain, on the contrary, was thoroughly* ***depraved*** *and had an eye* ***only to gain****…*

\- *Falvius Josephus* Jewish Antiquities 1:53-54[6]

…one of them exercises a business, and takes care of living creatures, although they are devoid of reason… but the other devotes his attention to ***earthly*** *and* ***inanimate objects****.* - *Works of Philo Judaeus* Questions and Answers on Genesis 1(59)[7]

The two seemed to have different *very* approaches to life; and *two* entirely different outlooks, here. Cain's was one of pride, feelings of superiority; and contempt for anything that seems to stand in front of him. Cain put out his vegetables and thought: "good enough." According to one source, Cain even *ate* the best of the flax (i.e. his vegetable sacrifice) he was to put out; and then left the *rest* to God.[8] How about that for reverence? How about *that* for obedience - obedience to the God who created you? There were major flaws in Cain's own perception of reality, and in life… and what *really* might be right or wrong.

His self-serving philosophies, in the end, wouldn't hold up for him, very well.

As though his offense had not been great enough in offering to God fruit of the ground which had been cursed by God! (Ginzberg, 1909, p. 107-8)[9]

Here, Cain's offering to God was of the very ground that God *cursed* in the first place! According to another source, Cain decided to allocate *the poorest* of his grains to God; or even *grains he trampled under his feet*![10] No wonder his sacrifice was going to be abhorred, and rejected.

Cain ***became*** *tiller of the ground, and, therefore, had* ***reason*** *to feel the curse in all its bitterness.* (Pember, 1975, p. 118)[11]

Cain's outlook on the world was *so* strange, compared to other people around! Cain enjoyed the *material* things of a cursed ground. He was too *proud* to follow anyone else's instruction. Cain's free will told him what he should do, and what his sacrifice should be. This was the first outward act of self-indulgence in our world - trying to please *one's own self*, over God; and looking to other things *of our world* for gratification and fulfilment. Cain thought there was nothing wrong with this, however.

"(Cain speaking to God)… according to ***my*** *righteous labors have I offered it to you."*
- Armenian Apocryphal Adam Literature Abel and Cain 9[12]

These "ways" - obviously *not* of God - would become the essence of something God universally hates: **idolatry**; or the act of putting other people, places, or things *above* God (including one's own self)!

Abel, on the other hand, did the opposite of Cain: he took the *best* of his lambs; turned it into a blood sacrifice; and made sure things were exactly how God wanted - all with the most important element of the sacrifice... a sense of humility, reverence, and overall love for his Creator! Cain offered haughtily; Abel offered with humility.[13] As a result, Abel's sacrifice was going to be accepted.[14]

A "Black Heart" - And a Whole Lot More?

And Cain was very wroth, **and** *his* **countenance** *fell.*
- *Gen.* 4:5 (KJV)

What happened next to Cain comes without any definitive written evidence - although a lot of different scriptural texts attempt to make some sense of what was about to happen. Theories abound on how God responded to Cain, for his actions.

It was now time for God to react to each sacrifice, individually. Abel's, obviously, went well:

Immediately a gentle breeze blew, and a light shone from heaven and illuminated the face of Abel. - *Armenian Apocryphal Adam Literature* Abel and Cain 12[15]

Something was going on, in Cain's world - something was about to happen to a person who almost continually assumes *his* ways are right:

A black cloud came over Cain's bundle (and) it thundered, and dust came forth from it, (and) it caused everything (to be) blown by the wind. It scattered the bundle, and destroyed everything.
- *Armenian Apocryphal Adam Literature* Abel and Cain 10[16]

There was definitely a different response, in regards to God's feelings, here. One common theory on what happened to Cain revolves around the following: if God was pleased with the sacrifice, burning fire would come down from the heavens, and consume it! The rising of burnt smoke, soon after, was considered the symbol of God's acceptance! God smelled the sweet savor (or smoke) of Abel's sacrifice, for example, and was pleased - the smoke rose up to the sky. With Cain's half-hazard attempt, however, the fire of God's approval did not come down to consume his sacrifice - it did just *the opposite*. The fire descended, and smoke did *not* go up into heaven. Instead, it went all around Cain, almost suffocating him to death! The diversion of this smoke clearly signified God's utter rejection.[17]

Everything around Cain "became dark." Many sources, here, state that Cain's face and body also became *blackened*, in a way, by the smoke.[18] It was somewhat like those other **angels** who had fallen around the time of Adam, as we recall - they all were "burnt." We are not sure if these angels were burnt to a crisp, or just, somehow, changed in their appearance. With Cain, however, he was not burnt to a crisp, and destroyed. As we'll see, this *blackening* of Cain could now have been looked upon in direct *contrast* to his once "heavenly-like" splendor. Once he had a bright countenance; now it was all gone.[19] At the very least, Cain, most probably, lost his heavenly shine; and began to look like every other human being around him.

It may even have gotten worse for Cain.

> *...in fact, it has been noticed in our day that men* ***who have lost the spirit*** *of the Lord, and from whom his blessings have been withdrawn, have turned* ***dark*** *to such an extent as to excite the comments of all who have known them.*
>
> ("Juvenile Instructor, Vol. 26", n. d., p. 635)[20]

This *darkness* of Cain could have been Cain going through some sort of transformation - being "darkened" on the outside, if you will; but there isn't too much ancient written evidence - beyond speculation - to back this up. But, there is another possibility to all of this: Cain could have become *blackened*, not really on the outside, but **on the inside**… a reflection of his *inner* character! This *darkness* of Cain's thoughts and attitudes could have become a great deal more noticeable to himself, as well as everyone around him. His *true* colors began to be revealed at this time - due to whatever emotional *blow* he might have felt, as result of his rejection. This theory seems to lead us back to the Bible:

> *And the LORD said unto Cain, Why art thou* ***wroth****? And why is thy* ***countenance*** *fallen?* - *Gen.* 4:6 (KJV)

After his sacrifice was rejected, God himself asked Cain why his countenance had "fallen". Assuredly, his shine - his heavenly, angelic countenance he once had - was now lost. His spirits also must have been "down in the dumps" - humiliated, depressed, and even enraged. Whether Cain *now* had a darkened, outer appearance still remains under conjecture.

The reason we get into this topic will, soon, be made clear. There would be those - in the ancient past and no-so-ancient past - who might want to claim that this was the point where Cain was physically turned "black as coal" - equating him with those, today, who have darker skin color:

> *He beat Cain's face with hail and blackened it like coal, and thus his face remained black.* - *Armenian Apocryphal Adam Literature* Abel and Cain 10[21]

It's understandable, based on reading texts such as the above - until we remember how the ancients probably wanted to describe *emotions*, among other things, within people; and probably had a hard time doing so. Could this "blackness," above, not really be describing Cain's skin color, but his *sullenness*; his permanently *negative* demeanor, now written all over his face, as result of his rejection. Why do we postulate this? Because, there are, actually, a number of *other* ancient texts which claimed Cain was not really *blackened* on the outside - he had blonde hair, ivory skin and a yellow beard… his blackness, indeed, only internal.

We easily could assume, though, that Cain was about to develop a "black" heart, as a result of his attempt… but it *was* his fault. Cain fell from God's grace because he wanted to do things his *own* way; and really didn't seem to care about any of God's ramifications for his actions. Maybe Cain was "turning a corner" - not learning the lessons that most other people around him might have learned, by now.

> *(God)... sent down smoke so that his face became dirty with soot. But Cain was **not ashamed** at God's displeasure.* (Frankel, 1989, p. 37)[22]

Instead, Cain seemed to move towards the *opposite* extremes of where he should be heading, *in his mind.*

Cain's Anger

God already knew that Cain was beginning to develop *darkened* thoughts and attitudes within himself; and He, then, confronted him:

> <u>*Gen.* 4:</u>
> 6 *And the LORD said unto Cain, Why art thou **wroth**? And why is thy countenance fallen?*
> 7 *If thou doest well, shalt thou not be accepted? and if thou doest not well, sin lieth at the door. And unto thee [shall be] his desire, and thou shalt rule over him.*

Obviously, the "evil inclination" and other worldly temptations were crouching at the door to Cain's *now-blackened* heart.

> *"(God speaking)... I have placed in your hand control over the evil **inclination**, and you shall rule over it, whether for better or for worse (whether to be guilty, or innocent)."* - *Genizah Manuscripts* Gen. 4:7[23]

> *And into thy hand have I delivered the power **over evil passion**, and unto **thee** shall be the inclination thereof, that thou mayest have authority over it to **become righteous**, or to sin.* - *Targum Pseudo-Jonathan* IV[24]

Although Cain could have chosen what was right, he openly began to accept those negative thoughts on the *inside*.[25] Unlike Abel, he seemed to begin to follow those attributes of his blood-born ancestor. Cain soon would set aside his inner restraints, and began to allow the Serpent's anger, envy, wrath and pride to continually penetrate his mind - leading him down into more of a *permanent* path of acting on negative attributes.

The Wrath of Cain

Now we see that there are still other meanings for the word *Cain*: "as nought" and "the wrathful one."[26]

> *Do not reveal to Cain the secret plan which you know, for he is a* ***son of wrath****.*
> - *Book of Adam* [23]3.2[27]

No matter what circumstances were in front of Cain, the denial of his sacrifice angered him to the utmost. He lost out; and didn't want to blame himself. Cain went to Abel about his situation, and openly griped:

> *...**I** perceive that the world was created in goodness, but it is not governed according to the fruit of good works, for there is respect to persons in judgment; therefore it is that thy offering was accepted, and mine not accepted* ***with good will****.*
> - *Targum Pseudo-Jonathan* IV[28]

Cain further griped about it - according to his *own* point of view:

> *...I perceive that the world was not created in* ***mercy*** *and that it is not being conducted according to the fruits* ***of good words****, and that there is* ***favoritism*** *in judgment.*
> - *Targum Neofiti* Gen. 4:8[29]

> *...nor will good reward be given to the* ***righteous****, nor vengeance be taken of the wicked.*
> - *Targum Pseudo-Jonathan* IV[30]

Continually assuming he knew it all, Cain continued: "The entire process is not fair."

Explaining his statement, Cain began with this argument: "We're all the same; our sacrifices were both the same, *overall* - mine was just not accepted for some unfair reason." Abel, however, did not agree; and had honest words for his brother: "Mine was accepted because I love God; yours was rejected because you hate Him."[31] Abel told him the *real* truth, and why his sacrifice wasn't accepted. Cain, however, didn't appreciate this honesty. He didn't want to hear the truth. It only prompted Cain to more and more *anger* - which allowed him to eventually *act* on these inner, *blackened* emotions.[32]

Now, it seemed, was the time for Cain to take action. According to one source, he was so upset with Abel he arrogantly blurted: "If I were to slay you today, who would demand your blood from me?" Abel, confident in his answer, replied: "Surely God will know your hiding place and will judge you for the evil you have proposed to do today!"[33] Another source stated that Abel already knew Cain was set out against him, and hid away. Once Cain learned of it, he sent word to the other people around him, and asked them to find Abel… and tell him everything was all right. Cain obviously lied to the people, and told them he abandoned any of his negative thoughts and emotions. This deception allowed him to catch up with Abel again, and confront him one final time.[34]

Once he caught up with his brother, down in some near-by valley, he used the same *subtleness* his father used to achieve *his* true intentions.[35] His rage slowly began to overtake him. And, in the middle of verbal confrontation, he began to show more of a *violent* side; wrestling Abel down. They both fell to the ground. Abel, however, quickly overpowered Cain, and jumped on top of him - Cain cried out, helplessly, underneath.

Some sources suggested that Abel, naturally, was stronger than Cain, and more powerful. Another source stated that God was watching out for Abel, the same as He did for Adam; and notified Abel that something was about to happen. God also may have encouraged Abel to severely *beat* Cain, if he ever got in this situation. The interesting parallel here is that: Adam fell because he listened to God; but listened to **Eve *more***. As we'll soon see, Abel probably did ***the same***, here! Both Adam and Abel didn't trust God enough. And, they both acted on decisions which were open to *their own interpretation*!

Upon hearing Cain's plea for mercy, Abel did what he thought was the *just* and *human* thing to do - he *compassionately* released his hold over Cain, now. While on top of him, Abel could have easily halted Cain's attempts of violence; but he didn't stay there. It was possibly the choice which cost Abel his life.[36]

This was Cain's opportunity to act on his twisted motives.

Lord Byron makes Lucifer say to Cain:
"First born of the first man
Thy present state of sin - and ***thou art evil****"...*
(Bristowe, 1927, p. 4)[37]

The Murder Occurs

This ***evil*** *in Cain (which destroys alike soul and body)* ***caused*** *him to kill Abel.*
- Yalkut Hadash[38]

First, adultery came into being, afterward murder. And ***he*** *was begotten in adultery, for he was* ***the child of the Serpent****. So he became a murderer,* ***just like his father****, and he killed his brother. Indeed, every act of sexual intercourse which has occurred between those unlike one another is adultery.* *- Gospel of Philip*[39]

The murder of Abel would be no accident. Cain took advantage of his brother's mercy and took a stick (or reed), a rock, or another tool, and hit, and hit, and *hit* Abel. He did whatever he could to kill another man. Another source stated that Cain could have even *bit* his brother like an *adder* (again, "like father, like son?").[40]

And Cain talked with Abel his brother: and it came to pass, when they were in the field, that Cain rose up against Abel his brother, and ***slew*** *him.*
- *Gen.* 4:8 (KJV)

One source stated that Cain was even able to tie up Abel with a grapevine, because he had difficulty finding how to kill him smoothly - after all, no one really killed anyone else before this; so he wasn't sure. He still was intent on accomplishing the deed, however. He spent over an hour hitting him with his weapon, anything to finally end his life![41] Another source stated that he used a sharpened rock, and stabbed Abel directly in the forehead.[42]

However it was finalized, Abel fell down, paralyzed with pain. As he was lying there, dying, he uttered a request:

*...while he was slaughtering him Abel said "I am gone out of the world, but you **gain** the heart of our parents."*
- *Armenian Apocryphal Adam Literature* Abel and Cain 33[43]

Cain didn't care. Good riddance. He, indeed, took *possession* of a lot more than his sister on that day.

After Cain eventually killed his brother, Abel's blood spilled all over the ground. Cain tried to hide his body, somewhere in the earth, and flee the entire scene. He didn't do a very good job at hiding it, however. The people around him found out what happened, and became very upset. God also knew (obviously); and was about to confront Cain.

Some of Cain's inner thoughts were of remorse. Yet, the majority of his thoughts were bent on helping him achieving a means to his *own* ends. In fact, he was somewhat *glad* he did it:

When he killed his brother, he went away cheerfully.
- *Armenian Apocryphal Adam Literature* Abel and Cain 34[44]

His Twisted Outlook

God would have none of this; and confronted Cain. A conversation arose

And the LORD said unto Cain, Where [is] Abel thy brother? And he said, I know not: [Am] I my brother's keeper? - *Gen.* 4:9 (KJV)

God knew he did it; and *Cain* knew he did it. In front of God, he *subtly* tried to get out of his shame with the "I didn't know" approach.[45] He also took the "victim" mentality position. He even started to act like a little child - and state that practically nothing was *really* his fault. In one excuse, he began to claim that he never saw a man die before, so how was *he* supposed to know the ways he struck a man could end his life? Despicable. Again, he said whatever *he could*, and did whatever he could, to try to weasel his way out of any responsibility. Everyone around him knew he really meant to do it, however.

Some people are truly sorry for their crimes; some people are only sorry when *they get caught* - these thoughts occur within a person's twisted, self-centered rationale. This was Cain… to a tee.

God wasn't about to buy it. His punishment was upon him:

> <u>Gen. 4</u>:
> 10 *And he said, What hast thou done? the voice of thy brother's blood crieth unto me from the ground.*
> 11 *And now [art] thou cursed from the earth, which hath opened her mouth to receive thy brother's blood from thy hand;*
> 12 *When thou tillest the ground, it shall not henceforth yield unto thee her strength; a fugitive and a vagabond shalt thou be in the earth.*
> 13 *And Cain said unto the LORD, My punishment [is] greater than I can bear.*

God patiently tried to reason with Cain, as with a willful child; but Cain was not about to accept any responsibility.[46] According to Cain, *God* was the one who was mean and unfair! He created the world. He did so much, here, in this world; yet He couldn't do anything as simple as overlook this one act? God banished Adam and Eve from the garden; and, now, He was about to banish Cain - how unfair of a God could He be? Couldn't God just absorb this *one* crime?

Cain could have tried to confront God, with an angle such as this:

> *"Thou bearest the whole world," he said, "and* ***my*** *sin* ***Thou canst not*** *bear? Verily, mine iniquity is too great to be borne! Yet, yesterday Thou didst banish my father from Thy presence, today, Thou dost banish me. In sooth, it will be said, it is* ***Thy way to banish****."* (Ginzberg, 1909, p. 111)[47]

God didn't care, according to Cain. With his twisted outlook on morality, Cain blurted out: "My punishment is greater than I can bear" (Gen. 4:13). This was probably not an admission of guilt; but proclaimed out, in a selfish, sarcastic manner! As we begin to understand how Cain's mind now began to work, his words were probably uttered for his *own* advantage. Here, he probably meant something more like: "My punishment is greater than I can bear - it's too much for *me.* God, how could you do this to *me*, anyhow? Why are you **so mean**? I can't handle this."

Cain, then, continued to reason within himself: "Is my iniquity *too great* to be forgiven by you, God?"[48]

> *My sins are too great to bear; but there is much [ability] before* ***You*** *to pardon and to remit.*
> - *Genizah Manuscripts* Gen. 4:13[49]

> *Nevertheless there is power before Thee to absolve and* ***forgive*** *me.*
> - *Targum Pseudo-Jonathan* IV[50]

When God confronted Cain, he said practically everything he could to divert the original cause of the problem: ***himself***. He did all he could to try to skew the original crime *he* committed; and to blunt the necessity for *any* punishment to be administered, here. Cain obviously never learned the value of **humility** (unlike *Adam*), as well as *introspection.*[51]

The Ultimate Complainer

> *When Cain saw that God had accepted his brother's sacrifice and not his, he began to* ***mock*** *God before Abel. "What an unjust God this is who rules strictly by* ***whim****! See, your sacrifice has been chosen over mine for no good reason! And to think that I used to believe that God ruled the world fairly!"* (Frankel, 1989, p. 37)[52]

Cain continued to go "off the deep end," in regards to his rationales; and continued to twist everything to the extreme. Cain eventually replied to God's request to subdue his anger, pride, and jealously… with a statement of blasphemy: "There is no **law** and no judge!"[53] In other words, "It *shouldn't* matter what we do - what we do is our *own* business. Nobody should judge me for just being **me**!"

He thought:

> *…(Cain speaking) There is neither Justice nor Judge; there is* ***no retribution*** *for the wicked* ***nor reward*** *for the just, nor is there another world.*
> - *Genizah Manuscripts* Gen. 4:8[54]

Wow, doesn't this sound similar to a lot of our *modern-day* thought? People, today, often seem so concerned with how *fair* something might be; or the emotional, or "compassionate," side of some story. A lot of progressive, democratic, and secular humanistic ideology seems to have basis in these same rationales.

Whenever he used these rationales, Cain's excuses started to become *vain* to God. It was getting old:

> *"This world was not created in* ***mercy****; neither is it* ***ruled by compassion****. Why else has your (Abel's) offering been accepted and mine rejected?"*
> (Graves and Patai, 1964, p. 91)[55]

> *"(Cain to God) What will people say of* ***You*** *when they see me... You will become known as a God who delights in exile!"* (Frankel, 1989, p. 38-9)[56]

Cain blamed his situation; he blamed God; he blamed almost everything and everyone *else* around him… but *himself*.[57] Doesn't this sound like a lot of people around us, today? Doesn't this sound like how so many people work, to get around guilt and personal responsibility? Would this "victim-mentality" be the antidote that Cain would utilize, in order to save himself?

We have an interesting commentary about those who eventually think with a lot of these same ways, today… and what their rationale *really* points one towards:

> *(You have) no reason to feel guilty. Your heart continues to tell you that you are the center of the universe. Your problems are somebody else's fault. This world owes you happiness. You are basically good and unselfish. You'll be happy if you get what you want. You will be happy when you follow your own heart...* ***You are under a curse****.*
> ("Have We Gone the Way of Cain?", n. d., p. 6-7)[58]

Could these ways of thought, those we see so often today - have originated from **this "seed of the Serpent?"** Could these actually work to become a curse to the individual, *over time*? This is so important to understand!

Although Cain was guilty - and he, deep down inside, *knew* it - he *still* refused to confess his guilt. He refused to admit liability. He refused to accept responsibility;

because of what inner rationales began to *perpetuate* in him. He, obviously, must not have had a lot of self-esteem (or worth); or else he would have been man enough to admit his faults. His pride caused Cain to leave out any honor, and integrity, within his thoughts/actions.

The Cynical One

The following, for example, is a style of thought which most probably originated with Cain himself: ***cynicism***. The name *Cain* is also considered the root of the word "Cynic," as well as "Canine."[59] Well; what do these mean? And, just what is *cynicism*?

cynical - 1. *distrustful of human nature: doubting or contemptuous of human nature or the motives, goodness, or sincerity of others.*
2. *sarcastic: mocking, scornful, or sneering.*[60]

The *Cynics* actually began as a Greek philosophical sect in the 4th century B.C. A disciple of Socrates was considered founder of the movement. These learned scholars were also known as *Canine* (or "dog-like"), by others in the ancient of times, because the **dog** was once symbolized as an animal who, apparently, had a **lack of shame**. These Cynics, then, "paraded their poverty, their antagonism to pleasure, and their indifference to others…" and they also "…rejected the social values of their time, often flouting conventions in shocking ways to prove their point."[61] In other words, they delighted in mocking other people and things; they enjoyed being scornful; contemptuous; and felt *superior* to others, in their own, vain ways.[62] Now, from what we already know about Cain, it's easy to see where these thoughts could have come from.

It is important to understand where people inherited certain ideals such as this, and what this means, in an overall construct. This *Cynic* movement - originating in **Cain** - is just one example of how we could peel back the deeper layers of what would be *Mystery Babylon*. We'll soon see how.

…historically speaking a connection between the words ***Cain****, Cynic and dog seems*

probable for, while the Epistle of Jude indicates that the evil character of Cain's later life was known to the Apostles, St. Paul and St. John head their lists of ***evildoers*** *with the word "dogs," which one modern translator of the Bible has changed into "Cynics," a more convincing rendering than "dogs," for obviously* ***men*** *and not animals* ***are referred to****. Cain's wickedness... was thus vividly remembered in Palestine in the Apostles' time...* (Bristowe, 1927, p. 111)[63]

Philologists agree that the word "Cynics"... given to certain Greek philosophers in the first century A.D. came from the Greek word for dog and that those philosophers were so-called because they were "prone to fall back into ***animalism*** *pure and simple"...* (Bristowe, 1927, p. 111)[64]

Obviously, these Cynics, through their thoughts and actions, "outraged the dictates of common decency."[65]

"In the Old and New Testaments the dog is spoken of almost with abhorrence; it ranked amongst the unclean beasts; traffic in it was considered as an abomination." The Cynics of Greece were evidently ***proud*** *of their opprobrious title for they adopted a dog as their emblem or badge... "They believed that Cain derived his existence from the* ***superior*** *power and Abel from the inferior power."*
(Bristowe, 1927, p. 112)[66]

...and, just *who or what* would have been that "superior power" that ***Cain*** **drew from**? Would it be *the Serpent*, himself?

Cain: The First "Free-Thinker?"

It is interesting to note that the Jews spoke of Cain as "the first free-thinker"...
(Bristowe, 1927, p. 79)[67]

Some people, in the ancient, considered Adam the first "thinker." Other people, even some ancient Jewish religious leaders, considered it to be Cain. Why... a different way of looking at ancient times, maybe? Maybe, we now see that this gives us an example of a *division* which was emanating between people. There would be people who would think the cultural, political, and religious ideologies of one forefather as the first (or correct) "free thinker;" and others who'd think of *someone else* as the same. Let's see how this all probably originated; and how it all went down.

Yet, we see that God confronted Cain, and even directly told him the reasons behind *why* he killed his brother - yet, Cain still thought *differently* about it. All of their exchange began to go down to one's *perceptions* on reality; and how one *looks* at things. God told it *as it was*, and made sure he knew that he committed a crime.

> *You are not his keeper; why did you become his murderer?*
> - *Armenian Apocryphal Adam Literature* Repentance 49[68]

Cain mind had, now, become a barrier to his overall understanding; as well as his desire to participate in any reconciliation with God. Through all of Cain's twisted thoughts, throughout all of his rationale, Cain ultimately acted on Abel because of something he truly hated, and did not want to face: *the truth.*[69]

Abel and God both gave Cain some insights to dwell upon, however. And, whatever was deep, deep, inside of Cain would not go **away** that easily. He couldn't rationalize away *everything* in his mind, however. That was his one problem with his mental stand. He *still* had a conscience. So, all of what happened on this day would further complicate Cain's mind, from then on - and an internal *battle* would begin, within.

> *[God] offers him [Cain] an* ***amnesty****, imposing a benevolent and kindly law concerning the first on all judges - not that they may not destroy evil men, but that by hesitating a little and showing patience, they may cleave to mercy...* ***forgiveness is wont to produce repentance****.*
> - *Works of Philo Judaeus* Questions and Answers on Genesis 1(76, 82)[70]

Half a Dose of Regret

> *...the penitence of Cain... was not sincere. He was filled with remorse, but it was mingled with* ***envy*** *and hatred...* (Baring-Gould, 1881, p. 76)[71]

As we previously stated: a young boy, sometimes, is truly sorry for his disobedience; other times, he's only sorry that *he was caught*. He bitterly bemoans the severity of his punishment. God was hoping Cain would cry out, repent - at least feel a little guilty - so He could give him *some* compassion.[72] Instead, with Cain, the *opposite* was true.

Yet, from all of his attempts to provide all manners of excuses, Cain, ultimately, couldn't get away from truth bellowing inside of him:

> *Thus we (Adam and his brethren) walked in Light, but Cain and his brethren walked in darkness and anguish of soul. And Cain wrestled within himself, for the voice of Jehovah continued to call unto him, Where is thy brother whose blood crieth unto me from the ground for vengeance? To which Cain replied, Am I my brother's keeper? Nevertheless, he* ***knew*** *that he was lost in darkness and his mind was blighted and he became a fugitive and a vagabond in the earth, forever fleeing his memories and the* ***darkness*** *which pursued him and* ***grew within him****.*
>
> - *Book of the Generations of Adam* 5:11[73]

The above could also represent an example of how Cain became *further* darkened, via his own internal, negative progression. The guilt in Cain's mind began to entrench itself into his psyche. He probably developed great inner conflicts; and had to *further* twist his new thoughts - in order to rationalize away, almost every single negative feeling which might enter his mind. Some of these thoughts became *overwhelming* to him, at times.

The Curses Upon Cain

God, as we know, didn't buy his manipulation attempts. Cain had to show *some* responsibility - whether he liked it or not. He had to show *some* remorse. As a result, there *would* be punishment soon on the horizon. The time was high for Cain to understand his place in the murder - at least to a degree.

> *(Cain) shares in the responsibility for every soul that is wrongfully killed. That is because he was the first to institute killing.*
>
> - *al-Tabari: The History of al-Tabari - Vol. I: General Introduction and From the Creation to the Flood* Cain and Abel 144[74]

We know that Cain, at one time, was exceptionally good at farming. After this deed, interestingly enough, he and his descendants now seemed to be *cursed* from the ground - cursed *even more* than Adam and the rest of the planet was, from now on.[75] Farming just didn't seem to be profitable for Cain and his kin, anymore.

> *The first curse was the judgment of God on the sin of Adam. Although the ground would bring forth thorns and thistles, its strength to produce abundant crops was not removed (Gen. 3:18). The second curse was the penalty of Cain's sin for shedding the righteous blood of Abel... And Cain was placed under a curse in which the ground was* ***no longer*** *able to yield its crops as it used to be. The harvest which were once plentiful had become barely sufficient.*
>
> ("The Mark of the Wicked Ones", n. d., p. 7)[76]

Cain and his progeny would not be alone, however. It seems that God dictated the rest of the human race would, also, be at least *somewhat* cursed from the bountifulness that the earth had before... a *universal* remembrance of Cain's deed.

> *...May you be cursed... (upon) ground where you shed your brother's blood... (and) till the ground in toil and fatigue... And the earth will not give you its fruit, for with the blood of the righteous have you colored it.*
>
> - *Armenian Apocryphal Adam Literature* Repentance 51-54[77]

Cain, and his seed, would still be *the least* able to derive benefit from the earth, because of this universal punishment... *even if* they may have worked hard at contributing positively to the planet![78] In other words, this was a curse: Cain and his progeny would probably have a hard time **making the world a better place**, compared to other people... even if they *wanted* to. This ***curse* of Cain** - a curse on the earth - was established because Cain, according to God, was the one who first made the ground to drink *blood* - the blood of Abel; and *this* was a serious offense to God.[79]

Half of a Fugitive and Vagabond

> *You see the foolishness of Cain... he answered God rudely and did not confess, so that he might* ***make expiation*** *and be* ***justified*** *(for killing Abel)... O, the* ***beast****, how foolishly did he respond!*
> - *Armenian Apocrypha Relating to Adam and Eve* Adam and his Grandsons 17[80]

After a half-hearted apology, God knew that Cain's remorse really wasn't too sincere.[81] As bad as Cain's attitude was, as diluted as Cain's repentance was, God bent over backwards to try to take *anything* he said as a heart-felt apology. God gave Cain *so* much leeway; but Cain really didn't bite. In the end, the Lord could only go so far - punishment was due.

What a merciful God, anyhow - to do His best try to help out people, here - *even* a **son of the Serpent**. Yet, Cain, still, was not impressed:

> *Behold, thou hast driven me out this day from the face of the earth; and from thy face shall I be hid; and I shall be a fugitive and a vagabond in the earth, and it shall come to pass, [that] every one that findeth me shall slay me.* - *Gen.* 4:14 (KJV)

Even though Cain perceived God as being brutal for his reprimand, God still tried to give Cain credit for - at least *half* - of an apology. God originally destined Cain to become a fugitive **and** vagabond (i.e. a wanderer), throughout the earth.[82] God knew he was going to be wanted for murder by a number of people around him - just like a fugitive would. Ancient sources tell us the people of the day - even the *animals* around Cain - wanted vengeance for this first death![83]

> *...wherever Cain went, swords sounded and flashed as though thirsting to smite him.*
> (Baring-Gould, 1881, p. 73)[84]

> *Adam said to Cain "Go away! You will always be afraid and not safe from anyone you see." Everyone... who passed by him shot (insults) at him.*
> - *al-Tabari: The History of al-Tabari - Vol. I: General Introduction and*

From the Creation to the Flood Cain and Abel 144[85]

So, God ended up removing only *half* of Cain's punishment, here. Now, he was only to be a vagabond on the earth - to roam aimlessly around, and never be satisfied, wherever he planted himself.[86] God, also, would **not** allow Cain to be hunted down and killed for Abel's murder. He was to continue to roam the earth in this way, in order for him to *think* about what he had done; and have it eat away at his soul.[87]

This way he, most likely, would not find peace, rest, or any inner satisfaction until rectified himself for his actions.[88]

No peace for him, no rest for him, treading the blood-drenched ground.
(Baring-Gould, 1881, p. 70)[89]

God was continually fair, even though Cain certainly was not. Cain was truly in need of a change of heart - whether he thought he did, or not.

Cain's Nervous Trembling

He shuddered continually, and he walked upon the earth shaking incessantly, night and day. - *Armenian Apocryphal Adam Literature* Repentance 60[90]

As part of his punishment, God made Cain to tremble and shake upon the earth, all the time he walked about.[91] The ground seemed to "shake" continually under him, on account of it (at least it seemed that way to him).[92] In other words, his body was condemned to such a "shuddering" - non-stop, back and forth, and side to side - that he could hardly even sit down peacefully, or even bring his hand to his mouth accurately.[93] Another source stated that Cain "shook like a tree in the wind." He could not stand still, nor stay in one place, for extended periods of time. We, today, might notice somewhat of this same type of shudder in someone, today, who acts extremely *guilty* or *nervous*; or wanders to and fro - as if mentally unsettled, or unstable.

*And He (God) said to him, "Where is thy brother?" To which he answered and said, "I know not." Then the Creator said to him, "Be trembling and quaking." Then Cain trembled and **became terrified**; and through this sign did God make him an example before all the creation, as the murder of his brother. And also did God bring trembling and terror upon him, that he might see the **peace** in which he was at first, and see also the trembling and terror he endured **at the last**; so that he might **humble** himself before God, and repent of his sin, and seek the peace he enjoyed at first... God was not seeking to kill Cain with the sword, but He sought to make him die of **fasting** and **praying** and **weeping by hard rule**, until the time that he was delivered from his sin... as to Cain, ever since he had killed his brother, he could not find rest in any place...*

- *First Book of Adam and Eve (The Conflict of Adam and Eve with Satan)* 79:24-28[94]

*"Quaking and quivering shalt thou (Cain) be in the earth." That is, thy **soul shall shake**, and thy body shall quiver.* - *Barhebraeus* Gen. 4:12[95]

Condemned in this way was Cain because he showed God **no** nervousness or trembling when he engaged God in conversation. Adam shuddered and feared God when He was talking to him; Cain did not. Adam was not condemned to any further punishment because he gave God a show of respect. God now *made* Cain to shake and shudder - to act like he *should* have, all along! From now on, this shudder would become a constant reminder - to Cain - of his former acts of criminality and disrespect![96]

...with his feet and hands and every single limb he shuddered like a yew-tree.
- *Armenian Apocryphal Adam Literature* Abel and Cain 41[97]

...May you shake like a tree in the winds... May you be tossed like the sea which is agitated by the waves.
- *Armenian Apocryphal Adam Literature* Repentance 55-56[98]

He, from now on, shook like a leaf; he blew like the wind. Cain seemed, also, to be extremely *paranoid*; with **constant suspicion** and **mistrust** of others around him.[99] Because of these curses, his life had truly become miserable; with constant insecurities; and without inner peace.

He, outwardly, had become a reflection of his *inner* guilt and turmoil.

*...and God said to him, "Thou tremblest and art in fear; this shall **be thy sign**."*
(Baring-Gould, 1881, p. 74)[100]

More Signs Upon Cain

There were more curses to Cain; such as, from now on, he:

- *toiled*
- *groaned*
- *was removed from God*
- *did not **profit***[101]

He also developed:

- *a voracious hunger, never to be satisfied*
- *disappointment in every desire*
- *a perpetual lack of sleep*
- *a life where no man should either befriend or kill him*[102]

Cain apparently had a hard time dealing with the simple things in everyday life, from then on. He had issues going on, with his own, general feelings of satisfaction with life - constantly - whenever he tried to do things; and in regards to most of his perceptions about reality. Some ancient sources stated that, no matter how much he ate, he wasn't satisfied (for example).[103] Assuredly, this didn't happen only with his food. It probably occurred with most things he *touched* or *dealt with*: material things, interpersonal relationships, etc.. He continually came up short - in his own mind - on most everything he tried to accomplish in his life. Essentially: he was never really satisfied.

His life would resonate with misery and anguish, overall, because of this:

But when Cain killed Abel, Cain was stricken... (and) cried "Woe!" and "Alas" bitterly. - *Armenian Apocryphal Adam Literature* Abel and Cain 57[104]

Some ancient sources stated that he remained incurable; and even wished to die.[105] Cain could not sleep very well. Yet, all of these factors, regarding Cain, are important to this book's theme, as we shall soon see. They all give us insight into the very soul of Cain, himself; this ancient side of that "Days of Noah" parallel; and *Mystery Babylon.*

Nod - The Land of Wandering

> *And Cain went out from the presence of the LORD, and dwelt in the land of **Nod**, on the east of Eden.* - *Gen.* 4:16 (KJV)

It was now time for Cain to make his way in the new world he helped to fashion. God forced him to dwell in the land (or forest) of *Nod*; which stands for "restlessness," "wandering," or "exile."[106]

Now, to seal His promise upon Cain, God provided *one* more thing to Cain, as part of his punishment: his ***mark***.

The Prophecy for Cain

To stifle any change of plans, God not only delivered the prophecy of Genesis 3:15 to Adam and Eve, He also delivered a *warning* to anyone who interfered with Cain's punishment, here:

> *And the LORD said unto him, Therefore whosoever slayeth Cain, vengeance shall be taken on him **sevenfold**...* - *Gen.* 4:15 (KJV)

Simply, this stated that: if somebody interrupted Cain's penance, he and his generations would be *punished* for a very long time - seventy-seven of his subsequent generations! Again, this was actually an order of **protection**, by God - to stop angry people around him from killing him. God wanted to make sure *nobody* killed Cain before his time - to make sure he was to forever contemplate what he had done.

The Mark of Cain

And the LORD set a mark upon Cain, lest any finding him should kill him.
- *Gen.* 4:15 (KJV)

On top of his wandering and shuddering, on top of other punishments he was given, God gave him the famous *mark* - the **mark of Cain**. No one knows for sure what this mark was. We *do* know it seemed to have an effect on others around him - to make people recognize, avoid, and - most importantly - to **not** kill him.[107] The mark of Cain actually was for his own protection - to allow him to walk around, throughout the lands he crossed, without being overwhelmingly afraid.

Theories abound about what it was; but nothing's definitive. In one opinion, it was a physical mark or *brand*, somewhere on his body - much like a slave of ancient times would have had. Cain, according to some, may have been branded this way in order to designate him a special protégé of God - and God alone… a brand to make sure everyone around him understood he was a ward of God; and was "off limits," here.[108]

Another thought which naturally might arise, here, is: just *who* would God need to protect Cain from, if he, Adam, and Eve were the only people on the earth, at this time? The land he was destined to go - *Nod* - could even be a form of the word *nomad*.[109] Were there, possibly, *nomads* - or pre-Adamites - **already** in the areas Cain was destined to roam?

> *Interestingly, we have further scriptural "proof" of pre-Adamites in the Bible a mark was put upon him as a protection against those people. This shows that, although we may assume that Adam was the first man into whom God breathed a "living soul," he was* ***not the first human being*** *upon the earth.* (Bristowe, 1927, p. 15)[110]

A couple of other interesting thoughts about this *mark* abound.

The Cross

One way that God could have marked Cain, according to some, was to brand him with the letter "**T**" (or *Tau*). Possibly, this letter was placed on Cain left arm, or even his forehead.[111] As the last letter of the Phoenician and Hebrew alphabet, the *Tav* was considered to be a **cross**. From the word *Tav* comes the Greek word *tau*. This *tau* was said to have inspired another interesting concept: **crucifixion**.[112]

> *The killing of Abel... could not but suggest to early Christians a parallel to the crucifixion - indeed, the specific mention of Abel's "blood(s)" implied a typological connection to "the sprinkled blood" of Jesus...* (Kugel, 1998, p. 168)[113]

We're aware of the prophecy of Genesis 3:15. Could this *mark* - a mark placed upon this seed of the Serpent - have been a symbol of what would *eventually be the modem of Jesus Christ* (and how he would conquer death)? Could a symbol of what would be used to crucify Jesus - to "bruise the heel" of the Serpent's power, in the future - actually be this mark of Cain? It seems the future might have been laid out since the beginning of our world; we're not sure.

Another interesting thought abounds:

> *One ancient rabbi thinks Cain killed Abel with* **wood** *- this was what Christ was crucified on.* (Baring-Gould, 1881, p. 72)[114]

Also, a symbol of the ancient pagan god *Tammuz* was *the cross*.[115] We'll soon see, in the next chapter, that the origin of this pagan god was, most probably, Cain's *own brother **Abel***. Could this *cross*, then, also be a symbol of *Abel* - as far as some sort of justification for his own murder? And, *why* was Jesus destined to die on this cross of wood - in order to justify all of what happened early on, here, in the book of Genesis?

There is another famous interpretation of this mark.

The Horn of Power

Beyond the *Tav*, another interesting and popular interpretation of Cain's mark involves a *horn*: according to some, God caused Cain to be hairy on the outside, and gave him an animal's **horn** - placed on the middle of his forehead![116] It was able to blow as a bugle.[117] Some even suggested this horn continually announced, "Cain the fratricide is coming!"[118] So, by this, it would continually alert the people around him, and how they should get *away* from him.

According to some, Cain became spiteful, because of his mark; and tried to compliment this horn by wearing animal skins, as clothing.[119] In a weak attempt, it was Cain's way to try to further *intimidate* anyone else around him, and shoo them away from him (and, at best, to give him a little bit more self-esteem, assuredly).

In whatever ways Cain was now about to use his horn, here, please try to think about this: imagine what a humbling experience Cain would have felt, at least in the beginning - noticing how everyone around him would want to avoid him. There are other sources which identify his mark as some "wild, ghastly look."[120] All of it would have given Cain an unmistakable - and very negative - fanfare to any, and all, of those around him.

There was more:

> *The mark or token, placed on his forehead, is said by the Rabbinical critics to have been a* **horn** *which grew on his head when the curse was pronounced, or, according to others, the sign consists only in the sun becoming brighter. Both sayings have the same meaning, for the horns of the sun are his rays, and it is clear that after the slaughter of the dawn brother, the sun (or* **son***) driven forth to wander over the* **earth becomes brighter***... as his "horn is exalted".* (Rogers, 1884, p. 12)[121]

This "horn" could actually stand for something *more*: Cain, according to some ancient sources, was famous for wearing a *horned* helmet. Throughout his attempts to further intimidate those around him, Cain tried to strengthen himself, and also became a *warrior*, or **war-like** individual. Soon, Cain's horn would become a symbol of this *power*. And, as we'll soon see, he would use any of his newfound power to his advantage.

There, still, could have been another interpretation of this horn. This *horn*, as we've already found out, symbolizes power; but, now, we see it also can symbolize another *form* of power - a "power" located *inside* the human mind! Also known as the ***psychic function***, this was a power of understanding, and using, things *beyond our natural world…* to aid us in our everyday lives. Cain, according to some, may have either gathered knowledge from his father, or from other terrestrial angelic beings around him, or may *have* ***even*** developed some of this *psychic* ability on his own! Interestingly enough, these *horns* were often positioned on a person *exactly* where one might think an individual would harbor such psychic abilities as this - on the middle of their forehead!

The "Horn" of the Mind

Could God have bestowed upon Cain some of this p*sychic* power - the "third-eye," if you will - to be able to assist him in his own protection efforts?[122]

> *Intellectually, Cain was as smart and cunning as his father, the Serpent. He had not only inherited the evil traits from the wicked one, the devil, but was also full of* ***worldly wisdom****... with his intellectual shrewdness he would be able to escape unscathed... With the mark set on him, Cain must have been more* ***subtle*** *than his Serpent father. His intellectual and sagacious mind must have helped him to outwit his pursuers in many situations when he was being hunted.*
>
> ("The Mark of the Wicked Ones", n. d., p. 10-11)[123]

Now, this **mark** could also relate to his ability to understand insights and introspection beyond this world. Cain not only could become an expert in "the ways of the world," but also a master *in the* ***occult***.

God even may have even allowed Cain to become a *lot* bigger, and taller; in order to aid in his attempt to intimidate others:[124]

> *Cain, a white man endowed with* ***superhuman knowledge*** *and* ***physique*** *and*

*rendered **invulnerable** by some divine talisman.*

(Bristowe, 1927, p. 15-16)[125]

All of this could have helped Cain to escape any persecution, or any rush to judgment, by anyone around him - continually keeping him "one step ahead" of any of those who might want to go after him.

Cain, with whatever *mark* he inherited, would really not use it all *to improve himself*, or to *go on to become a better person* - but *really* go in some complete, opposite direction:

*...the sign was that when he was going forward, he was **thrust backward**.*

- *Barhebraeus* Gen. 4:16[126]

The "Abused" One - Not a Murderer

He (God) made him an example for murderers... He made him an example to penitents... the Lord made Cain a sign (to others)... of the fear that haunts a murderer (and) of the saving power of repentance, which Cain displayed, so that God did not put him to death immediately. - *Genesis Rabbah* 22:12 (and notes)[127]

Whatever happened to Cain, overall, he took it all in *a negative way*. The mark was meant to protect Cain. He, at first, took it as something horrible; *disrespectful* to his own ego. This, as we'll see, would become the usual thought pattern of those who begin to adopt his ways of thinking, as well:

*...the paradox is that you can't bear the **mark** of God's grace without it reflecting the **marks of sin**. God's (protective) seal upon us should make us appreciative. But I am almost sure that Cain **only saw** the negative aspect of his mark. He only saw that he was **marked** as a murderer.*

("Sermon: Have We Gone in the Way of Cain?", n. d., p. 8)[128]

*His punishment, however, **far from being** taken as a warning, only served to **increase his vice**.* - *Falvius Josephus* Jewish Antiquities 1:59-64[129]

Instead of remorse, here, Cain became even more rebellious.

He (Cain) would never let anybody walk over him, or take an insult, or allow anyone to besmirch his imagined "honor". ("The Mark of Cain", n. d., p. 6)[130]

These thoughts began to lay the footsteps of whom Cain would, ultimately, begin to follow.

The "Son of Perdition"

<u>perdition</u> - *a state of final spiritual ruin*[131]
complete and irreparable loss, ruin
loss of the soul[132]

Interestingly enough, there is a *son of Perdition*, known throughout the Bible. Just who was he? The definition of perdition, besides meaning "eternal damnation" or "Hell," could also represent the *above*.

If we look at the meaning of *loss*, we see it could also stand for, "the act of *losing* possession."[133] Interestingly, we recall one of the meanings of the name *Cain*: "possession." Now, as a result of his negative thoughts, as well as his desperate attempts to acquire things, he was *not* destined to gather as many *possessions* as he wanted - but quite the opposite. He, now, was destined to *lose* a lot of what he had, over circumstance and time… now, he was cursed to eventual, utter *perdition*!

Cain and the Serpent - The Same "Perdition"

…Cain, who had been led by the adversary to break the law, and the murdered Abel (and) the ***perdition*** *brought on him and given through* ***the lawless one****.*
- *Apocalypse of Abraham* 24:5-6[134]

…and Cain, that Son of Darkness who had become ***Perdition****… ministered in them mysteries of darkness, showing himself to be god through satanic powers.*
- *Book of the Generations of Adam* 9:6[135]

As we see, the Serpent was also known as:

...***perdition*** *personified, like Sheol (Hell) and Abaddon.*
(Jung, 1974, p. 155)[136]

We see, here, that ***perdition***, also, becomes an important link between Cain and his father: the Serpent.[137]

Generations Ripe for Destruction

Some other definitions of *perdition* are: "eternal misery," "destruction," or "ruin" - other trademarks of how Cain, and his eventual followers, would eventually begin to affect others around them.[138]

Why doth they brother's blood cry from under the altar against thee? Behold, is not his blood upon they flesh, a mark which shall not be eradicated until the end of time? Thou wicked Cain, thou art Perdition and thy deeds shall follow thee for from thee shall flow murder and bloodshed, wars and contentions, until the earth shall hide her face from the wickedness and pollution of mankind. Depart from before my face, for ***thine existence is a pollution*** *to the sanctity of this spot. Nevertheless, no man shall slay thee, for thou shalt live to see the full measure flowing from thine iniquity, until the final destruction of the darkness of this world.*
- Book of the Generations of Adam 5:8[139]

As we see, in the above, wars and contention seem to flow easily from Cain, his progeny, and his conformists. The word *contention* is defined as, "verbal strife, dispute, argument, controversy, a statement or point that one argues for as true or valid." Vines Expository Dictionary of New Testament Words says this about - what the Bible calls - that "Son of Perdition:"

...(the) "son of perdition" signifies the proper destiny of the person mentioned; metaphorically of men ***persistent in evil****... vessels of wrath* ***fitted themselves for "destruction"****... of professing Christians, really enemies of the Cross of Christ... of professing... adherents who shrink back into unbelief...*
("Vines Expository Dictionary, *Perdition*", n. d., p. 1)[140]

God's Prophecy Set Into Motion

We all know that Cain spilled blood. We know Cain killed someone for an improper reason. And, we know that God set up a prophecy for Cain - to stop any of those who might want revenge, for these reasons:

> *And the LORD said unto him, Therefore whosoever slayeth Cain, vengeance shall be taken on him* ***sevenfold***... - *Gen.* 4:15 (KJV)

We'll soon discover how Cain's descendants - through their tendencies towards *perdition* - would, most probably, be more *prone* to destroy other people, places, and things around them; as well, destroy their *selves*. Would Cain survive, in this environment, to be *able* to serve out his punishment - or would he, himself, *fall*; becoming a statistic of those around him who are more *prone* to *destruction*?

We know that Cain opposed whatever punishment he had, in a major way; and ended up trying to go in the *opposite* moral direction of where God wanted him to go. He used almost every tool he had; not to remain *humble* (as would *Adam*), but to magnify *his* ways of living and thinking. This arrogance, however, would not last forever.

We'll soon look at what Cain did to influence the world around him; and bring others into adopt his Serpent-based "ways." We'll also discover how there would be members of Cain's ***own* family** - those who adopted these ways of life - who would interfere with what God's intended to happen to him. This, in turn, would bring on *so* many more problems to Cain, to his descendants, and to the rest of the world.

Chapter 10

"Raising Cain" - Founder of an Ancient Religion and Empire

*Was not Cain the **foremost** of all the "wandering stars for which the **blackness** of **darkness** hath been reserved for ever?"* (Bristowe, 1927, p. 153)[1]

Cain, his soon-to-be descendants, and other conformists about him, would all seem to fall under the domain of these negative (i.e. *darkened*) ways of living and thinking. Many would go on to, at least in part, *fulfill* one element of the Genesis 3:15 Prophecy (the *Protoevangelium*) - there would be descendants of this Serpent who would go on, to be at *enmity* with Adam and his descendants. We'll soon begin to look at the pathways Cain took; where he ended up; and how he was able to influence so many people after him… to, largely, be *against* Adam and his seed.

We'll soon look at one side of this "great division" of the Garden - the side of Cain (and his father, the Serpent) - by looking at the political and religious *empires* he/they were about to establish.

The World - According to Cain

As we know, there are almost always two sides to every story - the same in this case. The Bible has one story - and opinion - of Cain, and a number of other ancient texts out there seem to have another. So much of the world's ancient *mythological* and *pagan* writings seem to point towards Cain - not in a negative outlook, overall - but in a *positive*. Not only that, we'll see that most of these prefer, and point towards, the adoption of what *he* would believe, and the "ways" he would follow… believe it or not. An interesting modern book - *The Parthenon Code* - gives us some interesting explanations of how most of these ancient pagan/mythological views compare to the Bible:

Ancient Greek religion, what we call mythology, tells the same story as the Book of Genesis, except from the ***point of view*** *that the* ***serpent*** *is the enlightener of mankind rather than our deceiver.* (Johnson, 2004, p. 9)[2]

The Judeo-Christian tradition says God is the measure of all things; the ***Greek religious system says man*** *is the measure of all things. Both stem from* ***the same source****.* (Johnson, 2004, p. 26)[3]

This last quote is, oh, so *important*. We now see an ancient *rift* - ***two*** *theologies* of belief beginning to develop! A lot of ancient mythological and pagan lore often seems to say things very similar to the same story of Genesis - but, from their *own* perspective.[4] So, according to *these* sources, we now find that Cain was not really the bloody murderer the Bible portrays him as; but, more or less, a *hero*. But; *why*? *Why* would there be an expanding valley of difference, ever growing between the two?

It all depends on the origins of the story - *who* was telling it:

Two of the most recent writers upon the Babylonian inscriptions unintentionally support… that the Genesis stories came down in 'two streams,' and also my theory that one stream came down through the descendants of Seth (a true son of Adam) and the other through ***Cain*** *in Babylonia.* (Bristowe, 1927, p. 13)[5]

We are already beginning to see a *division* - or *enmity* - between the seeds of the Serpent and the seeds of Adam. We are already beginning to see the Genesis 3:15 Prophecy (i.e. the *Protoevangelium*) starting to unfold, and manifest itself, here! Cain and the Serpent's (false) "ways" would, now, begin to challenge the ways of God, and what He wanted for this post-Fall world. The *valley* of directly opposing differences between the two had now begun.

The descendants of Cain, and other people associated with them, contributed a large part in this "reinterpretation" of many Bible stories we all know, now. We'll soon see, because of these *other* points of view, Cain was **not** going to be turned into the lowest common human denominator, but one he would become of **the greatest, "god-like" heroes** of antiquity!

This was evident, even thousands of years later, in *Gnostic* thought:

The Cainites (descendents of Cain) are sometimes called libertine Gnostics for believing that true perfection, and hence salvation, comes only by ***breaking*** *all the laws of the Old Testament. The violation of biblical prescriptions was, therefore,* ***a religious duty****... the Cainites did not look for salvation in the created world but rather* ***escape from it****. Their subversion of biblical stories allowed them to use Sacred Scripture to support their dualist view of existence.*

("Britannica Online Encylopedia, *Cainite*", n. d., p. 5)[6]

(A Cainite also was considered a) member of a ***Gnostic*** *sect mentioned by Irenaeus and other early Christian writers as flourishing in the 2nd century AD... (The ancient theologian) Origen declared that the Cainites had "entirely abandoned Jesus." (The Gnostic) reinterpretation of Old Testament texts reflected the view that Yahweh (God)... was positively evil because His creation of the world was perversely designed to* ***prevent*** *the* ***reunion*** *of the* ***divine element in man*** *with the unknown perfect God (i.e. the Serpent). The Cainites also* ***reversed biblical values*** *by* ***revering*** *such rejected figures as Cain, Esau, and the Sodomites, all of whom were considered to be* ***bearers*** *of an esoteric, saving knowledge (gnosis).*

("Britannica Online Encylopedia, *Cainite*", n. d., p. 5)[7]

The Bible, for example, referred to certain people of antiquity as "giants;" not only because they were physically large, but also by reason of how influential their evil deeds were! Their popularity made them so very popular - these apostate "giants." The Bible, for example, does not refer to Noah, and other Adamites, as physical "giants;" but some non-Biblical sources state that *Noah* was a giant - a "giant" of character and moral fortitude.

There are also some non-Biblical sources which state the *Adamites* of old were "giants" - and portrayed them in a very *negative* tone.[8] Instead of being the *protagonists* of the Bible (because of the most famous one among them - *Adam*), instead of being looked upon as wonderful, God-fearing beings, they were the *troublemakers* - the antagonists. We'll delve more of this, as time goes on.

Once people began to follow the *other* "ways" of life - those instigated by **Cain** - the decline in morality also began, on a *grand* scale. These two points of view, flowing down two separate, and often *opposite*, "streams," began to make things very difficult for the average individual to weed through all of this rhetoric - hard for them to *truly* say what happened to their ancestors, here. It also became harder for them to decipher what truly is right, and what truly is wrong. Opposing viewpoints, on a grand scale such as this, often makes it difficult for someone to understand history - and, to Cain and his kind, this was probably meant to be this way *by design*.

With enough study, however, we, for the most part, **will be able to conglomerate one *real* story**, out of the combination of these two streams of information. We have enough ancient written evidence to put most of these ancient pieces together - and *that* is a major theme of this book.

So, let's, now, begin to decipher the *untold* story of Cain, assembled from the four corners of the ancient, written world; and discover what ancient history, here, *truly* might be telling us!

Cain Did Not Wander for Long

We know that, after God turned him into a vagabond, Cain didn't want to accept this as a punishment.[9] He didn't want to follow God's commandments to roam abroad; to contemplate what he did. Soon after his banishment, he began to strive for the *opposite* - to settle in one place, at least for a while… and not really be too concerned about the murder.[10] We already know how Cain, through his sacrifice, wanted things do be done his *own* way. In his own mind, he believed he was, in ways, *innocent* of the murder charge - for the most part, a ***victim*** of some extraneous circumstances. He also thought he could have even "pulled one over" on God, in ways.

> *...he threw the words behind him and went out, like one who would **deceive** the Almighty.* - *Genesis Rabbah* 22:13[11]

What he did to Abel was, now, becoming justified in his mind, in ways - even though evidence to the contrary was overwhelming:

> *...Cain was the only one of the first few Adamites to **rebel against** the sentence of death pronounced upon all mankind.* (Bristowe, 1927, p. 79)[12]

Cain had more of an effect on our world than most of us would ever guess. Not only would he physically go his own way, defiant of God's punishment, he was also the first to go his own way as far as a *religious* theology. These would be the first inklings of a counter belief system - contrary to God, since the Fall. This was an ideology, in part, based on the way Cain looked at the world; but, most probably based on **influences** of the fallen angels in the area… especially his father: the **Serpent**.[13] Cain also began to concentrate on the material elements of our world, with hopes to help him, and his confederates, the ability to gather feelings of divine sanctification and personal enlightenment. God, now, began to be "in the way" - starting to become their enemy.

On top of the establishment of some sort of *counter-religion*, Cain began to promote *his own* ways (and *ways of the Serpent*) by establishing an **empire** - sub-doing others in areas about him, and indoctrinating as many as possible. Cain was, soon, about to become a very cunning man, like his father (the **Serpent**) - a great leader of men into "wicked courses."[14]

The Most Famous Men of Ancient Times - "Sargon" and "Khan"

If we are to connect Cain with the origin of this counter-belief, this empire, and these new "ways" of thinking and living, we need to look at some ancient mythological and pagan accounts. Interestingly enough, we *can* seem to identify him with some of the most famous people of their day! Let's look at some of these connections between *Cain* and these famous individuals of old:

> *Another indication of the identity of Cain with the Babylonian **Sargon** is that the name variously rendered Sargon, Sargoni, Sarrukinu, Shargani, etc., may reasonably be taken as synonymous with "**King Cain**," the first syllable Sar or Shar meaning ruler or King in Babylonia and obviously the origin of Shah, Czar, Sahib, Sire, Sir, etc., while the second syllable gon, gani, gina or kinu, is very like Cain. George Smith writes: "Several of the other names of antediluvian patriarchs correspond with Babylonian words and roots such as Cain with gina and kinu." (Chaldean Genesis, p. 295. Early edition.)…* (Bristowe, 1927, p. 31)[15]

So, **Sargon** was one of the most famous people in the ancient land of **Babylonia** (e.g. modern Iraq), and was noted as one of the earliest *conquerors* in recorded history. This ancient land could easily have been the area where the ancient Garden of Eden was located; so it makes sense.

Many of us have, as well, heard of the famous "Genghis-Khan" - conqueror of western Asia. Interestingly enough, the word "Khan" could mean *ruler*. And, there seemed to be other "Khans" out there, in our ancient world, beyond him! The first probable conqueror - the original "Khan" - could, in actuality, have been **Cain**, himself:[16]

> *...the "**Kan**" or "**Gan**" of the Babylonian texts was 'obviously the historical origin of the "Cain" of the Hebrew Genesis, and that his father, King Adar or Adda or Addamu was the historical origin of "Adam" of the "Garden of Eden"'...*
> (Bristowe, 1950, p. 19)[17]

Some ancient sources stated that Cain, most probably, lived 700 years, or more - more than enough time to expand his influences to those around him![18] A lot of ancient people in Cain's day, according to the Bible, lived up to 900 years; or more. Could *Cain* have found ways, such as the conquering of other people around him, to give him more and more feelings of *self-importance*, and *relevance*? Could his extended years have given him enough time to establish the first **empire** of his homeland; *Khan* or *Sargon* - both famous ancient conquerors - being the earliest, pagan avatars for *Cain*?

> *...Sargon's date was about 3800 B.C., at which time Cain, according to the Bible dates, may have been alive.* (Bristowe, 1927, p. 150)[19]

Both *Cain* and *Sargon*, interestingly enough, were thought to have had a similar profession; as well as shared the same language:

> *(Sargon)... was a gardener when young... (and his) language (Ancient Babylonian) resembled Hebrew, which was presumably that of Cain.*
> (Bristowe, 1927, p. 22)[20]

God Maker... Developer of the First "Religion"

> *...Sargon is called in inscriptions "the first **high priest**."*
> (Bristowe, 1927, p. 84)[21]

After he murdered Abel, Cain *did* go out from the presence of the Lord, in ways - but Divine Providence tells us that God is everywhere; so what could this mean? Most probably, Cain went out from the presence of the Lord in his *thought* and *ideology*. He could never walk anywhere to get away from God, but he *did* step away in a religious sense. The birth of this first counterfeit, anti-God religion most probably originated at this time, with his dissidence. Interestingly enough, some sources state Cain's rebellious thoughts originated in the *very* field where he committed this unconscionable murder! How ironic! How telling!

So, even though Cain abandoned God - being *far* from God in thought and deed - he *still* gained a great deal of knowledge and worldly understanding. Some of it came from Adam and Eve; some from the Serpent, and some from other fallen angels around him. Most of his knowledge, of course, because twisted in favor of the Serpent's "ways;" allowing Cain the way to achieve his own, self-guided goals, here:[22]

> *Cain, type of the religious natural man, who believes in a God, and in "**religion**," but after his own **will**, and who rejects redemption by blood... the apostate teacher explains it away.* - *Schofield Reference Bible* Jude 1:11 (notes)[23]

> *These had so **perverted** the truth as to offer sacrifices unto Jehovah in the name of Satan, taking the fruit of the ground and offering it up in an unholy parody of the holy ordinance.* - *Book of the Generations of Adam* 5:5[24]

We know Sammael/Satan influenced the Serpent to *his* own ways. Now, the same probably happened with Cain - from *his* father. Thus became the foundation of **idolatry**: looking to one's own prideful self, or looking to other "gods," as a modem to one's own salvation, enlightenment, or ego gratification:

> *...Cain introduced that knowledge, and used it as the basis of idolatry by ascribing Divine attributes to the gods of his* ***own*** *invention.*
> (Bristowe, 1927, p. 117)[25]

So, just *where* did these "gods" of ancient, pagan belief come from?

Parents Turned Into Gods - The Origins of Ancestor Worship

> *The examination of names is the beginning of learning.*
> *- Socrates*[26]

A number of ancient sources stated that these earliest "gods" of pagan lore and religion were, at one time, *very* human:

> *Did not the pagans by attributing God-like qualities to* ***men****, change "the uncorruptible God into an image made like to corruptible man?"*
> (Bristowe, 1927, p. 63)[27]

> *...as early as the 4th century A.D. the Christian Bishop Augustine of Africa, wrote in his book, De Civita Dei: "Alexander the Great told his mother in a letter that even the higher gods were* ***men****"...* (Bristowe, 1950, p. 46)[28]

> *...the view propounded by Euemerus (316 B.C.), according to whom the* ***myths*** *were* ***history in disguise*** *and: "all gods* ***were once men*** *whose real feats have been decorated and distorted by later fancy" (Ency. Brit., Ed. II. Mythology)".*
> (Bristowe, 1927, p. 62-63)[29]

Cain was probably able to establish a belief system *based on whatever he knew around him*. He, obviously, would begin to establish his own "*gods*" - in defiance of the one, true God - by looking around, and deifying those important to his own life. Not only did Cain begin to turn one's veneration towards *material things* of this world, but also to those individuals *close* to him:

> *...Cain, armed with superhuman knowledge and power, came into Babylonia bringing with him the marvelous story of the Creation of the world and the Garden of*

> *Eden... No wonder the old times were perpetually harped upon in inscriptions in which are* ***veiled allusions*** *to Adam and Eve - the Fall of Adam - Eve's sorrow for Abel and her anger against Cain - the coming of Cain to Babylonia and his alliance with the Devil.* (Bristowe, 1927, p. 57)[30]

We can decipher, from ancient works of the past, that Cain probably had a great deal of respect for Adam and Eve - *especially* for his mother. His first move towards "deification" of those around seemed to begin with the conversation of *them* into a god and goddess. This, probably, was the true origin of **ancestor worship** - a widely held belief in most ancient cultures of old.

Adam, Eve, the Serpent, and Abel

> *These illusions are cloaked in the form of mythology which originated (as I hope to show) in Cain's travesty of the truth in transferring the Divine attributes of the Creator to* ***three false gods****, whom he called* ***Anu*** *and* ***Ea****, after his parents, and* ***Bel****, after the Devil.* (Bristowe, 1927, p. 57)[31]

> *The Professor tells us that the first Babylonian gods were a trio - "the supreme gods Anu, Mul-lil and Ea," and there was a fourth god called* ***Tammuz****. These four gods seem to be regarded by Assyriologists as the models from which* ***Adam****,* ***Eve****,* ***the Devil*** *and* ***Abel*** *were drawn, but my contention is that, on the contrary, they were the deified representatives of those Bible characters, and that it was Cain who deified their memories by transferring to them some of the attributes of God.*
> (Bristowe, 1927, p. 70)[32]

Sargon, we know, was probably another name for Cain. And, as we see, this ancient king established four major gods - "gods" originating with Adam, Eve, Abel, *and* the Serpent.[33] Hence, we have these first, four ancient *gods*, with even *more* ancient avatars springing out from them, for example:

Eve - a.k.a. the deities *Ea, Enki, Ishtar, Ashtoreth*[34]
Adam - a.k.a. the deities *Anu, Atum, Shamash, Zeus*[35]
The Serpent - a.k.a. the deities *Enlil, Mul-lil, Bel, Sin the moon god, Akki* [36]
Abel - a.k.a. the deity *Tammuz*[37]

Throughout the ages, these original gods had developed even *further*:

> *According to the Babylonian priests, several gods took part in the creation of the world, and the gods Anu, Ea and Bel at first, and in later times Shamas, Ishtar and Sin ruled the heavens, earth, sea and "the affairs of men".*
>
> (Bristowe, 1927, p. 115)[38]

Beginning in the ancient lands of Mesopotamia (a.k.a. Sumeria, Akkad, Babylonia, etc.), the story of Cain's new religion began to spread abroad, into all kinds of directions… spread, for the most part, via the new *empire* he also began to establish. Beyond these new names, they became transformed, over time, into a great deal of *other* gods and goddesses, since; and spread out, into most every ancient culture, religion, and empire, since then!

The Obscured Accounts of Old?

> *…the knowledge of God and of His laws was taken into Babylonia in the very earliest times and… that knowledge came to be* ***suppressed*** *or* ***travestied almost beyond recognition****.* (Bristowe, 1927, p. 151)[39]

> *…(the Sumerian story of the Creation) is only one of the* ***corrupt*** *versions of the Creation story handed down from the time of Cain by the Babylonian priests.*
>
> (Bristowe, 1927, p. 49)[40]

In ancient accounts, these gods were, sometimes, brother and sister; sometimes they were looked upon as mother and son; sometimes they were married, sometimes single; sometimes looked upon as male, sometimes female; etc.. There were a variety of reasons why facts surrounding these ancient gods had changed: sometimes time, sometimes inaccurate telling and retelling, sometimes inaccurate copying and recopying.

Also, a number of ancient gods and goddesses may have *intentionally* been blurred, over time![41] *Why*? We'll discover, with careful enough study, *how* and *why* someone may want to obscure the real truths, here! There are *reasons* why individuals of old may want to hide these real origins of this whole belief; there are reasons why people wouldn't want everyone to know that these "gods" originally were based Cain, the Serpent, and others of the day.

Whatever the "gods" developed into, since then - whatever direction this original story branched out into - it is important to understand how they, most probably, all had a similar origin.

Eve - The Goddess Mother

We have some revealing quotes on the probability of *Eve* being the origin of many early goddesses (and even gods):

> *...Sargon is called the son of* ***Ea*** *(Eve)...*
> (Bristowe, 1927, p. 151)[42]

> ***Ishtar's*** *countless titles include those of "Lady of Eden," "Goddess of the Tree of Life," "Mother of Mankind," and "Beloved of Anu (i.e. Adam)."*
> (Bristowe, 1950, p. 10)[43]

Under Mother's Care?

And, we recall that Cain seemed to have great respect for his mother. This is reflected in ancient lore, as well:[44]

> *...the Babylonians themselves attributed Sargon's superhuman knowledge to* ***his mother's teaching****.* (Bristowe, 1950, p. 5)[45]

> *...the following inscription refers to Cain's indebtness to his mother for his knowledge: "Moreover he... possessed all... Ea's wisdom;" "My child" Ea had said to him, "What is there that thou knowest not and what could I teach thee? What* ***I know thou knowest*** *also" (Mesopotamia, Delaporte, p. 141).*
> (Bristowe, 1927, p. 84)[46]

After the murder of Abel, things would begin to change between Eve and her son. Instead of great affection, Eve developed somewhat of a distain for her son, at least for a while. We see this in ancient mythology:

> *That Sargon is represented in inscriptions as the gardener of Anu (Adam), as Beloved of Ishtar (Eve) and* ***only loved by her for a certain period****, since he says: "When I was a gardener Ishtar loved me," which may refer to the fact that after the murder of Abel, Eve renounced Cain.* (Bristowe, 1927, p. 151)[47]

> *...another "Penitential Hymn"... was used as part of a temple ritual... and its great importance... is that it records Cain's first step in idolatry... in the very same words as he addresses to the Creator... We read:... "I knew not that I sinned. May Ishtar, my mother be appeased again, for I knew not that I sinned, God knoweth that I knew not... God, in the strength of his heart, has taken me, Ishtar, my mother, has seized me, and put me to grief."* (Bristowe, 1950, p. 40)[48]

We'll see how long this lasts.

Adam - The Father God

We have some reveling quotes on the possibility of *Adam* being the origin of a number of early gods, as well:

> *Abu (is the)... "Lord of the* ***Plants****"... It seems so obvious that "Abu," who's name means "father," represented Adam...* (Bristowe, 1950, p. 62)[49]

> *That Sargon (Cain) is represented in inscriptions as the* ***gardener*** *of Anu (Adam)...* (Bristowe, 1927, p. 151)[50]

> *...(an) inscription in which Anu and Ishtar are called lord and lady of the holy mound is probably an allusion to the Garden of Eden.* (Bristowe, 1927, p. 73)[51]

So, we see that Adam was known by names other than *Abu* or *Anu*. In ancient Egypt, Adam could have also been known as the god *Atum*. Atum apparently arose "out of these chaotic waters," and had a son named Seth.[52] Again, this seems to be similar to the Adam of the Bible - and how his soul was brought up from the *Darkness*; and also had a son named Seth.

The Greek *Zeus* could even be another title for Adam.

> *Zeus and Hera, a husband/wife and brother/sister pair, are pictures of Adam and Eve.* (Johnson, 2004, p. 9)[53]

> *The meaning of Zeus' name has led us directly back to the Garden of Eden, and to the time when Eve and Adam accepted the serpent's wisdom as their own... He (Adam) may very well have desired to possess the knowledge of good and evil for himself... Homer says that Zeus is "the father of men and gods"... (and) Athena is born out of Zeus just as Eve came out of Adam...* (Johnson, 2004, p. 173)[54]

The Serpent - Also Now a "God"

We also have revealing quotes on the possibility of **the Serpent** being the origin of a number of ancient gods:

> *King Sargina (Sargon)... listening obediently to the god **Enlil** (the Serpent)...* (Bristowe, 1950, p. 44)[55]

> *...the chief god was Enlil, whose name is translated... "lord of **demons**" by various authorities.* (Mackenzie, 1915, p. 35)[56]

We see that the god "Dati-Enlil" could even be where we get the word *devil*:

> ***Sargon** says in... (one) legend that he "knew not his father," while he elsewhere claims **Dati-Enlil** as his father.* (Bristowe, 1927, p. 95)[57]

> *That while St. John says that Cain was "of the wicked one," Sargon is called the "king-priest of Enlil" (the* Devil*); and is made to call his father "**Dati-Enlil**" (the **Devil**).* (Bristowe, 1927, p. 150)[58]

In ancient mythology, we've also heard a lot of references to the "dragon." And, we know the *dragon* could have been another symbol of the *Serpent*. So, could the god *Bel*, *Mul-lil*, the Serpent, and *this dragon* be one in the same?

> *Professor Sayce seems to identify the second god of the great trio with Satan by writing: "The supreme* ***Bel*** *was* ***Mul-lil*** *who was called the god of the lower world, his messengers were nightmares and demons of the night, and from whom came the plagues that oppressed mankind (Hibbert Lectures, p. 147)."*
>
> (Bristowe, 1927, p. 71)[59]

> *Neither in Hebrew nor Babylonian literature are Bel and the Dragon represented as antagonists. They are obviously, on the contrary, different forms of* ***the same god*** *and there is no authority, therefore, for concluding that this drawing represents a fight between the two. It is even possible that the word* ***Dragon*** *came from Dagon which, according to Professor Jastrow, was only another name for* ***Bel****... And Professor Sayce says... "Dagon is identified as Mul-lil" (Hibbert Lectures, 1887, p. 1888).*
>
> (Bristowe, 1927, p. 100)[60]

There is another ancient god, known as *Sin the Moon God*. This god was very popular in areas of the ancient Middle East. Interestingly enough, this god *also* seems to fulfill one's visual perception of the devil:

> *As Robert Browning wrote: "Note that the climax and the crown of things. Invariably is - the Devil appears himself - Armed, accoutered, horns and hoofs and tail." And sure enough those baneful signs are inseparable from the Babylonian religion; for in their drawings all their gods and heroes are represented with* ***horns*** *or* ***hoofs*** *or* ***tail****.*
>
> (Bristowe, 1927, p. 55)[61]

Another popular god of the land of Mesopotamia was *Akki*. The following, not only links *Akki* with the Serpent, but also might give us some insight into Sargon's (i.e. Cain's) early life:[62]

> *In the "Legend of* ***Sargon****" he (Sargon) calls his adopted father "****Akki,****" which is evidently another name for the Devil, for it is closely connected with the name of* ***Nakash*** *the Hebrew serpent - with Ahi, the water-god and serpent - with Ahri-man, who in the Persian religion is the "source of all evil, the devil" - with Agni, the Indian god of fire - with the Egyptian Naka, the serpent - with Naga, the Indian serpent-*

> *god... and with Agu or Acu, another name for the Babylonian moon-god, otherwise called* ***Sin****. The moon-god Sin is evidently* ***Bel*** *or* ***En-lil*** *under another name, for in later times the original trio Anu, Ea and Bel became Shamash, Sin and Ishtar (Shamash supplanting Anu, Ishtar supplanting Ea, and Sin, Bel).*
> (Bristowe, 1927, p. 93)[63]

It seems so much of this comes from the same source…

Cain - Now, Turned Into a "God" Himself

Cain, as well, seemed to have been transformed into a "god," here:

> *It can hardly be considered a coincidence that while St. John says that Cain was "of that wicked one," referring to the Devil, Sargon is described by the Babylonian priests as being the son or protégé of the Devil. This is one of the strongest indications of the identity of* ***Cain*** *with Sargon, who in different inscriptions is called "****son of Bel*** *the just," "the son of Itti-Bel," and the "son of Dati-Enlil," while Sargon's country is called the "realm of Enlil" (or Bel)...* (Bristowe, 1927, p. 93)[64]

> *...in a Babylonian text* ***Sargon*** *proclaims himself "The* ***Divine*** *Sargani, the illustrious king, a son of Bel the Just, the King of Agade, and of* ***the children of Bel****" (The First Bible, Conder).* (Bristowe, 1950, p. 8)[65]

In another title, Cain could have been known as a god mentioned in the Bible (i.e. in Jer. 50:2) - named *Merodach* (or *Marduk*).[66]

> *Nebuchadnezzar calls Merodach in inscriptions "the* ***first****-born, the glorious, the first-born of the gods, Merodach the prince," suitable titles, one would think, for the first-born of Adam's race... To crown their (the Babylonian scribes') inconsistencies, in the story of the Creation, Merodach's father is called, not Ea as elsewhere, but Anu. Since Anu represents Adam, and Ea and Ishtar represent Eve,* ***who could*** *Merodach their eldest born have represented but* ***Cain****?* (Bristowe, 1927, p. 80-81)[67]

As with Cain, Merodach was once known as a farmer:

> *..."Merodach" is described in another text as "Donor of* ***fruitfulness****, founder of agriculture and creator of grain and plants, who causes the green herb to spring forth" (Origin of Bible Traditions, p. 211, Clay).* (Bristowe, 1950, p. 66)[68]

Children of the "Sun" God

In the past, the words *son* and *sun* seemed to be close in meaning. Simply, a rounded disk - as with the *sun's* shape - was also the ancient symbol of a person's *own* son, or even a reincarnated soul.[69] So, whenever we hear of the *sun god*, we know it also could have referred to *the son* of someone very special... a *son* now turned into a god.

In our case, it's easy to see how *Cain* could be a part of this, since he was the *son* of the infamous Serpent.[70]

> *...the founder of the Babylonian empire was Cain and that he was flimsily disguised in mythology as Merodach, or Marduk the* ***Sun-god*** *who,* ***together*** *with* ***Bel (the serpent)****, was worshipped in Babylon up to the end of that city.*
> (Bristowe, 1950, p. 45)[71]

> *Merodach... is the solar hero who belongs* ***to the darkness*** *and not to the light.*
> (Sayce, 1898, p. 154)[72]

Interestingly, many ancient people have considered themselves ***Children of the Sun***. Could these people have thought of themselves as *descendants* of Cain; or, maybe, among those who had subscribed to his "ways," in some way?

> *...if Cain... was the human original of the Babylonian Sun-god whose followers spread a high grade of civilization all over the ancient world, the nature of the* ***religion*** *which accompanies that civilization* ***witnesses against him****. Wherever the "Children of the Sun" raised their pyramids and dolmens, their stately palaces and temples... all... as we have seen, can be traced back to* ***Sargon****.*
> (Bristowe, 1927, p. 127)[73]

The Greek "Lord of Light"

> *...the Greeks themselves not only adopted the ancient mythology of* ***Babylonia****, but added to it some even worse features...* (Bristowe, 1927, p. 64)[74]

The gods of *Greek* Mythology could, often, be thought of as *borrowed* from the ancient Babylonian gods of old. And, we know how Cain was probably connected to the "sun god" - one born with a "brilliant" countenance. The philosopher Socrates describes the Greek god *Hephaistos* as, "the princely lord of **light.**"[75] Zeus, of whom we now know was probably the Greek version of *Adam*, was considered the father of Hephaistos. Interesting. This god will become a lot more important to our story, as we move on.

Abel - Their Arch Enemy

> *Abel resolves into* ***Ab*** *(Snake) and* ***El*** *(God/shining)... and therefore he is a "snake* ***god****" or "shining snake."* (Gardiner, 2006, p. 18)[76]

So, as we recall, mythological and pagan accounts often considered the heroes of the Bible as *antagonists* - the *real* problem in the world; Abel was no exception. In reality, in some of these cases, Abel was even thought of as the god of "*enmity*" (which *even* seems to bring us back a reference of that Genesis 3:15 Prophecy). Interestingly enough, Abel seems to have had his place in ancient mythological lore, as well:

> *Professor Sayce says about the fourth god Tammuz, whom he calls the prototype of Abel: "The primitive home of Tammuz had been in that Garden of Eden or Edin... hence his mother... is called 'the lady of Edin.'" (Hibbert Lectures, p. 23.) He also says that like Abel, Tammuz was a* ***shepherd*** *and was killed when young.*
> (Bristowe, 1927, p. 70-71)[77]

> *In some inscriptions Tammuz also is called the son of Ea... and so is shown to be the brother of Merocach as* ***Abel*** *was of Cain...* (Bristowe, 1927, p. 81)[78]

And Cain (i.e. Sargon) was given credit for accomplishing one more thing:

> *...Sargon... is shown to be the brother of Tammuz (Abel) and (as the god Adar) to have* ***killed*** *Tammuz.* (Bristowe, 1927, p. 151)[79]

The Essence of Cain's Religion

We now know who had become the ancient pagan "gods" of old; and *how* they got there. Now, let's take a look at how Cain *further* twisted what were, once, the ways of God. In our first example, we see that: according to Cain, God was not the creator, protagonist, and benefactor of the world - *the Serpent* was!

> *...Greek poets and artists are telling us the same story from an* ***opposite*** *viewpoint - one that says that the serpent did not delude Adam and Eve in the ancient garden, but rather,* ***enlightened them****.* (Johnson, 2004, p. 7)[80]

The "True" Enlightener

Famous throughout ancient mythology, the "wisdom of the serpent" may also have its origins with the *Serpent* of the Garden of Eden. According to Cain, what *the Serpent* had brought to mankind was important - his angelic knowledge was important. This all, in fact, seems to stem from the Garden of Eden; and what happened, here:

> *In Genesis, the fruit of the tree was "good for food," brought a "yearning to the eyes," and was "to be coveted as the tree to* ***make one intelligent****." It is for embodying this last quality for which Athena (****Eve****), as goddess of the serpent's* ***wisdom****, was specifically and especially revered.* (Johnson, 2004, p. 189)[81]

The Serpent seduced Eve; and, through this, she acquired the "**Knowledge** of Good and Evil." This was the first incidence of the **Serpent's "knowledge,"** given to mankind.[82] Again, the whole incident of the Garden was twisted by these ancient, pagan mythological accounts. The moment Eve ate the fruit actually, according to *them*, pointed towards the point of gathering Serpent "enlightenment;" not disobedience to God. This *knowledge*, at least in God's eyes, was probably *not* meant for human beings; Cain claimed just the opposite.

Just as Eve was given credit for receiving this "enlightenment" from the Serpent, the ancients also stated that Adam was able to "*steal*" this same enlightenment from God - thanks, of course, to the Serpent's help.[83]

> *To the Greeks, the* ***serpent*** *freed mankind from bondage to an oppressive God, and was therefore a savior and illuminator of our race.* (Johnson, 2004, p. 12)[84]

The "Enlightened" Eve

Ancient mythologies, from Egypt to Persia, from Greece to Rome, contain "gods" that probably originated from the civilizations before them. Ultimately, most of them came from the lands surrounding the land of the Garden of Eden - in the general area of Mesopotamia or Babylonia. We also know how their ancient "gods" were probably based on the characters of early Genesis.

Eve, soon, became a huge part of this "illumination" concept:

> *Under the name of Nina or Nintu Ishtar is said to have divined all the mysteries of the gods - surely a reference to Eve's* ***acquisition of God-like knowledge*** *described in the Bible.* (Bristowe, 1927, p. 74)[85]

> *Athena's (Eve's) familiar and endearing intimacy with the serpent is undeniable, and it points* ***straight to Eden****. Her being is indissolubly coupled with the serpent: she is the goddess of* ***the serpent's wisdom****... (Athena) is the serpent's Eve, reborn and exhaulted... she is the new representative of Eve in the Greek age.*
> (Johnson, 2004, p. 6, 22)[86]

Also, that "Enlightened" Adam

Adam (a.k.a. Zeus) also probably had a part in this "illumination" process; even though it wasn't at prominent, here:[87]

> *The presence of snakes around the other gods indicated that they were part of the serpent's system of enlightenment and sacrifice. But* ***Zeus*** *is not a subordinate part of the serpent's system - he is the serpent... The Judeo-Christian viewpoint has Adam ashamed of himself after eating of the tree. But on... (one ancient) vase we have a picture of an* ***unashamed*** *Adam who has eaten its fruit. From the viewpoint of Zeus-religion, taking the fruit from the tree of the knowledge of good and evil did not bring shame, but* ***Victory****.* (Johnson, 2004, p. 171, 244)[88]

Cain loved Adam, and respected him as pseudo-father; even though he was not totally on board to what Cain was developing.

Again, we are starting to these ideologies developing into one of *two* major spiritual "**pathways to wisdom**." Again, this Genesis 3:15 *division* is being laid out. People would begin to, either, follow ways of the Serpent, or the ways of God (through *Adam*).

Cain - King of the Ancient World

And, we also begin to see that there are two different *viewpoints* of these early stories. According to Cain: Adam, Eve, the Serpent, and Cain were the real "gods;" ancestor worship and worship of the "sun god" was now to be the norm; the Serpent's "enlightenment" now represented the proper pathway to divine reconciliation, etc. Not only would Cain begin to control people through this new Serpent-based religion, he would also begin to control them *politically* - through the first "world *empire*."

> *...****Cain*** *(was)... the ancestor of all the impious generations that were* ***rebellious*** *toward God, and rose up against Him.* (Ginzberg, 1909, p. 105)[89]

The Fiery Beginning

Beyond the conquest of people via *religious* beliefs, Cain now began to conquer people in a military-like style. He began to establish an empire that would go on to influence future civilizations, from then on. Through this, Cain further began to stave people around him, in his mind (from gathering *revenge*, for Abel); and also further pervert others around him towards these Serpent "ways" of thinking.

In one example, Cain did not only use **fire** for an upright and worthy purpose, but began to use it for another, sinister, reason: he began to use it, as part of his method of worship![90]

Iblis (the Serpent?) came (to Cain) and said to him: "Abel's offering was accepted and consumed by fire because he used to serve and worship ***fire****. So, you, too, set up a fire for yourself and your descendents!" Cain thus built a fire temple. He was the first to set up and worship fire.*

- al-Tabari: The History of al-Tabari - Vol. I: General Introduction and From the Creation to the Flood Adam's Descendants to Jared 167[91]

These had so perverted the truth as to offer sacrifices unto Jehovah in ***the name of Satan****, taking the fruit of the ground and offering it up in an unholy parody of the holy ordinance.* *- Book of the Generations of Adam* 5:5[92]

The Blacksmith

Interestingly enough, another meaning of the name *Cain* is "smith."[93] In some areas of our ancient world, the occupation of a "smith" had certain stigmas attached to it. A smith was often considered to be an alien, intruder, or a "tinker" of the old world. He also could have been a magician, or performer in some "forbidden art."[94] We might even have gotten the word "blacksmith" because some "smiths" may have had the knowledge of dark, or *black*, arts - hence, the title.[95] This was probably one skill the Serpent, or some fallen angel, had taught Cain. Whatever the situation, the stigmas around the occupation of *smith* often seem to point towards its human originator: *Cain*.[96]

Also, interestingly enough, we also see that the Greek Hephaistos (of whom we already know was equated with Cain) as being the god of *techne* - a discipline of which we get the word *technology*.[97] Was Cain truly the originator of the art of metallurgy; and, ultimately, the force behind the technical or industrial advancements of the earliest people of our age?

The Opposite of Farmer

> *Cain, says Josephus, sought to gain livelihood by farming methods which depleted the soil... God put a stop to Cain's way - the way of* ***getting****. If Cain and his heirs had been allowed to continue their agricultural pursuits, soils all over the world would long ago have been rendered unfit for cultivation... The geological record tells us what God did to save the soil from utter depletion... Wherever Cain wandered his agricultural pursuits came to* ***naught****. When it should have rained, the weather turned dry. Just as he was about to reap the ripening crop, a storm blew in. Nothing turned out right... He and the generations who followed him eked out a wretched living.*
>
> (Hoeh, 1962, p. 9-10)[98]

Cain was a farmer. The faming methods most people used at the time no longer began to work with Cain and his progeny. We recall, he was cursed from the ground for the murder of Abel. Because it now became more difficult to cause his crops to grow, Cain began to devise ways to exploit the land *in other ways*. Instead of roaming, Cain thought it might be more advantageous to begin to create more permanent structures - solid buildings and the like. Through these, he would begin to diverge from the traditional, tent-dwelling ways of life people once had - a life of which God originally set up for His people.

Since Cain's thoughts were not on the ways of God above, he began to concentrate efforts on **shaping the world** around him… to his advantage, of course. He wished to satisfy his desires for solace and security by formulating organized living areas. He exploited the wealth of the land, as well as other people around him, all to mold life into something of which *he* considered better.[99]

The Builder of Large Structures

Cain, then, began to initialize a system of aqueducts and irrigation techniques; which helped deliver water to the masses.[100] The knowledge of measures and weights also were attributed to his promotion.[101] He, obviously, received a lot of knowledge from the Serpent, and other terrestrial angels, to be able to promote it all. He also used this knowledge to *further* defy God - and *not* wander like he was supposed to.

Beyond this, Cain was the first to initiate boundary stones around fields. Beyond the Garden, there were now fences sprouting up outside, in the areas around - to help secure one their own property border.[102] As far as Cain was concerned, he wanted to make sure that everyone around him knew what was theirs; and what was *his*. He was still paranoid of any angry people around him (for the murder of Abel), and felt the paranoid need to differentiate some areas as *his*. Eventually, he would move beyond his own boarders - to attempt to dominate other people, and their lands.[103]

This building of (Cain's) cities was a godless deed, for he surrounded them with a wall, forcing his family to remain within. All his other doings were equally impious. The punishment God had ordained for him did not effect any improvement... He also introduced a change in the ***simplicity*** *wherein men had lived before, and he was the author of measures and weights. And whereas men lived* ***innocently*** *while they knew nothing of such arts, he changed the world into cunning craftiness.*
(Ginzberg, 1909, p. 117)[104]

The innocent, tent-dwelling lives of many people - such as those who followed God's ways - were about to end.[105] The lifestyles of those who lived around Cain were, also, about to become a lot more complicated. Cain's desire to strip the land, to build things, as well as *possess* things, became foremost in his mind.

So, we now see there was *one* more undertaking which was said to have originated with Cain… something huge:

<u>*Gen.* 4</u>:
16 *And Cain went out from the presence of the LORD, and dwelt in the land of Nod, on the east of Eden.*
17 *And Cain knew his wife; and she conceived, and bare Enoch: and he builded a* ***city****...*

Again, we notice Cain took the *opposite* pathway that God wanted for him:

*As A.E. Knock has written, "****Cities*** *display the highest achievements of mortals and glorify mankind." The word city (****naked*** *in Hebrew) indicates that the ground has been denuded of vegetation. But living, growing plant life is God's achievement, and* *reminds us of his vital power, wisdom, and glory.* (Johnson, 2003, p. 54)[106]

As we know, Cain, probably, continually feared that he would end up *dead* for the murder of Abel, or dead from continual anguish… so he really didn't care too much about the consequences of what he did in life. He also wanted to continue on, within his smith occupation - buildings things; and gaining control over people. Quite possibly, the building of a city was Cain's **vain** attempt to even, somehow, immortalize himself, and his style of living.

It's obvious, Cain did seem to try to "immortalize his name" through the building of monuments and large structures.[107] And, interestingly enough, we do seem to have further proof that there were a lot *more* people on the earth at these early times. A city is quite a bit for one person to build - where did all of his help come from? We are not talking about a house here; or even a couple of neighborhoods - but a *city*.[108]

> *Poets and painters have depicted Cain as going into exile accompanied by an Adamite wife and family, but the Bible leads us to infer that before the birth of Seth only Cain and Abel had been born to Adam and Eve. We are prepared, therefore, to find that Cain had settled among a* ***non-Adamite*** *race when he built a city and founded a family…* (Bristowe, 1927, p. 14)[109]

Obviously, there really needed to be other groups of people on the earth - once located close to the Garden of Eden - but, now were beginning to work with Cain, and his goals. The people who began to flock to these cities of Cain's creation felt they, now, live luxuriously; and also felt they could begin to exploit whatever resources around them they wanted to, if need be.[110] Ancient sources stated Cain, not only, built one city, but *seven*.[111]

As in today, the cities of Cain's day would eventually become filled with violence and debauchery. Cain, and others who came to power, amassed wealth by the rapine of other groups of individuals.

> *A Jewish history says: "Cain dwelt in the earth trembling according as God had appointed him after he slew Abel his brother." But it adds "and he began to build cities" and "he founded seven cities," which indicates that new **courage** came to him; and the Babylonian inscriptions show whence it came. According to them it was the **Devil** who adopted Sargon and in exchange for his worship and obedience gave him **power** and **wealth**.* (Bristowe, 1927, p. 152)[112]

Cain's Power - Beginning at Eden?

One of the earliest cities of Sargon (i.e. Cain) was named ***Eridu*** - in southern Babylonia. Could this have actually been in the same area as *Eden*?

> *The primitive home of Tammuz had been in that Garden of Eden or Edin which Babylonian tradition placed in the immediate vicinity of **Eridu**. (Hibbert Lectures, p. 23.)... It was at **Eridu** that the Garden of the Babylonian Eden was placed.* (Bristowe, 1927, p. 70-71 (and notes))[113]

> *Sir Leonard Woolley... says "the Sumerians believed (Eridu) to be the **oldest city** upon the earth" (Ur of the Chaldees, p.13).* (Bristowe, 1950, p. 65)[114]

Beyond Eridu, the other cities built by Cain were called *Ur*, *Enoch*, and one other famous city, named ***Babylon***.[115]

> *...in the Encyclopedia Britannica we read: "The history of the city of **Babylon** can now be traced back to the days of **Sargon** of Agade (before 3000 B.C.), who appears to have given that city its name".* (Bristowe, 1927, p. 80)[116]

> *If we rule out the possibility of its having been built by the pre-Adamites, **Babylon** may have been one of the **seven cities** attributed to Cain in Jewish traditions.* (Bristowe, 1927, p. 80)[117]

Cain Ruled Over Groups of People

What about all of those *pre-Adamites* who lived around Cain; the ones he now was beginning to unite, in these cities?

*At **Babylon** there was a great resort of people... who... lived in a lawless manner like the **beasts of the field**.* - *Berossus* Of the Cosmology and Deluge [118]

One way or another, *Cain* probably made use of his angel-given knowledge, and his power, to become a swift and powerful leader. We recall that one interpretation of Cain's "mark" was a *horn* - could this *horn* have once been part of his warrior uniform?

*Perhaps the story of the horn arose from the fact that **Sargon** wore a horned helmet... Professor King says: "He wears a **helmet** adorned with the **horns** of a bull, and he carries a battle-axe and a bow and arrow."* (Bristowe, 1927, p. 142 (notes))[119]

With war-like aggression, Cain probably recruited a good number of holdouts to his side. According to ancient sources, Cain even conquered those with a number of different racial characteristics about them:

...the black race... (were the)... race of whom Cain was afraid. (Bristowe, 1950, p. 7)[120]

*If, as Professor Sayce thinks probable, Babylonia was the country to which Cain journeyed and if, as the same authority suggests, the first inhabitants of that country were **blacks**, it is easy to imagine Cain, a white man endowed with superhuman knowledge and physique and rendered invulnerable by some divine talisman, taking command over those pre-Adamites; and that he did so seems proved by the fact that he built a city and called it after his son Enoch.* (Bristowe, 1927, p. 15-16)[121]

And, yet again, we discover another meaning of the name *Cain*: or, a *spear*… yes, very war-like, indeed! Of course, he probably got a lot of his weapons of war from his knowledge at being a *smith*. It all ties together.

And, interestingly enough, the word for *spear*, above, is the Hebrew *Qayin*:

Qayin (7014) - *Kajin, the name of first child (Cain)... (and) an **Oriental** tribe*[122]

Could there have been a *variety* of people in the area, misplaced after the fall of Eden… now, beginning to be dominated by Cain? Could there have been a good number of *Adamites* and *pre-Adamites* volunteering to move to these cities; and willingly subjecting themselves?[123] Could this, also, begin to provide us a clue on what differentiated the different groups of Adamite and pre-Adamite groups, in Cain's day - differentiated by *how they looked*? More on that, later.

But, first, we see that:

> *Again, for straws show which way the wind blows, the* ***Chinese*** *Imperial title, Ruler of the Yellow, the coveted order of the Yellow Jacket, the Yellow titles of the Imperial palaces and the temples, the Yellow Imperial color and the Yellow River are all curiously suggestive considering that, for some unknown reason,* ***yellow is Cain's traditional color****. Shakespeare wrote: "a little beard, a* ***Cain****-colored beard;" and in ancient tapestries Cain's beard is always* ***yellow****.*
>
> (Bristowe, 1927, p. 148-149)[124]

This also seems to give us a little on what Cain might have looked like. Obviously, he wasn't turned *black* by God. He wasn't the father of black people - he *conquered* many of them, instead (along with Orientals, Adamites, and other people, as well). Sargon (a.k.a. Cain) was often described as light-skinned; having thick, prominent-looking, blonde hair; as well a most prominent beard of the same color. He really must have had a prominent look, overall - being the child of a terrestrial angel - standing out "like a sore thumb" to many others around him. With this semi-divine look, with his knowledge, and his overall-power, Cain probably made a grand entrance to fulfill his role as world-conqueror:

> *That while Sargon's subjects are called the black-heads, Merodach, whom I regard as the mythological representative of Cain, is said to have ruled... It must be remembered too, that the theory of Cain's presence in Babylonia offers the best explanation for the sudden arrival in that country of a marvelous civilization and culture, and relieves us of the necessity of believing that it was gradually evolved... that it seems to be the key to... the problem of the origin of idolatry - to the problem of the ancient civilizations attributed to the* ***Children of the Sun-god****...*
>
> (Bristowe, 1927, p. 151)[125]

The "Sun-God"… How the Idea Spread Throughout

After the beginning of Cain's empire, a number of people began to spread throughout the ancient world, into many areas; and probably passed on the influences of Cain to their descendants.[126]

> *…Cain was the* **human original** *of the Sun-god whose followers wandered into every clime, carrying with them the culture of the ancient Babylonians and the leaven of malice and wickedness as well.* (Bristowe, 1927, p. 129)[127]
>
> *In some far-off lands the Sun-god's name was "***Kane***" (The Children of the Sun. W. J. Perry, p. 167).* (Bristowe, 1927, p. 88 (notes))[128]

Now, we are beginning to see how *Cain* and *the Serpent* both began to influence the entire human race. How much more would the rest of the terrestrial, **fallen angels** of the time, as well as the Serpent himself, continue to expand *their influences* with more of the same?

Chapter 11

The "Other" Seed Line Expansion - Via the Nephilim

> ***Anu's*** *(Adam's?) only rivals in mythology were* ***Bel*** *(the Serpent?)...*
> (Bristowe, 1927, p. 72)[1]

The world, thanks to Cain and the Serpent, was about to go on steady decline; probably heading towards the same world which existed *before* the "Six-Day Creation" - with the same angels *of old* probably at the helm, turning it that way.

These terrestrial angels probably began to feel somewhat *vindicated*, at least in their minds. Adam and Eve were overthrown. Cain - the son of Perdition - was influencing developing societies. Cain, the Serpent, and these other fallen angels were beginning to be held in **high regard** because of all the knowledge they had. Now, the *rest* of these fallen, terrestrial angels began to take **their** place in the new world they helped to create.

Before, the fallen angels of the Garden trembled in Adam's presence. Now, **Adam** began to tremble before *them*, and became afraid of *them*.[2] The power grid had truly changed… and these fallen angels aimed to keep it that way.

The Separations of People

We recall the *Provoevangelium* - that prophecy, as stated by God, to the Serpent:[3]

> *And I will put enmity between thee and the woman, and between* ***thy seed*** *and* ***her seed****; it shall bruise thy head, and thou shalt bruise his heel...*
> - *Gen.* 3:15 (KJV)

The word *seed*, in this verse, can also stand for "semen virile;" hence one's "offspring," "posterity," or "descendants."[4] We already know there were groups of human beings - with only human blood (such as Adam's direct descendants)… no doubt about it. We also know how there began to be those with *mixed* blood out there - with the blood of the Serpent, himself… such as his descendant ***Cain***. Now, we'll see that, on the horizon, there would be a number of *other* individuals with angelic, mixed blood. This time, it would be the crossbred offspring of fallen angels and human beings. As we've already mentioned, these latter two groups of individuals would be, in some texts, known as *mixed multitudes*; or those with blood *from the Other Side*. Entirely new groups of people would emerge, here.

As imagination might suggest, *enmity* would begin develop between a number of these mixed-blood multitudes and pureblood human beings - *especially* the purebred descendants of Adam and Eve. As well, enmity would arise between those who began to follow the "*ways*" of Cain, the Serpent, and these other, terrestrial angels, against those who still wanted to follow the ways of God (via Adam's instruction). **The ways of life** of the two bloodlines and sympathizers would help to increase the *division* of theology Cain, and the Serpent, began… on a grand scale.

> *...while the other race of evil fame which trod the earth in Cain's lifetime is shown by both the Bible and Babylonian monuments to have been* ***half human - half spirit****. These people are called in the Bible the Nephilim, Rephaim, or Fallen Ones, and are said to have been the children of the fallen angels who took as wives the daughter of men. As Professor King points out, a parallel is provided in the Babylonian inscriptions: "... According to the traditions the records embody, the Sumerians looked back to a time when* ***gods*** *lived upon the earth with men... we read of two Sumerian heroes, also rulers of cities who were* ***divine*** *on the* ***father's or mother's side but not on both****" (Legends of Babylon and Egypt, p. 39).*
>
> (Bristowe, 1927, p. 101)[5]

Are These Types of Offspring Even Possible?

> *You saw also, he said, the six* ***men****, and in the middle of them that venerable great man… That tall man was the* ***Son of God****, and those six were his* ***angels*** *of most eminent dignity…* - *3 Hermas* 9:118-119[6]

The merging of terrestrial angels and human beings - into forming offspring - has been a heavily debated topic for centuries. Today, most scholars agree that these angels, often known as the *Sons of God*, weren't even angels, at all! They were nothing more than pious human beings; even human *judges* - but, **not angels**.[7] Many have even tried to disprove the existence of any angel - *especially* any of those who could, possibility, be able to take on human qualities. These same people, however, cannot deny the voracity of ancient written works to the contrary! Are so many of these ancient texts wrong, just because people don't believe things like this don't happen in our *modern* society? There are even a number of "interesting," human-*like* remains, found throughout the world.[8] They did not look *entirely* human. In fact, hardly anyone challenged the truth of these angelic unions until about the third or fourth century A.D.![9]

The Same "Estate"

We, however, have already assumed that there *could* have been angels who were forced to live a lot like *human beings*, because of their fall.

> *Aza and Azael, who rebelled above, and whom the Holy One, blessed be He, caused to fall from heaven, were forced to put on and to live with* ***the garments of the earth****. They could not divest themselves of these garments and could not return* ***to their former residence*** *with the rest of the angels. They remained forever on earth.*
> - *Zohar* Beresheet B69[10]

> *...the Evil Inclination gained sway over them as over the sons of men, and their forces and their strength were reduced to (the level of) man, and they became clothed with the* ***clod of the earth****...* (Jung, 1974, p. 113)[11]

Since some angelic beings were now considered terrestrial - on this same *plateau* as men, in ways - could they have been able to function on the same *estate* as man… mentally, emotionally, as well as *physically*?[12] The Bible states that angels could sleep, eat, and otherwise function, as most human individuals. Why can't their *other* functions, such as their sexual functions, work just as well?

The famous Catholic scholar, *Augustine*, wrote this about those fallen angels: "…their nature is **animal**, their mind rational, their soul subject to **passions**… (these things) they have in common with men…"[13] We recall the Serpent may have also lusted after *Eve* with these same emotional/sexual desires. On top of this, we are also given a number of *Biblical* examples of angels - and their ability to alternate between man and angel![14] One angel, for example, was considered to be a *man* (in Gen. 18:22) by others around him; and then went back to being considered an *angel* (in Gen. 19:1 and 19:15); and, then, back to being a *man* again (in Gen. 19:16). Also, three angels approached Abraham to announce the birth of his son, Isaac. Abraham looked at them *as human beings*, however… but understood, later on, that they were something *more*. Two angels visited Lot, and physically dragged him and his family away from the cities of Sodom and Gommorah. These angels also stayed with him the night before; and ate of his food. Lot, as well, knew that they were something *more*. There was even an angel who wrestled with Jacob. All of these could have been considered "men" - during bouts of time - to the ancients; even though these same ancients knew there was something *more* to them.

Apparently, the New Testament tells us there are might even be angels out there - *today* - who appear to be *so close* to men, that we may never know they were something *more*:

> *Be not forgetful to entertain strangers: for thereby some have entertained* ***angels unawares****.* - *Heb.* 13:2 (KJV)

Angelic beings, as we see, *did* seem to be able to manifest themselves into men, and go back to their original estate, at will. They could affect change upon their surroundings, and other people around them. What's so far-fetched about some being able to live like human beings, and *cohabitate*?

The Unmarriageable Ones?

There is a famous verse in the Bible which modern theologians often use to debunk the possibility of any cohabitation between angels and human beings.

> *For* ***in the resurrection*** *they neither marry, nor are given in marriage, but are as the angels of God in heaven.* - *Mat.* 22:30 (KJV)

If we look at this verse, it's apparent that Jesus was taking about the angelic beings, or those who would become angels, in the *future*. This, however, does **not** represent the circumstance, and *time frame*, of what we're really discussing, here. This refers to *future* times - after the resurrection of the dead (when Jesus returns to earth)… *not* these times of the past. Also, in the verse, the verse is referring to human beings who - in the future - would eventually become angels (in heaven); *not* those angelic beings who might have been **demoted** from their former angelic estates. Just because angels do not mate **after the resurrection** doesn't mean it never could have happened, or *has* happened, in the past.

> *The angels… no sooner had they rebelled against God and descended to earth than they lost their transcendental qualities, and were invested with sublunary bodies, so that a* ***union*** *with the daughter of men became possible.*
>
> (Ginzberg, 1909, p. 151)[15]

When certain groups of angels fell, they, according to the Bible, did *lose* their former angelic "estate":

> *And the angels which kept not their first estate, but left their own habitation…*
>
> - *Jude* 1:6 (KJV)

Male and Female Angels?

There is also a school of thought that states practically every angel has the *potential* to form into a male or a female, if necessary. All angels, however, are *male* in their original form (just as most angels in Bible stories are).[16] Adam, according to some Hebrew traditions, was even said to have, once, had much of this same potential. We know, from the Biblical story, that Eve was first *formed* from Adam's rib. Could this be the justification of why Eve was *so easily* taken out of Adam? Could this also be why Adam could have easily considered Eve "flesh of my flesh" - his female potential actually taken out of him? These concepts are actually a little beyond the scope of this book; what is relevant is that these fallen angels, of the past, might have even been able to become a man or woman, if needed. Azazel's famous companion *Aza* (or *Ozza*) could have been one of these, after his fall - now, a *female* earthbound angel.[17] What if these fallen angelic beings were able to mate with human beings of *both* sexes; doubling the potential for mixed offspring?

Regardless, as we'll see, this era of cross breeding - angel to human - would morph into a perilous time for our planet; known as the time of ***fornication***. This *fornication* would represent a genetic expansion of angelic sperm to the human gene pool on a grand scale - working to upstart, and threaten, God's "kind-after-kind" plan for our existence.[18]

"They Acted Like Beasts!"

Also, a number of people of the day were, now, beginning to act uncivilized; and debauchery began to ensue:

> *The mixed multitude consists of ignorant people, about whom it is written: "Cursed be he that lies with any manner of* ***beast****" (Devarim 27:21), because they come from the side of that* ***Serpent****...*
> - *Zohar* Beresheet A29[19]

A lot of fingers were pointed at those who had blood of these terrestrial angels. But, the bloodline of a person isn't necessarily determinate of their behavior, as most of us know. We remember the example of *Abel*. And, within these times of *fornication*, there was *another* reason why a good many people began to choose these Godless ways, beyond their genetics - they openly began to **choose** the attitudes, behaviors, and ways of Cain and the Serpent because they were, now, being made to look so appealing. Let's explain.

We already know that, when something was spoken of as a *beast* in the Bible, that it doesn't necessarily mean that they *were* animals.

> *If after the manner of men I have fought with* ***beasts*** *at Ephesus...*
> - *I Cor.* 15:32 (KJV)

Behold, the days come, saith the LORD, that I will ***sow*** *the house of Israel and the house of Judah with the seed of man (the* ***Adamite****?), and with the seed of* ***beast*** *(the* ***Behemah****?).* - *Jer.* 31:27 (KJV)

Now, the ancients began to place stigmas on other people, in regards to how their moral and spiritual development was. Actually, things were now *digressing*, and people were, seemingly, acting *less* than human.

For it is the style of the scripture to grasp the highest and lowliest... the lowest is the ***beast****.* - *Zohar* Tazria 22[20]

Beyond keeping the seed of Adam pure, interestingly enough, there seemed to be *another* reason why (as we'll see) God didn't really appreciate His children marrying human beings of other cultures - many of them began to act like "beasts:"

There are many evil kinds among Yisrael (Israel) that are called ***cattle*** *and* ***beasts****.* ***One is from the side*** *of the Serpent* ***and another from the*** *side of the idolatrous* ***nations****, who are like the animals and wild beasts.* - *Zohar* Beresheet A29[21]

Neither shalt thou lie with any beast (Behemah) to defile thyself therewith: neither shall any woman stand before a beast to lie down thereto: it [is] confusion. Defile not ye yourselves in any of these things: for in all these the ***nations are defiled*** *which I cast out before you.* - *Lev.* 18:23-24 (KJV)

And, the rationale against marrying foreign people, here, was simple: it was related to the probability that a foreign mate would work to cause their Godly partner to gravitate towards ***other*** - often pagan - "ways" (i.e. Deut. 7:3, Josh. 23:12)! A verse in Ephesians seems to mention a specific group of people who, often, follow these *other* ways - the "ways" of the Serpent

Wherein in time past ye walked ***according*** *to the course of the world,* ***according*** *to the prince and power of the air (Satan), the spirit that now worketh in the* ***children of disobedience****: Among whom also we all had our conversation in times past in the lusts of the flesh, fulfilling the desires of the flesh and of the mind; and were* ***by nature*** *the* ***children of wrath****, even as others.* - *Eph.* 2:3 (KJV)

Following these ways, then, could often bring out *beast-like* qualities in an individual - just like Cain possessed when he killed Abel.[22] Many of these same *ways* would become standard in Cain - and the Serpent's - new world.

The Nephilim Would "Divide" the World Even Further

*Azazel **still** walks out, pursuing women.*
(Jung, 1974, p. 105 (notes))[23]

As we recall, the Serpent (a.k.a. Azazel) and Aza both were known to have been the loudest complainers to God, in regards to Adam's formation. Because of their bickering, fifty to sixty angels were cast *down*, to the earth - we know of them as the *Nephilim* (or, the "fallen ones"). Apparently, through the time period of their "demotion," they were to serve as leaders, or managers, over other human groups in the garden… still angels, but forced to live, more or less, like any other human being on earth.

After Adam's fall, these same angels, then, approached God, and said something like: "See? We told you so! We told you Adam would sin; and now he did. So, now, we are *vindicated* - right? You should be able to pardon us for our previous grumblings about Adam - right?" Even though it was one of their own, or one close to them, who helped Adam sin; it really didn't matter, in their minds - they felt they should be vindicated, anyhow. They thought, now, they should get their old, angelic "estates" back, because God's plan for this earth was, now, *flawed*. We already know that the Serpent was punished by God, for what he did to bring this on - but the Serpent still thought in much the same way… he should, rather, have been freed from his "demotion." And, since Adam was now considered a being of *lower* stature (because he, now, was to be subjected to the ultimate reality of *death*), Aza and the other Nephilim also assumed *they* should be freed from their "demotion" - after all, *they* would never submit to temptation like man did. They are above all that. God, however, was ready to respond to all of what they were trying to accomplish; and soon had another challenge for them:

> *When he (Adam) sinned at the tree of knowledge, and was driven out of the Garden of Eden, those two celestial angels,* ***Aza*** *and* ***Azael****, said to the Holy One, blessed be He (God), "If it would have been us on earth, like man, we would have been* ***virtuous****." The Holy One, blessed be He, then asked them, "****Would you be able to overcome the evil inclination*** *that is in control on earth?" They said, "****We can****."*
> - *Zohar* Beresheet A50[24]

> *As soon as Adam was created and sinned, and left His (God's) presence with his judgment sentence, Aza and Azael approached. They said to Him, We have a redress to complain about to You. Here is the man that You created and he sinned against You. He replied to them, "If you would have been with them, you would have* ***been worse than him****."*
> - *Zohar* Balak 43[25]

Again, as the merciful God He is, the Lord Almighty was fair to these angels, and gave them a way to prove themselves. These angels claimed superiority; so if they fell to the temptations of the earth (just as Adam did), then they would be on *the same plane* as Adam and Eve were - as far as their future, and their destiny. In other words, if they failed, and fell from grace (just like Adam did), then they would *also* have to suffer the same, ultimate reality of ***death***, just like Adam did![26] They already were "demoted" once. Now, if they fell to the sins of the *flesh* (just like Adam and Eve), ***not only*** would they have to live like terrestrial human beings, but they'd also have to *die* like them.

There would be *one* difference between them, and human beings, in the afterlife: once they died, *none* would ever have a chance at God's redemption, or salvation! They wanted to get out of their "demotion" *so bad*, that they were willing to face such an ultimate price.

Well, as we'll see, the Nephilim (again) wouldn't fare very well. Just as Eve was seduced by one of their own, other human women could, soon, be able to have their *own* ways with them, using the same kind of temptations. *Fornication* would, again, be the tool used… to seduce even *them*:

> *When Aza and Azael fell from the place of their sanctity above, they* ***saw*** *the daughters of men, sinned with them…*
> - *Zohar* Beresheet A50[27]

God, however, *knew* that they would fail, and how *quickly* they would fall. Unbeknownst to them, these terrestrial angels started to have a hard time understanding how temptation in the world really works, as well as how to restrain themselves from the sins of the flesh. Most of us would probably be able to guess that they couldn't allow themselves, *wholly*, to escape these new-found, human-like passions.

Forbidden Knowledge for Sex

> *...they cast the world into ruins, were themselves driven from the world in ruin, and* ***caused the world to be ruined****...* - *Genesis Rabbah* 26:7[28]

The rest of these angels began to mate with other women around them, just as Azazel once had. And, soon after, they realized their futures were about to be futile - there was no way back. They have been "demoted" by God, once again. Now, because of their actions, they were destined to eventually *die* in this terrestrial world, without any chance for redemption.

So, because of this, they continually began to look for ways on this earth to make them feel at least *a little more* esteemed, in their minds. These *Nephilim*, for generations to come, would now begin to teach the mankind specific arts and sciences previously held only *for those above*. This occult **knowledge**, for the most part, was reserved for vastly superior, intelligent beings. So, to feel a little better about their new position in the world - as another *dying* breed - they began to use this knowledge as "bargaining chips"... *especially* in exchange for **sexual practices** with earthly women![29] It seems that sex seemed to have - and still has - some kind of *spiritual*, esteem-raising connection to it, beyond most things. Certain curious, power-hungry women had their bodies to offer; these angels were ready participants; thus began this *fornication* on a grand scale.

Those Up-And-Coming "Mixed Multitudes"

> *And the women also of the angels who went astray shall become* ***sirens****.*
> - *1 Enoch* 19:2[30]

Groups of people, once under Adam's moral authority (especially certain women), began to make deals with these fallen angels. Obviously, the esteem of these angels was (probably) pretty low, because they *knew* they were about to die, eventually (with nothing *more* to look forward to). And, they also understood how ***sex*** could (at least temporarily) give them a raised feeling of esteem (or worth). So, now, *sex* began to be used as their "go-to" modem of worldly gratification or actualization.

According to *Tertullianus* (A.D. 160-230), an early church father, early women were instructed to cover their heads; as not to excite wantonness in men. He also used the examples of **fallen angels** of the past - who lusted after unveiled women *with beautiful long hair*![31] One professor, named William Barclay, talked about an old rabbinic tradition that alleges "it was the beauty of women's long hair that attracted and tempted the angels in Genesis."[32] In the Bible, the same thing seems to be implied:

> *For if the woman be not covered, let her also be shorn... a man indeed ought not to cover [his] head... For this cause ought the woman to have power on [her] head because* ***of the angels****.*
> - *I Cor.* 11:6-10 (KJV)

Part of this "angelic seduction," beyond a woman's long hair, involved the uses of *make-up* and *cosmetics* in women. The Serpent Azazel, as we know, was instrumental in instructing Eve how to *sexually* seduce Adam. Now, it would be Azazel and these other angels who would begin to show *more* women how to use bracelets, ornaments, and antimony (the beautification of the eyelids); as well as how to wear all kinds of costly stones![33] Yes, it would these *very* angels who would be instrumental, in part, in their own destruction - as these *make-up* techniques would be a part of that "hidden knowledge" of which they would barter with! Certain women began to want *more* and *more* power - including how to make their selves appear *more* attractive, here - and bartered their bodies in order to get it. As a result:

> *All (the angels) were going astray after them.*
> - *Zohar* Acharei Mot 60[34]

The angels, obviously, made things a lot harder for themselves to resist, through some of this knowledge they were giving away. They, obviously, brought their punishment upon themselves, in the end. They did not trust God; and how harsh worldly temptation might be.

Power for Power

The Serpent was already cursed. And, since he was, why not bring as many of his fellow peers down with him? Most of these other Nephilim were now about to face their mortality. If they fell, *again*, and couldn't regain their original "estates" anymore, they figured they should do something of some kind of worth to them: maybe they could, at least, dominate the world, somehow, through some means. All they could do now was exploit everything and everyone around them - and take *most* of whatever they felt would make them feel good; to grasp any sort of a life they had left.

So, their "tricks" did give women knowledge; which, in turn, allowed certain woman to have a great deal of power over others. The angels "began to devise and deliver to the women the finery and ornaments by means of which women could allure men."[35] Many human women further prostituted their bodies, for the purpose of giving themselves *even* more of a place in their world! Soon, these exchanges became common to almost *all* of these angelic beings.

The Adulteration of the Human Race

> *Proceed against the bastards and the reprobates, and against the children of* ***fornication****...* - *1 Enoch* 10:9[36]

As we know, the mixed multitudes were offspring of people who had crossed bloodlines with the Nephilim… sometimes they turned beautiful, comely, and mentally stable; sometimes, not so much. As a result, many offspring were considered *adulterated* in some physical way, and even in some *mental/emotional* way!

<u>(to) adulterate</u> - *to make impure by adding **extraneous**, **improper**, or inferior ingredients*[37]

This angelic problem went beyond the adulterous situation between the Serpent and Eve. No more hybrid angelic-human offspring, such as Cain, created every *once in a while*. Now, mixed-breeding was all over. Certain women, probably, from every single human group out there were participating in exchanges via these fifty-or-so fallen angels; and this affected everyone, in some way. The Nephilim had now brought so many previously-constrained thoughts - and passions - out into the open.

According to ancient sources, after Cain killed Abel, Adam became quite distraught with Eve, and how the world was turning out; and really didn't want to cohabitate with her, very much, anymore. So, in the night, some angels seemed to be able to manifest themselves to Adam and Eve, probably while they were sleeping; and began to sexually seduce them (possibly, these were some of those strictly-spiritual *1/3*, who accompanied Sammael/Satan with *his* rebellion; or they were some other type; or were demons). Whatever seduced them, they fell to these night-time seductions; and even may have had *more* children, as a result.[38] Other people might have experienced these *same* night-terrors, as well. However these angels, now, begin to work on the human race, they were being proud to see that their seed was spreading… everywhere.

> *There is also mixed multitude from the side of the evil spirits, which are the souls of the wicked. These are **the actual evildoers in the world** and there is a **mixture** of demons, spirits and nightspirits as well.* - *Zohar* Beresheet A29[39]

The Serpent followed suit, as well; seducing as many women as he could. He may have even gone so far as to work on seducing *Eve*, again - more than once - to obtain *more* children through her![40]

According to a number of ancient sources, the Nephilim were said to have filled the world with *abortions*. In ancient times, the word *abortion* didn't necessarily mean the same as it does today. It probably meant an *untimely* or *improper birth* - something just not meant to be.[41] We also know the word *adulterate* probably meant something different back then, as well. These both may have been more connected with some angel-to-human cohabitation than anyone might have ever thought.

Along these same lines, *fornication*, today, has the simple definition of "sex outside of marriage." Again, beyond this common one, there could have been another, more *sinister* meaning of *fornication* - relating to the above topics.

Fornication

> *There is* ***a wholesale abandonment*** *of God and his righteous ways for women known to be in sin. This is what God calls* ***fornication****, not referring only to a sexual sin, but the* ***sin of mixing the righteous with the wicked, truth with evil****... This sin was so prevalent, and so blatant, a rejection of God that it could not be allowed to continue indefinitely.*
>
> ("There Were Giants on the earth… The Nephilim", n. d., p. 2)[42]

We recall that the Serpent used *fornication* to seduce Eve; and Eve used *fornication* to seduce Adam. A woman (or man) could commit fornication through some attempt to manipulate her man - to help her achieve her goals by one means or another - in this case, by using ***sex***. In this case of the Nephilim, women wanted occult knowledge and power - and used *fornication* to achieve this forbidden knowledge. The Nephilim, likewise, used *fornication* to get what *they* wanted. It's almost like they committed fornication with each other; both for a nefarious purpose.

These practices of **fornication** continued on, throughout the centuries, way beyond these 50-or-so angels. As a result, there were *many* human beings being born with angelic blood and genetic makeup, somewhere; and *many more* began to follow these sacrilegious, pagan dignitaries of the day; such as Cain. The world was definitely *not* moving in the direction of Adam and God.

> *The prohibition against marrying foreign peoples in the Bible is connected with the probability that the non-Israelite mate will cause their Israelite partner or whatsoever children of the union who are Israelite to go* ***in pagan ways****.*
>
> ("Race", n. d., p. 2)[43]

Another by-product of these affairs was on the horizon, however: angelic blood slowly was slowly *compromising* a majority of pure, human seed! This began to pose one huge problem to God! If these trends continued, it might even be able to, eventually, penetrate every blood-born descendant of Adam, himself… *negating* the prophecy of Genesis 3:15! A perfect God cannot make a prophecy and not have it fulfilled! That's not how it works. And, we know that this prophecy required a *pure* seed of Adam to be passed on to whoever would be the prophesied savior of Eve's descendants! Yet, now, most men - even Adam himself - were beginning to create offspring with mixed, angelic flesh… a serious problem, now, about to face the planet.

"Strange" Flesh

> *...giving themselves over to* ***fornication****, and going after* ***strange flesh****...*
> - *Jude* 1:7 (KJV)

In the past, the word *strange* could also mean something different than we're used to. These angelic beings - and their descendants - were both called *strange* because they possessed a **different**, or *strange*, kind of flesh:[44]

> *...Merrill F. Unger also interprets this... as cohabitation between "beings of a different* ***nature****" probably took place... For no creatures of a strange flesh ever lived on this earth except the evolved Nephilim...* (DeLoach, 1995, p. 4)[45]

We even have the name of one group of *strange* beings, here:

> *...the eagle of holiness (God)... shall spread his wings upon the mixed multitudes... (as well as the)* ***Amalekites****, and the evil multitudes of Yisrael (Israel), and devour them. And not one will remain, to fulfill that which is written about Yisrael: "so Hashem alone did lead him, and there was no* ***strange El*** *with him" (Devarim 32:12).*
> - *Zohar* Mishpatim 18[46]

The above *El* is another word for *god*.[47] One such group who originated from some strange "El" was the **Amalekites**. We recall that *Amalek* was just another name for the Serpent, himself - and the *Amalekites*, obviously, were probably the group offspring who sprung directly from the seed of the Serpent, himself![48] We recall, the Serpent was, also, still out on the prowl - seducing whoever he could, as well. It would be these groups of individuals, and/or their sympathizers, which would cause *so many* of the problems for any of pure blooded descendants of Adam, in the future.

We even have a number of examples of *strange* offspring in the Bible - mixed, angelic offspring… even these mixed-blooded Amalekites:

> *...thou mayest not set a* ***stranger*** *over thee, which [is]* ***not thy brother****.*
> - *Deut.* 17:15 (KJV)

> *And David said unto the young man that told him, Whence [art] thou? And he answered, I [am] the son of a* ***stranger****, an* ***Amalekite****.*
> - *II Sam.* 1:13 (KJV)

> *They have dealt treacherously against the LORD: for they have begotten* ***strange*** *children...*
> - *Ho.* 5:7 (KJV)

Interestingly, the Schofield Reference Bible (Ex. 17:8 (notes)) even identifies *Amalek* as one who was "born after the *flesh*." Now, we have another new word, here. Just what might the word *flesh* mean, in all of this?

> *...when these angels fell from Heaven, their strength and stature were reduced to those of mortals, and* ***their fire*** *changed into* ***flesh****.*
> (Graves and Patai, 1964, p. 105)[49]

Flesh is quite similar to *strange*, in ways; but stands for something a little more insidious. Not only is it thought of as the mixing of human and angelic seed, but it also could signify one's own *desire* to attain worldly things, rather than go after higher, *spiritual* (i.e. Godly) values.

> *For by the spirit of God they had been made angels of God and sons of God; but declining towards lower things, they are called men, a name of nature not of grace; and they are called **flesh**, as deserters **of the Spirit**.* (Jung, 1974, p. 108)[50]

> *And they (the Nephilim) shall produce on the earth giants not according to the **spirit**, but according to the **flesh**...* - *1 Enoch* 106:7[51]

These people wouldn't really mind utilizing *whatever they could* from the world around them, including *sex*, to achieve their own moral goals. Those who follow the *flesh* don't seem to mind going in ways *opposite* of what God might signify as His own; doing whatever *they* think is best.[52]

"Earth-Born" - An Ancient Mythological Term

Do we have evidence for people with this "mixed flesh" *outside* of the Bible? Absolutely *yes*.

> *As for the spirits of heaven, in heaven shall be their dwelling, but as for the spirits of the **earth** which were **born** upon the earth, on the earth shall be their dwelling.*
> - *1 Enoch* 15:10[53]

References to ***earth-born*** human beings are splashed throughout ancient mythology. The reason some ancient, pagan heroes were known as *earth-born* was because a number of ancients didn't really consider them a full-fledged god, but a *demi-god*: a mortal creature with some blood of a god.[54] This goes right back to our discussion on the unification of terrestrial angels and humans. Somewhat similar to the word *flesh*, the title of *earth-born* also seems to have a two-fold meaning: mixed individuals with angelic blood, *as well as* those concerned more with seeking **worldly pleasures** or **desires**.[55]

These *earth-born* beings - in ancient mythology, as well as in *the Bible* - were often known by *another*, more infamous title: the ***giants***.

The Giants of Scripture

The Greek Septuagint of the Bible renders the term *giant* as "*gigantes*;" a word that, also, could stand for "earth-born."[56] In other, non-Biblical works, we have quotes such as:

> *On the earth there once were **giants**.*
> - *Homer* (400 B. C.)[57]

Some of these mixed angel-human offspring may have looked "normal" - similar to almost any other human being. But, there were some who, not only carried the same shining countenance as an angel, but were also very *much different* in size than their human counterparts. As a result, some offspring were fairly small: the size of midgets; or they were very *large* - physical *giants*.[58] A good number, however, ended up as **giants** - even up to *9 feet* tall.[59]

In the past, as we've mentioned, a normal-sized human being could have even been thought of as a "giant" because they achieved some great feat, or had some vast amount of recognition or notoriety. A lot of the patriarchs of the Bible (including Noah, his son Shem, etc.) were thought to be *giants* (outside of the Bible), even though they probably did not physically have great height. But, that doesn't mean *real* giants - extremely large individuals - did not exist in the ancient world.

How Could This Occur?

How could there have been *giants* back then? And, if there was: why *then*, and not now? Why did a number of these offspring become giants in the first place?

> *...the fact that human beings can obtain larger than normal size through what amounts to a minor **flaw** in their **genetic code**, also bolsters the fact that giants could be the logical result from an alteration of human genetic traits as might result from a human/angel mating.* (Quayle, 2005, p. 124-125)[60]

> *The **climate** and **environment** both on the land and in the sea enabled creatures to live long ages and reach huge sizes.* (Gray, 2006, p. 11)[61]

Many believe a combination of the above allowed some of these individuals to become gigantic. A number of those who sprang strait from the Nephilim, especially, were thought to be physical giants. The more *human* blood that mixed into the genetic pools, however, the more *normal-sized* these angelic-human bloodlines may have ended up.

So, these early combinations, as well as those who continually bred with giant, hybrid *beings*, often continued on, in their large sizes.

> *...the first created men... received bodies of vast **size** reaching to a gigantic height, (and) must also of necessity have received more **accurate** (or advanced) senses...*
> - *Works of Philo Judaeus* Questions and Answers on Genesis 1(32)[62]

According to the ancient historian *Philo*, a variety of people on earth were once of gigantic size. They were superior to men in many ways. Even with gigantic size, and superiorities, it's obvious the giants, as a whole, would not survive on their own, very well, in this world. We'll soon see why. The Bible even states that, a couple of thousand years after Adam and Eve, most early giants who did were wiped out by a confederacy of human beings living around them. Either way, these giants, it seemed, were not destined to survive, for long.

Not Genetically Meant for This World?

As we'll also see, these early offspring seemed to have had *more* distinguishing physical characteristics about them. Some traits seemed to work them well; some really didn't. It might be beneficial for a giant individual to have a countenance similar to an angel, but having such a large size could, eventually, become a hindrance to anyone living in this world. Let's see how.

It has been calculated that nine feet is probably the ***maximum*** height for a human being to maintain effective mobility.[63] Anyone taller would probably have a hard time getting around; living day to day life. The pressure of weight, pressing on a nine-foot tall frame, would probably prove almost unbearable to the owner, over time (due to gravity). It would probably make one quite awkward, in the end. The giants, at best, probably ended up very miserable, and angry, because of their situations.

Along with feeling inner thoughts of anger and misery, in regards to their situation, many, then, could have easily wanted to adopt *Cain's* ways of life - Cain was angry at God; the Serpent was, obviously. Now, the giants easily could feel some of this anger and resentment about their live, and why they ended up the way they did (of course, their reason-to-be was because of their *parents*, or *ancestors*; and the choices that *they* made - not God).

The Giant Anakim

> *First they were called Nefilim, the fallen, at the time they were dropped down from heaven. After they joined up with the females of human kind and had children from them,* ***the children*** *were called* ***Anakim****...* - *Zohar* Shlach Lecha 10[64]

But, how did these offspring receive names, such as *the Anakim*? One theory involves a woman. As we've stated, already: there may have been *other* female angelic beings who visited Adam, after the Fall.[65] Most were intent on seducing him; and, quite often, were involved in bearing him offspring.[66] One such daughter was named ***Anak*** - a vile woman in her own right; often known as the first *witch*.[67] Whatever surrounded the birth of this Anak, she could have been the actual matriarch of one early group of mixed offspring - with blood strait from **Adam** himself - known as the *Anakim*. This could have been another attempt by the Serpent and/or the other fallen angels to try to *dilute* the significance of Adam's seed line, here… beginning with *Adam* himself.

"Those of the Necklace"

> *...Hebrew names are often based on common words, giving the names special meanings that relate it back to characteristics of the individual or thing being named. The word, Anaq, which was employed to name the Anak, used in other contexts means "a necklace so tight as to appear to be strangling" (James Strong, Exhaustive Concordance of the Bible).*
> (Quayle, 2005, p. 218)[68]

There are other thoughts about this name: the Anakim were often said to have had something in common - they were known as the "Long-Necked" or the "Wearers of Necklaces."[69] What does this mean? What were these necklaces; and why would they even want to wear them? These Anakim, as we'll see, seemed to be associated with *chains* for a few reasons:

> *...the Holy One, blessed be He (God), dropped them down* ***in chains****.*
> \- *Zohar* Beresheet A20[70]

The Anakim, possibly as a twisted *statement of honor* to their forefathers, could have begun to wear a number of ornamental *chains* as a **protest** to God - the One who did this to them. God, as we recall, punished the Nephilim to eternal *death*; because of their fornicating with women; soon to go down, in *chains*, to the *Darkness* - and never a chance for redemption. So, these chains *now* had become a symbol of their fore-father's suffering and "unfair" treatment. They began to wear these, proudly, as an outward show of their discontentment with God's (and Adam's) world.

On top of this sense of dissatisfaction and misery, they would begin to advance their own situation on earth by means of *force* and *deception*, rather than with Godly labor; by violence, rather than peace; by taking things, rather than bartering. In the end, most added no real value to the present order of society. They were even said to have lived off the work of others; stripping the natural world beyond capacity; creating no wealth, value, or anything to a productive order of things.[71] In short, they turned their entire world into a decadent place of chaos.

> ***Anakim*** *(giants) are the fifth group of the mixed multitude. They* **belittle the value** *of those, about whom it is written: "And* **chains** *(Heb. anakim) about your neck" (Mishlei 1:9)...* - *Zohar* Beresheet A20[72]

> *...they were loaded with chains ('anakim) upon chains...they increased the chains ('anakim) around the necks ('anakim) - they subjugated many people.*
> - *Genesis Rabbah* 26:7 (and notes)[73]

Ironically, because of all their actions, many Anakim actually *did* end up being a burden, or *chain*, to almost everyone around them![74] How fitting. These Anakim really didn't care, however. They even began to *wallow* in their destructive pride. Many walked around with a prideful attitude in their hearts; threatening others; and causing people around them to shiver in fear.[75]

Beyond their outward characteristics, this mixing of angelic and human blood also allowed some negative *mental* attributes to also develop. Some giants became known as, in today's terminology, individuals with bipolar personalities, schizophrenics, and originators of those who possessed suicidal thoughts.[76] There were all sorts of deviant things developing within their minds.

> *...the giants had been bred in such a way to be natural bipolar schizophrenics, so that in order to maintain their sanity it was necessary for them to direct their inner anger* ***outward****, in the form of warfare... seeking to conquor and destroy to fill the* ***emptiness*** *they felt inside.*
> ("*Giants in the Earth Part 4: Giants of Europe*", n. d., p. 16, 23)[77]

The World of Enosh - A Change for the Worse

Beyond the influences of these mixed giant offspring, the world began to change in other ways. The year was approximately 3550 B.C.; nearly 450 years after the fall of Adam.[78] During a 450-year span, even descendants of Adam, and other previously-pious groups, began to lose their faith in God - now, turning to the *flesh*. The attitudes the Anakim helped here - to seal the moral pathway of many people around them. *Enosh*, a grandson of Adam, and leader of a number of pious individuals at the time, wanted to keep people on the straight and narrow. Those who didn't want to go in the path of Cain, the Serpent, and now the Anakim, separated themselves from the corruption brewing. Even this separation would not last, for the most part.

In one story - a tale of *Enosh*, himself - actually might tell us about the beginning of the practices of ***idolatry***: there was a time when many chaste people of Enosh's day asked him about the great Adam (who was dead by this time) - what he was like, and how he was brought about, by God. They also wanted to know the proper ways to live in this world, now that it was being corrupted. Enosh began to show them how God created Adam from lowly dust. The name *Enosh* actually stands for "frail," "incurable," or "weak." And we'll see, now, he may have been named so *for good reason*:[79]

> *Enosh (Enos) took six clods of earth, mixed them, and molded them, and formed an image of dust and clay... He then assayed to show them how God breathed the breath of life into the nostrils of Adam, but when he began to blow his breath into the image he had formed, Satan entered it, and the figure walked, and the people of his time who had been inquiring these matters of Enosh* ***went astray after it****, saying, "What is the difference between* ***bowing down before this image*** *and paying* ***homage to a man****?"*
> (Ginzberg, 1909, p. 122-123)[80]

What a horrible failure, here - this attempt. The good people of Enosh's day wanted to do right. Instead, they began to question the very concept of an invisible God; and lose their faith in anything they couldn't see. The only thing left for them to do was to look to *other* things - things of the earth - for help and every-day guidance. How quickly people lose their faith. Now, the ways of Cain, the Serpent, and the Anakim began to look even *more* attractive.

In the days of Enosh, men, then, began to defile the name of God; and desisted from praying in His name.[81]

> *These had so perverted the truth as to offer sacrifices unto Jehovah in the name of Satan, taking the fruit of the ground and offering it up in an unholy parody of the holy ordinance.* *- Book of the Generations of Adam* 5:5[82]

This could be a good reason why Enosh meant "incurable" or "frail." Through his *frail* attempt at instruction, he became the unintentional contributor to the world's incurable condition of idolatry.[83] As a consequence, the countenances of those beyond the time of Enosh were no longer closer to the image of God.[84] People may have been better looking; with more of a healthier *glow* to them. Now, people, and the entire world, began to show signs of depravity; signs of sickness, or decay. A person's imperfections began to show a lot more easily.[85] Some of the land even became barren. Men began to feel ill, and *look a lot more like it* - all because *idolatry* was introduced to the world.[86]

A lot of the people - especially the *women* who, somehow, were related to those who had a hand in seducing the fallen angels - began to quickly show age and ugliness.[87] The out-of-control actions of Cain's world was beginning to come back to them.

And as for those who do (this) wickedness, their judgment is ready, and their ***error is lasting****.* - *Book of the Glory of Kings (Kerba Nagast)* 6[88]

Regardless, many of them maintained a stubborn stance against God. The people under the intellectual domain of Cain, the Serpent, and the Nephilim would look to them as "gods;" and perpetuate the concept of idolatry. The behaviors of the Anakim were also rising in popularity. People were even begin to worship these giants; seeking to have some of this "divine" blood as their own. Ancestor worship was on the rise. The whole world began to be perverted.

These sacrileges would continue on; the world would sink deeper and deeper into corruption. How long would this continue on, without causing the *total* population to succumb to corruption? How many *pious* people would fall short; and would any of them remain?

Chapter 12

The Cainites
And Their "Mark" on the World

...they knew that whoever was descended from Cain was doomed to annihilation.
(Ginzberg, 1909, p. 117)[1]

We know that Cain was the first to develop an empire, and a religion. We know the Nephilim continued to corrupt the world - through their affections for women - by producing giant offspring. Even their offspring - the *Anakim* - made the planet worse with their vengeful ways. Let's continue more with some of the more famous descendants of Cain - those mentioned in the Bible - and discover what "marks" they left on ancient society. These famous people brought on a good number of ways to destroy a society.

One who reads early Genesis might recall that *Enoch* was said to be a son of Cain; and even had a *city* named after him (by his father). Yet, there were a number of other descendents of Cain's family in the Bible, as well. One in particular would have a disastrous effect on the world to come; as we'll see:

And unto Enoch was born Irad: and Irad begat Mehujael: and Mehujael begat Methusael: and Methusael begat ***Lamech****.* - *Gen.* 4:18 (KJV)

It is the final one - *Lamech* - of whom we need to look deeper at. Something was in store for Cain's subsequent generations *after* the era of this one descendant. Why? *What happened*? Interestingly enough, God may have even spelled out the future of Cain's generations by the meaning of these subsequent names, above. Let's take a look.

Each of these names, interestingly enough, seems to have been a *prediction* of what would happen to Cain's progeny, in the future:[2]

Irad (meaning) - *"I shall **drive** them out of the world"*
Mehujael (meaning) - *"I shall **wipe** them out of the world"*
Methusael (meaning) - *"I shall **wear** them out from the world"*

Let's look at the final descendent of this chain, and the meaning behind *his* name:

Lamech (meaning) - *"Powerful or strong warrior"*[3]

Interestingly enough, the Bible seems to talk about this descendant more than any other offspring of Cain! So, in order to move further, let's take a look in this man, and see what he did… as well, the relevance *he* would have on his family tree, and even the entire *world*. In *one* act, this man probably changed the course of world history.

Lamech… And His Two Wives

> *And **Lamech took** unto him two wives: the name of the one was Adah, and the name of the other Zillah.* - *Gen.* 4:19 (KJV)

Although Lamech stood for "powerful and strong," he wasn't very positive in his actions. He would begin to go down a number of *negative* moral pathways, as many before him. How he ended up with these two wives - most might say, *today* - was not really a proper achievement. According to one ancient source, Lamech wanted *Enoch* - a famous descendant of Adam - **dead**. Enoch had become a very famous prophet of God, by this time. The ancient *Book of Enoch* was even attributed to him. Adamites and non-Adamites alike respected him, all throughout the ancient world.

Since Enoch taught the ways of God to so many around him, and tried to warn all of the people of God disfavor with what they were doing, this apparently got under Lamech's skin. Because of his stature amongst the Cainites, he also followed most of what Cain was about; and, therefore, had something against any dissidents.

Although he tried, Lamech was not able to destroy Enoch - nor his message - however; but he did manage to kill Enoch's own brother. Enoch reportedly ran from

Lamech, and hid in a cave. On top of killing his brother, Lamech also kidnapped Enoch's wife, and his brother's wife, in the process: these women were, apparently, **Adah** and **Zillah** (Gen. 4:19)![4]

There are a few other interesting elements to the story of Adah and Zillah: first off, beyond the many acts of decadence of these people of Cain, they also began to indulge in another interesting practice: *abortion*.[5]

> Book of Jasher 2:
> 19 *For in those days the sons of men began to trespass against God, and to transgress the commandments which he had commanded to Adam, to be fruitful and multiply in the earth.*
> 20 *And some of the sons of men caused their wives to drink a draught that would render them* ***barren****, in order that they might retain* ***their figures*** *and whereby their beautiful appearance might not fade.*
> 21 *And when the sons of men caused some of their wives to drink,* ***Zillah*** *drank with them.*
> 22 *And the child-bearing women appeared* ***abominable*** *in the sight of their husbands as widows, whilst their husbands lived, for to the barren ones only they were attached.*

In those days, it was very honorable for a woman to be a mother. Men were supposed to accept his wife *as she was*, and honor her position as his wife. It was common-place that women understood the prophecy of Genesis 3:15; and knew that one of them would bring forth the promised one. What a motivation to have children! The descendants of Cain, however, began to have other ideas.

The men of Lamech's era began to be intensive on achieving their *own* sexual pleasure, rather than treating their partners with dignity, and rather than worrying about any Genesis prophecy. They also really didn't care much about the family unit, or accepting the women in their lives at face value. Thus began abortion as common practice.[6]

As a result, each wife of Lamech began to be used in a slightly different way. Adah - a possible wife of Enoch - could have been turned into a woman "of the dawn" by Lamech.[7] In other words, she would be the "open" wife of Lamech - the one he walked around with; the one he used to portray in front of other people; the one who "brightened" the scene with her presence.[8] Since her name stood for "beauty" or "adornment," it's easy to conclude that they looked as if the perfect couple.[9] Lamech also placed her as the wife who, in his mind, would bare him children.

Zillah, on the other hand, was associated with the word "shadow." Being known as the "woman of the shadows," this was the wife Lamech really used for his *sexual* pleasure.[10] Being constantly decked out as a harlot, Zillah would have to entertain her husband luxuriously; open to her husband's every physical desire.[11] Even though Zillah probably had a wonderful figure, she probably felt sad that she was only considered a sex object; and was a little down. Lamech also kept her thin and good-looking through the drink mentioned above; a drink that would, in actuality, destroy her future pregnancies. Now, where would men have gotten those ideas? Where would they get the knowledge to use what herbs to make women barren?

We recall that there were those in this world who had a vast pool of often-forbidden knowledge; and we know who they are.[12] This was probably another tidbit of *angelic* influence, spreading throughout our ancient world on a grand scale - and the sons of Cain seemed to have more and more hunger for the taking.

Lamech did not treat his women well, overall. Eventually, he would get what was coming to him. Let's take a look at a few of the children his *wives* gave birth to, and how they would influence their ever-changing world around them.

Jabal and Jubal - "The Sons of Song"

Gen. 4:
20 *And Adah bare* ***Jabal****: he was the father of such as dwell in tents, and of such as have cattle.*
21 *And his brother's name was* ***Jubal****: he was the father of all such as handle the harp and organ.*

As we know, Adah was known as the "childbearing" mother. Her first son, *Jabal*, grew up as a professional shepherd. He began to dwell as a nomad; in shepherds' tents… and herd flocks on a large scale.[13] Her other son, *Jubal* (a.k.a. *Yubal*, or *Tubal*) was known as the "father of musicians."[14] He began to be involved with the invention of musical instruments, as in the harp, the psaltery, and the lute (a stringed musical instrument).[15] Jubal obviously had a passionate addiction to music. He wrote songs, practiced minstrelsy, and taught people how to play instruments of his own invention. Jubal also learned how to ferment wine - wine that, after he drank of it, allowed him, and others, to easily get up and dance.[16] He, his wine, and his music would soon have a **huge** impact on the world to come, just as these influences have on the world *today*.

We know these were children of Adah because, as we recall, her husband constantly made Zillah to be barren. It would not continue this way forever, though! Although Adah's children would go on to influence the world in a vast number of ways, Zillah would soon have her chance. Whatever Zillah's situation was, before, her opportunity to become a mother was on the horizon.

Tubal-Cain

Book of Jasher 2:
18 *...and Zillah... was barren in those days and had no offspring.*
23 *And in the end of days and years, when Zillah became old, the Lord opened her womb.*
24 *And she conceived and bare a son and she called his name **Tubal Cain**, saying, After I had withered away have **I obtained him from the Almighty God**.*

Gen. 4:
22 *And Zillah, she also bare **Tubalcain**, an instructor of every artificer in brass and iron...*

We see, in the above, that Zillah exclaims: "I obtained him from the Almighty God." Interesting, this was much the same thing *Eve* said soon after giving birth to Cain ("I have gotten a man from the LORD" (Gen. 4:1))! Could there have been some *outward* similarities between the two births, here? Could Zillah have also thought her child came *from the Lord*, or *an angel of the Lord*? Could Tubal-Cain have had a bright countenance, as well... possibly being sired of a fallen angel?

As we recall, Cain probably was born of the Serpent, and apparently had an outer, angelic-like countenance because of it. Could Zillah have had an affair with one of these Nephilim? It never states in the Bible that Lamech fathered Tubal-Cain; but states that,

"Zillah bare so-and-so" (Gen. 4:22). Might a fallen angel have seduced Zillah as well, after God opened her womb? Let's look at some possible reasons why.

Regardless - if it *did* or *did not* happen this way - this offspring turned out to be a fairly *important* descendant to the Cainites, it seems.

The Weapon Maker

> *Therefore, it is written, "The sons of Elohim saw that the daughters of men were fair" (Beresheet 6:2). All were going astray after them. There was one male, who was born* ***to the spirit*** *from the aspect of Cain, and he was named* ***Tuval Cain****...*
>
> - *Zohar* Acharei Mot 60[17]

The possibility, according to ancient sources, is that one of these ancient Nephilim understood the marital situation of Lamech, and got a hold of Zillah (possibly even against her will); having a child, through her. What was so important about Lamech, in this all, however? And, why would they even attempt such a thing, if they did? Zillah seemed to have been in a pivotal position, here, as we'll soon see.

With all of the abortion-inducing drinks Zillah had been taking, she really wasn't sure if she could ever become pregnant, anymore; yet, it seemed to have been happened! This "miracle-child" was called *Tubal-Cain*. Interestingly enough, the name actuality means "the completion (or perfection) of Cain."[18] Why? Years after Cain's birth, we will see that Tubal-Cain, in ways, *completed* the atrocities of his noted ancestor.

This son had become an expert in the forging of metal - becoming another blacksmith, and setting up a copper and iron smithery (a lot like Cain would have).[19] Tubal-Cain began to utilize his metallurgy even *further* - to provide advancements in farming implements, as well as allow farmers to turn their inundated, hard ground into some kind of *workable* ground.[20] Although this all seemed to be positive on the surface, his art began to take him beyond the direction of farming; and into the formation of other, more *dangerous*, implements:

> *This Tuval Cain introduced* ***weaponry*** *to the world, as he sharpened all earthenware, copper and iron.* - *Zohar* Acharei Mot 60[21]

The Serpent Azazel, as some ancient sources stated, was the one who showed people how to forge iron into swords of war, and spear-points. Could Tubal-Cain have gotten his information from the Serpent, as well? Tubal-Cain was known to become a *master* in the art of war.[22] And, to sum it all up: Cain killed another human being, but really lacked the necessary weapons for a quality slaying. **Tubal-Cain**, on the other hand, created - or *perfected* - these weapons of warfare and death… so, in this sense, he was credited for completing (or perfecting) Cain's work, here![23]

Going further: the Serpent (i.e. Azazel) was also given credit for introducing human beings to the brewing of beer; which may have allowed murder to be committed a lot more easily (when people were intoxicated). What about the other brothers of Tubal-Cain, and their inventions? Did he also have an effect on them… showing them nefarious ways to twist these things, as well? And, why does it all matter?

Going one step further, could the Serpent have even been the fallen, terrestrial angel who impregnated the mother of either Jubal or Tubal-Cain, *themselves*? It seems they were both heavily under the influence of the Serpent, since childhood; and we know the Serpent still went out, pursuing women.[24] There must have been something important about this whole situation with Lamech, here. Could these descendants have been pivotal in shaping the *directions* by which ancient societies were about to head?

The Musical "Arts"

> *Some say that… (Jubal) and Tubal-cain, who were of the family of Cain, were the first who invented the three tools of the art of working in iron, the* ***anvil****,* ***hammer*** *and* ***tongs****. The art of working in iron* ***is the mother and begetter of all arts****; as the head is to the body, so is it to* ***all other crafts****. And as all the limbs of the body cease to perform their functions if the head is taken away from it, so also all other arts would cease if the art of working in* ***iron*** *were to come to an end.*
>
> \- *Book of the Bee* 19[25]

Jubal's talent for designing, combined with Tubal-Cain's knowledge of the forge, helped to create musical instruments, and a musical revolution. As they discovered, a good deal of *power* - over their society - was about to be obtained through the use of these musical instruments! These pivotal Cainites, through their inventions, would begin to further complicate the **once-simple** lifestyles of most everyone around them.

The Self-Perceived "Down Trodden"

There is more. Times were extremely different back then, as one could guess. There was no TV, no Internet - nothing compared to what we have today. The Cainites, and those who began to follow him - and the *Serpent* - began to live out their lives according to what *their false* ideologies would be teaching. They began to get really angry at God. They began to become very defiant of Adam's teaching. They didn't want to do practically *anything* of God's ways; such as having to live in tents, having to work hard, and having to be a good neighbor to others (all with **God** being at the center of everything, of course)! Instead, the *opposite* began to take hold: many began to sit around idly, without direction, and without goals. Apparently, with these new devices on the horizon, there seemed to some other ways for them to *get out of* any of negative feelings they might have once felt, by their abandonment of God:

> *And how shall I occupy myself in times of idleness?*
> *In* ***music****, dancing, and song.*
> (Baring-Gould, 1881, p. 54) [26]

Throughout their new-found sloth, many of them might not have felt too good about their situations. It only made sense for them to do something of purpose (in their own minds) - something to make them feel a little better. Now, Jubal and Tubal-Cain had ways to provide them with some sort of temporary relief - playing/listening to *music* and experimenting with their newfound *wine*.

> *Thus did this Genun (another name for both Jubal and Tubal-Cain) thus multiply sin exceedingly; he (they) also acted with **pride**, and taught the children of Cain to commit all manner of the grossest wickedness, which they **knew not**; and put them up to manifold doings which they **knew not before**.*
>
> *- Second Book of Adam and Eve (The Conflict of Adam and Eve with Satan)* 20:6[27]

As the Anakim wore chains, in protest against the "unfairness" of the treatment of their ancestors, as Cain moaned and belly-ached about his punishments, many of these new Cainite-sympathizers began to feel the same. Much like their self-victimizing, cynical patriarch, Cain's descendants and followers began to take on his mannerisms to the *extreme*:

> *...because many operate out of **the subjective mind** there is a natural urge to get them involved in the charismatic practices perhaps to **validate** their own **sense of failures**. Therefore, they actively "evangelize" to spread their worship. To do this, it was necessary to "join the unity movement"... a weak man is always brought into judgment by a strong person who does not fall under the same spell. If the drunkard can get his teetotaler to take a sip then his own actions are validated and he feels **so much better**.* ("Jubal - Genun - Musical Worship", n. d., p. 15-16)[28]

> *Their need to dominate and destroy came out of the essential emptiness of their souls, which they sought in vain to fill with **earthly pleasures**. However, the more they stole, the emptier their souls became, and they had to conquer and plunder more and more to fill the emptiness inside them until all life on Earth was in peril of being destroyed. And even if they had conquered the whole world, they still would have lost their souls.* ("Giants of the Ancient Near East", 2003, p. 13)[29]

The more time had passed, the hungrier people became for this *earthly* knowledge and pleasure, which was fronted by Cain. Their desires became *especially* prevalent for what these angelic beings had to offer. If we think about it, metalworking, music, and other forms of technology - if used in the *proper* respect - could be a very positive addition to society. But, if used in the wrong respects, they could complicate human life a great deal; and turn a lot of people in *wrong* directions. And, this was *exactly* what was going on in those days.

Music and Alcohol - The Wrong Uses

> *One plays music because it is personally pleasing but it is not long before it is understood that the skilled musician has a powerful* ***tool*** *which may be used to amplify* ***other natural skills****. One has only to look at the physical appearance of many powerful musicians to understand that they may have gained control of a supernatural weapon.* ("Jubal - Genun - Musical Worship", n. d., p. 10)[30]

> *Music has been considered and defined as "the* ***effeminate*** *art." That is, music was primarily the tool of children and women because it* ***altered their lives*** *by appealing to the "right brain" or feminine nature. It also had the power to* ***suppress*** *the "left brain" or rational nature and allow fairly bright young men to be led into the irrational acts required by a warrior.*
> ("Jubal - Genun - Musical Worship", n. d., p. 11)[31]

Tubal-Cain had become a powerful man, surpassing most men around him in power and strength.[32] He might have even been the ancient equivalent of a "rock-star," today. One reason he was so popular was that his new-found devices had become a "means for satisfying the ***pleasures*** **of the body**…"[33] What kind of *pleasures* would we be talking about - some kind of *worldly* pleasures, maybe?

> *The speaking voice has only a single tone but the invention of various instruments showed how to create fantastic harmonies. It was not just the music itself but music has the power to* ***alter*** *the nature of singing so that sounds and combinations of sounds could actually create totally* ***new*** *sounds which did not come from the harp or the voice. Modern scientific studies have shown that sounds produced by various instruments are actually mixed and combined in the ear and brain to produce tones which did* ***not previously exist****. These combinations have the power to produce* ***endorphins*** *in the blood and actually alter the mind of the "worshiper" just as morphine would alter the mind of a drug addict.*
> ("Jubal - Genun - Musical Worship", n. d., p. 10)[34]

> *There is nothing wrong with a* ***revolver*** *but if* ***improperly aimed*** *it becomes the tool of great destruction. In the same way, the innocent instruments when combined into an orchestra actually* ***altered*** *the chemical balance of the brain so that it no longer functioned rationally. Wine and music is often grouped together because wine, too, is totally innocent but when put into the brain it* ***alters*** *that part of the mind which constructs barriers beyond which we will not ordinarily go. The* ***quiet*** *soloist cannot* ***always get the job done****.* ("Jubal - Genun - Musical Worship", n. d., p. 14)[35]

These offspring/sympathizers of Cain, as we know, could have become *heavily* influenced by this fallen-angelic knowledge. Interestingly enough, the very name *Nachash* (another name of the Serpent, as we recall) *also* seems to be connected to a brass musical instrument, in ways! We can also see know that, according to the Bible, Satan was even known as the *overseer of music*, in heaven, for a time. Maybe Satan could have had influences on the Serpent (i.e. *Nachash*, *Azazel*); and he, in turn, could have influenced Jubal, Tubal-Cain, and other famous Cainites.

Interestingly enough, we see (from the above) that certain musical sounds, used together, *don't* even seem to come from this world! Well, if they don't come from this world, just *what* world could they have come from? From where could the inspiration of an early Cainite musician, here, quite often, originate?

> *Yôbâl (Jubal) and Tôbalḵîn (Tubal-Cain), the two brethren, the sons of Lamech... invented and made all kinds of instruments of music. Yôbâl made reed instruments, and harps, and flutes, and whistles, and* ***the devils went and dwelt inside them****. When men blew into the pipes, the* ***devils*** *sang inside them, and sent out sounds from inside them. Tôbalḵîn made cymbals, and sistra, and tambourines (or drums).*
> - *Cave of Treasures* The Second Thousand Years[36]

Could some of these influences indeed come from the *supernatural* world - from some of Satan's fallen 1/3, maybe? According to Genesis 4:26, men eventually "became vulnerable" to demons, and "lax in praying," around this time - probably because of supernatural influences, such as these.[37] Look at how so many people are influenced by music, today; and the lifestyles of their performers? Where do these preforms get *their* influences, by the way?

There was more: there seemed, back then, to be plenty of people willing to jump "on the bandwagon" of what these early musicians were singing, and talking, about. Sound familiar… like *today*?

Interestingly enough, we discover that:[38]

...those who were ***beaten*** *came to... (Jubal and Tubal-Cain), took refuge with... (them), and he made them... (their)* ***confederates****.*
- *Second Book of Adam and Eve (The Conflict of Adam and Eve with Satan)* 20:9[39]

Anyone who thought they were being treated unfairly had a new someone, or something, to revere... *beyond* God. The human race finally felt they had their *own*, independent belief system! The trumped-up world of the Serpent and Cain's **religion** began to gather more and more followers.

How Music Became Related to Idolatry

...(the) people had agreed to do what God disapproves, committing wickedness, drinking wine, and letting their preoccupation with ***musical instruments*** *divert them from obedience to God.*
- *al-Tabari: The History of al-Tabari - Vol. I: General Introduction and From the Creation to the Flood* The Events That Took Place in Noah's Time 184[40]

Could their negative actions - along with *song* - help to give the people some element of **spiritual** gratification, here? People often sing in church. Yet, whatever they began to adopt things *of this world*, they found themselves not staying with the boundaries of what God wanted.

...(Tubal-Cain)... showed unto men arts in lead and tin and iron and copper and silver and gold: and then began the inhabiters of the earth to make ***graven images*** *and to worship them.* - *Pseudo Philo* 2:9[41]

God, soon, wasn't their friend, at all. A lot of people, deep down inside, began to think that God was inherently *unfair* to them; continually treating them wrongly. **Idolatry**, as we know, is the placing of *other* objects, or even other people, above God.[42] Many hoped to achieve their health, their strength, and their riches - even a long life - by providing *ritual* sacrifice to other gods of Cain and the Serpent. They wanted to please *their own* hearts - without having to go though any *spiritual* change of heart![43] The Cainites, and their sympathizers, may, now, have begun to imitate the music and singing they knew that *angels* would have directed towards God; and directing it their *own* pagan gods and sacrifices.[44]

> *And that accursed man Cain... multiplied evil, and his* ***seed*** *did likewise... They had not the fear of God before their eyes, and they never kept in mind that He had created them, and they never prayed to Him, and they never worshipped Him... nay, they ate, and they drank, and they* ***danced****, and they played upon stringed instruments, and sang lewd* ***songs*** *thereto...* - *Book of the Glory of Kings (Kerba Nagast)* 6[45]

Sex - The Ritual

It has been said that: if you don't make a conscious choice to follow God, you may have already made an **unconscious** choice to follow some *other* ways... of the world. What direction was their worship heading towards, *now*: Cain, the Serpent, and (ultimately) the prince and power of the present, *cursed* world... *Satan*?

> *In the days of Tubal (Jubal) and Tubal-cain, the sons of Lamech the blind,* ***Satan*** *entered and dwelt in them, and they constructed all kinds of musical instruments, harps and pipes. Some say that* ***spirits*** *used to go into the reeds and disturb them, and that* ***the sound from them was like the sound of singing and pipes****; and men constructed all kinds of musical instruments...* - *Book of the Bee* 19[46]
>
> *...Satan came into him (Jubal) in his childhood; and he made sundry trumpets and horns, and string instruments, cymbals and psalteries, and lyres and harps, and flutes; and he played them at all times and at every hour. And when he played on them, Satan came into them, so that from among them were heard beautiful and sweet sounds, that* ***ravished the heart****. Then he gathered companies upon companies to play on them; and when they played, it pleased* ***well*** *the children of Cain, who* ***inflamed themselves with sin*** *among themselves, and burnt as with fire; while Satan inflamed their hearts, one with another, and increased* ***lust among them****.*
> - *Second Book of Adam and Eve (The Conflict of Adam and Eve with Satan)* 20:2-4[47]

One's lusts soon began to take hold, over their character. Quite possibly, following some twisted model of the sexual occurrence at Eden, their sexual experiences now began to be turned into a *religious* ritual - a *celebration* of how the Serpent actually "freed"

Eve's mind by seducing her (at least, *according to them*). Now, eight hundred years after the Fall, sexual improprieties increased with the followers of Cain on *a grand scale*.[48]

> *...(Jubal and Tubal-Cain) was ruled by Azael (i.e. Azazel, the Serpent) from... (their) earliest youth, and invented all sorts of musical instruments.... (these) gave forth seductive* ***tunes*** *entrancing the hearts of all listeners... (they) would assemble companies of musicians, who inflamed one another with music until their* ***lust*** *burned bright like fire, and they* ***lay*** *together promiscuously.*
>
> (Graves and Patai, 1964, p. 103)[49]

> *And at that time, when they that dwelt on the earth had begun to do evil,* ***every one with his neighbour's wife, defiling them****, God was angry. And he began to* ***play*** *upon the lute (kinnor) and the harp and on every instrument of sweet psalmody (lit. psaltery), and to corrupt the earth.* - *Pseudo Philo* 2:8[50]

These practices truly helped bring the world into a state of anarchy and confusion. There were soon no real moral boundaries.[51]

> *Satan also taught... (Jubal and Tubal-Cain) to bring strong drink out of corn; and this... (they) used to bring together companies upon companies in drink-houses; and brought into their hands all manner of fruits and flowers; and they drank together... Then when they were drunk,* ***hatred and murder increased*** *among them; one man used violence against another to teach him evil taking his children and defiling them before them... Then sin increased among them greatly; until a man married his own sister, or daughter, or mother, and others; or the daughter of his father's sister, so that there was no more distinction of relationship, and they no longer knew what is* ***iniquity****...*
>
> - *Second Book of Adam and Eve (The Conflict of Adam and Eve with Satan)* 20:5-10[52]

Men went after the daughters of their own brothers.[53] One would have sex with his in-laws, his mother, even his own daughters.[54] People began to walk around naked in the streets.[55] They had sex, whenever and wherever they wanted. Older women were even more voracious than the young![56] No longer present were many of the early family values God had instilled in Adam. Many people of the day truly began to act like the **animals** which surrounded them.[57] God was not pleased.

Amalek - Their "New Idol"

As we recall:

> *These are all mixed among Yisrael, but none of them is cursed as Amalek, who is the evil Serpent, a Strange El: The one who uncovers all nakedness in the world. This means that it… causes* ***incest*** *(among other sexual transgressions) in the world. It is the* ***murderer****. From it, all murders in the world originate, and its spouse is the potion of death of* ***idol-worship****. So the three transgressions of idol-worship, incest and bloodshed derive from…* ***Amalek****, who is the serpent and another El. They are all related to the aspect of Samael (Sammael), who has many different aspects…*
>
> \- *Zohar* Beresheet A29[58]

As we notice (above), there were three attributes of which the Serpent (i.e. Amalek) had brought into this world. Obviously, he had major influences over the world ever since the Garden of Eden! The Serpent, even though he was cursed, *still* had become a powerful character in the world he inherited, overall:

> *…wherefore he is called Amalek, which signifies… a* ***Loose*** *People; or a people (consisting) of 130, because Amalek came with 130* ***chiefs*** *of Sammael…*
>
> (Eisenmenger, 1748, p. 206)[59]

He even had 130 spiritual chiefs (angels) of Sammael/Satan at his disposal, to help him influence the masses! Was *he* to soon become the major idol to these descendants, over time? We recall the **Serpent** *did* have a major part in the establishment of this early pagan religion - a religion, ultimately, devoted to Cain and *himself*. The fallen angels under the Serpent also probably convinced those around them to worship *them*, as well… instead of God. Thus Polytheism - the worship of *many* gods - began; and became the mainstay of pagan populations, from that point on.[60]

Josephus interpreted it something like this:

*(For many angels of God)... were overbearing and disdainful of every virtue; such **confidence** had they in their strength; in fact, the deeds that tradition ascribes to them resemble the audacious exploits told by the Greeks of the giants.*
- *Falvius Josephus* Jewish Antiquities I:72-76[61]

How long would God allow these angels to become so powerful, here? How long would idolatry continue along these same pathways? When would God put a stop to it?

As we'll soon see, it wasn't all that easy. To complicate things further, Lamech's wife, *Zillah*, would soon have another offspring. And this offspring - a female - could, quite possibly, have been *another* child of the Serpent himself (as we shall see)! If this did happen, one could assume there might have been reasons for him to continually seduce Zillah into coition. Maybe something ***big*** was about to happen, within Lamech's family, here. Maybe the Serpent also felt the desire to insert *himself* into the family tree, here, for some reason! Whatever happened, there would be another Cainite child born to Zillah - an important one. This woman, as with Tubal-Cain, would go on to possess a *major* role in further deteriorating her society. Yet, it wouldn't stop there.

It would, also, be during her lifetime that major **change** would occur, in this world. A terrible judgment - by God - was on the horizon. It was time for the population to pay for their depravities. Yet, this woman was, most probably, able to escape it all. How? And, if so, could this be *why* the Serpent was so interested in being with Zillah, and baring him this woman? So, just *who* was this woman; and *how* did she survive the punishment God plotted for all of mankind?

Naamah

...and the sister of Tubalcain was Naamah.
- *Gen.* 4:22 (KJV)

*And she (Zillah) conceived again and bare a daughter, and she called her name **Naamah**, for she said, After I had withered away have I obtained pleasure and delight.* - *Book of Jasher* 2:25

The name *Naamah* stands for "pleasant," or "lovely."[62] Naamah was last of these famous descendants of Cain in the Bible; and one of the most important.[63] Possibly, as we stated, she could have been a child of Zillah *and some angel* - the same as Tubal - Cain. Could they both have been children of the Serpent, as well? One ancient source stated that Naamah could have even been Tubal-Cain's *twin*:

> *Therefore, it is written, "The* ***sons of Elohim*** *saw that the daughters of men were fair" (Beresheet 6:2). All were going astray after them. There was one male, who was born to the spirit from the aspect of Cain, and he was named Tuval Cain.* ***A female was born with him****. People were going astray after her, and she was called* ***Na'amah****.*
>
> \- *Zohar* Acharei Mot 60[64]

Interestingly enough, she was also associated with the words "beauty" and "fatness." In those days, a *fat* person signified they lived a life somewhat luxuriously and comfortable. Obviously, Naamah must have also had beauty, because of the definition of her name. One might be able to assume, here, that she, not only had this beauty, but knew how to *use it* (to get all her luxuries). She got *fat*, in a way, because she obtained so much of what she desired:[65]

> *Because of her* ***beauty****, she led the sons of Elohim,* ***Aza*** *and* ***Azael*** *astray. She bore them all sorts of (descendants)...* ***Evil spirits*** *and* ***demons*** *spread out from her into the world.*
>
> \- *Zohar* Beresheet A9[66]

Quite possibly, for the sake of gain, Naamah could have gone down some improper pathways to achieve her goals. Did she involve herself, sexually, with fallen angels, as well - even up to the point of *incest* with the Serpent (Azazel) - her *own*, possible father? What *purpose* would this all of this be for, at least concerning the Serpent's motives? Let's see.

The "Final Straw" to Be Pulled

It's obvious: depravity began to rage in this newfound Cainite world; and God, obviously, wasn't going to take all of this sacrilege for long. Because He was a fair God, however, there would be advanced warning, given to people "in the know." So, those who *really* wanted to be pious, and still follow God, may have had an opportunity to escape His wrath.

Yet, this beautiful woman *also* seemed to have found out that God's judgment was on the cusp; and wanted a way out. Could *this* be why the fallen angels - especially *the Serpent*, himself - wanted to find a way to sire her; and wanted her to have children by him? Could there have been something *about* her, of which he knew, that showed him she would be able to survive God's up-and-coming judgment. Maybe the Serpent understood that his future *death* would be upon him, very quickly; and *desperately* wanted to provide himself, at least, *some* element of immortality… *in his descendants*! Let's see how it all went down.

Beyond corrupting herself with these fallen angels, Naamah could have also used one of the most **famous** characters in the Bible, in order to get her own way, here. We'll also soon learn who *he* was.

First, however, we need to discover *one* more element of the downfall of their present world. The previously mentioned depravities of the Cainites would not be enough to enact God's judgment *alone*; neither would it be because of the fornication of these fallen angels. There would be **one more** group of angelic individuals who, soon enough, would want to come onto the scene; and attempt to bring the world down *even further*. Their arrival would truly be the "final straw" of God's suffrage, in this case.

Let's see which group actually made up this "final straw."

Chapter 13

The Third Influx of Fallen Angels - The Watchers

Dan. 4:
13 *I saw in the visions of my head upon my bed, and, behold, a* **watcher** *and an holy one came down from heaven...*
17 *This matter [is] by the decree of the* **watchers**...

To add insult to injury, there would soon be *another* group of angels - destined to fall from grace, as well; *another* group who seemed to put the final "nail in the coffin," in regards to the world's depravity. These angels would also produce mixed offspring *just as illegitimate* and *rebellious* as the Nephilim - if not more. These two hundred or so angels could also be known as *the Shining Ones*, *the Holy Ones*, or the *Egregoroi*. Their most famous name, however, is *the Watchers* (the *Watchers of the Throne of God*).[1]

These Watchers, most probably, represented another group of angels who existed before the world's foundation.[2] Known as the *Sleepless Angels*, the Watchers were designated to "watch over" mankind almost *continually*.[3] They were also allowed, by God, to descend to the earth, and instruct people in a number of essential truths, core values, and moral ways of living.[4] They also worked to protect the people from many numerous *negative* factions they may have encountered in our post-Fall world (i.e. disease, sicknesses, poisonous plants and animals, etc.).[5] But, there was a problem: even *these* angels, with all of their helpful tips, would eventually be subjected to temptations in the world around them. No longer would they be there to help people - quite the opposite! Let's look at what brought on such a *change* in these angels, and why it angered God to the utmost.

The Third Group of Fallen Angels

So many groups of angels, here - how do we distinguish them? According to one ancient Jewish text (the *Genesis Apocryphon*, Frag. 2, Col. 2), an Adamite woman placed these fallen angels into, at least, three groups:

the Sons of Heaven **the Strangers** **the Watchers**

These three groups *could*, in actuality, be the following groups:

the ***Light*** (of Genesis 1) the ***Nephilim*** the ***Watchers***

The *Light* - angelic beings truly composed of *spirit* - could be the likes of Satan, those angels who accompanied God (as the Elohim) in the "Six-Day Creation," and others of the like… without corporeal bodies.

The *Strangers*, most probably, those of Nephilim statue: with the ability to shift into the image of a man, and back. We recall the earthly offspring of these fallen angels were known to be those with *strange* flesh.

The last group - the *Watchers* - represented a large group of angels (in physical appearance) who, along with the Nephilim, could become *corporeal*, if need be. Interestingly enough, these Watchers were *also* mentioned in the Bible (such as the above verse), and in a variety of ancient texts:

- *Book of Jubilees* 10:5, 4:15, 21-23
- *Testament of Amram* (The Dead Sea Scrolls) 4Q534
- *Genesis Apocryphon* (Dead Sea Scrolls) IQ20
- *Damascus (Zadokite) Document* (The Dead Sea Scrolls) CD, 4Q265-73, 5Q12, 6Q15
- *Testament of the Twelve Patriarchs (The Testament of Reuben: The First-Born Son of Jacob and Leah)* 2:18-19

Beyond various Apocrypha and Pseudepigrapha works, here, the Watchers were even mentioned in obscured pagan accounts of old (such as the *Book of the Dead*).[6] It's fairly obvious these giant were well known throughout ancient times. Let's discover what the Watchers did - how they contributed to this final outrage in the world… an outrage which set everything up for God's up-and-coming annihilation.

The Fall of the Watchers

For whatever reason, the Watchers didn't do the same as other angels - at the time of Adam's creation - and complain to God. We're not sure why; but for whatever reason, they weren't punished like the others. Whatever their circumstances, they seemed to have remained chaste throughout the years, all the way to this time (even through the rest of the world was succumbing to such depravity. Their time was to come, however: maybe it was the continual pressure of seeing so much sin underneath them; maybe things down there on earth were a little too much for most to handle.

Evil Times of Jared

> *…and she bare him a son in the third week of the sixth year, and he called his name* ***Jared****; for in his days the* ***angels*** *of the Lord descended on the earth, those who are named the* ***Watchers****…* - *Book of Jubilees* 4:15[7]

The time period the Watchers would descend to earth seemed to be prevalent during the life of *Jared*, father of that famous prophet, *Enoch*.[8] The year was approximately 3540-3544 B.C. that Jared was born (460 years after the formation of Adam).[9] The name *Jared*, in fact, means "descent" - a fitting name for the time the Watchers made their move.[10]

The Mount of Dissension

Many years seemed to have gone by, since the Watchers first began to descend to the earth, in order to instruct mankind. They may have even been instructing human beings way back to the time of Adam! It was around the time of Jared, however, that things went horribly wrong.

Five hundred years after Jared's birth (in approx. 3040 B.C.) the Watchers would, routinely, ascended and descended a tall mountain; and sing praises to God.[11] The mountain they used was called Mount *Hermon* (or *Armon*).[12] Interestingly enough, there *is* a mountain of the same name which exists at the northern tip of Israel. This mountain was also thought to be the place where Jesus himself communicated with those in the heavens![13]

Mount Hermon was also thought of as the "Mountain of the *Chief*." In this case, the "Chief" obviously stood for God himself![14] Other meanings for the *Hermon* are "Mount of the Oath," the mount of "Abomination," or the mountain "Devoted to Destruction."[15] Why? What "oath" or "abomination" could have taken place, here? What destruction might have happened?

As we'll see, a group of Watchers would, soon, bind themselves by an *oath*; an oath of which they made - under penalty of Herem (i.e. *abomination*).[16] Let's discover what was behind their oath; what they did wrong; and how it brought about further *destruction* to the planet at large.

Abomination and Failure

Up in the sky, the Watchers were able to look safely down upon the world; and notice the horrible atrocities going on below unscathed. Over time, they probably began to develop a condescending attitude towards the people doing all of these things. After witnessing so much of man's sinfulness, they decided they couldn't take it any more: they needed to complain to God - just like the *other* angels did, in the time of Adam.

They threw a hypothetical situation out to God: first, they claimed that Adam, and all of the other human beings around him, were really *destined* to fail… because of their physical make-up; and that God really shouldn't have put such a lowly man as *Adam* in charge of the entire world. Adam wasn't, and never *could* be, as "special" as they were. God, then, responded to them:

> *And God said unto them... "I created him (Adam) out of the dust... and I will not make my handiwork a laughingstock for his enemies." And those angels said, "Praise be unto thee, O Lord. For thou, the Knower of hearts, knowest that we have reviled Adam"... And (God)... answered them on behalf of Adam... "You have I created out of fire and air with the one intent (that ye should) praise (Me). Him have I created of twice as many elements as you - of dust and water, and of wind and fire; and he became (a being) of flesh and blood... And if his heart inciteth him to good, he walketh with good intent; and if the Devil seduceth him, he walketh with him on an evil path. As for you, ye have no other object in your minds but* ***praise of Me****, with the exception of that arrogant one (Satan) who produced evil, and became an evil being, and was driven forth from your assembly. And now, why do ye magnify yourselves over Adam? If ye were as he is, and I had created you of water and dust,* ***ye would have been flesh and blood****, and ye would have* ***transgressed*** *My commandment more than he hath done"...And the angels said unto him... "we will not oppose Thy word; for we are spiritual beings for life, and he is a creature of* ***dust (doomed) to folly****"... And straightway there were* ***given unto them****... flesh, and blood, and a heart of the children of men.* - *Book of the Glory of Kings (Kerba Nagast)* 100[17]

Apparently, the Watchers felt they needed to prove something. They thought, with their superior intellect, they would not allow themselves to fall the same way as their angelic predecessors. Confident in themselves, these angels even volunteered to "abandon their proper, former abode," to take on human form… to prove their point.[18] They were around this human depravity every day - how could *they* falter?

The Watchers should have had foresight - by looking at what happened to their predecessors - to understand the power of *temptation*. The women of the day, thanks to what they've learned over the years, would see *them* as targets, as well; and began to prepare themselves for the seduction. They began to scent themselves (i.e. to wear perfume), to fix their hair, and to dress seductively. They did all this to make themselves look irresistible to anyone around them. To the Watchers dismay, it *was* enough to take down even them.[19]

Many women went all out: they painted their eyes like harlots; they even walked around *naked*.[20] What was the reason for their actions? As we know… *power*. The

Watchers also had a vast amount of occult knowledge; and, as before, started to give away their knowledge for any sexual favors they may have wanted.

This segues into, probably, one of the most confusing set of verses in the Bible:

<u>Gen. 6:</u>
1 *And it came to pass, when Adam (the man) began to multiply on the face of the earth, and daughters were born unto them,*
2 *That the sons of God saw the daughters of Adam that they were fair; and they took them wives of all which they chose.*
3 *And the LORD said, My spirit shall not always strive with Adam (the man), for that he also is flesh: yet his days shall be an hundred and twenty years.*
4 *There were giants (Nephilim) in the earth in those days (at the time that marked 120 years before Adam's death); and after that (time), when the sons of God came in unto the daughters of men...*
(in retranslation)

On the surface, these verses might sound a little confusing. Accompanied with the detail we already know, however, we'll see they provide a *great* deal of information - straight from the Bible - about our ancient world. There seems, here, to have been *two* separate occurrences, with two separate angelic groups, being reported at once (as we'll see): first, the words "And it came to pass" probably summarized that a certain period of time had passed. Time passed, since the Fall.

And, because thc word for *man*, in the above verse, actually is represented by *The Adam*, we know (from Chapter 4, *The Adam is Formed*) the verse is referring to that *one* particular man - named ***Adam***; and *not* mankind, in general. So, we gather from this that: it must have been around the time of which Adam was very *old*; and it was God who made a statement about *his* end of days:

<u>Gen. 6:</u>
1 *And it came to pass, when Adam (the man) began to multiply on the face of the earth, and daughters were born unto them,*
3 *And the LORD said, My spirit shall not always strive with* **Adam** *(the man), for that he also is flesh: yet* **his days** *shall be an hundred and twenty years."*
(in retranslation)

We already know, from a previous chapter, what *flesh* often stood for (in ancient times). And, we already know that Adam probably participated in sexual exchanges with female fallen angels - he followed the *flesh*. These exchanged, often, created offspring who ended up - over time - wandering *away* from God; and going *after the flesh*. Even *Adam* had fallen, some, by these exchanges. And, eventually, God decided to end his life, at this time, because of it all. After all, Adam was supposed to be His viceroy - but, even *he* would fall, to a degree… in this present, evil world. It was now time for God to do something. He, first off, gave Adam about 120 more years to live. This set into motion God's plan of judgment.

The next piece of information, in these verses, probably involves *two* groups of fallen angels. Genesis 6:3 stated that these Nephilim (translated in the KJV as *giants*) were "in the earth" at that point Adam was destined to have 120 years left in his life:

Gen. 6:
4 *There were giants (Nephilim) in the earth* ***in those days****...*

And, it was **also** during this same time that another group of angels (the "Sons of God") came unto the daughters of men, and bore children by them. Guess who these were…

Gen. 6:
2 *That the* ***sons of God*** *(the* ***Watchers?****) saw the daughters of Adam that they were fair; and they took them wives of all which they chose.*
4 *...and after that (time)... the* ***sons of God*** *(the Watchers) came in unto the daughters of men...*
(in retranslation)

Could these "Sons of God" be the Watchers? We know they weren't the Nephilim because the Bible mentioned them previously! This was a *new* group of angelic beings, with an entirely *different* undertaking, about to commence. Could this have *also* represented the time of the Watcher's descent?

If we follow the assumption that there were two *individual* groups, here, the context of these verses becomes really clear.[21]

<u>*Gen.* 6:</u>
2 *...the **sons of God** (the **Watchers**) saw the daughters of Adam that they were fair; and they took them wives of all which they chose.*
(in retranslation)

<u>*Gen.* 6:</u>
4 *There were (already) giants (the **Nephilim**) in the earth in those days (the time that marked 120 years before Adam's death); and after that (point in time)... the sons of God (the **Watchers**) came in unto the daughters of men, and they bare children to them...*
(in retranslation)

The Third Dissension

So, we probably could conclude, here, that *this* was the point when the Watchers volunteered to go down to earth. They weren't *cast down* like their fallen, Nephilim counterparts; they *freely* chose to leave their former habitation, and show God what they were really "made of."[22]

As the Watchers began to challenge God, some of them came through as a little hesitant about their fortitude; others really didn't want to go at all... but a group of them *still* went.

> *...the Watchers are the **sons of God** (Genesis 6) sent from heaven to instruct the children of men; they fell after they descended to earth... But not all Watchers descended: those that remained are the **holy Watchers**...*
> ("A Dictionary of Angels", n. d., p. 10)[23]

We see that a division arose, here. Some truly began to be afraid that they would fall to temptation. Their leader, Shemhazai, wanted all of them to go through with this task. He caused 200 angels to take an oath: that *all* will go down at the same time, and try to upstart God's thoughts. And, if *some* began to have indecent thoughts about women, they

all would have to follow along.[24] Shemhazai obviously didn't want to fall alone, if he felt he was going to. An oath was **oath**; *all* or nothing.

The Evil Inclination Overcame Them

> *...As soon as they descended to earth, the **evil inclination** seized them...*
> - *Zohar* Beresheet A50[25]

When the 200 descended, they obviously didn't take into account the *human* element: *emotions* and other physical desires they may have inherited. They underestimated worldly temptation:

> ***Immediately**, "The sons of the Elohim (God) saw the daughters of man..." They were filled with passion for them...* - *Zohar* Beresheet A20[26]

So much for their superior intellect. As soon as they descended, the **evil inclination** quickly overpowered them.[27] Some sources stated that those angels who volunteered to go down to earth could *not* return to heaven… after being on the earth for seven days.[28] The Watchers - supposedly there to help people - began to subject themselves to the ways of the world; and helped *themselves* to more than they should have!

In the end, the Watchers ended up doing the exact *opposite* of what they thought they would, and fell even *worse* than their predecessors! No longer were they continually awake, "watching" over those below them. Now, they began to prostitute their forbidden arts and sciences - information by which God gave them for helping people (but, only in limited quantities, however) - to help gather them their *own* worldly favors.[29]

> *Rabbi Eleizar, in the 8th century... put the blame squarely upon the women. "The angels who fell from Heaven saw the daughters of Cain perambulating and displaying their private parts, their eyes painted with antimony in the manner of harlots, and, being seduced, took wives from among them" (Chapter 22). It is difficult to believe the angels were entirely innocent bystanders but they did prove to be highly vulnerable.* (Godwin, 1990, p. 85)[30]

Now, they began to teach human beings even more forbidden knowledge: spells, herbs, and other magical enchantments.

Two Working Together

And, through the eventual abuses of all this occult knowledge, the Watchers helped to drag the world down *even more*:[31]

> *The wickedness of these giants became so great that the earth complained [to God]. At this time (the angel) 'Azâz'êl taught men the art of working in **metals**, and the use of stibium, or **eye-paint**, and the art of **dyeing** stuffs in bright colours. 'Amêzârâk taught **enchantments** (i.e. magic) and the knowledge of **herbs**; 'Armârôs taught how **spells** were to be broken; Barak'âl taught **astrology**; Kôkab'êl taught the knowledge of **signs**; Tem'êl taught **astronomy**; and 'Asrâdêl taught concerning the moon...*
>
> \- *Cave of Treasures*, The Second Thousand Years[32]

People used this, and *other*, knowledge - and began to abuse it.

The "Men of Old"

Here, we continue with our reinterpretation of Genesis, Chapter 6:

> *...and they bare children to them, **the same** became mighty men which were **of old**...*
>
> \- *Gen.* 6:4 (KJV)

These words, though initially confusing, go right to the point: *the same* stands for *these same* offspring of the Watchers (as mentioned, before). Their particular descendants would be called the ***Mighty Men*** (the *Great Men*, the *Gever*, the *Gibborim*, etc.). We'll, also, see Biblical evidence that these descendants came from a group of angels who were reportedly *of old*, or who were around *from the foundation of our world.*

We already discovered the mixed offspring of the Nephilim were known as *Anakim*. The *Mighty Men* were a little different, though. Because the Watchers were large angels to begin with, their offspring were so-called because - when they grew into adulthood - they grew to a mighty, overbearing size![33] Their descendants ended up being anywhere from twelve to fourteen feet tall - three to four feet *taller* than those Anakim were!

The "Men of Renown"

> *...the same became mighty men which were of old,* ***men of renown****.*
> - Gen. 6:4 (KJV)

These angelic offspring would be lot more intimidating, however: they were intelligent; their deeds would make them look like *heroes* to almost everyone around them.[34] These Mighty Men were also called *men of renown* (or, the *men of name*). Even though popular, they didn't their reputations by living in proper, wholesome ways.[35] They utilized all of this highly-advanced knowledge - the knowledge that *God* had given to their forefathers - *without* giving any of the glory to Him! This segues, perfectly, into the next verse of Genesis:

> *And God saw that the wickedness of man was great in the earth, and that every imagination of the thoughts of his heart was only evil continually.*
> - *Gen.* 6:5 (KJV)

The evil deeds of these Mighty Men, however, would not come without a cost to themselves, and everyone else around. The Mighty Men, along with the Anakim, had an extremely hard time living in our world. Their huge sizes - measure for measure - would come back to haunt them, on many levels. On top of this, their evil deeds angered God - to the utmost.

Why These Offspring Didn't Work - Problems at Birth

> *Wherefore have ye (the Watchers) left the high, holy, and eternal heaven, and lain with women, and defiled yourselves with the daughters of men and taken to yourselves wives, and done like the children of earth, and begotten giants (as your)*

sons. And though ye were holy, spiritual, living the eternal life, you... have lusted after flesh and blood as those also who die and perish. Therefore have I given them (human beings) also wives that they might impregnate them, and beget children by them, that thus nothing shall be wanting to them on earth. But you were formerly spiritual... And therefore I have not appointed wives for you... (Your children), the giants, who are produced from the spirits and flesh, shall be called evil spirits upon the earth, and on the earth shall be their dwelling... because they are born from men, and from the holy watchers is their beginning and primal origin...

- *1 Enoch* 15:3-9[36]

Not only were the Mighty Men up to five feet taller than the Anakim, the birth of these individuals, often, seemed much more difficult to come about. Imagine one of these giant babies - how could it come out of a human womb effectively? There are ancient accounts of the horrible circumstances which surrounded the birth of these offspring:

And the daughters of Cain with whom the angels had companied conceived, but they were unable to bring forth their children, and they ***died****. And of the children who were in their wombs some died, and some came forth; having* ***split open the bellies*** *of their mothers they came forth by their navels. And when they were grown up and reached man's estate they became giants...*

- *Book of the Glory of Kings (Kerba Nagast)* 100[37]

As they grew, their 12-foot-plus sizes posed even more of a logistic problem:[38]

Our skills and behavior are finely attuned to our size. We could not be twice as tall as we are, for the kinetic energy of a fall would then be 16 to 32 times as great, and our sheer weight (increased eightfold) would be more than our legs could support. Human giants of eight to nine feet have either died young or been ***crippled early*** *by failure of joints and bones.* ("Sizing Up Human Intelligence", 1996-1997, p. 151-155)[39]

This was the beginning of their realization that their present world may not have been **meant** for them. This fact made the Mighty Men even *more* angry and resentful (to God) than the Anakim ever were; and soon began to take out their anger on anyone and *anything* that surrounded them.

Another Motivation to Breed With Women

Beyond the exchanges of sex with power-hungry women, here, there could have been *another* reason that the Nephilim and Watchers wanted to breed with so many women, and have as many children as possible - very *important* reasons (at least to them). First, we need to understand that these Watchers, after *their* fall, were not allowed a *second chance* for redemption; just like the Nephilim:[40]

> *...because man (Adam) definitely was destined to sin... as Aza and Azael said, as written "the woman whom you did give to be with me, she gave me of the tree, and I did eat"... He (God) replied... You, Aza and Azael, have laid accusations before me that go beyond those of all the hosts above. If you were better than man in your actions, you would have had a right to accuse him, but man is destined to sin only with one woman while you are destined to sin with* ***many women****. Therefore, your* ***sins are greater*** *than those of human beings... As man sinned, I prepared* ***atonement*** *for him to amend his sin, as repentance takes precedence in the world. But for the angels,* ***atonement has no effect at all****.* - *Zohar* Beresheet A16[41]

As with the Nephilim, they, now, had their reward right in front of them - *in this world*, already… and that's *all*:

> *(The) Nefilim... made themselves fall from their holiness, and they fornicated with women who were fair. Because of this, the Holy One, blessed be He, also eliminated them from the* ***world to come****, so that they may not have a portion there. And He* ***gave them their reward in this world****...* - *Zohar* Beresheet A20[42]

There's nothing really left for them, after their mortal run on this earth finally ends. After the Fall of Adam, the Nephilim *knew* that their lives would not continue forever. They would die, just as any other living being in this world. The Watchers were now in this same boat! After their deaths, God would sentence *all* of their souls down in *chains* - imprisoned in the debts of the earth… until the end of our era.[43] This was even mentioned in the Bible:

And the ***angels who kept not their first estate****, but left their own habitation, he hath reserved in everlasting* ***chains under darkness*** *unto the* ***judgment*** *of the great day. Even as Sodom and Gomorrah... giving themselves over to* ***fornication****.*
- *Jude* 1:6-7 (KJV)

Angels who are *truly* immortal do not really need to reproduce! Because human beings are mortal, however - and these fallen angels have *now* been made mortal - *this* could have been a huge reason behind their desire for coition, and pregnancies. By producing a child, one might feel at least *a part* of them could continue. So, by this, they may feel at least a little bit of "immortality," by way of their offspring.[44]

The following is a passage from a Jewish Midrash: a woman named Hannah was praying to God, in order to have a child. Notice what she says:

The ***celestials never die****, and they do not reproduce their kind. Terrestrial beings die, but they are fruitful and multiply. Therefore I pray: either make me* ***immortal****, or give me a* ***son****!* ("The Watchers & the Nephilim", n. d., p. 2)[45]

This is much like a person who lives *vicariously* through their children; as we so often see, today! These fallen angels now found themselves in a similar situation. Only terrestrial beings use methods such as these, in order to achieve some sort of immortal feelings; which would also be a reason why these angelic beings would develop such **insatiable** sexual appetites.

To Feel Better

Must of us know that sex feels good, and helps to create children; but it is *not* a *complete* pathway to personal gratification. It, temporarily, feels good; but one has to keep doing it - over and over again - in order to achieve a similar effect. That's not complete. That's not perfection. Regardless, many of these angels also felt the need to use *sex* as a way for them to a least feel *a little* better about themselves. Regardless of how many times it was done, back then, we know that even angels couldn't be *fully* satisfied with all of their worldly attempts... even though they did it *a lot*:[46]

> *...they were never satisfied from hunger because of their hybrid nature (1/2 Earthly - 1/2 Spirit), since their* ***Spiritual side was never fed****, since... (God) had no desire to accept these unwelcome offspring of the Watchers. They were considered no part of his Creation Scheme and therefore outside of his help, and they would not be able to take advantage of any redemption plan.*
>
> ("The Watchers of Heaven FAQ Page", n. d., p. 4)[47]

The Continual Hunger

Their over-extended sexual appetites began to expand, as in *other* appetites. The angels, and their mixed offspring, also began to be tormented with a continual hunger, and not only for sex.[48] They began to eat a lot of food; they even began to develop a taste for human flesh and blood![49] Nothing of this world really satisfied them; not for long! Much like a drug addiction, their thoughts became somewhat overwhelming:

> *These children grew up and became giants... and when they had* ***devoured*** *all the provisions which their neighbours had collected, they began to fight against men and to eat them, and at length they ate the flesh and drank the blood of* ***each other****...*
>
> - *Cave of Treasures* The Second Thousand Years[50]

Again, it seems they were trying to gather some sort of *immortality* through their overindulgences; no matter *what* they would manifest into. Their drives to consume more and more resources began to have some negative side-affects to the world around them: their habits helped to destroy things around them. God, responding to this, even tried to rain *manna* down from heaven, to give these individuals enough food to suffice their obsessions. Although He tried to help, He really did not want them to go beyond their normal diets, in any way. Nor did He did not want them to eat human flesh, or drink blood… that's for sure. God was a gracious God, even though these individuals were already becoming so misguided in their ways.

The giant offspring, especially, was intent on rejecting any help from God. Through their acts, they began to lead other people down these same pathways.[51] The world was going downhill, *fast*. Cannibalism was even becoming a normal part of human hunger; as well, a part of religious practice.[52] Eventually, the Anakim and Mighty Men became a *burden* to the world - even downright *dangerous*. There were reasons why God did not want these fallen angels to procreate.

Another Way to Avert Their Doom?

There may have even been, yet, *another* reason why these fallen angels *worked so hard* to pollute the earth with their own angelic sperm! We know the immortality of these angels had come and gone - their time on earth was upon them. Their next step would be eternal punishment. We also know the prophecy of which God gave to Adam and Eve: the savior would clearly be descended from a seed of *Adam* (Gen. 3:15). And, at the time of his arrival, the savior would disable *any* and *all* of holds these angelic beings might have had on the earth; and this includes Satan! He would **seal** their fate - pure and simple… and the angels knew it!

So, these angels thought: if they could, somehow, totally compromise the seed of Adam, at this time, it might be able disrupt God's prophecy, here. If they could totally prevent this Adamic seed from being passed on to the eventual savior, then he might never be born… thus, nullifying this prophecy![53] They would no longer be defeated! Through their rationale, they felt they could never be punished - if they only were able to accomplish this dastardly deed!

With this possibility in their view, the stage began to be set. The influx of angelic DNA into mankind's gene pool now seemed to take on a life of its own! This was also probably why the Serpent **worked so hard** to show women how to allure men to their physical/moral destruction!

Not only were these fallen angels having so much sex to raise their lowered feelings of self-esteem, and to feel some sort of "immortality" in having descendants, *now* they tried to disrupt the prophecy of Genesis 3:15!

These angels, and their mixed, giant offspring, became so sexually outrageous that they began to be known by another famous name - ***demons***.

"The Living Demons"

> *...(human) creatures were formed... whose bodies were not completed, namely* ***demons****. They joined the body of Adam (the Adamites), the male and the female... and* ***begot offspring in the world****. They are called the plagues of men...*
> - *Zohar* Tazria 22[54]

Now, we see that these fallen angels, and their offspring, were the *origin* of this "demonic" concept![55] Yes, demons, today, are mostly thought of as almost entirely *in spiritual form* - evil "spirits." Back then, however, these demons were considered to be *live*, terrestrial beings!

There are demons, known as the *incubus* and *succubus*, for example, who are considered to be *spiritual* entities; seducing men and women while they sleep. Yet, an interesting quote on these particular demons seems to give us a clue to their *real* origins, however:

> *According to one legend, the incubus, and its female counterpart, the succubus, were* ***fallen angels****. Union with an incubus was thought to produce demons, witches, and deformed children.* (Killian, n. d., p. 22)[56]

And, we know that the word *demon* comes from the Greek word *daio*; which means, "to divide" or "apportion." And, we also recall that Adam once called Eve the "divider of mankind." Because Eve may have produced a child with the Serpent, she bore offspring who would be at *enmity* with the seeds of Adam. These demons, because they also had seed of the Serpent and other fallen angels, would also, often, be at *enmity* with these same seeds of Adam - trying to *divide* a whole number of people away from God, and His ways.[57]

On top of being the world's "dividers," a *demon* could also be referred to as "an inferior deity (or "god")."[58] As we know, these angels and their offspring were becoming *so popular* that they tried to convince others around them to worship *them*, as **divine**:

> *It should be remembered, however, that **these antediluvian heroes** were thought to be something **more than human**, since they were so close to the beginning of the world... The length of their lives is therefore symbolic of their supra-human characters.* (Goldstein, 1933, p. 43)[59]

Now, we know them as they *really* were; and where they *really* came from. Along with their Nephilim and Watcher forefathers, a good number of these hybrid-offspring would *also* have their souls imprisoned in the bowels of the earth, after their death. One ancient source stated that up to *ten percent* of these original hybrid souls were not brought down to the *Darkness*, after their death - but destined to *remain* on the earth, and become the ***demons*** we know of today! They were, then, forever condemned to roam the earth, as *disembodied* spirits.[60]

> *These are descendants (of Adam), but the earlier ones were not [human] descendents. What then were they? **Demons**... Throughout the entire one hundred and thirty years during which Adam held aloof from Eve the **male demons** were made ardent by her and she bore, while the **female demons** were inflamed by Adam and they bore...*
> - *Genesis Rabbah* 24:6[61]

> *And now, the giants, who are produced from the spirits and flesh, **shall be called evil spirits** upon the earth, and on the earth shall be their dwelling. Evil spirits have proceeded from their bodies, because they are born from men, and from the holy watchers is their beginning and primal origin... And the **spirits** of the giants afflict, oppress, destroy, attack, do battle, and work destruction on the earth, and cause trouble: they take no food, but nevertheless hunger and thirst, and cause offences. And these spirits shall rise up against the children of men and against the women, because they **have proceeded from them**.* - *1 Enoch* 15:8-9, 15:11-12[62]

The destiny of these mixed descendants angered these **demons** even *more* than their terrestrial, angelic ancestors. And, these are the reasons why the demons of which we've heard of today are thought to be so *sexually* vivacious; and have so much anger.[63] They desperately wanted (in the past), and still want, to achieve the immortality they no longer have; and also want to bring *everyone* and *everything* they could down with them, as a result! Total pride dominates their thoughts.

An Ancient Parallel of Worldly Domination

The Nephilim, Watchers, and their mixed offspring were responsible for bringing even *more* deviant acts upon our world - those never done on such a grand scale.

> *...there emerge firm grounds to suggest that initiates and secret societies preserved, revered, even celebrated the forbidden knowledge that our most distant ancestors had gained their inspiration and wisdom, not from God or from the experiences of life, but* ***from a forgotten race remembered by us today only as fallen angels, demons, devils, giants and evil spirits****. Should such a view prove in any way correct, then it must indicate one of the greatest secrets ever* ***kept*** *from mankind.*
>
> (Collins, 1996, p. 10)[64]

From these demons, *really* deviant sexual acts, serial murders, and even a crossbreeding of different animal species had begun.[65] People probably didn't think too much about homosexuality and other alternative sexual practices until the angels (and their offspring) came upon the scene. They introduced orgies, sodomy, and other alternate sexual acts into the mix - now, as *mainstream*.[66] One ancient source, *The Book of Jubilees*, stated: "all of them corrupted their order ways and their orders."[67] At this time, deviations to both the human and animal kingdom - even acts of bestiality - became fashionable. The animal kingdom would not only be violated by men and angel, animals were crossbred, one species to another. The whole natural world, around these terrestrial individuals, was being manipulated - exploited *beyond* their natural means.

> *All acted corruptly... the dog (copulated) with the wolf, the fowl with the peacock; hence it is written, For all flesh had corrupted their way (Genesis 6:12).*
>
> - *Genesis Rabbah* 28:8[68]

Animals lost a lot of their natural tendencies. Some began to reject their own mates; others became increasingly violent and dangerous.[69] Sexuality truly lost a lot of its original uses and purposes. If these angels and their offspring were going to go down, they wanted to bring **the entire world** down with them; that's how they felt about it.

So many of the problems in our world, today, did not probably originate from some hormonal imbalance in human and animal; they probably didn't originate with some fluke, some genetic mutation, or natural selection - but genetic *manipulation*: a **deliberate** perversion of the flora and fauna on our planet… pure and simple.

We know the fallen Watchers were supposed to teach people *what **not** to do*; now they were beginning to do the opposite! No wonder why the world was becoming so rampant, as far as *deviant* actions, here - it was like a drug enforcement officer showing people how to *use* drugs!

The misdeeds of the *Watchers* and their *Mighty Men* descendants helped to devastate the world a lot more than any Nephilim could have dreamed. They might have totally destroyed most of the true orders of nature, if allowed to continue.[70]

"Spreading the Disease"

> *According to Persian legend, Arimanes, the Evil Spirit, by eating a certain kind of fruit, transformed himself into a serpent, and went gliding about on the earth to tempt human beings. His devs (demons) entered the bodies of men and produced all **manner of diseases**.* (Doane, 1882, p. 3)[71]

Now, mental problems, genetic deformities, and other physical and emotional human conditions began to take hold with the populous. According to the *Book of the Generations of Adam*, one corrupted daughter of Adam (named *Ammah*) now, even "manipulated the very fountain of life, until she had created new forms of beings dedicated to evil and the destruction of mankind. From then on, **sickness** and **disease** began to spread among the sons of men, bringing sorrow and death upon them."[72]

The Straw that Broke the Camel's Back

Because of all these problems, the world was going downhill… rapidly. The time frame for the world's self-destruction was upon them - there was almost no other way for mankind to go. Everyone who turned their back on God was almost drowned in these new "ways" of Cain and the Serpent. The actions of the Nephilim, the Cainites, and *now* the Watchers, almost brought to the world to the point of no return - unless God caused something drastic to happen.

Interestingly enough, thróughout this all, something seemed to be "in the air." People were beginning to have that feeling that some kind of change was soon to be upon them. There were even *Watchers*, and their descendants, who were beginning to have these feelings: feelings that they, no longer, would be able to live the *same* way they did, in the past… they just "felt it."[73]

> *Now, they will find neither peace nor pardon. For every time they take joy in their offspring, they shall see* ***the violent death*** *of their sons and sigh over the ruin of their children... Trembling seized upon them... for they could not speak with God as afore time, nor even raise their eyes heavenward, for shame on account of their sins.*
> (Ginzberg, 1909, p. 126)[74]

What would happen to all of those who adopted these "ways?" What about the pious, if any, who were to be left behind, after God's judgment? Could anything stop the world's downward spiral, here? And, most importantly, would there be something on the horizon to assure the survival of the Genesis 3:15 Prophecy… preserving, a least, a little of the untainted, Adamic seed, still left?

Chapter 14

The Sethites
Come Down the Mountain

And ***they*** *went up on the skirts of the mountain... and they became praisers and glorifiers of God in the place of that* ***host of devils*** *who fell from heaven... and they had nothing to do except to praise and glorify God, with the angels.*
- *Cave of Treasures* The Rule of Seth[1]

"The Appointed" Adamic Seed

And Adam knew his wife again; and she bare a son, and called his name ***Seth****: For God, said she,* ***hath appointed me*** *another seed instead of Abel, whom Cain slew.*
- *Gen.* 4:25 (KJV)

The name *Seth* stands for, "the appointed one," the "power," or the "replacement."[2] One ancient source stated that, after the birth of Seth, Eve exclaimed "God has heard my prayer, and has delivered me out of my affliction." Seth just seems to be *appointed* as Eve's emancipator for a number of reasons, here.[3] For one, Seth seemed to have been a son Adam was looking for - *appointed* to be as righteous as the best of individuals, such as Abel. For another, it seems that Seth was to be *appointed*, by God, to, first, take this prophesied seed of Adam, and pass it on.

The other women/angels (of whom Adam might have been with, *sexually*) could not have been the matriarch of this chosen seed line. Only ***Eve*** was to be (according to the Genesis 3:15 Prophecy, itself). There would be *no* mixed, angelic blood in his descendants… at all.

...All the children of Adam were ***breathless****, except only for Seth, for he was* ***son of the greatness of God****.*
- *Book of Adam* [47]38:4[4]

The word *breathless* simply implies that many other descendants of Adam probably had lacked that unique *image* and *likeness* of God's breath. Obviously, the seed was not what God wanted, in this case. This *breath* of God was said to have been inserted directly into Adam himself (Gen. 2:7), by God; and Adam and **Eve** *had* to get together again, to start the prophecy into motion. Seth and his further descendants *had* to be born, to allow the savior his chance to overcome the Serpent's hold on this planet! So, Seth, then, would become the **protector** of this chosen bloodline - in charge of the pious, after the time of Adam's dominion.

The Other Side of this "Seed Line" Prophecy - The Sethites

Let's look at the *anointed* son of Adam, the first child who - the Bible says - *actually* looked like him! Seth, according to one ancient source, had a *fair* countenance; which often meant a *light* or bright countenance - one similar to *an angel of God*, and what Adam might have originally had.[5]

The descendants of Seth were known as ***Sethites***. These Sethites - this special Adamic seed line - were required to stay righteous, and pass their untainted seed on the same as how Adam and Eve passed it on to Seth. Obviously, this would be a repeating cycle - to the one eventually who would become their savior. We'll see, however, that their attempts at keeping this going - and keeping righteous - would not go on, very well. Those within Seth's seed would begin to fall - to those around them - one by one.

130 Years of Image Loss

Soon after Adam's fall, as we recall, he lost his heavenly countenance. It seemed that he would lose a little more of this, and any of the magnificent, angelic-like appearance he might have been given, as time went on. This trend would continue *downward*; passing on through each subsequent generation… until there was hardly anything left which made Adam's seed special - *at least on the outside*![6]

For years - after the death of Abel - Adam and Eve might have been apart. Yet, eventually, Adam came to his senses; and realized what he must do. He knew, for the fulfilment of prophecy, he had eventually to go back to Eve. God, it was said, even gave him the strong desire to be with Eve, again - and her alone.[7] When they eventually reunited, Adam begot a son in *his own likeness* (i.e. his own "ways of thought"?), as well as his own *image*.[8]

> *And Adam lived an hundred and thirty years, and begat a son in* ***his own likeness****, and after* ***his image****; and called his name* ***Seth****...* - *Gen.* 5:3 (KJV)

Basically, this son seemed to have looked like he *belonged* to Adam; unlike Cain and Abel - who looked like, as Eve said, they belonged to (or were sired by) *an angel*. The child didn't only *look* like his father, but, as we now see, had similarities to him in *thought* and deed.

Their Voyage to Mount Hermon

Seth became a famous Adamite, along with the likes of the aforementioned Enosh, Jared, and Enoch. And, we also know times were beginning to get bad when Enosh was the patriarch of the family. By the time of Jared, the Watchers had already descended to the earth, and corrupted it more. Now, we'll see that there was *another* major event which took place in the 500th year of Jared's life - in approximately 2465 B.C.: almost *all* the Sethites were going to be seduced by a number of evil-loving Cainites surrounding them; this nullifying the Genesis 3:15 Prophecy.[9]

By the time of Jared's death, many children of Cain were totally steeped in corruption. They had also become successful in infiltrating most any of those who wanted to be stay pious. Some sources stated that the sons of Seth dwelled in mountains near the Garden of Eden, others stated that they eventually moved away from the Garden; to another land… to escape all of these problems they saw were going on.[10] In this *new* land, they were able to worship God freely… at least, for a while:

> *They were happy, innocent, without sudden fear, there was no jealously, no evil action, no hatred among them. There was no animal passion; from no mouth among them went forth either foul words or curse; neither evil counsel nor fraud... when men must swear, they swore by the blood of Abel the just.*
>
> - *Second Book of Adam and Eve (The Conflict of Adam and Eve with Satan)* 11:12[11]

According to ancient sources, the family line of Seth, as well as Adam himself, took leave of Eden; and went to the Cainite city of *Enoch*. From there, Adam and these Sethites traveled northwest, to what would now be known as the land of *Israel*.

> *(Adam talking to Seth) "Son, this is not our home, for this was the home of wild* ***beasts*** *and animals. Rather our home was in Eden towards the east, in the garden."*
>
> - *Armenian Apocryphal Adam Literature* The Words of Adam to Seth 1[12]

Although there were a lot of unsavory people and animals in most areas, Mount *Hermon* - the mount at the northern tip of Israel - would become their new home of peace and tranquility. Mount Hermon, as we also know, was also the mountain where the Watcher angels once would descend and ascend; singing praises to God. It seemed a perfect place for anyone who truly wanted to be closer to his Lord.[13]

Interestingly, Hermon was also believed to have housed a cave where Adam designated himself to be buried, when the time was to come (known as "The Cave of Treasures").[14] The Cainites, on the other hand, noticed there were other people moving in, here; and also noticed that they specifically wanted to move there to be *pious* and *separate*. Of course, the Cainites would have nothing of this: if *they were* going to go down in *morality*, then so was everyone else around them! Because of this, the Cainites seemed hell-bent on their destruction.

Another Separation

> *(Adam speaking)... my son Seth, governor of the sons of thy people... thou shalt rule them purely and holily in an the fear of God. And keep* ***ye offspring separate from the offspring*** *of Cain, the murderer.*
>
> - *Cave of Treasures* The Death of Adam[15]

The time had come for Adam's death. Adam, in his last breaths, tried to instruct his offspring in virtue, humility, and purity. Adam gave them one more instruction: Seth and his descendants were **not** to associate with the children of Cain, for any reason.[16] He wanted them to worship God in the proper manner - up in their mountain, and *away* from any temptation![17]

Cain's influence, however, was *strong* in most areas of the civilized world. The areas around the Garden of Eden, for example, were probably becoming too corrupt for this group of Sethites; and most anyone else wanting to remain chaste. So, the mountain proved to be a stronghold of faith and virtue, for those who wanted to be free to worship God again, and feel somewhat protected. This lasted for a while.[18]

But, some of the Cainites were starting to settle down in a valley, close to the mountain.[19] The Cainites also knew about the Sethites, and their intentions; and begun to press hard towards the filling of their *own* resolve. As long as the Sethites remained on the mountain, however, it seemed that God was helping them. It seemed as though He assured them they would be away from any Cainite wiles - as long as they stayed up there. The division between the two seemed clearly defined.

> *Now the generation of Seth... **drove** away the generation of Cain and did not mix with Cain's people... there was no way of mixing with Cain's generation.*
> - *Armenian Apocryphal Adam Literature* Tidings 9, 20[20]

For a while, every Sethite up there lived a very happy, spirit-filled life; praising God continuously. The pious of the world also began to look up to *these individuals*, as living on some shining beacon on a hill. That would not last for long, however.

The Watcher's Replacement?

After the fall of the Watchers, the Sethites seemed to have "taken their place," in a way. They began to worship God just like the choir of angels once did![21] Because of their holiness, and piety, the Sethites could have even been known, by some, as the "sons of

God" (i.e. "sons of the Elohim") - the *same* as once given to these Watchers![22] They truly acted angelic.

Interestingly enough, we'll soon see that Watchers and Sethites *both* may have been known as "sons of God" later on, throughout the centuries. This could have easily left room for confusion, on just "who was who," here. Why is this important? According to the Jerusalem Bible, for example: "Later Judaism and almost **all** the earliest ecclesiastical writers identify the 'sons of God' with the fallen angels; but from the 4th century onwards, as the idea of angelic natures **becomes less material**, the Fathers commonly take that *sons of God* to be **Seth's** descendants…"[23]

We might wonder why, today, so many people might find the stories of terrestrial angels - and those breeding with mortal women - fantastic. So many, today, probably don't even believe in angels! Could this be by design, over the years? And; *why*? Of course, the most correct answer to this is: *exposure*! As we'll see, soon enough, those who follow *Mystery Babylon* would certainly not want the *real* story of Cain and these fallen angels to be known… all of this sheds too much light on their plans. Although all of this might be passed off as fantasy, today, that doesn't mean all of this didn't happen.

Interestingly enough, the Old Testament never really referred to these *sons of God* as human beings at all - always **as angels**.[24] And, in Daniel 3:25, for example, we recall a famous story: king Nebuchadnezzar commanded to have three Israelites thrown into a huge furnace of fire. After they did, these people were never burned; not even close. They were actually *walking* around in the flames, unscathed. As Nebuchadnezzar looked into the flames, he even saw a *fourth* figure (i.e. an angel) inside the fire, with them. After he saw this, he exclaimed: "the form of the forth is like the **son of God**."

Any of those, today, who quickly might insist on these *sons of God* as being *only* righteous men may indeed be trying to decipher meanings of the Biblical text which really are *not* there. Human beings and angels *both* could have shared this honor; but - in the earliest parts of the Bible - this title was reserved *only* for angels. More on all of this, later.

The Trend Downward

> *The Sethites continued to live on the Mountain which is treated as somewhere between the earth and heaven. The Cainites lived down in the dark valley of the* ***true, physical earth****.* ("Jubal - Genun - Musical Worship", n. d., p. 2-3)[25]

Interestingly, one source stated that Cain may have even killed Abel *in a valley*; now we have Cainites living, and enjoying, themselves in *another valley*. Could, in an esoteric way, the **lowness** of these valleys parallel, in ways, with the **lowliness** of their values; the **darkness** of the soil correspond with the **darkness** of their souls; and their desires to be **so close** to the lowest part of earth also be reflected by their desires for lower, **material**, or **earthly**, things?[26]

> *...for they (the Cainites) began to be caught up again in the* ***ways of the world****, seeking after riches and gain for themselves... the people... did seek to excel in the good of the world, each striving to* ***possess*** *that which was above his neighbor.*
> - *Book of the Generations of Adam* 11:1[27]

As Cain was the *possessor*, many Cainites also strived to *possess* whatever earthly elements they could - their "ways" of living serving in constant remembrance of Cain's unholy example.

Idle Hands…

> *...nevertheless, they followed not after the ways of the evil combination whereby they murder and steal to* ***obtain*** *for themselves* ***the labors of other men's hands****.*
> - *Book of the Generations of Adam* 11:1[28]

Living in *low* lands *did* seem to have a number of advantages for the descendants of Cain; at least, in some respects: the soil was rich and fertile; the people could gain a livelihood without having to do a lot of work, etc..[29] Good for those of Cainite blood, who were cursed from, often, being able to farm in an efficient manner. Yet, the Cainites seemed to have enjoyed *this* type of lifestyle. Their easy, idle lives seemed to go hand in hand with their immorality. If one recalls the phrase, "Idle hands are the devil workshop," it seems to fit in perfectly, here.

The ancient historian *Philo*, for example, stated that the people of Cain committed all manner of immoral acts and deeds:

> *The inhabitants are the companions of impiety, ungodliness, self-love, haughtiness, falsehood, vain opinions; the men wise in their own conceit, the men who know not wisdom as relating to truth, the men who are full of ignorance, and stupidity, and folly; and all the other similar and kindred evils.*
>
> - *Works of Philo Judaeus* On the Posterity of Cain and His Exile 15(52)[30]

The "Carnival of Sin"

> *And lasciviousness and fornication increased among the children of Cain, and they* ***had nothing to occupy them except fornication****--now they had* ***no obligation [to pay] tribute*** *(taxes), and they had neither prince nor governor--and* ***eating****, and* ***drinking****, and lasciviousness, and* ***drunkenness****, and* ***dancing and singing to instruments of music****, and the wanton sportings of the devils, and the laughter which affordeth pleasure to the devils, and the sounds of the furious lust of men neighing after women. And Satan, finding [his] opportunity in this work of error, rejoiced greatly, because thereby he could compel the sons of Seth to come down from that holy mountain. There they had been made to occupy the place of that army [of angels] that fell, there they were beloved by God, there they were held in honour by the angels, and were called "sons of God," even as the blessed David saith in the psalm, I have said, "Ye are gods, and all of you sons of the Most High." (Psalms 82:6.) Meanwhile fornication reigned among the daughters of Cain, and without shame [several] women would run after one man. And one man would attack another, and they committed fornication in the presence of each other shamelessly. For all the devils were gathered together in that camp of Cain, and unclean spirits entered into the women, and took possession of them. The old women were more lascivious than the maidens, fathers and sons defiled themselves with their mothers and sisters, sons respected not even their own fathers, and fathers made no distinction between their sons [and other men]. And Satan had been made ruler (or prince) of that camp. And when the men and women were stirred up to lascivious frenzy by the devilish playing of the reeds which emitted musical sounds, and by the harps which the men played through the operation of the power of the devils, and by the sounds of the tambourines and of the sistra which were beaten and rattled through the agency of evil spirits, the sounds of their laughter were heard in the air above them, and ascended to that holy mountain.*
>
> - *Cave of Treasures* The Second Thousand Years[31]

To the dismay of the Sethites, these valley-dwelling Cainites would rather dance around, and enjoy music, than to do work, and be responsible. They would rather take the *easy way* towards accomplishing their deeds; rather than doing what's right. They also probably began to have a lot of sex, and get intoxicated - probably because there wasn't much better for them to do. The fallen Watchers and Nephilim also taught many how to turn certain plants into recreational drugs. Sound familiar - a lot like today? *Now* we are starting to see the *ancient* parallel of these "Days of Noah," compared to today.

The people of these ancient societies ate, and drank, a plenty. They even laughed, but not in a respectable manner (to others); their laughter was more hateful, spiteful, and condescending. It's much like a person who laughs at another person's expense, and belittles them (as one ancient source put it, "*like the neighing of steeds*").[32] They laughed really loud, so everyone around them could hear them.

They also played musical instruments; again, very loudly.[33] The reason so many of them acted in this way was, not because they were *really* happy, but because but wanted to prove to the world *their* ways were right; and prove how much they were having a "good" time. Some people are truly happy and fulfilled; others try to be loud and proud - just to show others; when, in reality, their world around them isn't really all that great, or allowing them all they need to be *spiritually* fulfilled.

Regardless, their outward shows of defiance and enjoyment were taken, by some, as being something other than weak attempts to fulfill an empty soul. This began to, slowly, put *pressure* on the Sethites who lived above them; to come down, and observe.

> *And the sons of Cain who wrought all this, and shone in beauty and gorgeous apparel, gathered together at the foot of the mountain in splendour, with horns and gorgeous dresses, and horse races, committing all manner of abominations.*
> - *Second Book of Adam and Eve (The Conflict of Adam and Eve with Satan)* 20:14[34]

> *Next Satan taught men how to dye their garments crimson and purple, and they arrayed themselves in* ***gaudy attire****, and began to race their horses...*
> - *Cave of Treasures* The Second Thousand Years (notes)[35]

Interestingly, Cainites were even thought to be the first who set up some kind of *amusement* area.[36] They wanted to show all the world what the "ways" of Cain and the Serpent were all about, and what it could bring. All of these improprieties - games and music playing - helped to turn the Cainite camp, below, into a "carnival of sin."[37]

A Chaos-In-The-Making

The more freely and unabatedly they utilized their music, dancing, mind-altering drugs, and alcohol, the more this allowed the populous to begin to act in *deviant* ways - caving to the *evil-inclination* inside; or any of their negative, pride-filled emotions.[38]

> *Satan appeared in the form of one... (man) and taught him to make horns and trumpets, stringed instruments, cymbals, psalteries, lyres, harps and flutes. Into these Satan himself entered, and made the music which came from them. (The man) made corn spirit, and established drinking booths, in which men assembled and drank and ate fruit. Then Satan taught... (the man) to make weapons of war out of* ***iron****, and when men were* ***drunk*** *they* ***killed each other with them****.*
> - *Cave of Treasures* The Second Thousand Years (notes)[39]

People soon began to participate in acts of robbery and other violent crimes - the same as today.[40] A lot of their world became chaotic.

> *Therefore, they did conspire together... taking upon themselves that combination which had been handed down from Cain, whereby they might murder and steal* ***to get gain****.*
> - *Book of the Generations of Adam* 12:3[41]

How about the Sethites, up in the mountain? What did they think about this all? Would they begin to come down, and "join the fun?"

Misery Loves Company

> *Little by little the children of Seth began to wish to join the sons of Cain...*
> - *Cave of Treasures* The Second Thousand Years (notes)[42]

The Cainites realized one thing, however: things were not really turning out too well, in regards to their world around them… because of all the depravity that was going on. It was just a fact… their "ways," although seductive, weren't really working out for their society, as a whole (in the end). These are just the facts of one leading an "anti-God" life!

So, noticing that things were slowly starting to fall apart, many people made this decision: if their whole world was going to go *down*, they'd, at least, feel a little better about themselves - and what they were doing - if *everyone else* fell down, in much the same ways! They didn't want to do these immoral acts by *themselves*, here. So, this cemented their newfound cause, and motives - with their targets, obviously, being the *Sethites*, up in the mountain.

If we notice, *envy* was the primary reason that Satan and the other fallen angels of Adam's day were so against Adam, himself; now their mixed-offspring and other sympathizers began to feel the *same* way about Adam's offspring, as well… like father, like son!

As we recall, angels used to come up and down the mountain; every morning and evening. We also know, now, that the Sethites did the same. A number of these Cainites could have used this as an opportunity to try to win them over. The Cainites came as close to the mountain as they *could* - when the Sethites came down the mountain - to try and get their attention. They waved their hands wildly; the women even began to take of some of their clothing… whatever might have worked. We know that Mount Hermon, previously, was known as the mount "devoted to destruction." Would Hermon, then, be the location of *another* era of desolation, here?

Eventually, the curiosity of the Sethites began to get the better of them. They noticed some of the things the Cainites were doing; and began to come closer and closer. Interestingly enough, some sources even stated the Sethites were *spiritually* protected, as long as they stayed farther up the mountain. Once they went beyond a certain point, it seemed their supernatural protection had vanished. No longer being protected, many of the Cainites - especially the women - were now able to physically walk up to them, and drag them away![43]

But after this, they (the Sethites) no longer kept His commandment, nor held by the promise He had made to their fathers... And they kept on gathering together on the top of the mountain, to look upon the children of Cain... After this a hundred men of the children of Seth gathered together, and said among themselves, "Come let us go down to the children of Cain, and see what they do, and ***enjoy*** *ourselves with them."*

- *Second Book of Adam and Eve (The Conflict of Adam and Eve with Satan)* 20:16, 24[44]

...and when the devils had shown them a way down the mountain, one hundred of them went down to the plain, and were led astray by the women whose hands and feet were stained with bright colours and whose faces had tattoo marks on them. When the Sethites tried to return to the top of the mountain, the stones turned into coals of fire, and they could not pass over them. Company after company of the children of Seth went down to the plain...

- *Cave of Treasures* The Second Thousand Years (notes) [45]

The strongest, most powerful men of Seth would come down from the mountain first, to see what was going on… and they were among the first to be taken away! Now, if the **strongest** Sethite men were the first to be taken away by these Cainites, imagine how easy it would soon be to seduce the rest of them? And, on top of it, one might ponder: why would these women really desire *these* men so badly?

Another Need for Sethite Men

The Biblical term "…and daughters were born unto them" (Gen. 6:1) could actually make reference to a significant *event* occurring, in their time: a massive *increase* in population, especially the increase of *one* sex, over another.[46] This verse might be implying such an imbalance: in those days, many *daughters* were born to the people; compared to sons born. This may have posed a *great* problem to the Cainites. The women may have wanted to nurture their female instincts: to breed, and have children… and there were not enough *men* among them, to suffice.

It was the Cainite's punishment to have a ***hundred daughters borne*** *them for each son; and this led to such husband-hunger that their women began to raid houses and carry off men. One day it pleased them to seduce the Sethites, after daubing their faces with rouge and powder, their eyes with antimony, and the soles of their feet with*

> *scarlet, dyeing their hair, putting on golden earrings, golden anklets, bracelets, and many-color garments... each caught hold of her victim and seduced him.*
> (Graves and Patai, 1964, p. 102-103)[47]

This could have even been another punishment set for Cain and his early descendants, by God. Whatever was the source of their affliction, in this case, the reality is that: the excessive number of women, over men, seemed to have "multiplied" their lusts inside! And, this led to such a husband-hunger that the women desired to get a man at almost any cost. The Cainite women, down in the valley, began to fight amongst themselves; many were forced to do whatever unsavory acts that were necessary (at least, in their minds) to be able act on their instincts, and mate with men. These Sethites, then, would become fresh meat because of it:

> *And when the children of Seth heard the noise, and uproar, and shouts of* ***laughter*** *in the camp of the children of Cain, about one hundred of them who were mighty men of war gathered together, and set their faces to go down to the camp of the children of Cain. When Yârêd (Jared) heard their words and knew their intention, he... said unto them, 'By the holy blood of Abel, I will have you swear that not one of you shall go down from this holy mountain. Remember ye the oaths which our fathers Seth, and Ânôsh, and Kainân, and Mahlâlâîl made you to swear'... But the children of Seth would neither hearken to the commandment of Yârêd... and they dared to transgress the commandment, and those hundred men, who were mighty men of war, went down [to the camp of Cain]. And when they saw that the daughters of Cain were beautiful in form and that they were* ***naked*** *and* ***unashamed****, the children of Seth became inflamed with the fire of lust. And when the daughters of Cain saw the* ***goodliness*** *of the children of Seth, they gripped them like ravening beasts and defiled their bodies... and having defiled their souls with the fire of fornication, God did not permit them to ascend to that holy place. And, moreover, very many others made bold and went down after them, and they, too, fell.*
> - *Cave of Treasures* The Second Thousand Years[48]

Their Best Efforts

We've already surmised: as soon as these women of Cain noticed the Sethites coming down to see what was going on, they began to use their bodies - most affectively - to lure them into joining their own "party." After soon seducing such a great number already, the women eventually focused their efforts on any Sethite "holdouts" - any of the pious still remaining:

> *But the maidens of Cain's generation invented carmine and flake white, (and) they reddened and whitened their faces. They plucked their eyebrows and painted their eyes... they adorned and beautified their bodies with other embellishments... they went to the mountains making merry... marching in a long procession and singing various songs...* - *Armenian Apocryphal Adam Literature* Tidings 21-22[49]

For almost 200 years, this depravity raged. Most of the Sethites began to give way:

> *And the race of Cain became* ***envious*** *because of (their) not having intercourse at all with them... And they made various sorts of musical instruments, and they adorned themselves and their daughters, and they went to mount Ahermon (Hermon). And after* ***two hundred years*** *of their ascesis, they, (i.e., the Cainite women), having seduced them, caused them to descend from the mountain, and they mingled them with themselves promiscuously.*
> - *Armenian Apocrypha Relating to Adam and Eve* Concerning the Flood 4-6[50]

The man in charge of these Sethites - *Jared* - chastised anyone still left; anyone who was thinking about going down:

> *...when Jared saw that they (many of the Sethites) did not receive his words, he said unto them... "you shall no longer be called 'children of God,' but 'children of the* ***devil****'"... And when they looked at the daughter of Cain, at their beautiful figures, and at their hands and feet dyed with colour, and tattooed in ornaments on their faces, the fire of sin was kindled in them. Then Satan made them look most beautiful before the sons of Seth, as he also made the sons of Seth appear of the fairest in the eyes of the daughters of Cain, so that the daughters of Cain lusted after the sons of Seth like ravenous beasts, and the sons of Seth after the daughters of Cain, until they committed abomination* ***with them****.*
> - *Second Book of Adam and Eve (The Conflict of Adam and Eve with Satan)* 20:26-32[51]

Around the year 3074 B.C., Adam finally died.[52] So, with Adam gone, the time of great change - the judgment of their evil world - seemed to be, quickly, on the *horizon*. Everyone seemed to have sensed it. The question was *when*. It was at this time that the patriarch Seth brought Enos, Cainan, Mahalaleel, Jared, and even Enoch (all of his direct descendants) together, into the Cave of Treasures, and made them all to swear an oath:[53]

> *I will make you to take an oath, and to swear by the holy blood of Abel, that none of you will go down from this holy mountain to the children of Cain, the murderer. For ye know well* ***the enmity*** *which hath existed between us and Cain from the day whereon he slew Abel.* - *Cave of Treasures* The Rule of Seth[54]

Interesting choice of words, here: as we know - through the Genesis 3:15 Prophecy - the seeds of Eve (via Adam) would be at *enmity* with seeds of the Serpent. Now, almost 1000 years after Adam's formulation, the descendants of Eve (through the **Sethites**) were *still* aware of this division; and what it all meant! And, they were aware of who the seeds of *enmity* were: the "ways" of the Serpent and the Cainites.

There was no "political correctness" back then. There were no campaigns of awareness. The Sethite men were not given lessons in tolerance, here. They knew the truth. They were not told that they should live with these other groups of sinful people and just look the other way. The Sethites were told, strait out, **not** to have anything to do with followers of Cain. Over time, however, it was their *awareness* (and eventual acceptance) of the "ways" of Cain and the Serpent which eventually led them down the same wrong paths… *permanently*.

The Corruption of All Flesh

> *When they (the Sethites) saw the daughters of Cain and their beauty… they committed fornication with them, and* ***destroyed their souls****.*
> - *Book of the Rolls (Kitab Al-Magall)* 10[55]

Sexual sins, because of their nature, are capable of destroying men physically and morally.[56] The men of Seth "slew their own souls" after they adulterated themselves with the Cainite women, here.[57] After becoming *physically* in close proximity to them, the **minds** of these Sethites would also become corrupted. We also know that fornication is not *only* defined as sexual intercourse outside the bonds of marriage, but also the use of sex (and other devices), by people, to achieve her own ungodly ends! And, it, as well, stands for the mixing of blood lines - mainly human blood with *angelic* blood.

> *And in these years the **handicraftsmen** of sin, and the disciples of Satan, appeared, for he was their teacher, and he entered in and dwelt in them, and he poured into them the spirit **of the operation of error**, through which the fall of the children of Seth was to take place.* - *Cave of Treasures* The Rule of Yared[58]

Sexual misconduct was everywhere; compliments of the Cainites and offspring of these fallen angels. The Sethites were falling to the same *error*. Everywhere on the mountain, people were willingly (and, sometimes, *inadvertently*) mixing with the people of the valley.

> *...all the others intermingled with them (Cain's generation) and became more wicked than they, and acted more shamefully than a **dog**.*
> - *Armenian Apocryphal Adam Literature* Tidings 23[59]

Many became as unclean as *dogs*; and, utterly, forgot God's laws.

Down From the Mountain Abode

> *...and at length only Yârêd (Jared) and a few others remained on the mountain.*
> - *Cave of Treasures* The Second Thousand Years (notes)[60]

Eventually, only a few *hardliners* would remain.[61] What effect could the Nephilim, the Watchers, and (now) these descendants/followers of Cain and the Serpent have on any of the pious remaining?

*Whenever they are united with that generation, your good children will become wicked, and all will **be punished together**.*
- *Armenian Apocryphal Adam Literature* Tidings 4[62]

Their Time Had Come - The Revelation of Fact

*...God would punish the descendants of Cain and **those who mixed** with them and were **sympathetic** to them...*
- *al-Tabari: The History of al-Tabari - Vol. I: General Introduction and From the Creation to the Flood* Enoch to Noah 177[63]

The newly-combined people of the valley (i.e. the Cainites and Sethites) were both, now, beginning to pollute the known world, beyond the point of no return - one morality and way of life was now being absorbed by another. No longer were the Sethites standing alone; they were part of the *system*. There, no longer, would be any *enmity* - they would become *one*. The seed of Adam was truly being compromised.

Interestingly, we know:

*What we tolerate today will be **embraced tomorrow**.*
- *unknown*

Scary… but true. Yet, this not going to go on, unchallenged… this was the final straw of God's tolerance. There would be hardly any pure Sethites left - no more Genesis 3:15 Prophecy. Some kind of action had to be taken, and *quick*. Would *this*, then, be the time for that prophesized savior to be born (to save them all), or was something *else* about to happen; which would, *forever*, change the **destiny** of their world, at hand?

Chapter 15

A Change in Destiny

***Enoch** knew full well that the only way to keep from losing one's mind is to hold onto it.* ("Jubal - Genun - Musical Worship", n. d., p. 34)[1]

Enoch Vs. Lamech

We recall a couple of famous people of this time: Enoch and Lamech. Enoch was, as we know from a previous chapter, a son of Jared; as well as a great prophet of God! Lamech, on the other hand, was a great-grandson of Cain - and the last of these famous Biblical Cainites. We also know he was a fairly mean and arrogant person; one who killed Enoch's brother, and also took two women - Adah and Zillah - as his wives.

Enoch, indeed, was, at the time, the "go-to" person about the up-and-coming future of mankind. He began to inform people and mixed multitudes alike that the end was near; and tried to make sure the masses knew what was about to happen.

The name *Lamech*, as we know, could have stood for "strong" and "powerful;" but, later, the name could have even stood for "to strike with a flat hand," "to look stealthily," or to look "sideways."[2] *These* attributes, as we'll see, would become a reflection of his attitude, as well as something he would, soon, do. Lamech would do something *so deviant* that it would change his entire world![3] Let's see how this all went down.

Enoch, the Sethite, judged and instructed people in the righteous ways of God; Lamech, on the other hand, became strong and powerful in his Cainite "ways." Thus began a struggle between two titans - *especially* in Lamech's mind.

Enoch, as we know, understood Lamech's intentions to murder him; and removed himself from other people… hiding in a cave. Because he wasn't able to fulfill his goal, quickly, this probably angered Lamech all the more. Eventually, God "took" Enoch up to heaven, to allow Enoch a way out of the struggle.

The Lord God transferred him (Enoch) to the garden which is immortal, Lest Lamech kill him, an ***embodiment*** *of maleficent* ***Satan****.* - *Yovhannes T'Ulkuranc'I*[4]

Next, Lamech - the evil tyrant - would, eventually, get what was coming to him.

This Time of Change

There was another interesting story, which relates to God's aforementioned "seventh-generation" prophecy to Cain:

Therefore whosoever slayeth Cain, vengeance shall be taken on him ***sevenfold****...*
- *Gen.* 4:15 (KJV)

According to this, Cain was *cursed* - in himself and his seed - for seven generations (of Adam), because of the murder. In other words, Cain's blood lines would have a curse placed upon them - their lives wouldn't work out really well; happiness would, most often, elude them, etc.. They, on the outside, acted like they were having a good time, and totally enjoying life, but - in reality - things weren't going all that great. But, this curse that God gave to Cain and his blood descendants was not to last forever. Everything seemed to hinge on the *seventh* man born of Adam's blood line - the *seventh* generation of Adam. Once this man would be born, Cain knew that the time of his curse would be over; and thing would start to get better, for him and his family.

The seventh generation of Adam had now come; and Cain was getting old. He was finally seeing the time for the curse to live out its life, here; and be fulfilled. All it took was for Cain to die *on his own*, from old age; and things would begin to be a little better for *all* of his subsequent generations.

And, at this same time, people were beginning to wonder *what* would happen at the time of this seventh generation. Would the **other** prophecy - the prophecy of Genesis 3:15 - *also* be fulfilled? Would the "savior," soon, be born, here? And, most importantly, would this be the *end of the world* they once lived in? People, with a lot of questions, had bombarded Enoch, the prophet. Even the wives of Lamech were scared of what's to come in this generation:

> *And Lamech said to his wives: Enter with me to the bed chamber, so that [I might] establish progeny through you... The wives refused, and said to him: We do not wish to become pregnant and give birth, only for [the child] to be devoured.*
> - *Genizah Manuscripts* Gen. 4:23[5]

Whatever timeline was upon them, God definitely had a schedule, here - no interference. Everything was being fulfilled, just as God prophesied. The seventh generation of Adam was upon them… the time was close. As we know, God also assured that anyone who interfered with His prophecies would be punished. Anyone who killed Cain before his time, here (for example), would, then, cause Cain's *entire* family line to be subjected to an extension of Cain's curse… a *sevenfold* extension!

> *...whosoever slayeth Cain, vengeance shall be taken on him* ***sevenfold****...*
> - *Gen.* 4:15 (KJV)

Simply, if anyone interfered with Cain's punishment, the curse on his family line would extend… **seventy** more generations! So, it was very obvious, to everyone around, *not* to interfere with Cain's destiny, at all - one doesn't mess with God! But, in actuality, someone *did* interfere with this judgment. Someone actually *brought on* more curses upon himself, and his family - and this person would be none other than ***Lamech*** himself!

The Trials of Lamech

One profound act of Lamech may have, indeed, changed our entire world. Part of this story even seems to be in the Bible! There are a couple of different versions of what may have happened, overall, however. What *is* important is for us to understand the story's major elements:

<u>Jasher 2</u>:
26 *And Lamech was old and advanced in years, and his eyes were dim that he could not see, and Tubal Cain, his son, was leading him and it was one day that Lamech went into the field and Tubal Cain his son was with him, and whilst they were walking in the field,* ***Cain*** *the son of Adam advanced towards them; for Lamech was very old and could not see much, and Tubal Cain his son was very young.*
27 *And Tubal Cain told his father to draw his bow, and with the arrows he smote Cain, who was yet far off, and he slew him, for he appeared to them to be an animal.*
28 *And the arrows entered Cain's body although he was distant from them, and he fell to the ground and died.*
30 *And it came to pass when Cain had died, that Lamech and Tubal went to see the animal which they had slain, and they saw, and behold Cain their grandfather was fallen dead upon the earth.*

As Lamech was leaning on the youth, his son [Tubal-Cain], and the youth was setting straight his father's arm in the direction in which he saw the quarry, he heard the sound of Cain moving about, backwards and forwards, in the forest. Now Cain was unable to stand still in one place and to hold his peace. And Lamech, thinking that it was a wild beast that was making a movement in the forest, raised his arm, and, having made ready, drew his bow and shot an arrow towards that spot, and the arrow smote Cain between his eyes, and he fell down and ***died****. And Lamech, thinking that he had shot game, spake to the youth, saying, "Make haste, and let us see what game we have shot." And when they went to the spot, and the boy of whom Lamech leaned had looked, and said unto him. "O, my lord, thou hast killed Cain." And Lamech moved his hands to smite them together, and as he did so he smote the youth and killed him also.* - *Cave of Treasures* The Rule of Anosh[6]

There is another variation of the story that - knowing *Lamech* - seems to make a lot more sense:

In those days lived Lamech the blind, who was of the sons of Cain. He had a son whose name was Atun (Jubal?), and they two had much cattle. But Lamech was in the habit of sending them (a.k.a. Jubal, Tubal-Cain, or Jubal's son?) to feed with a young shepherd, who tended them… (one day, the shepherd) said to them… "I cannot feed those cattle alone, lest one rob me of some of them, or kill me for the sake of them." For among the children of Cain there was much robbery, murder and sin. Then Lamech pitied him… (and he) arose, took a bow he had kept ever since he was a youth… and he took some large arrows… and a sling he had… and went to the field with the young shepherd, and placed himself behind the cattle; while the young shepherd watched the cattle. Thus did Lamech many days. Meanwhile Cain, ever since God had cast him off… could neither settle nor find rest in any one place; but wandered from place to place. In his wanderings he came to Lamech's wives, and asked them about him. They said to him, "He is in the field with the cattle." Then Cain went to look for him; and as he came into the field, the young shepherd heard the noise he made... Then said he to Lamech, "O my lord, is that a wild beast or a robber"... Then Lamech bent his bow... and when Cain came out from the open country, the shepherd said to Lamech "Shoot, behold, he is coming." Then Lamech shot at Cain with his arrow and hit him in his side. And Lamech struck him with a stone from his sling, that fell upon his face, and knocked out both his eyes; then Cain fell at once and died. Then Lamech and the young shepherd came up to him, and found him lying on the ground. And the young shepherd said to him, "It is Cain our grandfather, whom thou hast killed, O my lord!" Then was Lamech sorry for it, and from the bitterness of his regret, he clapped his hands together, and struck with his flat palm the head of the youth, who fell as if dead; but Lamech thought it ***was a feint*** *(i.e. a trick, ploy, or maneuver of the young shepherd); so he* ***smote*** *him, and smashed his head until he died.*

- *Second Book of Adam and Eve (The Conflict of Adam and Eve with Satan)* 13:1-13[7]

Either way, what *really* happened, here? What did Lamech do? Remember the warning God gave the entire world? Nobody was to kill Cain - nobody! He was to live out his punishment until the day of his death… as a vagabond, in a depressive state.

Now, that's all by the wayside. Lamech went hunting in the forest; possibly the same land (i.e. *Nod*) Cain was originally meant to roam! Whether by accident or not, Lamech did something to totally upstart God's entire time frame.

We know that Cain probably "walked upon the earth shaking incessantly" and "wandered around ceaselessly from morning to night… he did not remain in one place."[8] With this nervous way about him - dissatisfied with most every turn he took in life - Cain would constantly shake, back and forth.

When Cain was making his way towards Lamech - shaking from side to side - the nearly blind Lamech probably took the rustling sound of Cain's approach as something nefarious; possibly even an approaching *animal*. He might have even perceived Cain as some sort of criminal; coming to rob him (obviously, there was probably a lot of crime in the area). Lamech picked up an arrow, and took a shot. Cain may have even been wearing his horned helmet, or had been dressed in animal-skins (as Sargon was known to do). Whatever the circumstances, Lamech shot at what he thought was an animal; and took Cain's life.[9]

Cain's death, however, *now* posed a major problem. He was to live out his days - and die - on his own. Now what? The world, and everyone in it, seemed to have been going down the proverbial toilet, very quickly. The time might have even been ripe for the prophesized *savior* to be born - the one who was about to "crush the Serpent's head." All Cain needed to do was to die, on his own, and **both** prophecies might have even been fulfilled, at almost the same time! The act of Lamech, however, threw a "monkey wrench" into the whole, entire process! Now, it's obvious the savior probably could *not* be born at this time, because of this other discrepancy. With a perfect God, we know that discrepancies plainly **cannot** happen. Now, there had to be adjustments.

Interestingly enough, another meaning of the name *Lamech* is "humiliation."[10] Through his carelessness, Lamech did humiliate his entire seed line, for many generations to come. Let's take a look, now, at what *might* have happened if Cain died on his own; and what, most probably, *did* happen, because of Lamech.

Retribution to Lamech

As we recall, Lamech hated Enoch, and continually leaned towards glorifying evil. Things, however, have a way of coming back to people, it seems. Before he killed Cain, Lamech took young *Jubal* and *Tubal-Cain* and showed them how to do evil, as well. Apparently, it was time for Lamech to realize how all of what he did would come back to him:

> *Now Lamech said unto his wives Adah and Sella (Zillah): Hear my voice, ye wives of Lamech, give heed to my precept: for I have corrupted men for myself, and have taken away sucklings from the breasts,* ***that I might show my sons how to work evil****, and the inhabiters of the earth. And now shall vengeance be taken seven times of Cain, but of Lamech* ***seventy times seven****.* - *Pseudo Philo* 2:10[11]

After discovering it was *Cain* who had died, Lamech was unbelievably aghast and angry. He knew what he had done to his entire family tree. In disgust, Lamech then slapped his hands together, extremely hard. Some sources state the nearly blind Lamech did not know his young helper was in the middle of this display of anger; others say he did. Regardless, Lamech quickly brought both hands together and caught the youngster in a crushing blow. Now, we have the explanation to an otherwise *confusing* set of verses in the Bible:

> Gen. 4:
> 23 *And Lamech said unto his wives, Adah and Zillah, Hear my voice; ye wives of*
> *Lamech, hearken unto my speech: for **I have slain a man** (Cain?) **to my***
> ***wounding** (my blindness?), and **a young man** (the servant/Tubal-Cain?) **to my***
> ***hurt**.*
> 24 *If Cain shall be avenged sevenfold, truly Lamech **seventy and sevenfold**.*
> (in retranslation)

There is even *another* variant to this story. Even though it might not be the most accurate, here, it does display the treachery which was Lamech:

> *While Naamah was yet a child, great consternation fell upon the seed of Cain, for Irad the Son of Enoch, the son of Cain, had become a member of the secret combination and was privy to all it secrets until one night when the Lord appeared to him in a dream saying, Irad, thou hast done evil instead of good and hast followed after Satan rather than God; wherefore, I shall destroy thee and thine **house** when I send in the floods upon the earth. But Irad was pricked in his heart and pled with the Lord to show mercy and preserve **his seed** through the great flood. Seeing that his penitence was true, the Lord said to him, Irad, if thou wilt repent and reveal the evils of the secret combination unto the sons of Seth, I will have mercy upon thee and I will join thy seed unto the seed of Seth that it may be preserved through the great flood. Wherefore, Irad went forth and began to reveal the **secrets** of the sons of Cain unto the sons of Seth. **Lamech**, being Master Mahan at that time, found Irad sitting in his garden with Joram, the young son of Irad, and slew him. Thus Lamech slew Irad for the sake of the oath of the secret combination and he slew Irad's son with him. But Tubal Cain, the son of Lamech, had followed him and viewed his evil deed which he had committed and he revealed it unto his mother Zillah and she unto her sister Adah. Wherefore, Adah and Zillah confronted Lamech with his evil and cursed him in the name of the Lord for having slain Irad who had repented of his wickedness from among the sons of men. And Lamech said unto his wives Adah and Zillah, Hear my voice, ye wives of Lamech; hearken unto my speech, for I have slain a man **to my wounding** and **a young man to my hurt**. If Cain shall be avenged sevenfold, truly Lamech shall be seventy and seven fold. Lamech's wives, therefore, feared to confront him further, but Lamech repented **not** of his evil deeds and finding his son Tubal Cain at prayer, he **slew him** for having revealed his murders.*
>
> \- *Writings of Abraham* 13:1-11[12]

The "Song of the Sword"

After the two horrible acts of murder, Lamech sought out his wives, and cried openly to them.[13] In one interpretation, his wives were the ones who sought him out; and, after confronting him, Lamech cried aloud, in a sad, wail of a song:

Maid of dawn and maid of dust,
this my utterance hear;
Womenfolk of Lamech's tribe
to what I say give ear:
If e'er a grown man scratch me,
behold, I lay him low;
The same I do to merest boys
for but a single blow.
If injury unto a smith
men sevenfold requite,
sevenfold and seventy
is due a Lamechite![14]

This wailing poem was known as the *Song of the Sword*.[15] Apparently, because the wives of Lamech were praying, on behalf of him, God took pity:

But Lamech's wife was a good woman. She cried out to the Lord, and she wept in such a way that blood dropped from her eyes instead of tears. God saw the woman's weeping and supplications; God took pity on everyone and he cured Lamech's pain.
- *Armenian Apocryphal Adam Literature* Abel and Cain 50-51[16]

An interesting quote from the *Book of Jasher*, regarding this deed:

And the Lord requited Cain's evil according ***to his wickedness****, which he had done to his brother Abel, according to the word of the Lord which he had spoken.*
- *Book of Jasher* 2:29[17]

"An Eye for an Eye"

In whatever way it turned out, here, it seemed to end up as "an eye for an eye" for him. And, it's quite ironic to see, here, that the murderer of Cain was one of his most *evil* descendants. It's also quite ironic how this whole sequence of events, here, seemed to have avenged Abel's murder: Cain murdered someone, and he was also murdered.

So, from this situation, we might want to understand that we all live *by example*. What we do in our lives often can bring retribution to us, and our children. One ancient source makes it plainly clear that family *dishonor* was the reason behind Cain's untimely death:[18]

> *Doctors say that the son of a sickly man will be sickly... And similarly they say that Cain's first son (Enoch) shuddered like him... Lamech, the fifth descendant of Cain killed (him), on account of the* ***ignominy*** *of the race.*
> - *Armenian Apocrypha Relating to Adam and Eve* Abel and Other Pieces 5.3[19]

Just what is an *ignominy*? It is a "condition" or "stipulation." Maybe, if Cain would have lived a different life than he led after Abel's murder; if he would have **disciplined** his children enough; if he would have done what God told him… maybe the curse on him and his family would never have been **extended**. But, now, something had to be done; and done *differently*.

There is more to this whole story than just a morality play: when God makes a promise, it *has* to be fulfilled. God doesn't mess around. And, His prophecies are not to be taken *lightly*.

We also see this was a major reason God separated the sons of Seth and the sons of Cain. It wasn't *only* their bloodline, here: it was their ***culture*** - their exploits of greed, anger, and immorality. It was their *culture* that helped them become detrimental to themselves, as well as anyone around! And, the main reason God wanted the ancient descendants of Adam to stay away from these people was that - more often than not – they would find themselves being led into the following of *other* "ways;" including idolatry. **Abel**, as we recall, was most probably Cain's twin; and **both** of them had blood of the Serpent. Abel, though, retained a proper, positive attitude. The ways he lived his life was different - he did not go along with the "ways of Cain." Again, it is not where we come from, or our blood line… but what we *make* out of what we have! Lamech's ways of life were, now, about to come back to him.

A New and Different Route

We notice the seven generations since the beginning of our "Six-Day Creation:"

Each Generation Number	Patriarchs of the Serpent's Generation	Patriarchs of Adam's Generation
# 1	the Serpent	Adam
# 2	Cain	Seth
# 3	Enoch	Enos
# 4	Irad	Cainan
# 5	Mehujael	Mahalaleel
# 6	Methusael	Jared
# **7**	**Lamech**	**Enoch**

As we see (in the above), it was in the *seventh* generation of the Serpent that **Lamech** was born; and, in the *seventh* generation of Adam, **Enoch** was born - and we know that *both* were significant characters to our story. Cain's curse, as we know, probably would have been lifted at this time. But, we also know that, because of Lamech's act, his offspring would have to be cursed for *seventy* more generations.[20] So, the savior of this time was no longer able to be utilized. Seventy more generations had to pass, before the savior of the world was now to arrive - and, we'll see, that savior would be the one we now know as **Jesus Christ**.

> *"Because sevenfold Cain will be requited, but* ***Lamech*** *seventy and seven," i.e., generations, according to the gospel genealogy of Luke, which begins with God the father and ends with* ***the son*** *made flesh, who blots out sin.*
>
> - *Barhebraeus* Gen. 4:24[21]

> *Therefore Cain's sins were removed by the Flood, but Lamech's needed* ***the coming of Christ****, for he was found to be a murderer after (his) example. He was condemned to 77 vengeances, (and) Luke counts* ***77 patriarchs*** *up to Christ. But to Cain He gave 7 vengeances.*
>
> \- *Armenian Apocrypha Relating to Adam and Eve* Abel and Other Pieces 5.5[22]

Interestingly enough, Jesus *was* born in the seventy-seventh generation of God's viceroy, Adam! In one ancient account, Michael - the Archangel - was told by God to *chain* the souls of any and all of the fallen angels who died - interestingly enough… for **seventy generations**.[23] Why *this* specific amount of time? Could it all have been related to the sin of Lamech?

The important question might arise, in all of this: could God have originally have been on His way to *end* the present, sinful world at this time? Was the "savior" - Jesus Christ - about to be born… to fulfill the other prophecy of Genesis 3:15? Interesting things to ponder.

The Antediluvian "End-Times"?

One Encyclopedia provides an interesting difference between Lamech, the *Cainite*, and Enoch, the *Adamite*:

> *(There is a…) great difference between this descendant of Seth and the descendant of Cain. While the one was stimulated to a song of* ***defiance*** *by the* ***worldly inventions*** *of his sons, the other, in prophetical mood, expresses his sure* ***belief*** *in the* ***coming of better times****…* ("Int. Std. Bible Encyclopedia", n. d., p. 1824)[24]

The "end times" of the ancient world might have actually been set to occur at this time. The "savior" of the Sethites might have *almost* been born. Their world was about to be a better place, because of it. What if this was so?

And, in regards to the story of Jesus, most of us know that Mary was the one known as his virgin mother; and Joseph was her husband. Could there have been a "Mary" and "Joseph" character at this ancient time? Could the framework have already been laid out, back then?

The "Virgin Mother" - Horea

> *You (Horia), together with your offspring, belong to the primeval parent (Eve?); from above, out of the incorruptible light, their souls are come…*
> - *Reality of the Rulers* 96:19-22[25]

> *…there are other schools of thought that say there is a power whom they name* ***Horaia****. So, these (Sethians) say that… (there is a) power, whom others* ***esteem*** *and call Horaia…* - *The Sethians according to St. Epiphanius* 39.5.3[26]

As we recall, Eve made an exclamation about the birth Cain. We recall she might have even believed Cain was the promised "seed" of the Genesis 3:15 Prophecy already, by looking at him! When Cain was born, it seems obvious that Eve probably hoped Cain would have been born… to save her from misery. She may have even *welcomed* Cain as this promised "savior;" when, in actuality, he was *the direct opposite*. This could have also been a reason why Eve and Cain had such a close relationship, over the years.[27] Obviously, we know that Cain was not the "Christ" equivalent of these early times. And, we, on the same level, could probably assume Eve wasn't the "Mary" character, here, as well. Enter ***Horea*** (sometimes thought of as *Norea*) - another direct descendant of Eve. This woman, as we'll see, could have actually been the *one* apportioned to be the "virgin mother," or "Mary," of ancient times.[28] According to one ancient source, Eve became pregnant with Horea; and, then, made another one of her exclamations:

> *Again Eve became pregnant, and she bore (Horea). And she said, "He had begotten on [me a] virgin as an assistance [for] many generations of humankind." She is the* ***virgin*** *of whom the powers (the Nephilim?) did not defile.*
> - *Reality of the Rulers* 91:30-92:1[29]

Virgin? A number of ancient works have been written about Horea. According to ancient sources, she was apportioned to be a *virgin* throughout most of her long life. It was to be this way for a reason. Interesting. And, there are a number of ancient sources which state she was even the sister of *Seth* himself. I'm sure, here, that she may have figured out, over time, she was something special.[30]

If Horea was designated to be this "virgin" - the one to bring forth the Christ child - the next thing for her to do was to become impregnated by the Holy Spirit. Then, she would eventually meet up with whoever would become the "Joseph" character (of this whole story)… ultimately bearing the savior of the world, at *this* time.

The "Husband" - Enoch

We recall, in the seventh generation of Adam, *Enoch* was born:

Each Generation Number	Patriarchs of The Serpent's Generation	Patriarchs of Adam's Generation
# **7**	**Lamech**	**Enoch**

We know **Enoch** was a pivotal character of the ancient world, as well. He was a very, very wise prophet - a favorite of God, actually. In this era of peril, he was God's new spokesman on earth - who better to be the "Joseph" character? Even though many had lost their way because of these fallen angels, Enoch brought a good number of them *back* in the right direction. As a result, this man might have been singled out for, yet, *another* purpose: the husband of Horea.

There is one more interesting fact about Enoch, according to the Bible: he did *not* die; but was taken away to heaven, by God. Why not? Maybe, because of these new circumstances (through Lamech's sin), he was no longer needed.

Why, No Longer Needed?

Both of these characters could have been destined for the two roles; but, as we know, everything had now changed. God may have decided to take Enoch up to heaven, to allow him to *avoid* His upcoming judgment. Interestingly enough, ancient sources seemed to have stated that this *same* thing could have happened to Horea!

A lot of people in the day probably knew about the prophecy of Genesis 3:15; and word could have gotten out that *Horea* was the anointed "virgin" mother of the savior - the fallen angels, however, would be no exception. As we already know, there could have been attempts by some of these angels to *disrupt* the prophecy of Genesis 3:15. And, once the cat was "out of the bag" that she was the virgin mother-to-be, they probably devised that the easiest way to *stop* the fulfillment of this prophecy was to *compromise* this role of "Mary!" We know from history that King Herod tried to murder the babies of ancient Israel, when he heard of Jesus' upcoming birth. The pharaoh of Egypt also tried to kill all of the Israelite children, when he heard of Moses' upcoming birth. Couldn't this have been almost the same thing?

The angels wanted to dilute the significance of Horea's position, or *compromise* her ability to bear seed. As we'll soon see, there *were* fallen angels who tried a number of tactics to "upset this apple cart."

The "Type" and "Anti-Type"

One of their plots involved a "type" and "anti-type" of the person Horea. The Bible stated that, as well as there being a "Christ" in our world, there would also be an "anti-Christ," in the future. Along these same lines, there could have been a *real* Horea, and an "anti-Horea"... a human "plant" of these fallen angels. In other words, this was an attempt to dilute the significance of the virgin mother... by trying to confuse the populous. It's the same as how the *antichrist* would be able to confuse a great number of people, as well, in the future... by masquerading himself off as another "Christ."

We know many people followed Cain's way of life at the time; and many would listen to what these fallen angels, and their offspring, had told them. The *true* Horea, according to the Bible, would have been a descendant of Adam and Eve; the "anti-Horea" could have even been a descendant of some fallen angel... her *real* origins hidden from everyone around. By convincing those under Cain that this "virgin" was the correct one, these angels could have also begun to usher in their *own* "Horea" into the entire equation.

We'll soon see that this "anti-Horea" could have been known by another name: ***Norea***.[31] Now, we have the *true* **Horea**, and the *anti-Horea* - **Norea**; one being accepted by the followers of God, and the other being accepted by the followers of Cain.

Some sources even stated the Serpent, also, may have tried to manipulate (or *seduce*) Eve… *again*.[32] Could the Serpent even have been the father of Norea (the "anti-Horea")? And, could Eve have been the mother of both of them? This could add further credence to any false, trumped-up argument, here! We simply don't know for sure; but, if things *did* happen in these ways, those believing in Cain and the Serpent would, most probably, have no problem adopting *this* Horea as their own… secular/pagan Norea vs. God-following Horea.

We know how people often look at things according *to their own point of view*, as well as how it would benefit them the *most*, in the end. The same is true, here; it's human nature. Most probably, after *both* being convinced that they were the anointed "Mary," they probably began to act the part, over time. And, slowly, the fact of just "who was who" probably became quite blurry to a lot of the populous. In the end, because of so much political confusion, almost everyone wasn't sure which "Mary" to look up to - it was, now, really up to each individual.

Interestingly enough, there were even *two* ancient goddesses of the Middle East, for example, who seemed to parallel Horea and Norea: **Manat** and **Allat**. Let's look at some ancient mythology, in this example, and look at more information which might help us validate our theory.

The Serpent and Aza?

Early gods and goddesses of the Middle East, also, could give us hints to how the Serpent might have even been father of Norea. We already know two of the most famous fallen angels: the Serpent (i.e. Azazel) and *Aza*, his female counterpart.[33] There are a couple of ancient deities in the Middle East who seem to have been paired in this way: ***Hubal*** and ***Azza*** (or *Ozza*). A major god of pre-Islamic Arabia, *Hubal* was known as *The Moon God*. We already know, from an earlier chapter, that *the Moon God* was also known as the god *Sin* - and *Sin* was just another name for the **Serpent**! So, could Hubal be another ancient name for this same Serpent? It's quite possible.

Also, the daughters (or wives) of Hubal were known as *Manat*, *Allat*, and *Uzza*. Could these be *Horea*, *Norea*, and *Aza* (respectively)? We have ancient sources which equate the goddess *Al-Uzza* to the Serpent's female counterpart *Aza* (above)![34] The two also seem to be close in name. So, if we could establish *Uzza* as the Serpent's counterpart *Aza*, then that leaves the other two. Could the Serpent (a.k.a. Hubal or Azazel) be the "father" of Allat and Manat - the two other Arabian goddesses - at least in some *hypothetical* way?[35]

Allat - The "Anti-Horea?"

If so, let's break them both down. If we go one step further: could *Allat* (or *Al-Lat*) have been the equivalent of the Serpent's **Norea** (the "anti-Horea"):

> ***Allat**... is believed... to have been the moon goddess of North Arabia. If this is the correct interpretation of her character, she corresponded to the moon deity of South Arabia... **Sin** as he was called... Similarly, al-Uzza is supposed to come from Sinai, and to have been the goddess of planet Venus. As the **moon** and the evening star (Venus) are associated in the heavens, so too were **Allat** and al-Uzza together in religious belief...* (Finegan, n. d., p. 192, 482-485, 492)[36]

Allat has parallels in other ancient mythological accounts, as well; which give us further insight into the possibility she was Norea. Allat was thought to be equivalent to the goddesses Aphrodite, Ishtar, among many others.[37] And, the goddesses Athena, Ashtorah and Astarte - more of her avatars - were all thought to be goddesses of the sacred, crested **moon**.[38] So what (one might say)? Well, interestingly enough, we find that a number of the ancient gods and goddesses may have had a "good" or "evil" side to them. In the case of Allat, she was known as the *crane* goddess: goddess of the *new*, or waxing, moon.[39] In other words, she was the young, "beneficial" avatar. And, any of those following **Cain** and **the Serpent** would, obviously, have considered her to be "good!"

On the other side, there was also a goddess with qualities of sharp *contrast* to Allat… could this be because she was *Horea - God's* pick for the "Mary" character, of old?

Manat - The Real Horea!

If we continue along this same train of logic - if Horea was the moral *opposite* of Norea - then *Allat* should have an *opposite* avatar, as well. It apparently is true. We *do* seem to have a goddess in the Middle East (and, in other ancient areas) who was considered *opposite* of the "beneficial" goddess **Manat**.

Interestingly, the Qur'an states:

*Have ye seen (Al-)**Lat** and '**Uzza**,*
*And another, the third (goddess), **Manat**?*
- *Qur'an* An-Najm 053:019-020[40]

So, who was the *Manat*; this third goddess? The name *Manat* could have been derived from the Arabic *Maniya*, which stands for "fate," "destruction," "doom," and "death." Manat was also connected with the moon; but in a ***negative*** tone (of course). Manat's symbol was also the *waning* moon - which signifies the old, *crone* goddess.[41] Strikingly, the opposite. Could she have been the true "Mary" character of God's choosing - looked upon, with such negativity, by Cainites and pagans alike?

As we understand, further, many people of the day truly were led to *believe* that the God of Adam - and all he stood for - was *evil*, and wanted this other ideology destroyed, in one way or another. They may have begun to consider this true Horea - if she was God's potential mother of the "savior" - as a person who would help the savior bring on the "end times"… and halt their "ways" of life. She now became an enemy. They did not want to give up the atrocities they were doing, and be destroyed!

The Ascent of Horea - The Real Virgin

So, besides the attempt to insert some false "Mary" into the entire equation, here, there could have even been some attempts by fallen angels to halt Horea from ever continuing on, as **a virgin**. According to one source, it seemed around this same time the angels *Shemhazai* and *Azazel*, among other angels, continually looked for women to have sex with.[42] We already know that *Azazel* was the Serpent. So, it's easy to conclude that these angels knew about Horea, and what they were up against; and even tried to sexually seduce *her* at one time or another. Why not? Their very **futures** were at stake! We get hints, from ancient sources, to all of what might have happened around the time Horea was confronted by these fallen angels:

> *The rulers (fallen angels?) went to meet her intending to lead her astray. Their... chief said to her, "Your mother **Eve** came to us." But... (Horea?) turned to them and said to them, "It is you who are the rulers of the darkness; you are accursed. And you did not know (sexually) my mother; instead it was your **female counterpart** that you knew (Norea?). For I am not your descendant; rather, it is from the world above that I am come"... (Horea?) turned... (and) cried out (to God?)... "Rescue me from the rulers of **injustice** and **save** me from their clutches - immediately!"*
>
> \- *Reality of the Rulers* 92:18-93:1[13]

There are variant accounts to this story:[44]

> *(The leader of the **Watchers**) **Shemhazai** saw a maiden named Istehar (a.k.a. **Horea**?), and he lost his heart to her. She promised to surrender herself to him, if he first taught her the Ineffable Name, by means of which he raised himself to heaven. He assented to her condition. But once she knew it, she pronounced the Name, and herself **ascended to heaven**, without fulfilling her promise to the angel.*
>
> (Ginzberg, 1909, p. 149)[45]

She conned him. She had to, in order to survive! Now that she and Enoch both were able to ascend into heaven, the circuit was now complete: God was finished recanting His process of bringing on the savior at this time; and was going to do *something* with the world still left behind.

What Next?

The additional seventy-generation punishment of Cain's descendants **now** had to go in affect. Enoch and Horea, both, were removed. The world was **still** going down the proverbial toilet, however. And, this seed of Adam was being compromised around every corner. What to do? God's prophecy must come true. It could not, on present course. So, God's judgment would soon be on the horizon. It was time to right this wrongly-sailing ship. What would happen to those still on the earth?

And, what about *Norea* - the counterfeit "Mary" - who also remained? Would she be around there to do, still, further damage? Would she and these fallen angels *continue* to fool the populous into thinking she was someone special, and to fallow the Serpent's "ways?" And, would any of them be able to devise a way to save their selves from God's judgment; or, at least, allow some of *their* offspring to survive?

Chapter 16

The Flood of Lust & Judgment - The Pious to Survive

> *Through their prayers the Lord God will deliver all those who believe from the **flood of lust** for this world. Amen.*
> - *Armenian Apocryphal Adam Literature* Tidings 59[1]

The Nephilim, Cainites, and Watchers brought the world beyond the point of no return. The "Mary" and "Joseph" types were to be utilized; but, because of Lamech, were no longer needed. The whole world had to change; there were barely any Sethites to pass on Adam's seed to (whomever would be) the *next* savior. God's Judgment was upon them - there would soon be a devastating **flood**.[2] This would be the means God would use to *right* this entire wayward train. This flood is commonly known as the flood of **Noah**, today, and would change everything.

There are a variety of theories to *why* there had to be a flood: the most prominent (but not, necessarily, the most popular) being the **fornication** which occurred between the two seed lines. Whatever way people try to front it, however, it's obvious that *sin* was in the center stage.

Again, we recall another definition of fornication:

> *...a wholesale abandonment of God and his righteous ways for women known to be in sin. This is what God calls fornication, not referring only to a sexual sin, but **the sin of mixing the righteous with the wicked**, truth with evil... This sin was so prevalent, and so blatant, a rejection of God that it **could not be allowed to continue indefinitely**.* ("There Were Giants on the Earth… The Nephilim", n. d., p. 2)[3]

The human population was not going in the right direction - the time was ripe for some change.

During the whole lifetime of Adam the sons of Seth had not intermarried with the seed of Cain, but when Adam died they intermarried... for seven generations the descendants of Seth kept righteous, but thenceforwards they became wicked. It was for ***this reason*** *that God repented that He made man.*

- *Chronicles of Jerahmeel* 24:11[4]

The Time Had Come

And I will turn your feasts into mourning, and all your songs into lamentation...

- *Amos* 8:10 (KJV)

As one could guess, in the world they once lived, there were no real laws, no real punishment, and no real organization. Chaos was on the horizon. There needed to be some sort of divine intervention - *some* kind of assistance - to save the remaining Sethite seed from dwindling into obscurity! No longer would there be such depravity; no longer would there be such decadence; or such sin. Imagine what would happen to the pious generations of Adam if some sort of action *wasn't* taken at this time - there would soon be no *pureblooded* Adamites left; and no fulfillment of God's "Seed Line" Prophecy.

God, now, needed to assure *some* seeds of Adam would continue. He, as well, must assure some seeds of the Serpent would survive - to allow this "other side" of the Genesis 3:15 Prophecy to be fulfilled, obviously! So, if Noah and his immediate family were the only ones to survive the flood (as so many might assume, today), then *in what way* could God's prophecy be fulfilled, if no seeds of the Serpent were there?

If we were to assume that Noah and his family were the only eight who survived, there would be no Cainites, no Serpent-seeds, nor anyone else. We know that if the two prophecies of Genesis were to be fulfilled, things could not happen this way at all - there **had** to be other survivors of the flood! Some of each group had to make it through. Obviously, there may have been more to Noah's flood than many might have assumed.

Just what was going to happen, and who would be allowed to carry on through this time?

The Man of "Rest," And "Comfort"

Enter ***Noah*** - the man who (as most of us know) survived this great flood. But, just who was Noah? The name *Noah* actually stands for "rest," or "comfort." The time of *rest* had arrived for the Sethites who still remained - *rest* was in store for those wondering if their seed would ever survive; and *comfort* for those with anxious thoughts about their own future.[5]

At least a *few* with pure, Adamic blood were to survive; that's fairly obvious. But, by the time of Noah, this would prove *extremely* difficult. There weren't many pure Adamite souls left - probably just enough to be able to count, using one's *fingers*! There was so much crossbreeding between man, angel, and Cainite, that even the **father of Noah** had become suspicions of Noah - his own son! We will see, he thought his *own* wife had even committed fornication, the same way!

An Adamite named *Lamech* (not the Cainite Lamech) was Noah's father. It was common knowledge, throughout these ancient times, that any of the offspring with angelic blood often came out of the womb with a *shining* countenance, at least somewhat. Noah did come out as a *shining* baby, much like the other mixed giants of the day.

> *(Lamech speaking) Behold, I thought then within my heart that conception was (due) to the **Watchers**...* - *The Genesis Apocryphon (1Q20)* Col. II[6]

Lamech immediately thought Noah was conceived through some affair of his wife; and ran right over to Enoch - that great judge/prophet of the day.[7] God instructed Enoch to tell him that it was a ***good*** sign. Noah, in actually, was quite a unique baby - with a very special purpose - and not to worry. If a pure-bred Adamite *still* had that angelic "shine" by that time, he/she must have been someone special. Now, baby *Noah* became a sign for the Adamites - *the time had come* for their seed to escape the present, evil world (and Enoch knew it).

120 Years to Adam's Death

We recall the famous "120-year span" of the Bible:

And the LORD said, My spirit shall not always strive with man (the man, Adam), for that he also is flesh: yet his days shall be ***an hundred and twenty years****.*
- *Gen.* 6:3 (KJV)

And, we also know (in the above) that when the Hebrew word for "man" is used *in conjunction* with the article ("the"), then it usually stands for one man - *the one man* **Adam**. We also know this was the time the Watchers descended from heaven; never to return. Now, this "120-year span" seems to even have *another* meaning:

And the Lord granted them a period of ***one hundred and twenty years****, saying, if they will return, then will God repent of the evil, so as not to destroy the earth...*
- *Book of Jasher* 5:11[8]

This proclamation of God officially condemned Adam to fulfill the ultimate punishment given to him in the garden - *death*. On the other hand, God also used this time to allow all of those *evil* descendants on the earth a chance to repent.[9] As we'll see, the world, as a whole, wasn't really going to take heed of any of this.

Let's take a look *beyond* this "120-year" mark, and see how the Sethites would be allowed to escape all of this treachery with their "seed" still intact. Let's look at the flood of Noah.

The "End of All Flesh" Had Come

<u>*Gen.* 6:</u>
6 *And it repented the LORD that he had made the Adamites (i.e. man) on the earth, and it grieved him at his heart.*
7 *And the LORD said, I will destroy the Adamites (i.e. man) whom I have created from the face of the earth; both Adamite (i.e. man), and Behemah and Chay (i.e. beast), and the Remes (i.e. creeping thing), and the Owph (i.e. fowls) of the air; for it*

repenteth me that I have made them.
(in retranslation)

Some interesting things going on here: God was angry, and decided to destroy the Adamites, as well as every other group of human beings around. He, probably, was going to destroy animals in the area, as well, because the fallen angels had also tainted other elements of our world.[10]

But Noah Found Grace…

Gen. 6:
8 *But Noah found grace in the eyes of the LORD.*
9 *These are the generations of Noah: Noah was a just Adamite (i.e. man) and* ***perfect*** *in his generations, and Noah walked with God.*
10 *And Noah begat three sons, Shem, Ham, and Japheth.*
(in retranslation)

Here, *Noah* is first mentioned. Noah was considered "perfect" in his generations. What this probably meant was that he didn't have any *angelic* seed in him - absolutely **no** tainted flesh. His seed was pure.[11] Noah, along with his sons, would be asked by God to build a large boat - an *ark* - to survive His up-and-coming flood. This flood of water would save all inside from total annihilation.

The Warning in the Sky

Gen. 6:
11 *The earth also was corrupt before God, and the earth was filled with violence.*
12 *And God looked upon the earth, and, behold, it was corrupt; for all* ***flesh*** *had corrupted his way upon the earth.*

Acts of *flesh* tainted the known world. God tried to warn the people of what was about to happen.[12] According to ancient sources, God even warned the people in quite a unique way: He placed a huge *bow* in the sky (like the typical *rainbow* we see today).

Apparently, before the flood, this bow was also paired with an *arrow*: an arrow of war.[13] Imagine a huge bow and arrow, high in the sky - actually pointed *down* at them? This was symbolic of God making a proclamation of their upcoming destruction - a bow of **anger**, with the arrow of **wrath**![14] This would be enough to scare most anyone who looked at it, assuredly! Many of us recall, after the flood, that God also allowed a rainbow to appear in the sky, in remembrance of the flood. This time, the bow did *not* have an arrow - a sign that peace had now come to the people. Yet, even with a gigantic bow and arrow in the sky (before the flood), most of the people did not have much of a desire to change themselves.

Noah also pleaded to God. One source stated that Noah even asked God to give the people *seven more* days - beyond the day the flood was supposed to start - to allow people one more chance to repent. God agreed. And, in its stead, He provided a great show of thunder and lightning everywhere. It was horrifying! This now should, hopefully, scare all of the people into repentance.[15] Correct? Of course, nobody really budged.

In one final, mind-blowing attempt, God tried something different:

> *And on that day, the Lord caused the whole earth to* ***shake****, and the* ***sun darkened****, and the foundations of the world raged, and the whole earth was moved violently, and the lightning flashed, and the thunder roared, and all the fountains in the earth were broken up, such as was not known to the inhabitants before; and God did this mighty act, in order to terrify the sons of men, that there might be no more evil upon earth.*
>
> \- *Book of Jasher* 6:11

Of course, it was to no avail:

> *And still the sons of men would* ***not*** *return from their evil ways, and* ***they increased*** *the anger of the Lord at that time, and* ***did not even direct their hearts to all this****.*
>
> \- *Book of Jasher* 6:12

That was it. The followers of Cain, and the descendants of mixed blood, were so evil that most didn't even lift an eyebrow to what was going on around them! God, as merciful and patient as He was, would not put up with any more. The flood had to happen.

> *And God said unto Noah, The end of all flesh (those with this mixed angelic blood?) is come before me; for the earth is filled with violence through them; and, behold, I will destroy them with the earth.* - *Gen.* 6:13 (KJV)

Time for Heavenly Angels to Do Some Preliminary Damage

> *...those (Nephilim and Watchers) who had reviled and made a laughingstock of Adam were* ***conquered****.* - *Book of the Glory of Kings (Kerba Nagast)* 100[16]

It was at this time that some of God's most powerful angels were sent down to the earth, to make one more last-ditch attempt to heal the earth of its corruption. These angels tried to frustrate the current plans of any of these fallen angels and their mixed offspring around (as well as any of the spiritual angels of Sammael/Satan).[17] According to some sources, there were actual battles - spiritual "combat" - between the angels of God and these fallen angels![18]

> *Then Michael, Gabriel, Suriel, and Uriel looked down from heaven, and saw the wickedness which* ***Azazel*** *had done in the world, and they heard the appeal which the souls of the dead were making to heaven, and they reported the matter to the Most High... The God commanded Rafael to bind Azazel hand and foot... Gabriel was sent to destroy all the children of* ***fornication****; and Michael was sent to bind Semyaza (Shemhazai) and... (others, in order to)... imprison them under the mountains of the earth* ***for 70 generations****, after which time they were to be taken to the abyss of fire and tortured there for ever.* - *1 Enoch* 9:1-10:15[19]

It was also at this time that one of God's angels - *Raphael* - grabbed the Serpent (i.e. Azazel), and brought him down to the Abyss (i.e. the *Darkness of the Deep*). This is the spiritual "prison" of which the Bible speaks of:

By which he (Jesus) also he went and preached unto the spirits in ***prison****; Which sometime were disobedient, when once the longsuffering of God waited* ***in the days of Noah****...* - *I Pet.* 3:19-20 (KJV)

And God spared not the ***angels that sinned****, but cast them down to hell, and delivered them into* ***chains of darkness****, to be reserved unto judgment, And spared not* ***the old world****, but saved* ***Noah****...* - *II Pet.* 2:4-5 (KJV)

It's fairly easy to assume this was the *Darkness* - the holding place for fallen angelic (and human) souls. Interestingly enough, the Book of Revelation stated that an angel named *Abaddon* was in this abyss. This angel was also known as the "destroyer." Could Abaddon be the same as the Serpent (Azazel) - the fallen angel who help to *destroy* the world with weapons and tools of his introduction?[20]

And, we already know that up to *ten* percent of the hybrid, human offspring - upon their death - would have souls destined to *remain* on this earth after their deaths… to act as **demons**.[21] Those direct offspring of the fallen angels who died naturally, as well as those destroyed by the angels of God, would have their souls sent strait to the *Darkness*; and into these chains.

Eventually, the death of most of these sinful individuals was on the horizon. Some fallen angels - even **Shemhazai** himself (the leader of the Watchers) - repented to God, and pleaded for mercy.[22] Regardless of who may have sorry by this time, regardless of who might have had a change of heart, many of these sinful deeds have already been done; and those around began to understand what would be their fate. Whoever was chosen to survive this flood - on an *ark* - would, now, be entirely *up to God.*

Eight "Souls" to Survive the Flood

And all else from the wooden house
went forth
Into one place. And then, most just
of men,
Went Noah forth, the ***eighth****...*
- *Sibylline Oracles* Book. I, Line 331-341[23]

Most of us know the story: ***eight*** people survived Noah's flood… all of those, supposedly, were of Noah and his immediate family. According to a number of ancient sources, however, there may have been *more* than these on the ark! The Bible, believe it or not, might also seem to back this up. First, we already know that some sons of the Serpent (and Cainites) *had* to survive - to fulfil the Genesis 3:15 Prophecy. We also have to consider the possibility of *other* groups of human beings living at this time, and if God wanted some of them to survive. Why wouldn't He? Was He *that* mean - especially to the *other* groups of people - just because they may not be of that special **seed** of Adam? Could a good number *more* have gone aboard?

If there was a possibility for more people on the ark besides eight, then why were we always led to believe that there were only **eight** souls saved?[24] If we look at the Bible:

> *For if God spared not the angels that sinned, but cast them down to hell... And spared not the old world, but saved Noah the* ***eighth****, a preacher of righteousness, bringing in the flood upon the world of the ungodly...* - *II Pet.* 2:4-5 (KJV)

> *Which sometime were disobedient, when once the longsuffering of God waited in the days of Noah, while the ark was a preparing, wherein few, that is,* ***eight souls*** *were saved by water.* - *I Pet.* 3:20 (KJV)

In the Bible, this might sound like an open-and-shut case… only eight were allowed on board. Most people were also taught these eight were: **Noah**, **his wife**, **his three sons**, and **their wives**.[25] The above tow verses also seemed to *contradict* any chance of more people going aboard… right? Not necessarily.

First, we'll notice that the Bible (and other ancient sources) often might mention these eight persons in the terms of *souls*.[26] We see, in II Peter 2:5, the original Hebrew doesn't make references to human beings at all, just "*the eighth*"… the eighth what? I Peter 3:20 also refers to these eight in terms of *souls*. We are hard-pressed to locate most any reputable source of old which states anything other than human *souls*, here. Why? Ironically, the Bible is known to be the book of the *generations of Adam* (Gen. 5:1). Could this, *then*, give us an answer? The eight *souls* mentioned above could actually be referring to only the souls of a particular bloodline - the **bloodline of Adam**.[27] Since the

Bible is "the book of the generations of Adam," then we are to understand the flood truly only allowed eight *Adamic* souls to pass through it; pure and simple.

> *The number of people who came forth from the ark was* ***eight souls****, and they built the town of Themânôn after the name of the eight* ***souls****...*
> - *Book of the Bee* 20[28]

More Pious Allowed to Survive, However

> *At length, behold! there came Our command, and the fountains of the earth gushed forth! We said: "Embark therein, of each kind two, male and female, and your family - except those against whom the word has already gone forth, - and* ***the Believers****." but only* ***a few believed*** *with him.*
> - *The Qur'an* Hud 011:040[29]

Most probably, eight Adamic souls would be allowed to board the ark. Even so, this doesn't mean that *more* pious individuals weren't allowed to survive![30] As we recall, there were crossbred giants who actually listened to Enoch. Upon hearing his warnings, they believed in God, and what He had in store for them.[31] A number were sorry, repented to God, and flat-out accepted their fate. Some begged for mercy. Some pleaded for God to save them. A number truly had a change of heart. Could some of these have been allowed aboard?

And, with the possibility of the *Chay of the Field*, the *Owph of the Air*, the *Behemah*, and the *Remes that Creepeth* as **pre-Adamite** human groups, there could have also been pious individuals from these groups, as well. Assuredly, there are a number of *them* who wanted aboard, also. Interestingly enough, the Bible seems to mention these exact same groups as coming and going off the ark!

Beyond any speculation of mixed giants going aboard, beyond any speculation of these other groups as going aboard, we also have *more* ancient works which stated *a lot more* than eight individuals survived Noah's flood:[32]

> *Talmaiel: A descendent of the Grigori who managed to* ***escape*** *both* ***the flood*** *and the swords of the avenging angels.*
> (Godwin, 1990, p. 113)[33]

He (Noah) carried his three sons... and their wives, as well as ***six men*** *of those who believed in him...*
- *al-Tabari: The History of al-Tabari - Vol. I: General Introduction and From the Creation to the Flood* The Events That Took Place in Noah's Time 196[34]

He (Xisuthrus - the "Babylonian Noah") therefore enjoined... (to) take with him into it his ***friends*** *and relations... his wife, his children, and his friends...*
- *Berossus* Of the Cosmology and Deluge[35]

...they hid themselves in an ark... not only Noah, but ***many other people*** *from the immovable generation.* - *Apocryphon of John*[36]

A curious legend exists among the Slavonic nations... He (God) took from among Adam's daughters the ***three*** *finest... they were good and holy, and therefore did not perish in the Deluge, but entered with Noah into the ark and were saved.*
(Baring-Gould, 1881, p. 60)[37]

Noah and his family, together with a ***company*** *of other believers, the number of whom some say was six, others ten, twelve, and even* ***seventy-eight*** *or* ***eighty****, half of them* ***men*** *and half* ***women****... were saved...* (Hanauer, 2007, p. 14)[38]

There are even other ancient sources which state that Noah built a *city*, sometime after the flood; and the name of this city was *Themanon*. The name means, "city of the eight."[39] Yet, interestingly enough, this same name, in Arabic, could *also* mean "city of the **eighty.**"[40] Could there have been, not just *eight* Adamic souls aboard, but, possibly, a lot *more*... maybe even up to *eighty*?[41] Islamic sources tell us:

"Embark therein, of each kind two, male and female, and your family... and the Believers." but only a ***few*** *believed with him.*
- *The Qur'an*, Hud 011:040[42]

They were ***eighty****, referring to "the* ***few****" in God's word (the Qur'an): "But only a* ***few*** *believed with him"... Noah... built himself a village there which he called Thamanin ("Eighty") because he had built a house there for each of the* ***men*** *who were with him; they were* ***eighty****...*
- *al-Tabari: The History of al-Tabari - Vol. I: General Introduction and From the Creation to the Flood* The Events That Took Place in Noah's Time 195-196[43]

Groups Going Aboard Together

One was traditionally taught that there were a good number of animals, *also*, on board the ark. Through divine providence, God signaled to the specific animals He wanted aboard, and told them to travel to the ark by themselves.[44] One source stated that a number of animals walked up to the ark, and lied down. Then, God appointed the two He wanted to stand up, and walk towards the ark. Noah, then, permitted them to enter.

Many have been told the Bible says that there were two of each species allowed on board the ark. How about any *people*, here? Doesn't God care more about people, overall? Assuredly, animals are important to one's idea of compassion, and are important to the livelihood of our world; but *human beings* are the *real* elements of our planet which need to be of concern, here (as most will agree). *People* would (and should) be of the most importance - at least to God. Does the Bible talk about any of these groups *of people* going aboard the ark, besides just Noah?

<u>Gen. 6:</u>
17 *And, behold, I, even I, do bring a flood of waters upon the earth, to destroy all flesh, wherein is the breath (i.e.* ***human*** *souls?) of life, from under heaven; and every thing that is in the earth shall die.*
18 *But with thee will I establish my covenant; and thou shalt come into the ark, thou, and thy sons, and thy wife, and thy sons' wives with thee.*
19 ***And*** *of every living* ***Chay*** *(thing) of all flesh, two of every sort shalt thou bring into the ark, to keep them alive with thee; they shall be male and female.*
20 *Of* ***Owph*** *(fowls) after their kind, and of* ***Behemah*** *(cattle) after their kind, of every* ***Remes that Creepeth*** *(creeping thing) of the earth after his kind, two of every sort shall come unto thee, to keep them alive.*
(in retranslation)

If we look deeper into this, we see that these verses could not only refer to animals, but also to *human* beings. Could groups of people have been brought aboard, at this time? Assuredly, animals around them were important to them, in ways. Assuredly, animals were brought on board, too. That's not the argument. Maybe they even went aboard with these different groups of people. Or, maybe they want on board at some time of which the Bible didn't really notate! The significant thing, here, is how *people* were brought aboard the ark. After all, it was for the sake of the human race that God had to bring on a flood; and it was also for the sake of the human race that God wanted to build an ark in the first place! Animals are important, yes; but, really, not to the extreme of which they have been glamorized in traditional Bible stories… or, at least they shouldn't be.

Did animals go alongside these groups of human beings, here? The following verse seems to develop on our theorem, a little bit. Note the following differences, when the Bible spoke about these different groups going on board:

> *They, and every Chay of the Field (beast) after* ***his*** *kind, and all the Behemah (cattle) after* ***their*** *kind, and every Remes (creeping thing) that Creepeth upon the earth after* ***his*** *kind...* - *Gen.* 7:14 (in retranslation)

Note the use of the words *his* and *their*. Why were *different* words being used - with these different individual groups - here? Could the use of the word "their" refer to a combination of *human* and *animal*, here; and "his" only referring to a group of *human beings*? Why would we suggest this? Well, we've already postulated that the *Behemah* (i.e. *Cattle*) were that group of individuals who worked with the animals; the shepherds, animal caretakers, etc. This was unlike the *Chay of the Field*, who probably may have worked the fields, almost exclusively. The *Remes that Creepeth*, as we've also theorized, probably did not work with animals, either. And, since the *Behemah* once, traditionally, took care of animals as their *profession*, they, now, may have been given the awesome responsibility of taking care of animals while *aboard* Noah's ark (for the most part)! It all makes perfect sense: if animals *did* go aboard, many probably would have gone aboard *at this time*; along with, and under the care of, the *Behemah* who traditionally worked with them, in the past!

Besides, even if this *wasn't* the case (and if these groups were on*ly* animals), wouldn't it be **so much simpler** for the Bible to state something like "all the animals went aboard at this time;" rather than **divide up** animals into these specific groups, here? Why do this? It really doesn't make sense - except to help confuse. And, why would the Bible *continually* seem to mention these **same** group names - throughout Scripture? Why? The answer is probably that: the *truth* is a lot easier to read, here, than what certain individuals/translators *believe* we should see it say! It would be *so* much easier for the Bible to say, here, that "Noah and two of each animal entered"… if *that's* what it was *really* trying to say!

Along these same lines, we have:

> *They, and every… Owph of the Air after* **his** *kind, every* **bird** *of every sort.*
> - *Gen.* 7:14 (in retranslation)

Obviously, the *Owph of the Air*, here, was not a group of **birds**. If they were, the Bible would have absolutely **no** reason to mention these two groups individually. Right?

Two-by-Two Groups of People Go Aboard

> *And they went in unto Noah into the ark, two* **and** *two of all flesh, wherein is the* ***breath of life****.*
> - *Gen.* 7:15 (KJV)

In verse 15, we may even have more scriptural "proof" that God probably brought humans and animals *together*, in some instances. The above verse stated that two of each animal *and* two of each **who had the breath of life** went on board. Again, a human being is the only being who has this *breath of life* - this ***soul***.[45] That's what this means; the same as with the other verse, previously mentioned:

> *And, behold, I, even I, do bring a flood of waters upon the earth, to destroy all flesh, wherein is* ***the breath of life****, from under heaven; and every thing that is in the earth shall die.*
> - *Gen.* 6:17 (KJV)

Again, *why* does the Bible need to mention about animals having a *breath of life*? Surely, dead animals aren't about to walk aboard the ark. They wouldn't be needed! If Scripture is as perfect as many of us believe, then these words were inserted *for a reason*… and, probably, not for the reason so many might assume, now-a-days. It's all about mentioning those *with souls*… human souls!

Even non-Biblical works say something similar:

*All **the living beings** (the humans with **souls**?) that I had I loaded on it, I had all my kith (i.e. friends, neighbors, or relatives) and **kin** go up into the boat, all the **beasts** and **animals of the field** (i.e. the Chay and Behemah?) and the craftsmen I had go up.*
- *The Epic of Gilgamesh* Tablet XI[46]

With this in mind, let's postulate, further. As we see, one of the verses we already mentioned (above) also might even separate animals and humans into *two* groups - stating that they went aboard Noah's ark; side by side.[47] Let's see:

*And they went in unto Noah into the ark, two (i.e. animals?) <u>and</u> **two of all flesh, wherein is the breath of life** (i.e. people?).* - *Gen.* 7:15 (KJV)

So, when the animals *were* to come aboard the ark (such as the times when they were to be accompanied by *Behemah* caretakers, for example), they walked aboard; two by two… they, *and* their human counterparts!

There are some other, non-Biblical works which seem to separate animals and *humans* into two groups:

(God speaking) But do thou (Noah)
Make haste and enter with thy sons,
And wife,
And their wives. Call as many as I bid,
*The **tribes** of beasts (i.e. the Chay and Behemah?) and*
creeping things (i.e. the Remes?) and birds (i.e. the Owph?),
***<u>And</u>** in the **beasts** (the animals?) of such as I*
Ordain
To keep alive will I then strait
Impart
- *Sibylline Oracles* Book 1, line 242–248[48]

Animals don't really form into *tribes*… only humans do! In the non-Biblical account, below, the animals were brought aboard, *as well as* a group of "sentient" beings:

Early the next day he brought in the beasts and the cattle... In the middle of the day he brought in the birds and ***all the sentient beings****... At sunset Noah and his sons and his sons' wives entered...* *- Book of the Rolls (Kitab Al-Magall)* 28[49]

The word *sentient* means "conscious." What type of *beings* possesses a human-like consciousness… except human beings, themselves? Again, we see that *more*, sentient beings went aboard the ark… more "conscious" beings, beyond Noah and his family.

Gen. 7:
13 *In the selfsame day entered Noah, and Shem, and Ham, and Japheth, the sons of Noah, and Noah's wife, and the three wives of his sons with them, into the ark;*
16 *And they that went in, went in male and female* ***of all flesh****, as God had commanded him: and the LORD shut him in.*

Could *a number* of different groups of people have gone aboard Noah's ark… beyond the usual "eight?"

Different Strokes for Different Folks

...he (Noah) should make three stories to it. The lowest should be for the tame and the wild animals and the cattle (the Chay, Behemah, and, possibly, the Remes?), the middle one for the birds and their like (the Owph?), and the highest one for him and his children and his wife and his sons' wives.
- Book of the Rolls (Kitab Al-Magall) 24[50]

Could the people and animals *both* have been placed within different levels of Noah's ark - with each human group assigned to tend, or care for, different groups of animals?[51]

So, in conclusion, we might be able to assume that pious were allowed on board - some from *each* group - to repopulate the world. Why would God only want to allow *only* members of Noah's family to survive, here? Assuredly, there were other pious individuals from other creeds, races, or groups. Why wouldn't God have enough of a heart to allow some of every pious group, here?

Could the number of pious individuals aboard the ark be up to *eighty* in total… or even *more*? And, what about any of the not-so-pious individuals left? Would some of *them* be able to get themselves, or some of their seed, aboard the ark? Let's see.

The Great Deception

Although we know that *some* of those with mixed-blood could have survived the flood (to fulfill the prophecy of Genesis 3:15), there are many, today, who assume that *every* one of those who went aboard Noah's ark *had* to have been pious! Many have concluded that God wouldn't want *any* individuals who practiced evil to survive the flood. Makes sense.

And, obviously, *none* of the original fallen angels should have been allowed to survive; neither would any of the original Watchers. The Serpent, as we know, was, also, totally *unrepentant*. Their fate was in front of them. Yet, if they all knew they were going to die, *maybe* they could, somehow, immortalize themselves… through their descendants! *Maybe*, somehow, they could sneak some of *their own seed* on board. At least that would make them feel *a little better*. Maybe they felt they could "get back at" God, in their own little way. To do so, however, would have been a monumental task for these; but, that doesn't mean they wouldn't have even tried.

Apparently, a lot of these angels, including the Serpent, himself, *did* try to find a way "out" for their own seed; as well as keep their apostate causes going! They weren't going to just accept their futures; and welcome it with open arms. So, in order to accomplish this, they'd have to take almost *any* sinister route. *Now*, we'll see that there may have even been fallen angels who listened to Enoch for, yet, *another reason* - to find a way out for their own seed!

Now, a major goal of the Nephilim and Watchers left - if *they* couldn't get on board - would be to find a way to their *own* seed aboard; to continue on, with their anti-God "ways":

> *...if it (their desires) had been in them as it is in men, the Devils would not have left any one in the world alone without corrupting them, till not a* ***virgin*** *would have been left on the earth, for the foul Devils love corruption and fornication. As they cannot do this, they change their nature on account of it; they recommend it to men and make them love it.* *- Book of the Rolls (Kitab Al-Magall)* 25[52]

We can assume *why* these angels, and most of their immediate descendants, were not allowed to board the ark: they would not have a change of heart. There was *no way* they were going to change their natures. They were trying their hardest to figure out ways to do things *their own way*, here. How would they pull it off… if they could?

Well, we recall that many people might assume that Noah, his wife, his three sons, and their three wives were the **eight** Adamic souls who survived the flood… makes sense. And, the Bible seems to be correct in stating that *eight* Adamic souls went aboard the ark. So, that's not the issue. But, the question which arises, now, might be: were these *eight* the members of Noah's family? Just ***who*** these eight were might actually become the point of conjecture, now! If there would be any manipulation done… how about doing it with these *eight*? Could the fallen angels have even inserted their **own** seed into the immediate family of Noah?

We'll soon see that there *may have* been two or three people - out of the eight immediate members of Noah's family - who **didn't** have pure, Adamite blood, here… but had the blood of fallen, angelic beings!

Chapter 17

The Real Adamites to Go Aboard - The Flood Occurs

> *The first race he (Adam) supposed to have peopled the whole world... Adam was created with a spiritual soul, and that from Adam the Jewish race was descendents, whereas the Gentile nations issued from the loins of the pre-Adamites. Consequently the original sin of Adam weighed only on his descendants, and Peyreira supposed that it was his race* ***alone*** *which perished,* ***with the exception*** *of Noah and his family, in the Deluge...* (Baring-Gould, 1881, p. 28)[1]

When the Bible states that "everyone died" in the flood, could this mean that *the rest* of the *Adamites* died… except the *eight*; or could it mean that *everyone* died who wasn't aboard the ark; or *both*? We're not sure. We are not sure how specific the Bible goes, here… but we can assume, for sure, that those aboard the ark were saved.

We already know of ancient written texts which state that a number of people could have been aboard the ark, beyond those "eight." Now, what about these eight (Noah, his wife, his three sons, and their wives)… can we assume that they were *all* Adamites, and of this pure seed of Adam?

The Assumed Eight Survivors
Noah
Noah's Wife
Japheth
Japheth's Wife
Shem
Shem's Wife
Ham
Ham's Wife

We'll now see that, inside of these eight, there could have been a few discrepancies: two or three may, actually, ***not*** have had pure, Adamic blood. *Who* could have been these exceptions… and *what* may have really happened, here? Were these fallen angels involved, somehow?

The First Wife of Noah

According to ancient sources, Noah remained a virgin for almost 500 years.[2] He may have been afraid (as many people often were) that any of his offspring would perish in the up-and-coming flood. Close to the time the flood, however, God instructed Noah to marry anyhow.

> *All his contemporaries begot at a hundred or two hundred years, while he begot at five hundred years! The reason, however, is that (God)... said: "If they [Noah's sons] are to be wicked, I do not desire them to perish in the flood"... Therefore the Lord stopped his **fountain** and he begot at five hundred years.*
>
> \- *Genesis Rabbah* 26:2[3]

God wanted Noah's children to remain pious; so He allowed him to bear children *late* in life - so they would *not* be exposed to a lot of this worldly temptation, at the time.

Beyond this, Noah could have had at least two wives, over time. The first (in succession) could have been someone we already know of - a **virgin**. There were many names for this woman. Could it possibly the aforementioned "virgin" - that "Mary" character, of before?

By most accounts, his first wife of Noah was known as his "true love."[4] A few of her names were *Emzara*, *Amzara*, *Amzurah*, or even *Zara*.[5] Another name for her - *Azura* - was probably the most interesting one, here. The ancient historian *Tabari* stated that Azura could have been a sister of Seth; or another descendant of Adam and Eve.[6] And, we know ***Horea*** was a descendant of Adam and Eve, as well; and even was considered a sister of Seth, by some accounts. Now, could Azura be *Horea*: the direct descendent of Eve; and this *same* "virgin" mother?[7]

> *...(Noah's wife's) name was Noema (Norea/Horea?)... The Gnostics called her Noria...* (Baring-Gould, 1881, p. 123-124)[8]

If this *was* the case, then Horea, like Noah, were both virgins for a long, long time. After foiling the advancements of these fallen angels, and **before** her ascension into heaven, God could have held Horea over for one more task: to marry **Noah**! At least, if she wouldn't be allowed to be mother of the antediluvian "savior," maybe she could have at least married Noah; and had a couple of *his* children.

The first wife of Noah, according to sources, probably bore him his sons ***Japheth*** and ***Shem***. *Then*, at this time, she may have been allowed to ascend into heaven! Her role on earth was over. She did, at least, contribute to her society, *some*.

With the woman gone, Noah was now all by himself. What was next for him? Was Noah going to have any more children? Was he going to be alone, from then on?

And, what about that "anti-Horea" of their day - known as *Norea*? She was probably still around, at the time of Horea's departure. As we recall, Norea was, most probably, the *plant* of the fallen angels and the Cainites - their *own* version of "Mary." Both of these women lost their bids to become the mother of the promised savior. So, what might have been next for this "anti-Horea?" Word probably got around that Noah married the real "Mary" character; and even had children by her. So, many around may have realized that the "Mary" character of the day was granted this honor; which was beginning to expose the other "Mary" - the "anti-Horea" - as a *fraud*. Would she bow her head in utter defeat, due to this exposure; or would she go on, and attempt to do something about it?

From the ancient evidence, we know Noah had *another* wife; probably a second wife.[9] Interestingly enough, this was not *Norea*. It was a woman of whom we've mentioned before - ***Naamah***; the famous Cainite of the Bible! What a change of pace for the patriarch Noah, now. Why marry a Cainite? And, if this happened - if Norea didn't end up with Noah, as *she probably assumed* was her place - what did she, and her angelic supporters, attempt to do to Noah, as a *result*?

As we begin to discover these answers, let's first look at *Naamah*, and how she came into this whole picture.

Noah's Second Wife?

Because of two unfulfilled prophecies, some of those with *Cainite* blood had to go aboard Noah's ark, at this time; and that's without a doubt. There are a number of ancient accounts which state that Noah married someone of *Cain's* kin. It would be at this time that *Naamah* would have come onto the scene. This could have even been part of God's plan to have some of these Cainites go aboard the ark; we're not sure. Regardless, this woman, as we recall, could have even had blood of the *Nephilim* - even the Serpent himself! Why was she chosen?

A year-or-so after his first two sons were born, Noah could have married her:

> *And when Noah was for hundred and fifty years old, he begat a son and he called his name Japheth. Forty two years later he begat another son of her who was the* ***mother of Japheth****, and he called his name Shem.* ***Eight years*** *later Noah begat a son* ***of his wife Naamah****...* - *Writings of Abraham* 11:1-3 (also 12:1, 16:1)[10]

With the amount of ancient evidence, abroad, it's almost certain that Noah probably married Naamah; at least for a certain length of time.

> *And Noah took her on this wise: For the word of the Lord came unto Noah, saying, Take unto thyself* ***Naamah****, the daughter of Lamech, who dwelleth here in the city of thy fathers, for she hath been faithful to my gospel, wherefore I shall preserve through her the* ***seed of Cain*** *through the flood.*
> - *Writings of Abraham* 12:2 (also 16:1)[11]

> *Wherefore, let not my son Noah fear to take her to wife, for in so doing he shall be blessed for through him will* ***come*** *all* ***nations****.*
> - *Writings of Abraham* 14:3[12]

In conclusion, here, we now discover that Naamah, for whatever reason God wanted her, could have been the *first* member of these famous eight who really **didn't** have pure, Adamic blood!

Woman Corrupted

Naamah may have started *out* a wholesome woman:[13]

> *When Adah and Zillah, the wives of Lamech, learned of this, they took their remaining sons and daughters and went unto their father Cainan's city and revealed the remainder of the secrets of this evil combination among the sons of Adam. Thus did* ***Naamah*** *come to dwell among the sons of Adam and she grew up before the Lord* ***in righteousness*** *and was known for* ***her tender care*** *toward the sick and the* ***unfortunate****. Nevertheless, she had not husband because* ***she was of the forbidden race****.* - *Writings of Abraham* 13:12-14[14]

Naamah was, once, very well-known for how agreeable, and ***tender***, she was to others.[15] She also became famous for her *musical* ability: she sang to the timbrel - a musical invention of her brother *Jubal*. As with today, those who wrote music, and sang, back then, often had the ability to become *very* influential to people around them. Naamah, quickly, began to rise in popularity. She also was thought to have taught women the beautifying of themselves; as well as hairdressing.[16] Because of her overwhelming beauty and tenderness, as well as her abilities, she became famous to the masses.

And, as we recall, there were others who were interested in her - for *more* than just her positive talents:

> *..."And the sister of Tuval Kayin (Tubal-Cain) was Naamah" (Beresheet 4:22). Why do the scriptures mention her name, Naamah* ***(tender)****? It is because people were seduced by her overwhelming beauty and tenderness, and* ***spirits*** *and* ***demons*** *lusted after her... the sons of Elohim, Aza, and Azael were seduced by her. Because of those seductions, she was named Naamah...* - *Zohar* Beresheet B62[17]

Eventually, Naamah raised the eyebrows of many around her, *including* some of the most important fallen angels of the day. She had a lot, she knew a lot, and, now, could have begun to use all of this to her advantage.[18] She, soon, had fallen angels in her left hand, Noah in her *right* - and her desire to survive God's horrible flood in the middle! Things may have been changing in her mind, in regards to her feelings of "self-importance," and how to work the system. And, now, she really wasn't about to mind using *whatever it took* to achieve any of her end-goals, now.

The Hot One

After Shem and Japheth, Noah's younger son - ***Ham*** - was born. We know that Noah probably begat Japheth and Shem with his previous wife. Soon after this, Noah could have fathered a son with *Naamah*, now - his new wife. We recall:

> *And when Noah was for hundred and fifty years old, he begat a son and he called his name Japheth. Forty two years later he begat another son of her who was the mother of Japheth, and he called his name Shem. Eight years later Noah begat a son* ***of his wife Naamah****, who was of the seed of Cain, and he called his name* ***Ham****...*
>
> \- *Writings of Abraham* 11:1-3[19]

At the moment of Ham's birth, Naamah made a statement about *her* son, here; just as Eve had, a couple of times! We recall that:

> *...Noah begat a son of his wife Naamah, who was of the seed of Cain, and he called his name Ham, for she said,* ***Through him will the curse be preserved in the land****.*
>
> \- *Writings of Abraham* 11:1-3[20]

We also recall that one meaning of the name *Cain* is *possession*. And this, as we know, seems to be related to a circumstance of his birth: after he was born, he rose up, grabbed a stick or branch, and gave it to his mother. This desire to take, and *possess*, things of this earth seemed to follow Cain for the rest of his life. **Ham's** name, interestingly enough, could *also* have been a reflection of the kind of life *he* would live in the future:

> *Hebrew names are often based on common words, giving the names special meanings that relate it back to characteristics of the individual or thing being named.*
>
> (Quayle, 2005, p. 218)[21]

Well, what could *Ham* mean; and how would his name be associated with something about him, or his *future*? The name *Ham* comes from a Hebrew word meaning "*hot*." It could also mean "*warm*," or "passionate."[22]

We see, according to ancient sources, that when God refashioned our present world, *heat* seemed to have been involved in the process! He hovered over the waters of the *Darkness*, and the waters, below, became *hot*:

...the whole nature of the waters glowed with heat, and the leaven of creation was united to them. As the mother-bird maketh warm her young by the embrace of her closely covering wings, and the young birds acquire form through the ***warmth*** *of the heat which (they derive) from her, so through the operation of he Spirit of holiness... the leaven of the breath of life was united to the waters when He hovered over them.*
- *Cave of Treasures* The Creation: First Day, First Day[23]

From this, we discover:

...the Spirit of holiness... hovered over the waters, and through the hovering thereof over the face of the waters, the waters were blessed so that they might ***become producers of offspring****, and they became* ***hot****... And when the dust of the earth became* ***hot****, it brought forth all the trees, and plants, and seeds, and roots which had been conceived inside it...*
- *Cave of Treasures* The Creation: First Day, Fourth Day[24]

Heat - the sensation of feeling *hot* - often may also be connected with the act of coition, or *sexual* activity. The sexual act itself, as most know, could generate a good deal of *body* heat. What about *Ham* - and his role in this all?

One theory abounds: Noah could have noticed something a little different about Naamah, in regards to her coitus with him. It seemed that Naamah might have been much more sexually *voracious* than the other, non-Cainite - hence a reason for the name of their product, *Ham*.

The Vice of the Soul

And, we know Naamah was thought to have, once, been a very beautiful woman. Beyond being a Cainite, however, she might have even been the offspring of an angelic being, herself (as we speculated)! We know, around this time, that she may have begun to seek power for herself, and agree to affairs with certain fallen angels. Could these concepts of "heat" or "fire" be connected with her desire for coition with these angels, as well?

> *...The angels are flaming* ***fire****... (this same)* ***fire*** *came with the* **coition** *of flesh and blood, but did not burn the body...* - *Pirke deR. Eliezer* XXII[25]

After becoming corrupted by these encounters, she may have come to Noah with a pattern of sexual voraciousness and an almost-overbearing amount of passion:

> *..."****heat****"... (is) a sign of vice of the soul...*
> (Haynes, 2002, p. 26)[26]

The "Changeling"

Beyond any over-bearing sexual practices, Naamah could have indulged in *other* very questionable activities with fallen angels. What happened next is purely under speculation. We don't have ancient evidence to support the following in any definitive nature; but there *are* ancient written texts to support that this could have happened.

There are *two* theories that surround Ham, and how he got aboard Noah's ark. The Bible states that Noah begat his son Ham; and they both went aboard the ark - simple. And, it probably happened this way - in a *way*. There may have been some underlying variants to this whole story, however. The first thought was that Ham may have been switched at birth. Noah and Naamah *did*, indeed, bare a child Ham; but the Ham that went aboard the ark was not the same baby: it was a **changeling**. A *changeling* is defined as *another* baby, switched (or "secretly inserted") soon after the first baby's birth! In this case, the changeling was actually a mixed-blood offspring of a fallen angel… inserted to perpetuate their seed. There was no DNA back then. This ability to switch a newborn was, probably, much more prominent. How was Noah to know, for sure? In this case, Noah may have gone along with it, not knowing he was no longer the father.

As we now see, Naamah was, interestingly enough, also famous for something else:

> *...she (Naamah) was the mother of demons, being of the side of Kayin, and... she is responsible for the epileptic* ***death of babies****.* - *Zohar* Beresheet B62[27]

What if one of these angels did not want to accept his fate; and worked with Naamah to make a deal - and pass *his own seed* through the flood? What if they both agreed to switch a baby at birth? What if Naamah did it to fulfill some sort of obligation to her *own* family line; after all, she was a Cainite? Who knows? Maybe one of these angels even raped, or cohabited with, Naamah at the time she was married; and she felt shame by it; had a child through him (and not Noah) on the sly - we simply don't know for sure.[28] How would anyone know, for sure?

One ancient Gnostic work stated:

> *But in turn the angels* ***secretly introduced*** *Kham* ***(Ham)*** *into the ark, for* ***he belonged to their posterity****. For, they say that out of eight persons then saved in that 'coffer' of Noah seven belonged to the pure people, but one-namely Kham-belonged to the other power, having sneaked on board... And this plan, which was contrived by the angels, came out as follows. Now-they say-inasmuch as the angels recognized that their entire people was going to be obliterated by the flood, by trickery they secretly added the aforementioned Kham in order to preserve the* ***evil*** *people, which had been* ***made by them****. And as a result of this (people) there arose forgetfulness, error, sinful undisciplined passions, and evil promiscuity among humankind within the world. And thus the world turned back again to its original state of disorderliness and became filled with evils as it had been in the beginning before the flood.* - *The Sethians According to St. Epipanius* 39.3.2-4[29]

Whatever way it might have happened, the switch of one Ham by another "Ham" could have ensured the survival of, at least, *one* seed of a fallen angel, destined for death.

The second thought was that Ham had a brother; close to him, in name. Noah could have had a forth son at this time, named ***Yam***. One went aboard; the other didn't. Yam, like Horea, could also have been thought of as "type," and "anti-type," in a way... one being *true* and *just*; the other *imitation*. We, now, see ancient evidence to support *this* thought, as well.

The Four Who Persecuted Noah

God, as most of us know, instructed Noah to build an ark; an ark whose construction would take a long, long time. During this time of construction, Noah began to warn the people around him of God's impending doom. Some listened; many more didn't.

Ironically, the ark was said to have been built in the encampment of Cainites themselves - possibly because it gave Noah opportunities to witness to them; or it even began to serve as a test of *Noah's resolve*.[30] Regardless of the reason, this situation also allowed some of the Cainites to be able to speak their mind against Noah - to be disruptive to this whole ark-building progress.[31] Ancient sources commented on this disruption:

> *Noah was enjoined to tell no man that he was making the ark; and, miraculously, his tools made no noise when he worked at it. The devil, anxious to prevent the building, went in human form to Noah's wife and asked her where her husband spent his time so secretly. She could not tell. He effectually roused her jealousy and suspicion, and gave her certain grains. "These," he said, "if put in Noah's drink, will force him to tell you all about it." This happened: Noah gave away the secret, and next day, when he went out to work, the first blow of his axe resounded through all the countryside. An angel came to him and rebuked him for his want of caution.*
>
> - *Queen Mary's Prayerbook* (Brit. Mus. Royal 2. B. 7)[32]

> *And while he was building the ark, the* ***axe*** *cried out, the* ***hatchet*** *cried out, the* ***saw*** *cried out, <and> the* ***wood*** *cried out, "Behold, a flood is coming and it will destroy this world!" When Noah heard the cry of the axe, he went <and> related to everyone that a flood was coming, Every man scorned him... They would scorn and say, "Look at the ignorance of Noah, who says a flood is coming!"*
>
> - *Armenian Apocryphal Adam Literature* Tidings 37-38[33]

Probably during that "120 year" span God gave man to change his ways, He also directed Noah to minister to the people around him.[34] When Noah was 480 years old, it seems, he began to preach - all the way till his 600th year. A lot of people laughed at his warnings, and didn't do anything but mock him.[35] Some even became violent to him.[36]

According to one ancient source, *four* people continually tried to persuade everyone that Noah was wrong; even *mad*:

- Noah's wife (so named Wa'ileh)
- Ij ibn 'Anak (translated ***Og*** *the son of Anak*)
- ***Anak***
- Noah's own **son**

How would these people be related, in any way, to the eight Adamites who went aboard the ark? Let's see.

The "Fire Woman"

We recall that Noah's first wife was probably named *Azura* (or *Horea*). She was continually tempted by a couple of fallen angels; and, eventually - after bearing Shem and Japheth - ascended into heaven. The above woman - *Wa'ileh* - probably wasn't Horea… she had probably ascended into heaven already, by this time! She probably wasn't Naamah, as well. Naamah wouldn't really want to be too upset with her husband at this time, because she was *already* going on board. Yes, this probably was another name for the scorned ***Norea*** - the "plant" of these fallen angels.

And, we do recall that Norea was no longer in contention for this "Mary" character, because she no longer existed. She did not have much of a purpose in the world anymore; and now, was, probably, even more angry that Noah chose to take the other, *true* "Mary" as his wife. She was in the mood for action.

And, if we think about it, a lot of the Cainites and other people around her were wholly convinced that *she* was the *real*, anointed one - the mother of this "savior." It only made **sense** (to so many) that *she* should have, at least, been the one to marry Noah, and to survive the flood. Ancient Gnostic sources provide us with an interesting affirmation, here:

> *…when she wanted many times to be with Noah in the ark, her request was denied since -it says- the ruler (God?) who created the world wanted* ***to destroy her*** *in the flood along with all the others.*
>
> \- *The Sethians According to St. Epipanius* 26.1.7[37]

There are a number of ancient, mythological accounts which considered *Norea* as Noah's proper wife.[38] Ultimately, we could only place her as a scorned woman who considered herself as having a rightful heir.

And, interestingly enough, *Norea* was known for one more thing: in Greek mythological accounts, for example, the name *Noria* could have originated from *nura*, a word meaning "fire."[39] Another character of ancient mythology - *Deucalion* - was, often, considered to be the Greek's version of "Noah;" and this Deucalion was *also* said to have been married to *Pyrrha* - a woman with a name meaning "bright red," or "fire."[40] Why? Yet, another equivalent for *Norea*, in ancient mythology, is *Vesta* - the goddess of the forge.[41] Why all these associations with *fire*?

> *And-it says-she (Norea) laid siege to the "coffer" (i.e. the ark) and **burned** it, once, again, and a third time. Hence, indeed, the construction of Noah's 'coffer' went on for many years because it was **burnt many times** by her. For–it says-Noah put his trust in the ruler (God?), whereas Noria (Norea)... (supported those)... **opposed** to the ruler.*
>
> \- *The Sethians According to St. Epipanius* 26.1.8-9[42]

A scornful Norea probably did everything she could to *upstart* Noah's construction - including her attempts to burn the ark! Obviously, it wasn't very successful.

We recall the four people against Noah at this time:

- Noah's wife (so named Wa'ileh)
- Ij ibn 'Anak (translated ***Og** the son of Anak*)
- ***Anak***
- Noah's own **son**

We will learn more about Ij ibn 'Anak - or ***Og*** - in a future chapter. What we need to know about Og now is that he was considered a *Mighty Man* - one of those offspring of the Watchers and human women. One source states that the leader of these Watchers, *Shemhazai*, could have tried to allow his seed to survive, as well! And, according to the Bible, this same **Og** (and his brother Sihon) lived well beyond the flood - into the time of Moses, even. How could this be? If they were both alive *before* the flood occurred, as ancient texts tell us, then they *must* have survived the flood, somehow. But, now, what was so significant about Og at this time, regarding Noah, and the building of the ark?

Og was considered either the son, or grandson, of Shemhazai.[43] And, before the infamous **Ham** married his own wife, she either was raped, or had an affair with, a fallen angel (or even Shemhazai, himself)… and *Og* was the result. Then, when Ham eventually married her, he accepted Og as part of his family. So, near to the time of the flood, Ham's wife was raped, or seduced, by a fallen angel (or even Shemhazai) again; and became pregnant, once again.[44] Ham *pleaded* with Noah to take her aboard the ark, because it was obvious she was the mother of the mixed Og and Sihon. Noah reluctantly agreed. But, Ham may *not* have told him she was pregnant, yet again.[45]

Noah really didn't feel as if they should go on board in the first place; but, out of the generosity of his heart, he allowed all of them on board. Og (and probably Sihon) survived on top of the ark, holding onto a beam. And, Noah graciously put food and provisions out for him, on a daily basis.[46] As a statement of gratitude, Og *swore* that he would become a servant to Noah, and his posterity, from then on![47] This whole story did not have a happy ending, however; as we'll soon see. Og's attitude would not end up "too far from the tree," regardless of the gracious treatment he received by Noah, overall.

Next, as far as the third character - *Anak* - we are not sure. Could this have been a name for Ham's wife - the mother of Og? Possibly, she wasn't very happy that Noah had trepidations about wanting to welcome her, and her mixed sons.

Finally, the forth character (above) - one of Noah's sons - could have even been *Ham*, himself.[48] Possibly, Ham was also upset that Noah had trepidations about his choice of wife; we're not sure.

Whoever these four individuals were - those who began to protest Noah and all that he stood for (even without openly saying it) - we *do* have ancient evidence that Noah's own wife, Naamah, was a Cainite, who was beginning to fall to corruption. And, we also have her son *Ham* as another individual aboard the ark - a *second* individual who might *not* have been of pure, Adamic blood. Could there have been more?

Ham's Wife - Also a Cainite

Along with these two, there could have been *another* member of Noah's family who was a Cainite: Ham's ***wife***.[49] Possibly, as we know, Ham took compassion on this woman because he, himself, also had Cainite blood! Who knows?

> *Now Ham's wife was named Zeptah and she was also of the* ***seed of Cain****...*
> - *Writings of Abraham* 17:7[50]

Like minds think alike.

If so, now we have three - *three* souls without pure, Adamic blood! Since Naamah, Ham, and Ham's wife possibly did not have this pure seed of Adam, just *who* were the *real* eight souls that the Bible tallies, here?

The Real Eight Souls

We, now, recall the eight Adamites - along with the *three* who weren't totally pure-bred:

Noah
Noah's Wife (Naamah) ***- Non-Adamite***
Japheth
Japheth's Wife
Shem
Shem's Wife
Ham ***- Non-Adamite***
Ham's Wife ***- Non-Adamite***

And, we already may be able to assume there could have been *a number* of people going aboard Noah's ark; beyond just these eight. Noah could have asked personal servants, his friends - even his *concubines* - to board. So, looking at the above, we could assume that up to *three* of these other people could have been of pure, Adamite blood (to make the total *eight*, again):

> *The **nurse** of Noah was an important personage... She was named Sambethe, and was the first Sibyl... (This) Sibyl... was **of the race** of Noah.*
> (Baring-Gould, 1881, p. 123-124)[51]

> *...And Noah together with his sons, his **[wives]** and his son's wives... entered the ark...* - *Genizah Manuscripts* Gen. 7:7[52]

> *...he (Xisuthrus - the "Babylonian Noah") immediately quitted it with his wife, his **daughter**, and **the pilot**.* - *Berossus* Of the Cosmology and Deluge[53]

> *he invited **his people***
> *...to a feast*
> *...his family was brought on board.*
> - *Epic of Atrahasis*[54]

> 85. *I made to go up into the ship all my family and **kinsfolk**,*
> 86. *The **cattle** of the field, the beasts of the field, all **handicraftsmen** I made them go up into it...*
> 94. *I went into the ship and shut my door.*
> 95. *To the **pilot** of the ship, Puzur-Enlil the sailor*
> 96. *I committed the great house (the ark / ship), together with the contents thereof.*
> - *The Epic of Gilgamesh* The Loading of the Ship[55]

If we put these all together, the most rational "eight" could be:

Noah
Noah's Sister, Daughter, Daughter-in-Law, or Another Wife[56]
Japheth
Japheth's Wife
Shem
Shem's Wife
The Pilot
The Architect / Handicraftsman of the Ark

Ultimately, whoever they really were, there were probably eight Adamic *souls* saved from among the children of Seth (just as the Bible said):

All the children of Adam today trace their pedigree back to Seth. That is because the offspring of all the other children of Adam except those of Seth have completely disappeared, and not one of them remains.
- *al-Tabari: The History of al-Tabari - Vol. I: General Introduction and From the Creation to the Flood* Eve Giving Birth to Seth 153[57]

Now, Why Did It Have To Be a Flood?

And God said unto Noah, "Go about among the people and tell them that a ***flood*** *shall come and shall overwhelm them... build it (the ark)... in presence of the children of Cain... and if they will not repent they shall perish, and the blame shall rest on them."*
- *Third Book of Adam and Eve (The Conflict of Adam and Eve with Satan)* Ch. 2[58]

The *eight* Adamites were chosen. The year of Noah's flood was approximately 2370-2369 B.C.[59] Interestingly, the word *flood* comes from the same word as the word *abyss* (in Gen. 1:2, for example).[60] Would this devastating flood be not unlike the pre-Adamite devastation which once led so many human and angelic souls to the *Darkness*, or the abyss?

But, why would it have to be a flood, again? It might be for an *ironic* reason, here - God, assuredly, understood what was going on in the world below, and the people were about to get *back* what was coming to them - in some sort of *ironic* manner.[61] As we know, flagrant sexuality and illicit sexual practices were, often, considered the largest contributors to God's desire for judgment.[62] The "flood" of sin was about to have its impurities "washed away":

*The idea that the flood was essentially a purifying bath derives... from the very essence of the thing: bathing was, in ancient Israel, seen as a means of cleansing not only from actual dirt but from "****impurity****" as well - a concept in which the physical and metaphysical met.* (Kugel, 1997, p. 199)[63]

All of their "folly and impiety" were going to be "washed" away from human existence; much like a good *rain* would wash away any impurities on a plot of land.[64]

> *From Cain arose and were descended all the generations of the wicked, who rebel and sin... and they said: We do not need the* ***drops of Thy rain****, neither to walk in Thy ways, as it is said, "Yet they said unto God,* ***Depart from us****" (Job 21:14).*
> *- Pirke deR. Eliezer* XXII[65]

How cruel: many people of the day *still* did not think God was really serious; and/or really didn't *care*. They didn't want any "rain" of influence upon them, and what they were still doing - especially from *God*, Himself. So, it'll soon be easy for us to conclude that *water*, and a *flood*, would become a *perfect* retaliation for such a *flood* of immorality they were saturating the earth with. It was the perfect method used before Adam's formulation; and, now, seems the perfect method to use again (probably because the world before Adam had degenerated into much the *same* state of moral decadence and decay).

The "120 years" time frame, before the onset of the flood, were about to come to a close; with Noah using the last breaths he was allowed to reach anyone and everyone he could.[66] We also know that some of the hybrid offspring of his day (of these fallen angels) actually *did* listen to Enoch, and probably Noah, as well. And, as a result, some of these individuals might have *also* been allowed aboard! Yes, God wanted to be fair to everyone, it seems... regardless of the circumstances of their birth.

There were other individuals around who, half-heartedly, may have even *believed* that what they were doing could have been wrong, at least somewhat; and probably tried their *own* solutions to the societal problems brewing around them. They rationalized: "If there are so many problems in our society, today - which result from such open and unbound sexual practices - then we simply *won't do* certain things that might make things worse... such as produce as many mixed offspring as we did before, and the like! We will *intercept* our sperm at the point of orgasm, and divert it from our coitus. *That* should help solve things!"[67] As one interpretation of early Genesis goes: "*And God saw the earth, and behold it was* ***spilled***" (Gen. 6:12). In other words, a number of people *still* didn't want to change their ways, as far as stopping their sexual rampages, their orgies, and their perversions. And, they realized that having the offspring which resulted from these exchanges (as well as bringing on more Anakim and Mighty Men) was beginning to weigh on their society. The less responsibility they had (as far as time spent on raising children, etc.), the *more* time they had to commit their sexual atrocities and perversion, here! So, why have children, anyhow? Many no longer wanted to take the time and effort to raise children, if it was getting in the way of achieving their goals! Doesn't *this* sound a lot like much of the rationale so many people use, today? The real problem - according to them - is not *really* their actions, just the children which resulted from it! *That* was what's getting in their way… not their *own* actions. Doesn't this sound a lot like the rationale behind many of those who have **abortions**, today? People want to do their careless actions without any inconveniences resulting from. They did not want to give up any of their current habits; they just wanted to fix things *their own ways*. Again, we see that it's not *sexuality*, in itself, as being the problem; it's the way it was being used!

So, the people of the day began to abuse their "fountains" (i.e. their penises), on a grand scale. They poured their semen everywhere! They even spewed onto trees and stones.[68] Their sex did not decrease, however. There was no change to their actions… it was just that their sex, now, began to look a lot more open, and contrary. Interestingly enough, we *do* see - at the beginning of the flood - that the "fountains of the deep" were being broken up: *fountains* of water were gushing up, from beneath the earth. Why? When a flood normally occurs, *rain* usually falls, *first*… then, followed by the eventual overflow of water (on the surface of the ground). In Noah's flood, however, *the opposite* seemed to occur - the waters of the earth, *first*, came from the fountains of the deep; and *then* the rains came sometime after (Gen. 7:11). Why? Again, the reason was simple: if mankind thought they could spew their "fountains" wherever they wished, there would now be fountains *of the earth* spewing liquids right back at them! How ironic. This was judgment, again - in God's perfect way. As David (the psalmist) once wrote: "*Deep calleth unto deep…*" (Psa. 42:7).

In regards to this irony, there's *another* story which describes how the pious of God were told to go aboard the ark. Noah, according to one source, owned a brick oven (and old brick oven, once belonging to Eve, *herself*)! A sign, soon, came to him, from the midst of this oven:

The "oven" with the water boiling that God made a sign between Himself and Noah was an oven of stone that belonged to Eve... Noah was told: When you see the water ***boil*** *forth from the oven, go aboard, you and your companions!*
- al-Tabari: The History of al-Tabari - Vol. I: General Introduction and From the Creation to the Flood The Events That Took Place in Noah's Time 193[69]

Again, another taste of irony, here: the boiling of water of the oven would be another sign of the boiling water to come onto the world. Boiling water?

Hot Water for "Hot Times"

As their sensual desires had made them ***hot****, and inflamed them to immoral excesses, so they were chastised by means of* ***heated water****.*
(Ginzberg, 1909, p. 159)[70]

The eight pure-blooded Adamites were now on board; and so were the others. The ark was all ready to go. The doors to the outside world had just been closed. As the "fountains of the deep" began to open, here, water would begin to flood all of the areas around the ark - and those who were still outside. To make matters worse for those *outside* the ark, the water that fell from heaven came down hot - *boiling* hot.

The people in the generation of the Flood sinned with ***hot passion****, and with* ***hot water*** *they were punished...*
- Babylonian Talmud Mas. Zevachim 113b[71]

Since the people enjoyed *hot*, sensual times before the flood, it had now come back to them the same. According to one interpretation, God heated the deluge via "*the pit of hell's flames*," to punish their fiery lusts with scalding water. The rain of fire poured down on those evildoers.[72] Not only were these rains hot, but the "fountains of the deep," which came up from the earth, *also* scalded everything it came across![73] This made it extremely difficult for anyone trying to escape these rising waters. People may have tried, but no one could stand going near the holes which spewed this water out.[74]

> *They stretched out their feet, and stopped up all the holes of the abyss. But what did God? He made the waters of the abyss boiling hot, so that their flesh were scalded, and the skin came off...* (Eisenmenger, 1748, p. 78)[75]

> *The heat increases as we descend into the earth, and hence many scientific men have held that the interior of our globe is a reservoir of liquid fire... just as God broke up the fountains of the great deep to cause the Deluge, so will He command His stored fires to burst through the crust of the earth... A heat will then be developed so intense...* (Pember, 1975, p. 64)[76]

After these "rains of fire" fell, many people soon began to be convinced - that God wasn't kidding! But, now, it was too late! The ark, parked in its original stead, was slowly starting to rise… slowly being swept away with the floodwaters. The people around it desperately tried to get in. They banged on the ark's door; they tried to climb aboard. But, no one made it in, however - the heated water began to burn their skin, during their attempts… scalding all of their hopes away.[77]

No More Second Chances

One ancient source stated 700,000 people gathered around the ark, and implored Noah to give them protection.[78] When Noah said no (at God's direction), they wanted to enter the ark by force, in whatever way they could. Yet, even beyond this scalding water, this great multitude of people were faced with, yet, *another* obstruction: the animals - those of which were *not* allowed to enter - were still *encamped* around the huge boat. Through God's intervention, these animals began to keep watch over the ark; to guard it. As the multitude tried to approach the ark, they (the wolves, lions, bears, etc.) tore through hundreds of them - tearing them into pieces, and dispersing the rest.[79] It was even said that the birds of the area tore out the eyes of anyone who might have tried to swim towards it![80] Funny, these animals seemed to know who were chosen ones to go aboard, and honorably accepted their own fate. They seemed to have more dignity, honor, and respect than the rest of the human beings who lived around them. Ironically, the human race was supposed to be the most gifted, knowledgeable beings on the planet. Yet, these beings acted with less dignity than the lowly animals, here - no wonder why the earth was in such bad shape; and why, presently, it seems to be in the shape, today.

After realizing they couldn't force their way aboard the ark, a number of people attempted *other* ways to save their lives. Whenever they tried - creating a make-shift raft, or whatever - their actions became fruitless… they were all "tripped up" by God, in one way or another.[81] In one example, the flood swelled up to 15 cubits (approximately 14 feet) over the highest elevation around them… which was *just enough* to drown any 14 foot giant who might have survived, otherwise![82] The flood, in all of its dimensions, in all of the ways it came to be, seems to have went down the way it did for specific *reasons*.

Even though death and destruction is not a good thing, the people left probably had the *lowest* morals that most anyone would have ever dreamed. Not even up to the hour of their death did they feel remorse, nor suppress any of their vile instincts! We see that, for example, as the heated water began to come out of those inner springs of the earth, they began to toss their **own children** into the holes, *alive*, in some vain attempt to choke off the flood![83] Yes, their Cainite "ways" of life truly helped to create a number of vile, contemptuous individuals. These people truly became *evil* - not caring much about anyone or anything else, but their own, individual welfare. Their actions before the flood, and now, truly showed what they were made of, and why God *had* to do things the way He did. So many had died:

> *…(their bodies would) clog the river like dragonflies…*
> - *Epic of Atrahasis*[84]

Ham's Wife and the Ark

What about those on board? Some Cainite corruption, for example, may have manifested in the ark. As we recall,

> *In the selfsame day entered Noah, and Shem, and Ham, and Japheth, the sons of Noah, and Noah's **wife**, and **the three wives of his sons** with them, into the ark…*
> - *Gen.* 7:13 (KJV)

As we notice, in the above, Noah's family seemed to have entered the ark **separately** - the men *first*; and *then* the women. There was a reason for this, however: ancient sources tell us that God wanted no *intercourse* aboard the ark, during their stay. It didn't matter if anyone was married, or not. The reason, probably, was that flagrant misuses of *sexuality* were that which helped to devastate the world; and God didn't want any part of this to continue, on the ark.[85] This ark was now to be a place of *sanctity* and *purity* - the opposite of what the previous world had been. While the world around them was being destroyed, the people, inside, were to think about nothing, except for its replenishment. Again, it's often *measure for measure*, as far as God in concerned.[86]

> *...there was no procreation, either human or animal, in the ark, for it was not appropriate that creatures should indulge themselves in such pleasures while the rest of the world was plunged in tragedy.* (Goldstein, 1933, p. 47)[87]

Because of this proclamation, the women were to remain in the *west*-end of the ark; with the men in the *east*.[88] *Ham*, the Cainite, obviously knew that he was not supposed to go over to the other side, and have *sex* on the ark. Yet, he also knew about his wife being pregnant (via an angel), as we know.[89] No one else may have known about this pregnancy, however; and Ham wanted to conceal her pregnancy, as long as he could. Ancient sources tell us that Ham *did* eventually have sex with his wife, however - against God's orders.[90] And, there were a number of reasons (according to him) why he may have needed to disobey this order:

> *Ham sinned in order to save his wife from disgrace: had he not lain with her himself, Shem and Japheth would have known that she was already bearing a child to the fallen angel Shemhazai.* (Graves and Patai, 1964, p. 114)[91]

For whatever reason, Ham thought this act was *honorable*; yet, it was still **disobedience** to God! Just like Adam, just like Cain, just like a number of Biblical characters throughout history, Ham rationalized *to his self* what God's command might have meant *to him* - following his *own* interpretations on the matter. No matter. Some of these things are not for *us* to decide. God gave him an incredibly simple and straight forward command; and, for some pride-filled reason, he did not choose to follow it.

Let's look at more of how he disobeyed, here. There is another part to this story, which exposes Ham, and the use of some *mischievous* tactics, to achieve his end result. According to a number of ancient sources, Ham learned some forbidden, magical arts, from, most probably, one of these fallen angels of old; and began to use them *now*… to get what he wanted:[92]

> *...Ham, calling up a demon by magic art, crossed over* ***to his wife*** *and slept with her. The reason why the vehicle of the demon was used is that Noah had strewn ashes between them, by means of which he could observe the footprints of those crossing over to their wives. The others remained continent with their father; Ham alone through the service of the devil and the aid of his wife rendered himself to* ***his wife's embraces****. Because Noah persisted in his prayers the demon was unable to bring Ham back; blocked in his efforts by Noah's nocturnal orisons he fled. Ham therefore was compelled to walk back before daylight to the other brothers, and because of the scattered ashes he could not hide his guilt. Noah therefore detected his footprints, and he began to hate Ham for his disobedience.* - *Peter of Riga* Aurora[93]

Ham felt it more important to him *not* to follow the rules, the way they were laid out; or flat-out *didn't care*. This act of Ham, among other acts that he would do in the future, would have repercussions on - not only his family line - but for many, many of his generations to come.

All wasn't perfect that was aboard the ark.

Everything Died Around Them - Animal and Human

In regards to the world outside, the Bible clearly stated that everyone around them - who was not aboard the ark - was now dead:[94]

> *And all flesh died that moved upon the earth,* ***both*** *of Owph (fowl), and of Behemah (cattle), and of Chay (beast), and of every Remes (creeping thing) that creepeth upon the earth, and every* ***Adamite*** *(man)...* - *Gen.* 7:21 (in retranslation)

The rest of the Adamite and pre-Adamite groups around them did not survive… only those aboard.

Yet, life for those aboard the ark was not entirely pleasant. There were animals to feed; their close quarters brought on a number of diseases… apart from there being discomfort caused by the odor of animals and people aboard.[95] They survived, however - God made sure that they would.[96]

After a while, the tide would begin to change. Their peace was, soon, in front of them.

<u>*Gen.* 8:</u>
1 *And God remembered Noah, and every Chay (living thing), and all the Behemah (cattle) that was with him in the ark: and God made a wind to pass over the earth, and the waters asswaged;*
2 *The fountains also of the deep and the windows of heaven were stopped, and the rain from heaven was restrained;*
14 *And in the second month, on the seven and twentieth day of the month, was the earth dried.*
(in retranslation)

After the waters receded, dry land began to reappear. The flood was officially over. The time was nigh for these occupants to leave this ark. Again, these same *human* groups seem to have been mentioned as *coming off* the ark, as well:

<u>*Gen.* 8:</u>
15 *And God spake unto Noah, saying,*
16 *Go forth of the ark, thou, and thy wife, and thy sons, and thy sons' wives with thee.*
17 *Bring forth with thee* ***every living thing*** *that is with thee, of all flesh, both of* ***Owph*** *(fowl), and of* ***Behemah*** *(beast), and the every* ***Remes*** *(creeping thing)* ***that Creepeth*** *upon the earth…*
18 *And Noah went forth, and his sons, and his wife, and his sons' wives with him:*
19 *Every* ***Chay*** *(beast), every* ***Remes*** *(creeping thing), and every* ***Owph*** *(fowl), and whatsoever creepeth upon the earth (animal and human?), after their kinds, went forth out of the ark.*
(in retranslation)

These verses don't state that, "God brought forth Noah and all *of the animals*" - there were certain, **specific** groups of individuals who went in, and came out… there has to be something to these groups!

And, as we see: God's mercy *always* seems to show through. He remembered Noah, as well as *every* group of human and animal that He allowed aboard Noah's ark. He cared about *all* living creatures - even, probably, those with mixed blood. The Cainites had to make it through. *Other groups* (including mixed-blooded *Anakim* and *Mighty Men*) also seemed to have made it through - as we shall soon see! The Lord was merciful to *all*, regardless of their blood lines, or genetic predispositions. He just hoped there would be a *new*, moral standard in this post-flood world.

God wanted *all* who came out off of the ark - with mixed blood or without - to work *together*, in this brave, new world. Obviously, from noticing all of what's going on, today, we know that things didn't really pan out like He wanted. What happened? What would be the driving forces behind our world falling back *down*, morally, one more time?

Chapter 18

Reemergence of the Same World After the Flood

Like a dog that returns to its vomit is a fool who repeats his folly.
- *Prov.* 26:11 (KJV)

The Depravity Continues

The Bible does state that, after the flood, Noah and his immediate family went down from the ark; and tried to go back towards living their lives, again. Assuredly, Noah's family got it in their minds that God really wasn't kidding, in regards to what He wanted: He wanted people to live *morally*, now, after the flood… *not* the other way around. Well, if this was true, what about this? What about the *rest* of the people who were on board? What would happen to everyone who came off of the ark?

And, as well, do we have some scriptural evidence that shows us that the human groups which may have boarded the ark *also* went forth from the ark? How about these antediluvian giants (i.e. the Anakim and Mighty Men) of the pre-flood world? Did they survive, and thrive after the flood? And, if they did survive, did they remain *pious*? What about the Cainites (i.e. the sons of Cain) and the Amalekites (i.e. other sons of the Serpent)? Where were they, after the flood? Did they remain pious? Ultimately, the question to ask is: how did the world *come back* to the same states of corruption, again, in a lot of ways… if only the *pious* were able to survive? What may have gone on, here?

We already know that Naamah, Ham, and Ham's wife probably had the blood of *Cain*; possibly the blood of a major fallen angel! Did all of those once "pious" individuals aboard the ark hold onto their honor *after the flood*? Could identifying these *same* groups after the flood, as well as understanding what *moral* directions many of them might have taken, give us *further* credence to support this book's theme?

The Post-Flood Fall to Corruption

> *God blessed* ***Noah and his family*** *with: "Be fruitful, multiply, rule all* ***beasts, birds*** *and* ***creeping things****."* (Graves and Patai, 1964, p. 115)[1]

We know eight souls from Adam's pure, direct blood line survived the flood. As we've also discovered, a lot of written evidence may exist to show that there were *more* people aboard the ark, beyond just these eight. Do we also have ancient evidence, even *in the Bible*, which shows how every one of the above groups still lived, and thrived, *after* the flood? Apparently, yes.

After the flood, no longer was there that huge division of people, such as the *Cainites*, being down in a valley; and the *Sethites*, living up in a mountain. No longer was this *enmity* so well-defined, anymore. There would be a number of groups of people, going in a number of different directions - all to be developing varying agendas and ways of life. As with before the flood, seed lines were going to be mix; new groups of nations were about to be formed. Since God promised Noah, after the flood, that He would no longer execute His judgment on the earth with a *flood*, again, the above groups were able to head themselves in *many* different, and unfettered, directions (both physically and *ideologically*). As a result, things were going to become *a lot more* complicated than ever before - *especially* for those eight pure souls of Adam, and their attempts to preserve this promised seed. So, this would now become another *major* element to the world's complexity - the ability to distinguish one of the Serpent's seed from one with this Adamic **seed**! Yet, as we recall, it was *extremely* important - before the flood - to assure that some pure descendants of these Adamic souls to remain… but, the world was about to become very complex. What would God do, to assure continuity? We now discover why there had to have been a *chosen people* of God - known as the *Israelites* - after the flood… to preserve this seed! Yes, the *Israelites* were of this direct seed of Adam; and God wanted to make sure enough of them survived, throughout the ages, in pure of form. There are reasons for everything; and *this* was one major reason God went to Abraham, and informed him that he was about to be the patriarch of something very special. One could figure that it *also* had become part of Satan's plan - in the post-flood era - to *destroy* this seed line from off the face of the earth… hence, the major reason for the creation of the Israeli nation; and its struggle, throughout the ages.

Let's identify some of these *same* groups after the flood, and how the fulfillment of God's antediluvian prophecies had taken place.

The Same Groups… After the Flood?

We recall the five antediluvian human groups:

- The *Adamites*
- The *Chay* (or "Beasts") *of the Field*
- The *Behemah* (or "Cattle"/"Beasts")
- The *Remes* (or "Creeping Thing") *that Creepeth*
- The *Owph* (or "Fowl") *of the Air*

We'll now see written evidence to show that these groups may have still thrived *after the flood*, as well. Here is one possible example:

> *and Noah…*
> *And his sons with him, his wife, and their wives,*
> *And* ***creeping things*** *(Remes?), and* ***birds*** *(Owph?), and* ***quadrupeds*** *(i.e. beasts - Bahemah and Chay?);*
> ***And all else*** *from the wooden house*
> *went forth*
> *Into one place. And then, most just of* ***men*** *(Adamites?),*
> *Went Noah forth…*
> - *Sibylline Oracles* Book 1, Lines 325-328[2]

Here, the ancient *Sibylline Oracles* also seems to label these groups in a similar way. Again, if they were *only* animals, here, then wouldn't it be much simpler to just *lump* all of these groups of animals together - using the word "animals" to describe all that left the ark - rather than have to divide them up, here, into certain, individual groups? Makes no sense, really. Why would one waste their time doing this… if there wasn't something *more* to it all? If everything already mentioned in this, and previous chapters, have not already convinced the reader that there was something *more* to these groups, maybe the following examples will.

The Post-Flood Behemah

We recall the Hebrew word *Behemah* was often translated into English as either the words *cattle* or *beast*. One ancient source interprets the *Behemah* in this way:

> *There are many evil kinds among Yisrael that are called* **cattle** *and* **beasts***. One is from* ***the side of the Serpent*** *and another from* ***the side of the idolatrous nations****, who are* ***like the animals and wild beasts****.* - *Zohar* Beresheet A29[3]

Obviously, these are human beings. We also surmised that the *Behemah* were distinguished from other groups of human beings via their *occupation* - they were in charge of animal herding and domestication. One possible draw back to their occupation, however, could be that a number of them - if they began to *falter* in their moral code - could easily begin to act as *uncivilized* as the animals around them! They had the perfect teachers, right in front of them. Thus began the association of people with wildly uncivilized and decadent practices with untamed members of the animal kingdom. Not to say that all of the *Behemah* acted in this way… not even close; but, there were a *few* that did (just like in any other group). These acts of human savagery and indecency not only happened before the flood, but *after*.

Job, a famous prophet of the Bible, was once accused of acting immoral. Notice what he says, in response:

> *Wherefore are we counted as* **beasts***, and reputed vile in your sight?*
> - *Job* 18:3 (KJV)

Again, the word for *beasts*, here, in the above, is *Behemah*.

And, in another example, we see the Bible seems to separates *real* animals of the field from the actual human beings found *working* in the field (i.e. the Adamites **and** the *Behemah*):

> *Send therefore now, and gather thy* ***cattle, and all that thou hast in the field****; for upon every* ***Adam (man) and Behemah (beast) which shall be found in the field****, and shall not be brought home, the hail shall come down upon them, and they shall die.*
> - *Ex.* 9:19 (in retranslation)

The next set of verses involves the city of Ninevah. Almost a thousand years before the birth of Christ, the king of Ninevah became very remorseful, and wanted to plead to God, for mercy. He would go on to proclaim that all **men** under him - no matter who they were - would have to wear sackcloth; and plead to God for forgiveness. Notice how the below verses seem to also group the *Adamites* and *Behemah* together, and how they are differentiated from *real* groups of animals (found in a *herd* or *flock*):

> <u>*Jonah* 3:</u>
> 7 *And he caused it to be proclaimed and published through Ninevah by the decree of the king and his nobles, saying, Let neither* **Adam** *(man) nor* **Behemah** *(beast),* ***herd nor flock****, taste any thing: let them not feed, nor drink water.*
> (in retranslation)

The following verse also stated that men *and Behemah* were to, both, turn from their evil ways; and refrain from the violence they had once caused.

> <u>*Jonah* 3:</u>
> 8 *But let* **Adam** *(man) and* **Behemah** *(beast) be covered with sackcloth, and cry mightily unto God: yea, let them turn every one from* **his evil way***, and from the violence that is in their* ***hands****.*
> (in retranslation)

Now, what kind of large animal knows that their ways are *evil*? And, what kind of animal has ***hands***, none-the-less? Animals don't have hands or feet - they have paws and claws; the *Behemah*, however, *do*… just like other human being. There are more:

<u>*Ex.* 19:</u>
12 *And thou shalt set bounds unto the people round about, saying, Take heed to yourselves, that ye go not up into the mount, or touch the border of it: whosoever toucheth the mount shall be surely put to death:*
13 *There shall not* ***an hand*** *touch it, but he shall surely be stoned, or shot through; whether it be* ***Behemah*** *(beast) or* ***Adam*** *(man), it shall not live: when the trumpet soundeth long, they shall come up to the mount.*
14 *And Moses went down from the mount unto the people, and sanctified the people; and they washed their clothes.*
(in retranslation)

<u>*Gen.* 9:</u>
5 *And surely your blood of your lives will I require; at the* ***hand*** *of every beast will I require it...*

We also see that the *Behemah* have *feet*, unlike any animal:

No foot of man shall pass through it, nor ***foot of Behemah*** *(beast) shall pass through it, neither shall it be inhabited forty years.*
- *Ezek.* 29:11 (in retranslation)

And, unlike the animal kingdom, the *Behemah* seem to understand the concept of *work*:

For before these days there was no ***hire*** *for* ***Adam*** *(man),* ***nor any hire*** *for* ***Behemah*** *(beast); neither was there any* ***peace*** *to him that went out or came in because of the affliction: for I set all* ***men*** *every one against his neighbour.*
- *Zech.* 8:10 (in retranslation)

Would anyone need to hire an animal? And, how many animals understand what the concept of *peace* is? Also, how many animals consciously set out to turn themselves against their neighbors? These behaviors only refer to people, and what *people* do.

> *But the seventh day is the sabbath of the LORD they God; in it thou shalt not do any* ***work****, thou, nor thy son, nor thy daughter, thy manservant, nor thy maidservant,* ***nor thy cattle*** *(Bahemah), nor thy stranger that is within thy gates.*
>
> \- *Ex.* 20:10 (KJV)

As we see in the above, the verse seems to be referring *only* to working human beings.

We now see a number of examples that show us that there *could* have been a group of *human* individuals - known as *Behemah* - in the Bible. And we also understand that a group of *Behemah* might have even been around *before* the time of Adam's creation… as well as long after; surviving Noah's flood.

What about the *Chay of the Field*?

The Chay of the Post-Flood World

The word *Chay*, in its most basic meaning, stands for "living creature," "community," or "relative." We've already attested that they, as well, could have been another group of human beings out there; beginning before the time of Adam. And these could have been a group of humans who, since the time of Adam, worked *the fields*: as gardeners; field hands, harvesters, etc. Could they have survived the flood, too?

> Ex. 23:
>
> 10 *And six years thou shalt sow thy land, and shalt gather in the fruits thereof:*
>
> 11 *But the seventh year thou shalt let it rest and lie still; that the* ***poor of thy people*** *may eat: and what they leave the* **Chay** *(beasts)* ***of the Field*** *shall eat. In like manner thou shalt deal with thy vineyard, and with thy oliveyard.*
>
> (in retranslation)

Again, these verses seem to be referring to individuals who *work* - work in the vineyards and olive yards. If we think about it, who, by the way, would really want to let large, domesticated animals come into their vineyards, or olive yards, and trample on all of their vines? People could walk through these yards, however.

Again, as before, these verses go back to a time *after* the flood; which tells us that the Chay of the Field may have also survived.

The Owph of the Post-Flood World

The *Owph of the Air* could, very well, have been another group of pre-Adamites, here. In the following verses, an entire (Assyrian) nation, and its leader, was compared to a Cedar tree… so were other *people*, it seems:

Ezek. 31:
3 *Behold, the Assyrian was a cedar in Lebanon with fair branches, and with a shadowing shroud, and of an high stature; and his top was among the thick boughs.*
5 *Therefore his height was exalted above all the trees of the field, and his boughs were multiplied, and his branches became long because of the multitude of waters, when he shot forth.*
6 *All the* ***Owph of the Air*** *(fowls of heaven) made their nests in his boughs, and under his branches did all the* ***Chay*** *(beasts)* ***of the Field*** *bring forth their young, and under his shadow dwelt all great* ***nations****.*
(in retranslation)

These are definitely groups of *people*, here - and not animals.

We also see, in the following, that some of the *Owph of the Air* (as well as the *Behemah*) were looked upon as *heathen*, or *idolatrous*:

Lev. 20:
22 *Ye shall therefore keep all my statutes, and all my judgments, and do them: that the land, whither I bring you to dwell therein, spue you not out.*
23 *And ye shall not walk in* ***the manners of the nation, which I cast out*** *before you: for they committed all these things, and therefore I abhorred them.*
24 *But I have said unto you, Ye shall inherit their land, and I will give it unto you to possess it, a land that floweth with milk and honey: I am the LORD your God, which have separated you from other* ***people****.*
25 *Ye shall therefore put difference between clean* ***Behemah*** *(beasts) and unclean, and between unclean* ***Owph*** *(fowls) and clean: and ye shall not make your souls abominable by* ***Behemah*** *(beast), or by* ***Owph*** *(fowl), or by any manner of living thing that creepeth (from the Darkness) on the ground, which I have separated from* ***you as unclean****.*
26 *And ye shall be holy unto me: for I the LORD am holy, and have severed you from other* ***people****, that ye should be mine.*
(in retranslation)

So, what kind of animal would want to make another person's soul feel ***abominable*** by associating with them? The *Owph of the Air*, also, must have survived.

The Remes of the Post-Flood World

Even up to 1500 years after the flood, the Bible seems to mention these same pre-Adamites groups - in their *same*, original **titles**! The following verse - near the end of the Old Testament - describes how God had made a covenant with Israel… and (seemingly) with *other* groups of people:

> *And in that day will I make a covenant for them with the* ***Chay*** *(beasts)* ***of the Field*** *and with the* ***Owph of the Air*** *(fowls of heaven), and with the* ***Remes*** *(creeping things)* ***of the ground****: and I will break the bow and the sword and the battle out of the earth, and will make them to lie down safely.* - *Ho.* 2:18 (in retranslation)

Why would God make a covenant with ***animals***? Makes no sense.

And, in the book of Ezekiel, we see the same four groups mentioned *again*:

> *...the* ***Fowls of the Heaven****, and the* ***Beasts of the Field****, and all* ***Creeping Things that Creep*** *upon the earth, and all the* ***Adamites*** *(men) that are upon the face of the earth, shall shake at my presence, and the mountains shall be thrown down, and the steep places shall fall, and every wall shall fall to the ground.*
>
> - *Ezek.* 38:20 (in retranslation)

Again, wouldn't it much easier to state that, "all of the animals and men shall shake…"? But, it seems that God, in His word, clearly defined these as *individual* groups; and **not** just groups of animals.

Well, there seems to be a good number of scriptural, and non-scriptural, evidence alike which shows us that the same pre-Adamite groups lived before the flood; and could have survived *after*.

What about the antediluvian ***giants*** - those mixed offspring of humans and those fallen, terrestrial angels? Did any of the pious - or even some of those who *weren't so pious*, survive Noah's flood, as well?

The Giants - Also Survivors of the Flood

If, at the end of the day, it was found that no such evidence for the existence of a now lost race in the Bible lands could be discovered, then at least an age-old enigma would have been investigated thoroughly. On the other hand, if... angels and fallen angels once walked among mankind as beings of flesh and blood, no different from you or me, then ***it could change our perspective of world history for ever****.*
(Collins, 1996, p. 8)[4]

Evolutionary anthropologists generally **hate** *giants, because they upset their pet theories. However, the evidence points to* ***physical degeneration****, and not evolutionary* ***improvement****, as the story of life on Earth. Giants* **prove** *that the Bible account of history is the true one. And that's not a popular concept with men whose hearts are at* **enmity** *against the idea of God.* (Gray, 2006, p. 31)[5]

The mixed offspring of the Nephilim and the Watchers - collectively known as the *giants* - could have also survived the flood! Even though most may have been somewhat pious aboard the ark, the worldly states of immorality and corruption, reportedly, were on the rise, *again*.[6] By the time of Noah's death, there may have even been up to a *million* people on the earth. And, as before the flood, it seemed like a growing number of human individuals had some blood of these pre-flood angelic beings.[7] Were many of these post-flood giants beginning to act as they did before the flood?

The Post-Flood Anakims

...for all the sons of men have gone astray through the corruptions of those angels who fell from among the Gods and mingled their seed with the daughters of men and begat sons of ***great strength*** *and mighty* ***wickedness****.*
- *Writings of Abraham* 4:2[8]

As we'll soon discover, the descendants of the Nephilim - the ***Anakim*** - also, apparently, survived the flood… to go on to negatively influence the world in much the same way! Some looked a lot like the Anakim of *before*: up to 9-foot tall, even possessing their famous necklaces. These post-flood Anakim began to pull a number of people *right back* to the same states of desolation, decay, and towards utter revolution against God![9] They had, again, become a burden, or "chain," around the necks of many of the pious individuals settling around them - trying, once again, to live out their lives in normal, wholesome ways:

> *From the Other Side, they overcame Yisrael (Israel)… They* ***rob*** *them,* ***shattering*** *and* ***wasting their work****… (and)* ***destroyed*** *the earth as they expanded…*
>
> \- *Zohar* Beresheet A20[10]

Besides desolating the land - and people - around them, the Anakim began to be aggressive against their neighbors:[11]

<u>*Josh.* 14:</u>
12 *Now therefore give me this mountain, whereof the LORD spake in that day; for thou heardest in that day how the* ***Anakims*** *were there, and that the cities were great and fenced: if so be the LORD will be with me, then I shall be able to drive them out, as the LORD said.*

<u>*Deut.* 1:</u>
28 *Whither shall we go up? our brethren have discouraged our heart, saying, The people is* ***greater and taller*** *than we; the cities are great and walled up to heaven; and moreover we have seen the sons of the* ***Anakims*** *there.*

The Bible even says that these post-flood *Anakim* originated in the Nephilim!

<u>*Num.* 13:</u>
30 *And Caleb stilled the people before Moses, and said, Let us go up at once, and possess it; for we are well able to overcome it.*
31 *But the men that went up with him said, We be not able to go up against the people; for they are stronger than we.*
32 *And they brought up an evil report of the land which they had searched unto the children of Israel, saying, The land, through which we have gone to search it, is a*

land that eateth up the inhabitants thereof; and all the people that we saw in it are men of a ***great-stature****.*
33 *And there we saw the* ***Nephilim*** *(giants), the sons of* ***Anak****,* ***which come of*** *the* ***Nephilim*** *(giants): and we were in our own sight as grasshoppers, and so we were in their sight.*
(in retranslation)

This clearly shows us how the Nephilim's descendants probably survived the flood - as the Anakims.

The Rapha

The Bible also speaks of a group of individuals known as the *Rapha* (or the *Refaim*, the *Rephaim*, etc.) - as another group of *giants* who lived after the flood.[12] Who were *they*? Why do we have a group with *another*, post-flood name, here? Sometimes, it seems the Rapha were grouped together with other giants; other times they were separate.[13] Most probably, they were nothing but these *Mighty Men* of the post flood world - the giant, twelve to fourteen foot tall offspring of those unholy Watchers. We'll soon see how we come to this conclusion. But, why would they have a different name, *now*?

The name *Rapha*, in actuality, comes from a Hebrew word meaning to "seize," to "heal," or to "pluck out."[14] And, along these lines, we may now be able to conclude that the Rapha might have descended from those who had been "seized," or even "plucked," out of their once-worthy positions… as the Watchers once were! And, after the flood of Noah, the sinful acts of these angelic forefathers would now be "justified," or "healed," in their descendants (we shall soon see how).

To provide an answer, let's look at some interesting elements to this all. As we recall, there were a number of reasons why God *did not* want fallen angels to breed with human beings: it was because so many of their descendents would probably have some rough times surviving in this world - *especially*, as we'll see, in the *post-flood* world.

"The Dead Shall Not Rise"

Another meaning of the name *Rapha* is associated with those "shades living in Hades."[15] Now, why were the *Rapha* (or *Refaim*) associated with this? First off, the Rapha, interestingly enough, were also thought to be *the living dead*, after the flood. Why? Well, according to theory, there were *atmospheric changes* at the time of the flood which didn't allow human beings to live as they did before - to not live *as long*. Although they once lived up to 900 years, or *more*, life spans, eventually, would be reduced - down to 100 years… even *less*.

> *The climate and environment both on the land and in the sea enabled creatures to live long ages and reach huge sizes.* (Gray, 2006, p. 11)[16]

Now, because of these changes, the Rapha began to be associated with the *dead*:

> *Of them (the Refaim), it is written: "The shades of the* ***dead*** *(Heb. refaim) shall not rise" (Yeshayah (Isaiah) 26:14), meaning that they shall not rise at the* ***resurrection of the dead****.* - *Zohar* Beresheet A20[17]

> *They are* ***dead****, they shall not live; they are* ***of the Rapha*** *(i.e. deceased), they shall not rise: therefore hast thou visited and destroyed them, and made all their memory to perish.* - *Isa.* 26:14 (in retranslation)

What happened? Before the flood, the *Anakim* and *Mighty Men* (i.e. the pre-flood *Refaim*) were able to live very long lives; but **so did human beings**. After the flood, the giants apparently *still* had that ability. Not so for the human race. This would prove very *devastating* for the Anakim and Refaim, if we think about it.[18] One half of their **hybrid** bodies would, now, begin to die before the other. How horrifying!

> *How can you say that "Refaim" is from the linguistic root of lax, weak… The explanation is because those giants were from two sides, meaning from an angelic source and a human female source, and were made more* ***hopeless to exist*** *on the earth. Similarly, the* ***Refaim****… were even more despairing until they released themselves altogether from the above and were living long lives. When they became*

> ***weaker***, *half their body became weakened and died and half their body remained living - since they were composed half of angels that do not deteriorate and die, and half of humans that do eventually die. When half of their body was deceased, they used to pick herbs from the field grasses, meaning poisonous herbs, swallowed them and died. Because they wished to kill themselves, they were called Refaim, or* ***lax ones****, since they let themselves* ***loose*** *from life... They used to throw themselves into the great sea and drown, and they died. That is what it is written: "The shades (Heb. refaim) tremble; the waters beneath with the inhabitants thereof"...*
>
> \- *Zohar* Shlach Lecha 10[19]

Their human side began to die, only after a couple of hundred years; the other side still **lived on**. Now, these *Mighty Men* were slowly becoming *weak*; and *lax*. So, as once half of their physical body - their *human* side - began to pass on, many became so distraught that they wished to commit suicide (and often *did*). As we affirm, this half human, half angelic mixture, in the end, truly was *not* meant to be. God was right. Almost nothing but a *cursed* existence resulted from this.

The First in the Land

So, if this was so for the *Rapha*, then what about the other giants? What happened to them? Why don't we see any remnants of *these* individuals, today... or *do* we? Well, the post-flood giants would go on to settle many of the *same* lands their antediluvian ancestors once did. And *this*, as we'll soon see, posed a major problem to the post-flood world: there were lands dedicated to the Adamite *Shem* (a son of Noah) - a declaration made by Noah *himself*.[20] After the flood, Noah was made patriarch of the whole known world - allocating certain lands to certain descendants. Yet, in the land we now know as *Israel* or *Palestine*, a number of peoples - including these *giants* - defied Noah; and settled there, anyway. This is, most probably, one reason why there was so much conflict in these ancient lands, between the giants and other people around.

There were many examples of giants living in these areas... *after* the flood:[21]

> *From the earliest times, a three-mile-long vale that... stretches south along* ***the road to Bethlehem*** *was known as the "Valley of the* ***Rephaim****," or "Valley of the* ***Giants****." Today it is called the Baqa'.* (DeLoach, 1995, p. 109)[22]

Ta Neter - "the land of the ***Watchers****" - Also called "the land of* ***Shumer****" and "the land of Shin'ar".*
("The Geography of Heaven & Earth During the Antediluvian World", n. d., p. 3)[23]

*...**Bashan** was called the land of the **giants** (or **Rephaim**, Deut. 3:13), leaving us to conclude the cities were built by giants.* (DeLoach, 1995, p. 17)[24]

*Beit Jibrim means the "House of the **Gibborim**," i.e., of "the **Giants**." The town, which still exists even to this day... (is) on the road from **Jerusalem to Gaza**.*
(DeLoach, 1995, p. 25)[25]

Even one of the oldest cities in the area - the famous *Jericho* - was said to have once had "*Mighty Men*" within its walls (Josh. 6:2):

*In olden days it (**Jericho**) also became widely known as the "city of the **giants**" - because so many Gibborim once lived within its walls.*
(DeLoach, 1995, p. 159)[26]

The Unwelcome Ones

The giants were not favored in these lands they occupied - *especially* by those Adamic Semites (sons of Shem). Other people in the area hated them, as well; and attacked them, periodically. Even *hornets* and other natural elements seemed to be against them:

*The text (the Bible) seems to promote the idea that nature itself was fighting against the giants who... were **out of balance** with nature. As a result, the land was 'vomiting them out,' driving them out and destroying them little by little to the point where they were ripe for conquest.* ("Giants of the Ancient Near East", 2003, p. 26)[27]

It seemed the entire post-flood world knew that their days were numbered - including *themselves*. They weren't very popular, at all.

The Last of the Refaim - Og and Sihon

> *...God gave him (Og) his* ***reward in this world*** *(because the wicked shall have no reward in the world to come) and made him a king; and he was king of Bashan.*
> (Eisenmenger, 1748, p. 74)[28]

The post-flood world soon became the last stand for these giants. As we recall, **Og** and **Sihon** were Mighty Men of the antediluvian world; and managed to survive the flood, on Noah's ark.

Interestingly enough: although human life spans began to diminish after the flood, *Noah*, as well as anyone who came off of the ark, *still* probably had the ability to live a long life, after.[29] Not sure why. But, this was probably the reason that Og and Sihon *also* had the ability to live so long *after* the flood, as well. Through this, they truly had become "the Last of the Refaim."

> <u>*Josh.* 12:</u>
> 4 *And the coast of Og king of Bashan, which was of the remnant* ***of the Rapha*** *(giants), that dwelt at Ashtaroth and at Edrei...*
> (in retranslation)

> <u>*Deut.* 3:</u>
> 11 *For only Og king of Bashan remained of the remnant* ***of the Rapha*** *(giants); behold his* ***bedstead*** *was a bedstead of iron... nine cubits was the length thereof, and four cubits the breadth of it...*
> 13 *And the rest of Gilead, and all Bashan, being the kingdom of Og, gave I unto the half tribe of Manasseh... with all Bashan, which was called the land* ***of the Rapha*** *(giants).*
> (in retranslation)

Og was mentioned some 22 times in the Old Testament; as well as by other ancient writers such as *Josephus*... which seems to give us even *further* evidence for his existence.[30]

Og, after the flood, seemed to have had an interesting story about him. As we know, Og was allowed to survive the flood; with Noah granting them stay (by sitting atop of the ark). Because of Noah's graciousness, Og swore allegiance to him, and all of his descendants! He was going to be there for them. Og ended up living almost 900 years - well into the time of *Moses*. This was, again, because he had the *same* longevity of life as others born before the flood.

Beginning as a servant to Noah, he eventually ended up servant Noah's descendants - all the way to the famous ***Abraham***. Abraham's wife, Sarah, was reportedly barren for most of her life. Og, however, noticed that Sarah was a very beautiful woman; and truly desired her. He mocked her, while she was with Abraham - hoping she would "bear no fruit" with him. When God began to notice this, He "suffered him to live many years; and till the time that he **might flee their children's children**."[31] In other words, God made sure Og lived for a very long time, and not be killed - so that he could see his whole world collapse from under him… under the offspring of *none other* than the descendants of Abraham himself! And, according to the Bible, that's exactly *what* happened!

Og - King of the Amorites

Eventually, Og abandoned his role of servitude, and took position over other giants in the area. Og and Sihon both did not want to cease in their wickedness, however; nor refrain in this betrayal of honor. They simply didn't care, anymore. The two eventually became combative to any of Abraham's descendants… their Israeli contemporaries.

Og eventually became the leader of a group of giants, known as the *Amorites*.[32] The Amorites, and their leader Og, both joined forces to fight anyone in their way… *especially* those descendants of Abraham.

"Arad the Canaanite"

The name *Sihon* means "striking down" - a fitting name for one who ended up a war-like tyrant, as Sihon did.[33] Og's brother also became known as "the Canaanite," or "Arad the Canaanite" - ruling any lands he conquered with an iron fist.[34]

As with Og, Sihon was mentioned numerous times in the Old Testament - at least 37 times![35] They would even appear *together* in certain verses (in Josh. 2:10, 9:10, I Kings 4:19, Neh. 9:22 and Psa. 135:11):

> *And the LORD shall do unto them as he did to* ***Sihon*** *and to* ***Og****, kings of the* ***Amorites****, and unto the land of them, whom he destroyed.*
> - *Deut.* 31:4 (KJV)

They may have survived for a while, but the rest of the Refaim, over time, were almost *all* wiped out.

> *...Sichon (Sihon) was harder than a wall or tower; and harder than any other creature; and taller than any tower, when his feet touch'd the ground; and no creature could withstand him. What did God do? ... He cast him out of his place, and deliver'd him to the Israelites.* (Eisenmenger, 1748, p. 77)[36]

Other Biblical Giants

There is even *more* evidence of post-flood giants in the Bible, known by a number of titles. Not only do we have them as the *Anakim* or *Refaim*, but, they became known by other names (to people living around them):

- the *Zuzims* or *Zamzummims* (in Gen. 14:5, Deut. 2:20)
- the *Emims* (in Gen. 14:5, Deut. 2:10-11)
- the *Horite* (in Gen. 36:20)

Even the post-flood *Jebusites* and *Perizzites* were thought to have been giants (in Gen. 10:16, Ex. 33:2, Josh. 9:1, 11:3, etc.); or in some way, related to them.[37] According to some, the Philistines were even thought to have been of *Anakim* blood. Interestingly enough, this leads us to the introduction of, probably, the most famous *giant* of them all: ***Goliath***.[38] It seems very obvious that there were giants in the *post-flood* era, as well. Where did they come from, if they didn't, somehow, survive Noah's flood? And, what were they *now* doing - in *this* post-flood world - to cause so much distain and disfavor to all of those living around them? Were many of them trying to drag their world *right back* to the same states of decadence that it once was? It seems these giants, for the most part, had gone right back down the same moral pathways. They, as well, may have passed on a number of *genetic* problems to the individuals they helped to sire, over the years: including *physical* problems; negative *spiritual* leanings; as well as *mental* issues. It seems like people who inherited this adulterated, *genetic* material often ended up feeling as if they might have been more *cursed*, overall; over those who did not possess any.

The Purging of These Ancient Lands

The giants began to rule harshly over other people; and also built cities in the areas that they dominated. According to some, they even built twenty-nine of them.[39] Their domain over these lands, however, would not last forever.

> *For which reason they (the children of Israel) removed their camp to Hebron; and when they had taken it, they slew all the inhabitants. There were till then left the race of* ***giants****, who had bodies so* ***large****, and* ***countenances so entirely different*** *from other men, that they were surprising to the sight, and terrible to the hearing.*
>
> \- *Falvius Josephus* Jewish Antiquities 5.2.3[40]

Many people of the area began to work together, in order to annihilate them all. The Israeli *Joshua*, for example, made war with them in a city named Hebron, near Mount *Hermon* (yes, the *same* Mount Hermon their Watcher ancestors were said to have routinely ascended and descended)!

> *Josh.* 11:
> 21 *And at that time came Joshua, and cut off* ***the Anakims*** *from the mountains, from* ***Hebron****... Joshua destroyed them utterly with their cities.*
> 22 *There was none of* ***the Anakims*** *left in the land of the children of Israel: only in Gaza, in Gath, and in Ashdod, there remained.*

Interesting enough, these post-flood giants were thought to have possessed *six fingers* on each hand; as well as *six* toes on each foot - the same as the giants were said to have had, before the flood. This seemed to have been just one genetic remnant of these offspring with mixed, angelic blood:

<u>*2 Sam.* 21:</u>
18 *And it came to pass after this, that there was again a battle with the Philistines at Gob: then Sibbechai the Hushathite slew Saph, which was of the* ***sons of the Rapha*** *(giant).*
20 *And there was yet a battle in Gath, where was a man* ***of great stature****, that had on every hand* ***six fingers****, and on every foot* **six toes**, *four and twenty in number; and he also was born* ***to the Rapha*** *(giant).*
22 *These four were born to the Rapha (giant) in Gath, and fell by the hand of David, and by the hand of his servants.*
(in retranslation)

<u>*I Chr.* 20:</u>
5 *And there was war again with the Philistines; and Elhanan the son of Jair slew Lahmi the brother of* **Goliath** *the Gittite, whose spear staff was like a* ***weaver's beam****.*
6 *And yet again there was war at Gath, where was a man of great stature, whose* ***fingers*** *and* **toes** *were* ***four and twenty***, **six** *on each hand and* **six** *on each foot: and he also was the son* ***of the Rapha*** *(giant).*
7 *But when he defiled Israel, Jonathan the son of Shimea David's brother slew him.*

Many of these Rapha, just the Mighty Men before them, were absolutely *no* help to those who wanted to live a God-fearing life. They would rather give assistance to those who worshipped idols:

If they (the ***Refaim****) notice a time of distress coming upon the children of Yisrael, they* ***abandon*** *them. Even if they have the power to save them, they* ***do not want to do so****. They abandon the Torah (the first books of the Old Testament) and avoid those who study it. Instead,* ***they do favors to those who worship idols****.*

- *Zohar* Beresheet A20[41]

Sodom - Hub of Anakim Influence

As we mentioned, many people wanted to wipe out these giants, because of their impieties and improprieties. They just did not really belong… especially with their arrogance and corrupted moral leanings. We even see a Biblical account, below - led by a confederacy of post-flood kings - to do this very thing. Note a few of the nearby cities, listed here:

<u>*Gen.* 14:</u>
1 *And it came to pass in the days of Amraphel king of Shinar, Arioch king of Ellasar, Chedorlaomer king of Elam, and Tidal king of nations;*
2 *That these made war with Bera king of **Sodom**, and with Birsha king of **Gomorrah**... (and defeated them)*
4 *Twelve years... (the fallen people) served Chedorlaomer, and in the thirteenth year they rebelled.*
5 *And in the fourteenth year came Chedorlaomer, and the kings that were with him, and smote the Rephaims in Ashteroth Karnaim, and the Zuzims in Ham, and the Emins in Shaveh Kiriathaim,*
7 *And they returned, and... smote all the country of the **Amalekites**, and also the **Amorites**...*

These verses do not only help us to identify some of these ancient *groups* of giants, but also the areas where they once lived. As we see, they most probably settled in the areas around the cities of Sodom and Gomorrah.[42] Now, why would this matter? Most of us know what *Sodom* was famous for: immorality, indecency, and unbridled sex - especially homosexuality and/or **sodomy**. It's obvious, at first, that the kings of Sodom and Gomorrah were *against* these practices; and fought the immorality of these giants. But, as we'll soon see, immorality began to overtake them, over time; with the influences of those with angelic blood slowly beginning to take hold. Interestingly enough, we also notice, here, that there were descendants of Cain in these areas, as well:

> *And others say that Cain was from the superior realm of absolute power (i.e. the Serpent), and confess that Esau, Korah, the **Sodomites**, and all such persons are of **the same people** (or nation) as themselves...*
>
> - *"Other" Gnostic Teachings According to St. Irenaeus* 1.31.1[43]

> *For there are certain men crept in unawares, who were before of old ordained to this condemnation, ungodly men, turning the grace of our God into lasciviousness, and denying... Even as* ***Sodom*** *and* ***Gomorrha****, and the cities about them in like manner, giving themselves over to fornication, and going after* ***strange flesh****... but what they know naturally, as brute* ***beasts****, in those things they corrupt themselves. Woe unto them! for they have gone in the way of* ***Cain****...* - *Jude* 1:4-11 (KJV)

The word for *strange*, in the above, comes from the Greek word *heteros*; a word which could mean either "different" or "other." So, we can see the word *strange*, here, could also be describing *another* type of flesh. What type of flesh, may we conclude, was being *sought after* by the people, here? These verses tell us that the men of Sodom and Gomorrah, not only, went after other men in a homosexual fashion, but they also went after those of a *different* flesh - those with mixed, angelic blood!

The infamous cities of Sodom and Gomorrah eventually became strongholds of the ancient *Rephaim* and other giants; and their eventual destruction - by God - seemed to be a sign that they were sinning against the human race, through these genetic admixtures and the adoption of these corrupt, giant "ways."

It was also interesting to see that *Cain* was also mentioned, in these above verses! Why? Maybe some of his descendants - and their *"ways"* - will become a part of this increase in moral depravity. Returning to these above verses of Genesis, we also see that two *final* groups were mentioned:

> *And they returned, and... smote all the country of the* ***Amalekites****, and also the* ***Amorites****...* - *Gen.* 14:7 (KJV)

This last verse seems very important: it seems to set the stage for a couple more groups, here, to come on the scene - those of which would probably begin to *parallel*, or even *accentuate*, these depravities of the post-flood, angelic giants.

The *Amorites*, as we recall, was one group of these giant individuals. We now see that they were one of the last strongholds of the post-flood Anakim - led by the Mighty Men *Og* and *Sihon*. Yet, eventually, they, also, would be wiped out. Even though the days of the giants seemed numbered, the sons of Cain and the Serpent seemed to have survived *much* longer.

We've heard about the *Amalekites* before the flood, and that they were those who, in some way, had some blood *of the Serpent*. What about the above verse? Were these *Amalekites* of the same group? What about the *Cainites* who were allowed to survive the flood? What contributions could these Cainites and Amalekites have on our world to come, *beyond* the giants?

Final Blow to the Post-Flood World

We understood that climate changes drastically *reduced* the chances for those Anakim and Refaim to survive in this post-flood; not for very long. And, interestingly enough, ancient sources have even stated that the post-flood Anakim and Refaim would not really pose a huge problem to those in the future - the ***Amalekites*** would:

> *...(the) groups in the mixed multitude that mixed with Yisrael (Israel) caused the destruction of the temple... Nevertheless, the redemption of Yisrael does not depend on the destruction of the Refaim, but* **on the destruction of Amalek***, that is, until he who was referred to in the oath is destroyed, as it is written: "Because Yah has sworn by His throne that Hashem will have war with* **Amalek***"...*
>
> \- *Zohar* Beresheet A20[44]

The plot thickens. We know a little about these Amalekites - those with blood of the Serpent himself. We also know that the Cainites were, ultimately, the sons of the Serpent, as well (through Cain). And, we also might be able to surmise that the Serpent could have spread his seed, in one way or another, to other people, beyond Eve - even some of those famous Cainites who had survived the flood (such as *Naamah*, *Ham*, etc.). So, beyond these post-flood giants, *other* groups of individuals, having mixed blood - those with direct ***blood of the Serpent*** - would began to "take over the reins" of depravity and influence upon our world. These would, eventually, become the *major* problem to all who tried to live a Godly life, from then on. Let's take a look at them.

The Kenites

In the verses below, we see that God tells Abram (or Abraham) - the would-be father of Israel (and other people) - that his seed will inherit the land currently occupied by certain *other* people… firstly noted the ***Kenites***.[45]

Gen. 15:
18 *In the same day the LORD made a covenant with Abram, saying, Unto thy seed have I given* **this land**, *from the river of Egypt unto the great river, the river Euphrates:*
19 *The* **Kenites** *(i.e. Qeyniy), and the Kenizzites, and the Kadmonites…*

The word ***Kenite*** simply stands for a "son of Cain," as we'll see! The Hebrew *Qeyniy* (above) originates in the word *Qayin* - a word synonymous with the *Cain* of early Genesis! So, if these post-flood *Kenites* were remnants of the antediluvian *Cainites*, that gives us further evidence *they* survived the flood, as well. And, as we'll soon see, it seems they may have also considered *themselves* the descendants of this famous patriarch, as well!

> *Since the* **Kenites** *were therefore known to the Israelites both as nomads and city dwellers, and generally* **hostile**, *their legendary ancestor* **Cain** *could figure in myth as the first murderer, the first nomad, and the first city builder.*
>
> (Graves and Patai, 1964, p. 96)[46]

So, a lot like the *Cainites* of the pre-flood era, the post-flood *Kenites* also seemed to have assumed many of these *same* occupations as their antediluvian predecessors. The word *Kenite* could also originate in the Hebrew word ***Qeyniy***. The use of this word (in Judg. 1:16, I Sam. 30:29, etc.) alludes that these post-flood Kenites were also "*smiths*" - often known as *wandering* smiths.[47] We know that Cain once wandered about; and many of his descendants were often *blacksmiths*.

The *Easton's Bible Dictionary* has this to say about the Kenites:

> *They were wandering smiths, "the gypsies and traveling tinkers of the old Oriental world. They formed an important guild in an age when the art of metallurgy was confined* ***to a few****" (Sayce's Races, etc.).*
>
> \- *The Easton's Bible Dictionary* Kenites[48]

Also, the word *Cain* could also come from a Hebrew word, meaning *spear*:[49]

> *And Ishbibenob, which was of the sons of the giant, the weight of whose spear (****Qayin****) weighed three hundred shekels of brass in weight...*
>
> \- *II Sam.* 21:16 (KJV)

Interestingly enough, we know that the antediluvian Cainites were among the first to forge *spears*, and weapons of war.[50] Cain, also, might have been the first to use some sort of *sharp instrument* to commit his murder. Could the post-flood *Kenites* have knowledge of the *same*? It seems as if they parallel.

So, although the original Hebrew word for *Kenite* could mean both "spear" and "smith," it also has one more meaning. A couple of Hebrew words translated into the English *Kenite* or *Cain* are the words ***Qayin*** and ***Qanah*** - both used in the same, general sense: as a *possession*.[51]

> *And Adam knew Eve his wife; and she conceived, and bare Cain (i.e. Qayin), and said, I have* **gotten** *(i.e.* ***Qanah****) a man from the LORD.*
>
> \- *Gen.* 4:1 (KJV)

And, as we *also* recall, Cain often wanted to *possess* material things around him. And, at the time of Cain's sacrifice, he was punished for hoarding the *best* fruits for himself. He cared about material things around him, rather than sacrificing anything to God. A lot of what he possessed on earth, over time, he would eventually *lose*. The Kenites seemed to have had this *same* curse inflicted upon them, as well! No matter what they possessed, it never seemed enough to so many of them; or they ended up *losing* a lot of it.

The following account gives us an example of how the post-flood *Kenites* would lose *most* of what they once had; and were taken over by *other* groups of people who grew much stronger than them:

<u>*Num.* 24</u>:
21 *And he looked on the* ***Kenites*** *(i.e. Qeyniy), and took up his parable, and said,*
Strong is thy dwelling place, and thou puttest thy nest in a rock.
22 *Nevertheless the* ***Kenite*** *(i.e.* ***Qayin****) shall be* ***wasted****, until Asshur shall carry thee*
away captive.

These Kenites probably lived the same as their ancient Cainite counterparts - which helped, as a whole, to bring them *down*, to the same states of *misery* and *despair*. You live certain "ways" (against God), and God will make sure that things often don't work out for you, overall… *in the end.*

These Kenites, as with the giants, would also have *other* names in the post-flood world: the *Midianites* (in Gen. 37:38, Num. 31:2, Judg. 1:16, etc.); the *Rechabites* (in I Chr. 2:55), etc..[52]

So, according to all of this scriptural evidence, the Cainites, also, must have survived the flood... as the *Kenites*.

The Amalekites

> *There are five races* ***of mixed multitude****. These are the Nefilim (fallen), the Giborim (mighty), the Anakim (giants), the Refaim (shades) and the* ***Amalekim*** *(a.k.a. Amalekites).*
> - *Zohar* Beresheet A20[53]

Along with the giants, along with these Kenites, we have evidence that another group of antediluvian people survived - more of those with blood of the Serpent. One meaning of the name *Amalek* stands for, "a people that licks up."[54] Just what would the Amalekites "lick up," here? Probably, they would *consume* (or "lick up") much of the wealth and resources around them, in the areas of which they lived (a lot like the giants). We also know the antediluvian Cainites exploited their environment, as well. Now, we see the post-flood giants, the Kenites, and other of these sons of the Serpent would do much of the same… and suffer the consequences.

Were These Amalekites Really Sons of Esau?

Many scholars now scoff at the idea that these post-flood Amalekites were actually sons of the Serpent - mainly because of an *anomaly* in the Bible. There *was* a group of people descended from an individual named *Amalek*… who was a grandson of Esau (a descendant of Abraham); and they were *also* called the Amalekites. Well, which one was which? Were they the same?

These Amalekites, interestingly enough, were first mentioned in Genesis 36:13 (in the year, approximately, 1800 B.C.)… which was a full **400** years *after* the flood! Yet, we have verses (such as in Gen. 14:1) which mention an *Amalekite* group of individuals - a full **120** years *before* this grandson of Esau would have ever been born:

> *Gen.* 14:
> 1 *And it came to pass in the days of Amraphel king of Shinar, Arioch king of Ellasar, Chedorlaomer king of Elam, and Tidal king of nations;*
> 2 *That these made war…*
> 5 *…Chedorlaomer, and the kings that were with him… smote the Rephaims in Ashteroth Karnaim, and the Zuzims in Ham, and the Emins in Shaveh Kiriathaim,*
> 7 *And they returned, and… smote all the country* ***of the Amalekites****, and also the Amorites…*

The time of this was practically in the era of *Abraham* - Esau's grandfather! So, if this is true, then where did *this* above group of Amalekites come from? Yes, there seems to be *two* groups of them, out there. And, if *this* above group was the remnant of those pre-flood Amalekites, then they, obviously, must have been of an *older* nation. Interestingly enough, we *do* have Biblical evidence of a group of *Amalekites*, coming from a very *ancient* origin: *the beginning of the world*!

> *And when he looked on Amalek (Amaleq), he took up his parable, and said, Amalek (i.e. Amaleq)* ***was the first of the nations****; but his latter end shall be that he perish for ever.*
> \- *Num.* 24:20 (KJV)

It's interesting to find out *why* the Biblical character (Balaam) said such a thing, here. Truly the grandson of Esau wasn't there since the beginning. We know who were, though. Apparently, someone **already** knew how old this group of Amalekites was. And, if these Amalekites indeed were seeds of the Serpent (in one way or another), then they would have been able to be among the *first* of the worldly nations out there! It all makes sense.

As with before the antediluvian world, these post-flood Amalekites seemed to have kept close ties with the post-flood Kenites - probably because they **both** were of the same kin!

I Sam. 15:
5 *And Saul came to a city of* ***Amalek*** *(i.e. Amaleq), and laid wait in the valley.*
6 *And Saul said unto the* ***Kenites*** *(i.e. Qeyniy), Go, depart, get you down from among the* ***Amalekites*** *(i.e. Amaleq), lest I destroy you with them: for ye shewed kindness to all the children of Israel, when they came up out of Egypt. So the* ***Kenites*** *(i.e. Qeyniy) departed from among the* ***Amalekites****.*

Interestingly, another meaning of the word *Amalek* (or *Amalekite*), in its original Hebrew, is *Amaleq* - a "dweller in a valley."[55] Interesting: we already know that the *Cainites* dwelled in a **valley**, just before the flood (while they were trying to seduce the Sethites, up in a mountain). Just as most of the Anakim and Refaim did, did most of the post-flood *Kenites* and *Amalekites* fall to the same ways - as they did before the flood?

The Time Ripe for Destruction

The question of just *who* were the Kenites and Amalekites - and what they, *over time*, would manifest themselves into - would go on to be the most important tool towards our understanding of how the pre-flood world **relates to our own**… and understanding some things about *Mystery Babylon*! We know a bit about the Kenites (because we can relate them to the "ways" of their patriarch Cain), but we don't know too much about the Amalekites, however; until we dig further.

First off, we see that:

...the redemption of Yisrael (i.e. Israel) does not depend on the destruction of the Refaim, but ***on the destruction of Amalek****...* - *Zohar* Beresheet A20[56]

Interesting: it seems that these ancient Israelites, and other people in the land, wanted this particular group of ancient people to be controlled - if not *destroyed* (as one could already figure). In the following verses, we'll also see that the post-flood Amalekites lived in somewhat close proximity to the lands the Israelites would eventually end up living in - the "land of milk and honey" (i.e. Israel):

Num. 13:
27 *And they told him, and said, We came unto the land whither thou sentest us, and surely it floweth with milk and honey; and this is the fruit of it.*
29 *The* ***Amalekites*** *(i.e. Amaleq) dwell in the land of the south...*

After the children of Israel were liberated from their 400-year bout with Egyptian slavery, they were directed to *overtake* the lands of which God promised Abraham. We already know that *giants* and other people (such as the Kenites and Amalekites) lived in these lands; and they wouldn't go without a fight! One day, these Israelites met up with the Amalekites, and promptly decided to wage war with them. These next set of verses, interestingly enough, may also be able to give us some interesting information about these post-flood Amalekites:

Ex. 17:
8 *Then came Amalek (i.e. Amaleq), and fought with Israel in Rephidim.*
9 *And Moses said unto Joshua, Choose us out men, and go out, fight with Amalek: to morrow I will stand on the top of the hill with the rod of God in mine hand.*
10 *So Joshua did as Moses had said to him, and fought with Amalek: and Moses, Aaron, and Hur went up to the top of the hill.*
11 *And it came to pass, when Moses held up his hand, that Israel prevailed: and when he let down his hand, Amalek prevailed.*
12 *But Moses hands were heavy; and they took a stone, and put it under him, and he sat thereon; and Aaron and Hur stayed up his hands, the one on the one side, and the other on the other side; and his hands were steady until the going down of the sun.*
13 *And Joshua discomfited Amalek and his people with the edge of the sword.*
14 *And the LORD said unto Moses, Write this for a memorial in a book, and rehearse*

it in the ears of Joshua: for I will utterly put ***out the remembrance of Amalek*** *from under heaven.*
15 *And Moses built an altar, and called the name of it Jehovahnissi:*
16 *For he said, Because the LORD hath sworn that the LORD will* ***have war with Amalek from generation to generation****.*

Here, we see that the Amalekites weren't *entirely* wiped out, in these early days. God also made it known how much He **does not like *Amalek***: it seems that He will be at *war* with the **descendants of Amalek**, from **generation to generation**. They just won't go away! Why them? What's their significance to our whole story? Well, if they were only descendants of Esau it all wouldn't really matter. But, in regards to the **Genesis 3:15 Prophecy**, it makes a lot more sense. This group now seems to *epitomize* those who act *evil* or *unrighteous* - those who act as if they came from the Serpent himself. Now, we know that they probably *did*!

And, if they *truly* were of the Serpent, then everything is so much more understandable, now:

Deut. 25:
16 *For all that do such things, and all that do* ***unrighteously****, are an abomination unto the LORD thy God.*
17 *Remember what* ***Amalek*** *(Amaleq) did unto thee by the way, when ye were come forth out of Egypt;*
18 *How he met thee by the way, and smote the hindmost of thee, even all that were feeble behind thee, when thou wast faint and weary; and he* ***feared not God****.*
19 *Therefore it shall be, when the LORD thy God hath given thee rest from all thine enemies round about, in the land which the LORD thy God giveth thee for an inheritance to possess it, that thou shalt* ***blot out the remembrance of Amalek from under heaven****; thou shalt not forget it.*

It seems the *enmity* between the Adamite Hebrews (i.e. the promised seed of Adam) and the Amalekites (i.e. the seeds of the **Serpent**) would continue on, and on, and *on*. And, we know *why*: these were the **two seed lines**, prophesied in Genesis 3:15! Why would God seem to retain *such a vendetta* against this particular group of people, if they were *only* the offspring of Esau's grandson? Makes no sense. Obviously, there's something deeper to this all! As we recall, from the previously mentioned book of *Zohar*:

> *These are all mixed among Yisrael (i.e. Israel), but none of them is cursed as* ***Amalek****, who is* ***the evil Serpent****, a* ***Strange*** *El...* - *Zohar* Beresheet A29[57]

If anything, we now have scriptural proof of descendants - **direct** descendants - of *the Serpent* who had gone on, to survive the flood! No wonder why God was so against them! No wonder the Amalekites and others who lived and thoughts like them possessed so much dissension, so much anger, and so much hard-pressed wrath against the God who already had to destroy their ancestors once.

All this leads us to: what even *became* of these Kenites and Amalekites… once they began to be put on the "hit list" of so many people of their day? What did they manifest themselves off as, over the years? And, what *influences* did their ancient Serpent "ways" have on their world at hand, since the flood? Lastly, just who might these people be, in front of us, ***today***? And, how could we be able to recognize just "who's who" - if we even *can*?

Also, what might we be able to do with all of this information, as a *whole*? And, how could we use all of this knowledge to allow us a *tool* against the enemy… a tool of which, in the end, might help us to enrich *our* own lives, each and every day?

Chapter 19

Leading to the Modern Parallel of "The Days of Noah"

...the distinction between past, present, and future is only a ***stubbornly persistent illusion****.*
- *Albert Einstein*[1]

What Could it All Mean?

We've seen how the antediluvian giants survived the flood. And, we've also seen how so many of them went down this same, *dark* moral pathway, once again… as they did before. We've also seen how a number of them would begin to mix with the local people around them - again - and corrupt them, in *more ways than one*.

And, we also have ancient written evidence that the *Kenites* and the *Amalekites* (both sons of the Serpent) survived the flood, as well… many of whom would go on, and try to corrupt the world, *again*. Members of the *Behemah*, *Chay*, *Owph*, and *Remes* all seemed to have also survived. So what, about all of this? What does it all *mean*, anyhow? And why should we get into this *so much*? What would be the *significance* of all these groups in the whole scheme of *Mystery Babylon*, today? The reason why we concentrate so much on understanding just *who* these people were, and what their actions were *after* the flood, is fairly simple: as we recall, from the beginning of this book, there was a very important prediction, in regards to the *end* of our current age… a prediction given by *Jesus Christ* himself:

But as the ***days of Noe (Noah)*** *were, so shall also the coming of the Son of man be.*
- *Mat.* 24:37 (KJV)

This tells us so much; and is *so* very important to our understanding of *Mystery Babylon*. Many of these pre-flood people led certain "ways" of life; they defined a certain culture; they glorified certain attitudes; and they lived within certain societal boundaries.

Many of those who survived the flood *also* brought these *same* attitudes, cultures, and ways of life they once had to the *post-flood* world - ultimately, to *our* current world. *Both* of these eras - before and right after the flood - represent the ancient side of the *parallel* of which Jesus spoke!

So, now, if we truly want to understand what the Bible - *for sure* - claims is *good* or *evil*; if we want to really understand what's *right* from *wrong* (even in today's "politically correct" world)... **we can**! All we have to do is discover what went on in these early days, and go from there! These ancient "ways" could now become the fundamental elements of what's *wrong* with society, what's *wrong* with our cultures; and ways for us to *not* really want to live! And, if history truly *does* repeat itself, then having this *real* knowledge of our past gives us a powerful tool - a means for us to gather what is, and what should be (*in the future*), positive ways for us to live our lives.

A lot of our modern thought, however, has become so corrupted by ideological "smoke and mirrors," or so clouded by "political correctness," that we are, most often, left "in the dark" - confused, or disoriented. A lot of the ways to look at stories in this book have, most probably, become *obscured*, over time; most probably hidden from our view, even "tossed aside," in order to keep a campaign of disinformation alive. A lot of it doesn't fit too nicely into most of the modern-day narratives we have been exposed to.

The deeper meanings behind their manipulations are simple: ***exposure***. Some of their ways of "political correctness" might not be looked upon in a good light if this information gets out... and they can't have that. *Mystery Babylon* works hard to hide a great deal of information which might oppose it - that's why it's called a "*mystery*." Now, however, it's time to move beyond these "smoke and mirrors" - to help us identify just "who is who" and what's truly "right and wrong." Let's go.

The Five Groups - Revisited

To begin, let's take a look at those Adamite and pre-Adamite human groups, and what they might mean to us, today. These are *only* groups of human beings - who, for the most part, had come onto the scene in a neutral moral fashion. These are, quite often, those individuals who become *swayed*, in one way or another; thanks to the divisive "ways" of Cain and his father, the Serpent.

We recall the five groups of Genesis' "Six-Day Creation":

- **The *Adamites***
- **The *Chay* (or "Beasts") *of the Field***
- **The *Behemah* (or "Cattle"/"Beasts")**
- **The *Remes* (or "Creeping Thing") *that Creepeth***
- **The *Owph* (or "Fowl") *of the Air***

Who could they be, *today*? Can we identify these groups in our present time? And, if we could, what does it mean to us, as a *whole*… if anything? This answer may be a little more *difficult* than one might figure, here (due to lack of evidence)… difficult; but, not impossible. Let's look at one possible argument for their current identification, today: many of us might show consensus on the number of the accepted *races* in the world, as distinguished by individual, physical characteristics. Some of the more popular ones are:

- ***The Caucasoid***: the Mediterranean, European, or Caucus peoples; roughly considered "white" people or "anyone not Negroid or Mongoloid."[2]

- ***The Congoid** (as **Negroids**, etc.)*: the Subsaharan African peoples; roughly considered "black" people.[3]

- ***The Australoid***: the darker-skinned peoples of Australia, Southeast Asia, and also parts of India.[4]

- ***The Mongoloid***: those from China, Manchuria, Indochina, Mongolia, American Indians and other indigenous American peoples; roughly considered the "red" or "yellow" peoples, Orientals, and those with unique eye and facial features and yellowish skin.[5]

Could there be some kind of *racial* correlation between these ancient five groups and a few of these races, above? The theme of this book was not meant to go off on any tangent, promoting any racial stereotype, or try to show any racial superiority. That's simply *not* what this work is all about. It is about *answers* - possible *answers*. It is about *understanding*. Its purpose is to provide us with information - *ancient* information - to help us come up with possible, *alternate* conclusions… other than what we've been spoon-fed, all of these years. We'll provide the ancient evidence, we'll show the *other* side of things - it's up to each one of us to be the judge, here.

So, building on this above: what is, and what has always been, the easiest way to identify a person? We, often, could tell that a person is either *male* or *female* by looking at their face. We could also make fairly-intelligent conclusions about the approximate age range of a person, by just looking at their face. We, also, can tell, by looking at their ***face***, what race they are, for the most part. These ways of identification, obviously, must have been in use since ancient times! So, in order to distinguish the above groups, there *must* have been some manner of identifying features the ancients used. There had to be!

And, in regards to our comprehension of what *Mystery Babylon* is, the identification of these people, today, as compared to long ago, is *not* really a necessity! What does matter is that there, very well, could have been *a number* of human groups around, at this time of Adam. The races could have been there from the beginning! What really matters is that one human group didn't necessarily come from another, or come into existence by some "fluke" - they've been there *all along*. What's so evil, or *wrong*, about suggesting this?

And, with this angle, what we also see is that the early stories of Genesis might, *indeed*, be a lot *different* that so many of us have ever been taught, or have ever even *dreamed*! So, what really matters is that there was a special seed of one man - *Adam*. It doesn't really matter what group of individuals he came from. What really matters is: that this particular man's see had passed on, to, eventually, what would have been the savior of the entire world… fulfilling that special seed line prophecy of Genesis 3:15! **That's** the important thing, here.

So, if we could look to the possibility of *race* being, somehow, behind the identifying characteristics of each group of Adamites and pre-Adamites, then, in ways, we might be able to understand a few things about how some of these groups lived their lives; or their occupations. We also *know* that the souls of the *Chay of the Field*, the *Owph of the Air*, the *Remes that Creepeth*, the *Behemah*, and the *Adamites* swarmed in the *Darkness* - all together. We all, ultimately, had come from the same place (at least *spiritually*)… that's for sure. And, we also know that Adam was only *one* man; caught up in the middle of a major prophecy! Incidentally, the race of Adam, here, was not necessarily a great race, because of him; and, Adam was not necessarily a great person, because of his race. He was, pretty much, his *own* man; and on his own. God fashioned this man in a special way, for the most part, because of the way He wanted him to *think*! Adam's attitudes and ways of handling himself was the important thing, here.

So, if we begin to go down this same ideological pathway, some other thoughts might begin to emerge: if it didn't really matter what race he was (because he was his own person), then what *race* was he, now that we face this question? He had to be of *some* race! Well, one thing we could assume, by looking at the nation of Israel in *our present time*, as well as looking at examples *in the Bible*, the **Adamites** were probably of the Caucasian race.[6] We'll soon explain more about this, and the ramifications of this all… if there even *is any*! And, if the above might be, in fact, true, then what about the members of the *other groups*? What was their place? How were *they* relevant to this whole story? Now, this becomes the time when things do get a little *cloudy*, as far as Biblical reasoning; and, we may need to dig a little bit deeper, to begin to give us some answers.

First off, let's look at the *Remes that Creepeth* group. The Bible seems to add the word *every* before the mentioning of this group, quite often - possibly making the point that this particular group of individuals could stand for *everyone* else, or *every other* person - beyond those who worked in the Garden of Eden! They probably had some role, or purpose, in Adam's Garden of Eden… but, we're just not sure *what*. More to come on all of this, in Volume 2…

We do seem to have a little more about the other human groups, however. We may be able to assume that the rest of them directly helped to work in, and around, the Garden of Eden. How do we know? We've already hypothesized the *Chay of the Field* could have been a group of individuals whose major occupation was working the fields, around the Garden; and the *Behemah* could, for the most part, have been the ranchers, shepherds, or animal-caretakers. And, throughout the Bible, the *Chay of the Field* and the *Behemah*, often, seemed to be looked upon as *similar* to each other, in a number of ways!

Sometimes, the word *Behemah* was used to describe *both* groups, overall… as more of a *general* word for those who *worked the fields* in some manner (either in a pasturing capacity or farming capacity)! Since there are two closely-related members of darker-skinned races (i.e. the Congoid/Negroids and Australoids), could these be the *Chay of the Field* and the *Behemah*? Could there be a link? And, could the *Remes that Creepeth* - by default - actually be of the left-over *Mongoloid* race? And, what about the *Owph of the Air* group? As already stated, we are not sure about ways to cement this all. It's still, overall, a little cloudy… due to lack of ancient written evidence. But, there will, in the next volume, be *more* additional information to this all… which will further help us make sense of things. More to come…

Goliath and His Insults

Using what we presently *do* have - with a few, possible connections to these above groups - we need to return to the probability of Adam being of the *Caucasian* race; and what that all might really mean… if *anything*. The next set of verses seems to provide, not only further evidence for all of this, but also more evidence on the probability of these above five groups as being *human*. It, as well, gives us an interesting look to how the ancients might have viewed these different groups of human beings, as well! Let's see.

The following account is from the story of *David and Goliath* (I Sam. 17). David and Goliath (an *Anakim*) were about to fight each other. They stood there, facing each other; just before their engagement - throwing taunts at each other. This was also the time right before David ended up killed him, with a stone.

According to the ancient written evidence, these offspring of the Nephilim and Watchers were, often, thought to have golden blonde hair; and brilliant, white skin (*much more* brilliant and fair than any Caucasian human out there - literally, these terrestrial angels and their descendants were of a class *all by themselves*)! Anyhow, Goliath was, most probably, one of these mixed angelic offspring - with these special physical characteristics. When David approached him, Goliath noticed he was fair (for a human being); and, as with other Adamites of the day, also had the ability to show *red* in his face (i.e. he had the ability to blush). So, then, Goliath began to speak to David in a *condescending* manner, because his physical features were, of course, *nowhere* near as *brilliant* as his own:

<u>*I Sam.* 17:</u>
42 *And when the Philistine looked about, and saw David, he disdained him: for he was but a youth, and* ***ruddy*** *(i.e. blushing-faced), and of* ***a fair countenance*** *(i.e. white?).*
43 *And the Philistine said unto David, Am* ***I a dog****, that thou comest to me with staves? And the Philistine cursed David by his gods.*
44 *And the Philistine said to David, Come to me, and I will give thy flesh unto the* ***Owph*** *(fowls)* ***of the Air****, and to the* ***Behemah*** *(beasts)* ***of the field****.*
45 *Then said David to the Philistine, Thou comest to me with a sword, and with a spear, and with a shield: but I come to thee in the name of the LORD of hosts, the God of the armies of Israel, whom thou hast defied.*
46 *This day will the LORD deliver thee into mine hand; and I will smite thee, and take thine head from thee; and I will give the carcases of the host of the Philistines this day unto the* ***Owph*** *(fowls)* ***of the Air****, and to the* ***wild Chay*** *(beasts)* ***of the Earth****; that all the earth may know that there is a God in Israel.*
(in retranslation)

First, we see in verse 42, that Goliath looked at David, and made a *racist* comment, here! It wasn't David who started it all. Goliath blurted out (in paraphrase): "*What*? Do you think I'm some sort of lowly *dog* that you have to send this little white, rosy-cheeked *child* out here, to fight me"? Goliath obviously thought he was physically - and (assuredly) *racially* - superior!

And, in the above verses, Goliath also seemed to have perceived the ***Owph of the Air*** and ***Behemah*** were of a *lower*, social class to him, as well! This is why he said to David (in paraphrase): "I will give you to the lowly **Owph (Fowl) of the Air** and the **Behemah (Beasts) of the Field** - to those *cannibals* - so that they can make a *meal* out of you; and eat your carcass (I Sam. 17:44)!" Talk about a superiority complex.

David knew he would defeat Goliath, and replied (in paraphrase): "No. It is *I* who will give you to these **Owph (Fowl) of the Air** and to the **wild Chay (beasts) of the Earth**." As we see, his comment was close to Goliath's; but a little *different*. What's the reason for this? Maybe David was trying to "one up" Goliath, and his insult… as if to say, "I will even give *your* flesh to *farmers*… so *they* could eat your flesh" (even though farmers, for the most part, would, most probably, not be as prone to develop into practicing cannibalism as the *Behemah* might). Why? Again, the *Chay* were, for the most part, concerned with developing the *land*, farming the *fields*, etc.; while the *Behemah* worked a lot closer with the animal kingdom; and may have understood how the "laws of the jungle" worked, the partaking of animal flesh, etc.. Due to the *Chay* rarely being thought of as individuals progressing into meat-eating individuals, David's comment assuredly could have "one bettered" Goliath's, here. His suggestion would have been *much more of* a feat for these *Chay* to accomplish!

Now, we get some insight on how certain individuals within some groups may have desired to switch to *cannibalism*, through whatever circumstance. And, not only do we get some affirmation that some *Behemah* and *Owph of the Air* might have resorted to these cannibalistic practices, we also see that the *Chay of the Field* and the *Behemah* being considered *close* to each other, in ways. They had to have been - or they wouldn't have been able to be brought into the *same context*, in the above![7]

Could the people of antiquity have similar prejudices, as people do today? Does this story, and the rest of it, help us to understand just "who's who," here? The answer is… no. But, in actuality, possessing a *definitive* answer to "who's who" really *doesn't matter*, in the end… right? Now, why would it? What does a person's race definitively mean for the individual - if we, ultimately, have the *free will* to want to follow God, or not? What we *do* need to understand, here - for sure - is that there were probably different groups of human individuals who had existed, since the beginning of our world. These people had, most probably, even been around *before* Adam's formulation - as the pre-Adamites!

These **pre-Adamites**, assuredly, contributed to the world of the Garden; each in their *own* way! They *all* must have had some manner of purpose, even though we can't definitively identify all of the details. Even though we *all* come out of the *Darkness*, and we're different in a number of outward, *physical* aspects, that doesn't mean God likes, or cares for, one group *more* than the other. We also know that there was *one* individual - *Adam* - who was of major significance to God, in the most ancient of times… not necessarily what individual *group* he was from! In fact, the Bible hardly mentions *any other* members of this *Adamite* group, here… just ***Adam***, and his direct descendants (i.e. the Israelites).

We may be able to assume that a number of people of *one* group might have begun to go down certain pathways in life, in the past; while others in *another* group might have begun to go down another. That's not really the problem. The people of these groups, for the most part, probably had different, physical characteristics. That's *also* not the real problem. There is one thing, however, which is *very* important to God, in regards to which directions people take - and this is something God does **not** ignore: many people would begin to go down their *own* ***moral*** pathways, as well! Many would turn away from God. God **hates** idolatry, however; He is a jealous God - He does not desire, nor tolerate, anyone who chooses to worship *other* gods, or to go to things *of the earth*, for means of their spiritual fulfillment.

So, what we really **need** to concentrate on, now-a-days, are things we *can* change: we need to concentrate on the cultures, attitudes, and "ways" of life, promoted by certain individuals, to help us understand what might actually be *good* or *evil*; *right* or *wrong*. We need to concentrate on the *moral* implications of what has been brought to us, by these individuals of old - and how to deal with them, the most effectively, *today*.

Only Those With Genetic Tendencies…?

Even though *no* giants seem to remain on the earth, today; there *does* seem to be a lot of archaeological evidence which suggests giants did have a place on our earth, at one time. A number of giant human skeletons were discovered, which puzzled evolutionary scientists. What about people of short stature (i.e. midgets), today? Could *they* be genetic remnants of something like this? And, what about those with six fingers and six toes on each of their extremities? Where do genetic tendencies, such as these, come from?

Beyond outward appearances, could some people have the *predispositions* to **think or behave** in the same of these same ways as the fallen angels, and their descendants, once did? As we recall, many of those mixed, angelic offspring had *huge* sexual appetites (often perverted); had a taste for violence, decadence, and chaos; and also had a tendency to follow other gods (i.e. to participate in idolatry)! A number may have even had extremely superstitious or/and suicidal thoughts. Some were schizophrenic; some might have had bi-polar tendencies, as well. Could so many of these *other* behaviors have originated with these fallen angels, of old?

These mixed angelic offspring were also thought to have openly practiced homosexual activities, in ancient times. We also know how many giants lived amongst the people of Sodom and Gomorrah. Could our human society have received a number of genetic tendencies from the mixed offspring of these fallen angels? And, even though this all might have a kernel of truth, somewhere down the line, should we point fingers at *anyone* who might have inherited these genes?

Obviously, not…

What Does This All Mean - Racism, Hatred, Inequality?

Could we use these tidbits of information to make any assumption about anyone; or make generalizations on anything? Could we use any of this to promote ideas of hate and racism towards other people? Definitely **not**. As a good Christian should know, we just don't jump to conclusions about anything or anyone, even with this knowledge. We have to look at what's *really* important: moral integrity and character. As the old saying goes, we should be looking at what a person *can* change; what's inside an individual's heart. As we recall, **Abel** - the direct offspring of *the Serpent*, himself - *chose* to follow God, and make proper, moral choices. He did it… why can't others?

On the other extreme, there *are* reasons why the world is in the shape it is in, today - because people act upon *so many negative elements* of their human nature! Many people, yet today, act the same way as Cain, and the Serpent, did… so long ago. We live in the *real* world. This is the real world, today. We cannot just ignore the world the way it *really* is, today - and turn a "blind eye" to what's really dragging us down *morally*. We need to see things as they really are; and use all of this information to help us to move *further*.

It's interesting, about how so many elites try to concentrate on putting people into certain political factions, or certain "groups" (such as "African-Americans," "LGBTs," "Asian-Americans," "Disabled-Americans," etc.). Why do people feel that we have to *divide* ourselves into "groups" such as these - and allow attempts, by others around us, to push certain political agendas *within them*; rather than just trying to work *together*, as a sympathetic group of individuals? Can't we just concentrate on capitalizing on the *best* sides of each person, or group? The first successful heart surgery was performed by a black man. The first light bulb was invented by a white man. Gunpowder was invented by the Chinese. Can't we just accentuate *all* of these positives, here?

What we really need to concentrate on are the things *beyond* what a person cannot change, and focus on **all** of what they can. That is the real issue, here… especially in this book. People *can* pick and choose what they want, and what pathways they may *want* to follow - and this includes the elements of *culture* around them; the pathways one's society might make tempting; certain *attitudes*; particular thoughts and actions; even specific *religious* theologies and practices! The latter is the most important, here, in regards to our whole focus, here!

The Fulfilment of Prophecy

Regardless of all the temptations, regardless of all the other pathways in life for one to choose, and regardless of how the world is turning out because of it all, God does not want **anyone** left out of His plan! He had a prophecy, way back in the time of Genesis; which was eventually fulfilled; but the misunderstanding of this prophecy *still* seems to have an effect upon us, as a whole, *today*! Let's explain how.

Contrary to what a lot of people might try to tell us, in this day and age, the Bible *is* a book for all people; not just a privileged few. It is not about one race over another. It is not only a book for *Adamites*, or anyone *without* angelic blood. True, it's clearly stated in the Bible that it is the *book of the generations of Adam* (the man); but this was, in major part, for the reason of the Genesis 3:15 Prophecy! It's not only the generations of Adam that God cares about; and wants to be with Him.

Also, it's clear that the Bible says God has a *chosen* people - **Israel**. And, in this nation, He desired to keep the people's blood lines *pure*. But, yet again, we already *know* the reason for this - it wasn't necessarily to *downgrade* anyone else (in regards to one's nationality, for example; of which *they couldn't change*), but to **fulfill** this prophecy of early Genesis… simple:

> *And I will put enmity between thee and the woman, and between thy seed and her seed; it shall bruise thy head, and thou shalt bruise his heel…*
>
> - *Gen.* 3:15 (KJV)

Maintaining purity would *assure* that a pure seed of Adam and Eve would eventually be born; to allow this particular individual a means to bruise the head of the Serpent. Beyond anyone breeding with seed lines *outside* of their nation, God **also** did not want Israel to adopt any outside *moral* influences… no doubt about it. But, again, there was good reason for this - most of these *outside* ways had become extremely corrupted (and pagan); and turned out being *detrimental* to the individual, overall. Yep, we know *why*: most of these ways had originated with *Cain* and *the Serpent*!

These facts are so simple - and, to the point. But, there are *so many* individuals out there (who follow today's "politically correct" narratives) who *don't* want these reasons to sound easy to understand; they would rather have God, and the Bible, sound *insensitive*, *condescending* - or even *racist*! There are political motives to most everything people do. Yet, throughout this book, we were shown examples of how God loved *all* of the people in the world; and tried to be fair to everyone - **regardless** of what group they were from, what blood they might have inherited, or even what they may have done in the past! What matters are an individual's *current* choices - in regards to whether they want to *now* follow God, or not…

> *After this I beheld, and, lo, a great multitude… of* ***all nations****, and* ***kindreds****, and* ***people****, and* ***tongues****, stood before the throne… saying, Amen: Blessing, and glory, and wisdom, and thanksgiving, and honour, and power, and might, be unto our God…*
> - *Rev.* 7 9-12 (KJV)

> *And* ***the nations*** *of them* ***which are saved*** *shall walk in the light of it…*
> - *Rev.* 21:24 (KJV)

We know that God probably took some individuals from *each* of the five groups aboard the ark; as well as some of the *mixed* offspring - by reason of His compassion (and this reason *alone*). Obviously, one's own salvation depends upon what *their heart* chooses - one's individual choice:

> *Eccl. 3:*
> 17 *I said in mine heart, God shall judge the righteous and the wicked: for there is a time there for every purpose and for every work.*

18 *I said in mine heart concerning the estate of the* ***sons of Adam (men)****, that God*
might manifest them, and that they might see that ***they themselves are Behemah***
(beasts)*.*
19 *For that which befalleth the sons of Adam (men) befalleth Behemah (beasts); even*
one thing befalleth them: as the one dieth, so dieth the other; yea, they have ***all one***
breath *(i.e. spirit, smell); so that an Adam (man)* ***hath no preeminence above a***
Behemah *(beast): for all is* ***vanity****.*
20 *All go unto one place; all are of the dust, and all turn to dust again.*
21 *Who knoweth the spirit of Adam (man) that goeth upward, and the spirit of the*
Behemah (beast) that goeth downward to the earth?
22 *Wherefore I perceive that there is nothing better, than that an Adam (man) should*
rejoice in his own works*; for that is his portion: for who shall bring him to see*
what shall be after him?
(in retranslation)

As we see (in the above), an Adamite could become just as uncivilized as a Behemah might; and **vice versa**! We already know that, beyond Adam, we all have a similar soul (or *breath*) from the *Darkness* - no matter what group we originated in; and the purpose of this is to refrain one from claiming that he or she, *physically*, is superior in origin. We all should be *content* with who we are, and *where* we come from; and we should also desire to show the world whatever *positive* accomplishments *we* might be able to achieve, while in this world.

So… Why Uncover All of This, Anyhow?

Now, in order to give support for this book's theme, we needed to go a little *backwards* in thought and rationale. If the reader truly believes the words of the Bible *are* from something beyond this world, then we have scriptural evidence which suggests the world was **refashioned** about 6,000 years ago. We, as well, have scriptural evidence that shows the *Chay of the Field*, the *Owph of the Air*, the *Remes that Creepeth*, and the *Behemah* may be something **more** than just different groups of animals. Also, we also can conclude that one man - ***Adam*** - was of a special significance; and he had to have his seed passed down, to the savior of the world - Jesus Christ! And, on top of it, we see that it's really not about racial or national superiority in the Bible, but, a need for *blood line purity*… **in order** to allow this Genesis 3:15 Prophecy to come about! It's that simple.

And, since all of the other races were probably around, since the beginning of our world, this would "rock" many of the assumptions being thrown at us, today. But, maybe that's good for us, *overall* (as we'll see), to think about things differently! In reality, any other scenario about the origins of our races might, often, begin to put certain groups into a *bad* light. For example: with every group existing since the beginning of our world, black individuals didn't just, somehow, "devolve" from white individuals; nor did all of humanity, somehow, just "evolve" from a couple of "Adam-like" and "Eve-like" characters in Africa. The racial groups were here, all along. This way, *politicized* DNA science is debunked; evolution is debunked. We didn't "just emerge" from lowly apes; and, somehow, also begin to develop *souls* (from who-knows-where). God gave us *all* a soul. He had a hand in this whole creation process. We don't just get "something" from nothing.

And, on top of it, where did life, itself, originate from… according to *their* own theories? From *chemicals*? Science isn't even close to giving any possible answer to all of this… it just takes *faith* - faith in the means of intelligent design. Die hard evolutionists also might want us to believe that we are nothing but *mutations*… mutated beings of which, somehow, just keep getting better and better *on our own*. That's not a very good compliment, in regards to the entire human race - to think that we are nothing more than a number of sequential, and chance, *mutations*!

In Genesis - way back in the days of Adam and Eve - things just seemed to work. In the Garden of Eden, everything was very *good*. The whole process of the Garden worked out well… with members of each group having their own role, or occupation (for the most part). Everyone probably worked well with one other. Everyone seemed to get along. Everybody knew their place…

Now, because of the Serpent's subtle advances, and Adam and Eve's bad choices, we have the *Fall*. And, after this Fall, everything had now changed. Cain and the Serpent's seductive "ways" of thinking and living were beginning to sound *alluring* to individuals in **all** of these human groups (*including* the Adamites); those displaced, after the fall of the Garden. These false, pagan "ways" began to look like something *new* and *different* for many of them to follow… if they so desired. And, sorry to say, a vast number of individuals, here, *did* made free-and-clear choices to go after these "ways," and/or follow some other pagan "gods"… instead of God.

One may look at a lot of areas in our present world - in segments of Africa, in India, and in Asia (for example) - and see the multitudes upon multitudes of poverty-stricken, destitute individuals; and wonder *why* so many of these areas *end up* that way! Sure, there might have been a number of internal issues there, which may have developed, over time; and it's unfortunate… but we also have a **little-spoken of** element to this all, which seems to accompany these areas, as well! It seems that a vast majority of individuals in so many of these destitute areas (such as in the above) *deliberately* follow a **moral/religious pathway *away* from God**. That is the "elephant in the room," of which most people might not like to really talk about, now-a-days. Why? Of course, it's because this all would be something that an individuals *could* change, if they really wanted to… but they *didn't*. And, quite possibly, their present state of being *could have been* a result of their desire to follow other gods… period (simple; but not "politically correct," of course).

A personal *choice* of the majority to follow false gods is *so* prevalent in *so many* destitute areas: in Africa, for example, we have numerous tribal beliefs (which are almost *all* pagan); in India we have Hinduism as the major religion; in Asia we have Buddhism, etc.. These are *all* against God, and the Bible. And, it seems, they all seem to end up with the same, *paralleled* socio/cultural conditions.

We must remember: God *hates* idolatry; He absolutely *hates* it. Every person who looks to another pagan god of this world is, in reality, slapping the face of God… even though "political correctness" makes it clear we should "reach out" to those of other societies/cultures, and have attempts to *understand* them, to respect their practices - even to *celebrate* our differences! God, however, doesn't think of things in these same ways, though. And, we now see that it doesn't really matter what color a person's skin is, in regards to these areas, it doesn't matter their creed, nor their nationality… what really matters it's ***the gods*** that they worship! *That's* what helps to bring them down.

Idolatry is *idolatry*, no matter how "sugar-coated," or seemingly unrelated, people might try to make it all out to seem. The *first* commandment of God (in His *Ten Commandments*) concerns how He demands "no other gods before Him!" God is God. He wants what He wants, here. Assuredly, God doesn't really care if people do not approve; or if people think it's easier to look towards something *of this world* to venerate or worship. He doesn't desire to "celebrate" the religious differences of pagan societies. He doesn't want to be subjected to lessons in "tolerance" - He wants those other pagan, anti-God, practices ***out*** of the picture… period! It's not too hard to understand, here. Yet, it's hard for a lot of us to want to swallow. Ultimately, we see that it's *not* because of one's race, one's creed, one's nationality, or one's own ethnic origin that makes God want to curse them… it's their own, idolatrous *choices*!

Generally, things in most pagan societies probably don't turn out very well, *overall* in their world, because of this (as in the examples, above)! Of course, this is not the case with every individual; each person is different. But, *overall*, the chances are very good for a culture or society *not* turning out very good… when they follow certain practices. It's just an observable fact.

It's a lot like those *before the flood* who looked to follow *other* individuals (a.k.a. Cain, the Serpent, and the other fallen angels), adopting their "ways" and making "gods" out of them - in the end, looking for ways to make *them*, and their descendants, feel special… rather than **God**. This all ***really*** explains the background of so many of the problems we face, today, in our world! It's just funny, and *ironic*, how things seem to work out, here.

These fallen, terrestrial angels might all be gone, now. Even the giants, for the most part, may be all gone. But, there *still* elements of these individuals still around, today; which might become *very* problematic to our world, at hand. Their ancestors have been around, since the beginning. And, their subsequent likenesses - their genetic remnants surviving either in blood *or spirit* - are continuing on; trying to change our world into something more akin to *their* own "ways."

This is also the reason why we need to concern ourselves so much about *Cain*: what his "ways" were, how to spot them in our world, today; and, most importantly, exactly who and where these "ways" ***truly*** originated from! If we begin to accept all of the above as absolute possibilities, it would change *so much* of our thinking. So much of our understanding of the world would change. It might also help us to see differently on *why* things might have really turned out the ways they did, today! Most importantly, all of this would **expose** the true conflict we are presently in - a **moral** conflict between the **seeds** of the Serpent (and their sympathizers) and the **seeds** of Adam (and their sympathizers)!

Let's take more of a look at how this *enmity* still (subtly) continues.

To Mislead By Example

> *For the **grain of evil seed** hath been sown in the heart of Adam from the beginning, and how much ungodliness hath it brought up unto this time? And how much shall it bring forth until the time of **threshing** come?* - *4 Ezra (2 Esdras)* 4:30[8]

With all of this said and done, we need to take more of a detailed look into how the Genesis 3:15 Prophecy was actually fulfilled, and the circumstances surrounding all this. As well, we need to dig a little deeper into deciphering Jesus' statement about what "the days of Noah" meant.

First, what exactly would be this "time of threshing," in the above verse - a situation sown way back, in the era of Adam? If Cain was truly a *child of the wicked one* (the Serpent), he, obviously, would be considered the first Cainite (or Kenite). Ultimately, he would also become **the first Amalekite**, as well! We know Cain didn't exactly follow the moral pathways of God. We already know about most of his negative thoughts. So, how do we identify what these "ways of Cain" are, in our world, today? Just as we are supposed to stay away from evil, would the right ways to follow manifested by *the exact opposite* of the "ways" of Cain, and "ways" of his father, the Serpent? How come it's so hard to distinguish from the two, sometimes?

First off, Jesus gave his disciples the parable of the *Wheat and the Tares*. This gives us a very good starting point towards exposing the "ways of Cain," and the proper ways to follow, instead. Through his teaching, Jesus openly exposed who exactly had the *literal* blood of Cain, and the Serpent. Let's see:

> *Another parable put he forth unto them, saying The kingdom of heaven is likened unto a man which sowed good seed in his field: But while men slept, his enemy came and sowed **tares** among the **wheat**, and went his way. But when the blade was sprung up, and brought forth fruit, then appeared the tares also. So the servants of the*

householder came and said unto him, Sir, didst not thou sow good seed in they field? from whence then hath it tares... Wilt thou then that we go and gather them up? But he (the householder) said, Nay; lest while ye gather up the tares, ye ***root up also*** *the wheat with them. Let both grow together until the harvest: and in the time of harvest* ***I*** *will say to the reapers, Gather ye together first the tares, and bind them in bundles to burn them: but gather the wheat into my barn.* - *Mat.* 13:24-30 (KJV)

In these verses, Jesus compared the *wheat* to good, wholesome plants; and the *tares* to dark, strangling weeds. Bullinger, in his *Companion Bible*, explained the tares (or *zewan*), above, as thus:

While growing it looks like wheat, but when full grown the ears are long and the grains almost black. Each grain of zewan must be removed before grinding wheat, or the bread is ***bitter*** *and* ***poisonous****. Wheat is golden; but the tares* ***show their true colour*** *as they ripen.* - *The Companion Bible* Mat. 13:25 (notes)[9]

As we see, the two seeds often seem to grow right alongside one another! They look and act practically *the same* - at least, *at first*… for a *little* while. **Slowly**, over time, one begins to go "**its own way**," and then, ultimately, begins to **corrupt the other** wheat stalks, as well. The two plants seem to be symbols of two *different* kinds of people: two with very *ancient* origins; two with, ultimately, very *different* agendas; and, ultimately, two who end up having *very different* ways of looking at this world.

Jesus' disciples, then, asked him for an interpretation of this parable:

Declare unto us the parable of the tares of the field. He answered and said unto them, He that soweth the good seed is the Son of man; The field is the ***world****; the good seed the* ***children of the kingdom****; but the tares are the* ***children of the wicked one****; The enemy* ***that sowed them is the devil****; the harvest is the end of the world; and the reapers are the angels. As therefore the tares are gathered and burned in the fire; so shall it be in the end of this world.* - *Mat.* 13:36-40 (KJV)

As we see, the two easily represents the **two seed lines** of Genesis - the two that had originated all the way back in the time of Eden! The "tares" (or "Serpent Seeds") would eventually be gathered together at the end of our existence - the "time of **threshing.**"

Could the "tares" be, *literally*, the children of the *Serpent* - the "children of the wicked one" (i.e. the Amalekites and the Kenites)?

The Kenites Slither Their Way Into the Priesthood

Again, this book is not to point fingers at just *who* might be a "tare," here; but, rather, to expose the *attitudes*, *morals*, and accepted *ways of life* promoted by so many of them! This is the real **problem** with these sons of the Serpent. And, these are, truly, the things that a human being *could change*… but choose not to! These are those ways of life which end up imparting a **bitter taste** on the rest of us, trying to live out our lives in semi-decent ways.

According to the ancient Jewish work *The Midrash Rabbah*, Cain "went forth like one who shows **the cloven hoof**."[10] This term is most intriguing, here: the *hoof*, obviously, represents part of a pig's foot. Its *cloven* hoof remains hidden from the view of others - until the time the pig eventually wants to **lets it out** in the open! And, interesting enough, the *hoof* is also considered the *unclean* part of the pig. So, in other words, these "tares" will often parade around, like they are clean and honorable - and will try to show to others that their actions are "on the up and up." Eventually, however, their "cloven hoof" will begin to show through.[11] They will, then, try to convince others about how *just* and *right* they, *now*, begin to think that they are. Yet, at the end of the day, their world will start to collapse around them, in certain ways. They usually will not be satisfied, deep down inside, no matter what happens to them… even though they might outwardly proclaim, otherwise. Things will never seem to be enough. Their view of their world at hand, over time, will begin seem a lot less fulfilled, a lot less constructive, and even begin to be somewhat chaotic. It's just the result of abandoning God. Regardless of the eventual downward spiral, most will "double down" on their efforts; and continue even further to bring others along with them.

So, if they really want to "double down" on what they think is right, just how did those "tares," in the past, begin to *slither* into fractions our ancient world… to gather their power? First, Jesus made it clearly known that they began to follow other pathways in life - other ways *of the world* - as their own:

Then came the Jews round about him, and said unto him, How long dost thou make us to ***doubt****? If thou be the Christ, tell us plainly. Jesus answered them, I told you, and ye believed not: the works that I do in my Father's name, they bear witness of me. But ye believe not, because ye* ***are not of my sheep****.* - *John* 10:26 (KJV)

These people clearly did not want to believe in God, and His ways. In another Biblical example, here, Jesus began to be confronted by the Pharisees - the Jewish religious leaders of the day; and spoke out loud, back to them! He, again, exposed them for what they *really* were: **actual** remnants of the seed of Cain! He also exposed them as those who followed these "ways of Cain" - under the guise of Jewish religious theology!

As we'll discover, the Pharisees really *did* seem to have ancestors who were **Kenites**. Once, these Kenites were the scribes for priests of Moses' day. Over time, they ended up becoming the *priests* themselves. This trend continued, all the way down to Jesus' time! Simple.

It is so important to understand just *who* may have infiltrated the Jewish priesthood, so long ago; and how they accomplished this feat:

And the families of the ***scribes*** *which dwelt at Jabez; the Tirathites, the Shimeathites, and Suchathites. These are the* ***Kenites*** *that came of Hamath, the father of the house of* ***Rechab****.* - *I Chr.* 2:55 (KJV)

We know about the Kenites; just who were those of the house of Rechab? Settling among the Israelites, Amalekites, and Canaanites, the ***Kenites*** *apparently became* ***absorbed*** *into the tribe of Judah. Conservative groups of Kenites retained their nomadic way of life and beliefs and practices, however, and one such group, the Rechabites (2 Kings), fought alongside the rebel and future king of Israel... (they were a) conservative, ascetic Israelite sect that was named for* ***Rechab****... Though of obscure origin, the Rechabites apparently were related to the Kenites... (they were) separatists who refused to participate in agricultural pursuits... Believing that the semi-nomadic way of life was a religious obligation... According to later Jewish tradition, the Rechabites intermarried with the* ***Levites****, the* ***priestly class****.*
("The Gospel of Judas: Cain-Cainites-Kenite-Rechabites", n. d., p. 7-8)[12]

Eventually, the majority of Levite priests were not even *of* the Levite tribe!

> *...all True Levitical priests were replaced with* ***Kenite*** *scribes (who were the Nethanims (Ezra 2:43).* ("Study of the Kenite", n. d., p. 2)[13]

Even Moses - the great leader of Israel - had a father-in-law, thought to be *Kenite*: a man of whom had priestly duties!

> *The father-in-law of Moses, Jethro, was a* ***Kenite****, and as* ***priest****-leader of the tribe he led in the* ***worship of Yahweh*** *(i.e. God)... also called Rues, or Hobab, in the Old Testament... (he was a)* ***priest*** *of Midian of the* ***Kenite*** *clan...*
> ("The Gospel of Judas: Cain-Cainites-Kenite-Rechabites", n. d., p. 7)[14]

Josephus, the ancient historian, even said that the Pharisees and Sadducees (the different priests of Jesus' day) were *not* Israeli by birth:

> *...for there are three philosophical sects among the Jews. The followers of the first of whom are the* ***Pharisees****; of the second, the* ***Sadducees****; and of the third sect, who pretends to a severer discipline, are called Essenes.* ***These last*** *are* ***Jews by birth****, and seem to have a greater affection for one another than the other sects have.*
> - *Falvius Josephus* Jewish Antiquities 2.8.2[15]

Jesus all-out "blew their cover" when he spoke his mind, here; and exposed them for what they really were:

> *Fill ye up then the measure of your fathers. Ye serpents, ye* ***generation of vipers****... That upon you may come all the righteous blood shed upon the earth, (all the way) from the blood of righteous* ***Abel****.* - *Mat.* 23:32-35 (KJV)

> *Ye are of your father the* ***devil****,* ***and the lusts of your father*** *ye will do. He was a* ***murderer*** *from the beginning.* - *John* 8:44 (KJV)

As we see (in the above), Jesus even likened the ancestors of the Pharisees with the one **who killed Abel** - the first murderer! Who was that? We already *know* who that was: **Cain**, of course! The word *generation*, in the above phrase "ye generation of vipers," comes from the Greek word for *offspring*. Hence, Jesus obviously made it known that what he was saying was not just *symbolic* - they were the "(literal) **offspring** of vipers (or snakes)"… offspring of the *Serpent*![16]

Interestingly enough, the Pharisees responded to Jesus' accusation with:

> *We be not born of **fornication**!*
> - *John* 9:41 (KJV)

Funny… how they answered, in this way! We know that the word *fornication* does not just stand for "sex outside of marriage," but the **mixing** of one seed line with another, here! Obviously, these Pharisees knew what Jesus was talking about; and responded accordingly! They weren't just talking about morality, here. They weren't just talking about religious dogma. They were talking about their **own** ancestral bloodlines! Why did they get upset in the first place, if Jesus' accusations were nowhere *near* correct?

Through these accusations, Jesus, obviously, began to make waves with these priests. Their cover was full-blown. They, now, hated him.

Now, we see that the characters to make up the fulfillment of the Genesis 3:15 Prophecy all seemed to be in place - Jesus (the seed of Adam) and the Pharisees (the seeds of the Serpent)! Now, the time was nigh for a major event to occur, obviously… something which had been set in motion for a very long, *long* time:

> *(God speaking to Adam) And for thy sake I will be pleased to endure suffering. And for thy sake I will be pleased to hang on the **wood of the Cross**. All these things [will I do] for thy **sake**, O Adam.* - *Testamentum Adami*[17]

Prophecy Fulfilled

> *These words spake Jesus… and said, Father, the hour is come… While I was with them (the righteous) in the world, I kept them in thy name: those that thou gavest me I have kept, and none of them is lost, **but** the **son of perdition**; **that the scripture might be fulfilled**.* - *John* 17:1, 12 (KJV)

We **now** see the end-results; how the fulfillment of the prophecy of Genesis ended up:

And I will put enmity between thee and the woman, and between ***thy seed*** *and* ***her seed; it shall bruise thy head****, and thou shalt bruise his heel…*
- *Gen.* 3:15 (KJV)

We have both seed lines, right here! The seed of Adam was passed down to **Jesus**. The seed line of the Serpent (through Eve) resulted in Cain, and the Cainites. The Cainites, eventually, passed through the flood as the Kenites. The Kenites, eventually, passed their seed onto the Pharisees (among other peoples).

Jesus really didn't have a problem with those who had blood of the Serpent, but the corruption of the **religious leadership** of his day! As time passed, this corrupt priesthood began to use all of their power to control others; and **that's** what enraged Jesus. They, however, were now in a position to railroad Jesus to his execution, if they wanted. And, most of us know what happened next: they did have him **crucified**.

Although they did *hurt* Jesus Christ (i.e. they "bruised his heel"), their whole corrupted authority was about to be over turned by his death… because it would be his death, burial, and *resurrection*! Jesus defeated death, and the hold Satan and the Serpent had on the world. No longer did someone have to go to a priest, and follow strict adherence of the Jewish law, for their salvation. Now, there really wasn't any need for substitute animal sacrifices, anymore (as were done, *before*). Now, Jesus ***was*** the perfect, substitute sacrifice; being the son of God, himself (through the virgin birth). A perfect *God* would naturally yield a perfect *substitution*, here - a *gift*… a *gift* to all those who want it. As well, this *gift* would be allowed to *replace* any subsequent sacrifices the human race may have had to do, from then on! All of this allowed the individual to be able to go ***straight*** to God for their own, assured salvation. The price for Adam's sin (and all after him) had, now, been *paid*, through this. And, the religious *hold* these Pharisees once had, over the populous, was, *also*, overturned. It was *no longer* "their way or the highway." This was exactly how Jesus "crushed the head" of these old (corrupted) institutions:

…we have these words, "it shall bruise thy ***head****:" in this is signified the* ***work*** *of the Old Serpent.* (Eisenmenger, 1748, p. 191-192)[18]

People, once, relied on the clergy, and rituals… for almost *all* of the elements of their salvation. Had Jesus never been born, the Serpent, and his corruption over the world, would have continued on. This "second Adam" repaired the cursed state of the world, brought on the world - a long time ago - by the very "first."

These priests actually stood face to face with the one who would be their replacement; unbeknownst to them. This was why Jesus had to be *sacrificed* the way he was. This was why these priests acted what they did: prophecy **fulfilled**.

That Genesis 3:15 Prophecy - From a Pagan Point of View

We know a lot of ancient (pagan) mythology was under the assumption that the ways of God, obviously, were *wrong*; and the way of Cain and the Serpent were, ultimately, *right*. According to the book, *The Parthenon Code*, the ancient Greeks even considered their lineage as from the blood of Cain, himself! As a result:

> *They (the ancient Greeks) made the line of Seth look brutal ad uncivilized; and the line of Kain (Cain),* ***noble*** *and* ***victimized****.* (Johnson, 2004, p. 60)[19]

For example: the *Kentuar* - an ancient Greek symbol - represented a half man, half horse. The original Greek word for Kentuar, however, was *Kentauros*: meaning "a hundred." According to *The Parthenon Code*, the Kentaur, then, became a symbol of Seth's bloodline - the ultimate enemy of these sons of Cain![20] It also seemed to have stood for the hundred-year span, of which Noah tried to warn people about the flood.[21]

And, the following also explains why these Kentaurs were considered to be half man, half horse:

> *…in the Chaldean language from Babylon (is) where the image of the Kentaur originated… the Kentaurs were depicted as half-men/half-horses. A word that is pronounced almost identically in Chaldean,* ***cuwph****, means "terminate, or have* ***an end, perish****." The horse-part of the Kentaur may have been a homophonic word-picture which connected to the reason that the line of Cain* ***perished*** *during the flood.*
> (Johnson, 2004, p. 62)[22]

In other, this *Kentaur* was symbolic of those "terrible" Adamites, or Sethites: those that the Greeks deemed *responsible* for the death of so many of their Cainite ancestors (i.e. those who were not aboard Noah's ark)! Along these same lines, the Greeks also had their own opinion about the fulfillment of this Genesis 3:15 Prophecy (above):

> *The Greeks pictured this cataclysmic event (the flood) as... (a symbol of the) Kentaurs (i.e. the Adamites/Sethites) pounding a man named* ***Kaineus*** *into the ground with a rock. The artist of the Francois Vase wrote the name "Kaineus" next to the man being pounded into the earth by the Kentaurs. Kaineus means "pertaining to Kain," or more directly, "the line of* ***Cain****"... In Genesis, the line of Kain is considered to be the serpent's seed... It appears in Genesis 3:15... The Greeks looked back at the pounding of Kaineus into the ground by rock-blows to the head as the* ***fulfillment of this curse****. If that were the end of the story, there wouldn't be any Greek religion embracing the way of Kain. But that wasn't the end... The line of Kain* ***came back*** *into being after the Flood. Thus, the hurting of Kain's head* ***put an end*** *to the curse without putting an* ***end*** *to the line of Kain.* (Johnson, 2004, p. 19, 72)[23]

Again, we see more evidence that the Cainites survived the flood. Obviously, there were Greeks who believed the line of Cain was *no longer cursed*; because, through the flood, they considered the prophecy of Genesis 3:15 *as* being fulfilled! The flood actually crushed "the head" of a number of their Cainite ancestors; which (in their minds), most probably, had "resolved" all of God's anger. Good enough.

Any of whom survived, assuredly, went through *so much*, because of the flood (at least, in these Greek minds). Shouldn't they be, *now*, be vindicated (according to *their* assumptions)?

The Rise of the Serpent Seeds

So, we see that, after the flood, these Cainites (i.e. as the *Kenites*) began to go on their merry way, once more - continually believing *they were right* in thinking what they were thinking, every step of the way. They used whatever inner thoughts they could, to justify to themselves that they - and the "ways" they would began to follow *once again* - were the right ones:

He that committeth sin is of the devil; for the devil sinneth from the beginning. For this purpose the Son of God was manifested, that he might destroy the works of the devil. Whosoever is born of God doth not commit sin; for his (God's) seed remaineth in him: and he cannot sin, because he is born of God. In this the children of God are manifest, and the children of the devil: whosoever doeth not righteousness is not of God, neither he that loveth not his brother. ***For this is the message that ye heard from the beginning****...*
- *I John* 3:8-11 (KJV)

The above seems to be a Biblical comparison: the "children of the devil" to the "children of God." This *could* be words of pure symbolism - until we read the latter half of this group of verses:

...Not as ***Cain****, who was* ***of that wicked one****, and slew his brother. And wherefore skew he him? Because his own works were evil, and his brother's righteous.*
- *I John* 3:12 (KJV)

Also, again, we have the mention of *Cain*, here; and how *he* was literally *of* that wicked one - a *son* of! As we see, the English word *of*, in the above verse, comes from the Greek word *ek*.[24] This word *ek* represents:

- *a primary preposition denoting* ***origin*** *(the point whence action or motion proceeds),* ***from****,* ***out*** *(of place, time, or cause);* ***literal*** *or figurative*[25]

In other words, these above verses seem to label the beginning of our problems as the one who *came* from the beginning - the one, *literally*, from the devil.

Another source makes it even clearer:

The members of the mixed multitude ***are the children*** *of the primordial* ***Serpent*** *that seduced Chavah (Eve) by the tree of knowledge, so the mixed multitude is indeed the impurity that the Serpent injected into Chavah. From this impurity, which is considered the* ***mixed multitude****,* ***Kayin*** *(Cain) came forth...*
- *Zohar* Beresheet A28[26]

> *When a person diverts his ways from the Torah (the first five books of the Old Testament) he draws upon himself a spirit from* ***the Other Side****, which is the* ***unclean*** *side. That defiled side awakens from the side of the hole of the great abyss, wherein lie the wicked spirits that harm people and are called* ***the world's destroyers*** *that* ***originate in Cain****...* - *Zohar* Naso 3[27]

"The World's Destroyers"

Beyond the introduction of murder, Cain, his descendants, and their sympathizers, began to destroy the world in so many *other* ways:

> *After Adam and his wife sinned, and the serpent had intercourse with Eve and injected filth into her, Eve bore Cain. He had the shape from above* ***and from below****... Therefore, he was the first to bring* ***death*** *into the world, caused by his side, as he came from the filth of the serpent. The nature of the serpent* ***is to lurk*** *so* ***as to kill****, and his issue, Cain,* ***learned his ways****.* - *Zohar* Pekudei 21[28]

We now, however, have the means for deciphering the modern *parallel* of which Jesus spoke of! We know almost the **exact** ways *Cain* and his sympathizers lived in the past - all we have to do is to see the same parallels *today*. It's not too hard; in fact, it's fairly *easy*. Once we see these, it'll help us *truly* distinguish what God wanted - and wants - for His people. And, on top of this all, we'll even discover some of these modern parallels - given to us *straight* from the Bible, itself!

Chapter 20

What Are the Modern "Ways of Cain"

What is ***right is not always popular*** *and what is popular is* ***not always right****.*
- Albert Einstein[1]

How do we identify the "ways of Cain" in our modern times; and what does this all have to do with *Mystery Babylon*? And, what *really* is that concept the Bible talks about - *Mystery Babylon* - ultimately? Well, one could figure that it involves a *mystery* - something subtly being brought to us, or even hidden from us… until *we* could be brought to a point of figuring it all out. It's a mystery until we learn how it affects our culture; our societies; even *our whole world*.

Also, it involves *Babylon*: of one of the first cities in our world - a once, massively-***corrupt*** city. It represented a living center - a *culture*, or *organized society* - established by none-other than the son of the Serpent (or devil), himself… ***Cain***!

Put them both *together*, and we have a subtle "way" of looking at our world; subtle ways of living and doing things… often riding "under the radar" of one's own understanding to what it all *really* is; and where it all *really* comes from. And, it's *not* good! It's not God-like, at all! There are societal ways of living, and certain attitudes, being pushed upon us - often *under* the surface of conscious realization - which is targeted to turn us *away* from the *true* Creator of the world. And, *this* is a huge part of the *mystery* behind what is *Mystery Babylon*!

There *does* seem to be two layers to *Mystery Babylon*, however: one representing these societal/cultural entrenchments we've already seen in this book; the second, a *deeper* layer of internal corruption - often involving *deeper*, political/religious entrenchments, as well! In this first book, the question may arise: how could we be able to fight some of these ***primary,*** surface layers of *Mystery Babylon* from infecting all of us, from saturating our cultures; from manifesting itself in our societies; and, ultimately, from the ways of life once based on a Biblical, or Godly, moral code? **That** is the theme of this first volume.

There are so many ideologies out there, so many opinions, so many thoughts and attitudes to choose… there are so many *ways* for us to think and live, today. How do we know what's really *right* and *just*; and - most importantly - how do we know the ways *God* would probably want us to live? If we utilize the examples within these ancient *parallels*, we could, now, come up with some **solid** conclusions. It's now possible - even though there are so many "smoke and mirrors" out there, today, trying to block our paths; and direct us, otherwise.

And, to top it off: why was a good deal of information in this book seemingly *suppressed*, over the years? Why haven't many of us heard of these *alternate* views of Biblical history? Why have we been "spoon-fed" the *same old thing* - continually, continually - throughout the ages? The answer is simple: ***exposure***. Those with blood of the Serpent, as well as those who choose to follow his "ways," haven't, over the years, had the desire to allow *any* bit of this information out… because they're afraid people will see something *different* than what they may have been trying to promote, all along; or even *begin* to act upon all of it.

If we think about it, most of the information in this book *doesn't* really fit into the core of who these people are, and what *they* believe in. Enter the "Ways of Cain," today! Yet, if there could be something *to* the information in this book, then we see this *same* fight going on, to this day - those of the Serpent *against* those of Adam! If this could be true - and this *same* enmity is going on - then how could we able to *conclusively* identify who are true children of the Serpent (or, those who follow him)? How about the descendants of Cain? How about those with any fallen, angelic blood? Is there a way to know just "who's who," by looking at them, *physically*?

The answer is: we **cannot**, on the surface, really tell "who's who," for sure; sorry to say. The bloodlines have become so interwoven that it's next to impossible to openly discover, in this day and age. Continued adulteration of the human gene pool has infiltrated *most* of the human race. So many probably *do* have something of the above groups *genetically*; things they might be a little better off *not* having. But, that's the way of the world. And, this, of course, might be a reason *why* so many of us have some type of genetic or emotional problem, why so many of us might act strange, or act in sinful ways… it all comes from what's *inside*.

Might we be able to have *some way* to spot those who, on the inside, are more prone to live within these corrupted "ways"… those who might push it all onto the rest of us?

First off, we have a quote of Jesus:

Beware of false prophets, which come to you in sheep's clothing, but ***inwardly they are ravening wolves****. Ye shall know* ***them by their fruits****... Even so every good tree bringeth for the good fruit; but a corrupt tree bringeth forth evil fruit... Wherefore* ***by their fruits*** *ye shall know them.* - *Mat.* 7:15-20 (KJV)

We, now, *do* have ammunition to understand what makes a deeper part of a person: their motives; their ideologies, their deeper, hidden agendas. To accomplish this goal, however, we may have to bring our fight to a truly ***theological*** front.

Those "Fruits"

As we already may know, **Amalek** is another name for the Serpent. Interestingly enough, this name *Amalek* also stands for "a loose people."[2] Now, the word *loose* can also be defined as:

- *free from a state of confinement, restraint, or obligation*
- *lacking moral constraint*
- *lacking in... exactness, or care*
- *permitting freedom of interpretation*[3]

Doesn't this sound like how the ancient Cainites lived, before the flood; and their *ideologies*? We know that the Cainites did not really have a lot of restraint - their world often became violent and chaotic, as a result. The Cainites protested any restraint to their actions on so many levels - they wanted *freedom* from anything and anyone trying to tell them way God's ways were. They, of course, interpreted things according to *their own* points of view. They were truly self-absorbed, and prideful. In the end, however, these "ways" of life would come right back to them, and haunt them. Their "fruits" would bud into something extremely *negative*, and hollow, in the end… nothing really nourishing to the soul.

Predestined to Live Without Faith?

There is much more: the Bible, as the definitive, final authority on these ancient topics, acknowledges Cain only *three* times outside the book of Genesis. So, as one might guess, they all should, most probably, have some *significance* to our whole story, here!

Our first example, in *Hebrews*, Chapter 11, discusses the topic of *faith*. Faith, by definition, is, "the substance of things hoped for, the evidence of things not seen" (Heb. 11:1). And, we already know, from his sacrifice, **Abel** had total faith; Cain did not:

> *By* ***faith*** *Abel offered unto God a more excellent sacrifice than Cain, by which he obtained witness that he was righteous…* - *Heb.* 11:4 (KJV)

Cain, and those descended from him, would, most probably, be endowed with a tendency (or predestination) to want to live without faith; or even try to. It seems that most any mixed descendents of fallen angels and women really did not come with a built-in desire to want to run to *God* with their problems. In fact, their predispositions were more towards going in *the opposite* direction: many would rather look *towards the earth*, or to things *of the world*, to gather them their hope, knowledge, and guidance!

We also recall that Cain and his sympathizers often had a deep *cynicism* towards their world; and towards most everyone and everything they encountered. They would rather attempt to do things *on their own*, or their own way, and not utilize to the "tried and true" methods shown them… *especially* if *God* or *Adam* were in the equation!

God, as we know, clearly has rules - *His rules*. He has *His own ways* to go about this world. These ways require personal *faith* in them, to ensure a proper follow through! These ways are tried and true - even though mankind might not approve of them, overall. Salvation requires the shedding of *blood*, for example - not the sacrificing of fruit (as Cain interpreted it). He didn't approve of what God required. Cain, apparently, didn't believe what God told him from the beginning; or really didn't seem to care. His focus was on *himself*, his *own thoughts*, and *own interpretations*.

So, in conclusion, we could have one identifying feature of Cain's "ways:" a desire to do things according to **man's** imperfect and often-irrational rationale. *Man* as the measure of all things; what *man* perceives is important; and man, ultimately, is in control of his own destiny. God really has no part in what goes on in our world, compared to **man**. These thoughts emanate in a lot of today's pagan, humanistic, and secular theology.

...Of the Wicked One

In our second example, we recall a verse that describes Cain as being from "that wicked one:"

> *For this is the message that ye heard from the* ***beginning****... Not as* ***Cain****, who was* ***of that wicked one****, and slew his brother. And wherefore skew he him? Because his* ***own works were evil****, and his brother's righteous.* - *I John* 3:8-12 (KJV)

Cain's works were truly **evil**, compared to his brother. Cain truly adopted the lifestyles of the wicked one. As we know, this battle has raged on, since the beginning of our era.

When we identify the past lifestyles of the descendents of Cain, plus the following "hints" of Cain's ways in the future, we will begin to see their modern parallels. In our last example, the Bible actually gives us a blueprint towards understanding this future parallel. You'll see the evidence, you be the judge.

The third and final mentioning of Cain is, probably, the *most* important; because it gets more into what would be the modern parallel of these "ways of Cain" we came across, in this work, so much - the crux of this entire book.

The Modern "Ways of Cain"

> *...denying the Lord that bought them... many shall follow their pernicious* ***ways****; by reason of whom the way of truth shall be evil spoken of. And through covetousness shall they with feigned words make merchandise of you...*
>
> \- *II Pet.* 2:1-3 (KJV)

The *Zohar*, in regards to the above, also stated that the ancient Adamites *tried* to make these defiant descendants of Cain (and other mixed multitudes) understand their ways were not exactly God-following, and repent. They soon realized they could **not** convert most of them - these people, for the most part, wouldn't listen, anyway. It just seemed as though they were proud to *separate* themselves from the rest of those "goodie-goodies." So many of them didn't seem to understand what would be this logic of God. In the end, most would not budge - ideologically and morally - and also would despise anyone who tried to get anything through to them.

The descendants of Adam, soon, realized that these groups *had* to remain this way, and gave up - as well, because they represented **the other half** of this Genesis 3:15 Prophecy. Those who followed the "*ways of Cain*" seemed destined to be at **enmity** with those who follow the ways of God, throughout eternity. If Cain (and possibly others) were indeed seeds of this Serpent, than a number of these descendants, as well as those sympathetic to his ways, would **naturally** be "up in arms" against anything ***truly*** **from God**, and **the Bible**. And, we do, today, see a lot of this *enmity* towards Judeo/Christian beliefs today - undoubtedly.

In the Bible, we also seem to have two sets of verses which describe those, in *the future*, who would follow these "ways of Cain!" These two, seemingly, relate to each other; some of the elements overlap... but the message of the twain is almost the same. Let's see!

We even notice how the first part of this chain begins... as the perfect piece of evidence:

> *Woe unto them! for they have gone in* ***the way of Cain****... These are spots in your feasts of charity, when they feast with you, feeding themselves without fear: clouds without water, carried about of winds, trees whose fruit withereth, without fruit, twice dead, plucked up by the roots; Raging waves of the sea, foaming out their own shame; wandering stars, to whom is reserved the blackness of darkness for ever... These are murmurers, complainers, walking after their own lusts; and their mouth speaketh great swelling words, having men's persons in admiration because of advantage... there should be mockers in the last time, who should walk after their own ungodly lusts. These be they who separate themselves, sensual, having not the spirit.*
> - *Jude* 1:11-19 (KJV)

> *But chiefly them that walk after the flesh in the lust of uncleanness, and despise government, Presumptuous are they, selfwilled, they are not afraid to speak evil of dignities... But these, as natural brute beasts, made to be taken and destroyed, speak evil of the things that they understand not; and shall utterly perish in their own corruption; And shall receive the reward of unrighteousness, as they that count it pleasure to riot in the day time. Spots they are and blemishes, sporting themselves with their own deceivings while they feast with you; Having eyes full of adultery, and that cannot cease from sin... Which have forsaken the right way, and are gone astray... These are wells without water, clouds that are carried with a tempest... For when they speak great swelling words of vanity, they allure through the lust of the flesh, through much wantonness, those that were clean escaped from them... in error. While they promise them liberty, they themselves are the servants of corruption: for of whom a man is overcome, of the same is he brought in bondage. For if after they have escaped the pollutions of the world through the knowledge of the Lord and Savior Jesus Christ, they are again entangled therein...* - *II Pet.* 2:1-20 (KJV)

Since the Bible is valued so highly in this book - above any other ancient work, used in here - we'll use these two blocks of verses as the *definitive interpretations* of this modern-day parallel! To sum it up: what follows are a number of *key* words from both groups; combined together, according to relevance. Along with these words, there's a lot more ancient written evidence to back it all up. We'll soon see that those who follow this modern parallel of the "ways of Cain" might often act in, or promote, the following "ways":

 # 1.
- *there should be mockers*
- *these are murmurers*
- *complainers*

 # 2.
- *selfwilled*
- *presumptuous (arrogant) are they*
- *they speak great swelling words of vanity*
- *and their mouth speaketh great swelling words, having men's persons in admiration because of advantage*

 # 3.
- *walking after their own lusts*
- *who should walk after their own ungodly lusts*
- *but chiefly them that walk after the flesh in the lust of uncleanness*

 # 4.
- *speak evil of the things that they understand not*
- *they are not afraid to speak evil of dignities*
- *and despise government*
- *they that count it pleasure to riot in the day time*

 # 5.
- *these be they who separate themselves, sensual, having not the spirit*

 # 6.
- *having eyes full of adultery, and that cannot cease from sin… Which have forsaken the right way, and are gone astray*
- *as natural brute beasts*
- *they allure through the lust of the flesh, through much wantonness (decadence)*

 # 7.
- *while they promise them (other people) liberty, they themselves are the servants of corruption*
- *these are wells without water*
- *clouds without water*
- *trees whose fruit withereth, without fruit, twice dead, plucked up by the roots*

 # 8.
- *raging (violent) waves of the sea*
- *foaming out their own shame*

 # 9.
- *these are spots in your feasts of charity*
- *spots they are and blemishes*
- *when they feast with you, feeding themselves without fear*
- *sporting themselves with their own deceivings while they feast with you*

 # 10.
- *wandering stars*
- *clouds that are carried with a tempest*
- *carried about of winds*

Let's look at each one, *individually*:

Those who follow the *Way of Cain*, today, may often act in way: # 1.

- *there should be mockers*
- *these are murmurers*
- *complainers*

In the above, we see that many of these people might not want to particularly blame *themselves* for their own failures, nor want to accept responsibility for their *own* actions. Instead, they often try to blame *other* individuals, or even their society around them! It's usually not their fault. They are also, often, *very* cynical. They continually complain and murmur. And, they might continually seek to find another reason for any *fault* with their own personal place in life, or situation; mocking most everything and everyone around them, because of it. As we see, there really is *no* honor to their actions.

And, we see this, on a grand scale, with their patriarch: *Cain.*

> *Cain said to God, "Am I [**expected to be**] my brother's keeper? (Gen. 4:9). You (God) are the keeper of all creatures, yet You call me to account for him"... Accordingly, Cain's question is in fact a defiant assertion: I slew Abel - it was **You** who created in me the impulse to evil. But You are the keeper of all things- yet **You let me slay him**. It is **You who slew him**. Had **You accepted my offering** and You did his, I would not have been jealous of him... I never in my life knew or saw anyone slain. **How was I to know** that if I struck Able with a stone, he would die? Cain went on, "Is my sin so great that it **cannot be borne**? (Gen. 4:13)... The whole world, all of it, You bear, yet my sin You cannot bear!"* (Bialik and Ravnitzky.1992, p. 23-24)[4]

> *"...Cain went out from the presence of the Lord" (Gen. 4:16)... signifies that Cain left [his consciousness of] the Lord's presence by* ***tossing off*** *the words ["My sin is greater than can be forgiven"], as if by mouthing them he could* ***blunt*** *the Almighty's awareness of his sin... Or: Cain reversed his garment front to back and went out thinking that he had deceived [literally, stolen the mind of] the Holy One.*
> (Bialik and Ravnitzky.1992, p. 24 (and notes))[5]

How unbelievably irreverent, and cocky, was Cain to the Creator of the world! He played the victim. He openly cried out: "It's not my fault - the fault is in the world around me; and, since *You* fashioned the world, here, **You**, naturally, should be the one who's at fault, here!" Interestingly enough, he even reversed his garment (in the above) from front to back - he wore his clothes *backwards*, as a sign of this rebellion to God's "status quo."[6] Doesn't this sound familiar, in ways? Do you see people thinking and doing things seemingly "backward" in our society - as some "statement" against any status quo?

Cain did the *opposite* of what God (or even some Biblically-based society) might have wanted him to do, or follow. He also thought, by his words, that he had outsmarted God.

> *...For clever sinners always have* ***excuses*** *for their sins, and it is best to turn a deaf ear to their crafty words.* (Frankel, 1989, p. 30)[7]

His prideful, self-absorbed attitudes could be summed up as a person who believes the following:

> *...your heart seeks to tell you... you have no reason to feel guilty. You live in a world where our hearts continues to tell you that you are the center of the universe. Your problems are somebody else's fault. This world owes you happiness. You are* ***basically good*** *and* ***unselfish****. You'll be happy if you get what you want. You will be happy when you follow* ***your own heart****...* ***You are under a curse****...*
> (Davis, n. d., p. 6-7)[8]

What could this curse be… the "Curse of Cain?"

Those who follow the *Way of Cain*, today, may often act in way: # 2.

- *selfwilled*
- *presumptuous (arrogant) are they*
- *they speak great swelling words of vanity*
- *and their mouth speaketh great swelling words, having men's persons in admiration because of advantage*

These people might, often, go about their lives in a number of self-centered, narcissistic, or even arrogant ways. Many dwell in the swamp of their own vanities. While pretending to be interested in righteous ways and beliefs around them, their instincts often betray their outer agenda. In the end, their work usually ends up becoming directed towards the fulfilment of some *inner*, selfish means; instead of openly engaging in positive practices, which help *other* people *just as much* as they have been; or improves their society around them.

> *The inhabitants are the companions of impiety, ungodliness, self-love, haughtiness, falsehood, vain opinions...*
> - *Works of Philo Judaeus* On the Posterity of Cain and His Exile 15(52)[9]

The way of God is truly *humility* - loving thy neighbor as thyself, *not* self-absorbed bouts of vanity, and arrogance.

> *...Cain, the* ***arrogant*** *tyrant, the* ***divider of the kingdom****, [who] walked in the counsel of the Devil, who maketh evil to flourish. And he taught them everything that God* ***hated - pride****,* ***boastfulness of speech****,* ***self-adulation****, calumniation,* ***false accusation****, and the swearing of* ***false oaths****.*
> *- Book of the Glory of Kings (Kerba Nagast)* 7[10]

Those who follow the *Way of Cain*, today, may often act in way: # 3.

- *walking after their own lusts*
- *who should walk after their own ungodly lusts*
- *but chiefly them that walk after the flesh in the lust of uncleanness*

The Book of Jeremiah seems to contain some interesting, and relevant, words of prophecy, here. We see, in the following verses, how many people *in the future* will want to follow their *own* pathways; not wanting to hear any of the Word of God.

> *Jer. 6:*
> 16 *Thus saith the LORD, Stand ye in the ways, and see, and ask for the old paths, where is the good way, and walk therein, and ye shall find rest for your souls. But they said,* ***We will not walk therein****.*
> 17 *Also I set watchmen over you, saying, Hearken to the sound of the trumpet. But they said,* ***We will not hearken****.*
>
> *"And they (the descendants of Israel) heard the voice of Hashem Elohim (God)"... (Beresheet 3:8). This alludes to the time when the children of Yisrael approached Mount Sinai to receive the Torah... While the* ***mixed multitude****... could not* ***bear*** *to* ***hear the voice*** *of Elohim (God and his angels)...* - *Zohar* Beresheet A29[11]

Many don't really care about seeking some sort of Godly enlightenment; nor desire a number of Biblical standards; but seek to go after the *dainties* of this world - just like the Serpent did. They really don't care about understanding what is truly right and wrong - they do things, as long as it all fits into their *own* moral code.

This, again, is the opposite of what God wants. He wants reflection on what we think, and how we do things - rather than thinking how it will only benefit *us*, in the end. As we recall, **Adam** was considered the "thinker:" the one who wanted to use his *conscience* as his guide:

> *(These are the)... men wise* ***in their own conceit****, the men who* ***know not wisdom as relating to truth****, the men who are full of* ***ignorance****, and* ***stupidity****, and* ***folly****; and all the other similar and kindred evils.*
> - *Works of Philo Judaeus* On the Posterity of Cain and His Exile 15(52)[12]

The people who follow these ways often *act* ignorant of what their conscience might be telling them; even though, in actuality, they really aren't. They may even believe it's "in vogue" to be *unenlightened* to fundamental moral truths. It seems that people sympathetic to Amalek and Cain often believe it's even *glamorous* to wallow around - in a worldly *bliss* of willfully thought-of ignorance.

Those who follow the *Way of Cain*, today, may often act in way: # 4.

- *speak evil of the things that they understand not*
- *they are not afraid to speak evil of dignities*
- *and despise government*
- *they that count it pleasure to riot in the day time*

Many of these people adhere to the opinions of those prominent "movers and shakers" with their society, rather than follow tried and true ways, such as the Bible (or a traditional, Bible-based governmental authority):

> *If **demoralization** does not proceed from the leaders, it is not real demoralization.*
> \- *Genesis Rabbah* 26:5[13]

These "movers and shakers" often have the power to promote *one* way of life over another; and, most often, these are ultimately *against* the ways of God. Even in ancient times, many individuals of the past felt pretty good about adopting the same ways as *their* contemporary "movers and shakers!"

> *II Pet.* 2:
> 1 *But there* **were** *false prophets also among the people, even as there shall be false teachers among you, who privily shall bring in damnable heresies, even denying the Lord that bought them and bring upon themselves swift destruction.*
> 2 *And many shall follow their pernicious ways; by reason of whom the way of truth shall be evil spoken of...*
>
> *For from the least of them even unto the greatest of them every one is given to covetousness; and from the* **prophet** *even unto the* **priest** *every one dealeth* ***falsely***.[14]
> \- *Jer.* 6:13 (KJV)

These always seemed to be, and *still* are, among the most vocal voices against any incumbent authority out there:

<u>*Jer.* 8:</u>
8 *How do ye say, We are **wise**, and the **law of the LORD** is with us? Lo, certainly in vain made he it; the pen of the scribes is in **vain**.*
9 *The wise men are ashamed, they are dismayed and taken: lo, they have **rejected** the word of the LORD; and what wisdom is in them?*

Beyond their own thoughts on things - their *own* politics and policies - many of these same influential people might also try to promote a *different* look at history in our world, and/or provide a different interpretation to what *they* think things are really *all about*:

*Neither give heed to **fables** and **endless genealogies**, which minister questions, rather than godly edifying which is in **faith**...* - *I Tim.* 1:4 (KJV)

*For the time will come when they will not endure sound doctrine; but after their own lusts shall they heap to themselves teachers, having itching ears; And they shall turn away their ears from the truth, and shall be turned unto **fables**.*
- *II Tim.* 4:3-4 (KJV)

Many of these people are very educated; often considering themselves *elite* in stature. Regardless of their status, they, often, desire the pursuit of *worldly* desires and options, because they believe that the ways of ***man***, and the ways **of the world**, are the most worth sentiments to chase after.[15]

*...the **children of this world** are in their generation **wiser** than the **children of light**.*
- *John* 16:8 (KJV)

<u>Those who follow the *Way of Cain*, today, may often act in way: # 5.</u>

- *these be they who separate themselves, sensual, having not the spirit*

Because of their self-perceptions of worthiness, many individuals will often move to ***separate*** themselves from being under the umbrella of many societal confines - especially those not stemming from some *man-centered* perception of our world. As we recall:

> *...Cain, the arrogant tyrant, the* **divider** *of the kingdom...*
> - *Book of the Glory of Kings (Kerba Nagast)* 7[16]

> *...they hold fast deceit, they refuse to return. I hearkened and heard, but they spake not aright: no man repented him of his wickedness, saying, What have I done? Every* ***one turned to his course****, as the horse rusheth into the battle.*
> - *Jer.* 8:5-6 (KJV)

We know the sympathizers of Cain and the Serpent work to *separate*, or *divide*, other people away from God; and towards the ways *of the world*.[17]

> *...know ye not that the friendship of the* **world** *is* **enmity** *with God?*
> - *James* 4:4 (KJV)

Interesting choice of words, here: *enmity*? Doesn't this sound familiar?

We recall that Ham, most probably, had angelic blood, somewhere. The Biblical character *Cush* - also considered a son of Ham, after the flood - would also have the blood of a fallen angel, assumedly. Let's look at one description of how Cush, most probably, acted, in the past - as he began to expand on his own "anti-God" life:

> *...Chus (Cush)... having a nature truly* ***dissolute****, does not at all keep fast the* ***spiritual bond of the soul****, nor of nature, nor of consistency of* ***manners****, but rather like a giant born of the earth, prefers* ***earthly*** *to heavenly things, and thus appears to verify the ancient fable of the giants and Titans; for in truth he who is an emulator of earthly and corruptible things is* ***always*** *engaged* ***in a conflict with heavenly and admirable natures****, raising up earth as a bulwark against heaven; and those things which are below are* ***adverse*** *to those* ***which are above****.*
> - *Works of Philo Judaeus* Questions and Answers on Genesis 2(82)[18]

Cush's name could even stand for "*black*" or "*night*" - a reflection of the *darkened* "ways" he began to desire, overall, here? Philo goes on, a little further:

> *...unmitigated wickedness has no participation in light, but imitates* ***night*** *and* ***darkness****.* - *Works of Philo Judaeus* Questions and Answers on Genesis 2(82)[19]

Those who follow the *Way of Cain*, today, may often act in way: # 6.

- *having eyes full of adultery, and that cannot cease from sin... Which have forsaken the right way, and are gone astray*
- *as natural brute beasts*
- *they allure through the lust of the flesh, through much wantonness (decadence)*

We know how some people, in the past, would act like *beasts* - they acted *uncivilized*; closer to the *savage* earth; etc.. These actions, ultimately, help to destroy an individual, in the end; as well as everyone else, around them. The foundations of the way things used to work - such as the family unit, a "give" and "take" society, etc. - would, slowly, begin to crumble. These people, continually, would want more and *more* for their own selves, as well as desire to consume *more* and *more* of the resources around them - *more* than they, most often, could produce to counterbalance anything. They do this until most of the resources around them begin to dry up.

Their lives, often, become taken over by the desires for *excess*:

> *...he who lives among wild beasts wishes **to live the life** of a beast, and to be equal to the brutes in the vices of wickedness.*
> - *Works of Philo Judaeus* Questions and Answers on Genesis 2(82)[20]

> *Who knoweth the spirit of **man** that goeth upward, and the spirit of the **beast** that goeth **downward to the earth**?* - *Eccl.* 3:21 (KJV)

> *The bestial (soul)... **makes the vanities** of the world, the bestial (soul)... **speaks** of the vanities of the world, and the bestial (soul)... **harbors** all kinds of **meditations and thoughts** about the vanities of the world.* - *Zohar* Tzav 20[21]

Apparently, these "bestial" habits of people, such as these, will get the better of most of them, in the end:

> *The Cainites will tell you that their worship makes them feel very **spiritual** but in their hearts they may feel that they have **lost** their will to resist.*
> ("Jubal - Genun - Musical Worship", n. d., p. 18)[22]

> *But these, as natural brute beasts... speak evil of the things that they understand not; and shall utterly perish* ***in their own corruption****.* - *II Pet.* 2:12 (KJV)

A prime example of these excessive desires would be the variety of reasons for the use of *sexual* activity, today - especially the uses of *unbridled* sex! The result of unbridled and inappropriate sex - the same acts so many of these Cainites practiced, in the past - would often result in a good deal of *unplanned pregnancies*! And, in the end, this often ends up with **overpopulation** in so many areas. In conclusion, many of them who follow these "way of Cain" tend to end-up breeding in this way - *exponentially* - because of their lack of self-control and common sense. Of course, this usually doesn't help a society out, over all:

> *...(Cain's wife) bare him children, who in their turn began to multiply by* ***degrees*** *until they filled that place... By the time (Adam's grandson) Enos was eight hundred and twenty years old, Cain had a large progeny; for they married* ***frequently****, being given to* ***animal*** *lusts; until the land below the mountain was* ***filled*** *with them.*
> - *Second Book of Adam and Eve (The Conflict of Adam and Eve with Satan)* 1:8, 12:16[23]

There's nothing wrong with breeding; but, when it happens *a lot* more than the resources of the land can bear, *then*, it becomes a problem.

In the following set of verses, for example, God assists the children of Israel to work hard, towards their quest of conquering the Holy Land. He told them to destroy most of the people living there. In some instances, however, this was to be done *a little at a time*. Why? The reason was simple: there were a vast number of people - in this case, the *Chay of the Field* - living in these areas, as well as evil individuals. So, God instructed the Israelites to go fairly *slow*, because a good number of *this* group, also, probably adopted these *pagan* elements (as most everyone around them). They might, not necessarily, have been among those who were *heavily* into these "ways" of the Serpent, because God didn't want them destroyed, outright. Instead, most would probably be kept alive, to assist Israel in the everyday working lives. God, however, was aware that they would probably be more apt to act on their own human natures; and breed a lot, because of it (because they lived within societies which continually promoted this)... and *this* was what God didn't *want* to occur. It this happened, no longer would the *Chay of the Field* be a *positive* element to these Israelis. If they became overpopulated, and overwhelmed with the burdens of raising children, this would probably take them away from doing a majority of their work, given to them:

<u>*Ex. 23:*</u>
27 *I will send my fear before thee, and will destroy all the people to whom thou shalt come, and I will make all thine enemies turn their backs unto thee.*
28 *And I will send hornets before thee, which shall drive out the Hivite, the Canaanite, and the Hittite, from before thee.*
29 *I will not drive them out from before thee* ***in one year****; lest the land become* ***desolate****, and the* **Chay** *(beast)* ***of the Field*** *multiply* ***against thee****.*
30 ***By little and little*** *I will drive them out from before thee, until thou be increased, and inherit the land.*
(in retranslation)

Again, these *Chay of the Field* were, most probably, not animals, here; because there was a fear of them multiplying too quickly! Animals, in ancient times, were considered *wealth* - the more domestic animals one had, the more production they feel they could achieve; hence, more *wealth* for all. If these were solely animals, it would be a great thing for Israel to have a number of domestic animals around them. Only *human beings* might become a problem in an area, over time, if they multiplied too quickly - spending a majority of their time trying to raise children; competing for resources, etc.. When people multiply like there's no tomorrow, then problems will arise, that's for sure: unhealthy living conditions, disease, poverty, etc… that's just the way the world works; and, interestingly, that just what's going on in so many areas of our world, ***today***!

It's obvious that God didn't want the population to explode, here. But, beyond this all, these verses also teach us something else: if people do not follow specific moral codes, and/or just sit around idly (without some work), it's so easy to start engaging in the deeds which could create more and more babies, here, on top of it! Ultimately, God did not want these extreme states of population to pop up, and become a **burden** to the Israelite cause, here… simple. In the end, these practices might easily result in a world of confusion, and utter chaos, to everyone:

And the whole city was filled with ***confusion****...*
- *Acts* 19:29 (KJV)

This same command was even echoed in a later part of the Bible, as well:

<u>*Deut.* 7:</u>
20 *Moreover the LORD thy God will send the hornet among them, until they that are left, and hide themselves from thee, be destroyed.*
21 *Thou shalt not be affrighted at them: for the LORD thy God is among you, a mighty God and terrible.*
22 *And the LORD thy God will put out those nations before thee* ***by little and little****: thou mayest not consume them at once, lest the* ***Chay*** *(beasts)* ***of the Field*** *increase upon thee.*
(in retranslation)

Again, the more cattle and beasts Israel had, the more **wealth** they could obtain from their working the fields. Cattle and beasts of the field, usually, were not a burden to these ancient people - only *people*, holding onto these excessive worldly practices, could become this way, in these instances.

<u>Those who follow the *Way of Cain*, today, may often act in way: # 7.</u>

- *while they promise them (other people) liberty, they themselves are the servants of corruption*
- *these are wells without water*
- *clouds without water*
- *trees whose fruit withereth, without fruit, twice dead, plucked up by the roots*

The people who follow the "ways of Cain" often may become *at odds* with their own ways of thinking. They think one thing, while their *conscience* says another - often spawning their thoughts into a pool of indifference. Many continually compare their own, self-centered rationales to what they might, deep down inside, understand as truly *right*:

...And he (Cain) had children, and his descendants who live here to this day and ***have two heads****.* (Baring-Gould, 1881, p. 73)[24]

They have two heads, wherefore they can never arrive at a decision; they are always at ***loggerheads with themselves****. It may happen that they are* ***pious*** *now, only to be inclined to do* ***evil*** *the next moment.* (Ginzberg, 1909, p. 114)[25]

As a result, many might begin to feel a lot of fear and insecurity (even though they may not, openly, admit to it). Their mind, and their actions, becomes volatile and/or unpredictable. They may begin to act in somewhat of a *nervous* manner, or act in seemingly unstable ways, overall - much the same as their forefather, Cain:

Now ***Cain*** *was unable to stand still in one place and to hold his* ***peace****.*
- *Cave of Treasures* The Rule of Anosh[26]

...Cain, ever since God had cast him off, and had cursed him with trembling and terror, could neither settle nor find rest in any one place; but wandered from place to place.
- *Second Book of Adam and Eve (The Conflict of Adam and Eve with Satan)* 13:5[27]

In the end, their *actions* will speak louder than their words. Those unpredictable thoughts often begin to turn a person into their *own* worst enemy.

Those who follow the *Way of Cain*, today, may often act in way: # 8.

- *raging (violent) waves of the sea*
- *foaming out their own shame*

And, with attempts to hide any insecurity, fear, or even guilt they might have begun to accumulate, many of these same individuals could, easily, get *emotional*, as a result - and then *act* on these passions.

He (Cain) sinned in order to secure his own pleasure, though his ***neighbors suffered injury*** *nearby. He augmented his household substance by rapine and violence; he excited his acquaintances to procure pleasures and spoils by robbery, and he became a great leader of men into wicked courses.* (Ginzberg, 1909, p. 116)[28]

As we recall, Cain seemed to, easily, get *angry*; especially when confronting Abel about his sacrifice (before killing him in cold blood, of course):

*Reveal not the secret that thou knowest to Cain... for he is a **son of wrath**.*
- *Apocalypse of Moses / Apocalypsis Mosis* 3:2[29]

Those negative ways of *arrogance*, *cockiness*, and even all-out *aggressiveness*, often might accompany those individuals caught up in following Cain's example, here:

*Wherein in time past ye walked according to the course **of this world**, according to the prince and the power of the air, the spirit that **now** worketh **in the children** of disobedience: Among whom also we all had our conversation in times past in the lusts of our flesh, fulfilling the desires of the flesh and of the mind; and were **by nature** the **children of wrath**, even as others.* - *Eph.* 2:2-3 (KJV)

Violence and **destruction** may begin to spread throughout the lands that these people occupy. Their outward aggressions, again, are, so-often, the result of what may be going on with these people - *on the inside*:

*But his **punishment**, so far from proving of advantage to him, proved only a **stimulus to his violence and passion**; and he increased his wealth by rapine, and he encouraged his children and friends to live by robbery and in luxury.*
(Baring-Gould, 1881, p. 75)[30]

In the end, desolation and chaos begin to take hold:

*...as the deep cannot be sown to yield fruit, so the deeds of the wicked do not produce **fruit**, for if they produced fruit they would **destroy the world**.*
- *Genesis Rabbah* 33:1[31]

*That defiled side... (will) harm people and are called **the world's destroyers** that **originate in Cain**...* - *Zohar* Naso 3[32]

<u>Those who follow the *Way of Cain*, today, may often act in way: # 9.</u>

- *these are spots in your feasts of charity*
- *spots they are and blemishes*
- *when they feast with you, feeding themselves without fear*
- *sporting themselves with their own deceivings while they feast with you*

> *It was their care-free life that gave them space and leisure for their* ***infamies****... "God is patient with all sins save (except)* ***an immoral life****."* (Ginzberg, 1909, p. 153)[33]

Many of those who get into a number of life-predicaments (most often, initiated by their *own* destructive thoughts or actions) may, often, begin to look for some assistance *outside* of their own selves, or their own world (either seeking help from family or friends, or from some governmental channel). They might even begin to feel as though that they're ***entitled*** to get some help, here - just because of their humanity (but, in reality, it's because of their *prideful* thoughts, overall)!

In the end, however, their constant reliance on a **dependency** status really doesn't help out their situation, overall - because they never really seem to have a change of heart. To them, it's, often, easier for them to do the *wrong* things; and then use other people as a *crutch* - to get them right back to where they *once* were. *Then*, they do it all over again - nothing seems to change… their own, self-destructive ways don't change.

And, as a result of their, possibly, being *overwhelmed* with the number of sequential negative results (coming from this self-destructive pattern), these same people may end up heading down the pathway of *lethargy* or *sloth* - rather than trying to participate in satisfying, tenacious work. It just doesn't become "worth it," anymore... because they feel they will get into the "same old situation," every time. What they fail to do, for the most part, is to address the possibility that their "Ways of Cain" might, indeed, *be erroneous*. Their pride stops them from looking at that.

As the old saying goes, "idle hands are the *devil's* hands." Socialist ideals begin to creep into the scene, now - looking inviting to these individuals… because they think these ways might allow them to *benefit*, in some way. It's easier for them *not* to make attempts to be self-reliant, or work towards changing themselves for the better, if they feel things aren't going to work *in the end*, anyhow. So, it's easier to complain about their situation, and feel entitled to something. It's a lot easier.

But, in the end, their lack of *effort*, here, further helps to bring their spirits *down*; and allows them to feel even *more* lethargic or miserable. Soon, they may begin to lack most of their desire to do any positive thing with their lives - they become *stuck* in a cycle of cynicism, envy, complaining, entitlement, dissatisfaction… and, continual failure. Yet, this is **not** how God wanted human beings to exist, in our world. He wants us to be strong, self-sufficient, and as positive about life might be able to offer - being the best that we can be.

Continual cynicism, envy, and thoughts of entitlement are really *not* a part of God's divine plan for us… they manifested themselves with those who prefer to take on a *worldly* view of things, here. Even *heaven* was said to have a hierarchy - with each angel having their own, independent rank and role:

> *Heaven is hardly what might be considered a haven for* ***socialists****, or those who believe in the equality* ***of all angels****.*
>
> (Godwin, 1990, p. 113)[34]

Those who end up thinking as *Cain* would, here, are not going to really end up content with their world around them, for the most part - in fact, the *opposite* is more likely to be in store! Those who wallow in these cylindrical patterns of negativity will, usually, experience a great deal of unhappiness, and ***misery***. They won't be able to fill the number of *voids* continually opening up *inside of them*:

> *...the* ***sorrow*** *of the world worketh* ***death****.*
>
> - *II Cor.* 7:10 (KJV)

<u>Those who follow the *Way of Cain*, today, may often act in way: # 10.</u>

- *wandering stars*
- *clouds that are carried with a tempest*
- *carried about of winds*

> *Their inward thought is, that their houses shall continue for ever... (but) The flood will sweep them away in their houses, which will thus* ***become their graves****.*
> \- *Genesis Rabbah* 23:1 (and notes)[35]

Even when they may - temporarily - improve their lot in life in some way, these people usually will end up in their original position (at least, in their *mind*)… discontented, **miserable** in some way, etc.. It's because they wholly abandoned God; and would rather go about their lives *their own way* (living within the boundaries of an *imperfect* world)![36]

> *He pronounced an additional curse on* ***Cain and his posterity****, and declared that the ground should not henceforth yield to him its strength, though cultivated with the utmost labor and ingenuity.* (Oliver, 1843, p. 44)[37]

> *The midwife replied to him (Cain) and told him, "God is just that he did not at all leave you in my hands. For, you are Cain, the perverse one, killer of the good, for you are the one* ***who plucks up*** *the* ***fruit****-bearing tree, and* ***not him*** *who plants it. You are the* ***bearer of bitterness*** *and not of sweetness."* - *Book of Adam* 21.3b[38]

Many who adhere to the "ways of Cain" often want the "quick and easy" pathways towards personal fulfillment, rather than work towards any of those "tried and true" ways (which might prove a little more pressing or more difficult to pursue). As the old saying goes, "it's always easier to **destroy**, *than to create*." These false, Cainite ways, ultimately, prove *destructive* to the individual, and the world around them, over time.

> <u>*Jer.* 12:</u>
> 10 *Many pastors (or, those of the field) have* ***destroyed*** *my vineyard, they have* ***trodden my portion under foot, they*** *have made my* ***pleasant portion*** *a* ***desolate*** *wilderness.*
> 11 *They have made it desolate, and being desolate it mourneth unto me; the whole land is made desolate,* ***because no man layeth it to heart****.*

As we see, the reason why certain ways of life may become so *destructive* to a society is because the people causing the problems really don't *layeth it to heart* - they *don't really care* about what any their actions do to others (as long as their *own* needs are being fulfilled, in some way, of course). Because of these results, the areas of which many live no longer stays a *harmonious order*, *system*, or *arrangement* - it all, eventually, heads towards the *opposite* extreme.

> *And **void** refers to **Cain**, who desired to turn the world back to formlessness and emptiness... (Chaos being the inevitable result of lawlessness).*
>
> - *Genesis Rabbah* 2:3 (and notes)[39]

A Hopeless World, Full of Chaos...

> *...for in all evils there are some things which are perceived immediately, and some which are felt at **a later period**...*
>
> - *Works of Philo Judaeus* Questions and Answers on Genesis 1(72)[40]

As a result of this continual negativity, entire societies begin to depreciate... *as a whole*.

> *...he (Enosh, the son of Seth) set up two pillars against the sons of Cain, these are **hope** and **good** works, which they **did not have**.*
>
> - *Armenian Apocrypha Relating to Adam and Eve* History of the Forefathers 40[41]

> *...for there was no other cause for the corruption of mankind, except that, being **slaves to pleasure** and to **desire**, they did everything, and were anxious about everything for that reason only; moreover they passed a life of extreme **misery**.*
>
> - *Works of Philo Judaeus* Questions and Answers on Genesis 2(8)[42]

As we might also see, there's a reason for rules and laws, here - to keep people on "the straight and narrow!" If not, people might easily be able to fall *down*, in some way. It's a fact of this cursed, post-Fall world! God has laws He wants adherence to - in order to *stop* any negativity from rearing its ugly head; actually working to *protect* an individual, in the end! There's a rhyme to all of God's reasons.

Those Tell-Tale Signs of Their Identification?

> *The shew of their countenance doth witness* ***against them****; and they declare their sin as Sodom, they hide [it] not. Woe unto their soul! for they have* ***rewarded evil*** *unto themselves.*
> - *Isa.* 3:9 (KJV)

Now, could there be *other*, tell-tale signs of identifying individuals who might desire these "ways of Cain," beyond just looking at their resulting "*fruits*," overall? As we recall:

> *And I will put* ***enmity*** *between thee and the woman, and between* ***thy seed*** *and* ***<u>her</u> seed****; it shall bruise thy head, and thou shalt bruise his heel...*
> - *Gen.* 3:15 (KJV)

For one, there are many, *many* people in this world who believe the **Bible** is true - the *absolute* word of God. And, as we see in the above, there would be those who would also be at ***enmity*** - or *hostility*, *hate*, or *antagonism* - with these words of the Bible, as well as those who *might* promote it! And, this has been going on, since the beginning of our time. There will clearly be individuals who just won't accept any of these Judeo-Christian values as "tolerable;" or desire to "celebrate" what Christianity might have to offer them, in most *any* way. For some reason, almost *anything* of God just seems to rub them the "wrong way." Interestingly enough, the fallen, terrestrial angels of old *also* felt in exactly the same ways…

The Ability to Blush

Because of this *enmity*, many ancient Adamites, assuredly, would have become targets for these "forces of separation" in the past, here - probably because they were visually associated with the viceroy of the Garden - *Adam*. Although Adam was, apparently, also white-skinned, and was considered "ruddy" (i.e. had the ability to blush), the question now arises: do these elements of one's outward appearance *automatically* make them all

signs of an individual who ***doesn't*** want to have a desire to follow these "way of Cain?" Of course not!

No matter what a person looks like, we cannot tell, for sure, if they would eventually want to eventually be a God-follower, or not. There are absolutely a great number of *white*-skinned individuals who don't follow God; and don't want to. And, since this is absolutely true, this may lead us to ask another question: *why*, then, would Adam (and the Adamites) be endowed with these particular *outward* features, if they weren't meant to be a symbol of something? Well, maybe these outward features *were* put into place for *some* reason… it's just *not* the sign of one being *better* than others; or being superior. Let's see.

The ancient historian *Philo* seemed to summarize this all up:

> *...the man* ***(Adam)*** *who was created (in Paradise) was endowed with senses, therefore he naturally and properly proceeded into a* ***sensible*** *place...*
> - *Works of Philo Judaeus* Questions and Answers on Genesis 1(8)[43]

> *Why is it said that God breathed into his face the breath of life?... the sense is the fountain of the animal form, and* ***sense*** *resides* ***in the face****... man is created to be a partaker not only of a soul but also of a* ***rational*** *soul; and the head is the temple of the* ***reason****...* - *Works of Philo Judaeus* Questions and Answers on Genesis 1(5)[44]

In other words, Adam's features seem to have been more related to how God wants someone to *think* about things, overall. We already recall that Adam was known as *the thinker* - so named because he was instructed, by God, to have a serene, sensible, and rational way of looking at his world! He was supposed to be *humble*, almost to a fault, here! **These** are the qualities most probably associated with Adam's *outward* features, here:

> *...but he who sins, and who thus* ***blushes*** *and is* ***overwhelmed with shame****, is* ***near akin to him (God)****... for those persons who* ***pride themselves on their errors*** *as if they had not done wrong, are afflicted with a disease which is difficult to cure, or rather which is altogether incurable.*
> - *Works of Philo Judaeus* Questions and Answers on Genesis 1(65)[45]

Adam's skin color didn't really matter, here; it was his *style of thought* (as it always ends up **seeming to be**)! Adam *blushed* when guilty of a sin. He **showed** it *outwardly* (as well as *feeling* it, on the inside). From this thought, one might easily be able to conclude that those who desire these "ways of Cain" really **wouldn't** want to act in these serene, sensible, and rational ways, overall! As a result, many might *not desire to* (or even *could not be able to*) **blush**, because of it:

> *Were they ashamed when they had committed abomination? nay, they were* ***not at all ashamed****, neither could they* ***blush****: therefore they shall fall among them that fall...*
> - *Jer.* 6:15 (KJV)[46]

Apparently, these who follow Cain's "ways," often, do not show any outward ***shame*** when committing sins, or abominations. Their pride *dictates* this to be so. No matter what it takes, they, usually, find a way to talk themselves out of any feeling they may be doing something wrong.

The ability to **blush**, as one professor put it, "is not the result of climatic influence; it is due solely to the pigment (change of the skin)." We see, here: blushing is not *only* the result of some automated change in human blood pressure, in circulation, or some other normal bodily function - it's the result of one's *way of thinking*. Could it have been an outward show - an *ingrained trait* of Adam - that assures he *outwardly* shows his shame, embarrassment, and guilt? The lesson learned, here: we, like Adam, should possess enough human dignity to *openly* admit our faults, and want to. We should admit when we're wrong - and *let it show*, in some way - instead of trying to find ways to conceal it, to cover it up, or to rationalize it all away (as the typical *Cainite*-sympathizer might)!

The Bible is not saying that Adam, or any Caucasian Adamite, never commits an abomination; nor are they *better* than anyone else. This particular trait was to be an outward *example* of how we all should act - showing to others we're "big enough" to *outwardly* admit our faults, mistakes, or liabilities. We also need to be *humbly* attempting to work things out, with whomever or whatever may have been affected by any of our negative thoughts or actions.

Their Lack of Peace

Beyond the lack of a number of serene, sensible, or rational thoughts, we *do* seem to have another way to *outwardly* identify those who may desire to follow these "ways of Cain." We recall the famous verse:

*[There is] no **peace**, saith the LORD, unto the wicked.*
- *Isa.* 48:22 (KJV)

For those who desire the "ways of Cain," one thing that, often, seems to permeate their lives (and, often becomes *difficult* for many of them to escape) is that their ability to have peace - *true* **peace** - often would escape them.

*The **spoilers** are come upon all high places through the wilderness: for the sword of the LORD shall devour from the one end of the land even to the other end of the land: no flesh **shall have peace**.* - *Jer.* 12:12 (KJV)

*But the **wicked** are like **the troubled sea**, when it cannot **rest**, whose waters cast up mire and dirt.* - *Isa.* 57:20 (KJV)

It's because the "ways of Cain" often help to bring about more *negative* results, overall (such as the above)! It's simple. People, often, might claim they *want* peace; but, so often, it seems to be just beyond the reach of their needy clutches!

Yet, many still continue to *outwardly* proclaim this desire - to no avail:

*They have healed also the hurt of the daughter of my people slightly, saying, **Peace, peace**; when **there is no peace**.* - *Jer.* 6:14 (KJV)

The above is so alarming - especially *today*. Apparently, many of these "movers and shakers" (those who follow the "ways of Cain") will go around proclaiming "peace, peace"... when, in fact, the situations they often might originate from, and the lifestyles they often might promote, don't really end up to be **peaceable** at all! Ultimately, things end up going in quite the *opposite* extremes.

Outwardly promoting peace, their *inner* "ways" of Cainite thought are those which continually end up betraying them, on a daily basis![47]

Heading Towards "Perdition"

We assume that most who want to follow Cainite "ways" probably do not care too much about the Bible; or want any Biblically-based laws to preside over them. In fact, all they seem to want is "freedom"... freedom to do whatever "strikes their fancy." And, since we *all* are irrational, unpredictable, and otherwise sin-filled humans, we need to have **laws** presiding over us; at least *some*. We cannot just have total freedom - without any restraint... because this, quite easily, could lead one to a world of *chaos*:

> *Samael's fathering of Cain is intended to explain the origin of evil. In the early generations the evil Cainites and the pious Sethites formed separate branches of the human family. When however the daughters of Cain succeeded in seducing the sons of Seth,* ***both good and evil*** *became parts of man's heritage. The two strains were considered to be* ***continually fighting for supremacy*** *in every* ***human heart****: only* ***knowledge of and obedience to the law could keep Cain's blood in check****.*
> (Graves and Patai, 1964, p. 88)[48]

When we are seeing some of the *same* patterns today, as practiced in the days of Cain, it gives us strong clues to what they're all *really* about, and where they all *really* come from:

> *All things return to the element,* ***from where they came****. Unless* ***Cain*** *came from that side of the serpent, he would have not behaved so towards his brother.*
> \- *Zohar* Pekudei 21[49]

> *Like a dog that* ***returns to its vomit*** *is a fool who repeats his folly.*
> \- *Prov.* 26:11 (KJV)

Cain obviously came from *the Serpent* - on, oh, *so many* levels! The protégé's of these "ways" of Cain, and the Serpent (his father), were, in actuality, mentioned in a couple of areas of the Bible: it refers to the two as "*Perdition*" (i.e. **the Serpent**) and the "*Son of Perdition*" (i.e. **Cain**). Why? It's quite simple: we see that the Bible makes it clear that *the two* are actually the ones who easily could lead us *down*, towards the states of perdition (i.e. **worthlessness**), by following their "ways"... no doubt about it!

There is an old Biblical saying: "be in the world, but not ***of*** the world." What this means is simple: most of us know that we have to live close to other people around us. It's unavoidable, at times. But, that's okay. We shouldn't just run away from any encounters with people who don't love God. What we *should* do is to bear witness to our faith - showing everyone around us the proper ways to act - by *living* the example. *We* are put on the earth to know, to understand, and to outwardly show other people what the ways of God *really* are! After all, it was Christ who said:

> *For in the days* ***before the flood****, people were eating and drinking, marrying and giving in marriage, up to the day Noah entered the ark.* ***And they knew nothing about*** *what would happen until the flood came and took them away.*
>
> \- *Mat.* 24:37 (KJV)

Most, today, have fallen into states of domestic "bliss," blindly losing themselves beneath the thresholds of Cain's "ways." As we begin to notice his "ways," all around us, **today**, we also need to understand what God wants us to do - to keep our own "backyards" clean! We cannot change the *free will* of others, nor force anyone to see God's "light," here - all we can do is to just live the example. The rest of the world's judgment is in God's hands:

> *Thou shalt not* ***avenge****, nor bear any* ***grudge*** *against the children of thy people, but thou shalt* ***love thy neighbour*** *as thyself: I am the LORD.* - *Lev.* 19:18 (KJV)

> *Thus saith the LORD against all mine evil neighbours, that touch the inheritance which I have caused my people Israel to inherit; Behold, I will pluck them out of their land... And it shall come to pass, after that I have plucked them out I will return, and have* ***compassion*** *on them, and will bring them again, every* ***man to his heritage****, and every man to his* ***land****.* - *Jer.* 12:14-15 (KJV)

Abel, As the "Key"

One thing to, perhaps, dwell upon (in regards to this book's theme) is what the **thoughts** and **behaviors** - those condemned in the "days of Noah" - *really* are, and where they *really* come from! The story of Cain's sacrifice provides us a premier example of what this is all about. As we recall, it was ***Abel*** who, most probably, had blood of *the Serpent*; in fact, he was thought to be the ***direct*** *descendant* of this evil Serpent (as well as with Cain, here)… you can't get much closer to the source than that! Yet, Abel had a *good* mindset, however - he followed the ways of God. But, Cain, however, did *not*. Why? How could there be such a difference, here? Obviously, it wasn't Cain's *genetic* composition, it wasn't his blood line, nor was it anything he *couldn't* change, which helped **spell out his destiny**, here… it was *him*! It's a perfect life-lesson: our lives really have nothing to do with where we come from, or what we are - even if we came from the *Serpent*, himself… it's what we *make* out of what we have!

Most Christians, all over the world, accept the fact that *Jesus* is the *major* player - and *major* focus - of the New Testament. He is the son of God; the Way, the Truth, and the Life… no doubt about all of it! *He* was the fulfilment of the Genesis 3:15 Prophecy. Yet, interestingly enough, it seems that there may be *another* important player to the Bible, here. And, that person was *Abel*! *Really*… Abel? Yes. And, let's see why.

Many of us know that Jesus was sent to earth to ***rectify*** the problem of the Garden - to "right" the wrong Adam and Eve helped bring to the world. The story of the Fall was huge, for this reason. Yet, it seems that (in certain ways) Jesus might have come to earth to "right the wrong" of *another*, substantial outrage to God's program for mankind - a much *less-known* situation. This story could be *almost* as important as the Fall - but, for different reasons. This other situation was, none other than what happened between *Cain and Abel*! Let's see how.

Interestingly enough, Jesus was known as the "last Adam" - most probably because he rectified the sin of the Garden of Eden! Makes sense, in this case. But, he also seemed to have things in common with the shepherd *Abel*, as well. He even brought up Abel in Scripture! So, what's there about this story of Cain and Abel that may *need* rectifying, or reconciling, here? How does Abel need to be *redeemed*, in any way… if he even does?

The event of Abel's murder was an outrage to God, in a whole number of ways. Although we know that the Fall was the major atrocity which started it all, *Abel's* murder really seemed to be *another*, world-shaking event. The entire earth was cursed in *both* instances! God cursed the planet after the Fall, in order to give Adam a little "competition," if you will. Thorns and thistles began to spring up at this time; competing with Adam's plants, and causing Adam's effort to grow crops a little more *trying*. Adam also had to *sweat* a lot more, while working the fields - something he never had to do, before.

God cursed the earth, *once again*, after Abel's murder. This time, God made the earth lose most of its "strength" - as far as the planet's ability to bring forth fruit (in other words, it lost most of its ability to allow human beings to grow something as big and healthy as they *once* did). Now, a number of things would "just happen," in the world, to help *stifle* the ability of plants to grow efficiently - a good number of planetary areas became infertile, even *sterile* (due to planetary conditions or changes soon on the horizon); the **weather**, also, would help impede plant growth (in a whole number of ways); and, most importantly, the ability of ***an individual*** to easily grow something will not seem to "work out," as well! Fruits and vegetables wouldn't get anywhere *near* as big as they once did, or, be as robust and healthy as they once were. The *entire* earth, it seemed, would be against any individual trying to grow anything *beneficial* to them; or, for their *own* good. Call it "karma;" call it "cosmic irony;" whatever. It just "wouldn't do it," anymore!

Interestingly enough, the curse of the *Fall* seemed to, in ways, relate to our everyday, natural world: *sin* and *death* entered the physical planet; all sorts of depravity descended upon the earth. The atrocity of *Abel's* murder, however, could have been thought of as more of a *spiritual* atrocity (in some ways): our world never had any *human* blood spilled upon it… at least, not until this time. Now, after Cain killed his brother, *human* blood was spilled all *over the ground*. This was something which abhorred God, a great deal, obviously - and became an outrage to His planet, at large.

Human blood is a *very* important commodity; at least, in the spiritual realm. The spilling of blood represents one's own *soul* being released, slowly, from their body - resulting in one's *premature* death. In the case of Abel, it represented the beginning of his untimely death - *not* because he did anything wrong… but, because he chose to *follow* God! It's a huge thing. Abel didn't commit an abomination against God, here - he only told Cain that what he did wrong *was* wrong!

It's true, sometimes, that God would call on people to be killed; but there is a *huge* difference between a person who, honestly, is against God, or hates Him, and those who were actually forced to die *on account of* Him. Cain, assuredly, was supposed to "love thy neighbor" - not to *kill* him. All of this was what made it a *major* event, and major *atrocity*.

Jesus even seemed to have knowledge of the importance of this event; and spoke out about it:

Mat. 23:
29 *Woe unto you,* ***scribes and Pharisees****, hypocrites…* ***ye are the children of them which killed the prophets****.*
32 *Fill ye up then the measure of* ***your fathers****.*
33 *Ye* ***serpents****, ye generation of vipers…*
35 *That upon you may come all the righteous blood shed upon the earth, from the blood of righteous* ***Abel*** *unto the blood of Zacharias son of Barachias…*

Luke 11:
50 *That the blood of all the prophets, which was shed from the foundation of the world, may be* ***required of this generation****;*
52 *Woe unto you… for ye have* ***taken away the key of knowledge****: ye entered not in yourselves, and* ***them that were entering in ye hindered****.*

In the above, Jesus *called out* these scribes and Pharisees for what they *were*. He called them out; and made it known to them - these descendants of *Cain* - that *their ancestors* were the ones who had begun all of this killing! It started, *first*, with the murder of the righteous one… ***Abel***! He also said the ***remedy*** to all the sacrilege, here, was upon them. All of their control and manipulation over the religious world was about to come to a head… *in their generation*! Yes, what that means is simple: Jesus was now *there*; and *his* sacrifice would be the tool of redemption, here - redeeming the world of *all* the corruption and depravity they helped to bring about! The solution to the situation in the Garden of Eden *and* with the spilling of Abel's blood was at standing there - right in front of their eyes.

We, now, see the importance of *Abel*, and the *ways of God* of which he followed. This all *does* seem to matter, at least *in the Bible*. There are ways of life that just seem to *work*; and there are those that clearly don't, over time. That's why they call certain pathways "beaten." And, there are things the Bible says we just shouldn't do - *regardless* if many around us might claim it's against some *human* rationale, or it doesn't really make sense to them (or that it even might sound somewhat *insensitive*). There's a reason for *all* of what God commands… everything. Beyond our flawed, human rationales, there *has* to be a higher reason for all of it. God, assuredly, knows the answers (even when we don't).

We don't have to be "politically incorrect" *all the time* - obviously, because most of us know, already, where so many of those "politically correct" thoughts *really* come from: a ***man-centered*** world. And, Cain was among the **first** who really valued what a *man* thinks - the "ways" *he* thought were correct - over what his Creator, God, had tried to give him.

Now, we see how there could have been more than *one* reason why Jesus came to earth, and brought with him *a new covenant* for believers.

> *And to **Jesus** the mediator of the **new covenant**, and to the blood of sprinkling, that speaketh better things than that of **Abel**.* - *Heb.* 12:24

How about if we begin to take into account the *moral* example of Abel, and his role in the whole scheme of things, here? Let's, first, go back in time. As we've already seen (in Chapter 10, *Raising Cain - Founder of an Ancient Religion and Empire*), Abel was, most probably, equated to the pagan god *Tammuz* (as inspired by Cain, of course)! Yet, if we look deeper into the story behind this Tammuz, we'll soon discover how Cain (for the most part) twisted the entire murder of Abel around, and used these twists to help form the foundations of what would be the Serpent's new pagan religion.

Let's see how it was all done.

Tammuz, interestingly enough, has long been a deity to be *wept after*. This custom was even in the Bible (in Ezek. 8:14). Why, then, would a pagan god need to be mourned in a repetitive way, such as this? The reason, as we'll discover, comes, not only from the Bible, but other ancient written accounts from the land of Babylonia. Abel (a.k.a.

Tammuz) died; and his mother, Eve, cried incessantly. Assuredly, she would have done most anything she could to get her son back. Cain noticed all of this, and even used some of this as the basis for his up-and-coming religion.

Cain, in true serpentine form, tried to manipulate all of what happened into something which made him, and what he did, look almost *wholesome* - even, to be a necessity! Most anyone would assume that this murder of Abel was an atrocity to God; and, also, it was something that Cain, in no way, could undo. Abel's lifeless body was, now, just lying there, waiting for someone to come by, and see what happened. Cain had a huge dilemma. He was even desperate… he never understood what happened to a human body, after death. He, now, needed to know what to do next, with this corpse! Assuredly, his goal was to find a way to "bury the evidence," here, somehow. But, how?

He eventually received insight (not from God, of course) on how to bury his brother, inside the earth. Yet, there was more to it all: this *unnatural* death, as we'll soon see, would become the first major event in the post-Fall world - something of grave consequence to our planet, ever since.

In an esoteric way, the planet could be thought of as a "living entity," of sorts. A number of ancient religious accounts state this, as well. If one thinks of that "Mother Gaia" concept, of modern paganism, we'll discover that this is quite similar, in concept, in a number of ways. In Christian literature, we find accounts claiming that our earth (in that same spiritual, or esoteric, way) *did not* want to assist Cain in this disposal of the body. He didn't want to allow Abel to be buried… period! And, to make a long story short, Sammael/Satan was the one who actually "whispered in Cain's ear," here, assuring him of the way to bury Abel's corpse… and be done with it. Of course, the earth, in a sense, would be looked upon as "giving in" - allowing Abel to be buried; and being a part of it all. Where we are going, here, with this is: we already *know* how Sammael/Satan is considered the "god of this world" - one who took over the spiritual reins of the planet, as result of the Fall. And, because of the Fall, he, quite often, has the power and ability to infiltrate, or manipulate, a lot of what actually goes on, down here… in a number of ways:

> *...the **god of this world** hath blinded the minds of them which believe not, lest the light of the glorious gospel of Christ, who is the image of God, should shine unto them.*
> - *II Cor.* 4:4 (KJV)

...this includes the physical planet, itself. The earth really seemed at the point of heading one way, or another. And, Satan would be more than willing to help out Cain, by making a recruit of his possession, here - the *earth*:

> *...(the earth) desiring to shield its master Cain, the ground opened its mouth and swallowed every drop of Abel blood within its reach...*
> (Eichhorn, 1957, p. 68)[50]

This dirty deed of Cain seemed to have a few collaborators, in total. The ground did eventually "give in," and Abel was concealed, in the ground. God, however, would not be fooled that easily. He saw all of what actually went down, here. And, then, He called things out for what they were, and rebuked the *ground*, here... because it allowed Abel's burial to continue. And, now, because of what happened, the world seemed to be *further* cursed, overall... because Cain was able to use it, in this way, for his own benefit.[51] Because Cain seemed to put more faith in material, *worldly* things of the world - right from the start - Sammael/Satan, most probably, assured that it all ended up to be some kind of "quick pro quo."

Now, to find a way to explain the entire story, Cain (with the Serpent's help) began to find ways to turn the bad into sounding "good," and the sin into something it was *not*. First, the ground, according to Cain, was rebuked, cursed, or utterly "malnourished" (in an esoteric way) by Abel's death... which, actually, it was, by God (as we know). And, because of this, the entire *world* needed be nourished again, or "brought back to life," via another sacrifice, or some new manner of bloodshed. Yes, this began the pagan practices of sacrifice and bloodshed... a "copy cat" version of what God had originally dictated for those who follow His ways. Not only would these pagan sacrifices help "heal" any of the blighted conditions of our world, they might, also, be able to appease the pagan spirits, or "gods," who might, also, roam the planet (the ones bringing on these changes in the world)! Of course, these routine acts of sacrifice would, ultimately, be directed in the direction of that *god of this world*, as well as founders of this pagan religion.

So, what comes out of this all, now, is: that once-horrible, violent act of murder was the symbol of *a new beginning*. This sacrifice, now, was turned into a "necessary evil." It seems that Abel, now, *had* to have been martyred, here, in order to enact this whole "copycat" system into action.[52] Cain and the Serpent successfully hijacked the entire means of *sacrifice*, and *bloodshed*, to God; and redirected the petitioners to direct their sacrifices, now, in *other directions*. The reality of Cain (and his kind) would, now, be to generate *material* wealth, enlightenment, etc. - all of which *the world* might be able to offer them; all the fulfillments and enlightenments the *world* might be able to give one. Again, this all seems to be a part of that great "quick pro quo."

And, to top it off - to help bring new converts into the belief - it became fairly easy for Cain to inject a *goddess* into his new religion, as well. Apparently, God didn't really have any stars of the faith of the *female* sex… at least, not yet. He had Adam; He had (the now deceased) Abel. Eve, at best, fornicated with Adam, and was punished a little bit more severely than Adam was, for her actions. And, that's about all we have, in regards to Eve, and women. That doesn't mean God felt less love for Eve, or women, in general… it's just how it all transpired, here. Cain, however, inserted a *goddess* into it all… as a way to gather even *more* sympathizers and converts.

Well, how did this addition all come about? As we recall, Eve was crying hysterically, after she learned what had happened to her son. The time was nigh for Cain to gather sympathy of this situation, and twist it all around. Abel's dead soul, according to him, went back into the *underworld* (i.e. the Darkness). And, Eve's crying and pleading actually may have helped things out for Abel - quite a bit. Now, up-and-coming mandates of the pagan religion also required one to prove their *intent*. Routinely weeping over a dead pagan god, here, was a good start. Trying to appease the *worldly* "gods" - for the sake of bringing back anything (or anyone) up, from the underworld - was a good start.

With proper appeasement, then, Abel's soul could have been granted *leave* from this underworld, and become something more. In other words, not only could the world - with proper appeasement - again, become a prosperous and fertile planet (evidenced in the waning of winter, and the "rebirth" of spring, everywhere), people, also, could be "regenerated," in similar fashion! Now - by following the pagan religion - a human being could, eventually, keep being "reborn," again and again (*spiritually*). This was the beginning of the concept of *reincarnation* - one being able to, continually, rise *upward*, in spiritual rank, until they reach the status of deity (the same way *Abel* was, supposedly, able to reach).

If we think about it, Cain may have even felt a little *sorry*, here, for the murder; but, not for the reasons one might think. And, to justify any of the negativities which may have actually come into his mind, he began to turn it all into something that - for the most part - *had* to have been done! Abel *had* to have been sacrificed… for the sake of humankind! It was all, actually, a great chain of events, here! Yet, how many of us really believe that Cain would (in any way) want to honor *Abel*, here… especially in ways, such as his morality and character? Absolutely not! In reality, putting Abel on the pagan pedestal, here, *really* stems from Cain's own envy of his brother (the same way his father, the Serpent, possessed *envy* towards Adam and Eve)![53]

The elevation of Abel into *deity* status also stemmed from Cain's desire to take out any competition, here. By the way things were heading, before this, Abel (and his future descendants) were on their way to becoming a strong and powerful force for *God*… if everything was only kept on their present course, however. A son of the Serpent… as the very first warrior for God? Incredible… and great embarrassment to Satan and the Serpent! They both knew something had to be done, by Cain, here… to stop all of this sacrilege from "catching on." It, also, would have slowed *Cain's* march towards his great quest for material wealth, and world domination. Cain, ultimately, wanted to *possess it all* (just like his father). And, now, with Abel's murder, Cain and any of his sympathizers could pursue this desire - to gather *all* of what the earth had to offer… unabated.

As well, anything which may have been set aside for Abel's inheritance (in this world) would have also been seized by Cain. With his pride, he *wasn't* about to take a "back seat" to anyone, here… or play a secondary role in world affairs! This whole struggle - between Cain and Abel - would become the prototype of a struggle between two different *mindsets* of people, as well… from then on! It would be the battle of the ages; one for moral control and authority over the world, and one we see going on, today!

If one really thinks about it, this whole pagan religion also became a twisted, "copycat" version of **Jesus'** reason-to-be, on earth! The Serpent, most probably, knew what was ahead of him (and his descendants), as a result of his earlier sins. Sammael/Satan, as well, knew that his hold on the world wouldn't be there, forever. If they, both, could be a little "ahead" of the game, and insert their *own* twist of Jesus' up-and-coming sacrifice, here, then maybe it might confuse enough of the followers of God - looking for Jesus, in the future. Maybe, it could, even, put a *dent* in their fate! It was worth a shot. What did they have to lose?

So, they also enacted their "paganized" interpretation of what would be the savior of the world… but, early on. What happened to Abel, here, was similar, in ways, to what would go down in the future - with Jesus Christ. There "needed" to be the sacrifice of Abel, just the same as how Jesus needed to be sacrificed. And, to top it off, Cain would have been seen to beginning something *monumental*, here - he brought on that sacrifice, which allowed the people to find *another* route to salvation! What an honor. Regardless of whether he wanted to or not, **Abel** had become "the ever-dying, ever-reviving… prototype of the resurrected savior."[54]

So, now, one could begin to see how much significance *Abel* had in pagan belief, as well as Judeo/Christian belief - a lot more than most of us probably ever dreamed! It's interesting how pivotal to the rest of the Bible he was, here, as well. Abel/Tammuz was called *"the shepherd"* or *"lord of the sheepfolds;"* Jesus, of course, was the *Good Shepherd* to the entire world.

> *By whom Christ was killed, the shepherd of the flock of people, who was prefigured in Abel, the shepherd of the flock of sheep...* (Delaney, 1996, p. 182)[55]

The kicker, here, was something that Cain, the Serpent, and any of those partial to this new pagan religion, might have wanted to cover up: even though Abel was the son of the Serpent, he was the first, *real* role-model of obedience and servitude to God! The ways of God - that Abel followed - were not to be known, or absorbed. Even Adam, supposedly, thought this about Abel's morality: "…this son Abel was a source of joy unto us, for he was filled with the Love of the Eloheim (i.e. God) and true to the dedication wherewith we did consecrate him unto Jehovah."[56] Abel, as we already know, offered *blood* because he knew God required shed blood (of animals) to cover sin.

> *Abel by contrast, notices in shepherding a process analogous to leadership, both spiritual and public, since the shepherd oversees and facilitates the natural and desirable development of lambs into maturity...* (Delaney, 1996, p. 141)[57]

He cared enough - beyond what his own perceptions - to do it God's way; and offered it up with humility, as well.[58] These, of course, are all the ways of working that God wanted. How utterly counter-productive for the entire pagan cause, however! Abel proved that: no matter who *you* were, you could *still* follow God, be loved, and be approved by Him… if you simply follow the ways He wants you to. Simple, but very exposing…

So, now, Abel became the "number one" threat to Cain, as well as Sammael/Satan and the Serpent - all right out of the "starting gate!" And, it would be up the *other* son of the Serpent - Cain - to step in, here, and make it all "right." With Abel dead, it was almost like "killing two birds with one stone," here. First, it worked to compromise an important mystery of God, here. Second, it served as a way to usher in an entirely *counterfeit* religion, as well - luring millions upon millions away from truths that would be God. People, then, could be able to focus on material things *of the world*: wealth, earnings, personal power, ego gratification; as well as look to other "gods," for their spiritual knowledge and salvation. This is a major reason *why* Abel was so important to this book… as well as how important the, overall, moral lessons, associated with him, were.

We all have free will. We all have a choice. We just have to make the right ones. Most of the correct answers are out there - it's up to us - just as it was with Abel: to want them, to study them, and have faith in them! *God* isn't the source of improper moral choices. He, also, isn't responsible for all of the negative results - on our world - that free-will choices might have had… *human beings* are!

So, now, we see that: it was around this time when so much "twisting" was going on - the whole plethora of Cain's twisted "ways" had, also, become the *backbone* of the entire system of *Mystery Babylon*, as we'll see (with more of the deciphering of *Mystery Babylon*, here, in Volume II)!

The Conclusion

Ultimately, we may need to acknowledge just *who* or *what* originally promoted a certain "way of life" - one we might face, today, in *our present world.* Especially, we need to look at ways which might seem a little *different* - even contrary - to the Word of God. We also need to understand that the world is, in reality, *destined* to be the way it turning out, now, because the Bible said it would. And, as we also know, Jesus said:

> *But as* ***the days of Noe (Noah)*** *were, so shall also* ***the coming of the Son of man*** *be.*
> \- *Mat.* 24:37 (KJV)

So, things, naturally, have to lean towards these "ways." But, just because some prophecy needs to be fulfilled, that doesn't mean *we* couldn't still do our best - utilizing the knowledge about it all that we presently have. Assuredly, those who *don't* want to eventually succumb to these "ways of Cain," today, are still in **good** hands. God takes good care of His own:[59]

> *While the concepts of a fallen race of now-depraved humanity and a ruined creation are depressing concepts, the* ***Bible*** *assures us that God sustains the universe moment by moment, guiding directing and governing in* ***all*** *the affairs of men, angels and nature.* (Dolphin, n. d., p. 5)[60]

The author personally accepts that *true* and proper ways to live are still out there, even *today* - and that they are laid out for us, in one way or another. As well, answers exist in the understanding of what *truly* might have gone on in **these "days of Noah."** So, we have what we need…

Jesus, also, said:

*But take ye heed: behold, I have fortold you **all** things...*
- *Mark* 13:23 (KJV)

The answers are out there. We, sometimes, need to understand the *negative* in order to help us to accentuate all of what's, really, *the positive*! Hopefully, this book provided enough information to help us begin, here. Use all of what you have! Research even further. Utilize some of the *older* versions of the Bible (such as what came out around the King James Version, or even *before*)… those with a minimum of "politically correct" additions! Even (if possible) try to look at what the *original* Hebrew and Greek words of the Bible might be trying to portray. As they say, "the farther you are away from the *originals*, the farther you are away from the **truth**."

Yes, truth is, slowly, being diluted away from us... far away. Deep down inside, most people, however, *do* have some sort of understanding of what's truly right or wrong; but will let their own egos, their own self-interests, and also peer-pressure from other groups of individuals to get in their way. Don't fall for this massive, yet subtle, cover-up going on today. Understand what these "ways of Cain" *really* are - and do the **opposite** of them… it's that simple! If we are able to take all of this information, and achieve the above goal, then we should be well-off enough to walk into most any worldly *fire* that might come upon us… and walk out, virtually *unscathed.*

May God richly guide all of us, on the pathways we choose to walk upon…

…there is so *much* more to all of this in Volume 2: *The Rise of Mystery Babylon: The Tower of Babel (Part I).*

Endnotes

Preface

[1] Thinkexist.com, *Dr. Carl Sagan quotes*, http://en.thinkexist.com/quotes/Dr._Carl_Sagan/ (accessed Dec. 22, 2009).
[2] *Luke* 17:26 (KJV).
[3] J. Preston Eby, *The World System*, 2, http://www.theshop.net/giess/world.html (accessed Aug. 17, 2000) 4.
[4] Andrew Collins, *From the Ashes of Angels* (Rochester, Vermont: Bear & Company, 1996), 20.

Chapter 1

[1] Robert Graves and Raphael Patai, *Hebrew Myths: The Book of Genesis* (Garden City, New York: Doubleday & Company, 1964), 45.
[2] *Targum Neofiti 1: Genesis / Translated, With Apparatus and Notes*, 3:24, trans. Martin McNamara (Collegeville, Minnesota: Liturgical Press, 1992), 63; James L. Kugel, *Traditions of the Bible* (Cambridge, Massachusetts: Harvard University Press, 1998), 57.
[3] *The First Earth Age*, 1-2, http://www.adamqadmon.com/nephilim/firstearthage.html (accessed Dec. 7, 2000); Stephen Quayle, *Genesis 6 Giants: The Master Builders of Prehistoric and Ancient Civilizations* (Bozeman, Montana: End Time Thunder Publishers, 2005), 10-16, 23.
[4] J. Preston Eby, *The World System*, 1, http://www.theshop.net/giess/world.html (accessed Aug. 17, 2000); Strong's G2889 - *kosmos*, http://www.blueletterbible.org/lang/lexicon/lexicon.cfm?Strongs=G2889&t=KJV.html (accessed Dec. 23, 2009).
[5] *The Book of the Mysteries of the Heavens and the Earth and Other Works of Bakhayla Mikael (Zosimas)*, trans. E.A. Wallis Budge (London: Oxford University Press, 1935), 8.
[6] Stephen Quayle, *Genesis 6 Giants: The Master Builders of Prehistoric and Ancient Civilizations* (Bozeman, Montana: End Time Thunder Publishers, 2005), 12, 14, 20-22.
[7] Strong's H7725 - *re'shiyth*, http://www.blueletterbible.org/lang/lexicon/lexicon.cfm?Strongs=H7225&t=KJV.html (accessed Dec. 23, 2009).
[8] The Bible, Genesis & Geology, *Understanding the Biblical Difference Between the Words "World" and "Earth"*, http://www.kjvbible.org/theworlds.html (accessed Dec. 23, 2009).
[9] Strong's G104 - *aei*, http://www.blueletterbible.org/lang/lexicon/lexicon.cfm?Strongs=G104&t=KJV.html (accessed Dec. 23, 2009).
[10] Strong's H8414 - *tohuw*, http://www.blueletterbible.org/lang/lexicon/lexicon.cfm?Strongs=H8414&t=KJV.html (accessed Dec. 23, 2009).
[11] Strongs's H922 - *bohuw*, http://www.blueletterbible.org/lang/lexicon/lexicon.cfm?Strongs=H922&t=KJV.html (accessed Dec. 23, 2009).
[12] Strong's H1961 - *hayah*, http://www.blueletterbible.org/lang/lexicon/lexicon.cfm?Strongs=H1961&t=KJV.html (accessed Dec. 23, 2009).
[13] Robert Bowie Johnson, Jr., *The Parthenon Code: Mankind's History in Marble* (Annapolis, Maryland: Solving Light Books, 2004), 205.
[14] J. Preston Eby, *The World System*, 5, http://www.theshop.net/giess/world.html (accessed Aug. 17, 2000 **4**); *The Companion Bible*, Appendix 146 (Grand Rapids, Michigan: Kregel Publications, 1990), 171; Robert Bowie Johnson, Jr., *The Parthenon Code: Mankind's History in Marble* (Annapolis, Maryland: Solving Light Books, 2004), 206.
[15] Strong's G2602 - *katabole*, http://www.blueletterbible.org/lang/lexicon/lexicon.cfm?Strongs=G2602&t=KJV.html (accessed Dec. 23, 2009).
[16] The Bible, Genesis & Geology, *Understanding the Biblical Difference Between the Words "World" and "Earth"*, http://www.kjvbible.org/theworlds.html (accessed Dec. 23, 2009).
[17] Greg Killian, *The Days of Noah*, 29-30, www.adamqadmon.com/nephilim/gkillian000 (accessed Dec. 6, 2000).
[18] Robert Bowie Johnson, Jr., *The Parthenon Code: Mankind's History in Marble* (Annapolis, Maryland: Solving Light Books, 2004), 45.
[19] The Bible, Genesis & Geology, *Understanding the Biblical Difference Between the Words "World" and "Earth"*, 5, http://www.kjvbible.org/theworlds.html (accessed Dec. 23, 2009).
[20] *The First Earth Age*, 4, http://www.adamqadmon.com/nephilim/firstearthage.html (accessed Dec. 7, 2000).
[21] *Pseudo - Philo (The Biblical Antiquities of Philo)*, 3:9, trans. M. R. James (1917), 81, http://www.sacred-texts.com/bib/bap/bap19.htm (accessed July 13, 2006).
[22] *The Works of Philo Judaeus*, Questions and Answers on Genesis II, 54, trans. C. D. Yonge (London: H. G. Bohn, 1854-1855).
[23] *Saltair na Rann*, 2437-2340, trans. David Greene.
[24] Stephen Quayle, *Genesis 6 Giants: The Master Builders of Prehistoric and Ancient Civilizations* (Bozeman, Montana: End Time Thunder Publishers, 2005), 52.
[25] The Bible, Genesis & Geology, *Subject: 12,000-Year-Old Human Hair DNA Has No Match With Modern Humans*, 3, http://www.kjvbible.org/earthfilesstory.html (accessed Dec. 11, 2007).

[26] Stephen Quayle, *Genesis 6 Giants: The Master Builders of Prehistoric and Ancient Civilizations* (Bozeman, Montana: End Time Thunder Publishers, 2005), 57-58.

Chapter 2

[1] *The Sibylline Oracles, Translated from the Greek into English blank Verse*, First Fragment (Notes), trans. Milton S. Terry (New York: Hunt & Eaton, 1890).

[2] *The First Book of Adam and Eve (The Conflict of Adam and Eve with Satan)*, 27:10, trans. S. C. Malan (London: Williams and Norgate, 1882).

[3] Augustine, *The City of God*, Book 11, Chapter 9 - What the Scriptures Teach Us To Believe Concerning the Creation of the Angels, http://www.newadvent.org/fathers/120111.htm (accessed Dec. 15, 2009).

[4] Answers.com, *light*, 1, http://www.answers.com/topic/light (accessed Oct. 3, 2005).

[5] Rabbi Leo Jung, Ph. D., *Fallen Angels in Jewish, Christian and Mohammedan Literature* (New York: KTAV Publishing House, 1974), 99.

[6] Robert Graves and Raphael Patai, *Hebrew Myths: The Book of Genesis* (Garden City, New York: Doubleday & Company, 1964), 102; James L. Kugel, *The Bible As It Was*, (Cambridge, Massachusetts: Harvard University Press, 1997), 58, 60; *The Book of the Rolls (Kitab Al-Magall)*, 6, trans. Margaret Dunlop Gibson, Apocrypha Arabica (London: C.J Clay and Sons, 1901), 3; Christian Geology: Science and Scripture, *Introduction: Beyond Gap Theory Interpretation of Genesis*, 8, http://kjvbible.org/gap_theory.html (accessed Aug. 29, 2005); *The Lebor Gabala Erren*, 2, http://www.ancienttexts.org/library/celtic/irish/lebor.html (accessed May 26, 2005); James L. Kugel, *Traditions of the Bible* (Cambridge, Massachusetts: Harvard University Press, 1998), 76; *The Book of Jubilees*, 2:2, trans. R. H. Charles, The Apocrypha and Pseudepigrapha of the Old Testament (Oxford, Clarendon Press, 1913).

[7] *The Shepherd of Hermas*, First Book: Visions, Third Vision, Ch. IV, 6, Roberts-Donaldson English Translation, http://www.earlychristianwritings.com/text/shepherd.html (accessed Dec. 16, 2009).

[8] *The Book of the Cave of Treasures*, The First Thousand Years: Adam to Yared (Jared), The Creation, First Day, trans. Sir E. A. Wallis Budge (London: The Religious Tract Society, 1927), 43-46.

[9] *The Book of Jubilees*, 2:2 (also 2:8), trans. R. H. Charles, The Apocrypha and Pseudepigrapha of the Old Testament (Oxford: Clarendon Press, 1913).

[10] Louis Ginzberg, *The Legends of the Jews Volume I: From the Creation to Jacob* (Baltimore, Maryland: The Johns Hopkins University Press, 1909), 135.

[11] *2 Enoch (The Book of the Secrets of Enoch)*, 25:1, trans. W. R. Morfill, M. A. (Oxford: Clarendon Press, 1896).

[12] Louis Ginzberg, *The Legends of the Jews Volume I: From the Creation to Jacob*, trans. Henrietta Szold (Baltimore, Maryland: The Johns Hopkins University Press, 1909), 135.

[13] *The Book of the Bee*, Chapter 2: Of the Creation of the Seven Natures (Substances) in Silence, trans. Earnest A. Wallis Budge, M.A., http://www.sacred-texts.com/chr/bb/bb02.htm (accessed Dec. 23, 2009).

[14] *The Penitence of our Forefather Adam*, Adam and Abel's Funerary Rites [47]39.3, trans. Gary A. Anderson and Michael E. Stone, http://www2.iath.virginia.edu/anderson/viat/english/vita.arm.html (accessed Dec 26, 2009).

[15] Augustine, *The City of God*, Book XI, Chapter 9 - What the Scriptures Teach Us To Believe Concerning the Creation of the Angels, http://www.newadvent.org/fathers/120111.htm (accessed Dec. 15, 2009).

[16] *The Book of Jubilees*, 2:2, trans. R. H. Charles, The Apocrypha and Pseudepigrapha of the Old Testament (Oxford: Clarendon Press, 1913).

[17] *The Book of the Mysteries of the Heavens and the Earth and Other Works of Bakhayla Mikael (Zosimas)*, trans. E.A. Wallis Budge (London: Oxford University Press, 1935), 12.

[18] Answers.com, *dark*, 1, http://www.answers.com/topic/dark (accessed Oct. 3, 2005).

[19] Watchmen Bible Study Group, *When Was the Beginning?*, 6, http://biblestudysite.com/begin.html (accessed Dec. 6, 2006).

[20] Answers.com, *night*, 1, http://www.answers.com/topic/night (accessed Oct. 3, 2005).

[21] Stephen Quayle, *Genesis 6 Giants: The Master Builders of Prehistoric and Ancient Civilizations* (Bozeman, Montana: End Time Thunder Publishers, 2005), 16; G. H. Pember, M. A., *Earth's Earliest Ages and their Connection With Modern Spiritualism, Theosophy, and Buddhism* (Grand Rapids, Michigan: Kregel Publications, 1975), 69.

[22] Answers.com, *black and white dualism*, 1, http://www.answers.com/topic/black-and-white-dualism (accessed Feb. 9, 2010).

[23] Answers.com, *chthonic*, 1-2, http://www.answers.com/topic/chthonic (accessed Feb. 9, 2010).

[24] *The Book of the Mysteries of the Heavens and the Earth and Other Works of Bakhayla Mikael (Zosimas)*, trans. E.A. Wallis Budge (London: Oxford University Press, 1935), 13.

[25] Stephen Quayle, *Genesis 6 Giants: The Master Builders of Prehistoric and Ancient Civilizations* (Bozeman, Montana: End Time Thunder Publishers, 2005), 16; *On the Origin of the World*, 1-2, http://www.earth-history.com/Judaism/origin-world.htm (accessed May 10, 2007).

[26] Stephen Quayle, *Genesis 6 Giants: The Master Builders of Prehistoric and Ancient Civilizations* (Bozeman, Montana: End Time Thunder Publishers, 2005), 16-17.

[27] Wikipedia, the Free Encyclopedia, *Pre-existence*, 1-4, http://en.wikipedia.org/wiki/Pre-existence (accessed May 14,

2007).
[28] Watchmen Bible Study Group, *When Was the Beginning?*, 8-12, http://biblestudysite.com/begin.html (accessed Dec. 6, 2006).
[29] *Welcome to 3 World Ages*, 1, http://www.geocities.com/Vienna/6787/word4.html (accessed Oct. 21, 2005).
[30] *The Book of the Cave of Treasures*, The First Thousand Years: Adam to Yared (Jared), The Creation, First Day, trans. Sir E. A. Wallis Budge (London: The Religious Tract Society, 1927), 43-46.
[31] *3 Enoch (The Hebrew Book of Enoch)*, 43:1, trans. Hugo Odeberg (New York, Ktav Publishing House, Inc., 1973), 132-135 (and notes).
[32] *The Book of the Cave of Treasures*, The First Thousand Years: Adam to Yared (Jared), The Creation of Adam (notes), trans. Sir E. A. Wallis Budge (London: The Religious Tract Society, 1927), 51-55; *Genesis 6*, 1, http://www.adamqadmon.com/watchers/sonsofgod006.html (accessed Dec. 29, 2000).
[33] Welcome to 3 World Ages, *Let's try to find out WHO or WHAT caused that destruction*, 2, http://www.geocities.com/Vienna/6787/word3.html?200521 (accessed Oct. 21, 2005).
[34] Graham Hancock, *Fingerprints of the Gods* (New York: Three Rivers Press, 1995), 381.
[35] Corinne Heline, *Mythology and the Bible* (Oceanside, California: New Age Press, 1941), 7.
[36] Corinne Heline, *Mythology and the Bible* (Oceanside, California: New Age Press, 1941), 7.
[37] Robert Bowie Johnson, Jr., *The Parthenon Code: Mankind's History in Marble* (Annapolis, Maryland: Solving Light Books, 2004), 204.
[38] Corinne Heline, *Mythology and the Bible* (Oceanside, California: New Age Press, 1941), 7; Robert Bowie Johnson, Jr., *The Parthenon Code: Mankind's History in Marble* (Annapolis, Maryland: Solving Light Books, 2004), 199, 201.
[39] *The Book of Jubilees*, 2:4, 2:8, trans. R. H. Charles, The Apocrypha and Pseudepigrapha of the Old Testament (Oxford: Clarendon Press, 1913).
[40] The Bible, Genesis & Geology, *The 4th Day - Paradox of the Sun and Stars*, http://www.kjvbible.org/paradox_of_the_sun_and_stars.html (accessed Dec. 23, 2009); The Bible, Genesis & Geology, *Introduction: Beyond Gap Theory Interpretation of Genesis*, 3, http://www.kjvbible.org/gaptheory.html (accessed Sept. 29, 2005).
[41] G. H. Pember, M. A., *Earth's Earliest Ages and their Connection With Modern Spiritualism, Theosophy, and Buddhism* (Grand Rapids, Michigan: Kregel Publications, 1975), 63.
[42] The Bible, Genesis & Geology, *The Firmament, Third Heaven, and Structure of Things Biblical*, 1-2, http://www.kjvbible.org/firmament.html (accessed Dec. 23, 2009).
[43] The Bible, Genesis & Geology, *Understanding the Biblical Difference Between the Words "World" and "Earth"*, 4, http://www.kjvbible.org/theworlds.html (accessed Sept. 29, 2005).
[44] *The Book of Jubilees*, 2:7, trans. R. H. Charles, The Apocrypha and Pseudepigrapha of the Old Testament (Oxford: Clarendon Press, 1913).
[45] G. H. Pember, M. A., *Earth's Earliest Ages and their Connection With Modern Spiritualism, Theosophy, and Buddhism* (Grand Rapids, Michigan: Kregel Publications, 1975), 65.
[46] The Bible, Genesis & Geology, *Introduction: Beyond Gap Theory Interpretation of Genesis*, 3, http://www.kjvbible.org/gaptheory.html (accessed Sept. 29, 2005).
[47] James L. Kugel, *Traditions of the Bible* (Cambridge, Massachusetts: Harvard University Press, 1998), 77; *The First Earth Age*, 11, http://www.adamqadmon.com/nephilim/firstearthage.html (accessed Dec.7, 2000); *The Book of Enoch*, 21:6, trans. R. H. Charles (Montana: Kessinger Publishing, 1912).
[48] James L. Kugel, *The Bible As It Was*, (Cambridge, Massachusetts: Harvard University Press, 1997), 59.

Chapter 3

[1] *Genizah Manuscripts of Palestinian Targum to the Pentateuch Volume One*, Genesis 2:20, trans. Michael L. Klein (Cincinnati: Hebrew Union College Press, 1986), 2.
[2] *The Companion Bible*, Appendix 13 (Grand Rapids, Michigan: Kregel Publications, 1990), 19.
[3] *The Zohar*, Volume 11, Safra Det'zniuta, Section 3. Third Chapter, 38, https://www2.kabbalah.com/k/index.php/p=zohar/zohar&vol=22&sec=816 (accessed March 16, 2010).
[4] *The Babylonian Talmud*, Jews' College / Soncino English Translation, Yebamoth 98a, http://www.halakhah.com/yebamoth/yebamoth_98.html (accessed Dec. 28, 2010).
[5] *The Writings of Abraham*, 29:8, http://www.earth-history.com/Pseudepigrapha/Mormonism/writings-abraham-1.htm (accessed May 10, 2007); *Armenian Apocrypha Relating to the Patriarchs and Prophets*, The Words of Adam To Seth 1, 16, 18, trans. Michael E. Stone (Jerusalem: The Israel Academy of Sciences and Humanities, 1982), 12-13.
[6] Bible Hub, *Genesis 7:14*, 2, http://biblehub.com/text/genesis/7-14.htm (accessed June 5, 2017); Bible Hub, *5775. oph*, 1, http://biblehub.com/hebrew/5775.htm (accessed June 5, 2017).
[7] *The Midrash Rabbah*, Bereshith (Genesis) 1:3 (& notes), trans. Rabbi Dr. H. Freedman and Maurice Simon (London: The Soncino Press, 1961).
[8] *The Book of Adam*, 19:2, trans. J. P. Mahe, http://www.pseudepigrapha.com/pseudepigrapha/TheBookOfAdam.htm (accessed June 27, 2005).
[9] Johann Andreas Eisenmenger, *The Traditions of the Jews, Contained in the Talmud and other Mystical Writings*

(London: J. Robinson, 1748), 130-131; Mrs. Sydney Bristowe, *Sargon the Magnificent* (London: The Covenant Publishing Co., 1927), 102; Andrew Collins, *From the Ashes of Angels* (Rochester, Vermont: Bear & Company, 1996), 57-59; *The Penitence of our Forefather Adam*, Separation of Adam and Eve 20.2, trans. Gary A. Anderson and Michael E. Stone, http://www2.iath.virginia.edu/anderson/viat/english/vita.arm.html (accessed Dec 26, 2009).
[10] *The Book of Adam*, 20:2, trans. J. P. Mahe, http://www.pseudepigrapha.com/pseudepigrapha/TheBookOfAdam.htm (accessed June 27, 2005).
[11] http://av1611.com/kjbp/kjv-dictionary/wing.html
[12] The King James Bible Page, *KJV Dictionary Definition: wing*, 1, http://av1611.com/kjbp/kjv-dictionary/wing.html (accessed June 5, 2017).
[13] Bob Curran, *Dark Fairies* (Pompton Plaines, New Jersey: The Career Press, Inc., 2010), 65.
[14] *Jer*. 9:10 (KJV); *Job* 35:11 (KJV).
[15] Blue Letter Bible, *Strong's H8064 - shamayim*, 1, https://www.blueletterbible.org/lang/lexicon/lexicon.cfm?Strongs=H8064&t=KJV (accessed Dec. 23, 2016).
[16] Dictionary.com, *behemoth*, 3, http://dictionary.reference.com/search?r=2&q=behemoth (accessed May 16, 2007).
[17] Mrs. Sydney Bristowe, *Sargon the Magnificent* (London: The Covenant Publishing Co., 1927), 105.
[18] *Acts 17:26*, 1, http://biblehub.com/text/acts/17-26.htm (accessed Dec. 23, 2016).
[19] Blue Letter Bible, *Acts 17:26*, 1, https://www.blueletterbible.org/kjv/act/17/1/t_conc_1035026 (accessed Dec. 23, 2016); Blue Letter Bible, Strong's G129 - *haima*, 1, https://www.blueletterbible.org/lang/lexicon/lexicon.cfm?Strongs=G129&t=KJV (accessed Dec. 23, 2016).
[20] (From Dr. William Boyd, *Races and People* (1955), 145) *Was Adam the First Man?*, 5, http://www.seek-info.com/adam.htm (accessed Sept. 10, 2000).
[21] Wikipedia, the free encyclopedia, *Polygenism*, 1, http://en.wikipedia.org/wiki/Polygenism (accessed Nov. 21, 2006).

Chapter 4

[1] *The Sibylline Oracles, Translated from the Greek into English blank Verse*, Second Fragment, Lines 13-18, trans. Milton S. Terry (New York: Hunt & Eaton, 1890).
[2] Mrs. Sydney Bristowe, *Sargon the Magnificent* (London: The Covenant Publishing Co., 1927), 17.
[3] *The Zohar*, Volume 15, Tazria, Section 22, Man, person, 107, https://www2.kabbalah.com/k/index.php/p=zohar/zohar&vol=30&sec=1090 (accessed Feb. 26, 2010).
[4] S. Baring-Gould, *Legends of the Patriarchs and Prophets and Other Old Testament Characters* (New York: American Book Exchange, 1881), 28.
[5] *The Companion Bible*, Appendix 14 (Grand Rapids, Michigan: Kregel Publications, 1990), 21; *Gen.* 1:26, 2:5, 5:1 (KJV).
[6] *The Companion Bible*, Appendix 14 (Grand Rapids, Michigan: Kregel Publications, 1990), 21; *Gen.* 2:7, 2:8, 2:15 (KJV).
[7] *The Companion Bible*, Genesis 2:7, Appendix 14 (Grand Rapids, Michigan: Kregel Publications, 1990), 5, 21.
[8] *The Companion Bible*, Appendix 14, Appendix 24 (Grand Rapids, Michigan: Kregel Publications, 1990), 21, 27; Mrs. Sydney Bristowe, *Sargon the Magnificent* (London: The Covenant Publishing Co., 1927), 17.
[9] *Targum Pseudo-Jonathan (Targum of Palestine / Targum of Jonathan Ben Uzziel)*, On the Book of Genesis, Section 3, Berashith, http://targum.info/pj/pjgen1-6.htm (accessed Oct. 2, 2009).
[10] *The History of al-Tabari - Volume I: General Introduction and From the Creation to the Flood*, The Story of Adam, 87, trans. Franz Rosenthal (Albany: New York Press, 1989), 258.
[11] *The History of al-Tabari - Volume I: General Introduction and From the Creation to the Flood*, The Story of Adam, 91, trans. Franz Rosenthal (Albany: New York Press, 1989), 263.
[12] *The Bible, The Koran, and the Talmud (Biblical Legends of the Mussulmans)*, Adam (A Mohammedan Legend), trans. Dr. G. Weil (New York, 1863), 22.
[13] Mrs. Sydney Bristowe, *Sargon the Magnificent* (London: The Covenant Publishing Co., 1927), 16-17.
[14] S. Baring-Gould, *Legends of the Patriarchs and Prophets and Other Old Testament Characters* (New York: American Book Exchange, 1881), 28.
[15] *Saltair na Rann*, 1789-1796, trans. David Greene.
[16] Strongs's H6754 - *tselem*, http://www.blueletterbible.org/lang/lexicon/lexicon.cfm?Strongs=H6754&t=KJV.html (accessed Dec. 17, 2009).
[17] Stephen Quayle, *Genesis 6 Giants: The Master Builders of Prehistoric and Ancient Civilizations* (Bozeman, Montana: End Time Thunder Publishers, 2005), 23-4.
[18] Strong's G444 – *anthropos*, http://www.blueletterbible.org/lang/lexicon/lexicon.cfm?Strongs=G444&t=KJV.html (accessed Dec. 17, 2009).
[19] *The Book of the Bee*, 14, trans. Earnest A Wallis Budge, M.A., http://www.sacred-texts.com/chr/bb/bb14.htm (accessed Oct. 10, 2004); *Armenian Apocrypha Relating to Adam and Eve*, 9, 13, 25, trans. Michael E. Stone (Leiden: E. J. Brill, 1996), 33, 35, 45; James L. Kugel, *Traditions of the Bible* (Cambridge, Massachusetts: Harvard University Press, 1998), 114-5; *Barhebraeus' Scholia on the Old Testament Part I: Genesis - II Samuel*, Genesis 2:25, trans. Martin Sprengling and William Creighton Graham (Chicago, Illinois: University of Chicago Press, 1931), 25.

[20] *The Book of the Mysteries of the Heavens and the Earth and Other Works of Bakhayla Mikael (Zosimas)*, trans. E. A. Wallis Budge (London: Oxford University Press, 1935), 21; Mrs. Sydney Bristowe, *Sargon the Magnificent* (London: The Covenant Publishing Co., 1927), 83; *The Chronicles of Jerahmeel* (*The Hebrew Bible Historiale*), 6:16, trans. M. Gaster, Ph. D. (London: The Royal Asiatic Society, 1899), 18; *The Armenian Apocryphal Adam Literature*, History of the Creation and Transgression of Adam 18, trans. William Lowndes Lipscomb (Ann Arbor, Michigan: University Microfilms International, 1983), 121; Ellen Frankel, *The Classic Tales: 4000 years of Jewish Lore* (Northvale, New Jersey: Jason Aronson Inc., 1989), 29.

[21] *An Historical Treatise of the Travels of Noah Into Europe: Containing the first inhabitation and peopling thereof*, trans. Richard Lynche (1601), http://www.annomundi.com/history/travels_of_noah.htm (accessed Dec. 7, 2007).

[22] E. S. G. Bristowe, *Cain - An Argument* (Leicester: Edgar Backus, 1950), 91-92.

[23] *Targum Pseudo-Jonathan (Targum of Palestine / Targum of Jonathan Ben Uzziel)*, On the Book of Genesis, Section 2, Berashith, http://targum.info/pj/pjgen1-6.htm (accessed Oct. 2, 2009).

[24] E. S. G. Bristowe, *Cain - An Argument* (Leicester: Edgar Backus, 1950), 7; *The First Book of Adam and Eve (The Conflict of Adam and Eve with Satan)*, 34:14, trans. S. C. Malan (London: Williams and Norgate, 1882).

[25] *The Book of the Mysteries of the Heavens and the Earth and Other Works of Bakhayla Mikael (Zosimas)*, trans. E.A. Wallis Budge (London: Oxford University Press, 1935), 8.

[26] *The History of al-Tabari - Volume I: General Introduction and From the Creation to the Flood*, The Story of Adam, 91, trans. Franz Rosenthal (Albany: New York Press, 1989), 263.

[27] Mrs. Sydney Bristowe, *Sargon the Magnificent* (London: The Covenant Publishing Co., 1927), 16-17.

[28] *2 Enoch (The Book of the Secrets of Enoch)*, 65:2, trans. W. R. Morfill, M. A. (Oxford: Clarendon Press, 1896).

[29] *The First Book of Adam and Eve (The Conflict of Adam and Eve with Satan)*, 34:8, trans. S. C. Malan (London: Williams and Norgate, 1882).

[30] *The Words of the Heavenly Lights* (The Dead Sea Scrolls), (4Q504), Fr. 8 recto, trans. Geza Vermes, *The Complete Dead Sea Scrolls in English* (New York: Penguin Books, 1997), 367.

[31] *Targum Pseudo-Jonathan (Targum of Palestine / Targum of Jonathan Ben Uzziel)*, On the Book of Genesis, Section 2, Berashith, http://targum.info/pj/pjgen1-6.htm (accessed Oct. 2, 2009).

[32] *The Book of Jubilees*, 4:15, trans. R. H. Charles, The Apocrypha and Pseudepigrapha of the Old Testament (Oxford: Clarendon Press, 1913).

[33] *The Companion Bible*, Gen. 2:7, Appendix 14 (Grand Rapids, Michigan: Kregel Publications, 1990) 5, 21.

[34] *The Book of the Cave of Treasures*, The First Thousand Years: Adam to Yared (Jared), The Revolt of Satan, and the Battle in Heaven, trans. Sir E. A. Wallis Budge (London: The Religious Tract Society, 1927) 55-59; *The Armenian Apocryphal Adam Literature*, History of the Repentance of Adam and Eve, the First Created Ones, and How They Did It 21, trans. William Lowndes Lipscomb (Ann Arbor, Michigan: University Microfilms International, 1983), 224; *Saltair na Rann*, 2245-2248, trans. David Greene; *The History of al-Tabari - Volume I: General Introduction and From the Creation to the Flood,* The Story of Adam, 87, trans. Franz Rosenthal (Albany: New York Press, 1989), 258-259.

[35] *The Book of the Cave of Treasures*, The First Thousand Years: Adam to Yared (Jared), The Creation of Adam, trans. Sir E. A. Wallis Budge (London: The Religious Tract Society, 1927), 51-55.

[36] *The Book of Adam*, [37]10.3, trans. J. P. Mahe, http://www.pseudepigrapha.com/pseudepigrapha/TheBookOfAdam.htm (accessed June 27, 2005).

[37] Strong's H119 - *adam*, http://www.blueletterbible.org/lang/lexicon/lexicon.cfm?Strongs=H119&t=KJV (accessed Dec. 17, 2009).

[38] Wikipedia, the Free Encyclopedia, *Adam*, 5, http://en.wikipedia.org/wiki/Adam (accessed Aug 28, 2007).

[39] E. S. G. Bristowe, *Cain - An Argument* (Leicester: Edgar Backus, 1950), 60.

[40] *Saltair na Rann*, 1401-1412, trans. David Greene; Wikipedia, the Free Encyclopedia, *Adam*, 5, http://en.wikipedia.org/wiki/Adam (accessed Aug 28, 2007).

[41] *The Book of Enoch*, 106:2, trans. R. H. Charles (Montana: Kessinger Publishing, 1912).

[42] Strong's H119 - *adam*, http://www.blueletterbible.org/lang/lexicon/lexicon.cfm?Strongs=H119&t=KJV (accessed Dec. 17, 2009).

[43] *Barhebraeus' Scholia on the Old Testament Part I: Genesis - II Samuel*, Genesis 2:7, trans. Martin Sprengling and William Creighton Graham (Chicago, Illinois: University of Chicago Press 1931), 19.

[44] Gesenius's Lexicon - *aphar*, http://www.blueletterbible.org/lang/lexicon/lexicon.cfm?Strongs=H6083&t=KJV (accessed Dec. 17, 2009).

[45] *The Apocalypse of Moses / Apocalypsis Mosis*, 6:2, 9:3, trans. R. H. Charles, http://www.pseudepigrapha.com/pseudepigrapha/aprmose.htm (accessed June 27, 2005); *The Book of Adam*, [36]9.3, trans. J. P. Mahe, http://www.pseudepigrapha.com/pseudepigrapha/TheBookOfAdam.htm (accessed June 27, 2005).

[46] Star Wars, *Lesson Seven - The Serpent*, 1, http://usa-the-republic.com/religion/star%20wars/Star%20Wars%20-%20Lesson%20Seven.htm (accessed April 23, 2005).

[47] Strong's H6635 - *tsaba*, http://www.blueletterbible.org/lang/lexicon/lexicon.cfm?Strongs=H6635&t=KJV# (accessed Jan. 4, 2010); Lambert Dolphin, *The Ruin of Creation*, 1, http://www.adamqadmon.com/nephilim/dolphin-ruin.html (accessed Dec 5, 2000).

[48] *The Sibylline Oracles, Translated from the Greek into English blank Verse*, Second Fragment, Lines 13-18, trans.

Milton S. Terry (New York: Hunt & Eaton, 1890).
[49] Mrs. Sydney Bristowe, *Sargon the Magnificent* (London: The Covenant Publishing Co., 1927), 29.
[50] *The Chronicles of Jerahmeel* (*The Hebrew Bible Historiale*), 6:14, trans. M. Gaster, Ph. D. (London: The Royal Asiatic Society, 1899) 17.
[51] *The Chronicles of Jerahmeel* (*The Hebrew Bible Historiale*), 6:14, trans. M. Gaster, Ph. D. (London: The Royal Asiatic Society, 1899), 17.
[52] *The Book of the Generations of Adam*, 1:3, 3:1, http://www.earth-history.com/Pseudepigrapha/generations-adam.htm (accessed May 5, 2007).

Chapter 5

[1] Andrew Collins, *From the Ashes of Angels* (Rochester, Vermont: Bear & Company, 1996), 151; *The Theme of Paradise*, 1, http://www.adamqadmon.com/watchers/paradise.html (accessed Feb. 10, 2001); Wikipedia, the Free Encyclopedia, *Garden of Eden*, 2, http://en.wikipedia.org/wiki/Garden_of_Eden (accessed April 23, 2007); James L. Kugel, *Traditions of the Bible* (Cambridge, Massachusetts: Harvard University Press, 1998), 110.
[2] Ezekiel 28:14 (KJV); James L. Kugel, *Traditions of the Bible* (Cambridge, Massachusetts: Harvard University Press, 1998), 162; Robert Graves and Raphael Patai, *Hebrew Myths: The Book of Genesis* (Garden City, New York: Doubleday & Company, 1964), 73, 105.
[3] Wikipedia, the Free Encyclopedia, *Garden of Eden*, 2, http://en.wikipedia.org/wiki/Garden_of_Eden (accessed April 23, 2007); Andrew Collins, *From the Ashes of Angels* (Rochester, Vermont: Bear & Company, 1996), 151.
[4] Andrew Collins, *From the Ashes of Angels* (Rochester, Vermont: Bear & Company, 1996), 151; *The Theme of Paradise*, 1, http://www.adamqadmon.com/watchers/paradise.html (accessed Feb. 10, 2001).
[5] *The Penitence of our Forefather Adam*, Serpent's Approach to Paradise [44]17.3, trans. Gary A. Anderson and Michael E. Stone, http://www2.iath.virginia.edu/anderson/viat/english/vita.arm.html (accessed Dec 26, 2009).
[6] *The Book of Adam*, [32]7.3b-[33].1, trans. J. P. Mahe, http://www.pseudepigrapha.com/pseudepigrapha/TheBookOfAdam.htm (accessed June 27, 2005).
[7] Andrew Collins, *From the Ashes of Angels* (Rochester, Vermont: Bear & Company, 1996), 69.
[8] *The Armenian Apocryphal Adam Literature*, History of the Creation and Transgression of Adam 1, trans. William Lowndes Lipscomb (Ann Arbor, Michigan: University Microfilms International, 1983), 118.
[9] *The First Book of Adam and Eve (The Conflict of Adam and Eve with Satan)*, 13:4, trans. S. C. Malan (London: Williams and Norgate, 1882).
[10] *The History of al-Tabari – Volume I: General Introduction and From the Creation to the Flood*, The Story of Iblis, 81, trans. Franz Rosenthal (Albany: New York Press, 1989), 252.
[11] *2 Enoch (The Book of the Secrets of Enoch)*, 31:1-5, trans. W. R. Morfill, M. A. (Oxford: Clarendon Press, 1896).
[12] Robert Graves and Raphael Patai, *Hebrew Myths: The Book of Genesis* (Garden City, New York: Doubleday & Company, 1964), 85; *The Penitence of our Forefather Adam*, Fall of Satan 12.1, trans. Gary A. Anderson and Michael E. Stone, http://www2.iath.virginia.edu/anderson/viat/english/vita.arm.html (accessed Dec 26, 2009).
[13] *The History of al-Tabari - Volume I: General Introduction and From the Creation to the Flood*, The Story of Iblis, 84, 81, trans. Franz Rosenthal (Albany: New York Press, 1989), 252-253, 255
[14] *The Midrash Rabbah*, Bereshith (Genesis) 26:7, trans. Rabbi Dr. H. Freedman and Maurice Simon (London: The Soncino Press, 1961).
[15] *The Armenian Apocryphal Adam Literature*, History of the Creation and Transgression of Adam 1-4, trans. William Lowndes Lipscomb (Ann Arbor, Michigan: University Microfilms International, 1983), 118-119.
[16] *Saltair na Rann*, 1729-1752, 1777-1784, 1821-1844, 1865-1880, trans. David Greene; *The Armenian Apocryphal Adam Literature*, History and Sermon: Concerning the Creation of Adam and the Incarnation of Christ Our God 1-5, trans. William Lowndes Lipscomb (Ann Arbor, Michigan: University Microfilms International, 1983), 261.
[17] G. H. Pember, M. A., *Earth's Earliest Ages and their Connection With Modern Spiritualism, Theosophy, and Buddhism* (Grand Rapids, Michigan: Kregel Publications, 1975), 37.
[18] *The History of al-Tabari - Volume I: General Introduction and From the Creation to the Flood*, The Story of Adam, 85-86, trans. Franz Rosenthal (Albany: New York Press, 1989), 256-257.
[19] *The Book of the Cave of Treasures*, The First Thousand Years: Adam to Yared (Jared), The Creation of Adam (notes), The Revolt of Satan, and the Battle in Heaven, trans. Sir E. A. Wallis Budge (London: The Religious Tract Society, 1927), 55-59; *The History of al-Tabari - Volume I: General Introduction and From the Creation to the Flood*, The Story of Iblis, 80, trans. Franz Rosenthal (Albany: New York Press, 1989), 251.
[20] S. Baring-Gould, *Legends of the Patriarchs and Prophets and Other Old Testament Characters* (New York: American Book Exchange, 1881), 21.
[21] E. S. G. Bristowe, *Cain - An Argument* (Leicester: Edgar Backus, 1950), 39.
[22] Mrs. Sydney Bristowe, *Sargon the Magnificent* (London: The Covenant Publishing Co., 1927), 120; *The Armenian Apocryphal Adam Literature*, The History of the Creation and Transgression of Adam 5, 9, trans. William Lowndes Lipscomb (Ann Arbor, Michigan: University Microfilms International, 1983), 119.
[23] *The Armenian Apocryphal Adam Literature*, History of the Creation and Transgression of Adam 1, trans. William Lowndes Lipscomb (Ann Arbor, Michigan: University Microfilms International, 1983), 119.

[24] *The History of al-Tabari - Volume I: General Introduction and From the Creation to the Flood*, The Story of Adam, 86, trans. Franz Rosenthal (Albany: New York Press, 1989), 257.
[25] *The Zohar*, Volume 1, Beresheet A, Section 20. The five types of the mixed multitude, 226, https://www2.kabbalah.com/k/index.php/p=zohar/zohar&vol=2&sec=41 (accessed Feb. 24, 2010).
[26] *The History of al-Tabari - Volume I: General Introduction and From the Creation to the Flood*, The First House on Earth, 130, trans. Franz Rosenthal (Albany: New York Press, 1989), 300.
[27] *Pirke De Rabbi Eliezer*, Chapter 13: The Serpent in Paradise (15A.ii.), trans. Gerald Friedlander (New York: Sepher-Hermon Press, 1981), 91.
[28] *The History of al-Tabari - Volume I: General Introduction and From the Creation to the Flood*, The First House on Earth, 130, trans. Franz Rosenthal (Albany: New York Press, 1989), 300.
[29] *The Book of the Cave of Treasures*, The First Thousand Years: Adam to Yared (Jared), The Creation of Adam, trans. Sir E. A. Wallis Budge (London: The Religious Tract Society, 1927), 51-55.
[30] *The Chronicles of Jerahmeel* (*The Hebrew Bible Historiale*), 6:13, trans. M. Gaster, Ph. D. (London: The Royal Asiatic Society, 1899), 17.
[31] Johann Andreas Eisenmenger, *The Traditions of the Jews, Contained in the Talmud and other Mystical Writings* (London: J. Robinson, 1748), 25.
[32] *The Chronicles of Jerahmeel* (*The Hebrew Bible Historiale*), 6:12, trans. M. Gaster, Ph. D. (London: The Royal Asiatic Society, 1899), 14.
[33] S. Baring-Gould, *Legends of the Patriarchs and Prophets and Other Old Testament Characters* (New York: American Book Exchange, 1881), 26.
[34] S. Baring-Gould, *Legends of the Patriarchs and Prophets and Other Old Testament Characters* (New York: American Book Exchange, 1881), 26.
[35] S. Baring-Gould, *Legends of the Patriarchs and Prophets and Other Old Testament Characters* (New York: American Book Exchange, 1881), 15.
[36] *The Chronicles of Jerahmeel* (*The Hebrew Bible Historiale*), 7:1, trans. M. Gaster, Ph. D. (London: The Royal Asiatic Society, 1899), 18; Rabbi Leo Jung, Ph. D., *Fallen Angels in Jewish, Christian and Mohammedan Literature* (New York: KTAV Publishing House, 1974), 75.
[37] Johann Andreas Eisenmenger, *The Traditions of the Jews, Contained in the Talmud and Other Mystical Writings* (London: J. Robinson, 1748), 195.
[38] James L. Kugel, *Traditions of the Bible* (Cambridge, Massachusetts: Harvard University Press, 1998), 121.
[39] *The Book of Jubilees*, 2:17-21 (notes), trans. R. H. Charles, The Apocrypha and Pseudepigrapha of the Old Testament (Oxford: Clarendon Press, 1913); James L. Kugel, *Traditions of the Bible* (Cambridge, Massachusetts: Harvard University Press, 1998), 121; *The History of al-Tabari - Volume I: General Introduction and From the Creation to the Flood*, The Story of Iblis, 82, The Story of Adam, 90, trans. Franz Rosenthal (Albany. New York Press, 1989), 253, 62-63; *The Book of Adam*, [44]16.3b, trans. J. P. Mahe, http://www.pseudepigrapha.com/pseudepigrapha/TheBookOfAdam.htm (accessed June 27, 2005); *The Qur'an* (Yusufali), 7. Al-Araf (The Heights), 007.011, http://www.usc.edu/schools/college/crcc/engagement/resources/texts/muslim/quran/007.qmt.html (accessed Dec. 30, 2010).
[40] *The History of al-Tabari - Volume I: General Introduction and From the Creation to the Flood*, The Story of Iblis, 81, trans. Franz Rosenthal (Albany: New York Press, 1989), 252; Psalms 104:4 (KJV); James L. Kugel, *Traditions of the Bible* (Cambridge, Massachusetts: Harvard University Press, 1998), 75.
[41] *The Qur'an* (Yusufali), 15. Al-Hijr (Al-Hijr, Stoneland, Rock City), 015.027, http://www.usc.edu/schools/college/crcc/engagement/resources/texts/muslim/quran/015.qmt.html (accessed Dec. 30, 2010).
[42] Johann Andreas Eisenmenger, *The Traditions of the Jews, Contained in the Talmud and Other Mystical Writings* (London: J. Robinson, 1748), 192.
[43] *The History of al-Tabari - Volume I: General Introduction and From the Creation to the Flood*, The Story of Adam, 93, trans. Franz Rosenthal (Albany: New York Press, 1989), 264; *The Silence of the Hosts of Angels*, 4, http://adamqadmon.com/nephilim/acollins2.html (accessed Dec. 5, 2000); *The Qur'an* (Yusufali), 15. Al-Hijr (Al-Hijr, Stoneland, Rock City), 015.026 - 015.035, http://www.usc.edu/schools/college/crcc/engagement/resources/texts/muslim/quran/015.qmt.html (accessed Dec. 30, 2010).
[44] *The Book of the Cave of Treasures*, The First Thousand Years: Adam to Yared (Jared), The Revolt of Satan, and the Battle in Heaven, trans. Sir E. A. Wallis Budge (London: The Religious Tract Society, 1927), 55-59.
[45] *The Book of the Cave of Treasures*, The First Thousand Years, The Revolt of Satan, and the Battle in Heaven, trans. Sir E. A. Wallis Budge (London: The Religious Tract Society, 1927), 55-59.
[46] *The First Book of Adam and Eve (The Conflict of Adam and Eve with Satan)*, 13:14, trans. S. C. Malan (London: Williams and Norgate, 1882).
[47] *The Armenian Apocryphal Adam Literature*, Concerning the Creation of Adam and the Incarnation of Christ Our God 10, trans. William Lowndes Lipscomb (Ann Arbor, Michigan: University Microfilms International, 1983), 262;

Johann Andreas Eisenmenger, *The Traditions of the Jews, Contained in the Talmud and other Mystical Writings* (London: J. Robinson, 1748), 195; Rabbi Leo Jung, Ph. D., *Fallen Angels in Jewish, Christian and Mohammedan Literature* (New York: KTAV Publishing House, 1974), 76; Stephen Quayle, *Genesis 6 Giants: The Master Builders of Prehistoric and Ancient Civilizations* (Bozeman, Montana: End Time Thunder Publishers, 2005), 30.

48 *Vita Adae Et Evae (The Life of Adam and Eve)*, 13:2-15:3, trans. R. H. Charles, *The Apocrypha and Pseudepigrapha of the Old Testament* (Oxford: Clarendon Press, 1913).

49 *The Book of the Cave of Treasures*, The First Thousand Years, The Revolt of Satan, and the Battle in Heaven, trans. Sir E. A. Wallis Budge (London: The Religious Tract Society, 1927), 55-59.

50 *The First Book of Adam and Eve (The Conflict of Adam and Eve with Satan)*, 6:7, trans. S. C. Malan (London: Williams and Norgate, 1882).

51 *The First Book of Adam and Eve (The Conflict of Adam and Eve with Satan)*, 13:2-5, trans. S. C. Malan (London: Williams and Norgate, 1882).

52 *The Penitence of our Forefather Adam*, Fall of Satan 12.1-16.2, trans. Gary A. Anderson and Michael E. Stone, http://www2.iath.virginia.edu/anderson/viat/english/vita.arm.html (accessed Dec 26, 2009).

53 S. Baring-Gould, *Legends of the Patriarchs and Prophets and Other Old Testament Characters* (New York: American Book Exchange, 1881), 18.

54 James L. Kugel, *Traditions of the Bible* (Cambridge, Massachusetts: Harvard University Press, 1998), 124; *The Armenian Apocryphal Adam Literature*, The History of the Creation and Transgression of Adam 11, trans. William Lowndes Lipscomb (Ann Arbor, Michigan: University Microfilms International, 1983), 120; *The History of al-Tabari - Volume I: General Introduction and From the Creation to the Flood*, The Story of Iblis, 81, 82, The Story of Adam, 93 (and notes), trans. Franz Rosenthal (Albany: New York Press, 1989), 252, 253, 264-265; S. Baring-Gould, *Legends of the Patriarchs and Prophets and Other Old Testament Characters* (New York: American Book Exchange, 1881), 39.

55 S. Baring-Gould, *Legends of the Patriarchs and Prophets and Other Old Testament Characters* (New York: American Book Exchange, 1881) 23, 39; *The Armenian Apocryphal Adam Literature*, History of the Creation and Transgression of Adam 11, trans. William Lowndes Lipscomb (Ann Arbor, Michigan: University Microfilms International, 1983), 120.

56 S. Baring-Gould, *Legends of the Patriarchs and Prophets and Other Old Testament Characters* (New York: American Book Exchange, 1881), 16.

57 Johann Andreas Eisenmenger, *The Traditions of the Jews, Contained in the Talmud and other Mystical Writings* (London: J. Robinson, 1748), 196; Alan Unterman, *Dictionary of Jewish Lore and Legend* (London: Thames and Hudson, 1991), 170; S. Baring-Gould, *Legends of the Patriarchs and Prophets and Other Old Testament Characters* (New York: American Book Exchange, 1881), 16.

58 Johann Andreas Eisenmenger, *The Traditions of the Jews, Contained in the Talmud and other Mystical Writings* (London: J. Robinson, 1748), 190, 192-193.

59 Alan Unterman, *Dictionary of Jewish Lore and Legend* (London: Thames and Hudson, 1991), 170; Johann Andreas Eisenmenger, *The Traditions of the Jews, Contained in the Talmud and other Mystical Writings*, By (London: J. Robinson, 1748), 188; Rabbi Leo Jung, Ph. D., *Fallen Angels in Jewish, Christian and Mohammedan Literature* (New York: KTAV Publishing House, 1974), 80.

60 *3 Enoch (The Hebrew Book of Enoch*), 26:12 (notes), trans. Hugo Odeberg (New York: KTAV Publishing House, Inc., 1973), 93; *Azazel and Atonement (No. 214)*, 6, http://www.adamqadmon.com/me[jo;o,/huie003.html (accessed Dec. 5, 2000); Johann Andreas Eisenmenger, *The Traditions of the Jews, Contained in the Talmud and other Mystical Writings* (London: J. Robinson, 1748), 186, 188.

61 *Zech.* 3:1-7 (KJV); *3 Enoch (The Hebrew Book of Enoch*), Chapter 26:12 (and notes), trans. Hugo Odeberg (New York: KTAV Publishing House, Inc., 1973), 93.

62 G. H. Pember, M. A., *Earth's Earliest Ages and their Connection With Modern Spiritualism, Theosophy, and Buddhism* (Grand Rapids, Michigan: Kregel Publications, 1975), 52, 56; *Rev.* 12:10 (KJV).

63 Johann Andreas Eisenmenger, *The Traditions of the Jews, Contained in the Talmud and Other Mystical Writings* (London: J. Robinson, 1748), 189.

64 Philip Gardiner and Gary Osborn, *The Shining Ones: The World's Most Powerful Secret Society Revealed* (London: Watkins Publishing, 2006), 145.

65 Philip Gardiner and Gary Osborn, *The Shining Ones: The World's Most Powerful Secret Society Revealed* (London: Watkins Publishing, 2006), 134.

66 Philip Gardiner and Gary Osborn, *The Shining Ones: The World's Most Powerful Secret Society Revealed* (London: Watkins Publishing, 2006), 146.

67 Strong's H1711 - *dagah*, http://www.blueletterbible.org/lang/lexicon/lexicon.cfm?Strongs=H1711&t=KJV# (accessed Jan. 5, 2010).

68 Gesunius's Lexicon - *dagah*, http://www.blueletterbible.org/lang/lexicon/lexicon.cfm?Strongs=H1711&t=KJV# (accessed Jan. 5, 2010).

69 Donald Mackenzie, *Myths of Babylonia and Assyriai,* Chapter 2 (1915), 28.

70 S. Baring-Gould, *Legends of the Patriarchs and Prophets and Other Old Testament Characters* (New York: American Book Exchange, 1881), 47-48.

[71] *The Zohar*, Volume 10, Mishpatim, Section 18. Two Messiahs, 482, www2.kabbalah.com/k/index.php/p=zohar/zohar&vol=20&sec=702 (accessed Feb. 24, 2010),

[72] Johann Andreas Eisenmenger, *The Traditions of the Jews, Contained in the Talmud and Other Mystical Writings* (London: J. Robinson, 1748), 193.

[73] *The Zohar*, Volume 10, Mishpatim, Section 18. Two Messiahs, 482, www2.kabbalah.com/k/index.php/p=zohar/zohar&vol=20&sec=702 (accessed Feb. 24, 2010),

[74] Johann Andreas Eisenmenger, *The Traditions of the Jews, Contained in the Talmud and other Mystical Writings*, By (London: J. Robinson, 1748), 205-206.

[75] Johann Andreas Eisenmenger, *The Traditions of the Jews, Contained in the Talmud and other Mystical Writings*, By (London: J. Robinson, 1748), 187.

[76] Johann Andreas Eisenmenger, *The Traditions of the Jews, Contained in the Talmud and other Mystical Writings*, By (London: J. Robinson, 1748), 186-187.

[77] Robert Graves and Raphael Patai, *Hebrew Myths: The Book of Genesis* (Garden City, New York: Doubleday & Company, 1964), 65.

[78] *Genizah Manuscripts of Palestinian Targum to the Pentateuch Volume One*, Genesis 2:20, trans. Michael L. Klein (Cincinnati: Hebrew Union College Press, 1986), 2.

[79] Strong's H3335 - *yatsar*, http://www.blueletterbible.org/lang/lexicon/lexicon.cfm?Strongs=H3335&t=KJV (accessed Jan. 5, 2010).

[80] Johann Andreas Eisenmenger, *The Traditions of the Jews, Contained in the Talmud and Other Mystical Writings* (London: J. Robinson, 1748), 22.

[81] *The Chronicles of Jerahmeel* (*The Hebrew Bible Historiale*), 23:1, trans. M. Gaster, Ph. D. (London: The Royal Asiatic Society, 1899), 48.

[82] James L. Kugel, *Traditions of the Bible* (Cambridge, Massachusetts: Harvard University Press, 1998), 113.

[83] J. E. Hanauer, *Folklore of the Holy Land: Moslem, Christian and Jewish*, II: Our Father Adam (London: BiblioBazaar, 2007), 9; James L. Kugel, *Traditions of the Bible* (Cambridge, Massachusetts: Harvard University Press, 1998), 113-114.

[84] J. E. Hanauer, *Folklore of the Holy Land: Moslem, Christian and Jewish*, II: Our Father Adam (London: BiblioBazaar, 2007), 9.

[85] Robert Graves and Raphael Patai, *Hebrew Myths: The Book of Genesis* (Garden City, New York: Doubleday & Company, 1964), 65.

[86] J. E. Hanauer, *Folklore of the Holy Land: Moslem, Christian and Jewish*, II: Our Father Adam (London: BiblioBazaar, 2007), 9.

[87] J. E. Hanauer, *Folklore of the Holy Land: Moslem, Christian and Jewish*, II: Our Father Adam (London: BiblioBazaar, 2007), 9.

[88] S. Baring-Gould, *Legends of the Patriarchs and Prophets and Other Old Testament Characters* (New York: American Book Exchange, 1881), 34.

[89] S. Baring-Gould, *Legends of the Patriarchs and Prophets and Other Old Testament Characters* (New York: American Book Exchange, 1881), 34.

[90] Louis Ginzberg, *Legends of the Jews: Volume 1*, trans. Henrietta Szold (Baltimore, Maryland: The Johns Hopkins University Press, 1909), 62.

[91] *The Chronicles of Jerahmeel* (*The Hebrew Bible Historiale*), 22:1, trans. M. Gaster, Ph. D. (London: The Royal Asiatic Society, 1899), 46.

[92] Hyman E. Goldin, *The Book of Legends: Tales From the Talmud and Midrash* (New York: The Jordan Publishng Co., 1929), 16; *The History of al-Tabari - Volume I: General Introduction and From the Creation to the Flood*, Adam is Taught All the Names, 98-99, trans. Franz Rosenthal (Albany: New York Press, 1989), 270-271; *The Armenian Apocryphal Adam Literature*, History and Sermon: Concerning the Creation of Adam and the Incarnation of Christ Our God 9, trans. William Lowndes Lipscomb (Ann Arbor, Michigan: University Microfilms International, 1983), 262; *Pirke De Rabbi Eliezer*, Chapter 13: The Serpent in Paradise [15A. ii.], trans. Gerald Friedlander (New York: Sepher-Hermon Press, 1981), 91.

[93] S. Baring-Gould, *Legends of the Patriarchs and Prophets and Other Old Testament Characters* (New York: American Book Exchange, 1881), 23; *Pirke De Rabbi Eliezer*, Chapter 13: The Serpent in Paradise [15A. ii.], trans. Gerald Friedlander (New York: Sepher-Hermon Press, 1981), 91.

[94] *Pirke De Rabbi Eliezer*, Chapter 13: The Serpent in Paradise [15A.ii.], trans. Gerald Friedlander (New York: Sepher-Hermon Press, 1981), 91.

[95] Ellen Frankel, *The Classic Tales: 4000 years of Jewish Lore* (Northvale, New Jersey: Jason Aronson Inc., 1989), 27.

[96] *The Chronicles of Jerahmeel* (*The Hebrew Bible Historiale*), 22:1, trans. M. Gaster, Ph. D. (London: The Royal Asiatic Society, 1899), 46.

[97] Robert Graves and Raphael Patai, *Hebrew Myths: The Book of Genesis* (Garden City, New York: Doubleday & Company, 1964), 62.

[98] *The Zohar*, Volume 19. Balak, Section 43. Aza and Azael, "falling down, but having his eyes open", 416, 419, https://www2.kabbalah.com/k/index.php/p=zohar/zohar&vol=43&sec=1518 (accessed Feb. 24, 2010); *3 Enoch (The*

Hebrew Book of Enoch), 40:3, trans. Hugo Odeberg (New York: KTAV Publishing House, Inc., 1973), 126; *The Chronicles of Jerahmeel* (*The Hebrew Bible Historiale*), 6:3, trans. M. Gaster, Ph. D (London: The Royal Asiatic Society, 1899); S. Baring-Gould, *Legends of the Patriarchs and Prophets and Other Old Testament Characters* (New York: American Book Exchange, 1881), 17.
[99] *The History of al-Tabari - Volume I: General Introduction and From the Creation to the Flood*, The Story of Iblis, 84, trans. Franz Rosenthal (Albany: New York Press, 1989), 255.
[100] *The Babylonian Talmud*, Book VII, Tract Sandhedrin, Part II (Haggada), Chapter XI, 369, trans. by Michael L. Rodkinson, http://www.sacred-texts.com/jud/t08/t0814.htm (accessed Jan 31, 2011).
[101] Louis Ginzberg, *Legends of the Jews: Volume 1*, trans. Henrietta Szold (Baltimore, Maryland: The Johns Hopkins University Press, 1909), 53.
[102] *The Zohar*, Volume 2, Beresheet B, Section 69. "The Nefilim were on the earth", 423, https://www2.kabbalah.com/k/index.php/p=zohar/zohar&vol=3&sec=142 (accessed Feb. 24, 2010).
[103] Louis Ginzberg, *Legends of the Jews: Volume 1*, trans. Henrietta Szold (Baltimore, Maryland: The Johns Hopkins University Press, 1909), 151.
[104] *The Zohar*, Volume 1, Beresheet A, Section 20. The five types of the mixed multitude, 227, https://www2.kabbalah.com/k/index.php/p=zohar/zohar&vol=2&sec=41 (accessed Feb. 24, 2010).
[105] *Pirke De Rabbi Eliezer*, Chapter 22: The Fall of the Angels [26A. i.], trans. Gerald Friedlander, 160.
[106] *The Zohar*, Volume 2. Beresheet B, Section 69. "The Nefilim were on the earth", 423-424, https://www2.kabbalah.com/k/index.php/p=zohar/zohar&vol=3&sec=142 (accessed Feb. 24, 2010); *The Zohar*, Volume 1. Beresheet A, Section 20. The five types of the mixed multitude, 226, https://www2.kabbalah.com/k/index.php/p=zohar/zohar&vol=2&sec=41 (accessed Feb. 24, 2010). *The Zohar*, Volume 1. Beresheet A, Section 50. Aza and Azael, 464, https://www2.kabbalah.com/k/index.php/p=zohar/zohar&vol=2&sec=71 (accessed Feb. 24, 2010).
[107] *The Zohar*, Volume 2, Beresheet B, Section 69. "The Nefilim were on the earth", 423, https://www2.kabbalah.com/k/index.php/p=zohar/zohar&vol=3&sec=142 (accessed Feb. 24, 2010).
[108] Malcolm Godwin, *Angels: An Endangered Species* (New York: Simon & Schuester, 1990), 86.
[109] *The Zohar*, Volume 1. Beresheet A, Section 20. The five types of the mixed multitude, 226, https://www2.kabbalah.com/k/index.php/p=zohar/zohar&vol=2&sec=41 (accessed Feb. 24, 2010); *Sefer 'Uza Wa-'Aza(z)el: Exploring Early Jewish Mythologies of Evil*, 1, http://www.religiousstudies.uncc.edu/jcreeves/sefer_uzza_waazazel.htm (accessed July 1, 2005).
[110] *The Zohar*, Volume 2. Beresheet B, Section 69. "The Nefilim were on the earth", 423, https://www2.kabbalah.com/k/index.php/p=zohar/zohar&vol=3&sec=142 (accessed Feb. 24, 2010). *The Zohar*, Volume 1. Beresheet A, Section 50. Aza and Azael, 466, https://www2.kabbalah.com/k/index.php/p=zohar/zohar&vol=2&sec=71 (accessed Feb. 24, 2010).
[111] *Pirke De Rabbi Eliezer*, Chapter 13: The Serpent in Paradise [15A.ii.], trans. Gerald Friedlander, 91.

Chapter 6

[1] *Vita Adae Et Evae (The Life of Adam and Eve)*, 16:4, trans. R. H. Charles, *The Apocrypha and Pseudepigrapha of the Old Testament* (Oxford: Clarendon Press, 1913).
[2] *The Book of the Cave of Treasures*, The First Thousand Years: Adam to Yared (Jared), The Symbolism of Eden, trans. Sir E. A. Wallis Budge (London: The Religious Tract Society, 1927), 62-63.
[3] *The Apocalypse of Moses / Apocalypsis Mosis (The Life of Adam and Eve)*, 15:3, trans. R. H. Charles, http://www.pseudepigrapha.com/pseudepigrapha/aprmose.htm (accessed June 27, 2005); *The Book of Adam*, trans. J. P. Mahe, [32]7.3b, [44]15.3, [44]17.3, http://www.pseudepigrapha.com/pseudepigrapha/TheBookOfAdam.htm (accessed June 27, 2005); *The Bible, The Koran, and the Talmud (Biblical Legends of the Mussulmans)*, Adam (A Mohammedan Legend), trans. Dr. G. Weil (New York, 1863), 2.
[4] *The Book of the Cave of Treasures*, The First Thousand Years, The Making of Eve (notes), trans. Sir E. A. Wallis Budge (London: The Religious Tract Society, 1927), 61.
[5] David Goldstein, *Jewish Legends (Library of the World's Myths and Legends)* (New York: Peter Bedrick Books, 1933), 4.
[6] Mrs. Sydney Bristowe, *Sargon the Magnificent* (London: The Covenant Publishing Co., 1927), 120.
[7] *The Book of Adam*, trans. J. P. Mahe, [38]11.1, http://www.pseudepigrapha.com/pseudepigrapha/TheBookOfAdam.htm (accessed June 27, 2005).
[8] *Saltair na Rann*, 1193-1196, trans. David Greene.
[9] Malcolm Godwin, *Angels: An Endangered Species* (New York: Simon & Schuester, 1990), 71.
[10] Johann Andreas Eisenmenger, *The Traditions of the Jews, Contained in the Talmud and other Mystical Writings* (London: J. Robinson, 1748), 189.
[11] Andrew Collins, *From the Ashes of Angels* (Rochester, Vermont: Bear & Company, 1996), 59.
[12] *The Life of Adam and Eve (The Apocalypse of Moses / Apocalypsis Mosis)*, 26:3, trans. R. H. Charles, http://www.pseudepigrapha.com/pseudepigrapha/aprmose.htm (accessed June 27, 2005); Alan Unterman, *Dictionary of Jewish Lore and Legend* (London: Thames and Hudson Ltd., 1991), 176.

[13] Andrew Collins, *From the Ashes of Angels* (Rochester, Vermont: Bear & Company, 1996), 103.
[14] Alan Unterman, *Dictionary of Jewish Lore and Legend* (London: Thames and Hudson Ltd., 1991), 176.
[15] Rabbi Leo Jung, Ph. D., *Fallen Angels in Jewish, Christian and Mohammedan Literature* (New York: KTAV Publishing House, 1974), 115.
[16] *Timeline of Nephilim Movement Through the World*, 1-2, http://www.ziarah.net.timeline.html (accessed March 19, 2007).
[17] *The Book of Enoch*. 87:2, trans. R. H. Charles (Montana: Kessinger Publishing, 1912).
[18] *2 Enoch (The Book of the Secrets of Enoch)*, 1:6, trans. W. R. Morfill, M.A. (Oxford: Clarendon Press, 1896).
[19] Andrew Collins, *From the Ashes of Angels* (Rochester, Vermont: Bear & Company, 1996), 48.
[20] *The Testament of Amram* (The Dead Sea Scrolls), (4Q544) Fr. 1, trans. Geza Vermes, *The Complete Dead Sea Scrolls in English* (New York: Penguin Books, 1997), 535.
[21] Louis Ginzberg, *The Legends of the Jews Volume V: Notes for Volume One and Two*, II. Adam, 124, trans. Henrietta Szold (Baltimore, Maryland: The Johns Hopkins University Press, 1909), 131; Andrew Collins, *From the Ashes of Angels* (Rochester, Vermont: Bear & Company, 1996), 156, 158.
[22] *Gates of Hell: The Descent of Ishtar to the Netherworld*, 3 (*Ancient Near Eastern Texts*, trans. E. A. Speiser and George A. Barton), http://www.piney.com/Ishtar.html (accessed Dec. 30, 2010).
[23] *The Testament of Amram* (The Dead Sea Scrolls), (4Q544) Fr. 1, trans. Geza Vermes, *The Complete Dead Sea Scrolls in English* (New York: Penguin Books, 1997), 535.
[24] Andrew Collins, *From the Ashes of Angels* (Rochester, Vermont: Bear & Company, 1996), 255-256, 258-261, 268; *Timeline of Nephilim Movement Through the World*, 1-2, www.ziarah.net/timeline.html, (accessed March 19, 2007).
[25] *The Apocalypse of Abraham*, 23:7, translator unknown, http://www.pseudepigrapha.com/pseudepigrapha/Apocalypse_of_Abraham.html (accessed Oct 5, 2006); Louis Ginzberg, *The Legends of the Jews Volume V: Notes for Volume One and Two*, II. Adam, 117, trans. Henrietta Szold (Baltimore, Maryland: The Johns Hopkins University Press, 1909), 121; *The Writings of Abraham*, 23:7, 23:35, http://www.earth-history.com/Pseudepigrapha/Mormonism/writings-abraham-1.htm (accessed May 10, 2007); Strong's G1404 - *drakon*, http://www.blueletterbible.org/lang/lexicon/lexicon.cfm?Strongs=G1404&t=KJV (accessed Dec 29, 2010).
[26] Strong's H8314 - *seraph*, http://www.blueletterbible.org/lang/lexicon/lexicon.cfm?Strongs=H8314&t=KJV, (accessed Jan. 12, 2010); *dragon*, 1, https://www.blueletterbible.org/search/search.cfm?Criteria=dragon&t=KJV#s=s_primary_0_1 (accessed Dec. 29, 2016).
[27] Johann Andreas Eisenmenger, *The Traditions of the Jews, Contained in the Talmud and Other Mystical Writings* (London: J. Robinson, 1748), 187-189.
[28] Kingdom Bible Studies: Studies in End-Time Revelation, *The Heavens Declare Part 18: Scorpio - the Scorpion*, 1, http://www.sigler.org/eby/heavens18.html (accessed Sept. 11, 2000).
[29] Adam Clarke, *Nachash, The Serpent*, 3, http://wesley.nnu.edu/wesleyctr/books/0901-1000/HDM0999.PDF (accessed Jan. 5, 2010).
[30] *The Gospel of Judas: Cain-Cainites-Kenite-Rechablites*, 1, http://www.piney.com/Cain.html (accessed April 19, 2007).
[31] *The Companion Bible*, Appendix 19 (Grand Rapids, Michigan: Kregel Publications, 1990), 24-25.
[32] *Satan's Seed*, 1, http://www.thetruword.com/satansseed.htm (accessed Sept. 11, 2000); *The Doctrine of Original Sin Part I: The Garden of Eden (No. 246)*, 8, 24, http://www.adamqadmon.com/nephilim/gardeneden/html (accessed Feb. 10, 2001).
[33] Gary Osborn, *Shining Ones*, http://garyosborn.moonfruit.com/#/shining-ones-notes/4519248692 (accessed Dec. 30, 2010).
[34] Andrew Collins, *From the Ashes of Angels* (Rochester, Vermont: Bear & Company, 1996), 50; *The Doctrine of Original Sin Part I: The Garden of Eden (No. 246)*, 8, http://www.adamqadmon.com/nephilim/gardeneden/html (accessed Feb. 10, 2001); Louis Ginzberg, *The Legends of the Jews Volume V: Notes for Volume One and Two*, II. Adam, 131, trans. Henrietta Szold (Baltimore, Maryland: The Johns Hopkins University Press, 1909), 124.
[35] Andrew Collins, *From the Ashes of Angels* (Rochester, Vermont: Bear & Company, 1996), 41, 52-53; *The Doctrine of Original Sin Part I: The Garden of Eden (No. 246)*, 8, 24, http://www.adamqadmon.com/nephilim/gardeneden/html (accessed Feb. 10, 2001); G. H. Pember, M. A., *Earth's Earliest Ages and their Connection With Modern Spiritualism, Theosophy, and Buddhism* (Grand Rapids, Michigan: Kregel Publications, 1975), 112; Malcolm Godwin, *Angels: An Endangered Species* (New York: Simon & Schuester, 1990), 25-26; *The Silence of the Hosts of Angels*, 4, http://www.adamqadmon.com/nephilim/acollins2/html (accessed Dec. 5, 2000).
[36] *3 Enoch (The Hebrew Book of Enoch)*, 26:8 (notes), trans. Hugo Odeberg (New York: KTAV Publishing House, Inc., 1973), 92.
[37] Malcolm Godwin, *Angels: An Endangered Species* (New York: Simon & Schuester, 1990), 25.
[38] Encyclopedia Mithica, *Seraphim*, 1, http://www.pantheon.org/mythica/articles/seraphim.html (accessed July 1, 2000).
[39] *The Book of the Mysteries of the Heavens and the Earth and Other Works of Bakhayla Mikael (Zosimas)*, trans. E.A.

Wallis Budge (London: Oxford University Press, 1935), 17.
[40] *The Apocalypse of Abraham*, 23:11-2, translator unknown, http://www.pseudepigrapha.com/pseudepigrapha/Apocalypse_of_Abraham.html (accessed Oct 5, 2006).
[41] Louis Ginzberg, *The Legends of the Jews Volume V: Notes for Volume One and Two*, II. Adam, 131, trans. Henrietta Szold (Baltimore, Maryland: The Johns Hopkins University Press, 1909), 123; *The Apocalypse of Abraham*, 23:35-36, translator unknown, http://www.pseudepigrapha.com/pseudepigrapha/Apocalypse_of_Abraham.html (accessed Oct 5, 2006).
[42] Malcolm Godwin, *Angels: An Endangered Species* (New York: Simon & Schuester, 1990), 112.
[43] Hitchcock's Bible Name Dictionary, *Azaz*, 7, http://www.adamqadmon.com/nephilim/definitions/biblenames.html (accessed March 8, 2001); *Azazel and Atonement (No. 214)*, 32, http://www.adamqadmon.com/nephilim/huie003.html (accessed Dec. 5, 2000).
[44] *Azazel and Atonement (No. 214)*, 32, http://www.adamqadmon.com/nephilim/huie003.html (accessed Dec. 5, 2000).
[45] Louis Ginzberg, *The Legends of the Jews Volume V: Notes for Volume One and Two*, II. Adam, 121, trans. Henrietta Szold (Baltimore, Maryland: The Johns Hopkins University Press, 1909), 117; Wikipedia, the Free Encyclopedia, *Azazel*, 2, http://en.wikipedia.org/wiki/Azazel (accessed Oct. 05, 2006).
[46] Louis Ginzberg, *The Legends of the Jews Volume V: Notes for Volume One and Two*, II. Adam, 121, trans. Henrietta Szold (Baltimore, Maryland: The Johns Hopkins University Press, 1909), 117; Malcolm Godwin, *Angels: An Endangered Species* (New York: Simon & Schuester, 1990), 113.
[47] *The Book of Enoch*, 69:4-12, trans. R. H. Charles (Montana: Kessinger Publishing, 1912); Louis Ginzberg, *The Legends of the Jews Volume V: Notes for Volume One and Two*, II. Adam, 131, IV. Noah, 10, trans. Henrietta Szold (Baltimore, Maryland: The Johns Hopkins University Press, 1909), 124, 170-1; Malcolm Godwin, *Angels: An Endangered Species* (New York: Simon & Schuester, 1990), 113.
[48] *The Book of Enoch*, 69:6, trans. R. H. Charles (Montana: Kessinger Publishing, 1912); Malcolm Godwin, *Angels: An Endangered Species* (New York: Simon & Schuester, 1990), 113; Louis Ginzberg, *The Legends of the Jews Volume V: Notes for Volume One and Two*, II. Adam, 121, trans. Henrietta Szold (Baltimore, Maryland: The Johns Hopkins University Press, 1909), 116.
[49] *The Book of Enoch*, 69:4-12, trans. R. H. Charles (Montana: Kessinger Publishing, 1912); Louis Ginzberg, *The Legends of the Jews Volume V: Notes for Volume One and Two*, II. Adam, 121, trans. Henrietta Szold (Baltimore, Maryland: The Johns Hopkins University Press, 1909), 116; Malcolm Godwin, *Angels: An Endangered Species* (New York: Simon & Schuester, 1990), 113; *The Apocalypse of Abraham*, 22:33, 23:34, 23:36, translator unknown, http://www.pseudepigrapha.com/pseudepigrapha/Apocalypse_of_Abraham.html (accessed Oct 5, 2006).
[50] Jayim Nahman Bialik and Yehoshua Hana Ravnitzky, *The Book of Legends (Sefer Ha-Aggadah): Legends from the Talmud and Midrash* (New York: Shocken Books, 1992), 22; *The Chronicles of Jerahmeel* (*The Hebrew Bible Historiale*), 6:4, 6:13, 7:2, trans. M. Gaster, Ph. D. (London: The Royal Asiatic Society, 1899), 15, 17, 18.
[51] Hyman E. Goldin, *The Book of Legends: Tales From the Talmud and Midrash* (New York: The Jordan Publishing Co., 1929), 20.
[52] Johann Andreas Eisenmenger, *The Traditions of the Jews, Contained in the Talmud and Other Mystical Writings* (London: J. Robinson, 1748), 196.
[53] Ellen Frankel, *The Classic Tales: 4000 Years of Jewish Lore* (Northvale, New Jersey: Jason Aronson Inc., 1989), 28.
[54] Rabbi Leo Jung, Ph. D., *Fallen Angels in Jewish, Christian and Mohammedan Literature* (New York: KTAV Publishing House, 1974), 69.
[55] Johann Andreas Eisenmenger, *The Traditions of the Jews, Contained in the Talmud and Other Mystical Writings* (London: J. Robinson, 1748), 198.
[56] Merriam-Webster Dictionary, *Dainty*, http://www.merriam-webster.com/dictionary/dainty (accessed Feb. 3, 2010).
[57] Rabbi Leo Jung, Ph. D., *Fallen Angels in Jewish, Christian and Mohammedan Literature* (New York: KTAV Publishing House, 1974), 73-74.
[58] *Barhebraeus' Scholia on the Old Testament Part I: Genesis - II Samuel*, Genesis 3:1, trans. Martin Sprengling and William Creighton Graham (Chicago, Illinois: University of Chicago Press 1931), 25.
[59] *Star Wars, Lesson Seven*, 6, http://usa-the-republic.com/religion/star%20wars/Star%20Wars%20-%20Lesson%20Seven.htm (accessed April 23, 2005).
[60] *The History of al-Tabari - Volume I: General Introduction and From the Creation to the Flood*, The Story of Iblis, 83, trans. Franz Rosenthal (Albany: New York Press, 1989), 254.
[61] Shira Halevi, *The Life Story of Adam and Havah*, Genesis 3:1a (Northvale, New Jersey: Jason Aronson, Inc., 1997), 166.
[62] *Genizah Manuscripts of Palestinian Targum to the Pentateuch Volume One*, Genesis 3:1, trans. Michael L. Klein (Cincinnati: Hebrew Union College Press, 1986), 3.
[63] Merriam-Webster Dictionary, *Shrewd*, http://www.merriam-webster.com/dictionary/shrewd (accessed Feb. 3, 2010).
[64] *Star Wars, Lesson Seven*, 7, http://usa-the-republic.com/religion/star%20wars/Star%20Wars%20-%20Lesson%20Seven.htm (accessed April 23, 2005).
[65] Louis Ginzberg, *The Legends of the Jews Volume V: Notes for Volume One and Two*, II. Adam, 117, trans. Henrietta

Szold (Baltimore, Maryland: The Johns Hopkins University Press, 1909), 121.
[66] *The History of al-Tabari - Volume I: General Introduction and From the Creation to the Flood*, The Story of Adam, 91, trans. Franz Rosenthal (Albany: New York Press, 1989), 262.
[67] *The History of al-Tabari - Volume I: General Introduction and From the Creation to the Flood*, The Story of Iblis, 83, trans. Franz Rosenthal (Albany: New York Press, 1989), 254.
[68] *The History of al-Tabari - Volume I: General Introduction and From the Creation to the Flood*, The Story of Iblis, 83, trans. Franz Rosenthal (Albany: New York Press, 1989), 254; *The History of al-Tabari - Volume I: General Introduction and From the Creation to the Flood*, The Story of Iblis, 80, trans. Franz Rosenthal (Albany: New York Press, 1989), 250-251.
[69] *The History of al-Tabari - Volume I: General Introduction and From the Creation to the Flood*, The Story of Iblis, 80, trans. Franz Rosenthal (Albany: New York Press, 1989), 250-251.
[70] *The First Book of Adam and Eve (The Conflict of Adam and Eve with Satan)*, 46:4, trans. S. C. Malan (London: Williams and Norgate, 1882).
[71] *Pirke De Rabbi Eliezer*, Chapter 13: The Serpent in Paradise [15A.ii.], trans. Gerald Friedlander (New York: Sepher-Hermon Press, 1981), 91.
[72] *The Book of Adam*, [44]16.3a-16.4, trans. J. P. Mahe, http://www.pseudepigrapha.com/pseudepigrapha/TheBookOfAdam.htm (accessed June 27, 2005).
[73] *Pirke De Rabbi Eliezer*, Chapter 13: The Serpent in Paradise [15A. ii.], trans. Gerald Friedlander (New York: Sepher-Hermon Press, 1981), 92; *The Apocalypse of Moses / Apocalypsis Mosis*, 16:5, 17:4, trans. R. H. Charles, http://www.pseudepigrapha.com/pseudepigrapha/aprmose.htm (accessed June 27, 2005); James L. Kugel, *Traditions of the Bible* (Cambridge, Massachusetts: Harvard University Press, 1998), 124-125.
[74] *The Penitence of our Forefather Adam*, Temptation of Eve [44]18.3, trans. Gary A. Anderson and Michael E. Stone, http://www2.iath.virginia.edu/anderson/viat/english/vita.arm.html (accessed Dec. 26, 2009); *The History of al-Tabari - Volume I: General Introduction and From the Creation to the Flood*, God's Testing of Adam, 105, 109, trans. Franz Rosenthal (Albany: New York Press (1989), 276, 281; *The Book of Adam*, [44]16.1-4, trans. J. P. Mahe, http://www.pseudepigrapha.com/pseudepigrapha/TheBookOfAdam.htm (accessed June 27, 2005).
[75] Louis Ginzberg, *The Legends of the Jews Volume V: Notes for Volume One and Two*, II. Adam, 131, trans. Henrietta Szold (Baltimore, Maryland: The Johns Hopkins University Press, 1909), 124.
[76] *The History of al-Tabari - Volume I: General Introduction and From the Creation to the Flood*, The Story of Iblis, 83, trans. Franz Rosenthal (Albany: New York Press (1989), 254.
[77] *The Apocalypse of Moses / Apocalypsis Mosis*, 16:1-18:6, trans. R. H. Charles, http://www.pseudepigrapha.com/pseudepigrapha/aprmose.htm (accessed June 27, 2005).
[78] *Barhebraeus' Scholia on the Old Testament Part I: Genesis - II Samuel*, Genesis 3:1-4, trans. Martin Sprengling and William Creighton Graham (Chicago, Illinois: University of Chicago Press 1931), 25.
[79] *The Book of Enoch*, 10:9, trans. R. H. Charles (Montana: Kessinger Publishing, 1912).

Chapter 7

[1] *2 Enoch (The Book of the Secrets of Enoch)*, 31:5, trans. W.R. Morfill, M.A. (Oxford: Clarendon Press, 1896).
[2] Rabbi Leo Jung, Ph. D., *Fallen Angels in Jewish, Christian and Mohammedan Literature* (New York: KTAV Publishing House, 1974), 68-69.
[3] *The Apocalypse of Moses / Apocalypsis Mosis*, 15:3 (notes), trans. R. H. Charles, http://www.pseudepigrapha.com/pseudepigrapha/aprmose.htm (accessed June 27, 2005); Andrew Collins, *From the Ashes of Angels* (Rochester, Vermont: Bear & Company, 1996), 40.
[4] Andrew Collins, *From the Ashes of Angels* (Rochester, Vermont: Bear & Company, 1996), 40; J. E. Hanauer, *Folklore of the Holy Land: Moslem, Christian and Jewish*, 2: Our Father Adam (London: BiblioBazaar, 2007), 10; Alan Unterman, *Dictionary of Jewish Lore and Legend* (London: Thames and Hudson Ltd., 1991), 176.
[5] Dominick McClausland, *Adam and the Adamite; or, The Harmony of Scripture and Ethnology* (London, Richard Bentley and Son, 1872), 130.
[6] Robert Graves and Raphael Patai, *Hebrew Myths: The Book of Genesis* (Garden City, New York: Doubleday & Company, 1964), 85; James L. Kugel, *Traditions of the Bible* (Cambridge, Massachusetts: Harvard University Press, 1998), 122.
[7] Greg Killian, *The Days of Noah*, 19-20, http://www.adamqadmon.com/nephilim/gkillian000 (accessed Dec. 6, 2000); James L. Kugel, *Traditions of the Bible* (Cambridge, Massachusetts: Harvard University Press, 1998), 110.
2[8] 4 Maccabees 18:7-8 (Revised Standard Version), http://quod.lib.umich.edu/cgi/r/rsv/rsv-idx?type=DIV1&byte=4496061 (accessed Jan. 31, 2011).
[9] *Pirke De Rabbi Eliezer*, Chapter 13: The Serpent in Paradise [15A. ii.], trans. Gerald Friedlander (New York: Sepher-Hermon Press, 1981), 94.
[10] *Pirke De Rabbi Eliezer*, Chapter 13: The Serpent in Paradise [15A. ii.], trans. Gerald Friedlander (New York: Sepher-Hermon Press, 1981), 94.
[11] Shira Halevi, *The Life Story of Adam and Havah*, Genesis 3:5 - 3:6a (Northvale, New Jersey: Jason Aronson, Inc., 1997), 167-168.

[12] *The Book of Adam*, [44]15:3-4, trans. J. P. Mahe, http://www.pseudepigrapha.com/pseudepigrapha/TheBookOfAdam.htm (accessed June 27, 2005).

[13] *The Book of Adam*, [44]18.1, 19.1-20.5, trans. J. P. Mahe, http://www.pseudepigrapha.com/pseudepigrapha/TheBookOfAdam.htm (accessed June 27, 2005); *Vita Adae Et Evae (The Life of Adam and Eve)*, 4:2, trans. R. H. Charles, *The Apocrypha and Pseudepigrapha of the Old Testament* (Oxford: Clarendon Press, 1913); *Saltair na Rann*, 1233-1240, trans. David Greene.

[14] Johann Andreas Eisenmenger, *The Traditions of the Jews, Contained in the Talmud and other Mystical Writings* (London: J. Robinson, 1748) 193; Robert Graves and Raphael Patai, *Hebrew Myths: The Book of Genesis* (Garden City, New York: Doubleday & Company, 1964), 78.

[15] *The Book of Adam*, [44]18.3, trans. J. P. Mahe, http://www.pseudepigrapha.com/pseudepigrapha/TheBookOfAdam.htm (accessed June 27, 2005).

[16] *The First Book of Adam and Eve (The Conflict of Adam and Eve with Satan)*, 13:16, trans. S. C. Malan (London: Williams and Norgate, 1882).

[17] *The Book of Adam*, [44]19.1-3, [44]20.4-5, trans. J. P. Mahe, http://www.pseudepigrapha.com/pseudepigrapha/TheBookOfAdam.htm (accessed June 27, 2005).

[18] *Armenian Apocrypha Relating to Adam and Eve*, 9 (notes), trans. Michael E. Stone (Leiden: E. J. Brill, 1996), 31.

[19] G. H. Pember, M. A., *Earth's Earliest Ages and their Connection With Modern Spiritualism, Theosophy, and Buddhism* (Grand Rapids, Michigan: Kregel Publications, 1975), 127.

[20] Louis Ginzberg, *The Legends of the Jews Volume V: Notes for Volume One and Two*, II. Adam, 131, trans. Henrietta Szold (Baltimore, Maryland: The Johns Hopkins University Press, 1909), 124; Robert Graves and Raphael Patai, *Hebrew Myths: The Book of Genesis* (Garden City, New York: Doubleday & Company, 1964), 86-87.

[21] Bentley Layton, *The Gnostic Scriptures*, "Other" Gnostic Teachings According to St. Irenaeus (New York: Doubleday, 1995), 181; Rabbi Leo Jung, Ph. D., *Fallen Angels in Jewish, Christian and Mohammedan Literature* (New York: KTAV Publishing House, 1974), 75-76; Robert Graves and Raphael Patai, *Hebrew Myths: The Book of Genesis* (Garden City, New York: Doubleday & Company, 1964), 85.

[22] Schatzhohle, III (Rabbi Leo Jung, Ph. D., *Fallen Angels in Jewish, Christian and Mohammedan Literature* (New York: KTAV Publishing House, 1974), 79).

[23] Johann Andreas Eisenmenger, *The Traditions of the Jews, Contained in the Talmud and Other Mystical Writings* (London: J. Robinson, 1748), 21.

[24] *The Zohar*, Volume 13, Pekudei, Section 21. Breastplate and Efod, 203, https://www2.kabbalah.com/k/index.php/p=zohar/zohar&vol=26&sec=912 (accessed Feb. 24, 2010).

[25] Alan Unterman, *Dictionary of Jewish Lore and Legend* (London: Thames and Hudson Ltd., 1991), 150.

[26] Wikipedia, the Free Dictionary, *Eve*, 4, http://en.wikipedia.org/wiki/Eve_%28Bible%29 (accessed Oct. 23, 2007).

[27] Greg Killian, *The Days of Noah*, 4, http://www.adamqadmon.com/nephilim/gkillian000 (accessed Dec. 6, 2000); Alan Unterman, *Dictionary of Jewish Lore and Legend* (New York: Thames and Hudson 1991), 176.

[28] Louis Ginzberg, *The Legends of the Jews Volume V: Notes for Volume One and Two*, II. Adam, 119, III. The Ten Generations, 3, trans. Henrietta Szold (Baltimore, Maryland: The Johns Hopkins University Press, 1909), 121, 133; James L. Kugel, *Traditions of the Bible* (Cambridge, Massachusetts: Harvard University Press, 1998), 130-131; Alan Unterman, *Dictionary of Jewish Lore and Legend* (London: Thames and Hudson Ltd., 1991), 150.

[29] *The Apocalypse of Moses / Apocalypsis Mosis*, 19:3, trans. R. H. Charles, http://www.pseudepigrapha.com/pseudepigrapha/aprmose.htm (accessed June 27, 2005).

[30] Andrew Collins, *From the Ashes of Angels: The Forbidden Legacy of a Fallen Race* (Rochester, Vermont: Bear and Company, 1996), 25.

[31] *The Book of Enoch*, 10:8, trans. R.H. Charles (Montana: Kessinger Publishing, 1912).

[32] Rabbi Leo Jung, Ph. D., *Fallen Angels in Jewish, Christian and Mohammedan Literature* (New York: KTAV Publishing House, 1974), 76.

[33] Merriam-Webster Dictionary, *Lasciviousness*, http://www.merriam-webster.com/dictionary/lasciviousness (accessed July 28, 2010); Rabbi Leo Jung, Ph. D., *Fallen Angels in Jewish, Christian and Mohammedan Literature* (New York: KTAV Publishing House, 1974), 78.

[34] Johann Andreas Eisenmenger, *The Traditions of the Jews, Contained in the Talmud and other Mystical Writings* (London: J. Robinson, 1748), 194; *The Armenian Apocryphal Adam Literature*, The History of the Creation and Transgression of Adam 20-26, History and Sermon: Concerning the Creation of Adam and the Incarnation of Christ Our God 19-31, trans. William Lowndes Lipscomb (Ann Arbor, Michigan: University Microfilms International, 1983), 122, 263; *The Book of Adam*, [44]19.1, trans. J. P. Mahe, http://www.pseudepigrapha.com/pseudepigrapha/TheBookOfAdam.htm (accessed June 27, 2005); *The Chronicles of Jerahmeel* (*The Hebrew Bible Historiale*), 22:4-5, trans. M. Gaster, Ph. D. (London: The Royal Asiatic Society, 1899), 47.

[35] *Pirke De Rabbi Eliezer*, Chapter 13: The Serpent in Paradise [15A. ii.], trans. Gerald Friedlander (New York: Sepher-Hermon Press, 1981), 93.

[36] *The Book of Adam*, [45]32.2, trans. J. P. Mahe, http://www.pseudepigrapha.com/pseudepigrapha/TheBookOfAdam.htm (accessed June 27, 2005).

[37] *The Book of Adam*, [38]11.1-[38]11.2, trans. J. P. Mahe, http://www.pseudepigrapha.com/pseudepigrapha/TheBookOfAdam.htm (accessed June 27, 2005).
[38] *The Book of Adam*, [44]21.2, trans. J. P. Mahe, http://www.pseudepigrapha.com/pseudepigrapha/TheBookOfAdam.htm (accessed June 27, 2005).
[39] G. H. Pember, M. A., *Earth's Earliest Ages and their Connection With Modern Spiritualism, Theosophy, and Buddhism* (Grand Rapids, Michigan: Kregel Publications, 1975), 112; Malcolm Godwin, *Angels: An Endangered Species* (New York: Simon & Schuester, 1990), 26, 28, 104.
[40] *Saltair na Rann*, 1301-1316, trans. David Greene.
[41] *There Were Giants on the earth... The Nephilim*, 2, http://biblelight.net/nephilim.htm (accessed Feb. 3, 2010).
[42] *There Were Giants on the earth... The Nephilim*, 2, http://biblelight.net/nephilim.htm (accessed Feb. 3, 2010).
[43] Philo, *On the* Creation 151-152 (also 165-166) (James L. Kugel, *The Bible As It Was* (Cambridge, Massachusetts: Harvard University Press, 1997), 75).
[44] *The Gospel of Philip*, trans. Wesley W. Isenberg, http://www.gnosis.org/naghamm/gop.html (accessed Feb. 4, 2010).
[45] *The History of al-Tabari - Volume I: General Introduction and From the Creation to the Flood,* Adam and Eve's Place on Earth, 121, trans. Franz Rosenthal (Albany: New York Press, 1989), 292.
[46] *The First Book of Adam and Eve (The Conflict of Adam and Eve with Satan)*, 13:6-7, trans. S. C. Malan (London: Williams and Norgate, 1882).
[47] *The First Book of Adam and Eve (The Conflict of Adam and Eve with Satan)*, 32:7, 37:1, trans. S. C. Malan (London: Williams and Norgate, 1882).
[48] *The Apocalypse of Moses / Apocalypsis Mosis*, 24:4, trans. R. H. Charles, http://www.pseudepigrapha.com/pseudepigrapha/aprmose.htm (accessed June 27, 2005); *The Book of Adam*, [44]24:4, trans. J. P. Mahe, http://www.pseudepigrapha.com/pseudepigrapha/TheBookOfAdam.htm (accessed June 27, 2005); *The Armenian Apocryphal Adam Literature*, The History of the Repentance of Adam and Eve, the First Created Ones, and How They Did It 87-90, trans. William Lowndes Lipscomb (Ann Arbor, Michigan: University Microfilms International, 1983), 231.
[49] *The Book of the Bee*, 20, trans. Earnest A. Wallis Budge, M. A., http://www.sacred-texts.com/chr/bb/bb20.htm (accessed Oct. 10, 2004); *The Book of Adam*, [44]24.4, trans. J. P. Mahe, http://www.pseudepigrapha.com/pseudepigrapha/TheBookOfAdam.htm (accessed June 27, 2005).
[50] *The Armenian Apocryphal Adam Literature*, The History of the Repentance of Adam and Eve, The First Created Ones, and How They Did It 20, trans. William Lowndes Lipscomb (Ann Arbor, Michigan: University Microfilms International, 1983), 223-224.
[51] *The Babylonian Talmud*, Jews' College / Soncino English Translation, Sanhedrin 59a, http://www.halakhah.com/sanhedrin/sanhedrin_59.html (accessed Feb 3, 2010).
[52] *The Midrash Rabbah*, Bereshith (Genesis) 34.12, trans. Rabbi Dr. H. Freedman and Maurice Simon (London: The Soncino Press, 1961).
[53] *The Testimony of Truth*, trans. Soren Giversen and Birger A. Pearson, http://www.gnosis.org/naghamm/testruth.html (accessed Feb 3, 2010).
[54] *The Armenian Apocryphal Adam Literature*, History of the Creation and Transgression of Adam 41, trans. William Lowndes Lipscomb (Ann Arbor, Michigan: University Microfilms International, 1983), 125.
[55] *Saltair na Rann*, 1449-1456, trans. David Greene.
[56] *The Companion Bible*, Genesis 3:18 (notes) (Grand Rapids, Michigan: Kregel Publications, 1990), 8; Targum Neofiti 1: Genesis / translated, with apparatus and notes, 3:18, trans. Martin McNamara (Collegeville, Minnesota: Liturgical Press, 1992), 62; *The Armenian Apocryphal Adam Literature*, The Words of Adam to Seth 13, The History of the Repentance of Adam and Eve, the First Created Ones, and How They Did It 20, trans. William Lowndes Lipscomb (Ann Arbor, Michigan: University Microfilms International, 1983), 209, 224.
[57] Ellen Frankel, *The Classic Tales: 4000 Years of Jewish Lore* (Northvale, New Jersey: Jason Aronson Inc., 1989), 32.
[58] James L. Kugel, *Traditions of the Bible* (Cambridge, Massachusetts: Harvard University Press, 1998), 142; Johann Andreas Eisenmenger, *The Traditions of the Jews, Contained in the Talmud and other Mystical Writings* (London: J. Robinson, 1748), 23-24; Rabbi Leo Jung, Ph. D., *Fallen Angels in Jewish, Christian and Mohammedan Literature* (New York: KTAV Publishing House, 1974), 75.
[59] Rabbi Leo Jung, Ph. D., *Fallen Angels in Jewish, Christian and Mohammedan Literature* (New York: KTAV Publishing House, 1974), 75.
[60] James L. Kugel, *Traditions of the Bible* (Cambridge, Massachusetts: Harvard University Press, 1998), 142; Johann Andreas Eisenmenger, *The Traditions of the Jews, Contained in the Talmud and other Mystical Writings* (London: J. Robinson, 1748), 24; Rabbi Leo Jung, Ph. D., *Fallen Angels in Jewish, Christian and Mohammedan Literature* (New York: KTAV Publishing House, 1974), 75; Hyman E. Goldin, *The Book of Legends: Tales From the Talmud and Midrash* (New York: The Jordan Publishing Co., 1929), 25.
[61] *The Babylonian Talmud*, Jews' College / Soncino English Translation, Sotah 9a-9b, http://halakhah.com/sotah/sotah_9.html (accessed Jan. 31, 2011).
[62] *The Companion Bible*, Appendix 19 (Grand Rapids, Michigan: Kregel Publications, 1990), 24-25.
[63] *Psa.* 72:9 (KJV), *Isa.* 49:23 (KJV), Sherry Shriner, *Serpent Seedline*, 7-8, http://www.serpentseedline.com/

(accessed Sept. 5, 2007).
[64] Johann Andreas Eisenmenger, *The Traditions of the Jews, Contained in the Talmud and Other Mystical Writings* (London: J. Robinson, 1748), 198.
[65] *The Companion Bible*, Appendix 19 (Grand Rapids, Michigan: Kregel Publications, 1990), 24-25.
[66] *Psa.* 44:25 (KJV); Sherry Shriner, *Serpent Seedline*, 8, http://www.serpentseedline.com/ (accessed Sept. 5, 2007); *The Companion Bible*, Genesis 3:14 (notes) (Grand Rapids, Michigan: Kregel Publications, 1990), 7; *Prov.* 20:17 (KJV); *Psa.* 72:8 (KJV).
[67] *The Apocalypse of Moses / Apocalypsis Mosis*, 26:1-4, trans. R. H. Charles, http://www.pseudepigrapha.com/pseudepigrapha/aprmose.htm (accessed June 27, 2005).
[68] *Barhebraeus' Scholia on the Old Testament Part I: Genesis - II Samuel*, Genesis 3:14, trans. Martin Sprengling and William Creighton Graham (Chicago, Illinois: University of Chicago Press 1931), 27.
[69] S. Baring-Gould, *Legends of the Patriarchs and Prophets and Other Old Testament Characters* (New York: American Book Exchange, 1881), 43.
[70] Rabbi Leo Jung, Ph. D., *Fallen Angels in Jewish, Christian and Mohammedan Literature* (New York: KTAV Publishing House, 1974), 71; S. Baring-Gould, *Legends of the Patriarchs and Prophets and Other Old Testament Characters* (New York: American Book Exchange, 1881), 18.
[71] Shira Halevi, *The Life Story of Adam and Havah*, Genesis 3:15 (Northvale, New Jersey: Jason Aronson, Inc., 1997), 204.
[72] Rabbi Leo Jung, Ph. D., *Fallen Angels in Jewish, Christian and Mohammedan Literature* (New York: KTAV Publishing House, 1974), 71.
[73] S. Baring-Gould, *Legends of the Patriarchs and Prophets and Other Old Testament Characters* (New York: American Book Exchange, 1881), 16.
[74] Josephus, J*ewish Antiquities*, Book 1, 45-50, trans. H. ST. J. Thackeray (London: William Heinemann Ltd. 1961), 23.
[75] *Targum Pseudo-Jonathan (Targum of Palestine / Targum of Jonathan Ben Uzziel)*, On the Book of Genesis, Section III, Berashith, http://targum.info/pj/pjgen1-6.htm (accessed Oct. 2, 2009).
[76] Shira Halevi, *The Life Story of Adam and Havah*, Genesis 3:16 (Northvale, New Jersey: Jason Aronson, Inc., 1997), 204.
[77] *The Armenian Apocryphal Adam Literature*, History and Sermon: Concerning the Creation of Adam and the Incarnation of Christ Our God 42, trans. William Lowndes Lipscomb (Ann Arbor, Michigan: University Microfilms International, 1983), 261.
[78] *The Apocalypse of Moses / Apocalypsis Mosis*, 25:1-4, trans. R. H. Charles, http://www.pseudepigrapha.com/pseudepigrapha/aprmose.htm (accessed June 27, 2005).
[79] *The Apocalypse of Moses / Apocalypsis Mosis*, 25:2, trans. R. H. Charles, http://www.pseudepigrapha.com/pseudepigrapha/aprmose.htm (accessed June 27, 2005); *The Armenian Apocryphal Adam Literature*, 42, trans. William Lowndes Lipscomb (Ann Arbor, Michigan: University Microfilms International, 1983), 125.
[80] Robert Graves and Raphael Patai, *Hebrew Myths: The Book of Genesis* (Garden City, New York: Doubleday & Company, 1964), 87; *The History of al-Tabari - Volume I: General Introduction and From the Creation to the Flood*, God's Testing of Adam, 109, trans. Franz Rosenthal (Albany: New York Press, 1989), 280-281.
[81] *The History of al-Tabari - Volume I: General Introduction and From the Creation to the Flood*, God's Testing of Adam, 107, trans. Franz Rosenthal (Albany: New York Press, 1989), 278.
[82] *The Book of Adam*, [44] 25.1-4, trans. J. P. Mahe, http://www.pseudepigrapha.com/pseudepigrapha/TheBookOfAdam.htm (accessed June 27, 2005).
[83] S. Baring-Gould, *Legends of the Patriarchs and Prophets and Other Old Testament Characters* (New York: American Book Exchange, 1881), 43.
[84] James L. Kugel, *Traditions of the Bible* (Cambridge, Massachusetts: Harvard University Press, 1998), 143.
[85] James L. Kugel, *Traditions of the Bible* (Cambridge, Massachusetts: Harvard University Press, 1998), 143.
[86] Andrew Collins, *From the Ashes of Angels* ((Rochester, Vermont: Bear & Company, 1996), 40-41; *Armenian Apocrypha Relating to Adam and Eve*, History of the Forefathers, Adam and His Sons and Grandsons 32, trans. Michael E. Stone (Leiden: E. J. Brill, 1996), 196; Louis Ginzberg, *The Legends of the Jews Volume V: Notes for Volume One and Two*, III. The Ten Generations, 3, trans. Henrietta Szold (Baltimore, Maryland: The Johns Hopkins University Press, 1909), 134; Philip Gardiner, *Secrets of the Serpent: In Search of the Secret Past* (Foresthill Ca.: Reality press, 2006), 15, 17.
[87] *The Midrash Rabbah*, Bereshith (Genesis) 23:2, trans. Rabbi Dr. H. Freedman and Maurice Simon (London: The Soncino Press, 1961).
[88] *Saltair na Rann*, 1401-1404, trans. David Greene.
[89] *The Garden of Eden Bible Study*, 22, http://www.frank.germano.com/gardenofeden.htm (accessed Nov. 15, 2006).
[90] *Vita Adae Et Evae (The Life of Adam and Eve)*, 18:1-2, trans. R. H. Charles, *The Apocrypha and Pseudepigrapha of the Old Testament* (Oxford: Clarendon Press, 1913).
[91] *Vita Adae Et Evae (The Life of Adam and Eve)*, 18:3, trans. R. H. Charles, *The Apocrypha and Pseudepigrapha of*

the Old Testament (Oxford: Clarendon Press, 1913).

Chapter 8

[1] Shira Halevi, *The Life Story of Adam and Havah*, Genesis 3:13 (Northvale, New Jersey: Jason Aronson, Inc., 1997), 203.
[2] *The Book of the Mysteries of the Heavens and the Earth and Other Works of Bakhayla Mikael (Zosimas)*, trans. E.A. Wallis Budge (London: Oxford University Press, 1935), 26; G. H. Pember, M. A., *Earth's Earliest Ages and their Connection With Modern Spiritualism, Theosophy, and Buddhism* (Grand Rapids, Michigan: Kregel Publications, 1975), 100-101, 120.
[3] *The Book of Adam*, [44]26.3-4, trans. J. P. Mahe, http://www.pseudepigrapha.com/pseudepigrapha/TheBookOfAdam.htm (accessed June 27, 2005).
[4] *The Book of the Rolls (Kitab Al-Magall)*, trans. Margaret Dunlop Gibson, Apocrypha Arabica (London: C.J Clay and Sons, 1901), 10.
[5] Ed Tarkowski, *War of the Ages: 6000 Year Overview: Satan's Effort to Hinder God's Plan*, 3-4, http://www.adamqadmon.com/watchers/warofages.html (accessed Dec. 11, 2000).
[6] *The Companion Bible*, Appendix 19 (Grand Rapids, Michigan: Kregel Publications, 1990), 25.
[7] Rabbi Leo Jung, Ph. D., *Fallen Angels in Jewish, Christian and Mohammedan Literature* (New York: KTAV Publishing House, 1974), 70-71; Shira Halevi, *The Life Story of Adam and Havah*, Genesis 3:13 (Northvale, New Jersey: Jason Aronson, Inc., 1997), 203.
[8] *Targum Pseudo-Jonathan (Targum of Palestine / Targum of Jonathan Ben Uzziel)*, On the Book of Genesis, Section 3, Berashith, http://targum.info/pj/pjgen1-6.htm (accessed Oct. 2, 2009).
[9] Strong's G444 - *anthropos*, http://www.blueletterbible.org/lang/lexicon/lexicon.cfm?Strongs=G444&t=KJV.html (accessed Dec. 17, 2009).
[10] Garbiel Alvarez, *Historia Ecclesiae Antediluviana*, Madrid, 1713.
[11] *Luke* 3:23 (notes) (KJV (Scofield Reference Version)).
[12] Timothy Unruh, *The Days of Noah and the "Sons of God"*, 11, https://www.adamqadmon.com/watchers/sonsofgod002 (accessed Dec. 11, 2000).
[13] *2 Enoch (The Book of the Secrets of Enoch)*, 31:5, trans. W. R. Morfill, M. A. (Oxford: Clarendon Press, 1896).
[14] *The Zohar*, Volume 1. Beresheet A, Section 28. Hevel-Moshe, 286, https://www2.kabbalah.com/k/index.php/p=zohar/zohar&vol=2&sec=49 (accessed Feb. 24, 2010).
[15] *Book of the Glory of Kings (Kerba Nagast)*, 7. Concerning Noah, trans. Sir. E. A. Wallis Budge (London: Humphrey Milford, 1932).
[16] S. Baring-Gould, *Legends of the Patriarchs and Prophets and Other Old Testament Characters* (New York: American Book Exchange, 1881), 59.
[17] *Pirke De Rabbi Eliezer*, Chapter 21: Cain and Abel [25A. i.] (notes), trans. Gerald Friedlander (New York: Sepher-Hermon Press, 1981), 152.
[18] *The Book of Adam*, 21.2, trans. J. P. Mahe, http://www.pseudepigrapha.com/pseudepigrapha/TheBookOfAdam.htm (accessed June 27, 2005).
[19] Strong's H3045 - *yada*, http://www.blueletterbible.org/lang/lexicon/lexicon.cfm?Strongs=H3045&t=KJV (accessed Aug. 11, 2010); Strong's H853 - *eth*, http://www.blueletterbible.org/lang/lexicon/lexicon.cfm?Strongs=H853&t=KJV (accessed Aug. 11, 2010); Strong's H226 - *owth*, http://www.blueletterbible.org/lang/lexicon/lexicon.cfm?Strongs=H226&t=KJV (accessed Aug. 11, 2010); Strong's H2029 - *harah*, http://www.blueletterbible.org/lang/lexicon/lexicon.cfm?Strongs=H2029&t=KJV (accessed Aug. 16, 2010).
[20] James L. Kugel, *The Bible As It Was*, (Cambridge, Massachusetts: Harvard University Press, 1997), 86.
[21] *Pirke De Rabbi Eliezer*, Chapter 21, Cain and Abel [25A. i.], trans. Gerald Friedlander (New York: Sepher-Hermon Press, 1981), 151.
[22] *The Apocalypse of Moses / Apocalypsis Mosis*, 3:2, trans. R. H. Charles, http://www.pseudepigrapha.com/pseudepigrapha/aprmose.htm (accessed June 27, 2005).
[23] Johann Andreas Eisenmenger, *The Traditions of the Jews, Contained in the Talmud and Other Mystical Writings* (London: J. Robinson, 1748), 198.
[24] *Gen.* 1:1 (notes) (KJV (Scofield Reference Version)).
[25] James L. Kugel, *The Bible As It Was*, (Cambridge, Massachusetts: Harvard University Press, 1997), 86.
[26] *Targum Pseudo-Jonathan (Targum of Palestine / Targum of Jonathan Ben Uzziel)*, On the Book of Genesis, Section 2, Berashith, http://targum.info/pj/pjgen1-6.htm (accessed Oct. 2, 2009).
[27] *The Midrash Rabbah*, Bereshith (Genesis) 24:6, trans. Rabbi Dr. H. Freedman and Maurice Simon (London: The Soncino Press, 1961).
[28] James L. Kugel, *Traditions of the Bible* (Cambridge, Massachusetts: Harvard University Press, 1998), 157; Bentley Layton, *The Gnostic Scriptures*, The Holy Book of the Great Invisible Spirit, Mythic Characters: III. Humankind (New York: Doubleday, 1995), 103; Rabbi Leo Jung, Ph. D., *Fallen Angels in Jewish, Christian and Mohammedan Literature* (New York: KTAV Publishing House, 1974), 78; *Saltair na Rann*, 1961-1964, trans. David Greene; Alan

Unterman, *Dictionary of Jewish Lore and Legend* (London: Thames and Hudson Ltd., 1991), 44, 173.

[29] *The Works of Philo Judaeus*, Questions and Answers on Genesis 1, 81, trans. C. D. Yonge (London: H. G. Bohn, 1854-1855).

[30] Bentley Layton, *The Gnostic Scriptures*, The Reality of the Rulers, Cain and Abel, 11-29 (and notes) (New York: Doubleday, 1995), 72).

[31] *The Zohar*, Volume 5, Vayishlach, Section 28. "… who found Yemim in the wilderness", 261, https://www2.kabbalah.com/k/index.php/p=zohar/zohar&vol=10&sec=380 (accessed Feb. 24, 2010).

[32] Johann Andreas Eisenmenger, *The Traditions of the Jews, Contained in the Talmud and other Mystical Writings* (London: J. Robinson, 1748), 197; Rabbi Leo Jung, Ph. D., *Fallen Angels in Jewish, Christian and Mohammedan Literature* (New York: KTAV Publishing House, 1974), 92.

[33] Rabbi Leo Jung, Ph. D., *Fallen Angels in Jewish, Christian and Mohammedan Literature* (New York: KTAV Publishing House, 1974), 79.

[34] Johann Andreas Eisenmenger, *The Traditions of the Jews, Contained in the Talmud and Other Mystical Writings* (London: J. Robinson, 1748), 197.

[35] *The Book of Enoch*, 69:12, trans. R.H. Charles (Montana: Kessinger Publishing, 1912); Andrew Collins, *From the Ashes of Angels* (Rochester, Vermont: Bear & Company, 1996), 41.

[36] Rabbi Leo Jung, Ph. D., *Fallen Angels in Jewish, Christian and Mohammedan Literature* (New York: KTAV Publishing House, 1974), 78.

[37] *Pirke De Rabbi Eliezer*, Chapter 22: The Fall of the Angels [26A. i.], trans. Gerald Friedlander (New York: Sepher-Hermon Press, 1981), 158.

[38] Johann Andreas Eisenmenger, *The Traditions of the Jews, Contained in the Talmud and Other Mystical Writings* (London: J. Robinson, 1748), 198.

[39] Rabbi Leo Jung, Ph. D., *Fallen Angels in Jewish, Christian and Mohammedan Literature* (New York: KTAV Publishing House, 1974), 78.

[40] *Vita Adae Et Evae (The Life of Adam and Eve)*, 19.3, trans. R. H. Charles, The Apocrypha and Pseudepigrapha of the Old Testament (Oxford: Clarendon Press, 1913).

[41] *The Book of Adam*, 21.3a, trans. J. P. Mahe, http://www.pseudepigrapha.com/pseudepigrapha/TheBookOfAdam.htm (accessed June 27, 2005).

[42] Louis Ginzberg, *The Legends of the Jews Volume V: Notes for Volume One and Two*, III. The Ten Generations, 6, trans. Henrietta Szold (Baltimore, Maryland: The Johns Hopkins University Press, 1909), 135; Robert Graves and Raphael Patai, *Hebrew Myths: The Book of Genesis* (Garden City, New York: Doubleday & Company, 1964), 85.

[43] *The Apocalypse of Moses / Apocalypsis Mosis*, 21:3 (notes), trans. R. H. Charles, http://www.pseudepigrapha.com/pseudepigrapha/aprmose.htm (accessed June 27, 2005).

[44] *Targum Pseudo-Jonathan (Targum of Palestine / Targum of Jonathan Ben Uzziel)*, On the Book of Genesis, Section 4, Berashith, http://targum.info/pj/pjgen1-6.htm (accessed Oct. 2, 2009).

[45] Johann Andreas Eisenmenger, *The Traditions of the Jews, Contained in the Talmud and Other Mystical Writings* (London: J. Robinson, 1748), 198.

[46] Robert Bowie Johnson, Jr., *The Parthenon Code: Mankind's History in Marble* (Annapolis, Maryland: Solving Light Books, 2004), 193; *The World Before the Flood, and the History of the Patriarchs*, Chapter 1, 5, http://www.adamqadmon.com/watchers/pre-flood000.html (accessed Feb 10, 2001); James L. Kugel, *The Bible As It Was*, (Cambridge, Massachusetts: Harvard University Press, 1997), 87.

[47] James L. Kugel, *The Bible As It Was* (Cambridge, Massachusetts: Harvard University Press, 1997), 85.

[48] James L. Kugel, *The Bible As It Was* (Cambridge, Massachusetts: Harvard University Press, 1997), 87.

[49] *The Gospel of Judas: Cain - Cainites - Kenite - Rechabites*, 15, http://www.piney.com/Cain (accessed April 19, 2007).

[50] *The World Before the Flood and The History of the Patriarchs*, 5-6, www.adamqadmon.com/watchers/pre-flood000 (accessed Feb. 10, 2001).

[51] *The Penitence of our Forefather Adam*, 21.3a, trans. Gary A. Anderson and Michael E. Stone, http://www2.iath.virginia.edu/anderson/viat/english/vita.arm.html (accessed Dec 26, 2009).

[52] *The Book of Adam*, 21.3a, trans. J. P. Mahe, http://www.pseudepigrapha.com/pseudepigrapha/TheBookOfAdam.htm (accessed June 27, 2005).

[53] James L. Kugel, *The Bible As It Was* (Cambridge, Massachusetts: Harvard University Press, 1997), 85.

[54] *The Book of Adam*, 21.3a, trans. J. P. Mahe, http://www.pseudepigrapha.com/pseudepigrapha/TheBookOfAdam.htm (accessed June 27, 2005).

[55] Louis Ginzberg, *The Legends of the Jews Volume V: Notes for Volume One and Two*, III. The Ten Generations, 20, trans. Henrietta Szold (Baltimore, Maryland: The Johns Hopkins University Press, 1909), 140; Robert Graves and Raphael Patai, *Hebrew Myths: The Book of Genesis* (Garden City, New York: Doubleday & Company, 1964), 92.

[56] Louis Ginzberg, *The Legends of the Jews Volume V: Notes for Volume One and Two*, III. The Ten Generations, 7, trans. Henrietta Szold (Baltimore, Maryland: The Johns Hopkins University Press, 1909), 135.

[57] *The Book of Adam*, 21:3b-21:3c, trans. J. P. Mahe, http://www.pseudepigrapha.com/pseudepigrapha/TheBookOfAdam.htm (accessed June 27, 2005).

[58] *Barhebraeus' Scholia on the Old Testament Part I: Genesis - II Samuel*, Genesis 3:17, trans. Martin Sprengling and William Creighton Graham (Chicago, Illinois: University of Chicago Press 1931), 27.
[59] Bentley Layton, *The Gnostic Scriptures*, The Archontics According to St. Epiphanius, Cain and Abel, 40.5.3-4 (New York: Doubleday, 1995), 197.
[60] *The History of al-Tabari - Volume I: General Introduction and From the Creation to the Flood*, Cain and Abel, 137, 139, 146, trans. Franz Rosenthal (Albany: New York Press, 1989), 308, 310, 317; *Saltair na Rann*, 1969-1972, 2493-2496, trans. David Greene; *Barhebraeus' Scholia on the Old Testament Part I: Genesis - II Samuel*, Genesis 4:4, trans. Martin Sprengling and William Creighton Graham (Chicago, Illinois: University of Chicago Press 1931), 31; Louis Ginzberg, *The Legends of the Jews Volume I: From the Creation to Jacob*, trans. Henrietta Szold (Baltimore, Maryland: The Johns Hopkins University Press, 1909), 108; *The Armenian Apocryphal Adam Literature*, This Is the History of Abel and Cain the Sons of Adam 3-4, trans. William Lowndes Lipscomb (Ann Arbor, Michigan: University Microfilms International, 1983), 157-158.
[61] Robert Graves and Raphael Patai, *Hebrew Myths: The Book of Genesis* (Garden City, New York: Doubleday & Company, 1964), 99; *Pirke De Rabbi Eliezer*, Chap. 21: Cain and Abel [25A. i.], trans. Gerald Friedlander (New York: Sepher-Hermon Press, 1981), 152; *The History of al-Tabari - Volume I: General Introduction and From the Creation to the Flood,* Cain and Abel 137, 139-140, 147, trans. Franz Rosenthal (Albany: New York Press, 1989), 308, 310, 317; *The Garden of Eden Bible Study*, 17, http://www.frank.germano.com/gardenofeden.htm (accessed Nov. 15, 2006).
[62] *Pirke De Rabbi Eliezer*, Chapter 22: The Fall of the Angels [26A. i.] (notes), trans. Gerald Friedlander (New York: Sepher-Hermon Press, 1981), 158.
[63] *Pirke De Rabbi Eliezer*, Chap. 21: Cain and Abel [25A. i.], trans. Gerald Friedlander (New York: Sepher-Hermon Press, 1981), 152.
[64] *The Midrash Rabbah*, Bereshith (Genesis) 22:3, trans. Rabbi Dr. H. Freedman and Maurice Simon (London: The Soncino Press, 1961); *The Garden of Eden Bible Study*, 5, 17, http://www.frank.germano.com/gardenofeden.htm (accessed Nov. 15, 2006).
[65] Philip Gardiner, *Secrets of the Serpent: in Search of the Secret Past* (Foresthill Ca: Reality press, 2006), 18.
[66] *Gen.* 4:3-5 (KJV); *Sons of Cain: They Survived Noah's Flood*, 2, http://www.nfis.com/~danelady/sonsofcain.html (accessed June 5, 2000).
[67] Bentley Layton, *The Gnostic Scriptures*, The Secret Book According to John, Mythic characters II - III (New York: Doubleday, 1995), 25).
[68] *The Apocalypse of Moses / Apocalypsis Mosis*, 3:1 (notes), trans. R. H. Charles, The Apocrypha and Pseudepigrapha of the Old Testament, Volume Two (Berkeley, Ca.: Apocryphile Press, 2004).
[69] *Star Wars, Lesson Eight*, 4-5, http://usa-the-republic.com/religion/star%20wars/Star%20Wars%20-%20Lesson%20Eight.htm (accessed April 23, 2005).
[70] Richard Gan, *The Mark of the Wicked Ones*, 17, http://www.porpheticrevelation.net/w-ones.htm (accessed Aug. 22, 2007).
[71] William F. Dankenbring, *The Mark of Cain*, 2, http://www.triumphpro.com/the_mark_of_cain.htm (accessed Aug. 8, 2007).
[72] *The Zohar*, Volume 13, Pekudei, Section 21. Breastplate and Efod, 203, https://www2.kabbalah.com/k/index.php/p=zohar/zohar&vol=26&sec=912 (accessed Feb. 24, 2010).
[73] *The Zohar*, Volume 1, Beresheet A, Section 28. Hevel-Moshe, 285, https://www2.kabbalah.com/k/index.php/p=zohar/zohar&vol=2&sec=49 (accessed Feb. 24, 2010).
[74] Johann Andreas Eisenmenger, *The Traditions of the Jews, Contained in the Talmud and Other Mystical Writings* (London: J. Robinson, 1748), 197.
[75] *The World Before the Flood, and the History of the Patriarchs*, 6, http://www.adamqadmon.com/watchers/preflood000.htm (accessed Feb. 10, 2001); James E. Thorold, *Bible Folk-lore; A Study in Comparative Mythology* (London: Kegan Paul, Trench and Co, 1884), 11;
James L. Kugel, *The Bible As It Was*, (Cambridge, Massachusetts: Harvard University Press, 1997), 87; G. H. Pember, M. A., *Earth's Earliest Ages and their Connection With Modern Spiritualism, Theosophy, and Buddhism* (Grand Rapids, Michigan: Kregel Publications, 1975), 117.
[76] *Book of the Glory of Kings (Kerba Nagast)*, 3. Concerning the Kingdom of Adam, 4. Concerning Envy, trans. Sir. E. A. Wallis Budge (London: Humphrey Milford, 1932).
[77] *The Book of the Rolls (Kitab Al-Magall)*, trans. Margaret Dunlop Gibson, Apocrypha Arabica, (London: C.J. Clay and Sons, 1901), 11.
[78] *Book of the Glory of Kings (Kerba Nagast)*, 4. Concerning Envy, trans. Sir. E. A. Wallis Budge (London: Humphrey Milford, 1932).
[79] *The Book of the Cave of Treasures*, The First Thousand Years: Adam to Yared (Jared), Adam's Expulsion from Paradise, trans. Sir E. A. Wallis Budge (London: The Religious Tract Society, 1927), 68-70.

Chapter 9

[1] answers.com, *basilisk*, http://www.answers.com/topic/basilisk (accessed Feb. 4, 2010).
[2] Johann Andreas Eisenmenger, *The Traditions of the Jews, Contained in the Talmud and other Mystical Writings*

(London: J. Robinson, 1748), 197-198.

[3] *The Bible, The Koran, and the Talmud (Biblical Legends of the Mussulmans)*, Adam (A Mohammedan Legend), trans. Dr. G. Weil (New York, 1863), 10; Robert Graves and Raphael Patai, *Hebrew Myths: The Book of Genesis* (Garden City, New York: Doubleday & Company, 1964), 92; S. Baring-Gould, *Legends of the Patriarchs and Prophets and Other Old Testament Characters* (New York: American Book Exchange, 1881), 68; *The History of al-Tabari - Volume I: General Introduction and From the Creation to the Flood*, Cain and Abel, 138, 141, trans. Franz Rosenthal (Albany: New York Press, 1989), 308, 311.

[4] G. H. Pember, M. A., *Earth's Earliest Ages and their Connection With Modern Spiritualism, Theosophy, and Buddhism* (Grand Rapids, Michigan: Kregel Publications, 1975), 118.

[5] G. H. Pember, M. A., *Earth's Earliest Ages and their Connection With Modern Spiritualism, Theosophy, and Buddhism* (Grand Rapids, Michigan: Kregel Publications, 1975), 118.

[6] Josephus, *Jewish Antiquities*, Book 1, 53-4, trans. H. ST. J. Thackeray (London: William Heinemann Ltd. 1961), 25.

[7] *The Works of Philo Judaeus*, Questions and Answers in Genesis 1, 59, trans. C. D. Yonge (London: H.G Bohn, 1854-1855).

[8] Louis Ginzberg, *The Legends of the Jews Volume I: From the Creation to Jacob*, trans. Henrietta Szold (Baltimore, Maryland: The Johns Hopkins University Press, 1909), 107.

[9] Louis Ginzberg, *The Legends of the Jews Volume I: From the Creation to Jacob*, trans. Henrietta Szold (Baltimore, Maryland: The Johns Hopkins University Press, 1909), 107-108.

[10] S. Baring-Gould, *Legends of the Patriarchs and Prophets and Other Old Testament Characters* (New York: American Book Exchange, 1881), 69; *The Armenian Apocryphal Adam Literature*, The History of Cain and Abel 7, trans. William Lowndes Lipscomb (Ann Arbor, Michigan: University Microfilms International, 1983), 270-271.

[11] G. H. Pember, M. A., *Earth's Earliest Ages and their Connection With Modern Spiritualism, Theosophy, and Buddhism* (Grand Rapids, Michigan: Kregel Publications, 1975), 118.

[12] *The Armenian Apocryphal Adam Literature*, This is the History of Abel and Cain the Sons of Adam 9, trans. William Lowndes Lipscomb (Ann Arbor, Michigan: University Microfilms International, 1983), 159.

[13] Louis Ginzberg, *The Legends of the Jews Volume V: Notes for Volume One and Two*, III. The Ten Generations, 12, trans. Henrietta Szold (Baltimore, Maryland: The Johns Hopkins University Press, 1909), 136; *The History of al-Tabari - Volume I: General Introduction and From the Creation to the Flood*, Cain and Abel, 140, trans. Franz Rosenthal (Albany: New York Press, 1989), 311.

[14] *Pirke De Rabbi Eliezer*, Chapter 21: Cain and Abel [25A. i.], trans. Gerald Friedlander (New York: Sepher-Hermon Press, 1981), 153-154.

[15] *The Armenian Apocryphal Adam Literature*, This is the History of Abel and Cain the Sons of Adam 12, trans. William Lowndes Lipscomb (Ann Arbor, Michigan: University Microfilms International, 1983), 160.

[16] *The Armenian Apocryphal Adam Literature*, This is the History of Abel and Cain the Sons of Adam 10, trans. William Lowndes Lipscomb (Ann Arbor, Michigan: University Microfilms International, 1983), 160.

[17] James L. Kugel, *Traditions of the Bible* (Cambridge, Massachusetts: Harvard University Press, 1998), 159.

[18] Louis Ginzberg, *The Legends of the Jews Volume V: Notes for Volume One and Two*, III. The Ten Generations, 13, trans. Henrietta Szold (Baltimore, Maryland: The Johns Hopkins University Press, 1909), 137; *Saltair na Rann*, 1957-1960, trans. David Greene; Shira Halevi, *The Life Story of Adam and Havah*, Genesis 4:5b (Northvale, New Jersey: Jason Aronson, Inc., 1997), 248; Wikipedia, the Free Encyclopedia, *Curse and Mark of Cain*, 2, http://en.wikipedia.org/wiki/Curse_and_mark_of_Cain (Oct. 09, 2007).

[19] Louis Ginzberg, *The Legends of the Jews Volume V: Notes for Volume One and Two*, III. The Ten Generations, 13, trans. Henrietta Szold (Baltimore, Maryland: The Johns Hopkins University Press, 1909), 137; *The Third Book of Adam and Eve (The Conflict of Adam and Eve with Satan)*, Chapter 4, trans. S. C. Malan (London: Williams and Norgate, 1882); *Saltair na Rann*, 1661-1664, trans. David Greene; Bentley Layton, *The Gnostic Scriptures*, Confrontation of Norea and the Rulers, 92 (New York: Doubleday, 1995), 73; *Targum Neofiti 1: Genesis / Translated, With Apparatus and Notes*, Genesis 4:7 (notes), trans. Martin McNamara (Collegeville, Minnesota: Liturgical Press, 1992).

[20] *Juvenile Instructor*, Vol. 26, p. 635.

[21] *The Armenian Apocryphal Adam Literature*, This is the History of Abel and Cain the Sons of Adam 10, trans. William Lowndes Lipscomb (Ann Arbor, Michigan: University Microfilms International, 1983), 160.

[22] Ellen Frankel, *The Classic Tales: 4000 Years of Jewish Lore* (Northvale, New Jersey: Jason Aronson Inc., 1989), 37.

[23] *Genizah Manuscripts of Palestinian Targum to the Pentateuch Volume One*, Genesis 4:7, trans. Michael L. Klein (Cincinnati: Hebrew Union College Press, 1986), 6.

[24] *Targum Pseudo-Jonathan (Targum of Palestine / Targum of Jonathan Ben Uzziel)*, On the Book of Genesis, Section 4, Berashith, http://targum.info/pj/pjgen1-6.htm (accessed Oct. 2, 2009).

[25] G. H. Pember, M. A., *Earth's Earliest Ages and their Connection With Modern Spiritualism, Theosophy, and Buddhism* (Grand Rapids, Michigan: Kregel Publications, 1975), 119.

[26] Louis Ginzberg, *The Legends of the Jews Volume V: Notes for Volume One and Two*, III. The Ten Generations, 7, trans. Henrietta Szold (Baltimore, Maryland: The Johns Hopkins University Press, 1909), 135.

[27] *The Book of Adam*, [23]3.2, trans. J. P. Mahe, http://www.pseudepigrapha.com/pseudepigrapha/TheBookOfAdam.htm (accessed June 27, 2005).

[28] *Targum Pseudo-Jonathan (Targum of Palestine / Targum of Jonathan Ben Uzziel)*, On the Book of Genesis, Section 4, Berashith, http://targum.info/pj/pjgen1-6.htm (accessed Oct. 2, 2009).
[29] *Targum Neofiti 1: Genesis / Translated, With Apparatus and Notes*, Genesis 4:8, trans. Martin McNamara (Collegeville, Minnesota: Liturgical Press, 1992).
[30] *Targum Pseudo-Jonathan (Targum of Palestine / Targum of Jonathan Ben Uzziel)*, On the Book of Genesis, Section 4, Berashith, http://targum.info/pj/pjgen1-6.htm (accessed Oct. 2, 2009).
[31] Robert Graves and Raphael Patai, *Hebrew Myths: The Book of Genesis* (Garden City, New York: Doubleday & Company, 1964), 91.
[32] *The History of al-Tabari - Volume I: General Introduction and From the Creation to the Flood,* Cain and Abel, 138, trans. Franz Rosenthal (Albany: New York Press, 1989), 308.
[33] Mikal Bin Gorion, *Mimekor Yisrael - Volume I,* Cain and Abel (Bloomington, Indiana: University Press, 1976), 7.
[34] Louis Ginzberg, *The Legends of the Jews Volume V: Notes for Volume One and Two*, III. The Ten Generations, 19, trans. Henrietta Szold (Baltimore, Maryland: The Johns Hopkins University Press, 1909), 139.
[35] James L. Kugel, *Traditions of the Bible* (Cambridge, Massachusetts: Harvard University Press, 1998), 162.
[36] Robert Graves and Raphael Patai, *Hebrew Myths: The Book of Genesis* (Garden City, New York: Doubleday & Company, 1964), 92.
[37] Mrs. Sydney Bristowe, *Sargon the Magnificent* (London: The Covenant Publishing Co., 1927), 4.
[38] *Yalkut Hadash* (Rabbi Leo Jung, Ph. D., Fallen Angels in Jewish, Christian and Mohammedan Literature (New York: KTAV Publishing House, 1974), 78).
[39] *The Gospel of Philip*, trans. Wesley W. Isenberg, http://www.gnosis.org/naghamm/gop.html (accessed Feb. 4, 2010).
[40] Robert Graves and Raphael Patai, *Hebrew Myths: The Book of Genesis* (Garden City, New York: Doubleday & Company, 1964), 92; Louis Ginzberg, *The Legends of the Jews Volume V: Notes for Volume One and Two*, III. The Ten Generations, 20, trans. Henrietta Szold (Baltimore, Maryland: The Johns Hopkins University Press, 1909), 139.
[41] James L. Kugel, *Traditions of the Bible* (Cambridge, Massachusetts: Harvard University Press, 1998), 160; *The Armenian Apocryphal Adam Literature*, This is the History of Abel and Cain the sons of Adam 18-29, 32-33, trans. William Lowndes Lipscomb (Ann Arbor, Michigan: University Microfilms International, 1983), 162-165.
[42] Shira Halevi, *The Life Story of Adam and Havah*, Genesis 4:8a (Northvale, New Jersey: Jason Aronson, Inc., 1997), 250.
[43] *The Armenian Apocryphal Adam Literature*, This is the History of Abel and Cain the Sons of Adam 33, trans. William Lowndes Lipscomb (Ann Arbor, Michigan: University Microfilms International, 1983), 165.
[44] *The Armenian Apocryphal Adam Literature*, This is the History of Abel and Cain the Sons of Adam 34, trans. William Lowndes Lipscomb (Ann Arbor, Michigan: University Microfilms International, 1983), 165.
[45] *The Armenian Apocryphal Adam Literature*, The History of the Repentance of Adam and Eve, the First Created Ones, and How They Did It 46, trans. William Lowndes Lipscomb (Ann Arbor, Michigan: University Microfilms International, 1983), 228.
[46] G. H. Pember, M. A., *Earth's Earliest Ages and their Connection With Modern Spiritualism, Theosophy, and Buddhism* (Grand Rapids, Michigan: Kregel Publications, 1975), 119.
[47] Louis Ginzberg, *The Legends of the Jews Volume I: From the Creation to Jacob*, trans. Henrietta Szold (Baltimore, Maryland: The Johns Hopkins University Press, 1909), 111.
[48] *The Companion Bible*, Genesis 4:13 (notes) (Grand Rapids, Michigan: Kregel Publications, 1990), 9; *Targum Neofiti 1: Genesis / Translated, With Apparatus and Notes*, Genesis 4:13, trans. Martin McNamara (Collegeville, Minnesota: Liturgical Press, 1992).
[49] *Genizah Manuscripts of Palestinian Targum to the Pentateuch Volume One*, Genesis 4:13, trans. Michael L. Klein (Cincinnati: Hebrew Union College Press, 1986), 7.
[50] *Targum Pseudo-Jonathan (Targum of Palestine / Targum of Jonathan Ben Uzziel)*, On the Book of Genesis, Section 4, Berashith, http://targum.info/pj/pjgen1-6.htm (accessed Oct. 2, 2009).
[51] William Dankenbring, *The Mark of Cain*, 5, http://www.triumphpro.com/the_mark_of_cain.htm (accessed Aug. 22, 2007).
[52] Ellen Frankel, *The Classic Tales: 4000 Years of Jewish Lore* (Northvale, New Jersey: Jason Aronson Inc., 1989), 37.
[53] Robert Graves and Raphael Patai, *Hebrew Myths: The Book of Genesis* (Garden City, New York: Doubleday & Company, 1964), 91.
[54] *Genizah Manuscripts of Palestinian Targum to the Pentateuch Volume One*, Genesis 4:8, trans. Michael L. Klein (Cincinnati: Hebrew Union College Press, 1986), 10.
[55] Robert Graves and Raphael Patai, *Hebrew Myths: The Book of Genesis* (Garden City, New York: Doubleday & Company, 1964), 91.
[56] Ellen Frankel, *The Classic Tales: 4000 Years of Jewish Lore* (Northvale, New Jersey: Jason Aronson Inc., 1989), 38-39.
[57] Ellen Frankel, *The Classic Tales: 4000 years of Jewish Lore* (Northvale, New Jersey: Jason Aronson Inc., 1989), 38.
[58] James R. Davis, *Have We Gone the Way of Cain?*, 6-7, http://www.focusongod.com/cain (accessed March 3, 2001).
[59] E. S. G. Bristowe, *Cain - An Argument* (Leicester: Edgar Backus, 1950), 59.
[60] Dictionary - MSN Encarta, *cynical*, http://www.encarta.msn.com/dictionary_/cynical (accessed Feb. 4, 2010).

[61] answers.com, *Cynics*, 1-2, http://www.answers.com/topic/cynic-1 (accessed Oct 18, 2007).
[62] *Cynical*, 1, http://encarta.msn.com/dictionary_/cynical.html (accessed Feb. 4, 2010); *Cynics*, 1-2, http://www.answers.com/topic/cynic-1 (accessed Oct 18, 2007).
[63] Mrs. Sydney Bristowe, *Sargon the Magnificent* (London: The Covenant Publishing Co., 1927), 111.
[64] Mrs. Sydney Bristowe, *Sargon the Magnificent* (London: The Covenant Publishing Co., 1927), 111.
[65] Mrs. Sydney Bristowe, *Sargon the Magnificent* (London: The Covenant Publishing Co., 1927), 111.
[66] Mrs. Sydney Bristowe, *Sargon the Magnificent* (London: The Covenant Publishing Co., 1927), 112.
[67] Mrs. Sydney Bristowe, *Sargon the Magnificent* (London: The Covenant Publishing Co., 1927), 79.
[68] *The Armenian Apocryphal Adam Literature*, The History of the Repentance of Adam and Eve, the First Created Ones, and How They Did It 49, trans. William Lowndes Lipscomb (Ann Arbor, Michigan: University Microfilms International, 1983), 228.
[69] Mikal Bin Gorion, *Mimekor Yisrael - Volume I*, 7. Cain and Abel (Bloomington, Indiana: University Press, 1976), 9.
[70] James L. Kugel, *Traditions of the Bible* (Cambridge, Massachusetts: Harvard University Press, 1998), 165.
[71] S. Baring-Gould, *Legends of the Patriarchs and Prophets and Other Old Testament Characters* (New York: American Book Exchange, 1881), 76.
[72] *The Armenian Apocryphal Adam Literature*, This is the History of Abel and Cain the sons of Adam 36, History of Cain and Abel 37, trans. William Lowndes Lipscomb (Ann Arbor, Michigan: University Microfilms International, 1983), 165, 271.
[73] *The Book of the Generations of Adam*, 5:11, http://www.earth-history.com/Pseudepigrapha/generations-adam.htm (accessed May 5, 2007).
[74] *The History of al-Tabari - Volume I: General Introduction and From the Creation to the Flood*, Cain and Abel, 144, trans. Franz Rosenthal (Albany: New York Press, 1989), 315.
[75] Mikal Bin Gorion, *Mimekor Yisrael - Volume I*, 7. Cain and Abel (Bloomington, Indiana: University Press, 1976), 9.
[76] Richard Gan, *The Mark of the Wicked Ones*, 7, http://www.propheticrevelation.net/w-ones.htm (accessed Aug. 22, 2007).
[77] *The Armenian Apocryphal Adam Literature*, The History of the Repentance of Adam and Eve, The First Created Ones, and How They Did It 51-54, trans. William Lowndes Lipscomb (Ann Arbor, Michigan: University Microfilms International, 1983), 228.
[78] *The History of al-Tabari - Volume I: General Introduction and From the Creation to the Flood*, Cain and Abel 142, trans. Franz Rosenthal (Albany: New York Press, 1989), 312; *Barhebraeus' Scholia on the Old Testament Part I: Genesis - II Samuel*, Genesis 4:15, trans. Martin Sprengling and William Creighton Graham (Chicago, Illinois: University of Chicago Press 1931), 33.
[79] Mikal Bin Gorion, *Mimekor Yisrael - Volume I*, 7. Cain and Abel (Bloomington, Indiana: University Press, 1976), 9; *Barhebraeus' Scholia on the Old Testament Part I: Genesis - II Samuel*, Genesis 4:11, trans. Martin Sprengling and William Creighton Graham (Chicago, Illinois: University of Chicago Press 1931), 31.
[80] *Armenian Apocrypha Relating to Adam and Eve*, History of the Forefathers, Adam and His Sons and Grandsons 17, trans. Michael E. Stone (Leiden: E. J. Brill, 1996), 188-189.
[81] Louis Ginzberg, *The Legends of the Jews Volume V: Notes for Volume One and Two*, III. The Ten Generations, 26, trans. Henrietta Szold (Baltimore, Maryland: The Johns Hopkins University Press, 1909), 141.
[82] Mikal Bin Gorion, *Mimekor Yisrael - Volume I*, 7. Cain and Abel (Bloomington, Indiana: University Press, 1976), 9; *The History of al-Tabari - Volume I: General Introduction and From the Creation to the Flood*, Cain and Abel, 142, trans. Franz Rosenthal (Albany: New York Press, 1989), 312.
[83] Louis Ginzberg, *The Legends of the Jews Volume I: From the Creation to Jacob*, trans. Henrietta Szold (Baltimore, Maryland: The Johns Hopkins University Press, 1909), 111; Ellen Frankel, *The Classic Tales: 4000 years of Jewish Lore* (Northvale, New Jersey: Jason Aronson Inc., 1989), 39.
[84] S. Baring-Gould, *Legends of the Patriarchs and Prophets and Other Old Testament Characters* (New York: American Book Exchange, 1881), 73.
[85] *The History of al-Tabari - Volume I: General Introduction and From the Creation to the Flood*, Cain and Abel, 144, trans. Franz Rosenthal (Albany: New York Press, 1989), 315.
[86] Louis Ginzberg, *The Legends of the Jews Volume I: From the Creation to Jacob*, trans. Henrietta Szold (Baltimore, Maryland: The Johns Hopkins University Press, 1909), 111; Mikal Bin Gorion, *Mimekor Yisrael - Volume I*, 7. Cain and Abel (Bloomington, Indiana: University Press, 1976), 9.
[87] *The First Book of Adam and Eve (The Conflict of Adam and Eve with Satan)*, 79:24-26, trans. S. C. Malan (London: Williams and Norgate, 1882), 59.
[88] Mikal Bin Gorion, *Mimekor Yisrael - Volume I*, 7. Cain and Abel (Bloomington, Indiana: University Press, 1976), 9.
[89] S. Baring-Gould, *Legends of the Patriarchs and Prophets and Other Old Testament Characters* (New York: American Book Exchange, 1881), 70.
[90] *The Armenian Apocryphal Adam Literature*, The History of the Repentance of Adam and Eve, The First Created Ones, and How They Did It 60, trans. William Lowndes Lipscomb (Ann Arbor, Michigan: University Microfilms International, 1983), 229.
[91] James L. Kugel, *Traditions of the Bible* (Cambridge, Massachusetts: Harvard University Press, 1998), 163-164;

Armenian Apocrypha Relating to Adam and Eve, History of the Forefathers, Adam and his Sons and Grandsons 7, trans. Michael E. Stone (Leiden: E. J. Brill, 1996), 185.

[92] Louis Ginzberg, *The Legends of the Jews Volume I: From the Creation to Jacob*, trans. Henrietta Szold (Baltimore, Maryland: The Johns Hopkins University Press, 1909), 111.

[93] *Armenian Apocrypha Relating to Adam and Eve*, History of the Forefathers, Adam and his Sons and Grandsons 21, trans. Michael E. Stone (Leiden: E. J. Brill, 1996), 191; S. Baring-Gould, *Legends of the Patriarchs and Prophets and Other Old Testament Characters* (New York: American Book Exchange, 1881), 74.

[94] *The First Book of Adam and Eve (The Conflict of Adam and Eve with Satan)*, 79:24-28, trans. S. C. Malan (London: Williams and Norgate, 1882).

[95] *Barhebraeus' Scholia on the Old Testament Part I: Genesis - II Samuel*, Genesis 4:12, trans. Martin Sprengling and William Creighton Graham (Chicago, Illinois: University of Chicago Press 1931), 31.

[96] *The First Book of Adam and Eve (The Conflict of Adam and Eve with Satan)*, 79:24-26, trans. S. C. Malan (London: Williams and Norgate, 1882), 59.

[97] *The Armenian Apocryphal Adam Literature*, This is the History of Abel and Cain the Sons of Adam 41, trans. William Lowndes Lipscomb (Ann Arbor, Michigan: University Microfilms International, 1983), 166.

[98] *The Armenian Apocryphal Adam Literature*, The History of the Repentance of Adam and Eve, The First Created Ones, and How They Did It 55-56, trans. William Lowndes Lipscomb (Ann Arbor, Michigan: University Microfilms International, 1983), 228.

[99] *Book of the Glory of Kings (Kerba Nagast)*, 4. Concerning Envy, trans. Sir. E. A. Wallis Budge (London: Humphrey Milford, 1932).

[100] S. Baring-Gould, *Legends of the Patriarchs and Prophets and Other Old Testament Characters* (New York: American Book Exchange, 1881), 74.

[101] *Barhebraeus' Scholia on the Old Testament Part I: Genesis - II Samuel*, Genesis 4:16, trans. Martin Sprengling and William Creighton Graham (Chicago, Illinois: University of Chicago Press 1931), 33.

[102] Robert Graves and Raphael Patai, *Hebrew Myths: The Book of Genesis* (Garden City, New York: Doubleday & Company, 1964), 93.

[103] *The Armenian Apocryphal Adam Literature*, This is the History of Abel and Cain the Sons of Adam 42-43, trans. William Lowndes Lipscomb (Ann Arbor, Michigan: University Microfilms International, 1983), 167.

[104] *The Armenian Apocryphal Adam Literature*, This is the History of Abel and Cain the Sons of Adam 57, trans. William Lowndes Lipscomb (Ann Arbor, Michigan: University Microfilms International, 1983), 170.

[105] *The Armenian Apocryphal Adam Literature*, This is the History of Abel and Cain the Sons of Adam 44, 6, trans. William Lowndes Lipscomb (Ann Arbor, Michigan: University Microfilms International, 1983), 167.

[106] J. Preston Eby, *The World System*, 3, http://www.theshop.net/giess/world.html (accessed Aug. 17, 2000); *The Book of the Cave of Treasures*, The First Thousand Years: Adam to Yared (Jared), Adam's Expulsion from Paradise, trans. Sir E. A. Wallis Budge (London: The Religious Tract Society, 1927), 68-70; *The World Before the Flood, and the History of the Patriarchs: Chapter 1*, 7, http://www.adamqadmon.com/watchers/pre-flood000.html (accessed Feb. 10, 2001); Moses Aberbach and Bernard Grossfield, *Targum Onkelos to Genesis: A Critical Analysis Together with an English Translation of the Text*, Genesis 4:16 (KTAV Publishing House, Inc., 1995), 42.

[107] *The Armenian Apocryphal Adam Literature*, The History of the Repentance of Adam and Eve, the First Created Ones, and How They Did It 57, trans. William Lowndes Lipscomb (Ann Arbor, Michigan: University Microfilms International, 1983), 228; Sir James George Frazer, *Folk-lore in the Old Testament: Studies in Comparative Religion, Legend and Law* (London: Macmillan and Co., Limited, 1923), 38.

[108] Theodor Gaster, *Myth, Legend, and Custom in the Old Testament* (New York: Harper & Row, 1969), 55; Sir James George Frazer, *Folk-lore in the Old Testament: Studies in Comparative Religion, Legend and Law* (London: Macmillan and Co., Limited, 1923), 38; *The Companion Bible*, Genesis 4:5 (notes) (Grand Rapids, Michigan: Kregel Publications, 1990), 9.

[109] Dick Fischer, *In Search of the Historical Adam*, 6, http://www.asa3.org/ASA/PSCF/1993/PSCF12-93Fischer.html (accessed April 12, 2005).

[110] Mrs. Sydney Bristowe, *Sargon the Magnificent* (London: The Covenant Publishing Co., 1927), 15.

[111] *Pirke De Rabbi Eliezer*, Chapter 21: Cain and Abel [25A. i.], trans. Gerald Friedlander (New York: Sepher-Hermon Press, 1981), 156; Robert Graves and Raphael Patai, *Hebrew Myths: The Book of Genesis* (Garden City, New York: Doubleday & Company, 1964), 96-97.

[112] Robert Graves and Raphael Patai, *Hebrew Myths: The Book of Genesis* (Garden City, New York: Doubleday & Company, 1964), 96-97; James L. Kugel, *Traditions of the Bible* (Cambridge, Massachusetts: Harvard University Press, 1998), 168-169.

[113] James L. Kugel, *Traditions of the Bible* (Cambridge, Massachusetts: Harvard University Press, 1998), 168.

[114] S. Baring-Gould, *Legends of the Patriarchs and Prophets and Other Old Testament Characters* (New York: American Book Exchange, 1881), 72.

[115] Rev. Alexander Hislop, *The Two Babylons* (Neptune, Jew Jersey: Loizeaux Brothers, 1959), 197-199.

[116] S. Baring-Gould, *Legends of the Patriarchs and Prophets and Other Old Testament Characters* (New York: American Book Exchange, 1881), 74; Alan Unterman, Dictionary of Jewish Lore and Legend (New York: Thames and

Hudson 1991) 43-44.
[117] *Armenian Apocrypha Relating to Adam and Eve*, History of the Forefathers, Adam and his Sons and Grandsons 22, trans. Michael E. Stone (Leiden: E. J. Brill, 1996), 191-192; S. Baring-Gould, *Legends of the Patriarchs and Prophets and Other Old Testament Characters* (New York: American Book Exchange, 1881), 74.
[118] *Armenian Apocrypha Relating to Adam and Eve*, History of the Forefathers, Adam and his Sons and Grandsons 22, trans. Michael E. Stone (Leiden: E. J. Brill, 1996), 192.
[119] *The Armenian Apocryphal Adam Literature*, This is the History of Abel and Cain the Sons of Adam 47, trans. William Lowndes Lipscomb (Ann Arbor, Michigan: University Microfilms International, 1983), 167.
[120] Colin Kidd, *The Forging of Races: Race and Scripture in the Protestant Atlantic World, 1600-2000* (Cambridge, New York: Cambridge University Press 2006), 75.
[121] James E. Thorold Rogers, *Bible Folk-Lore; a Study in Comparative Mythology* (London: Kegan Paul, Trench and Co., 1884), 12.
[122] James L. Kugel, *The Bible As It Was* (Cambridge, Massachusetts: Harvard University Press, 1997), 85; *Fallen Angels and Genetic Science*, 3, http://www.angelfire.com/home/thefaery/hafgan.html (accessed Sept. 13, 2007).
[123] Richard Gan, *The Mark of the Wicked Ones*, 10-1, http://www.propheticrevelation.net/w-ones.htm (accessed Aug. 22, 2007).
[124] E. S. G. Bristowe, *Cain - An Argument* (Leicester: Edgar Backus, 1950), 75; Mrs. Sydney Bristowe, *Sargon the Magnificent* (London: The Covenant Publishing Co., 1927), 83; Richard Gan, *The Mark of the Wicked Ones*, 10-11, http://www.propheticrevelation.net/w-ones.htm (accessed Aug. 22, 2007).
[125] Mrs. Sydney Bristowe, *Sargon the Magnificent* (London: The Covenant Publishing Co., 1927), 15-16.
[126] *Barhebraeus' Scholia on the Old Testament Part I: Genesis - II Samuel*, Genesis 4:16, trans. Martin Sprengling and William Creighton Graham (Chicago, Illinois: University of Chicago Press 1931), 33.
[127] *The Midrash Rabbah*, Bereshith (Genesis) 22:12 (and notes), trans. Rabbi Dr. H. Freedman and Maurice Simon (London: The Soncino Press, 1961).
[128] James R. Davis, *Have We Gone the Way of Cain?*, 8, http://www.focusongod.com/cain (accessed March 3, 2001).
[129] Josephus, J*ewish Antiquities*, Book 1, 59-64, trans. H. ST. J. Thackeray (London: William Heinemann Ltd. 1961), 29.
[130] William F. Dankerbring, *The Mark of Cain*, 6, www.triumphro.com (accessed Aug. 22, 2007).
[131] Dictionary.com, *perdition*, http://www.dictionary.reference.com/browse/perdition (accessed Feb. 4, 2011).
[132] Your Dictionary.com, *perdition*, http://www.yourdictionary.com/perdition (accessed Feb. 4, 2010).
[133] Merriam-Webster Online Dictionary, *Loss*, 1, http://www.m-w.com/dictionary/loss (accessed June 7, 2007).
[134] *The Apocalypse of Abraham*, 24:5-6, translator unknown, http://www.pseudepigrapha.com/pseudepigrapha/Apocalypse_of_Abraham.html (accessed Oct 5, 2006).
[135] *The Book of the Generations of Adam*, 9:6, http://www.earth-history.com/Pseudepigrapha/generations-adam.htm (accessed May 5, 2007).
[136] Rabbi Leo Jung, Ph. D., *Fallen Angels in Jewish, Christian and Mohammedan Literature* (New York: KTAV Publishing House, 1974), 155.
[137] *The Writings of Abraham*, 40:2-4, http://www.earth-history.com/Pseudepigrapha/Mormonism/writings-abraham-1.htm (accessed May 10, 2007); *The Armenian Apocryphal Adam Literature*, The History of the Repentance of Adam and Eve, the First Created Ones, and How They Did It 14, trans. William Lowndes Lipscomb (Ann Arbor, Michigan: University Microfilms International, 1983), 222.
[138] Strongs's G684 - *apoleia* (Thayer's Lexicon), http://www.blueletterbible.org/lang/lexicon/lexicon.cfm?Strongs=G684&t=KJV# (accessed Dec. 30, 2010); Greg Killian, *The Days of Noah*, 20, http://www.adamqadmon.com/nephilim/gkillian000.html (accessed Dec. 6, 2000).
[139] *The Book of the Generations of Adam*, 5:8, http://www.earth-history.com/Pseudepigrapha/generations-adam.htm (accessed May 5, 2007).
[140] Vines Expository Dictionary of New Testament Words, *Perdition*, 1, http://www.blueletterbible.org/lang/lexicon/lexicon.cfm?Strongs=G684&t=KJV (accessed May 5, 2007).

Chapter 10

[1] *Jude* 1:13 (Mrs. Sydney Bristowe, *Sargon the Magnificent* (London: The Covenant Publishing Co., 1927), 153).
[2] Robert Bowie Johnson, Jr., *The Parthenon Code: Mankind's History in Marble* (Annapolis, Maryland: Solving Light Books, 2004), 9.
[3] Robert Bowie Johnson, Jr., *The Parthenon Code: Mankind's History in Marble* (Annapolis, Maryland: Solving Light Books, 2004), 26.
[4] Mrs. Sydney Bristowe, *Sargon the Magnificent* (London: The Covenant Publishing Co., 1927), 160; Robert Bowie Johnson, Jr., *The Parthenon Code: Mankind's History in Marble* (Annapolis, Maryland: Solving Light Books, 2004), 192.
[5] Robert Bowie Johnson, Jr., *The Parthenon Code: Mankind's History in Marble* (Annapolis, Maryland: Solving Light Books, 2004), 13.
[6] Britannica Online Encylopedia, *Cainite*, 5, www.members.eb.com/Ebchecked/topics/88487/Cainites (accessed

March 2, 2010).

[7] Britannica Online Encyclopedia, *Cainite*, 5, www.members.eb.com/Ebchecked/topics/88487/Cainites (accessed March 2, 2010).

[8] *An Historical Treatise of the Travels of Noah Into Europe: Containing the first inhabitation and peopling thereof*, (also Summary, p. 2), trans. Richard Lynche (1601), http://www.annomundi.com/history/travels_of_noah.htm (accessed Dec. 7, 2007); Robert Bowie Johnson, Jr., *The Parthenon Code: Mankind's History in Marble* (Annapolis, Maryland: Solving Light Books, 2004), 80-81; Robert Bowie Johnson, Jr., *Noah in Ancient Greek Art* (Annapolis, Maryland: Solving Light Books, 2007), 44-46.

[9] Josephus, *Jewish Antiquities*, Book 1, 59-64, trans. H. ST. J. Thackeray (London: William Heinemann Ltd. 1961), 29.

[10] Robert Bowie Johnson, Jr., *The Parthenon Code: Mankind's History in Marble* (Annapolis, Maryland: Solving Light Books, 2004), 17.

[11] *The Midrash Rabbah*, Bereshith (Genesis) 22:13, trans. Rabbi Dr. H. Freedman and Maurice Simon (London: The Soncino Press, 1961).

[12] Mrs. Sydney Bristowe, *Sargon the Magnificent* (London: The Covenant Publishing Co., 1927), 79.

[13] William F. Dankenbring, *The Mark of Cain*, 5, http://www.triumphpro.com/the_mark_of_cain.htm (accessed Aug. 22, 2007).

[14] William F. Dankenbring, *The Mark of Cain*, 3, http://www.triumphpro.com/the_mark_of_cain.htm (accessed Aug. 22, 2007).

[15] Mrs. Sydney Bristowe, *Sargon the Magnificent* (London: The Covenant Publishing Co., 1927), 31.

[16] Mrs. Sydney Bristowe, *Sargon the Magnificent* (London: The Covenant Publishing Co., 1927), 21.

[17] E. S. G. Bristowe, *Cain - An Argument* (Leicester: Edgar Backus, 1950), 19.

[18] E. S. G. Bristowe, *Cain - An Argument* (Leicester: Edgar Backus, 1950), 18; Mrs. Sydney Bristowe, *Sargon the Magnificent* (London: The Covenant Publishing Co., 1927), 26.

[19] Mrs. Sydney Bristowe, *Sargon the Magnificent* (London: The Covenant Publishing Co., 1927), 150.

[20] Mrs. Sydney Bristowe, *Sargon the Magnificent* (London: The Covenant Publishing Co., 1927), 22.

[21] Mrs. Sydney Bristowe, *Sargon the Magnificent* (London: The Covenant Publishing Co., 1927), 84.

[22] Mrs. Sydney Bristowe, *Sargon the Magnificent* (London: The Covenant Publishing Co., 1927), 89.

[23] *Jude* 1:11 (notes) (KJV (*The Schofield Reference Bible*)).

[24] *The Book of the Generations of Adam*, 5:5, http://www.earth-history.com/Pseudepigrapha/generations-adam.htm (accessed May 5, 2007).

[25] Mrs. Sydney Bristowe, *Sargon the Magnificent* (London: The Covenant Publishing Co., 1927), 117.

[26] Socrates (Mrs. Sydney Bristowe, *Sargon the Magnificent* (London: The Covenant Publishing Co., 1927), 70).

[27] Mrs. Sydney Bristowe, *Sargon the Magnificent* (London: The Covenant Publishing Co., 1927), 63.

[28] E. S. G. Bristowe, *Cain - An Argument* (Leicester: Edgar Backus, 1950), 46.

[29] Mrs. Sydney Bristowe, *Sargon the Magnificent* (London: The Covenant Publishing Co., 1927), 62-63.

[30] Mrs. Sydney Bristowe, *Sargon the Magnificent* (London: The Covenant Publishing Co., 1927), 57.

[31] Mrs. Sydney Bristowe, *Sargon the Magnificent* (London: The Covenant Publishing Co., 1927), 57.

[32] Mrs. Sydney Bristowe, *Sargon the Magnificent* (London: The Covenant Publishing Co., 1927), 70.

[33] Mrs. Sydney Bristowe, *Sargon the Magnificent* (London: The Covenant Publishing Co., 1927), 67, 70, 72-73, 75-77; Robert Bowie Johnson, Jr., *The Parthenon Code: Mankind's History in Marble* (Annapolis, Maryland: Solving Light Books, 2004), 11, 185; E. S. G. Bristowe, *Cain - An Argument* (Leicester: Edgar Backus, 1950), 41.

[34] Mrs. Sydney Bristowe, *Sargon the Magnificent* (London: The Covenant Publishing Co., 1927), 54, 72-76, 81, 84, 106, 166; Wikipedia, the free encyclopedia, *Eve*, 1, http://en.wikipedia.org/wiki/Eve_%28Bible%29 (accessed Oct. 23, 2007).

[35] E. S. G. Bristowe, *Cain - An Argument* (Leicester: Edgar Backus, 1950), 47, 62, 63; Mrs. Sydney Bristowe, *Sargon the Magnificent* (London: The Covenant Publishing Co., 1927), 72.

[36] E. S. G. Bristowe, *Cain - An Argument* (Leicester: Edgar Backus, 1950), 8.

[37] Mrs. Sydney Bristowe, *Sargon the Magnificent* (London: The Covenant Publishing Co., 1927), 76-7, 81, 91; E. S. G. Bristowe, *Cain - An Argument* (Leicester: Edgar Backus, 1950), 17, 41.

[38] Mrs. Sydney Bristowe, *Sargon the Magnificent* (London: The Covenant Publishing Co., 1927), 115.

[39] Mrs. Sydney Bristowe, *Sargon the Magnificent* (London: The Covenant Publishing Co., 1927), 151.

[40] Mrs. Sydney Bristowe, *Sargon the Magnificent* (London: The Covenant Publishing Co., 1927), 49.

[41] E. S. G. Bristowe, *Cain - An Argument* (Leicester: Edgar Backus, 1950), 3, 69; Mrs. Sydney Bristowe, *Sargon the Magnificent* (London: The Covenant Publishing Co., 1927), 39, 58-60, 66-67, 70, 87, 94, 103-104, 112, 161-162.

[42] Mrs. Sydney Bristowe, *Sargon the Magnificent* (London: The Covenant Publishing Co., 1927), 151.

[43] E. S. G. Bristowe, *Cain - An Argument* (Leicester: Edgar Backus, 1950), 10.

[44] Robert Bowie Johnson, Jr., *The Parthenon Code: Mankind's History in Marble* (Annapolis, Maryland: Solving Light Books, 2004), 194.

[45] E. S. G. Bristowe, *Cain - An Argument* (Leicester: Edgar Backus, 1950), 5.

[46] Mrs. Sydney Bristowe, *Sargon the Magnificent* (London: The Covenant Publishing Co., 1927), 84.

[47] Mrs. Sydney Bristowe, *Sargon the Magnificent* (London: The Covenant Publishing Co., 1927), 151.

[48] E. S. G. Bristowe, *Cain - An Argument* (Leicester: Edgar Backus, 1950), 40.
[49] E. S. G. Bristowe, *Cain - An Argument* (Leicester: Edgar Backus, 1950), 62.
[50] Mrs. Sydney Bristowe, *Sargon the Magnificent* (London: The Covenant Publishing Co., 1927), 151.
[51] Mrs. Sydney Bristowe, *Sargon the Magnificent* (London: The Covenant Publishing Co., 1927), 73.
[52] *Creation Mythology: Atum the Creator*, http://www.egyptartsite.com/crea.html (accessed Aug. 12, 2010).
[53] Robert Bowie Johnson, Jr., *The Parthenon Code: Mankind's History in Marble* (Annapolis, Maryland: Solving Light Books, 2004), 9.
[54] Robert Bowie Johnson, Jr., *The Parthenon Code: Mankind's History in Marble* (Annapolis, Maryland: Solving Light Books, 2004), 173.
[55] E. S. G. Bristowe, *Cain - An Argument* (Leicester: Edgar Backus, 1950), 44.
[56] Donald Mackenzie, *Myths of Babylonia and Assyria*, Chapter 10 (1915), 35.
[57] Mrs. Sydney Bristowe, *Sargon the Magnificent* (London: The Covenant Publishing Co., 1927), 95.
[58] Mrs. Sydney Bristowe, *Sargon the Magnificent* (London: The Covenant Publishing Co., 1927), 150.
[59] Mrs. Sydney Bristowe, *Sargon the Magnificent* (London: The Covenant Publishing Co., 1927), 71.
[60] Mrs. Sydney Bristowe, *Sargon the Magnificent* (London: The Covenant Publishing Co., 1927), 100 (and notes).
[61] Mrs. Sydney Bristowe, *Sargon the Magnificent* (London: The Covenant Publishing Co., 1927), 55.
[62] Mrs. Sydney Bristowe, *Sargon the Magnificent* (London: The Covenant Publishing Co., 1927), 150.
[63] Mrs. Sydney Bristowe, *Sargon the Magnificent* (London: The Covenant Publishing Co., 1927), 93.
[64] Mrs. Sydney Bristowe, *Sargon the Magnificent* (London: The Covenant Publishing Co., 1927), 93.
[65] E. S. G. Bristowe, *Cain - An Argument* (Leicester: Edgar Backus, 1950), 8.
[66] E. S. G. Bristowe, *Cain - An Argument* (Leicester: Edgar Backus, 1950), 45.
[67] Mrs. Sydney Bristowe, *Sargon the Magnificent* (London: The Covenant Publishing Co., 1927), 80-81.
[68] E. S. G. Bristowe, *Cain - An Argument* (Leicester: Edgar Backus, 1950), 66.
[69] Mrs. Sydney Bristowe, *Sargon the Magnificent* (London: The Covenant Publishing Co., 1927), 151; E. S. G. Bristowe, *Cain - An Argument* (Leicester: Edgar Backus, 1950), 45.
[70] Philip Gardiner, Secrets of the Serpent: in Search of the Secret Past (Foresthill Ca: Reality press, 2006), 42.
[71] E. S. G. Bristowe, *Cain - An Argument* (Leicester: Edgar Backus, 1950), 45.
[72] A. H. Sayce, *Hibbert Lectures, 1887: Lectures on the Origin and Growth of Religion* (Williams and Northgate, 1898), 154.
[73] E. S. G. Bristowe, *Cain - An Argument* (Leicester: Edgar Backus, 1950), 127.
[74] Mrs. Sydney Bristowe, *Sargon the Magnificent* (London: The Covenant Publishing Co., 1927), 64.
[75] Robert Bowie Johnson, Jr., *The Parthenon Code: Mankind's History in Marble* (Annapolis, Maryland: Solving Light Books, 2004), 17.
[76] Philip Gardiner, *Secrets of the Serpent: in Search of the Secret Past* (Foresthill Ca.: Reality press, 2006), 18.
[77] Mrs. Sydney Bristowe, *Sargon the Magnificent* (London: The Covenant Publishing Co., 1927), 70-71.
[78] Mrs. Sydney Bristowe, *Sargon the Magnificent* (London: The Covenant Publishing Co., 1927), 81.
[79] Mrs. Sydney Bristowe, *Sargon the Magnificent* (London: The Covenant Publishing Co., 1927), 151.
[80] Robert Bowie Johnson, Jr., *The Parthenon Code: Mankind's History in Marble* (Annapolis, Maryland: Solving Light Books, 2004), 7.
[81] Robert Bowie Johnson, Jr., *The Parthenon Code: Mankind's History in Marble* (Annapolis, Maryland: Solving Light Books, 2004), 189.
[82] Robert Bowie Johnson, Jr., *The Parthenon Code: Mankind's History in Marble* (Annapolis, Maryland: Solving Light Books, 2004), 244.
[83] Robert Graves and Raphael Patai, *Hebrew Myths: The Book of Genesis* (Garden City, New York: Doubleday & Company, 1964), 75.
[84] Robert Bowie Johnson, Jr., *The Parthenon Code: Mankind's History in Marble* (Annapolis, Maryland: Solving Light Books, 2004), 12.
[85] Mrs. Sydney Bristowe, *Sargon the Magnificent* (London: The Covenant Publishing Co., 1927), 74.
[86] Robert Bowie Johnson, Jr., *The Parthenon Code: Mankind's History in Marble* (Annapolis, Maryland: Solving Light Books, 2004), 6, 22.
[87] Robert Bowie Johnson, Jr., *The Parthenon Code: Mankind's History in Marble* (Annapolis, Maryland: Solving Light Books, 2004), 12, 99, 169-170.
[88] Robert Bowie Johnson, Jr., *The Parthenon Code: Mankind's History in Marble* (Annapolis, Maryland: Solving Light Books, 2004), 171, 244.
[89] Louis Ginzberg, *The Legends of the Jews Volume I: From the Creation to Jacob*, trans. Henrietta Szold (Baltimore, Maryland: The Johns Hopkins University Press, 1909), 105.
[90] S. Baring-Gould, *Legends of the Patriarchs and Prophets and Other Old Testament Characters* (New York: American Book Exchange, 1881), 75.
[91] *The History of al-Tabari - Volume I: General Introduction and From the Creation to the Flood*, Adam's Descendants to Jared, 167, trans. Franz Rosenthal (Albany: New York Press, 1989), 337.
[92] *The Book of the Generations of Adam*, 5:5, http://www.earth-history.com/Pseudepigrapha/generations-adam.htm

(accessed May 5, 2007).
[93] Theodor Gaster, *Myth, Legend, and Custom in the Old Testament* (New York: Harper & Row, 1969), 51.
[94] Theodor Gaster, *Myth, Legend, and Custom in the Old Testament* (New York: Harper & Row, 1969), 51-52.
[95] Theodor Gaster, *Myth, Legend, and Custom in the Old Testament* (New York: Harper & Row, 1969), 52; Wikipedia, the Free Encyclopedia, *Lamech*, 2, http://en.wikipedia.org/wiki/Lamech (accessed Aug. 28, 2007).
[96] Robert Bowie Johnson, Jr., *The Parthenon Code: Mankind's History in Marble* (Annapolis, Maryland: Solving Light Books, 2004), 16-18, 192; James E. Thorold Rogers, *Bible Folk-Lore: A Study in Comparative Mythology* (London: Kegan Paul, Trench & Co., 1884), 11.
[97] Robert Bowie Johnson, Jr., *The Parthenon Code: Mankind's History in Marble* (Annapolis, Maryland: Solving Light Books, 2004), 192.
[98] Herman L. Hoeh, *Compendium of World History*, Volume 2, Chapter 18, 9-10, www.earth-history.com/Various/Compendium/hhc2ch18 (accessed July 12, 2007).
[99] Mrs. Sydney Bristowe, *Sargon the Magnificent* (London: The Covenant Publishing Co., 1927), 126.
[100] E. S. G. Bristowe, *Cain - An Argument* (Leicester: Edgar Backus, 1950), 66; Mrs. Sydney Bristowe, *Sargon the Magnificent* (London: The Covenant Publishing Co., 1927), 152.
[101] Josephus, *Jewish Antiquities*, Book 1, 59-64, trans. H. ST. J. Thackeray (London: William Heinemann Ltd. 1961), 29; Louis Ginzberg, *The Legends of the Jews Volume V: Notes for Volume One and Two*, III. The Ten Generations, 41, trans. Henrietta Szold (Baltimore, Maryland: The Johns Hopkins University Press, 1909), 144.
[102] Robert Graves and Raphael Patai, *Hebrew Myths: The Book of Genesis* (Garden City, New York: Doubleday & Company, 1964), 94; *The Chronicles of Jerahmeel* (*The Hebrew Bible Historiale*), 24:1, trans. M. Gaster, Ph. D. (London: The Royal Asiatic Society, 1899), 50.
[103] Rev. G. Oliver, *The Antiquities of Freemasonry; Comprising Illustrations of the Five Grand Periods of Masonry, From The Creation of the World to the Dedication of King Solomon's Temple* (London: Richard Spencer, 1843), 46; *The Chronicles of Jerahmeel* (*The Hebrew Bible Historiale*), 24:1, trans. M. Gaster, Ph. D. (London: The Royal Asiatic Society, 1899), 50.
[104] Louis Ginzberg, *The Legends of the Jews Volume I: From the Creation to Jacob*, trans. Henrietta Szold (Baltimore, Maryland: The Johns Hopkins University Press, 1909), 117.
[105] S. Baring-Gould, *Legends of the Patriarchs and Prophets and Other Old Testament Characters* (New York: American Book Exchange, 1881), 75.
[106] Robert Bowie Johnson, Jr., *Athena and Kain: The True Meaning of Greek Myth* (Annapolis, Maryland: Solving Light Books, 2003), 54.
[107] Louis Ginzberg, *The Legends of the Jews Volume I: From the Creation to Jacob*, trans. Henrietta Szold (Baltimore, Maryland: The Johns Hopkins University Press, 1909), 115.
[108] *Pseudo-Philo (The Biblical Antiquities of Philo)*, 2:3-4, trans. M. R. James (1917), http://www.sacred-texts.com/bib/bap/bap19.htm (accessed July 13, 2006); Mrs. Sydney Bristowe, *Sargon the Magnificent* (London: The Covenant Publishing Co., 1927), 151.
[109] Mrs. Sydney Bristowe, *Sargon the Magnificent* (London: The Covenant Publishing Co., 1927), 14.
[110] Josephus, *Jewish Antiquities*, Book 1, 59-64, trans. H. ST. J. Thackeray (London: William Heinemann Ltd. 1961), 29; *The Chronicles of Jerahmeel* (*The Hebrew Bible Historiale*), 24:1, trans. M. Gaster, Ph. D. (London: The Royal Asiatic Society, 1899), 50.
[111] *The Chronicles of Jerahmeel* (*The Hebrew Bible Historiale*), 26:11, trans. M. Gaster, Ph. D. (London: The Royal Asiatic Society, 1899), 55.
[112] Mrs. Sydney Bristowe, *Sargon the Magnificent* (London: The Covenant Publishing Co., 1927), 152.
[113] Mrs. Sydney Bristowe, *Sargon the Magnificent* (London: The Covenant Publishing Co., 1927), 70-71 (and notes).
[114] E. S. G. Bristowe, *Cain - An Argument* (Leicester: Edgar Backus, 1950), 65.
[115] *Gen.* 4:17 (KJV); E. S. G. Bristowe, *Cain - An Argument* (Leicester: Edgar Backus, 1950), 5, 9; Mrs. Sydney Bristowe, *Sargon the Magnificent* (London: The Covenant Publishing Co., 1927), 27, 53-54, 72, 80, 150; Mysterious World: *Ah, Osiria! Part III: Nimrod Hunting*, 13, http://www.mysteriousworld.com/Journal/2003/Autumn/Osiria/ (accessed July 12, 2007).
[116] Mrs. Sydney Bristowe, *Sargon the Magnificent* (London: The Covenant Publishing Co., 1927), 80.
[117] Mrs. Sydney Bristowe, *Sargon the Magnificent* (London: The Covenant Publishing Co., 1927), 80.
[118] I. P. Cory, *Ancient Fragments* (1832), Berossus, Of the Cosmology and Deluge, http://www.sacred-texts.com/cla/af/index.htm (accessed Aug. 14, 2007).
[119] Mrs. Sydney Bristowe, *Sargon the Magnificent* (London: The Covenant Publishing Co., 1927), 142 (notes).
[120] E. S. G. Bristowe, *Cain - An Argument* (Leicester: Edgar Backus, 1950), 7.
[121] Mrs. Sydney Bristowe, *Sargon the Magnificent* (London: The Covenant Publishing Co., 1927), 15-16.
[122] Strong's Exhaustive Concordance, *Qayin (7014)*, 1, http://www.strongsnumbers.com/hebrew/7014 (accessed March 17, 2010),
[123] Mrs. Sydney Bristowe, *Sargon the Magnificent* (London: The Covenant Publishing Co., 1927), 144, 148-149; E. S. G. Bristowe, *Cain - An Argument* (Leicester: Edgar Backus, 1950), 58.
[124] Mrs. Sydney Bristowe, *Sargon the Magnificent* (London: The Covenant Publishing Co., 1927), 148-149.

[125] Mrs. Sydney Bristowe, *Sargon the Magnificent* (London: The Covenant Publishing Co., 1927), 151.
[126] Mrs. Sydney Bristowe, *Sargon the Magnificent* (London: The Covenant Publishing Co., 1927), 129; James L. Kugel, *Traditions of the Bible* (Cambridge, Massachusetts: Harvard University Press, 1998), 169.
[127] Mrs. Sydney Bristowe, *Sargon the Magnificent* (London: The Covenant Publishing Co., 1927), 129.
[128] Mrs. Sydney Bristowe, *Sargon the Magnificent* (London: The Covenant Publishing Co., 1927), 88 (notes).

Chapter 11

[1] Mrs. Sydney Bristowe, *Sargon the Magnificent* (London: The Covenant Publishing Co., 1927), 72.
[2] *The First Book of Adam and Eve (The Conflict of Adam and Eve with Satan)*, 36:5, trans. S. C. Malan (London: Williams and Norgate, 1882).
[3] Louis Ginzberg, *The Legends of the Jews Volume V: Notes for Volume One and Two*, II. Adam, 131, trans. Henrietta Szold (Baltimore, Maryland: The Johns Hopkins University Press, 1909), 124.
[4] Strong's H2233 - *zera*, http://www.blueletterbible.org/lang/lexicon/lexicon.cfm?Strongs=H2233&t=KJV (accessed Aug. 12, 2010).
[5] Mrs. Sydney Bristowe, *Sargon the Magnificent* (London: The Covenant Publishing Co., 1927), 101.
[6] *The Third Book of Hermas, Which is Called His Similitude*, 9:118-119, trans. by Rutherford H. Platt, Jr., http://www.sacred-texts.com/bib/lbob/lbob28.htm (accessed Aug. 12, 2010).
[7] *The Chronicles of Jerahmeel* (*The Hebrew Bible Historiale*), 26:20, trans. M. Gaster, Ph. D. (London: The Royal Asiatic Society, 1899), 56.
[8] Andrew Collins, *From the Ashes of Angels* ((Rochester, Vermont: Bear & Company, 1996), 67.
[9] James L. Kugel, *Traditions of the Bible* (Cambridge, Massachusetts: Harvard University Press, 1998), 209-210; Andrew Collins, *From the Ashes of Angels* (Rochester, Vermont: Bear & Company, 1996), 9-10, 20, 29, 38-39; Creationism & the Early Church, *Chapter 5: The 'Sons of God' (Genesis 6:1-4)*, 2, http://www.robibrad.domon.co.uk/Chapter5.htm (accessed June 3, 2000); A Personal UPDATE Article, *As The Days of Noah Were*, 1, http://www.adamqadmon.com/nephilim/daysofnoah.html (accessed Dec. 6, 2000).
[10] *The Zohar*, Volume 2, Beresheet B, Section 69. "The Nefilim were on the earth", 424, www2.kabbalah.com/k/index.php/p=zohar/zohar&vol=3&sec=142 (accessed Feb. 24, 2010).
[11] Rabbi Leo Jung, Ph. D., *Fallen Angels in Jewish, Christian and Mohammedan Literature* (New York: KTAV Publishing House, 1974), 113.
[12] *The Book of Enoch*, 17:1, trans. R. H. Charles (Montana: Kessinger Publishing, 1912); *The Book of the Giants*, 69, trans. W.B. Henning (1943); S. Baring-Gould, *Legends of the Patriarchs and Prophets and Other Old Testament Characters* (New York: American Book Exchange, 1881), 34-35.
[13] Augustine of Hippo, *City of God and Christian Doctrine: Nicene and Post-Nicene Fathers of the Christian Church Part 2*, Book 9: Chapter 13, trans. Rev. Marcus Dods, D. D. (Whitefish, MT.: Kessinger Publishing, 2004).
[14] Andrew Collins, *From the Ashes of Angels* ((Rochester, Vermont: Bear & Company, 1996), 46-47.
[15] Louis Ginzberg, *The Legends of the Jews Volume I: From the Creation to Jacob*, trans. Henrietta Szold (Baltimore, Maryland: The Johns Hopkins University Press, 1909), 151.
[16] *The Apocryphon of John*, 25, trans. Michael Waldstein and Frederik Wisse, http://www.gnosis.org/naghamm/apocjn-long.html (accessed Aug. 27, 2007).
[17] *Uzza's Origins*, 1, http://www.geocities.com/mabcosmic/essays/utheory.html?200719 (accessed April 19, 2007); *Al-Uzza and Lilith*, 1-2, http://lilithgate.atspace.org/essays/uzlil.html (accessed April 19, 2007); *Zech.* 5:5-11 (KJV); *Mormon View of the Nephilim*, 1, http://www.adamqadmon.com/nephilim/mormonnephilim.html (accessed Feb. 2, 2001); Ellen Frankel, *The Classic Tales: 4000 years of Jewish Lore* (Northvale, New Jersey: Jason Aronson Inc., 1989), 28; *The Midrash Rabbah*, Bereshith (Genesis) 24:6, trans. Rabbi Dr. H. Freedman and Maurice Simon (London: The Soncino Press, 1961).
[18] Falvius Josephus, *Jewish Antiquities*, Book 1, 72-76, trans. H. ST. J. Thackeray (London: William Heinemann Ltd. 1961), 35; Chris Ward, *The Origin of Demons*, 2, http://www.adamqadmon.com/watchers/nephilim019.html (accessed Dec. 5, 2000); *The Book of the Cave of Treasures*, The First Thousand Years: Adam to Yared (Jared), The Rule of Enoch (notes), trans. Sir E. A. Wallis Budge (London: The Religious Tract Society, 1927), 95-98.
[19] *The Zohar*, Volume 1, Beresheet A, Section 29. Evil admixtures, 290, www2.kabbalah.com/k/index.php/p=zohar/zohar&vol=2&sec=50 (accessed Feb. 24, 2010).
[20] *The Zohar*, Volume 15, Tazria, Section 22. Man, person, 122, www2.kabbalah.com/k/index.php/p=zohar/zohar&vol=30&sec=1090 (accessed Feb. 24, 2010).
[21] *The Zohar*, Volume 1, Beresheet A, Section 29. Evil Admixtures, 290, www2.kabbalah.com/k/index.php/p=zohar/zohar&vol=2&sec=50 (accessed Feb. 24, 2010).
[22] *The Book of Jubilees*, 5:9-12, trans. R. H. Charles, The Apocrypha and Pseudepigrapha of the Old Testament (Oxford: Clarendon Press, 1913); *The Second Book of Adam and Eve (The Conflict of Adam and Eve with Satan)*, 12:16, trans. S. C. Malan (London: Williams and Norgate, 1882).
[23] Rabbi Leo Jung, Ph. D., *Fallen Angels in Jewish, Christian and Mohammedan Literature* (New York: KTAV Publishing House, 1974), 105 (notes).
[24] *The Zohar*, Volume 1, Beresheet A, Section 50. Aza and Azael, 464,

www2.kabbalah.com/k/index.php/p=zohar/zohar&vol=2&sec=71 (accessed Feb. 24, 2010).
[25] *The Zohar*, Volume 19, Balak, Section 43. Aza and Azael, "falling down, but having his eyes open", 423, www2.kabbalah.com/k/index.php/p=zohar/zohar&vol=43&sec=1518 (accessed Feb. 24, 2010),
[26] *The Zohar*, Volume 19, Balak, Section 43. Aza and Azael, "falling down, but having his eyes open", 417, www2.kabbalah.com/k/index.php/p=zohar/zohar&vol=43&sec=1518 (accessed Feb. 24, 2010).
[27] *The Zohar*, Volume 1, Beresheet A, Section 50. Aza and Azael, 464, www2.kabbalah.com/k/index.php/p=zohar/zohar&vol=2&sec=71 (accessed Feb. 24, 2010).
[28] *The Midrash Rabbah*, Bereshith (Genesis) 26:7, trans. Rabbi Dr. H. Freedman and Maurice Simon (London: The Soncino Press, 1961).
[29] Flavius Josephus, *The Antiquities of the Jews*, Book 1.3.1, trans. William Whiston (1737), http://www.ccel.org/j/josephus/works/ant-1.htm (accessed Feb. 4, 2011).
[30] *The Book of Enoch*, 19:2, trans. R. H. Charles (Montana: Kessinger Publishing, 1912).
[31] Tertullian, *Ante-Nicene Fathers Vol. 4*, III. On The Veiling of Virgins, Chapter 7, trans. Leipzig Oehler (1853), http://www.tertullian.org/anf/anf04/anf04-09.htm#P545_113997 (accessed Jan. 5, 2011).
[32] Kenneth S. Wuest, *Word Studies in the Greek N.T Vol. 4* (Grand Rapids, Michigan: Wm. B. Eerdmans Publishing Co., 1966), 241; *Enoch & The Nephilim: Liber VII*, 47, http://www.adamqadmon.com/nephilim/bbcwatchers.html (accessed Feb. 6, 2001).
[33] *The Book of Enoch*, 8:1, trans. R. H. Charles (Montana: Kessinger Publishing, 1912); Malcolm Godwin, *Angels: An Endangered Species* (New York: Simon & Schuester, 1990), 86.
[34] *The Zohar*, Volume 15, Acharei Mot, Section 60. Lilit and Na'amah, 360, www2.kabbalah.com/k/index.php/p=zohar/zohar&vol=32&sec=1178 (accessed Feb. 24, 2010).
[35] Louis Ginzberg, *The Legends of the Jews Volume I: From the Creation to Jacob*, trans. Henrietta Szold (Baltimore, Maryland: The Johns Hopkins University Press, 1909), 149.
[36] *The Book of Enoch*, 10:9, trans. R. H. Charles (Montana: Kessinger Publishing, 1912).
[37] American Heritage Dictionary, *adulterate*, dictionary.reference.com/browse/adulterate (accessed March 17, 2010).
[38] *The Midrash Rabbah*, Bereshith (Genesis) 24:6, trans. Rabbi Dr. H. Freedman and Maurice Simon (London: The Soncino Press, 1961); Johann Andreas Eisenmenger, *The Traditions of the Jews, Contained in the Talmud and other Mystical Writings* (London: J. Robinson, 1748), 22-23.
[39] *The Zohar*, Volume 1, Beresheet A, Section 29. Evil admixtures, 291, www2.kabbalah.com/k/index.php/p=zohar/zohar&vol=2&sec=50 (accessed Feb. 24, 2010).
[40] Louis Ginzberg, *The Legends of the Jews Volume 5: Notes for Volume One and Two*, III. The Ten Generations, 3, trans. Henrietta Szold (Baltimore, Maryland: The Johns Hopkins University Press, 1909), 133; Bentley Layton, *The Gnostic Scriptures* (New York: Doubleday, 1995), 176; *Saltair na Rann*, 1661-1696, trans. David Greene; Louis Ginzberg, *The Legends of the Jews Volume I: From the Creation to Jacob*, trans. Henrietta Szold (Baltimore, Maryland: The Johns Hopkins University Press, 1909), 105.
[41] Rabbi Leo Jung, Ph. D., *Fallen Angels in Jewish, Christian and Mohammedan Literature* (New York: KTAV Publishing House, 1974), 115; *Who are the Nephilim?*, 4, http://www.adamqadmon.com/watchers/nephilim009.html (accessed Feb. 11, 2001); Strong's H5307 - *naphal*, http://www.blueletterbible.org/lang/lexicon/lexicon.cfm?Strongs=H5307&t=KJV (accessed Dec. 21, 2010); *Notes on the Demi-gods of Genesis 6: Part 1. Who are the Nephilim*, http://www.ldolphin.org/nephilim2.html (accessed Dec. 21, 2010).
[42] *There Were Giants on the earth... The Nephilim*, 2, http://biblelight.net/nephilim.htm (accessed Feb. 3, 2010).
[43] *Race*, 4, www.britam.org/Questions/QuestRace.html (accessed Feb. 4, 2010).
[44] Charles DeLoach, *Giants: A Reference Guide from History, the Bible, and Recorded Legend* (Metuchen, N. J.: The Scarecrow Press, Inc., 1995), 4; *Enoch & the Nephilim: Liber VII*, 46, http://www.adamqadmon.com/nephilim/bbcwatchers.html (accessed Feb. 6, 2001); *The B.B.C.: Going After Strange Flesh*, 1, http://www.adamqadmon.com/nephilim/bbcstrange.html (accessed Feb. 25, 2001).
[45] Charles DeLoach, *Giants: A Reference Guide from History, the Bible, and Recorded Legend* (Metuchen, N. J.: The Scarecrow Press, Inc., 1995), 4.
[46] *The Zohar*, Volume 10, Mishpatim, Section 18. Two Messiahs, 486, www2.kabbalah.com/k/index.php/p=zohar/zohar&vol=20&sec=702 (accessed Feb. 24, 2010).
[47] *The Companion Bible*, Appendix 4 (Grand Rapids, Michigan: Kregel Publications, 1990), 6.
[48] Johann Andreas Eisenmenger, *The Traditions of the Jews, Contained in the Talmud and other Mystical Writings* (London: J. Robinson, 1748), 192.
[49] Robert Graves and Raphael Patai, *Hebrew Myths: The Book of Genesis* (Garden City, New York: Doubleday & Company, 1964), 105.
[50] Rabbi Leo Jung, Ph. D., *Fallen Angels in Jewish, Christian and Mohammedan Literature* (New York: KTAV Publishing House, 1974), 108.
[51] *The Book of Enoch*, 106:7, trans. R. H. Charles (Montana: Kessinger Publishing, 1912).
[52] *Barhebraeus' Scholia on the Old Testament Part I: Genesis - II Samuel*, Genesis 6:3, trans. Martin Sprengling and William Creighton Graham (Chicago, Illinois: University of Chicago Press, 1931), 35.

[53] *The Book of Enoch*, 15:10, trans. R. H. Charles (Montana: Kessinger Publishing, 1912).
[54] *Oxford Annotated Bible, Revised Standard Version, edited by Herbert G. May and Bruce M. Metzger* (Clare Gregory, *Understanding the True Origins of Mormonism - The Incredible Story of a Race of Celestial Beings that once Came to the Earth…*, 1-2, http://www.adamqadmon.com/nephilim/fallen.html (accessed Dec. 6, 2000).
[55] *The Nephilim*, 7, http://www.adamqadmon.com/watchers/nephilim013.html (accessed Dec. 7, 2000); Clare Gregory, *Understanding the True Origins of Mormonism - The Incredible Story of a Race of Celestial Beings that once Came to the Earth…*, 3, http://www.adamqadmon.com/nephilim/fallen.html (accessed Dec. 6, 2000).
[56] *As the Days of Noah Were*, 1, http://www.adamqadmon.com/nephlim/daysofnoah.html (accessed Dec. 6, 2000).
[57] Stephen Quayle, *Genesis 6 Giants: The Master Builders of Prehistoric and Ancient Civilizations* (Bozeman, Montana: End Time Thunder Publishers, 2005), 181; Andrew Collins, *From the Ashes of Angels* (Rochester, Vermont: Bear & Company, 1996), 3.
[58] Louis Ginzberg, *The Legends of the Jews Volume I: From the Creation to Jacob*, trans. Henrietta Szold (Baltimore, Maryland: The Johns Hopkins University Press, 1909), 114; *The Midrash Rabbah*, Bereshith (Genesis) 37:5, trans. Rabbi Dr. H. Freedman and Maurice Simon (London: The Soncino Press, 1961).
[59] *The Midrash Rabbah*, Bereshith (Genesis) 26:7, Deuteronomy 1:28, trans. Rabbi Dr. H. Freedman and Maurice Simon (London: The Soncino Press, 1961); *The Babylonian Talmud*, Jews' College/Soncino English Translation, Yoma 10a, http://www.halakhah.com/pdf/moed/Yoma.pdf (accessed Dec. 30, 2010); Charles DeLoach, *Giants: A Reference Guide from History, the Bible, and Recorded Legend* (Metuchen, N. J.: The Scarecrow Press, Inc., 1995), 46; Jonathan Gray, *Lost World of Giants*, (Teach Services, Inc., 2006), 46; Andrew Collins, *From the Ashes of Angels* (Rochester, Vermont: Bear & Company, 1996), 51; *The Sibylline Oracles, Translated from the Greek into English blank Verse*, Book I, Line 146, trans. Milton S. Terry (New York: Hunt & Eaton, 1890).
[60] Stephen Quayle, *Genesis 6 Giants: The Master Builders of Prehistoric and Ancient Civilizations* (Bozeman, Montana: End Time Thunder Publishers, 2005), 124-125.
[61] Jonathan Gray, *Lost World of Giants*, (Teach Services, Inc., 2006), 11.
[62] *The Works of Philo Judaeus*, Questions and Answers on Genesis 1, 32, trans. C. D. Yonge (London: H. G. Bohn, 1854-1855).
[63] Hugh Ross Ph. D., *Sons of God… Who Are They?*, 1, http://www.adamqadmon.com/wtchers/ross-sonsofgod.html (accessed Dec. 5, 2000).
[64] *The Zohar*, Volume 18, Shlach Lecha, Section 10. The spies, 73, www2.kabbalah.com/k/index.php/p=zohar/zohar&vol=40&sec=1411 (accessed Feb. 24, 2010),
[65] Robert Graves and Raphael Patai, *Hebrew Myths: The Book of Genesis* (Garden City, New York: Doubleday & Company, 1964), 98.
[66] Robert Graves and Raphael Patai, *Hebrew Myths: The Book of Genesis* (Garden City, New York: Doubleday & Company, 1964), 98.
[67] J. E. Hanauer, *Folklore of the Holy Land: Moslem, Christian and Jewish*, 3: Noah and Og (London: BiblioBazaar, 2007), 13.
[68] Stephen Quayle, *Genesis 6 Giants: The Master Builders of Prehistoric and Ancient Civilizations* (Bozeman, Montana: End Time Thunder Publishers, 2005), 218.
[69] Robert Graves and Raphael Patai, *Hebrew Myths: The Book of Genesis* (Garden City, New York: Doubleday & Company, 1964), 106; Mysterious World: Winter 2003, *Giants in the Earth Part 4: Giants of Europe*, 13, http://www.mysteriousworld.com/Journal/2003/Winter/Giants/ (accessed July 20, 2007); Stephen Quayle, *Genesis 6 Giants: The Master Builders of Prehistoric and Ancient Civilizations* (Bozeman, Montana: End Time Thunder Publishers, 2005), 217-218.
[70] *The Zohar*, Volume 1, Beresheet A, Section 20. The five types of the mixed multitude, 227, www2.kabbalah.com/k/index.php/p=zohar/zohar&vol=2&sec=41 (accessed Feb. 24, 2010).
[71] Charles DeLoach, *Giants: A Reference Guide from History, the Bible, and Recorded Legend* (Metuchen, N. J.: The Scarecrow Press, Inc., 1995), 47.
[72] *The Zohar*, Volume 1, Beresheet A, Section 20. The five types of the mixed multitude, 231, www2.kabbalah.com/k/index.php/p=zohar/zohar&vol=2&sec=41 (accessed Feb. 24, 2010).
[73] *The Midrash Rabbah*, Bereshith (Genesis) 26:7 (and notes), trans. Rabbi Dr. H. Freedman and Maurice Simon (London: The Soncino Press, 1961).
[74] Charles DeLoach, *Giants: A Reference Guide from History, the Bible, and Recorded Legend* (Metuchen, N. J.: The Scarecrow Press, Inc., 1995), 47.
[75] *Pirke De Rabbi Eliezer*, Chapter 22: The Fall of the Angels [26A. i.], trans. Gerald Friedlander (New York: Sepher-Hermon Press, 1981), 161; Stephen Quayle, *Genesis 6 Giants: The Master Builders of Prehistoric and Ancient Civilizations* (Bozeman, Montana: End Time Thunder Publishers, 2005), 216-217; Rabbi Leo Jung, Ph. D., *Fallen Angels in Jewish, Christian and Mohammedan Literature* (New York: KTAV Publishing House, 1974), 113.
[76] Mysterious World: Winter 2003, *Giants in the Earth Part 4: Giants of Europe*, 16, 23, http://www.mysteriousworld.com/Journal/2003/Winter/Giants/ (accessed July 20, 2007); *"Biblical Information of Giants (8,500 B.C. to 1,300 B.C.)"*, 2, http://www.mazzaroth.com/ChapterThree/BiblicalInfoOfGiants.htm (accessed June 28, 2000).

[77] Mysterious World, *Giants in the Earth Part 4: Giants of Europe*, 16, 23, www.mysteriousworld.com/Journal/2003/Winter/Giants/ (accessed July 20, 2007).
[78] *The Book of Jubilees*, 4:15, trans. R. H. Charles, The Apocrypha and Pseudepigrapha of the Old Testament (Oxford: Clarendon Press, 1913); Earth's Ancient History, *The Generation Table (the Cain Line)*, 2, http://www.earth-history.com/_toplevel/Generation.htm (accessed May 10, 2007).
[79] *The Companion Bible*, Genesis 4:26 (Grand Rapids, Michigan: Kregel Publications, 1990), 9.
[80] Louis Ginzberg, *The Legends of the Jews Volume I: From the Creation to Jacob*, trans. Henrietta Szold (Baltimore, Maryland: The Johns Hopkins University Press, 1909), 122-123.
[81] Louis Ginzberg, *The Legends of the Jews Volume V: Notes for Volume One and Two*, III. The Ten Generations, 54, 56, trans. Henrietta Szold (Baltimore, Maryland: The Johns Hopkins University Press, 1909), 151, 153; *The Midrash Rabbah*, Bereshith (Genesis) 23:6 (and notes), trans. Rabbi Dr. H. Freedman and Maurice Simon (London: The Soncino Press, 1961); *Armenian Apocrypha Relating to Adam and Eve*, History of the Forefathers, Adam and His Sons and Grandsons 35, trans. Michael E. Stone (Leiden: E. J. Brill, 1996), 197; Merrill F, Unger, *Biblical Demonology* (Wheaton, Illinois: Van Kampen Press, 1952), 59.
[82] *The Book of the Generations of Adam*, 5:5, http://www.earth-history.com/Pseudepigrapha/generations-adam.htm (accessed May 5, 2007).
[83] G. H. Pember, M. A., *Earth's Earliest Ages and their Connection With Modern Spiritualism, Theosophy, and Buddhism* (Grand Rapids, Michigan: Kregel Publications, 1975), 122.
[84] Louis Ginzberg, *The Legends of the Jews Volume I: From the Creation to Jacob*, trans. Henrietta Szold (Baltimore, Maryland: The Johns Hopkins University Press, 1909), 123.
[85] *The Midrash Rabbah*, Bereshith (Genesis) 23:6, trans. Rabbi Dr. H. Freedman and Maurice Simon (London: The Soncino Press, 1961).
[86] Louis Ginzberg, *The Legends of the Jews Volume V: Notes for Volume One and Two*, III. The Ten Generations, 54, trans. Henrietta Szold (Baltimore, Maryland: The Johns Hopkins University Press, 1909), 151.
[87] Louis Ginzberg, *The Legends of the Jews Volume V: Notes for Volume One and Two*, III. The Ten Generations, 55, trans. Henrietta Szold (Baltimore, Maryland: The Johns Hopkins University Press, 1909), 152.
[88] *Book of the Glory of Kings (Kerba Nagast)*, 6. Concerning the Sin of Cain, trans. Sir. E. A. Wallis Budge (London: Humphrey Milford, 1932).

Chapter 12

[1] Louis Ginzberg, *The Legends of the Jews Volume I: From the Creation to Jacob*, trans. Henrietta Szold (Baltimore, Maryland: The Johns Hopkins University Press, 1909), 117.
[2] Greg Killiam, *The Days of Noah*, 6, http://www.adamqadmon.com/nephilim/gkillian000.html (accessed Dec. 6, 2000).
[3] James E. Thorold Rogers, *Bible Folk-Lore; a Study in Comparative Mythology* (London: Kegan Paul, Trench and Co., 1884), 15.
[4] *Armenian Apocrypha Relating to Adam and Eve*, Abel and Other Pieces 5.4, trans. Michael E. Stone (Leiden: E. J. Brill, 1996), 153-154.
[5] *The Midrash Rabbah*, Bereshith (Genesis) 23:2, trans. Rabbi Dr. H. Freedman and Maurice Simon (London: The Soncino Press, 1961).
[6] Louis Ginzberg, *The Legends of the Jews Volume I: From the Creation to Jacob*, trans. Henrietta Szold (Baltimore, Maryland: The Johns Hopkins University Press, 1909), 117.
[7] *The History of al-Tabari - Volume I: General Introduction and From the Creation to the Flood*, Enoch to Noah, 176, trans. Franz Rosenthal (Albany: New York Press, 1989), 346.
[8] Theodor Gaster, *Myth, Legend, and Custom in the Old Testament* (New York: Harper & Row, 1969), 78; *Rashi*, (Bereishit) Genesis 4:19, http://www.chabad.org/library/bible_cdo/aid/8168/showrashi/true (accessed Oct. 27, 2010); *The Midrash Rabbah*, Bereshith (Genesis) 23:2, trans. Rabbi Dr. H. Freedman and Maurice Simon (London: The Soncino Press, 1961); Wikipedia, the Free Encyclopedia, *Lamech*, 2, http://en.wikipedia.org/wiki/Lamech (accessed Aug. 28, 2007).
[9] James E. Thorold Rogers, *Bible Folk-Lore; a Study in Comparative Mythology* (London: Kegan Paul, Trench and Co., 1884), 15; G. H. Pember, M. A., *Earth's Earliest Ages and their Connection With Modern Spiritualism, Theosophy, and Buddhism* (Grand Rapids, Michigan: Kregel Publications, 1975), 121.
[10] The Works of Philo Judaeus, *On the Posterity of Cain and His Exile* 33, 112, trans. C. D. Yonge (London: H. G. Bohn, 1854-1855).
[11] Robert Graves and Raphael Patai, *Hebrew Myths: The Book of Genesis* (Garden City, New York: Doubleday & Company, 1964), 102.
[12] *The Zohar*, Volume 2, Beresheet B, Section 69. "The Nephilim were on the earth", 424, www2.kabbalah.com/k/index.php/p=zohar/zohar&vol=3&sec=142 (accessed Feb. 24, 2010).
[13] *Pseudo-Philo (The Biblical Antiquities of Philo)*, 2:6-7, trans. M. R. James (1917), http://www.sacred-texts.com/bib/bap/bap19.htm (accessed July 13, 2006); Josephus, *Jewish Antiquities*, Book 1, 64-67, trans. H. ST. J. Thackeray (London: William Heinemann Ltd. 1961), 31; G. H. Pember, M. A., *Earth's Earliest Ages and their*

Connection With Modern Spiritualism, Theosophy, and Buddhism (Grand Rapids, Michigan: Kregel Publications, 1975), 121. *The Chronicles of Jerahmeel* (*The Hebrew Bible Historiale*), 24:5, trans. M. Gaster, Ph. D. (London: The Royal Asiatic Society, 1899), 51.

[14] *Armenian Apocrypha Relating to Adam and Eve*, History of the Forefathers, Adam and His Sons and Grandsons 12, trans. Michael E. Stone (Leiden: E. J. Brill, 1996), 187.

[15] Josephus, *Jewish Antiquities*, Book 1, 64-67, trans. H. ST. J. Thackeray (London: William Heinemann Ltd. 1961), 31; The Works of Philo Judaeus, On the Posterity of Cain and His Exile 32, 111, trans. C. D. Yonge (London: H. G. Bohn, 1854-1855); *The Midrash Rabbah*, Bereshith (Genesis) 23:3, trans. Rabbi Dr. H. Freedman and Maurice Simon (London: The Soncino Press, 1961); *The Chronicles of Jerahmeel* (*The Hebrew Bible Historiale*), 24:6, trans. M. Gaster, Ph. D. (London: The Royal Asiatic Society, 1899), 51.

[16] S. Baring-Gould, *Legends of the Patriarchs and Prophets and Other Old Testament Characters* (New York: American Book Exchange, 1881), 98; *Armenian Apocrypha Relating to Adam and Eve*, The Sethites and the Cainites 10, trans. Michael E. Stone (Leiden: E. J. Brill, 1996), 205.

[17] *The Zohar*, Volume 15, Acharei Mot, Section 60. Lilit and Na'amah, 360, www2.kabbalah.com/k/index.php/p=zohar/zohar&vol=32&sec=1178 (accessed Feb. 24, 2010).

[18] Louis Ginzberg, *The Legends of the Jews Volume I: From the Creation to Jacob*, trans. Henrietta Szold (Baltimore, Maryland: The Johns Hopkins University Press, 1909), 118.

[19] *Armenian Apocrypha Relating to Adam and Eve*, History of the Forefathers, Adam and His Sons and Grandsons 13, trans. Michael E. Stone (Leiden: E. J. Brill, 1996), 187.

[20] James E. Thorold Rogers, *Bible Folk-Lore; A Study in Comparative Mythology* (London: Kegan Paul, Trench and Co., 1884), 10, 17; *The Chronicles of Jerahmeel* (*The Hebrew Bible Historiale*), 24:8, trans. M. Gaster, Ph. D. (London: The Royal Asiatic Society, 1899), 51.

[21] *The Zohar*, Volume 15, Acharei Mot, Section 60. Lilit and Na'amah, 361, www2.kabbalah.com/k/index.php/p=zohar/zohar&vol=32&sec=1178 (accessed Feb. 24, 2010).

[22] Josephus, *Jewish Antiquities*, Book 1, 64-67, trans. H. ST. J. Thackeray (London: William Heinemann Ltd. 1961), 31.

[23] *The Midrash Rabbah*, Bereshith (Genesis) 23:3 (notes), trans. Rabbi Dr. H. Freedman and Maurice Simon (London: The Soncino Press, 1961); The Works of Philo Judaeus, On the Posterity of Cain and His Exile 33, 114, trans. C. D. Yonge (London: H. G. Bohn, 1854-1855).

[24] Robert Graves and Raphael Patai, *Hebrew Myths: The Book of Genesis* (Garden City, New York: Doubleday & Company, 1964), 103.

[25] *The Book of the Bee*, Chapter 19: Of the Invention of the Instruments for Working in Iron, trans. Earnest A. Wallis Budge, M. A., http://www.sacred-texts.com/chr/bb/bb19.htm (accessed Oct. 10, 2004).

[26] S. Baring-Gould, *Legends of the Patriarchs and Prophets and Other Old Testament Characters* (New York: American Book Exchange, 1881), 54.

[27] *The Second Book of Adam and Eve (The Conflict of Adam and Eve with Satan)*, 20:2-4, trans. S. C. Malan (London: Williams and Norgate, 1882).

[28] *Jubal - Genun - Musical Worship*, Book of Adam and Eve, 15-16, http://www.piney.com/MuGenun2.html (accessed Aug. 17, 2010).

[29] Mysterious World: Spring 2003, *Giants in the Earth Part I: Giants of the Ancient Near East*, 13, http://www.mysteriousworld.com/Journal/2003/Spring/Giants/ (accessed July 12, 2007).

[30] *Jubal - Genun - Musical Worship*, Book of Adam and Eve, 10, http://www.piney.com/MuGenun2.html (accessed Aug. 17, 2010).

[31] *Jubal - Genun - Musical Worship*, Book of Adam and Eve, 11, http://www.piney.com/MuGenun2.html (accessed Aug. 17, 2010).

[32] Josephus, *Jewish Antiquities*, Book 1, 64-67, trans. H. ST. J. Thackeray (London: William Heinemann Ltd. 1961), 31.

[33] Josephus, *Jewish Antiquities*, Book 1, 64-67, trans. H. ST. J. Thackeray (London: William Heinemann Ltd. 1961), 31; The Works of Philo Judaeus, On the Posterity of Cain and His Exile 34, 119, trans. C. D. Yonge (London: H. G. Bohn, 1854-1855).

[34] *Jubal - Genun - Musical Worship*, Book of Adam and Eve, 10, http://www.piney.com/MuGenun2.html (accessed Aug. 17, 2010).

[35] *Jubal - Genun - Musical Worship*, Book of Adam and Eve, 14, http://www.piney.com/MuGenun2.html (accessed Aug. 17, 2010).

[36] *The Book of the Cave of Treasures*, The Second Thousand Years: Yared to the Flood, Of the Transmission of the Art of Playing the Harp, That is to Say, of Music, and Singing and Dancing, trans. Sir E. A. Wallis Budge (London: The Religious Tract Society, 1927), 87-95.

[37] Moses Aberbach and Bernard Grossfield, *Targum Onkelos to Genesis: A Critical Analysis Together with an English Translation of the Text*, Genesis 4:26 (New York: KTAV Publishing House, Inc., 1995), 46.

[38] Robert Graves and Raphael Patai, *Hebrew Myths: The Book of Genesis* (Garden City, New York: Doubleday & Company, 1964), 106.

[39] *The Second Book of Adam and Eve (The Conflict of Adam and Eve with Satan)*, 20:9, trans. S. C. Malan (London: Williams and Norgate, 1882).
[40] *The History of al-Tabari - Volume I: General Introduction and From the Creation to the Flood*, The Events That Took Place in Noah's Time, 184, trans. Franz Rosenthal (Albany: New York Press, 1989), 354.
[41] *Pseudo-Philo (The Biblical Antiquities of Philo)*, 2:9, trans. M. R. James (1917), http://www.sacred-texts.com/bib/bap/bap19.htm (accessed July 13, 2006).
[42] *The Chronicles of Jerahmeel* (*The Hebrew Bible Historiale*), 24:9, 26:18, trans. M. Gaster, Ph. D. (London: The Royal Asiatic Society, 1899), 51, 56.
[43] *Nimrod's Babylonian Musical Worship Teams*, 4-5, http://www.piney.com/MuBabylo.html (accessed July 2, 2000).
[44] *The Book of the Cave of Treasures*, The Second Thousand Years: Yared to the Flood, Of the Transmission of the Art of Playing the Harp, That is to Say, of Music, and Singing and Dancing, trans. Sir E. A. Wallis Budge (London: The Religious Tract Society, 1927), 89-94; *The Midrash Rabbah*, Bereshith (Genesis) 26:4, trans. Rabbi Dr. H. Freedman and Maurice Simon (London: The Soncino Press, 1961).
[45] *Book of the Glory of Kings (Kerba Nagast)*, 6. Concerning the Sin of Cain, trans. Sir. E. A. Wallis Budge (London: Humphrey Milford, 1932).
[46] *The Book of the Bee*, Chapter 19: Of the Invention of the Instruments for Working in Iron, trans. Earnest A. Wallis Budge, M. A., http://www.sacred-texts.com/chr/bb/bb19.htm (accessed Oct. 10, 2004).
[47] *The Second Book of Adam and Eve (The Conflict of Adam and Eve with Satan)*, 20:2-4, trans. S. C. Malan (London: Williams and Norgate, 1882).
[48] *Armenian Apocrypha Relating to Adam and Eve*, Question 5, trans. Michael E. Stone (Leiden: E. J. Brill, 1996), 119.
[49] Robert Graves and Raphael Patai, *Hebrew Myths: The Book of Genesis* (Garden City, New York: Doubleday & Company, 1964), 103.
[50] *Pseudo-Philo (The Biblical Antiquities of Philo)*, 2:8, trans. M. R. James (1917), http://www.sacred-texts.com/bib/bap/bap19.htm (accessed July 13, 2006).
[51] *The History of al-Tabari - Volume I: General Introduction and From the Creation to the Flood*, Adam's Descendants to Jared, 165, trans. Franz Rosenthal (Albany: New York Press, 1989), 338.
[52] *The Second Book of Adam and Eve (The Conflict of Adam and Eve with Satan)*, 20:5-10, trans. S. C. Malan (London: Williams and Norgate, 1882).
[53] *Armenian Apocrypha Relating to Adam and Eve*, Question 5, trans. Michael E. Stone (Leiden: E. J. Brill, 1996), 119.
[54] *Pirke De Rabbi Eliezer*, Chapter 22: The Fall of the Angels [26A. i.], trans. Gerald Friedlander (New York: Sepher-Hermon Press, 1981), 159.
[55] Johann Andreas Eisenmenger, *The Traditions of the Jews, Contained in the Talmud and other Mystical Writings* (London: J. Robinson, 1748), 73.
[56] *The Book of the Cave of Treasures*, The Second Thousand Years: Yared to the Flood, Of the Transmission of the Art of Playing the Harp, That is to Say, of Music, and Singing and Dancing, trans. Sir E. A. Wallis Budge (London: The Religious Tract Society, 1927), 87-94.
[57] *Pirke De Rabbi Eliezer*, Chapter 22: The Fall of the Angels [26A. i.], trans. Gerald Friedlander (New York: Sepher-Hermon Press, 1981), 160.
[58] *The Zohar*, Volume 1, Beresheet A, Section 29. Evil admixtures, 291, www2.kabbalah.com/k/index.php/p=zohar/zohar&vol=2&sec=50 (accessed Feb. 24, 2010).
[59] Johann Andreas Eisenmenger, *The Traditions of the Jews, Contained in the Talmud and Other Mystical Writings* (London: J. Robinson, 1748), 206.
[60] *The Book of Jasher*, 2:3-5, trans. Albinus Alcuin (Pomeroy, Washington: Health Research, 1966); *The Midrash Rabbah*, Bereshith (Genesis) 28:8, trans. Rabbi Dr. H. Freedman and Maurice Simon (London: The Soncino Press, 1961).
[61] Josephus, *Jewish Antiquities*, Book 1, 72-76, trans. H. ST. J. Thackeray (London: William Heinemann Ltd. 1961), 35.
[62] Robert Graves and Raphael Patai, *Hebrew Myths: The Book of Genesis* (Garden City, New York: Doubleday & Company, 1964), 69; Wikipedia, the Free Encyclopedia, *Lamech*, 2, http://en.wikipedia.org/wiki/Lamech (accessed Aug. 28, 2007); Louis Ginzberg, *The Legends of the Jews Volume V: Notes for Volume One and Two*, III. The Ten Generations, 45, trans. Henrietta Szold (Baltimore, Maryland: The Johns Hopkins University Press, 1909), 147.
[63] *Armenian Apocrypha Relating to Adam and Eve*, History of the Forefathers, Adam and His Sons and Grandsons 13, trans. Michael E. Stone (Leiden: E. J. Brill, 1996), 187; *The Zohar*, Volume 1, Beresheet A, Section 50. Aza and Azael, 466, www2.kabbalah.com/k/index.php/p=zohar/zohar&vol=2&sec=71 (accessed Feb. 24, 2010).
[64] *The Zohar*, Volume 15, Acharei Mot, Section 60. Lilit and Na'amah, 360, www2.kabbalah.com/k/index.php/p=zohar/zohar&vol=32&sec=1178 (accessed Feb. 24, 2010).
[65] The Works of Philo Judaeus, On the Posterity of Cain and His Exile 35, 120, trans. C. D. Yonge (London: H. G. Bohn, 1854-1855).
[66] *The Zohar*, Volume 1, Beresheet A, Section 9. "Let there be lights", 102,

www2.kabbalah.com/k/index.php/p=zohar/zohar&vol=2&sec=30 (accessed Feb. 25, 2010).

Chapter 13

[1] *The Book of Enoch*, 6:1-8, Trans. R. H. Charles (Montana: Kessinger Publishing, 1912); *The Book of Jubilees*, 10:4-5, trans. R. H. Charles, The Apocrypha and Pseudepigrapha of the Old Testament (Oxford: Clarendon Press, 1913); Robert Graves and Raphael Patai, *Hebrew Myths: The Book of Genesis* (Garden City, New York: Doubleday & Company, 1964), 84.

[2] Robert Graves and Raphael Patai, *Hebrew Myths: The Book of Genesis* (Garden City, New York: Doubleday & Company, 1964), 84.

[3] Paula O'Keefe, *Leviathan Chained*, 2, http://www.adamqadmon.com/nephilim/leviathanchained.html (accessed Dec. 6, 2000).

[4] *The Book of Enoch*, 6:6 (notes), trans. R. H. Charles (Montana: Kessinger Publishing, 1912); *The Book of Jubilees*, 4:15, trans. R. H. Charles, The Apocrypha and Pseudepigrapha of the Old Testament (Oxford: Clarendon Press, 1913); Louis Ginzberg, *The Legends of the Jews Volume V: Notes for Volume One and Two*, III. The Ten Generations, 57, trans. Henrietta Szold (Baltimore, Maryland: The Johns Hopkins University Press, 1909), 154.

[5] Paula O'Keefe, *Leviathan Chained*, 2, http://www.adamqadmon.com/nephilim/leviathanchained.html (accessed Dec. 6, 2000).

[6] *The Book of the Dead*, The Papyrus of ANI – 240 B.C., trans. E. A. Wallis Budge, http://www.pseudepigrapha.com/geypitan/BookOfTheDead.htm (accessed Aug. 12, 2010).

[7] *The Book of Jubilees*, 4:15, trans. R. H. Charles, The Apocrypha and Pseudepigrapha of the Old Testament (Oxford: Clarendon Press, 1913).

[8] Louis Ginzberg, *The Legends of the Jews Volume V: Notes for Volume One and Two*, III. The Ten Generations, 57, trans. Henrietta Szold (Baltimore, Maryland: The Johns Hopkins University Press, 1909), 154; *The Book of Jubilees*, 4:15, trans. R. H. Charles, The Apocrypha and Pseudepigrapha of the Old Testament (Oxford: Clarendon Press, 1913); *The Book of the Cave of Treasures*, The First Thousand Years: Adam to Yared (Jared), The Rule of Yared, trans. Sir E. A. Wallis Budge (London: The Religious Tract Society, 1927), 84-86.

[9] Earth's Ancient History, 1, *The Generation Table (the Cain line)*, http://www.earth-history.com/_toplevel/Generation.htm (accessed May 5, 2007); T*he History of al-Tabari - Volume I: General Introduction and From the Creation to the Flood*, Adam's Descendants to Jared, 167 (notes), The Rule of Oshahanj, 170, trans. Franz Rosenthal (Albany: New York Press, 1989), 337, 341.

[10] James E. Thorold Rogers, *Bible Folk-Lore; a Study in Comparative Mythology* (London: Kegan Paul, Trench and Co., 1884), 14.

[11] *...in the days of Seth*, 4, http://www.adamqadmon.com/nephilim/daysofseth.html (accessed Feb. 9, 2001); *The Book of Adam*, [44]17.1, trans. J. P. Mahe, http://www.pseudepigrapha.com/pseudepigrapha/TheBookOfAdam.htm (accessed June 27, 2005).

[12] Andrew Collins, *From the Ashes of Angels* (Rochester, Vermont: Bear & Company, 1996), 23-24; *Mount Hermon*, 1, http://www.adamqadmon.com/nephilim/mounthermon.html (accessed March 5, 2001).

[13] *Mount Hermon*, 1, http://www.adamqadmon.com/nephilim/mounthermon.html (accessed March 5, 2001); Andrew Collins, *From the Ashes of Angels* (Rochester, Vermont: Bear & Company, 1996), 24.

[14] *Mount Hermon*, 1, http://www.adamqadmon.com/nephilim/mounthermon.html (accessed March 5, 2001).

[15] Louis Ginzberg, *The Legends of the Jews Volume I: From the Creation to Jacob*, trans. Henrietta Szold (Baltimore, Maryland: The Johns Hopkins University Press, 1909), 124-125; Andrew Collins, *From the Ashes of Angels* (Rochester, Vermont: Bear & Company, 1996), 24.

[16] Louis Ginzberg, *The Legends of the Jews Volume I: From the Creation to Jacob*, trans. Henrietta Szold (Baltimore, Maryland: The Johns Hopkins University Press, 1909), 124 -125; *The Book of Enoch*, 6:6, trans. R. H. Charles (Montana: Kessinger Publishing, 1912).

[17] *Book of the Glory of Kings (Kerba Nagast)*, 100, Concerning the Angels who Rebelled, trans. Sir. E. A. Wallis Budge (London: Humphrey Milford, 1932).

[18] *The Lost Books of the Bible and the Forgotten Books of Eden*, Reuben 2:18, Naphtali 1:27, trans. Rutherford H. Platt, Jr. (Alpha House, 1927).

[19] *Book of the Glory of Kings (Kerba Nagast)*, 100. Concerning the Angels who Rebelled, trans. Sir. E. A. Wallis Budge (London: Humphrey Milford, 1932).

[20] *Pirke De Rabbi Eliezer*, Chapter 22: The Fall of the Angels [26A. i.], trans. Gerald Friedlander (New York: Sepher-Hermon Press, 1981), 160.

[21] *The Zohar*, Volume 1, Beresheet A, Section 50. Aza and Azael, 466, www2.kabbalah.com/k/index.php/p=zohar/zohar&vol=2&sec=71 (accessed Feb. 24, 2010).

[22] *The Lost Books of the Bible and the Forgotten Books of Eden*, Naphtali 1:27, trans. Rutherford H. Platt, Jr. (Alpha House, 1927); James L. Kugel, *Traditions of the Bible* (Cambridge, Massachusetts: Harvard University Press, 1998), 197; Clare Gregory, *Understanding the True Origins of Mormonism - The Incredible Story of a Race of Celestial Beings that once Came to the Earth…*, 6, http://www.adamqadmon.com/nephilim/fallen.html (accessed Dec. 6, 2000).

[23] *1. The Sumerian Watchers*, 10, http://www.earth-history.com/Various/Sons%20of%20god.htm (accessed May 10,

2007).

[24] Louis Ginzberg, *The Legends of the Jews Volume I: From the Creation to Jacob*, trans. Henrietta Szold (Baltimore, Maryland: The Johns Hopkins University Press, 1909), 124.

[25] *The Zohar*, Volume 1, Beresheet A, Section 50. Aza and Azael, 468, www2.kabbalah.com/k/index.php/p=zohar/zohar&vol=2&sec=71 (accessed Feb. 24, 2010).

[26] *The Zohar*, Volume 1, Beresheet A, Section 20. The five types of the mixed multitude, 227, www2.kabbalah.com/k/index.php/p=zohar/zohar&vol=2&sec=41 (accessed Feb. 24, 2010).

[27] Rabbi Leo Jung, Ph. D., *Fallen Angels in Jewish, Christian and Mohammedan Literature* (New York: KTAV Publishing House, 1974), 113.

[28] Louis Ginzberg, *The Legends of the Jews Volume V: Notes for Volume One and Two*, IV. Noah, 12, trans. Henrietta Szold (Baltimore, Maryland: The Johns Hopkins University Press, 1909), 172; S. Baring-Gould, *Legends of the Patriarchs and Prophets and Other Old Testament Characters* (New York: American Book Exchange, 1881), 91-92.

[29] *The Book of Enoch*, 6:6 - 7:1, trans. R. H. Charles (Montana: Kessinger Publishing, 1912).
The Book of the Cave of Treasures, The Second Thousand Years: Yared to the Flood, Of the Transmission of the Art of Playing the Harp, That is to Say, of Music, and Singing and Dancing (notes), trans. Sir E. A. Wallis Budge (London: The Religious Tract Society, 1927), 87-94.

[30] Malcolm Godwin, *Angels: An Endangered Species* (New York: Simon & Schuester, 1990), 85.

[31] *The Book of Enoch*, 7:1-3, trans. R. H. Charles (Montana: Kessinger Publishing, 1912); *The Lost Books of the Bible and the Forgotten Books of Eden*, Reuben 2:19, trans. Rutherford H. Platt, Jr. (Alpha House, 1927).

[32] *The Book of the Cave of Treasures*, The Second Thousand Years: Yared to the Flood, Of the Transmission of the Art of Playing the Harp, That is To Say, of Music, and Singing and Dancing, trans. Sir E. A. Wallis Budge (London: The Religious Tract Society, 1927), 87-95.

[33] *The Zohar*, Volume 1, Beresheet A, Section 50. Aza and Azael, 466, www2.kabbalah.com/k/index.php/p=zohar/zohar&vol=2&sec=71 (accessed Feb. 24, 2010); *The Midrash Rabbah*, Bereshith (Genesis) 26:7, trans. Rabbi Dr. H. Freedman and Maurice Simon (London: The Soncino Press, 1961).

[34] *The Zohar*, Volume 18, Shlach Lecha, Section 6. Joshua and Caleb, 40, www2.kabbalah.com/k/index.php/p=zohar/zohar&vol=40&sec=1407 (accessed Feb. 25, 2010); *The Zohar*, Volume 11, Safra Detzniuta, Section 5. Fifth Chapter, 65, www2.kabbalah.com/k/index.php/p=zohar/zohar&vol=22&sec=818 (accessed Feb. 25, 2010); *The Zohar*, Volume 1, Beresheet A, Section 20. The five types of mixed multitude, 229, www2.kabbalah.com/k/index.php/p=zohar/zohar&vol=2&sec=41 (accessed Feb. 24, 2010).

[35] *The Zohar*, Volume 1, Beresheet A, Section 50. Aza and Azael, 466, www2.kabbalah.com/k/index.php/p=zohar/zohar&vol=2&sec=71 (accessed Feb. 24, 2010).

[36] *The Book of Enoch*, 15:3-9, trans. R. H. Charles (Montana: Kessinger Publishing, 1912).

[37] *Book of the Glory of Kings (Kerba Nagast)*, 100. Concerning the Angels who Rebelled, trans. Sir. E. A. Wallis Budge (London: Humphrey Milford, 1932).

[38] *The Zohar*, Volume 3, Vaera, Section 29. "And Hashem visited Sarah", 418, www2.kabbalah.com/k/index.php/p=zohar/zohar&vol=6&sec=253 (accessed Feb. 25, 2010).

[39] *Who are the Nephilim?*, 5, http://www.adamqadmon.com/watchers/nephilim009.html (accessed Feb. 11, 2001).

[40] *B. B. C.: Enoch and the Nephilim*, 52, www.adamqadmon.com/nephilim/bbcwatchers.html (accessed Feb. 6, 2001).

[41] *The Zohar*, Volume 1, Beresheet A, Section 16. "Let us make man" (Part Two), 179, www2.kabbalah.com/k/index.php/p=zohar/zohar&vol=2&sec=37 (accessed Feb. 25, 2010).

[42] *The Zohar*, Volume 1, Beresheet A, Section 20. The five types of the mixed multitude, 228, www2.kabbalah.com/k/index.php/p=zohar/zohar&vol=2&sec=41 (accessed Feb. 25, 2010).

[43] *The Book of Jubilees*, 5:6, 5:10, trans. R. H. Charles, The Apocrypha and Pseudepigrapha of the Old Testament (Oxford: Clarendon Press, 1913).

[44] *The Watchers & Nephilim: Accounts of the Fall of the Angels*, 2, http://www.adamqadmon.com/nephilim/angels000.html (accessed Feb. 25, 2001).

[45] *The Watchers & the Nephilim: Accounts of the Fall of the Angels*, 2, http://www.adamqadmon.com/nephilim/angels000 (accessed Feb. 25, 2001).

[46] Mysterious World: Summer 2003, *Giants in the Earth Part II: Giants of the Americas*, 37, http://www.mysteriousworld.com/Journal/2003/Summer/Giants/ (accessed July 7, 2007).

[47] *The Watchers of Heaven FAQ Page*, 4, http://www.adamqadmon.com/watchers/watchersfaq.html (accessed Dec. 7, 2000).

[48] *The Clementine Homilies*, 8:15, trans. Rev. Thomas Smith, D. D. (Edinburgh, 1871-2); Robert Graves and Raphael Patai, *Hebrew Myths: The Book of Genesis* (Garden City, New York: Doubleday & Company, 1964), 101; *The Watchers of Heaven FAQ Page*, 4, http://www.adamqadmon.com/watchers/watchersfaq.html (accessed Dec. 7, 2000).

[49] *The Book of Enoch*, 7:6, trans. R. H. Charles (Montana: Kessinger Publishing, 1912); *The Clementine Homilies*, 8:15-6, trans. Rev. Thomas Smith, D. D. (Edinburgh, 1871-1872); Robert Graves and Raphael Patai, *Hebrew Myths: The Book of Genesis* (Garden City, New York: Doubleday & Company, 1964), 101; *The Watchers of Heaven FAQ Page*, 4, http://www.adamqadmon.com/watchers/watchersfaq.html (accessed Dec. 7, 2000).

[50] *The Book of the Cave of Treasures*, The Second Thousand Years: Yared to the Flood, Of the Transmission of the Art

of Playing the Harp, That is To Say, of Music, and Singing and Dancing, trans. Sir E. A. Wallis Budge (London: The Religious Tract Society, 1927), 87-94.

[51] Robert Graves and Raphael Patai, *Hebrew Myths: The Book of Genesis* (Garden City, New York: Doubleday & Company, 1964), 101.

[52] Stephen Quayle, *Genesis 6 Giants: The Master Builders of Prehistoric and Ancient Civilizations* (Bozeman, Montana: End Time Thunder Publishers, 2005), 60-61; *The Book of Enoch*, 7:4, trans. R. H. Charles (Montana: Kessinger Publishing, 1912).

[53] *The Armenian Apocryphal Adam Literature*, Concerning the Expulsion of Adam and Eve from the Garden 23-26, trans. William Lowndes Lipscomb (Ann Arbor, Michigan: University Microfilms International, 1983), 269; *The Book of the Cave of Treasures*, The Third Thousand Years: From the Flood to the Reign of Reu, Shem Carries the Body of Adam to Golgotha, trans. Sir E. A. Wallis Budge (London: The Religious Tract Society, 1927), 126-129; *The Companion Bible*, Appendix 23 (Grand Rapids, Michigan: Kregel Publications, 1990), 26-27; *The B. B. C.: Enoch & the Nephilim*, 52, http://www.adamqadmon.com/nephilim/bbcwatchers.html (accessed Feb. 6, 2001).

[54] *The Zohar*, Volume 15, Tazria, Section 22. Man, person, 117, www2.kabbalah.com/k/index.php/p=zohar/zohar&vol=30&sec=1090 (accessed Feb. 24, 2010).

[55] Tom Brown, *Origins of Demons*, 2, http://www.adamqadmon.com/watchers/origindemons000.html (accessed Dec. 6, 2000); *The Book of Jubilees*, 10:1, trans. R. H. Charles, The Apocrypha and Pseudepigrapha of the Old Testament (Oxford: Clarendon Press, 1913).

[56] Greg Killian, *The Days of Noah*, 22, http://www.adamqadmon.com/nephilim/gkillian000 (accessed Dec. 6, 2000).

[57] G. H. Pember, M. A., *Earth's Earliest Ages and their Connection With Modern Spiritualism, Theosophy, and Buddhism* (Grand Rapids, Michigan: Kregel Publications, 1975), 57; Catholic Encyclopedia, *Demons*, 1, www.adamqadmon.com/nephilim/definitions/catdemon.html (accessed March 5, 2001).

[58] Tom Brown, *Origins of Demons*, 3, www.adamqadmon.com/watchers/origindemons000.html (accessed Dec. 6, 2000).

[59] David Goldstein, *Jewish Legends (Library of the World's Myths and Legends)* (New York: Peter Bedrick Books, 1933), 43.

[60] G. H. Pember, M. A., *Earth's Earliest Ages and their Connection With Modern Spiritualism, Theosophy, and Buddhism* (Grand Rapids, Michigan: Kregel Publications, 1975), 58-59.

[61] *The Midrash Rabbah*, Bereshith (Genesis) 24:6, trans. Rabbi Dr. H. Freedman and Maurice Simon (London: The Soncino Press, 1961).

[62] *The Book of Enoch*, 15:8-9, 15:11-12, trans. R. H. Charles (Montana: Kessinger Publishing, 1912).

[63] *The Third Book of Adam and Eve (The Conflict of Adam and Eve with Satan)*, Chapter 4, trans. S. C. Malan (London: Williams and Norgate, 1882).

[64] Andrew Collins, *From the Ashes of Angels* (Rochester, Vermont: Bear & Company, 1996), 10.

[65] Andrew Collins, *From the Ashes of Angels* (Rochester, Vermont: Bear & Company, 1996), 25; *Armenian Apocrypha Relating to Adam and Eve*, Question 8, trans. Michael E. Stone (Leiden: E. J. Brill, 1996), 121; *Book of the Glory of Kings (Kerba Nagast)*, 6. Concerning the Sin of Cain, 7. Concerning Noah, trans. Sir. E. A. Wallis Budge (London: Humphrey Milford, 1932).

[66] Louis Ginzberg, *The Legends of the Jews Volume V: Notes for Volume One and Two*, IV. Noah, 26, trans. Henrietta Szold (Baltimore, Maryland: The Johns Hopkins University Press, 1909), 178; *Armenian Apocrypha Relating to Adam and Eve*, Question 8, trans. Michael E. Stone (Leiden: E. J. Brill, 1996), 121.

[67] *The Book of Jubilees*, 5:2, trans. R. H. Charles, The Apocrypha and Pseudepigrapha of the Old Testament (Oxford: Clarendon Press, 1913).

[68] *The Midrash Rabbah*, Bereshith (Genesis) 28:8, trans. Rabbi Dr. H. Freedman and Maurice Simon (London: The Soncino Press, 1961).

[69] Louis Ginzberg, *The Legends of the Jews Volume I: From the Creation to Jacob*, trans. Henrietta Szold (Baltimore, Maryland: The Johns Hopkins University Press, 1909), 160.

[70] *The Watchers & Nephilim (Naphidim): Accounts of the Fall of the Angels*, 7, www.adamqadmon.com/nephilim/angels000.html (accessed Feb. 25, 2001).

[71] T. W. Doane, *Bible Myths and Their Parallels in Other Religions: Being a Comparison of the Old And New Testament Myths and Miracles With Those of Heathen Natioins of Antiquity Considering Also Their Origin and Meaning* (New York: University Books, 1882), 3 (notes).

[72] *The Book of the Generations of Adam*, 6:5, http://www.earth-history.com/Pseudepigrapha/generations-adam.htm (accessed May 5, 2007).

[73] *The Book of Enoch*, 12:6, 16:4, trans. R. H. Charles (Montana: Kessinger Publishing, 1912).

[74] Louis Ginzberg, *The Legends of the Jews Volume I: From the Creation to Jacob*, trans. Henrietta Szold (Baltimore, Maryland: The Johns Hopkins University Press, 1909), 126.

Chapter 14

[1] *The Book of the Cave of Treasures*, The First Thousand Years: Adam to Yared (Jared), The Rule of Seth, trans. Sir E. A. Wallis Budge (London: The Religious Tract Society, 1927), 74-77.

---

[2] *The History of al-Tabari - Volume I: General Introduction and From the Creation to the Flood*, From Jayumart to Oshahanj, 152, trans. Franz Rosenthal (Albany: New York Press, 1989), 324; *The Second Book of Adam and Eve (The Conflict of Adam and Eve with Satan)*, 2:3, trans. S. C. Malan (London: Williams and Norgate, 1882).

[3] Robert Graves and Raphael Patai, *Hebrew Myths: The Book of Genesis* (Garden City, New York: Doubleday & Company, 1964), 98.

[4] *The Book of Adam*, [47]38:4, trans. J. P. Mahe, http://www.pseudepigrapha.com/pseudepigrapha/TheBookOfAdam.htm (accessed June 27, 2005).

[5] *The Second Book of Adam and Eve (The Conflict of Adam and Eve with Satan)*, 5:2, trans. S. C. Malan (London: Williams and Norgate, 1882); *The Book of Adam*, [39]12.2, trans. J. P. Mahe, http://www.pseudepigrapha.com/pseudepigrapha/TheBookOfAdam.htm (accessed June 27, 2005); *Book of the Glory of Kings (Kerba Nagast)*, 4. Concerning Envy, trans. Sir. E. A. Wallis Budge (London: Humphrey Milford, 1932).

[6] Louis Ginzberg, *The Legends of the Jews Volume I: From the Creation to Jacob*, trans. Henrietta Szold (Baltimore, Maryland: The Johns Hopkins University Press, 1909), 123.

[7] Robert Graves and Raphael Patai, *Hebrew Myths: The Book of Genesis* (Garden City, New York: Doubleday & Company, 1964), 98.

[8] *The Book of Adam*, [23]4.1, trans. J. P. Mahe, http://www.pseudepigrapha.com/pseudepigrapha/TheBookOfAdam.htm (accessed June 27, 2005).

[9] *The Book of the Cave of Treasures*, The First Thousand Years: Adam to Yared (Jared), Rule of Yared, trans. Sir E. A. Wallis Budge (London: The Religious Tract Society, 1927), 84-86.

[10] Robert Graves and Raphael Patai, *Hebrew Myths: The Book of Genesis* (Garden City, New York: Doubleday & Company, 1964), 73; *Armenian Apocrypha Relating to the Patriarchs and Prophets*, The Words of Adam To Seth 1, 16, trans. Michael E. Stone (Jerusalem: The Israel Academy of Sciences and Humanities, 1982), 12.

[11] *The Second Book of Adam and Eve (The Conflict of Adam and Eve with Satan)*, 11:12, trans. S. C. Malan (London: Williams and Norgate, 1882).

[12] *The Armenian Apocryphal Adam Literature*, The Words of Adam to Seth 1, trans. William Lowndes Lipscomb (Ann Arbor, Michigan: University Microfilms International, 1983), 208.

[13] *Armenian Apocrypha Relating to Adam and Eve*, Sermon Concerning the Flood, From the Words of Moses, The Prophet Who Spoke with God 3, trans. Michael E. Stone (Leiden: E. J. Brill, 1996), 176-177; Robert Graves and Raphael Patai, *Hebrew Myths: The Book of Genesis* (Garden City, New York: Doubleday & Company, 1964), 73; *Barhebraeus' Scholia on the Old Testament Part I: Genesis - II Samuel*, Genesis 6:2, trans. Martin Sprengling and William Creighton Graham (Chicago, Illinois: University of Chicago Press, 1931), 35.

[14] *The Second Book of Adam and Eve (The Conflict of Adam and Eve with Satan)*, 11:2, trans. S. C. Malan (London: Williams and Norgate, 1882); *Armenian Apocrypha Relating to Adam and Eve*, Question 6 (notes), trans. Michael E. Stone (Leiden: E. J. Brill, 1996), 120.

[15] *The Book of the Cave of Treasures*, The First Thousand Years: Adam to Yared (Jared), The Death of Adam, trans. Sir E. A. Wallis Budge (London: The Religious Tract Society, 1927), 71-73.

[16] *The Second Book of Adam and Eve (The Conflict of Adam and Eve with Satan)*, 8:15, 10:4, 12:1-11, trans. S. C. Malan (London: Williams and Norgate, 1882); *Armenian Apocrypha Relating to Adam and Eve*, Question 6, trans. Michael E. Stone (Leiden: E. J. Brill, 1996), 120; *Saltair na Rann*, 2397-2400, 2421-2424, trans. David Greene.

[17] *Armenian Apocrypha Relating to Adam and Eve*, History of the Forefathers, Adam and His Sons and Grandsons 45, trans. Michael E. Stone (Leiden: E. J. Brill, 1996), 200; *The Book of the Rolls (Kitab Al-Magall)*, trans. Margaret Dunlop Gibson, Apocrypha Arabica, (London: C. J. Clay and Sons, 1901), 19, 21. *The Armenian Apocryphal Adam Literature*, Concerning the Good Tidings of Seth, to Which We Ought to Give Ear 17, 20, trans. William Lowndes Lipscomb (Ann Arbor, Michigan: University Microfilms International, 1983), 192-193.

[18] *The Book of the Cave of Treasures*, The First Thousand Years: Adam to Yared (Jared), The Burial of Adam, trans. Sir E. A. Wallis Budge (London: The Religious Tract Society, 1927), 73-74; Robert Graves and Raphael Patai, *Hebrew Myths: The Book of Genesis* (Garden City, New York: Doubleday & Company, 1964), 102.

[19] *The Second Book of Adam and Eve (The Conflict of Adam and Eve with Satan)*, 12:16, trans. S. C. Malan (London: Williams and Norgate, 1882); *Armenian Apocrypha Relating to Adam and Eve*, Question 6 (and notes), trans. Michael E. Stone (Leiden: E. J. Brill, 1996), 120.

[20] *The Armenian Apocryphal Adam Literature*, Concerning the Good Tidings of Seth to Which We Ought to Give Ear 9, 20, trans. William Lowndes Lipscomb (Ann Arbor, Michigan: University Microfilms International, 1983), 191, 193.

[21] *Armenian Apocrypha Relating to Adam and Eve*, History of the Forefathers, Adam and His Sons and Grandsons 45, trans. Michael E. Stone (Leiden: E. J. Brill, 1996), 200; *The Book of the Rolls (Kitab Al-Magall)*, trans. Margaret Dunlop Gibson, Apocrypha Arabica (London: C. J. Clay and Sons, 1901), 18.

[22] *Pirke De Rabbi Eliezer*, Chapter 22: The Fall of the Angels [26A. i.], trans. Gerald Friedlander (New York: Sepher-Hermon Press, 1981), 161 (and notes); *The Book of the Cave of Treasures*, The First Thousand Years: Adam to Yared (Jared), The Rule of Seth, The Second Thousand Years: Yared to the Flood, Of the Transmission of the Art of Playing the Harp, That is to Say, of Music, and Singing and Dancing, trans. Sir E. A. Wallis Budge (London: The Religious Tract Society, 1927), 74-77, 87-94; *Armenian Apocrypha Relating to Adam and Eve*, History of the Forefathers, Adam and His Sons and Grandsons 45, Abel and Other Pieces 4.5, trans. Michael E. Stone (Leiden: E. J. Brill, 1996), 200,

151; *The Second Book of Adam and Eve (The Conflict of Adam and Eve with Satan)*, 20:15, trans. S. C. Malan (London: Williams and Norgate, 1882).

[23] *A Look at the Biblical 'Sons of God' Passage*, by Tim Hagemeister, 2, http://www.adamqadmon.com/watchers/nephilim020.html (accessed Dec 5, 2000).

[24] *Job* 1:6, 2:1, 38:7 (KJV).

[25] *Jubal - Genun - Musical Worship*, Book of Adam and Eve, 2-3, http://www.piney.com/MuGenun2.html (accessed Aug. 17, 2010).

[26] *The Second Book of Adam and Eve (The Conflict of Adam and Eve with Satan)*, 20:1, trans. S. C. Malan (London: Williams and Norgate, 1882).

[27] *The Book of the Generations of Adam*, 11:1, http://www.earth-history.com/Pseudepigrapha/generations-adam.htm (accessed May 5, 2007).

[28] *The Book of the Generations of Adam*, 11:1, http://www.earth-history.com/Pseudepigrapha/generations-adam.htm (accessed May 5, 2007).

[29] Louis Ginzberg, *The Legends of the Jews Volume I: From the Creation to Jacob*, trans. Henrietta Szold (Baltimore, Maryland: The Johns Hopkins University Press, 1909), 153; Louis Ginzberg, *The Legends of the Jews Volume V: Notes for Volume One and Two*, III. The Ten Generations, 1, IV. Noah, 132, trans. Henrietta Szold (Baltimore, Maryland: The Johns Hopkins University Press, 1909), 15, 173.

[30] *The Works of Philo Judaeus*, On the Posterity of Cain and His Exile 15(52), trans. C. D. Yonge (London: H. G. Bohn, 1854-1855).

[31] *The Book of the Cave of Treasures*, The Second Thousand Years: Yared to the Flood, Of the Transmission of the Art of Playing the Harp, That is to Say, of Music, and Singing and Dancing, trans. Sir E. A. Wallis Budge (London: The Religious Tract Society, 1927), 87-95.

[32] *The Book of the Rolls (Kitab Al-Magall)*, trans. Margaret Dunlop Gibson, Apocrypha Arabica (London: C. J. Clay and Sons, 1901), 22.

[33] *The Second Book of Adam and Eve (The Conflict of Adam and Eve with Satan)*, 20:11-12, trans. S. C. Malan (London: Williams and Norgate, 1882); *The Book of the Cave of Treasures*, The Second Thousand Years: Adam to Yared (Jared), Of the Transmission of the Art of Playing the Harp, That is to Say, or Music, and Singing and Dancing, trans. Sir E. A. Wallis Budge (London: The Religious Tract Society, 1927), 87-94.

[34] *The Second Book of Adam and Eve (The Conflict of Adam and Eve with Satan)*, 20:14, trans. S. C. Malan (London: Williams and Norgate, 1882).

[35] *The Book of the Cave of Treasures*, The Second Thousand Years: Yared to the Flood, Of the Transmission of the Art of Playing the Harp, That is to Say, of Music, and Singing and Dancing (notes), trans. Sir E. A. Wallis Budge (London: The Religious Tract Society, 1927), 87-95.

[36] *The Book of the Rolls (Kitab Al-Magall)*, trans. Margaret Dunlop Gibson, Apocrypha Arabica (London: C. J. Clay and Sons, 1901), 21.

[37] *The History of al-Tabari - Volume I: General Introduction and From the Creation to the Flood*, Adam's Descendants to Jared, 168, trans. Franz Rosenthal (Albany: New York Press, 1989), 339 (also notes); *The Book of the Rolls (Kitab Al-Magall)*, trans. Margaret Dunlop Gibson, Apocrypha Arabica (London: C. J. Clay and Sons, 1901), 21.

[38] *Nimrod's Babylonian Musical Worship Teams*, 3, http://www.piney.com/MuBabylo.html (accessed July 2, 2000).

[39] *The Book of the Cave of Treasures*, The Second Thousand Years: Yared to the Flood, Of the Transmission of the Art of Playing the Harp, That is to Say, of Music, and Singing and Dancing (notes), trans. Sir E. A. Wallis Budge (London: The Religious Tract Society, 1927), 87-95.

[40] *The Midrash Rabbah*, Bereshith (Genesis) 31:1, trans. Rabbi Dr. H. Freedman and Maurice Simon (London: The Soncino Press, 1961), 239; *The Babylonian Talmud*, Jews' College / Soncino English Translation, Sanhedrin 108a, http://www.halakhah.com/sanhedrin/sanhedrin_108.html (accessed Dec. 28, 2010); Josephus, J*ewish Antiquities*, Book 1, 64-67, trans. H. ST. J. Thackeray (London: William Heinemann Ltd. 1961), 31.

[41] *The Book of the Generations of Adam*, 12:3, http://www.earth-history.com/Pseudepigrapha/generations-adam.htm (accessed May 5, 2007).

[42] *The Book of the Cave of Treasures*, The Second Thousand Years: Yared to the Flood, Of the Transmission of the Art of Playing the Harp, That is to Say, of Music, and Singing and Dancing (notes), trans. Sir E. A. Wallis Budge (London: The Religious Tract Society, 1927), 87-95.

[43] Robert Graves and Raphael Patai, *Hebrew Myths: The Book of Genesis* (Garden City, New York: Doubleday & Company, 1964), 102.

[44] *The Second Book of Adam and Eve (The Conflict of Adam and Eve with Satan)*, 20:16, 20:24, trans. S. C. Malan (London: Williams and Norgate, 1882).

[45] *The Book of the Cave of Treasures*, The Second Thousand Years: Yared to the Flood, Of the Transmission of the Art of Playing the Harp, That is to Say, of Music, and Singing and Dancing (notes), trans. Sir E. A. Wallis Budge (London: The Religious Tract Society, 1927), 87-95.

[46] Robert Graves and Raphael Patai, *Hebrew Myths: The Book of Genesis* (Garden City, New York: Doubleday & Company, 1964), 102; *The Midrash Rabbah*, Bereshith (Genesis) 26:4, trans. Rabbi Dr. H. Freedman and Maurice Simon (London: The Soncino Press, 1961), 212; *The Armenian Apocryphal Adam Literature*, Concerning the Good

Tidings of Seth, to Which We Ought to Give Ear 18, trans. William Lowndes Lipscomb (Ann Arbor, Michigan: University Microfilms International, 1983), 193; *The Second Book of Adam and Eve (The Conflict of Adam and Eve with Satan)*, 12:16, trans. S. C. Malan (London: Williams and Norgate, 1882).

[47] Robert Graves and Raphael Patai, *Hebrew Myths: The Book of Genesis* (Garden City, New York: Doubleday & Company, 1964), 102-103.

[48] *The Book of the Cave of Treasures*, The Second Thousand Years: Yared to the Flood, Of the Transmission of the Art of Playing the Harp, That is to Say, of Music, and Singing and Dancing, trans. Sir E. A. Wallis Budge (London: The Religious Tract Society, 1927), 87-95.

[49] *The Armenian Apocryphal Adam Literature*, Concerning the Good Tidings of Seth to Which We Ought to Give Ear 21-22, trans. William Lowndes Lipscomb (Ann Arbor, Michigan: University Microfilms International, 1983), 193-194.

[50] *Armenian Apocrypha Relating to Adam and Eve*, Sermon Concerning the Flood, From the Words of Moses, The Prophet Who Spoke with God 4-6, trans. Michael E. Stone (Leiden: E. J. Brill, 1996), 177–178.

[51] *The Second Book of Adam and Eve (The Conflict of Adam and Eve with Satan)*, 20:26-32, trans. S. C. Malan (London: Williams and Norgate, 1882).

[52] Wikpedia, the Free Encyclopedia, *Adam*, http://en.wikipedia.org/wiki/Adam (accessed Dec. 14, 2010); *...in the Days of Adam*, 5, http://www.adamqadmon.com/nephilim/daysofadam.html (accessed Feb. 9, 2001).

[53] *The Book of the Cave of Treasures*, The First Thousand Years: Adam to Yared (Jared), The Rule of Anosh, trans. Sir E. A. Wallis Budge (London: The Religious Tract Society, 1927), 77-80.

[54] *The Book of the Cave of Treasures*, The First Thousand Years: Adam to Yared (Jared), The Rule of Seth, trans. Sir E. A. Wallis Budge (London: The Religious Tract Society, 1927), 74-77.

[55] *The Book of the Rolls (Kitab Al-Magall)*, trans. Margaret Dunlop Gibson, Apocrypha Arabica (London: C. J. Clay and Sons, 1901), 10.

[56] Stephen Quayle, *Genesis 6 Giants: The Master Builders of Prehistoric and Ancient Civilizations* (Bozeman, Montana: End Time Thunder Publishers, 2005), 47.

[57] *The Book of the Cave of Treasures*, The Second Thousand Years: Adam to Yared (Jared), Of the Transmission of the Art of Playing the Harp, That is to Say, of Music, and Singing and Dancing, trans. Sir E. A. Wallis Budge (London: The Religious Tract Society, 1927), 87-94.

[58] *The Book of the Cave of Treasures*, The First Thousand Years: Adam to Yared (Jared), The Rule of Yared: And in the Fortieth Year of Yared The First Thousand Years, From Adam to Yared, Came to an End, trans. Sir E. A. Wallis Budge (London: The Religious Tract Society, 1927), 86.

[59] *The Armenian Apocryphal Adam Literature*, Concerning the Good Tidings of Seth to Which We Ought to Give Ear 23, trans. William Lowndes Lipscomb (Ann Arbor, Michigan: University Microfilms International, 1983), 195.

[60] *The Book of the Cave of Treasures*, The Second Thousand Years: Yared to the Flood, Of the Transmission of the Art of Playing the Harp, That is to Say, of Music, and Singing and Dancing (notes), trans. Sir E. A. Wallis Budge (London: The Religious Tract Society, 1927), 87-94.

[61] *The Second Book of Adam and Eve (The Conflict of Adam and Eve with Satan)*, 22:10, trans. S. C. Malan (London: Williams and Norgate, 1882).

[62] *The Armenian Apocryphal Adam Literature*, Concerning the Good Tidings of Seth to Which We Ought to Give Ear 4, trans. William Lowndes Lipscomb (Ann Arbor, Michigan: University Microfilms International, 1983), 190.

[63] *The History of al-Tabari - Volume I: General Introduction and From the Creation to the Flood*, Enoch to Noah, 177, trans. Franz Rosenthal (Albany: New York Press, 1989), 346.

Chapter 15

[1] *Jubal - Genun - Musical Worship*, Book of Adam and Eve, 34, http://www.piney.com/MuGenun2.html (accessed Aug. 17, 2010).

[2] James R. Davis, *Have We Gone the Way of Cain?*, 9, http://www.focusongod.com/cain.htm (accessed March 3, 2001); Robert Graves and Raphael Patai, *Hebrew Myths: The Book of Genesis* (Garden City, New York: Doubleday & Company, 1964), 109.

[3] Louis Ginzberg, *The Legends of the Jews Volume V: Notes for Volume One and Two*, III. The Ten Generations, 42, trans. Henrietta Szold (Baltimore, Maryland: The Johns Hopkins University Press, 1909), 145.

[4] *Literature on Adam and Eve: Collected Essays*, trans. Gary Anderson, Michael Stone and Johannes Tromp (Leiden: Brill, 2000), 213.

[5] *Genizah Manuscripts of Palestinian Targum to the Pentateuch Volume One*, Genesis 4:23, trans. Michael L. Klein (Cincinnati: Hebrew Union College Press, 1986), 14.

[6] *The Book of the Cave of Treasures*, The First Thousand Years: Adam to Yared (Jared), The Rule of Anosh, trans. Sir E. A. Wallis Budge (London: The Religious Tract Society, 1927), 77-80.

[7] *The Second Book of Adam and Eve (The Conflict of Adam and Eve with Satan)*, 13:1-13, trans. S. C. Malan (London: Williams and Norgate, 1882).

[8] *Armenian Apocrypha Relating to Adam and Eve*, History of the Forefathers, Adam and His Sons and Grandsons 15 (notes), trans. Michael E. Stone (Leiden: E. J. Brill, 1996), 187.

[9] *The Book of the Cave of Treasures*, The First Thousand Years: Adam to Yared (Jared), The Rule of Anosh, trans. Sir

E. A. Wallis Budge (London: The Religious Tract Society, 1927), 77-80; Ellen Frankel, *The Classic Tales: 4000 years of Jewish Lore* (Northvale, New Jersey: Jason Aronson Inc., 1989), 39; The Works of Philo Judaeus, Questions and Answers on Genesis 1, 77, trans. C. D. Yonge (London: H. G. Bohn, 1854-1855); *The History of al-Tabari - Volume I: General Introduction and From the Creation to the Flood*, Cain and Abel, 144, trans. Franz Rosenthal (Albany: New York Press, 1989), 315.
[10] *The Works of Philo Judaeus*, On the Posterity of Cain and His Exile 13, 46, trans. C. D. Yonge (London: H. G. Bohn, 1854-1855).
[11] *Pseudo-Philo (The Biblical Antiquities of Philo)*, 2:10, trans. M. R. James (1917), http://www.sacred-texts.com/bib/bap/bap19.htm (accessed July 13, 2006).
[12] *The Writings of Abraham*, 13:1-11, http://www.earth-history.com/Pseudepigrapha/Mormonism/writings-abraham-1.htm (accessed May 10, 2007).
[13] *Targum Pseudo-Jonathan (Targum of Palestine / Targum of Jonathan Ben Uzziel)*, On the Book of Genesis, Section 4, Berashith, http://targum.info/pj/pjgen1-6.htm (accessed Oct. 2, 2009).
[14] Theodor Gaster, *Myth, Legend, and Custom in the Old Testament* (New York: Harper & Row, 1969), 78.
[15] Wikipedia, the Free Encyclopedia, *Lamech*, 1, http://en.wikipedia.org/wiki/Lamech (accessed Aug. 28, 2007).
[16] *The Armenian Apocryphal Adam Literature*, The History of Cain and Abel 50-1, trans. William Lowndes Lipscomb (Ann Arbor, Michigan: University Microfilms International, 1983), 274-275.
[17] *The Book of Jasher*, 2:29, trans. Albinus Alcuin (Pomeroy, Washington Health Research, 1966).
[18] *Armenian Apocrypha Relating to Adam and Eve*, Abel and Other Pieces, Enoch's Virtue 5.3 (notes), trans. Michael E. Stone (Leiden: E. J. Brill, 1996), 153.
[19] *Armenian Apocrypha Relating to Adam and Eve*, Abel and Other Pieces, Enoch's Virtue 5.3, trans. Michael E. Stone (Leiden: E. J. Brill, 1996), 153.
[20] *The Midrash Rabbah*, Bereshith (Genesis) 23:4, trans. Rabbi Dr. H. Freedman and Maurice Simon (London: The Soncino Press, 1961).
[21] *Barhebraeus' Scholia on the Old Testament Part I: Genesis - II Samuel*, Genesis 4:24, trans. Martin Sprengling and William Creighton Graham (Chicago, Illinois: University of Chicago Press 1931), 35.
[22] *Armenian Apocrypha Relating to Adam and Eve*, Abel and Other Pieces, Enoch's Virtue 5.5, trans. Michael E. Stone (Leiden: E. J. Brill, 1996), 154.
[23] *The Book of Enoch*, 10:12, trans. R. H. Charles (Montana: Kessinger Publishing, 1912); *The Book of the Cave of Treasures*, The First Thousand Years: Adam to Yared (Jared), The Rule of Enoch, trans. Sir E. A. Wallis Budge (London: The Religious Tract Society, 1927), 95-98; Robert Graves and Raphael Patai, *Hebrew Myths: The Book of Genesis* (Garden City, New York: Doubleday & Company, 1964), 103.
[24] *Int. Std. Bible Encyclopedia*, 1824 (*Jubal - Genun - Musical Worship*, Book of Adam and Eve, 7, http://www.piney.com/MuGenun2.html (accessed Aug. 17, 2010)).
[25] Bentley Layton, *The Gnostic Scriptures*, The Reality of the Rulers, Promise of salvation for Norea's offspring 93:17-22 (New York: Doubleday, 1995), 75).
[26] Bentley Layton, *The Gnostic Scriptures*, The Sethians according to St. Epipanius 39.5.3 (New York: Doubleday, 1995), 190).
[27] E. S. G. Bristowe, *Cain - An Argument* (Leicester: Edgar Backus, 1950), 5, 40, 56; Mrs. Sydney Bristowe, *Sargon the Magnificent* (London: The Covenant Publishing Co., 1927), 84.
[28] Bentley Layton, *The Gnostic Scriptures*, The Holy Book of the Great Invisible Spirit (New York: Doubleday, 1995), 103; Robert Graves and Raphael Patai, *Hebrew Myths: The Book of Genesis* (Garden City, New York: Doubleday & Company, 1964), 111.
[29] Bentley Layton, *The Gnostic Scriptures*, The Reality of the Rulers, Seth and Norea 91:30-92:1 (New York: Doubleday, 1995), 72.
[30] *The Chronicles of Jerahmeel* (*The Hebrew Bible Historiale*), 26:1, trans. M. Gaster, Ph. D. (London: The Royal Asiatic Society, 1899), 54.
[31] S. Baring-Gould, *Legends of the Patriarchs and Prophets and Other Old Testament Characters* (New York: American Book Exchange, 1881), 82; Bentley Layton, *The Gnostic Scriptures*, The Reality of the Rulers, Confrontation of Norea and the Rulers 24, 25 (New York: Doubleday, 1995), 73.
[32] Louis Ginzberg, *The Legends of the Jews Volume I: From the Creation to Jacob*, trans. Henrietta Szold (Baltimore, Maryland: The Johns Hopkins University Press, 1909), 105-106.
[33] Margi B., *Al-Uzza and 'Uzza - Hisorical Origins and Theory*, 1, http://www.geocities.com/mabcosmic/essays/utheory.html?200719 (accessed April 19, 2007).
[34] Margi B., *Al-Uzza and 'Uzza - Hisorical Origins and Theory*, 1, http://www.geocities.com/mabcosmic/essays/utheory.html?200719 (accessed April 19, 2007).
[35] *Chapter Eleven: Religion of Pagan Arabia*, 10-11, voi.org/books/htemples2/ch11.htm (accessed Jan. 14, 2008).
[36] *Al-Uzza and Lilith - Sisters of a Paradigm*, 4, www.geocities.com/mabcosmic/essays/uzil (accessed April 19, 2007).
[37] Margi B. *Istahar/'Asterah and Lilith's Origins*, 2, http://www.geocities.com/mabcosmic/essays/istahar.html?200719 (accessed April 19, 2007); *The Arab Triple Goddess*, 2, http://www.thaliatook.com/AMGG/arabtriple.html (accessed Sept. 6, 2007).

[38] *The Arab Triple Goddess*, 2, http://www.thaliatook.com/AMGG/arabtriple.html (accessed Sept. 6, 2007); Charles DeLoach, *Giants: A Reference Guide from History, the Bible, and Recorded Legend* (Metuchen, N. J.: The Scarecrow Press, Inc., 1995), 7.
[39] *Hubal*, 1, open-encyclopedia.com/Hubal (accessed Sept. 6, 2007).
[40] *The Qur'an* (Yusufali), An-Najm (The Star) 053:019-020, http://www.usc.edu/schools/college/crcc/engagement/resources/texts/muslim/quran/053.qmt.html (accessed Jan. 31, 2011).
[41] *The Arab Triple Goddess*, 2, http://www.thaliatook.com/AMGG/arabtriple.html (accessed Sept. 6, 2007).
[42] Rabbi Leo Jung, Ph. D., *Fallen Angels in Jewish, Christian and Mohammedan Literature* (New York: KTAV Publishing House, 1974), 92.
[43] Bentley Layton, *The Gnostic Scriptures*, The Reality of the Rulers, Confrontation of Norea and the rulers 92:18-93:1 (New York: Doubleday, 1995), 73.
[44] Rabbi Leo Jung, Ph. D., *Fallen Angels in Jewish, Christian and Mohammedan Literature* (New York: KTAV Publishing House, 1974), 112; Louis Ginzberg, *The Legends of the Jews Volume I: From the Creation to Jacob*, trans. Henrietta Szold (Baltimore, Maryland: The Johns Hopkins University Press, 1909), 149.
[45] Louis Ginzberg, *The Legends of the Jews Volume I: From the Creation to Jacob*, trans. Henrietta Szold (Baltimore, Maryland: The Johns Hopkins University Press, 1909), 149.

Chapter 16

[1] *The Armenian Apocryphal Adam Literature*, Concerning the Good Tidings of Seth to Which We Ought to Give Ear 59, trans. William Lowndes Lipscomb (Ann Arbor, Michigan: University Microfilms International, 1983), 282.
[2] *The Book of the Mysteries of the Heavens and the Earth and Other Works of Bakhayla Mikael (Zosimas)*, trans. E. A. Wallis Budge (London: Oxford University Press, 1935), 29.
[3] *There Were Giants on the earth... The Nephilim*, 2, http://biblelight.net/nephilim.htm (accessed Feb. 3, 2010).
[4] *The Chronicles of Jerahmeel* (*The Hebrew Bible Historiale*), 24:11, trans. M. Gaster, Ph. D. (London: The Royal Asiatic Society, 1899), 52.
[5] James L. Kugel, *Traditions of the Bible* (Cambridge, Massachusetts: Harvard University Press, 1998), 217.
[6] *The Genesis Apocryphon* (The Dead Sea Scrolls), (1Q20) Col. II, trans. Geza Vermes, *The Complete Dead Sea Scrolls in English* (New York: Penguin Books, 1997), 449.
[7] *The Genesis Apocryphon* (The Dead Sea Scrolls), (1Q20) Col. II, trans. Geza Vermes, *The Complete Dead Sea Scrolls in English* (New York: Penguin Books, 1997), 449.
[8] *The Book of Jasher*, 5:11, trans. Albinus Alcuin (Pomeroy, Washington: Health Research, 1966).
[9] Louis Ginzberg, *The Legends of the Jews Volume I: From the Creation to Jacob*, trans. Henrietta Szold (Baltimore, Maryland: The Johns Hopkins University Press, 1909), 153; *Rashi*, (Bereishit) Genesis 6:3, http://www.chabad.org/library/bible_cdo/aid/8168/showrashi/true (accessed Oct. 27, 2010).
[10] *The Book of Jubilees*, 5:2, trans. R. H. Charles, The Apocrypha and Pseudepigrapha of the Old Testament (Oxford: Clarendon Press, 1913); *The Babylonian Talmud*, Jews' College / Soncino English Translation, Sanhedrin 108a, http://www.halakhah.com/sanhedrin/sanhedrin_108.html (accessed Dec. 28, 2010); Louis Ginzberg, *The Legends of the Jews Volume I: From the Creation to Jacob*, trans. Henrietta Szold (Baltimore, Maryland: The Johns Hopkins University Press, 1909), 160.
[11] *The Companion Bible*, Appendix 26 (Grand Rapids, Michigan: Kregel Publications, 1990), 28.
[12] Louis Ginzberg, *The Legends of the Jews Volume I: From the Creation to Jacob*, trans. Henrietta Szold (Baltimore, Maryland: The Johns Hopkins University Press, 1909), 154, 158; Mendel G. Glenn, *Jewish Tales and Legends* (New York: Star Hebrew Book Co., 1929), 27.
[13] *The Book of the Cave of Treasures*, The Third Thousand Years: From the Flood to the Reign of Reu, Noah founds Themanon, the city of the "Eight", trans. Sir E. A. Wallis Budge (London: The Religious Tract Society, 1927), 116-118.
[14] *The Book of the Rolls (Kitab Al-Magall)*, trans. Margaret Dunlop Gibson, Apocrypha Arabica (London: C. J. Clay and Sons, 1901), 13, 30.
[15] Mendel G. Glenn, *Jewish Tales and Legends* (New York: Hebrew Publishing Co., 1929), 27.
[16] *Book of the Glory of Kings (Kerba Nagast)*, 100. Concerning the Angels who Rebelled, trans. Sir. E. A. Wallis Budge (London: Humphrey Milford, 1932).
[17] *3 Enoch (The Hebrew Book of Enoch)*, 26:12, trans. Hugo Odeberg (New York: KTAV Publishing House, Inc., 1973), 94.
[18] Andrew Collins, *From the Ashes of Angels* ((Rochester, Vermont: Bear & Company, 1996), 28; Mysterious World: Summer 2003, *Giants in the Earth Part II: Giants of the Americas*, 26, http://www.mysteriousworld.com/Journal/2003/Summer/Giants/ (accessed July 20, 2007); Malcolm Godwin, *Angels: An Endangered Species* (New York: Simon & Schuester, 1990), 111.
[19] *The Book of Enoch*, Chapter 10 (*The Book of the Cave of Treasures*, The Second Thousand Years: Yared to the Flood, Of the Transmission of the Art of Playing the Harp, That is to Say, of Music, and Singing and Dancing, The Rule of Enoch (notes), trans. Sir E. A. Wallis Budge (London: The Religious Tract Society, 1927), 95-98).

---

[20] *Azazel and Atonement*, 39-40, http://www.adamqadmon.com/nephlim/huie003.html (accessed Dec. 5, 2000); Mysterious World: Summer 2003, *Giants in the Earth Part II: Giants of the Americas*, 26, http://www.mysteriousworld.com/Journal/2003/Summer/Giants/ (accessed July 20, 2007).
[21] *The Book of Jubilees*, 10:4-14, trans. R. H. Charles, The Apocrypha and Pseudepigrapha of the Old Testament (Oxford: Clarendon Press, 1913).
[22] *The Book of Enoch*, 13:4, trans. R. H. Charles (Montana: Kessinger Publishing, 1912).
[23] *The Sibylline Oracles, Translated from the Greek into English blank Verse*, Book I, Line 331-341, trans. Milton S. Terry (New York: Hunt & Eaton, 1890), 27.
[24] *The Second Book of Adam and Eve (The Conflict of Adam and Eve with Satan)*, 8:10, trans. S. C. Malan (London: Williams and Norgate, 1882); *Book of the Glory of Kings (Kerba Nagast)*, 8. Concerning the Flood, trans. Sir. E. A. Wallis Budge (London: Humphrey Milford, 1932).
[25] *The Book of the Cave of Treasures*, The Third Thousand Years: From the Flood to the Reign of Reu, The Flood, trans. Sir E. A. Wallis Budge (London: The Religious Tract Society, 1927), 112-115; *The Sibylline Oracles, Translated from the Greek into English blank Verse*, Frag. 1, Line 330, trans. Milton S. Terry (New York: Hunt & Eaton, 1890).
[26] *Book of the Glory of Kings (Kerba Nagast)*, 8. Concerning the Flood, trans. Sir. E. A. Wallis Budge (London: Humphrey Milford, 1932).
[27] *Saltair na Rann*, 2433-2436, 2513-2516, trans. David Greene; *Were there any pre adamic humans in the ark?*, 2, http://www.truebiblecode.com/understanding238.html (accessed Sept. 7, 2005).
[28] *The Book of the Bee*, Chapter 20: Of Noah and the Flood, trans. Earnest A. Wallis Budge, M. A., http://www.sacred-texts.com/chr/bb/bb20.htm (accessed Oct. 10, 2004).
[29] *The Qur'an*, number. Hud (Hud), 011.040, http://www.usc.edu/schools/college/crcc/engagement/resources/texts/muslim/quran/011.qmt.html (accessed Jan 31, 2011).
[30] *The Bible, The Koran, and the Talmud (Biblical Legends of the Mussulmans)*, Noah, Hud, and Salih, trans. Dr. G. Weil (New York, 1863), 1.
[31] *The Book of Enoch*, 10:10 (notes), 12:1-6, 13:6 (notes), 14:6, trans. R. H. Charles (Montana: Kessinger Publishing, 1912).
[32] Targum Neofiti 1: Genesis / Translated, With Apparatus and Notes, Genesis 7:3 (notes), trans. Martin McNamara (Collegeville, Minnesota: Liturgical Press, 1992); *The History of al-Tabari - Volume I: General Introduction and From the Creation to the Flood*, The Events That Took Place in Noah's Time, 195, trans. Franz Rosenthal (Albany: New York Press, 1989), 365; Louis Ginzberg, *The Legends of the Jews Volume V: Notes for Volume One and Two*, IV. Noah, 75, trans. Henrietta Szold (Baltimore, Maryland: The Johns Hopkins University Press, 1909), 197; J. E. Hanauer, *Folklore of the Holy Land: Moslem, Christian and Jewish*, 3. Noah and Og (London: BiblioBazaar, 2007), 14.
[33] Malcolm Godwin, *Angels: An Endangered Species* (New York: Simon & Schuester, 1990), 113.
[34] *The History of al-Tabari - Volume I: General Introduction and From the Creation to the Flood*, The Events That Took Place in Noah's Time 196, 190, trans. Franz Rosenthal (Albany: New York Press, 1989), 366, 360.
[35] I. P. Cory, *Ancient Fragments* (1832), Berossus, Of the Cosmology and Deluge, 2-3, http://www.sacred-texts.com/cla/af/index.htm (accessed Aug. 14, 2007).
[36] *The Apocryphon of John*, trans. Frederik Wisse, http://www.pseudepigrapha.com/apocrypha_nt/apocjn.html (accessed Aug. 19, 2005).
[37] S. Baring-Gould, *Legends of the Patriarchs and Prophets and Other Old Testament Characters* (New York: American Book Exchange, 1881), 60.
[38] J. E. Hanauer, *Folklore of the Holy Land: Moslem, Christian and Jewish*, 3. Noah and Og (London: BiblioBazaar, 2007), 14.
[39] *Armenian Apocrypha Relating to Adam and Eve*, Question 10 (notes), trans. Michael E. Stone (Leiden: E. J. Brill, 1996), 122.
[40] *The Book of the Cave of Treasures*, The Third Thousand Years, From the Flood to the Reign of Reu, Noah Founds Themanon, The City of the "Eight." (and notes), trans. Sir E. A. Wallis Budge (London: The Religious Tract Society, 1927), 116-118; *The History of al-Tabari - Volume I: General Introduction and From the Creation to the Flood*, The Events That Took Place in Noah's Time, 196, trans. Franz Rosenthal (Albany: New York Press, 1989), 366.
[41] J. E. Hanauer, *Folklore of the Holy Land: Moslem, Christian and Jewish*, 3. Noah and Og (London: BiblioBazaar, 2007), 14; Robert Bowie Johnson, Jr., *The Parthenon Code: Mankind's History in Marble* (Annapolis, Maryland: Solving Light Books, 2004), 145.
[42] *The Qur'an*, number. Hud (Hud), 011.040, http://www.usc.edu/schools/college/crcc/engagement/resources/texts/muslim/quran/011.qmt.html (accessed Jan. 31, 2011).
[43] *The History of al-Tabari - Volume I: General Introduction and From the Creation to the Flood*, The Events That Took Place in Noah's Time, 195-196, trans. Franz Rosenthal (Albany: New York Press, 1989), 365-366.
[44] *Pirke De Rabbi Eliezer*, Chapter 23: The Ark and the Flood [26B. ii.], trans. Gerald Friedlander (New York: Sepher-Hermon Press, 1981), 166.
[45] *2 Enoch (The Book of the Secrets of Enoch)*, 58:4-6, trans. W. R. Morfill, M. A. (Oxford: Clarendon Press, 1896).

[46] *The Epic of Gilgamesh*, Tablet XI: The Story of the Flood, 2, http://ancienttexts.org/library/mesopotamian/gilgamesh/tab11.htm (accessed Aug 13, 2010).
[47] Targum Neofiti 1: Genesis / Translated, With Apparatus and Notes, 7:2 (notes), trans. Martin McNamara (Collegeville, Minnesota: Liturgical Press, 1992).
[48] *The Sibylline Oracles, Translated from the Greek into English Blank Verse*, Book 1, Line 242-248, trans. Milton S. Terry (New York: Hunt & Eaton, 1890), 24.
[49] *The Book of the Rolls (Kitab Al-Magall)*, trans. Margaret Dunlop Gibson, Apocrypha Arabica (London: C. J. Clay and Sons, 1901), 28.
[50] *The Book of the Rolls (Kitab Al-Magall)*, trans. Margaret Dunlop Gibson, Apocrypha Arabica (London: C. J. Clay and Sons, 1901), 24.
[51] *The Book of the Cave of Treasures*, The Second Thousand Years: Yared to the Flood, The Building of the Ark, trans. Sir E. A. Wallis Budge (London: The Religious Tract Society, 1927), 100-101.
[52] *The Book of the Rolls (Kitab Al-Magall)*, trans. Margaret Dunlop Gibson, Apocrypha Arabica (London: C. J. Clay and Sons, 1901), 24.

Chapter 17

[1] S. Baring-Gould, *Legends of the Patriarchs and Prophets and Other Old Testament Characters* (New York: American Book Exchange, 1881), 28.
[2] Louis Ginzberg, *The Legends of the Jews Volume I: From the Creation to Jacob*, trans.. Henrietta Szold (Baltimore, Maryland: The Johns Hopkins University Press, 1909), 159; *The Book of the Rolls (Kitab Al-Magall)*, trans. Margaret Dunlop Gibson, Apocrypha Arabica (London: C. J. Clay and Sons, 1901), 23; *The Book of the Cave of Treasures*, The Second Thousand Years: Yared (Jared) to the Flood, The Rule of Noah, trans. Sir E. A. Wallis Budge (London: The Religious Tract Society, 1927), 98-99.
[3] *The Midrash Rabbah*, Bereshith (Genesis) 26:2, trans. Rabbi Dr. H. Freedman and Maurice Simon (London: The Soncino Press, 1961).
[4] *... in the days of Noah*, 4, http://www.adamqadmon.com/nephilim/daysofnoah.html (accessed Feb. 9, 2001).
[5] *The Genesis Apocryphon* (The Dead Sea Scrolls), (1Q20) Col. IV, trans. Geza Vermes, *The Complete Dead Sea Scrolls in English* (New York: Penguin Books, 1997), 450; *Armenian Apocrypha Relating to Adam and Eve*, History of Adam and His Grandsons, trans. Michael E. Stone (Leiden: E. J. Brill, 1996), 91; *The History of al-Tabari - Volume I: General Introduction and From the Creation to the Flood*, Enoch to Noah, 177, trans. Franz Rosenthal (Albany: New York Press, 1989), 347.
[6] *The History of al-Tabari - Volume I: General Introduction and From the Creation to the Flood*, Cain and Abel, 146, Eve Giving Birth to Seth, 153, trans. Franz Rosenthal (Albany: New York Press, 1989), 317, 324.
[7] *Sefer Uzza Wa-Aza(z)el: Exploring Early Jewish Mythologies of Evil*, 2, http://www.religiousstudies.uncc.edu/jcreeves/sefer_uzza_waazazel.htm (accessed July 1, 2005).
[8] S. Baring-Gould, *Legends of the Patriarchs and Prophets and Other Old Testament Characters* (New York: American Book Exchange, 1881), 123-124.
[9] *The Book of the Cave of Treasures*, The Second Thousand Years: Yared to the Flood, The Rule of Noah (notes), trans. Sir E. A. Wallis Budge (London: The Religious Tract Society, 1927), 98-99.
[10] *The Writings of Abraham*, 11:1-3 (also 12:1, 16:1), http://www.earth-history.com/Pseudepigrapha/Mormonism/writings-abraham-1.htm (accessed May 10, 2007).
[11] *The Writings of Abraham*, 12:2 (also 16:1), http://www.earth-history.com/Pseudepigrapha/Mormonism/writings-abraham-1.htm (accessed May 10, 2007).
[12] *The Writings of Abraham*, 14:3, http://www.earth-history.com/Pseudepigrapha/Mormonism/writings-abraham-1.htm (accessed May 10, 2007).
[13] *The Writings of Abraham*, 12:1, http://www.earth-history.com/Pseudepigrapha/Mormonism/writings-abraham-1.htm (accessed May 10, 2007).
[14] *The Writings of Abraham*, 13:12-4, http://www.earth-history.com/Pseudepigrapha/Mormonism/writings-abraham-1.htm (accessed May 10, 2007).
[15] *Hitchock's Bible Names Dictionary*, 38, http://www.adamqadmon.com/nephilim/definitions/biblenames.html (accessed March 8, 2001).
[16] *Barhebraeus' Scholia on the Old Testament Part I: Genesis - II Samuel*, Genesis 4:20-2, trans. Martin Sprengling and William Creighton Graham (Chicago, Illinois: University of Chicago Press, 1931), 33.
[17] *The Zohar*, Volume 2, Beresheet B, Section 62. "Kayin killed Hevel", 353, www2.kabbalah.com/k/index.php/p=zohar/zohar&vol=3&sec=135 (accessed Feb. 25, 2010).
[18] *The Midrash Rabbah*, Bereshith (Genesis) 23:3, trans. Rabbi Dr. H. Freedman and Maurice Simon (London: The Soncino Press, 1961); Louis Ginzberg, *The Legends of the Jews Volume V: Notes for Volume One and Two*, III. The Ten Generations, 45, trans. Henrietta Szold (Baltimore, Maryland: The Johns Hopkins University Press, 1909), 148.
[19] *The Writings of Abraham*, 11:1-3, http://www.earth-history.com/Pseudepigrapha/Mormonism/writings-abraham-1.htm (accessed May 10, 2007).
[20] *The Writings of Abraham*, 11:1-3, http://www.earth-history.com/Pseudepigrapha/Mormonism/writings-abraham-

1.htm (accessed May 10, 2007).

[21] Stephen Quayle, *Genesis 6 Giants: The Master Builders of Prehistoric and Ancient Civilizations* (Bozeman, Montana: End Time Thunder Publishers, 2005), 218.

[22] *Genesis 10 - the Table of Nations*, 6, http://www.biblebelievers.org.au/bb000319.htm (accessed Aug. 9, 2000).

[23] *The Book of the Cave of Treasures*, The First Thousand Years: Adam to Yared (Jared), The Creation. First Day, trans. Sir E. A. Wallis Budge (London: The Religious Tract Society, 1927), 43-46.

[24] *The Book of the Cave of Treasures*, The First Thousand Years: Adam to Yared (Jared), The Creation. Fourth Day, trans. Sir E. A. Wallis Budge (London: The Religious Tract Society, 1927), 49-50.

[25] *Pirke De Rabbi Eliezer*, Chapter 22: The Fall of the Angels [26A. i.], trans. Gerald Friedlander (New York: Sepher-Hermon Press, 1981), 160.

[26] Stephen R. Haynes, *Noah's Curse: The Biblical Justification of American Slavery* (Oxford: University Press, 2002), 26.

[27] *The Zohar*, Volume 2, Beresheet B, Section 62. "Kayin killed Hevel", 354, www2.kabbalah.com/k/index.php/p=zohar/zohar&vol=3&sec=135 (accessed Feb. 25, 2010).

[28] Louis Ginzberg, *The Legends of the Jews Volume I: From the Creation to Jacob*, trans. Henrietta Szold (Baltimore, Maryland: The Johns Hopkins University Press, 1909), 150; Louis Ginzberg, *The Legends of the Jews Volume V: Notes for Volume One and Two*, III. The Ten Generations, 45, IV. Noah, 10, trans. Henrietta Szold (Baltimore, Maryland: The Johns Hopkins University Press, 1909), 147, 171; S. Baring-Gould, *Legends of the Patriarchs and Prophets and Other Old Testament Characters* (New York: American Book Exchange, 1881), 17.

[29] Bentley Layton, *The Gnostic Scriptures*, The Sethians According to St. Epipanius, Kham preserves an unrighteous strain within Noah's ark, 39.3.2-4 (New York: Doubleday, 1995), 189.

[30] *The Third Book of Adam and Eve (The Conflict of Adam and Eve with Satan)*, Chapter 2, trans. S. C. Malan (London: Williams and Norgate, 1882).

[31] *The Book of the Cave of Treasures*, The Second Thousand Years: Yared (Jared) to the Flood, The Building of the Ark, trans. Sir E. A. Wallis Budge (London: The Religious Tract Society, 1927), 99-100; *The Book of the Rolls (Kitab Al-Magall)*, trans. Margaret Dunlop Gibson, Apocrypha Arabica (London: C. J. Clay and Sons, 1901), 24.

[32] Montague Rhodes James, *The Lost Apocrypha of the Old Testament: their Titles and Fragments Collected, Translated and Discussed*, Queen Mary's Prayerbook (Brit. Mus. Royal 2. B. 7), 13, www.sas.upenn.edu/religious_studies/rak/publics/mrjames/jamesnew.htm (accessed Oct. 8, 2010).

[33] *The Armenian Apocryphal Adam Literature*, Concerning the Good Tidings of Seth to Which We Ought to Give Ear 37-38, trans. William Lowndes Lipscomb (Ann Arbor, Michigan: University Microfilms International, 1983), 198.

[34] *The History of al-Tabari - Volume I: General Introduction and From the Creation to the Flood*, Enoch to Noah, 179, trans. Franz Rosenthal (Albany: New York Press, 1989), 348.

[35] *Pirke De Rabbi Eliezer*, Chapter 22: The Fall of the Angels [26A. i.] (notes), trans. Gerald Friedlander (New York: Sepher-Hermon Press, 1981), 162.

[36] J. E. Hanauer, *Folklore of the Holy Land: Moslem, Christian and Jewish*, 3. Noah and Og (London: BiblioBazaar, 2007), 13.

[37] Bentley Layton, *The Gnostic Scriptures*, The Gnostics According to St. Epipanius, Noria and Noah 26.1.7 (New York: Doubleday, 1995), 204.

[38] S. Baring-Gould, *Legends of the Patriarchs and Prophets and Other Old Testament Characters* (New York: American Book Exchange, 1881), 102; Bentley Layton, *The Gnostic Scriptures*, The Gnostics According to St. Epiphanius, The Book "Noria", 203 (New York: Doubleday, 1995), 201.

[39] Bentley Layton, *The Gnostic Scriptures*, The Gnostics According to St. Epiphanius, Noria and Noah, 26.1 (New York: Doubleday: 1995), 204.

[40] Robert Graves and Raphael Patai, *Hebrew Myths: The Book of Genesis* (Garden City, New York: Doubleday & Company, 1964), 118.

[41] S. Baring-Gould, *Legends of the Patriarchs and Prophets and Other Old Testament Characters* (New York: American Book Exchange, 1881), 102.

[42] Bentley Layton, *The Gnostic Scriptures*, The Gnostics According to St. Epiphanius, Noria and Noah, 26.1.8-9 (New York: Doubleday: 1995), 204.

[43] Louis Ginzberg, *The Legends of the Jews Volume V: Notes for Volume One and Two*, IV. Noah, 10, trans. Henrietta Szold (Baltimore, Maryland: The Johns Hopkins University Press, 1909), 170; *The Babylonian Talmud*, Jews' College / Soncino English Translation, Niddah 61a, http://www.halakhah.com/niddah/niddah_61.html (accessed Aug. 13, 2010).

[44] Johann Andreas Eisenmenger, *The Traditions of the Jews, Contained in the Talmud and other Mystical Writings* (London: J. Robinson, 1748), 73; Robert Graves and Raphael Patai, *Hebrew Myths: The Book of Genesis* (Garden City, New York: Doubleday & Company, 1964), 114; Stephen R. Haynes, *Noah's Curse: The Biblical Justification of American Slavery*, Peter of Riga, *Aurora* (Oxford, University Press, 2002), 31.

[45] Johann Andreas Eisenmenger, *The Traditions of the Jews, Contained in the Talmud and other Mystical Writings* (London: J. Robinson, 1748), 73; S. Baring-Gould, *Legends of the Patriarchs and Prophets and Other Old Testament Characters* (New York: American Book Exchange, 1881), 92.

[46] Johann Andreas Eisenmenger, *The Traditions of the Jews, Contained in the Talmud and other Mystical Writings* (London: J. Robinson, 1748), 81; *The Babylonian Talmud*, Jews' College / Soncino English Translation, Niddah 61a, http://www.halakhah.com/niddah/niddah_61.html (accessed Aug. 13, 2010).
[47] Robert Graves and Raphael Patai, *Hebrew Myths: The Book of Genesis* (Garden City, New York: Doubleday & Company, 1964), 112; S. Baring-Gould, *Legends of the Patriarchs and Prophets and Other Old Testament Characters* (New York: American Book Exchange, 1881), 100.
[48] J. E. Hanauer, *Folklore of the Holy Land: Moslem, Christian and Jewish*, 3. Noah and Og (London: BiblioBazaar, 2007), 13; *The History of al-Tabari - Volume I: General Introduction and From the Creation to the Flood*, The Events That Took Place in Noah's Time, 190-191, trans. Franz Rosenthal (Albany: New York Press, 1989), 360-361.
[49] *The History of al-Tabari - Volume II: Prophets and Patriarchs*, An Account of Biwarasb, That Is, al-Azdahaq, 212, trans. William M. Brinner (Albany: State University of New York Press, 1987), 11; Journal of Discourses, Vol. 22, p. 304.
[50] *The Writings of Abraham*, 17:7, http://www.earth-history.com/Pseudepigrapha/Mormonism/writings-abraham-1.htm (accessed May 10, 2007).
[51] S. Baring-Gould, *Legends of the Patriarchs and Prophets and Other Old Testament Characters* (New York: American Book Exchange, 1881), 123-124.
[52] *Genizah Manuscripts of Palestinian Targum to the Pentateuch Volume One*, Genesis 7:7, trans. Michael L. Klein (Cincinnati: Hebrew Union College Press, 1986), 18.
[53] I. P. Cory, *Ancient Fragments* (1832), Berossus, Of the Cosmology and Deluge, 2-3, http://www.sacred-texts.com/cla/af/index.htm (accessed Aug. 14, 2007).
[54] *The Epic of Atrahasis*, Boarding of the Ark, [ii.40], 6, http://www.livius.org/as-as/atrahasis/atrahasis.html (accessed Aug. 13, 2010).
[55] E. A. Wallis Budge, *The Babylonian Story of the Deluge and the Epic of Gilgamish* (1929), 35, http://www.sacred-texts.com/ane/gilgdelu.htm (accessed Sept. 14, 2007).
[56] *The Writings of Abraham*, 16:2, http://www.earth-history.com/Pseudepigrapha/Mormonism/writings-abraham-1.htm (accessed May 10, 2007); *Saltair na Rann*, 2481-2484, trans. David Greene; J. E. Hanauer, *Folklore of the Holy Land: Moslem, Christian and Jewish*, 3. Noah and Og (London: BiblioBazaar, 2007), 16.
[57] *The History of al-Tabari - Volume I: General Introduction and From the Creation to the Flood*, Eve Giving Birth to Seth, 153, trans. Franz Rosenthal (Albany: New York Press, 1989), 325.
[58] *The Third Book of Adam and Eve (The Conflict of Adam and Eve with Satan)*, Chapter 2, trans. S. C. Malan (London: Williams and Norgate, 1882).
[59] Herman L. Hoeh, *Compendium of World History*, Volume 2, Chapter 8, http://www.earth-history.com/Various/Compendium/hhc2ch08.htm, (accessed Dec. 19, 2007), 5.
[60] *The Companion Bible*, Genesis 7:11 (notes) (Grand Rapids, Michigan: Kregel Publications, 1990), 12.
[61] Michael E. Stone and Theodore A. Begren, *Biblical Figures Outside the Bible* (Harrisburg, Pennsylvania: Trinity Press International, 1998), 134; *The Midrash Rabbah*, Bereshith (Genesis) 32:7, trans. Rabbi Dr. H. Freedman and Maurice Simon (London: The Soncino Press, 1961).
[62] *The Midrash Rabbah*, Bereshith (Genesis) 32:7, trans. Rabbi Dr. H. Freedman and Maurice Simon (London: The Soncino Press, 1961); The Works of Philo Judaeus, Questions and Answers on Genesis 2, 18, trans. C. D. Yonge (London: H. G. Bohn, 1854-5); *The Babylonian Talmud*, Jews' College / Soncino English Translation, Sanhedrin 108a, http://www.halakhah.com/sanhedrin/sanhedrin_108.html (accessed Dec. 28, 2010).
[63] James L. Kugel, *Traditions of the Bible* (Cambridge, Massachusetts: Harvard University Press, 1998), 199.
[64] James L. Kugel, *Traditions of the Bible* (Cambridge, Massachusetts: Harvard University Press, 1998), 199; James L. Kugel, *The Bible As It Was*, The Testament of Adam 3:5 (Cambridge, Massachusetts: Harvard University Press, 1997), 99, 118-119; *The Book of Enoch*, 10:4-7, 10:20, trans. R. H. Charles (Montana: Kessinger Publishing, 1912); Michael E. Stone and Theodore A. Begren, *Biblical Figures Outside the Bible* (Harrisburg, Pennsylvania: Trinity Press International, 1998), 133; *The Sibylline Oracles, Translated from the Greek into English blank Verse*, Book I, Line 216, trans. Milton S. Terry (New York: Hunt & Eaton, 1890); Wikipedia, the Free Encyclopedia, *Noah's Ark*, 3, http://en.wikipedia.org/wiki/Noah%27s_Ark (accessed Aug. 31, 2007).
[65] *Pirke De Rabbi Eliezer*, Chapter 22: The Fall of the Angels [26A. i.], trans. Gerald Friedlander (New York: Sepher-Hermon Press, 1981), 159.
[66] *Pirke De Rabbi Eliezer*, Chapter 22: The Fall of the Angels [26A. i.], trans. Gerald Friedlander (New York: Sepher-Hermon Press, 1981), 161-162.
[67] *Pirke De Rabbi Eliezer*, Chapter 22: The Fall of the Angels [26A. i.], trans. Gerald Friedlander (New York: Sepher-Hermon Press, 1981), 162.
[68] *The Midrash Rabbah*, Bereshith (Genesis) 32:7 (notes), trans. Rabbi Dr. H. Freedman and Maurice Simon (London: The Soncino Press, 1961).
[69] *The History of al-Tabari - Volume I: General Introduction and From the Creation to the Flood*, The Events That Took Place in Noah's Time, 193, trans. Franz Rosenthal (Albany: New York Press, 1989), 363.
[70] Louis Ginzberg, *The Legends of the Jews Volume I: From the Creation to Jacob*, trans. Henrietta Szold (Baltimore, Maryland: The Johns Hopkins University Press, 1909), 159.

[71] *The Babylonian Talmud*, Jews' College / Soncino English Translation, Mas. Zevachim 113b, http://www.halakhah.com/ (accessed Aug. 13, 2010).
[72] Robert Graves and Raphael Patai, *Hebrew Myths: The Book of Genesis* (Garden City, New York: Doubleday & Company, 1964), 113.
[73] Louis Ginzberg, *The Legends of the Jews Volume I: From the Creation to Jacob*, trans. Henrietta Szold (Baltimore, Maryland: The Johns Hopkins University Press, 1909), 159; S. Baring-Gould, *Legends of the Patriarchs and Prophets and Other Old Testament Characters* (New York: American Book Exchange, 1881), 100.
[74] *Pirke De Rabbi Eliezer*, Chapter 22: The Fall of the Angels [26A. i.], trans. Gerald Friedlander (New York: Sepher-Hermon Press, 1981), 162.
[75] Johann Andreas Eisenmenger, *The Traditions of the Jews, Contained in the Talmud and Other Mystical Writings* (London: J. Robinson, 1748), 78.
[76] G. H. Pember, M. A., *Earth's Earliest Ages and their Connection With Modern Spiritualism, Theosophy, and Buddhism* (Grand Rapids, Michigan: Kregel Publications, 1975), 64.
[77] *The Midrash Rabbah*, Bereshith (Genesis) 28:8, trans. Rabbi Dr. H. Freedman and Maurice Simon (London: The Soncino Press, 1961).
[78] Louis Ginzberg, *The Legends of the Jews Volume I: From the Creation to Jacob*, trans. Henrietta Szold (Baltimore, Maryland: The Johns Hopkins University Press, 1909), 158; Mendel G. Glenn, *Jewish Tales and Legends* (New York: Star Hebrew Book Co., 1929), 27.
[79] Robert Graves and Raphael Patai, *Hebrew Myths: The Book of Genesis* (Garden City, New York: Doubleday & Company, 1964), 113.
[80] Robert Graves and Raphael Patai, *Hebrew Myths: The Book of Genesis* (Garden City, New York: Doubleday & Company, 1964), 113.
[81] *The Midrash Rabbah*, Bereshith (Genesis) 31:12, trans. Rabbi Dr. H. Freedman and Maurice Simon (London: The Soncino Press, 1961).
[82] *Armenian Apocrypha Relating to Adam and Eve*, Abel and Other Pieces, 7.3, trans. Michael E. Stone (Leiden: E. J. Brill, 1996), 156.
[83] Louis Ginzberg, *The Legends of the Jews Volume I: From the Creation to Jacob*, trans. Henrietta Szold (Baltimore, Maryland: The Johns Hopkins University Press, 1909), 159; Robert Graves and Raphael Patai, *Hebrew Myths: The Book of Genesis* (Garden City, New York: Doubleday & Company, 1964), 113.
[84] *Atrahasis*, 5, http://www.earthhistory.org.uk/genesis-6-11-and-other-texts/flood-texts-from-mesopotamia (accessed Jan. 31, 2011).
[85] Louis Ginzberg, *The Legends of the Jews Volume V: Notes for Volume One and Two*, IV. Noah, 17, 26, trans. Henrietta Szold (Baltimore, Maryland: The Johns Hopkins University Press, 1909), 173, 178; James L. Kugel, *Traditions of the Bible* (Cambridge, Massachusetts: Harvard University Press, 1998), 195, 196; *Fragments of the Book of Noah (The Book of Enoch)*, 8:2, 106:13-16, trans. R. H. Charles (Montana: Kessinger Publishing, 1912); *The Book of the Mysteries of the Heavens and the Earth and Other Works of Bakhayla Mikael (Zosimas)*, trans. E. A. Wallis Budge (London: Oxford University Press, 1935), 29.
[86] The Works of Philo Judaeus, Questions and Answers on Genesis 2, 49, trans. C. D. Yonge (London: H. G. Bohn, 1854-1855); Louis Ginzberg, *The Legends of the Jews Volume V: Notes for Volume One and Two*, IV. Noah, 54, trans. Henrietta Szold (Baltimore, Maryland: The Johns Hopkins University Press, 1909), 188.
[87] David Goldstein, *Jewish Legends (Library of the World's Myths and Legends)* (New York: Peter Bedrick Books, 1933), 47.
[88] *The Third Book of Adam and Eve (The Conflict of Adam and Eve with Satan)*, Chapter 7, Chapter 11, trans. S. C. Malan (London: Williams and Norgate, 1882); Louis Ginzberg, *The Legends of the Jews Volume V: Notes for Volume One and Two*, IV. Noah, trans. Henrietta Szold (Baltimore, Maryland: The Johns Hopkins University Press, 1909), 188.
[89] Johann Andreas Eisenmenger, *The Traditions of the Jews, Contained in the Talmud and other Mystical Writings* (London: J. Robinson, 1748), 73; Robert Graves and Raphael Patai, *Hebrew Myths: The Book of Genesis* (Garden City, New York: Doubleday & Company, 1964), 114; Louis Ginzberg, *The Legends of the Jews Volume V: Notes for Volume One and Two*, IV. Noah, 10, trans. Henrietta Szold (Baltimore, Maryland: The Johns Hopkins University Press, 1909), 170; *The Babylonian Talmud*, Jews' College / Soncino English Translation, Niddah 61a, http://www.halakhah.com/niddah/niddah_61.html (accessed Aug. 13, 2010).
[90] *The History of al-Tabari - Volume I: General Introduction and From the Creation to the Flood*, The Events That Took Place in Noah's Time, 195, trans. Franz Rosenthal (Albany: New York Press, 1989), 365; *An Historical Treatise of the Travels of Noah Into Europe: Containing the first inhabitation and peopling thereof*, trans. Richard Lynche (1601), http://www.annomundi.com/history/travels_of_noah.htm (accessed Dec.7, 2007).
[91] Robert Graves and Raphael Patai, *Hebrew Myths: The Book of Genesis* (Garden City, New York: Doubleday & Company, 1964), 114.
[92] Steven R. Haynes, *Noah's Curse: The Biblical Justification of American Slavery* (Oxford: Oxford University Press, 2002), 30; *An Historical Treatise of the Travels of Noah Into Europe: Containing the first inhabitation and peopling thereof*, trans. Richard Lynche (1601), http://www.annomundi.com/history/travels_of_noah.htm (accessed Dec.7, 2007); S. Baring-Gould, *Legends of the Patriarchs and Prophets and Other Old Testament Characters* (New York:

American Book Exchange, 1881), 109-110, 124.
[93] Stephen R. Haynes, *Noah's Curse: The Biblical Justification of American Slavery*, Peter of Riga, *Aurora* (Oxford: University Press, 2002), 31.
[94] *The Companion Bible*, Genesis 7:23 (Grand Rapids, Michigan: Kregel Publications, 1990), 13.
[95] Louis Ginzberg, *The Legends of the Jews Volume V: Notes for Volume One and Two*, IV. Noah, 75, trans. Henrietta Szold (Baltimore, Maryland: The Johns Hopkins University Press, 1909), 197.
[96] David Goldstein, *Jewish Legends (Library of the World's Myths and Legends)* (New York: Peter Bedrick Books, 1933), 48.

Chapter 18

[1] Robert Graves and Raphael Patai, *Hebrew Myths: The Book of Genesis* (Garden City, New York: Doubleday & Company, 1964), 115.
[2] *The Sibylline Oracles, Translated from the Greek into English Blank Verse*, Book 1, Lines 325-328, trans. Milton S. Terry (New York: Hunt & Eaton, 1890).
[3] *The Zohar*, Volume 1, Beresheet A, Section 29. Evil admixtures, 291, www2.kabbalah.com/k/index.php/p=zohar/zohar&vol=2&sec=50 (accessed Feb. 24, 2010).
[4] Andrew Collins, *From the Ashes of Angels* (Rochester, Vermont: Bear & Company, 1996), 8.
[5] Jonathan Gray, *Lost World of Giants* (Teach Services, Inc., 2006), 31.
[6] *Pseudo-Philo (The Biblical Antiquities of Philo)*, 4:8, trans. M. R. James (1917), http://www.sacred-texts.com/bib/bap/bap19.htm (accessed July 13, 2006).
[7] *Pseudo-Philo (The Biblical Antiquities of Philo)*, 5:3-8, trans. M. R. James (1917), http://www.sacred-texts.com/bib/bap/bap19.htm (accessed July 13, 2006).
[8] *The Writings of Abraham*, 4:2, http://www.earth-history.com/Pseudepigrapha/Mormonism/writings-abraham-1.htm (accessed May 10, 2007).
[9] The Zohar, Volume 1, Beresheet A, Section 20. The five types of the mixed multitude, 231, http://www2.kabbalah.com/k/index.php/p=zohar/zohar&vol=2&sec=41 (accessed Feb. 24, 2010).
[10] *The Zohar*, Volume 1, Beresheet A, Section 20. The five types of the mixed multitude, 229, www2.kabbalah.com/k/index.php/p=zohar/zohar&vol=2&sec=41 (accessed Feb. 24, 2010).
[11] Charles DeLoach, *Giants: A Reference Guide from History, the Bible, and Recorded Legend* (Metuchen, N. J.: The Scarecrow Press, Inc., 1995), 46.
[12] The Zohar, Volume 1. Beresheet A, Section 20. The five types of the mixed multitude, 231, http://www2.kabbalah.com/k/index.php/p=zohar/zohar&vol=2&sec=41 (accessed Feb. 24, 2010); Deuteronomy 2 10-11 (KJV); *The Book of Jubilees*, 10:1, trans. R. H. Charles, The Apocrypha and Pseudepigrapha of the Old Testament (Oxford: Clarendon Press, 1913).
[13] The Zohar, Volume 1. Beresheet A, Section 20. The five types of the mixed multitude, 231, http://www2.kabbalah.com/k/index.php/p=zohar/zohar&vol=2&sec=41 (accessed Feb. 24, 2010); *Hypertext Webster Gateway*, From Easton's 1897 Bible Dictionary, 2, http://www.adamqadmon.com/nehilim/definitions/defgiants.html (accessed March 8, 2001).
[14] *Mysterious World: Spring 2003: Giants in the Earth Part I: Giants of the Ancient Near East*, 19, http://www.mysteriousworld.com/Journal/2003/Spring/Giants/ (accessed July 12, 2007).
[15] Strong's H7498 - *rapha*, http://www.blueletterbible.org/lang/lexicon/lexicon.cfm?Strongs=H7498&t=KJV (accessed Aug. 16, 2010).
[16] Jonathan Gray, *Lost World of Giants* (Teach Services, Inc., 2006), 11.
[17] *The Zohar*, Volume 1, Beresheet A, Section 20. The five types of the mixed multitude, 230, www2.kabbalah.com/k/index.php/p=zohar/zohar&vol=2&sec=41 (accessed Feb. 24, 2010).
[18] *The Book of Enoch*, 10:10, trans. R. H. Charles (Montana: Kessinger Publishing, 1912).
[19] *The Zohar*, Volume 18, Shlach Lecha, Section 10. The spies, 74, www2.kabbalah.com/k/index.php/p=zohar/zohar&vol=40&sec=1411 (accessed Feb. 24, 2010).
[20] *Book of the Glory of Kings (Kerba Nagast)*, 12. Concerning Canaan, trans. Sir. E. A. Wallis Budge (London: Humphrey Milford, 1932).
[21] Flavius Josephus, *The Antiquities of the Jews*, Book 7.4.1, trans. William Whiston (1737), http://www.ccel.org/j/josephus/works/ant-7.htm (accessed Feb. 4, 2011); A. H. Sayce, *The Races of the Old Testament* (London: The Religious Tract Society, 1891), 120.
[22] Charles DeLoach, *Giants: A Reference Guide from History, the Bible, and Recorded Legend* (Metuchen, N. J.: The Scarecrow Press, Inc., 1995), 109.
[23] *The Geography of Heaven & Earth During the Antediluvian World*, 3, http://bookofthenephilim.blogspot.com/2009/02/geography-of-heaven-earth-during.html (accessed Jan. 31, 2011).
[24] Charles DeLoach, *Giants: A Reference Guide from History, the Bible, and Recorded Legend* (Metuchen, N. J.: The Scarecrow Press, Inc., 1995), 17.
[25] Charles DeLoach, *Giants: A Reference Guide from History, the Bible, and Recorded Legend* (Metuchen, N. J.: The Scarecrow Press, Inc., 1995), 25.

[26] Charles DeLoach, *Giants: A Reference Guide from History, the Bible, and Recorded Legend* (Metuchen, N. J.: The Scarecrow Press, Inc., 1995), 159.
[27] Mysterious World: Spring 2003, *Giants in the Earth Part I: Giants of the Ancient Near East*, 26, www.mysteriousworld.com/Journal/2003/Spring /Giants/ (accessed July 12, 2007).
[28] Johann Andreas Eisenmenger, *The Traditions of the Jews, Contained in the Talmud and Other Mystical Writings* (London: J. Robinson, 1748), 74.
[29] *The Book of the Bee*, 20: Of Noah and the Flood, trans. Earnest A. Wallis Budge, M. A., http://www.sacred-texts.com/chr/bb/bb20.htm (accessed Oct. 10, 2004); Mrs. Sydney Bristowe, *Sargon the Magnificent* (London: The Covenant Publishing Co., 1927), 33-34; Robert Bowie Johnson, Jr., *The Parthenon Code: Mankind's History in Marble* (Annapolis, Maryland: Solving Light Books, 2004), 31-33.
[30] Josephus, J*ewish Antiquities*, Book 4, 97-102, trans. H. ST. J. Thackeray (London: William Heinemann Ltd., 1961), 525; Flavius Josephus, *The Antiquities of the Jews*, Book 4.5.3, trans. William Whiston (1737), http://www.ccel.org/j/josephus/works/ant-4.htm (accessed Feb. 4, 2011).
[31] Johann Andreas Eisenmenger, *The Traditions of the Jews, Contained in the Talmud and other Mystical Writings* (London: J. Robinson, 1748), 86.
[32] Charles DeLoach, *Giants: A Reference Guide from History, the Bible, and Recorded Legend* (Metuchen, N.J.: The Scarecrow Press, Inc., 1995), 151.
[33] The Easton's Bible Dictionary, *Sihon*, http://refbible.com/s/sihon.htm (accessed Aug. 16, 2010).
[34] *Num.* 21:1 (KJV); Charles DeLoach, *Giants: A Reference Guide from History, the Bible, and Recorded Legend* (Metuchen, N.J.: The Scarecrow Press, Inc., 1995), 263; Jewish Encyclopedia, *Sihon*, http://www.jewishencyclopedia.com/view.jsp?artid=706&letter=S&search=sihon (accessed Aug. 16, 2010).
[35] Josephus, J*ewish Antiquities*, Book 4, 85-89, 89-93, trans. H. ST. J. Thackeray (London: William Heinemann Ltd., 1961), 519, 521.
[36] Johann Andreas Eisenmenger, *The Traditions of the Jews, Contained in the Talmud and Other Mystical Writings* (London: J. Robinson, 1748), 77.
[37] Charles DeLoach, *Giants: A Reference Guide from History, the Bible, and Recorded Legend* (Metuchen, N. J.: The Scarecrow Press, Inc., 1995), 145, 156, 234; *The Companion Bible*, Genesis 10:16 (notes) (Grand Rapids, Michigan: Kregel Publications, 1990), 16; A. H. Sayce, *The Races of the Old Testament* (London: The Religious Tract Society, 1891), 111, 122.
[38] *Hypertext Webster Gateway*, From Easton's 1897 Bible Dictionary, 2, http://www.adamqadmon.com/nehilim/definitions/defgiants.html (accessed March 8, 2001); Jim A. Cornwell, *The Alpha and the Omega - Chapter 3*, 4, http://www.mazzaroth.com/ChapterThree/BiblicalInfoOfGiants.htm (accessed June 28, 2000); Greg Killian, *The Days of Noah*, 38, http://www.adamqadmon.com/nephilim/gkillian000.htm (accessed Dec. 6, 2000).
[39] Charles DeLoach, *Giants: A Reference Guide from History, the Bible, and Recorded Legend* (Metuchen, N. J.: The Scarecrow Press, Inc., 1995), 45.
[40] Flavius Josephus, *The Antiquities of the Jews*, Book 5.2.3, trans. William Whiston (1737), http://www.ccel.org/j/josephus/works/ant-5.htm (accessed Feb. 4, 2011).
[41] *The Zohar*, Volume 1, Beresheet A, Section 20. The five types of the mixed multitude, 230, www2.kabbalah.com/k/index.php/p=zohar/zohar&vol=2&sec=41 (accessed Feb. 24, 2010).
[42] *Mysterious World: Summer 2003: Giants in the Earth Part II: Giants of the Americas*, 37, http://www.mysteriousworld.com/Journal/2003/Summer/Giants/ (accessed July 20, 2007); *The Book of Jubilees*, 20:5, trans. R. H. Charles, The Apocrypha and Pseudepigrapha of the Old Testament (Oxford: Clarendon Press, 1913); Charles DeLoach, *Giants: A Reference Guide from History, the Bible, and Recorded Legend* (Metuchen, N. J.: The Scarecrow Press, Inc., 1995), 4.
[43] Bentley Layton, *The Gnostic Scriptures*, "Other" Gnostic Teachings According to St. Irenaeus 1.31.1 (New York: Doubleday, 1995), 181.
[44] *The Zohar*, Volume 1, Beresheet A, Section 20. The five types of the mixed multitude, 231, www2.kabbalah.com/k/index.php/p=zohar/zohar&vol=2&sec=41 (accessed Feb. 24, 2010).
[45] Robert Graves and Raphael Patai, *Hebrew Myths: The Book of Genesis* (Garden City, New York: Doubleday & Company, 1964), 96.
[46] Robert Graves and Raphael Patai, *Hebrew Myths: The Book of Genesis* (Garden City, New York: Doubleday & Company, 1964), 96.
[47] A. H. Sayce, *The Races of the Old Testament* (London: The Religious Tract Society, 1891), 118-119.
[48] The Easton's Bible Dictionary, *Kenites*, 1, http://refbible.com/k/kenites.htm (accessed Aug. 16, 2010).
[49] Strong's H7013 - *qayin*, http://www.blueletterbible.org/lang/lexicon/lexicon.cfm?Strongs=H7013&t=KJV (accessed Aug. 16, 2010).
[50] *Study of the Kenite*, 2, http://biblestudies.org/kjvstudies/kenite.htm (accessed Aug. 11, 2000).
[51] *Hitchcock's Bible Names Dictionary*, 32, http://www.adamqadmon.com/nephilim/definitions/biblenames.html (accessed March 8, 2001).
[52] Mrs. Sydney Bristowe, Sargon the Magnificent (London: The Covenant Publishing Co., 1927), 12; *Study of the*

Kenite, 2, http://biblestudies.org/kjvstudies/kenite.htm (accessed Aug. 11, 2000). *I Chr.* 2:55 (KJV); *The Gospel of Judas: Cain-Cainites-Kenite-Rechabites*, 7-8, http://www.piney.com/Cain.html (accessed April 19, 2007).

[53] *The Zohar*, Volume 1, Beresheet A, Section 20. The five types of the mixed multitude, 224, www2.kabbalah.com/k/index.php/p=zohar/zohar&vol=2&sec=41 (accessed Feb. 24, 2010).

[54] *Hitchcock's Bible Names Dictionary*, 4, http://www.adamqadmon.com/nephilim/definitions/biblenames.html (accessed March 8, 2001).

[55] Easton's Bible Dictionary, *Amalek*, http://refbible.com/a/amalek.htm (accessed Aug. 8, 2010).

[56] *The Zohar*, Volume 1, Beresheet A, Section 20. The five types of the mixed multitude, 231, www2.kabbalah.com/k/index.php/p=zohar/zohar&vol=2&sec=41 (accessed Feb. 24, 2010).

[57] *The Zohar*, Volume 1, Beresheet A, Section 29. Evil admixtures, 291, www2.kabbalah.com/k/index.php/p=zohar/zohar&vol=2&sec=50 (accessed Feb. 24, 2010).

Chapter 19

[1] Thinkexist.com, *Albert Einstein*, 1, http://thinkexist.com/quotation/the_distinction_between_past-present-and_future/184152.html (accessed Jan. 31, 2011).

[2] *Races*, 5-6, http://www.geocities.com/zakus_1999/Races.html?200710 (accessed Oct. 10, 2007).

[3] *Races*, 5-6, http://www.geocities.com/zakus_1999/Races.html?200710 (accessed Oct. 10, 2007).

[4] *Australoid*, 1, https://en.rightpedia.info/w/Australoid (accessed March 22, 2018).

[5] *Races*, 5-6, http://www.geocities.com/zakus_1999/Races.html?200710 (accessed Oct. 10, 2007).

[6] *I Sam.* 16:12 (KJV), *I Sam.* 17:42 (KJV), *Song of Sol.* 5:10 (KJV), *Lam.* 4:7 (KJV).

[7] *Jer.* 7:33, 16:4, 19:7, 34:20 (KJV); *Ezek.* 34:5, 8 (KJV).

[8] *4 Ezra (2 Esdras)*, 4:30, 2, http://etext.lib.virginia.edu/etcbin/toccer-new2?id=Kjv4Ezr.sgm&images=images/modeng&data=/texts/english/modeng/parsed&tag=public&part=4&division=div2 (accessed Jan. 31, 2011).

[9] *The Companion Bible*, Matthew 13:25 (notes) (Grand Rapids, Michigan: Kregel Publications, 1990).

[10] *The Midrash Rabbah*, Bereshith (Genesis) 22:13, trans. Rabbi Dr. H. Freedman and Maurice Simon (London: The Soncino Press, 1961).

[11] *The Midrash Rabbah*, Bereshith (Genesis) 22:13 (notes), trans. Rabbi Dr. H. Freedman and Maurice Simon (London: The Soncino Press, 1961).

[12] *The Gospel of Judas: Cain-Cainites-Kenite-Rechabites*, 7-8 (http://www.piney.com/Cain.html (accessed April 19, 2007).

[13] *Study of the Kenite*, 2, http://biblestudies.org/kjvstudies/kenite.htm (accessed Aug. 11, 2000).

[14] *The Gospel of Judas: Cain-Cainites-Kenite-Rechabites*, 7 (http://www.piney.com/Cain.html (accessed April 19, 2007).

[15] Flavius Josephus, *The Wars of the Jews*, Book 2.8.2, trans. William Whiston (1737) http://www.ccel.org/j/josephus/works/war-2.htm (accessed Aug. 16, 2010).

[16] *Sons of Cain: They Survived Noah's Flood!*, 5, http://www.nfis.com/~danelady/sonsofcain.html (accessed June 5, 2000).

[17] *Testamentum Adami (The Book of the Cave of Treasures)*, Adam Foretells the Coming of Christ, trans. E. A. Wallis Budge, http://www.sacred-texts.com/chr/bct/bct10.htm (accessed Jan. 22, 2010).

[18] Johann Andreas Eisenmenger, *The Traditions of the Jews, Contained in the Talmud and Other Mystical Writings* (London: J. Robinson, 1748), 191-192.

[19] Robert Bowie Johnson, Jr., *The Parthenon Code: Mankind's History in Marble* (Annapolis, Maryland: Solving Light Books, 2004), 60.

[20] Robert Bowie Johnson, Jr., *The Parthenon Code: Mankind's History in Marble* (Annapolis, Maryland: Solving Light Books, 2004), 19, 62-63.

[21] Robert Bowie Johnson, Jr., *The Parthenon Code: Mankind's History in Marble* (Annapolis, Maryland: Solving Light Books, 2004), 19, 62.

[22] Robert Bowie Johnson, Jr., *The Parthenon Code: Mankind's History in Marble* (Annapolis, Maryland: Solving Light Books, 2004), 62.

[23] Robert Bowie Johnson, Jr., *The Parthenon Code: Mankind's History in Marble* (Annapolis, Maryland: Solving Light Books, 2004), 19, 72.

[24] Strong's G1537 - *ek*, http://www.blueletterbible.org/lang/lexicon/lexicon.cfm?Strongs=G1537&t=KJV (accessed Aug. 16, 2010).

[25] Strong's G1537 - *ek*, http://www.blueletterbible.org/lang/lexicon/lexicon.cfm?Strongs=G1537&t=KJV (accessed Aug. 16, 2010).

[26] *The Zohar*, Volume 1, Beresheet A, Section 28. Hevel-Moshe, 285, www2.kabbalah.com/k/index.php/p=zohar/zohar&vol=2&sec=49 (accessed Feb. 24, 2010).

[27] *The Zohar*, Volume 17, Naso, Section 3. "To do trespass against Hashem", 17, www2.kabbalah.com/k/index.php/p=zohar/zohar&vol=38&sec=1302 (accessed Feb. 25, 2010).

[28] *The Zohar*, Volume 13, Pekudei, Section 21. Breastplate and Efod, 203,

www2.kabbalah.com/k/index.php/p=zohar/zohar&vol=26&sec=912 (accessed Feb. 24, 2010).

Chapter 20

[1] Goodreads.com, *Albert Einstein*, 1, http://www.goodreads.com/quotes/show/67533 (accessed Jan. 31, 2011).
[2] Johann Andreas Eisenmenger, *The Traditions of the Jews, Contained in the Talmud and other Mystical Writings* (London: J. Robinson, 1748), 205-206.
[3] merriam-webster.com, *loose*, http://www.merriam-webster.com/dictionary/loose (accessed Aug. 17, 2010).
[4] Jayim Nahman Bialik and Yehoshua Hana Ravnitzky, *The Book of Legends (Sefer Ha-Aggadah): Legends of the Talmud and Midrash*, 101 (New York: Shocken Books,.1992), 23-24.
[5] Jayim Nahman Bialik and Yehoshua Hana Ravnitzky, *The Book of Legends (Sefer Ha-Aggadah): Legends of the Talmud and Midrash*, 104 (and notes) (New York: Shocken Books,.1992), 24.
[6] Jayim Nahman Bialik and Yehoshua Hana Ravnitzky, *The Book of Legends (Sefer Ha-Aggadah): Legends of the Talmud and Midrash*, 104 (New York: Shocken Books,.1992), 24 (notes).
[7] Ellen Frankel, *The Classic Tales: 4000 Years of Jewish Lore* (Northvale, New Jersey: Jason Aronson Inc., 1989), 30.
[8] James R. Davis, Have We Gone the Way of Cain?, 6-7, www.focusongod.com/cain (accessed March 3, 2001) 60.
[9] *The Works of Philo Judaeus*, On the Posterity of Cain and His Exile 15, 52, trans. C. D. Yonge (London: H. G. Bohn, 1854-1855).
[10] *Book of the Glory of Kings (Kerba Nagast)*, 7. Concerning Noah, trans. Sir. E. A. Wallis Budge (London: Humphrey Milford, 1932).
[11] *The Zohar*, Volume 1, Beresheet A, Section 29. Evil admixtures, 290, www2.kabbalah.com/k/index.php/p=zohar/zohar&vol=2&sec=50 (accessed Feb. 24, 2010).
[12] *The Works of Philo Judaeus*, On the Posterity of Cain and His Exile 15, 52, trans. C. D. Yonge (London: H. G. Bohn, 1854-1855).
[13] *The Midrash Rabbah*, Bereshith (Genesis) 26:5, trans. Rabbi Dr. H. Freedman and Maurice Simon (London: The Soncino Press, 1961).
[14] *Jer.* 8:10 (KJV).
[15] The Works of Philo Judaeus, On the Posterity of Cain and His Exile 34, 116, trans. C. D. Yonge (London: H.G Bohn, 1854-1855).
[16] *Book of the Glory of Kings (Kerba Nagast)*, 7. Concerning Noah, trans. Sir. E. A. Wallis Budge (London: Humphrey Milford, 1932).
[17] *The Zohar*, Volume 1, Beresheet A, Section 28. Hevel-Moshe, 286, http//www2.kabbalah.com/k/index.php/p=zohar/zohar&vol=2&sec=49 (accessed Feb. 24, 2010).
[18] *The Works of Philo Judaeus*, Questions and Answers on Genesis 2, 82, trans. C. D. Yonge (London: H. G. Bohn, 1854-1855).
[19] *The Works of Philo Judaeus*, Questions and Answers on Genesis 2, 82, trans. C. D. Yonge (London: H. G. Bohn, 1854-1855).
[20] *The Works of Philo Judaeus*, Questions and Answers on Genesis 2, 82, trans. C. D. Yonge (London: H. G. Bohn, 1854-1855).
[21] *The Zohar*, Volume 14, Tzav, Section 20. Burning of holy things, 146, www2.kabbalah.com/k/index.php/p=zohar/zohar&vol=48&sec=1042 (accessed Feb. 25, 2010).
[22] *Jubal - Genun - Musical Worship*, Book of Adam and Eve, 18, http://www.piney.com/MuGenun2.html (accessed Aug. 17, 2010).
[23] *The Second Book of Adam and Eve (The Conflict of Adam and Eve with Satan)*, 1:8, 12:16, trans. S. C. Malan (London: Williams and Norgate, 1882).
[24] S. Baring-Gould, *Legends of the Patriarchs and Prophets and Other Old Testament Characters* (New York: American Book Exchange, 1881), 73.
[25] Louis Ginzberg, *The Legends of the Jews Volume I: From the Creation to Jacob*, trans. Henrietta Szold (Baltimore, Maryland: The Johns Hopkins University Press, 1909), 114.
[26] *The Book of the Cave of Treasures*, The First Thousand Years: Adam to Yared (Jared), The Rule of Anosh, trans. Sir E. A. Wallis Budge (London: The Religious Tract Society, 1927), 77-80.
[27] *The Second Book of Adam and Eve (The Conflict of Adam and Eve with Satan)*, 13:5, trans. S. C. Malan (London: Williams and Norgate, 1882).
[28] Louis Ginzberg, *The Legends of the Jews Volume I: From the Creation to Jacob*, trans. Henrietta Szold (Baltimore, Maryland: The Johns Hopkins University Press, 1909), 116.
[29] *The Apocalypse of Moses / Apocalypsis Mosis*, 3:2, trans. R. H. Charles, http://www.pseudepigrapha.com/pseudepigrapha/aprmose.htm (accessed June 27, 2005).
[30] S. Baring-Gould, *Legends of the Patriarchs and Prophets and Other Old Testament Characters* (New York: American Book Exchange, 1881), 75.
[31] *The Midrash Rabbah*, Bereshith (Genesis) 33:1, trans. Rabbi Dr. H. Freedman and Maurice Simon (London: The Soncino Press, 1961).
[32] *The Zohar*, Volume 17, Naso, Section 3. "To do trespass against Hashem", 17,

www2.kabbalah.com/k/index.php/p=zohar/zohar&vol=38&sec=1302 (accessed Feb. 25, 2010).
[33] Louis Ginzberg, *The Legends of the Jews Volume I: From the Creation to Jacob*, trans. Henrietta Szold (Baltimore, Maryland: The Johns Hopkins University Press, 1909), 153.
[34] Malcolm Godwin, *Angels: An Endangered Species* (New York: Simon & Schuester, 1990), 113.
[35] *The Midrash Rabbah*, Bereshith (Genesis) 23:1 (and notes), trans. Rabbi Dr. H. Freedman and Maurice Simon (London: The Soncino Press, 1961).
[36] *The Book of the Rolls (Kitab Al-Magall)*, trans. Margaret Dunlop Gibson, Apocrypha Arabica (London: C. J. Clay and Sons, 1901), 22; S. Baring-Gould, *Legends of the Patriarchs and Prophets and Other Old Testament Characters* (New York: American Book Exchange, 1881), 15.
[37] Rev. G. Oliver, *The Antiquities of Free-Masonry; Comprising Illustrations of the Five Grand Periods of Masonry, From the Creation of the World to the Dedication of King Solomon's Temple* (London: Richard Spencer, 314, High Holborn, 1843), 44.
[38] *The Book of Adam*, 21.3b, trans. J. P. Mahe, http://www.pseudepigrapha.com/pseudepigrapha/TheBookOfAdam.htm (accessed June 27, 2005).
[39] *The Midrash Rabbah*, Bereshith (Genesis) 2:3 (and notes), trans. Rabbi Dr. H. Freedman and Maurice Simon (London: The Soncino Press, 1961).
[40] *The Works of Philo Judaeus*, Questions and Answers on Genesis 1, 72, trans. C. D. Yonge (London: H. G. Bohn, 1854-1855).
[41] *Armenian Apocrypha Relating to Adam and Eve*, His Sons and Grandsons 40, trans. Michael E. Stone (Leiden: E. J. Brill, 1996), 198.
[42] *The Works of Philo Judaeus*, Questions and Answers on Genesis 2, 8, trans. C. D. Yonge (London: H. G. Bohn, 1854-1855).
[43] *The Works of Philo Judaeus*, Questions and Answers on Genesis 1, 8, trans. C. D. Yonge (London: H. G. Bohn, 1854-1855).
[44] *The Works of Philo Judaeus*, Questions and Answers on Genesis 1, 5, trans. C. D. Yonge (London: H. G. Bohn, 1854-1855).
[45] *The Works of Philo Judaeus*, Questions and Answers on Genesis 1, 65, trans. C. D. Yonge (London: H. G. Bohn, 1854-1855).
[46] *Jer.* 8:12 (KJV).
[47] *Jer.* 8:11 (KJV).
[48] Robert Graves and Raphael Patai, *Hebrew Myths: The Book of Genesis* (Garden City, New York: Doubleday & Company, 1964), 88.
[49] *The Zohar*, Volume 13, Pekudei, Section 21. Breastplate and Efod, 205, www2.kabbalah.com/k/index.php/p=zohar/zohar&vol=26&sec=912 (accessed Feb. 24, 2010).
[50] David Max Eichhorn, *Cain: Son of the Serpent* (New York: Whittier Books, Inc., 1957), 68.
[51] Louis Ginzberg, *The Legends of the Jews Volume I: From the Creation to Jacob*, trans. Henrietta Szold (Baltimore, Maryland: The Johns Hopkins University Press, 1909), 111
[52] Joseph Campbell, *The Masks of God: Occidental Mythology* (New York: The Viking Press), 14
[53] *Book of the Glory of Kings (Kerba Nagast)*, 4. Concering Envy, trans. Sir. E. A. Wallis Budge (London: Humphrey Milford, 1932).
[54] *Ancient Near East (Babylonia) Glossary and Texts*, 16, http://www.piney.com/BabGloss.html (accessed June 5, 2017).
[55] David Kevin Delaney, *The Sevenfold Vengeance of Cain: Genesis 4 in Early Jewish and Christian Interpretation* (University of Virginia, 1996), 182.
[56] *The Book of the Generations of Adam*, 5.1, http://www.earth-history.com/Pseudepigrapha/generations-adam.htm (accessed May 5, 2007).
[57] David Kevin Delaney, *The Sevenfold Vengeance of Cain: Genesis 4 in Early Jewish and Christian Interpretation* (University of Virginia, 1996), 141.
[58] Louis Ginzberg, *The Legends of the Jews Volume V: Notes for Volume One and Two*, trans. Henrietta Szold (Baltimore, Maryland: The Johns Hopkins University Press, 1909), 136.
[59] Lambert Dolphin, *The Ruin of Creation*, 7, http://ldolphin.org/Ruin.html (accessed Dec. 5, 2000).
[60] Lambert Dolphin, *The Ruin of Creation*, 5, http://ldolphin.org/Ruin.html (accessed Dec. 5, 2000).

48552541R00302

Made in the USA
Columbia, SC
09 January 2019